COMMUNICATING
PREJUDICE

COMMUNICATING
PREJUDICE

Michael L. Hecht
Editor

SAGE Publications
International Educational and Professional Publisher
Thousand Oaks   London   New Delhi

For information:

SAGE Publications, Inc.
2455 Teller Road
Thousand Oaks, California 91320
E-mail: order@sagepub.com

SAGE Publications Ltd.
6 Bonhill Street
London EC2A 4PU
United Kingdom

SAGE Publications India Pvt. Ltd.
M-32 Market
Greater Kailash I
New Delhi 110 048 India

Printed in the United States of America

Library of Congress Cataloging-in-Publication Data

Main entry under title:

Communicating prejudice / [edited by] Michael L. Hecht.
    p. cm.
  Includes bibliographical references and index.
  ISBN 0-7619-0124-8 (cloth: acid-free paper). —
  ISBN 0-7619-0125-6 (pbk.: acid-free paper)
    1. Toleration. 2. Prejudices. 3. Prejudices—United States.
  4. Communication—Social aspects. 5. Communication—Social aspects—
United States. 6. Intergroup relations. 7. Intergroup relations—
United States. I. Hecht, Michael L.
  HM276.C625 1998
  303.3′85—dc21   97-33906

98 99 00 01 02 03   10 9 8 7 6 5 4 3 2 1

Acquiring Editor: Margaret H. Seawell
Editorial Assistant: Renée Piernot
Production Editor: Michèle Lingre
Production Assistants: Lynn Miyata/Karen Wiley
Typesetter/Designer: Janelle LeMaster
Cover Designer: Ravi Balasuriya
Print Buyer: Anna Chin

Contents

PART V: Interventions

PART VI: Conclusion

Acknowledgments

There are so many people to thank for this book. There is Ann, more diverse than her Iowa farm girl appearance would suggest, for her support, love, ideas, and lifelong companionship. You provide a true sounding board. Jim and Rebecca provide constant generational challenges along with love and support. Lamont Hawkins Mitchell, wherever you are, thanks for accepting me in my naïveté. Thanks go to Joe DeVito, who taught me so much and provides a model for what a friend, scholar, and companion should be; to Sidney Ribeau, Michael Sedano, and Howie Giles, who have challenged my assumptions while accepting and caring for me; to T. A. Niles for keeping me from being lazy and helping me explore ideas of identity, culture, and communication in my intellectual and personal lives; to Linda Larkey, John Baldwin, and Sheryl Lindsley for teaching me as we learned together; and to Dan Strouse, Sandra Petronio, Flavio Marsiglia, Eric Margolis, and Cristina González, who have taken on portions of the challenge of supporting me during some difficult moments. Special thanks also go to Mary Fran Draisker for her meticulous copy editing and overall layout help when preparing this manuscript; to Janet Soper for her help with so many of my projects; and to Sophy Craze, my editor when this project began, and Margaret Seawell, who saw it to completion.

PART I   Introduction

1 Introduction

Michael L. Hecht

Is prejudice like the air and the ground, a basic structure of human existence? Is it like the light, an indelible part of the human viewpoint? Or, is it a germ that has polluted the waters of our bodily fluids and can be extinguished or expelled? Is it inevitably part of our connecting? Does it derive from our heredity, biology, or social structures? How does prejudice function as a form of expression in the social world? Our goal in writing this book is to further our understanding of prejudice and its communication, focusing mainly on U.S. culture. We cannot hope to answer all of these questions, but we can hope to discuss prejudice, particularly its expression, and suggest ways of understanding and dealing with these issues.

The chapters in this book describe prejudice in a variety of ways. These definitions, however, seem to coalesce around four central metaphors for prejudice:

Prejudice as fear of difference or the unknown (difference as threat)

Prejudice as dislike of difference or the unknown (difference as aversive)

Prejudice as competition with difference for scarce resources (difference as competition)

Prejudice as hierarchical and structure (prejudice as hierarchy)

These metaphors may be explained in a variety of ways including *biologically* through evolutionary theory, *economically* (or in *power relationships*) through Marxism or other critical theories, *cognitively* or *emotionally* through social-psychological approaches, or *socially* through the social constructionist approach. They may focus on the individual, the family and social circle, the culture or society, or the species. The diversity of society is reflected in these approaches.

3

■ The Pervasiveness of Prejudice

Although not a new social issue, prejudice is highly salient in modern society. Diversity issues seem to have erupted as the demographic character of U.S. culture evolves from one numerically dominated by European Americans and as resources no longer seem unbounded. Recent research suggests not only that the United States is more ethnically diverse than ever before but also that people overestimate that diversity—projecting, for example, many more African Americans in the population than their actual presence (Morris, 1995).

Unfortunately, these diversity issues seem to have intensified prejudice rather than manifesting themselves in an era of tolerance or even the embracing of difference. As images of the "melting pot" disappear from the American consciousness—a myth that never really reflected the reality of life in U.S. culture—no positive images of diversity have emerged to replace them. Instead, class, race/ethnic, religious, sexual preference, age, and other distinctions seem to have become even more polarized and negatively emotionalized.

There is no question that prejudice is a serious problem in contemporary society. News reports document increasing numbers of hate groups (e.g., "Hate Groups Increasing," 1992). It surprises many U.S. citizens to learn that gay men are now the number one target of hate crimes (Hamilton, 1994; see also Nakayama's chapter in this volume [Chapter 6]), with Blacks and Jews second and third. The growing rate of attacks on Asian Americans may reflect a trend to victimizing this group (Dubin, 1991). Lest one think that these problems are limited to certain segments of the population, articles document the pervasiveness of prejudice in "yuppies" (Lowy, 1991) and among high school students ("Racism Prevalent," 1990). In fact, young people who probably have experienced more "integration" than have other age cohorts are particularly pessimistic about race relations in the United States (Collison, 1992). Prejudice, in the form of racism, also appears prevalent among some of those who claim a "Christian" religious identity (McLemee, 1994), a religion predicated on Christ's teachings of love and acceptance. Moon and Rolison (Chapter 7 in this volume) discuss the myth that good, typical, middle class people are not prejudiced—that prejudice is only for deviants.

The problem of determining how much prejudice or discrimination exists is exacerbated by the personal/group discrimination discrepancy. Personal/group discrimination discrepancy is the label applied to the observation that individuals perceive more discrimination toward their groups than toward themselves as individuals (Taylor, Wright, & Porter, 1994). This discrepancy has been found across a wide number of groups and does not appear to result from sampling bias (i.e., sampling only relatively privileged members of any group), the way questions are worded, or other methodological factors (Taylor et al., 1994). Instead, it seems to occur when people deny or minimize personal discrimination and this and other coping mechanisms are developed to deal with the blows to the human spirit from discrimination. Others have suggested that this discrepancy results from trying to resolve the dissonance between perceiving discrimination and failing to take actions against the discriminator, media coverage of discrimination that tends to be highly dramatic, and possibly an accurate perception of more general prejudice toward groups than discrimination toward individuals (Taylor et al., 1994).

■ The Causes of Prejudice

Many trace recent manifestations of prejudice to the economic or market climate ("Economic Ills," 1991; Reinhold, 1991; Tzeng & Jackson, 1994; see also one of Lindsley's chapters in this volume [Chapter 10]), a conclusion that would not surprise Marxists and many other critical theorists. The purchasing power of most workers no longer is rising and, in fact, has been experiencing declines in most sectors of the economy. Many fear the exodus of jobs to other countries (Is this code for fear of "them," "others," or "difference," as some have suggested?) and the decrease in well-paid, middle management, and industrial sector jobs. Downsizing threatens even long-term, entrenched workers, and when "stable" companies (e.g., IBM) conduct mass layoffs and others (e.g., America West) lay off large numbers of workers right before the Christmas holidays, people begin to become apprehensive about their prosperity.

There is no question that women and minorities have suffered from the economic impact of prejudice. Comparably educated women earn about two thirds of the amounts earned by White males, even with college degrees, and Black men earn about three fourths of what comparably educated White males might make ("College-Educated Blacks' Earnings," 1991). The predominance of White males in certain occupations still eludes nonracist explanations (Shao, 1995). For example, why do White males comprise 88% of construction workers, 56% of sales representatives, 49% of janitors, 87% of automobile mechanics, and 81% of truck drivers? Although one could argue that the lingering effects of previous prejudice have disadvantaged some groups in pursuing "degreed" jobs such as medical doctors, this does not explain why White males dominate the previously referenced occupations.

Are economic conditions the only cause, or even the primary cause, of prejudice? No clear answer has emerged to explain these causes, although it is likely that there are different types of prejudice manifesting from a variety of causes (Brewer, 1994). One of the earliest attempts to specify causes is Sherif's (1966) functional approach, which argues that realistic conflict over scarce resources leads to intergroup conflict. His theory, "realistic conflict theory," received some empirical support (Brown, 1988). However, other studies show that conflicting interests are not a necessary condition for intergroup antagonism. Instead, the mere categorization of people into two groups is enough to foster intergroup discrimination (Bourhis, 1994; Tajfel, 1981b). These categorizations define in-groups and out-groups with resulting pro-in-group bias and anti-out-group attitudes and behaviors.

Based on social identity (Tajfel & Turner, 1986) and self-categorization (Turner, Hogg, Oakes, Reicher, & Wetherall, 1987) theories, the social categorization approach is based on two premises (Brewer, 1996):

1. Individuals organize their world into discrete categories or classes by transforming continuous variables.

2. Social categorization implies in-group/out-group (we/they, us/them) distinctions.

Once social categories are set up, they act as intergroup schemata, resulting in *intergroup accentuation* (i.e., assimilation of people within categories and contrast among groups), *in-group favoritism,* and *social competition* including intergroup-social comparisons. The result of these categorization processes is the preferential treatment of in-group members along with out-group bias and competition. Recent research suggests that the most salient factor is pro-in-group bias (Gaertner, Dovidio, & Bachman, 1996), which inhibits people from expanding their circles of inclusion and thus out-group contact (Gaertner, Dovidio, Banker, Rust, Nier, Mottola, & Ward, in press).

Recent theories have been developed to further explain these processes. Arguing that older explanations including psychoanalytic theory (projection, scapegoating), personality trait approaches (authoritarianism, self-esteem, ethnocentrism), demographic approaches (age, education, gender, socioeconomic status), and sociocultural approaches (institutional and historical factors) have not worked well, Stephan and Stephan (1996) offer the *radial network model,* which focuses on four types of threats. *Realistic* threats challenge a group's existence or economic/political power. *Symbolic* threats endanger a group's way of life (e.g., through value conflicts). *Intergroup* threats involve the anxiety associated with interacting with out-groups and tend to be high if there has been little prior contact with out-group members, a history of conflict, ethnocentricity, the perception that the other group is "different," little knowledge about the out-group, and interaction in a relatively unstructured, competitive situation where one's own group is in a minority or low-status position. The final category of threats is *negative stereotypes.*

Research using this perspective has produced a number of interesting findings. We have learned, for example, that dominant group prejudices are based more on intergroup threats and negative stereotypes, whereas subordinate group prejudices are based on all four types. We also know that with low intergroup contact, prejudice typically is based on negative stereotypes and intergroup threat/anxiety, whereas with high intergroup contact, prejudice usually is based on quality of contact. Stephan and Stephan (1996) believe that voluntary, equal status, personal, and positive contact should dissipate intergroup anxiety and negative stereotypes, whereas negative or conflictive contact leaves all four types of threat.

A second approach is called *social dominance theory* (Sidanius, Levin, & Pratto, 1996). This theory posits that intergroup discrimination develops out of a universal desire to form and preserve intergroup status differences within hierarchies. This desire is supported by social ideologies and policies justifying hierarchical inequalities through devices such as "legitimizing myths." There are both myths common to a culture and those not shared by people in different strata. These are called consensual (shared) and dissensual (not shared) myths. Consensual myths are shared to some degree by all status groups. Individual variation in support for group-based inequality is called social dominance orientation (SDO). There is more support for inequality and the ideology underlying it in high-status groups (Sidanius et al., 1996). Even where there is consensus, the SDO scores of Whites have a different pattern of correlations with social beliefs than do those of Blacks. Thus, "the psychosocial significance of consensually held beliefs might be systematically different for different groups within the social hierarchy" (p. 404).

Other writers point to the structural properties of prejudice. González (Chapter 12 in this volume) attributes prejudice to hierarchy, a structural property. Others, such as Hall (1981a), discuss how class relations and class domination are constructed and reproduce inequalities. These hierarchical relations are ideological and become ingrained in a society's worldview and expressed through practices such as segregation, inequitable educational and workplace opportunities, and treatment by the legal system and other strata of society (Wieviorka, 1995).

These theories, then, point to a variety of causes of prejudice. Brewer (1994) argues that some prejudice has its origin in personal needs and values or generalizations of personal experiences with group members, whereas other forms of prejudice are expressions of shared group beliefs. This has its parallel in findings that treatments of individuals and social groups are not always consistent (personal/group discrimination discrepancy). In addition, we must examine structural and historical factors. Rather than a single cause, we find multiple causes across individual, group, and societal levels that manifest themselves in a variety of prejudicial processes.

Although prejudice may have many causes and certainly pervades all layers of U.S. society, there are differences over the issue of who may be prejudiced. Some claim that only the empowered mainstream, with most of the power, can subjugate and, therefore, has the ability to "be prejudiced." Wallis (1991), for example, argues,

> Racism has to do with the power to dominate and enforce oppression, and that power in America is in White hands. Therefore, while there are instances of Black prejudice against Whites in the United States today (often in reaction to White racism), there is no such thing as Black racism. Black people in America do not have the power to enforce that prejudice. (p. 30)

This view is not shared by all voices, not even within this book. One can argue, as do Mathabane and Page (1991), that the statement that minorities cannot be racist implies that they have no structural power, a statement that does not accurately reflect their hard-earned economic and political gains. One also may take a more situational and individualistic view of power. There may be situations in which these "others" have power over the mainstream group. For example, on many of the basketball courts in our cities, Black culture prevails. Does this mean that in these settings, Blacks may be prejudiced toward Whites, Latinos, and other groups given that they hold normative power? Brewer (1994) argues that assuming that prejudice is unilateral conflates the social psychology of prejudice with the social psychology of power and dominance. In her analysis, power is treated as one among many cognitive and motivational bases for intergroup prejudice. Brewer argues for complex, bidirectional relationships between the psychological and structural dimensions, pointing to research derived from Tajfel's (1981b) social identity theory using the minimal intergroup paradigm, which shows that power provides a means of expression of in-group favoritism in reward allocation rather than its motivational basis. But this work also shows that power and status differentials are salient factors. A recent poll reports *minority* bias toward Anglos and each other ("Minorities Admit Bias," 1994), and Whites are the fourth most frequent victims of hate crimes in recent statistics (Hamilton, 1994). Others discuss bias within racial groupings, and classifying these practices as bias has been supported by recent court rulings ("Color Bias," 1989). Still others are concerned with the role of subordinate groups in legitimizing oppression (Wolf, 1986), and, although it is convenient to blame the victim for victimage, a relational perspective[1] would argue that participation in subordination be fully explored. Laboratory studies show that low-power groups discriminate but that groups with no power can discriminate only in unstable situations (Bourhis, 1994). Furthermore, Bourhis's (1994) work shows that males and females discriminate equally, thus supporting the notion that it is sociocultural rather than dispositional factors that are most salient. In addition, in some situations people from low-power groups can discriminate if the situation gives them the opportunity and resources to do so. However, it also is true in this work that those from high-power, high-status groups discriminated more than did those from low-power, low-status groups.

■ Forms of Prejudice

There have been many discussions of the forms of prejudice. The reader may have noticed terms such as discrimination and stereotyping conflated with prejudice. For some, this conflation is troublesome, and they seek to separate these terms. For these people, the three terms represent very different constructs.

Prejudice often is thought of as an attitude consisting of the combination of affect and belief or at least the affective or evaluative reaction to group differences (Brewer, 1994; Lott, 1995; Schütz & Six, 1996). It sometimes is seen as having three levels: prejudgment, prejudgment with evaluation, and prejudgment with a negative evaluative component (Gardner, 1994).

Stereotypes are the well-learned, widely shared, socially validated general beliefs or cognitions about disempowered groups that reinforce or justify prejudice and reduce ambiguity (Maluso, 1995; Neuberg, 1994; Schütz & Six, 1996). The common view of stereotypes is that they are consensual beliefs about a group with behavioral implications. Stereotypes often are seen as "facts" by those who hold them and receive much social support. Schütz and Six (1996) say that stereotypes involve consensual beliefs, unjustified beliefs, and beliefs that distinguish one category from another. But not all stereotypes are consensual; in-group and out-group stereotypes may invoke different cognitive processes (Gardner, 1994), and stereotypes appear to be triggered automatically. For example, most White people are aware of stereotypes of ethnic minorities, and these stereotypes are activated automatically in the presence of their targets. Less prejudiced Whites appear to substitute other thoughts for the stereotypes (Maluso, 1995).

A number of writers attempt to compare stereotypes to prejudice. Neuberg (1994) believes that both are expectancies. He writes that stereotypes tell us what a group is like, whereas prejudice tells us how we are likely to feel about that group. Schütz and Six (1996) note that both stereotypes and prejudice have behavioral intentions and overt behaviors associated with them. For most people, these behaviors are labeled *discrimination*.

Discrimination is the overt actions to exclude, avoid, or distance (Brewer, 1994; Lott, 1995). Lott argues that whereas prejudice and stereotyping are "deplorable," discrimination is the "social problem."

The relationships between and among these three components have been the subject of much discussion. Empirical studies find that the relationship between prejudice and discrimination is not very strong in general (the average correlation is .29) and varies across categories of behavior (Schütz & Six, 1996). Schütz and Six's (1996) meta-analysis also concludes that correlations are higher if behavior is under volitional control and that prejudice has a higher correlation with intention (.37) than with the other constructs. However, this analysis also concludes that the direction of causality is not known and probably is bidirectional.

Similarly, the empirical relationship between stereotyping and prejudice has been small (e.g., .05, .15, .16) (Duckitt, 1993). But if one considers the interaction between the stereotype (cognitive belief that a group has a certain trait) and the evaluation (positive/negative affect toward the trait), then the relationship is more substantial (e.g., average correlation of .36). Duckitt (1993) argues that prejudice and discrimination may not be related in situations with clear and salient normative criteria for equitable and fair behavior but are related in informal social interaction, and this may have important implications for intervention.

Brewer (1994) reviews this work and concludes that the "cognitive, affective, and behavioral orientations to individuals and social groups represent different, independent response systems whose interrelationships are more complex than previously thought" (Brewer, 1994, p. 321). She suggests that the observed discontinuities among the constructs be reexamined by separating preconscious and conscious processing (see also Neuberg, 1994). However, the observed relationship among these constructs is troubling given their conceptual definitions. For example, in addition to the studies reported previously, Crosby, Bromley, and Saxe (1980) conclude that discrimination toward Blacks by Whites is more prevalent than what would be expected based on attitudes. Others have noted that males' attitudes toward women are more egalitarian than their behaviors (Kahn, 1984).

Perhaps these problems are associated with the basic reductionistic assumptions that underlie the conceptualizations. By looking for the three constructs as *separate* or discrete but related entities, this approach has chopped up the holistic nature of human experience. If the entire human action—whether called prejudice or discrimination—is examined, there may be cognitive, emotional, and behavioral elements to it, and these should be placed within the social and historical context of intergroup relations, economic conditions, and the wide array of factors discussed as causes of prejudice. Although the conscious/unconscious continuum may be useful in understanding the cognitive functioning of an individual in a specific situation, to fully understand what is occurring among[2] people and among groups in society, as well as around the world, we need to treat things more holistically or at least place them in a more holistic context as we move back and forth between tightly focused studies of individuals and more social understandings of these processes.

Distinctions among terms are not the only discussion salient to forms of prejudice. Others are concerned about the levels of prejudice. For example, Lott (1995) distinguishes between *interindividual* (face-to-face) and *institutional* discrimination, and Maluso (1995) extends this by distinguishing among *institutional, collective,* and *interpersonal* racism. She defines institutional racism as the denial of equal participation in stable, organized, systematic associations or procedures such as electoral processes and formal education. Collective racism is based on less formal group and societal norms that reinforce collective acts against groups (e.g., exclusion from neighborhoods, demonstrations), and interpersonal racism occurs one-on-one. Similarly, Brewer (1994) argues that some prejudice originates in personal needs, values, and experiences, whereas other prejudice is grounded in shared group beliefs. She argues that this distinction has important implications for designing interventions, and I agree.

Another recent issue is the directness of forms of expression. Allport (1954/1979) places discrimination on a continuum from antilocution to extermination (midpoints include avoidance, active exclusion, and physical attack). Following this analysis, Lott (1995) talks about a range of sexist discrimination including humor, put-downs, pornography, institution exclusion, personal distancing, insults, harassment, intimidation, sexual coercion, abuse (sexual and physical), and murder. However, this range must be extended to even subtler forms of discrimination than that described by Allport (1954/1979). These include failure to make eye contact or to interact verbally, negative voice tone, and failure to respect personal space (Maluso, 1995, p. 52). For example, active and passive behaviors are used for "distancing from and avoidance and exclusion of persons in low-status social categories by persons with greater power" (Lott & Maluso, 1995, p. 3). Terms used to describe these subtle forms include aversive racism, symbolic racism, modern racism, regressive racism, and ambivalent racism (Maluso, 1995).

A strong argument has been made for increasingly indirect modes of expression in the United States throughout the decade of the 1980s and beyond (Gaertner & Dovidio, 1986; Giles & Evans, 1986; Hecht, Collier, & Ribeau, 1993; Hecht, Ribeau, & Alberts, 1989; Pettigrew, 1981, 1985; Terkel, 1992; Zatz, 1987). For example, Zatz (1987) concludes that the effect of race on court sentencing is moderated by variables such as bail status. Whereas van Dijk (1987) finds direct expression of prejudice in topics of conversations when those conversations are held within the boundaries of an ethnic group (e.g., minorities as criminal or lazy), less direct expressions are found in argument forms (e.g., arguments about immigration, affirmative action, or learning English). Interestingly, this indirectness also is found outside the United States (Stern, 1991; van Dijk, 1987; Wodak, 1991). Has the recent rise in hate crimes and electronic expressions of prejudice reversed this trend? What are the differences between these forms of expression in function and impact? Holton (Chapter 16 in this volume) believes that the more direct forms have had less deleterious psychological effects in her life. She argues that it is psychologically easier for her to cope when one knows where one stands in the face of direct prejudice. In addition, indirect prejudice creates a difficult rhetorical position. If one directly addresses the implied prejudice, then indirect messages have "deniability." A person who does not address the prejudice may be left feeling that he or she participated in the prejudice, what Wolf (1986) refers to as "legitimizing oppression." Wood Holten tells us about her daily experiences of these indirect forms, recalling a job in which she was placed for a long period at the desk for those "on trial," which continually implied that her talents were suspect and under scrutiny. Are racial nicknames, particularly American Indian terms (e.g., Washington Redskins, Cleveland Indians, Atlanta Braves) or cheers (e.g., tomahawk chop) for sports teams direct or indirect expressions? What is the role of hate speech (Whillock & Slayden, 1995)? Calvert (1997) separates the transmission and ritual effects of hate speech. *Transmission* effects examine the immediate and typically interpersonal impacts of hate speech. What effect does calling someone a name have on the target? Calvert summarizes research showing that these effects are real, including physical symptoms, but that courts are inclined to recognize harm only if the effects are physical. Conversely, *ritual* effects are those embedded in society including the continued subordination of certain groups and the reinforcement of stereotyping and discrimination. Racist hate speech, for example, perpetuates the view that race matters and that certain groups are different and inferior. Calvert argues that ritual effects are the basis for judicial judgments about the effects of hate speech in workplace harassment suits.

Regardless of the form of prejudice, it is clear that its effects are quite troublesome for individuals and society. Recent studies have chronicled the health hazards of routine, interpersonal discrimination (Williams & Collins, 1995), and the economic effects have been widely documented.

It is into this personal, historical, and cultural setting that we introduce this book on prejudice. It is our hope that our writings contribute to a constructive dialogue about prejudice by helping people understand what prejudice is and by providing a lexicon for discussing the issues that lead to appreciation for diversity of all types. We hope to expand the discussion from race/ethnicity to other "isms" to encourage people to think broadly about exclusion, discrimination, stereotyping, and other aspects of prejudice as well as to focus on their intersections and syntheses.

More specifically, the book focuses on the expression or communication of prejudice. Juxtaposed with increases in the extreme, overt, and direct forms of prejudice are the indirect forms of expression. Both of these forms are painted across a growing divide in the life experiences, values, and opinions of members of various groups who have increased daily contact. Mix in the issues of empowerment, context, and level of analysis, and we are presented with a puzzling picture of a culture in which prejudice is highly salient and its expression is suppressed to a point and then explodes into violence and other forms of extremist expression. The fragmented and contradictory images of prejudice that exist often war with each other, lending clarity only to "true believers" and leading to separation of camps into in-groups and out-groups of ideas or approaches, each with its own forms of prejudice toward others and their ideas. In many ways, these scholarly groups reflect the societal structures and processes that they set out to study with exclusion, in-group loyalties, out-group derogation, and intergroup ignorance characterizing discussions of prejudice. Status hierarchies within scholarly communities take on the structural properties of societal discriminatory practices. Thus, to understand the expression of prejudice, it is first necessary to articulate a synthetic framework, one that brings people together and promotes discussion, that treats difference as a positively valenced value and polarity or opposition as inherent in life rather than as "tense" or essentially negative.

We start the book with a chapter describing previous approaches to prejudice and then a chapter articulating a new layered perspective. These two chapters attempt to lay out the contours of the discussion—the perspectives that scholars have used to explain prejudice and a new stance from which to engage these perspectives in a constructive dialogue.

The first of these, John Baldwin's Chapter 2, describes four overall approaches to prejudice: evolutionary theories, group-level theories, individual-level theories, and message-based (rhetorical/critical) theories. *Evolutionary* theories focus on biological and evolutionary processes, often discussing the inborn or biologically programmed aspects of prejudice. *Group-level* and *structural* approaches stress the allocation of resources, structural issues, and groups as social entities. Some people who take this approach focus on the power relations and institutional dynamics and hierarchies. *Individual-level* approaches discuss the processes by which individuals come to perceive persons and groups as others or outsiders and their treatment of these people. *Linguistic* and *critical* approaches stress the role of language, with the critical camp adding an emphasis on power and hierarchy. Others taking this linguistic/critical perspective are concerned more generally with exclusionary processes, and they fall into the approach labeled *moral exclusion.*

After reviewing these theories, we were dissatisfied with their explanatory power. It seemed to us that each theory has limitations that could not be overcome with patching or piecemeal modifications. Instead, reflecting our value of appreciating diversity, we attempted to articulate a theoretical approach to prejudice that embraces and values difference. The resulting *layered theory of prejudice* is presented in Chapter 3. Michael Hecht and John Baldwin attempt to explain how the very differences in the perspectives articulated in Chapter 2 can be used theoretically as a model of how differences in society can lead to appreciation rather than intolerance. In other words, we attempt to build a metatheoretical perspective that mirrors our societal goals, one in which differences are valued and treated as opportunities for insight, experience, and growth rather than eliminated in service to the theoretical gods of logical consistency and parsimony.

The layered perspective starts with the metatheoretical construct of layering and then identifies four sensitizing constructs for understanding prejudice: stances, spheres, levels of analysis, and types or ways of understanding. *Layering* is a theoretical device for integrating and juxtaposing alternative experiences of the social world. We discuss a holographic character to this layering to avoid linearity. Dialectical thinking, for example, is one way of layering polarities in the social world and points us to the goal of problematizing or making problematic and uncertain. This approach may be layered on the competing goals of clarifying and making certain that arise out of more deterministic thinking. By layering these approaches, our perspective points to the value in both stabilizing and destabilizing. The layered perspective also "centers" the intersections and synthesis of ideas, contexts, process, and identities. These locales provide opportunities for insight at the borders, cross sections, and integrations of theories, processes, and groups. They also avoid the problems of reducing people to a single aspect of their identity that essentializes them as that element and of recreating the categories and associated problems we hope to redress. Ono's chapter in this volume (Chapter 11) provides a shining example of looking for new locales at intersections to avoid recreating the very divisions we seek to study when we isolate and essentialize a single identity. Thus, layering may be applied to descriptions of social experiences, theories, and methods.

Four sensitizing constructs help us identify the salient layers of prejudice. *Stances* refer to the levels of acceptance of an out-group or of an out-group member (intolerance, tolerance, appreciation). *Spheres* are group-based identities along with which prejudice exists (e.g., the "isms" of racism, sexism, ageism, heterosexism/homophobia, classism). *Levels or layers of analysis* describe the foci where social phenomena occur and can be studied (e.g., individual, interaction, relationship, community). *Types of understanding* refer to the various ways of seeing the world (both ontological and epistemological).

Once the groundwork has been laid in Part I, the book proceeds through three sections to describe prejudice and its expression using the layered perspective as a linguistic and descriptive system. Part II discusses the spheres of prejudice ("isms"), Part III explores the contexts of prejudice, Part IV presents personal narratives, and Part V addresses interventions designed as responses to prejudice.

■ Part II: Spheres of Prejudice

In Part II, we explore the spheres or "isms" (e.g., racism, sexism, heterosexism/homophobia, ageism, classism). We recognize that these are not totally independent. Instead, navigating the dialectic of separation and connection between and among the spheres, each chapter in this section uses an "ism" as an organizing lens, focusing on it alone as well as in intersection and overlap with other spheres. We also recognize that not all spheres are centered or even explored. Among the more obvious, perhaps glaring exclusions is religious prejudice. Political commentators note the role of religious intolerance in the politics of hate (Means, 1994), whereas others explore specific religious prejudices (Wodak, 1991).

Less obvious prejudices also have been confronted in society but are not directly dealt with here. For example, Crandall (1994) argues that overt expressions of prejudice against "fat people" are minimally affected by current social norms about cultural sensitivity. Prejudice against "large people" has spawned a series of self-help books such as Schroeder's (1992) *Fat Is Not a Four-Letter Word* and Lauderback's (1970) *Fat Power.* An entire industry has developed to serve the needs of this group including clothing (e.g., The King Size Co. in Massachusetts and Phoenix Big and Tall in

Arizona), sports equipment (e.g., Skin Diver Wetsuits in Washington and Men of Measure in St. Louis, MO [a telemarketing firm]), jewelry (e.g., The Right Touch in New York), and furniture (e.g., Select Comfort Furniture in Minnesota and Attitudes in Virginia). Other prejudices (e.g., against the physically challenged) also are not focused on in this book. I acknowledge these shortcomings and regret them.

In Chapter 4, Molefi Asante discusses *racism.* Asante focuses his chapter on racist language. He begins by sounding the optimistic note of a promise for a new beginning. However, he also notes the political nature of communication and quickly shifts to a discussion of offensive speech, commenting on the entanglement of racism in "the most intricate patterns of our conversation and language." Asante, using Afrocentrism, argues that, when applied to Black-White relationships, the "communication of racism is fundamentally the communication of Whiteness as status property" and Blackness as "a lack of status." The chapter then goes on to discuss the contexts in which racist speech occurs and its directness or indirectness, the power dynamics that underlie racist language (e.g., through definitions, initiation rites, and stifling opposition), speech acts (e.g., opinion, belief, fact), and the role of racism in the structure of knowledge in U.S. culture.

Lana Rakow and Laura Wackwitz address the communication of sexism in Chapter 5. Rakow and Wackwitz discuss sexism as one *belief system* about gender and examine the "layered ways in which sexism is communicated to create and maintain its status as a primary belief system." *Feminism* is articulated as an oppositional belief system. Various forms of sexist belief systems are then discussed (e.g., grounding in the perceived origins of difference such as religion, biology, and social order) and critiqued from a feminist way of understanding. In the process, various layers or branches of feminism are brought into play. The authors then examine the intersection of racism and sexism, the double jeopardy faced by women of color, and the sexist redefinition of cultural beliefs with and between these racial groups. The chapter then shifts its focus to examine *sexist language* beginning with an assertion that sexism is built into structure, content, and usage; sexism in *interaction* including the categories of "male" and "female" and interactional patterning; and *sexism in representational systems* such as media news. Rakow and Wackwitz end by suggesting strategies for change; discussing language, feminist politics, and sexual harassment; and noting feminist political activism and the attendant reactionary backlash.

Thomas Nakayama focuses his remarks in Chapter 6 on homophobia/heterosexism. He structures his chapter to reflect the layering of contemporary society and current thinking by providing news reports about heterosexism as well as discursive text. His discursive treatment begins by juxtaposing definitions of *homophobia* and *heterosexism* as two layers of intolerance. Like Rakow and Wackwitz, Nakayama treats heterosexism as a *belief system.* Whereas sexism privileges maleness, heterosexism privileges certain sexual practices. Nakayama reserves homophobia for emotional reactions and questions which term has more rhetorical force. He then moves to the communication practices that support these forms. Starting with *heteronormity,* which has its parallel in Rakow and Wackwitz's discussion of assumed or centered maleness, Nakayama unpacks the role of *silence* on individual and social levels. Echoing Corey's decrying the silence in his life and relationships (see Chapter 15 in this volume), Nakayama looks at laws and social practices surrounding marriage, domestic violence, rape, and taxes. He then moves on to examine stereotypes, starting with the problem of essentializing[3] people in terms of their sexual activities. Nakayama argues that the term *homosexual* defines gays only in terms of their sexual activities, poignantly asking how it would look if heterosexuals were similarly defined only in terms of their sexuality. Nakayama ends by returning to the relentlessness of heterosexism and a call for opposition.

Classism is the central topic of Dreama Moon and Garry Rolison in Chapter 7. They begin with the argument that class is not purely economic but rather is cultural as well. They are concerned about the cultural messages about class that are communicated particularly to the poor and the working class. Moon and Rolison illustrate how class is inscribed in verbal and nonverbal messages through two examples: the trailer park and fashion. They talk about how these discussions naturalize classism by treating class differences as if they were a natural part of community. The chapter then shifts to a discussion of how class operates by rendering nondominant class members invisible or hypervisible through discourses that define ego- and alter-ideology (i.e., through defining who we are and who we are not), and by unidirectionally marking difference downward. Poor people often are rendered invisible (e.g., the janitor whose name we forget) or hypervisible through stereotypes. This discussion examines how class and classism are marked and how they stigmatize or devalue lower classes and things lower class. In this discussion, Moon and Rolison critique the "culture of poverty" position because it ignores the structural aspects of economics and blames the victims. They use this discussion to emphasize the importance of both structural and "ordinary" (e.g., interpersonal, attitudinal) elements and to examine welfare reform as classism. The chapter also examines the intolerance myth that only social extreme types (e.g., "skinheads") are classist and that typical middle class people are not. They note that whereas class prejudice may be experienced by anyone, classism is only downward. This stand is one of the contested elements in the general discourse about prejudice: Who can be prejudiced, and who can discriminate? Moon and Rolison conclude by noting methodological issues in the study of class (e.g., the use of checklists) and critiquing the position that classism is primarily an attitude rather than an expression of unequal structural relations. They encourage researchers to take up the study of class from the joint lenses of structural, media, and interpersonal (ordinary discourse and individual attitudes) perspectives within a historical context.

Angie Williams and Howard Giles examine ageism in Chapter 8. They begin with the assumption, supported by research, that older people are communicated with in a way that reflects pervasive negative stereotypes. Media portrayals of the old reinforce these stereotypes, which present older people as frail, weak, unattractive, and useless, and older women often suffer the consequences of "double jeopardy." All stereotypes, however, are not inherently negative. Older people also are "appreciated" as worthy and deserving. Examining communication between older people and other groups as "intergroup communication," Williams and Giles characterize communication to the elderly as often patronizing, depersonalized, and disrespectful. They then summarize research on the perception of older people, concluding that older speech is recognizable and stereotyped. When older and younger people talk, older people typically do not adjust or accommodate to the younger communicators, whereas younger communicators tend to "overaccommodate" or adjust too much, often trying too hard and appearing condescending. Finally, Williams and Giles address responses to ageism, examining older people's participation in the ageism or taking advantage of it as well as oppositional strategies such as conversational avoidance of unwanted social comparisons, topic switching, dominating the conversation, and social change strategies at the group and communal levels.

■ Part III: Contexts of Prejudice

Part III cuts across the "isms" to explore the levels or contexts of prejudicial communication: personal relationships, organizations, the media, and the state. Although there are other ways of defining levels of analysis, these chapters seem to conform to research frames (e.g., people who study personal relationships are different from those who study organizations) as well as the practical experiences of everyday life (e.g., people commonly separate their personal relationships from their job-related experiences). As before, I apologize for any exclusion that offends or fails to inform adequately.

What happens when prejudice pervades personal relationships? In Chapter 9, Stanley Gaines, Julie Chalfin, Mary Kim, and Patrick Taing explore this context of prejudice. Gaines and colleagues start with the observation that the field of personal relationships rarely has dealt with the spheres of prejudice other than sexism, using the metaphor of relationships as "islands unto themselves" to describe how these studies have deflected consideration of these issues. They argue that this study must be grounded in an understanding of the relationship context (e.g., family relationships, friends) and cultural norms and values, using relationships as a "conceptual bridge" between individualistic and societal levels of prejudice. They then apply communication accommodation theory to this context, focusing on processes of divergence and convergence, under- and overaccommodation, and in-group/out-group bias to make predictions about when overt and covert expressions of prejudice should be manifested. The chapter then discusses situations in which the spheres are more or less likely to be present and the role of power differentials. The chapter ends with an exemplar of Black-Jewish friendships, drawing on the dialogue between Cornel West and Michael Lerner.

Earlier in the present chapter, I discussed prejudice's pervasive economic impact. Perhaps the primary arena for this effect is organizational life in the United States. Sheryl Lindsley draws on her research and personal experience in organizations to describe how prejudice functions in our businesses and industries in Chapter 10. Lindsley begins with a discussion of equality and its implications for organizational life including government policies and organizational practices. She describes historical trends in equal employment opportunity laws and economic changes over the past three decades. Economic trends are then linked to intergroup tensions, with increased intergroup disparities and divisiveness arising out of worsening economic conditions and increased competition for scarce resources. Lindsley then describes mass-mediated images of diversity in organizations, pointing to coverage of race and gender "wars" that polarize opinions and media images that trivialize tolerance movements and, in so doing, attenuate their effectiveness. Lindsley then explores the negative effects of affirmative action programs that may stigmatize protected groups and also discusses how organizations, themselves, enact prejudicial actions. The chapter includes an examination of the stigma that White males feel is attached to the intersection of their gender and ethnicity.

The effects of media are felt in all areas of our lives. Televisions, radios, and telephones have penetrated into almost all U.S. households, and the effects of newspapers, movies, and computers are felt throughout the culture. In Chapter 11, Kent Ono writes about how prejudice is communicated in the media. Ono focuses his discussion on representations of race and seeks an analytic frame that avoids recreating the system it attempts to critique. In other words, Ono seeks to articulate a lens for explicating media that neither embraces racialization and racial divisions nor accepts a priori racial definitions that maintain existing hierarchies. After reviewing the predominant trends in research on media representations of race (good/bad representations, discrimination, pedagogy about race, audience reception, images and stereotypes, and uses and gratifications), Ono describes recent trends that examine Whiteness, diaspora, exhilic experiences, and "otherness." From these trends, Ono builds his discussion based on the assumption that media representations are sites of political contestation involving disparities of power. He is concerned with how media images participate in the construction of political realities in addition to reflecting social practice. To accomplish these goals, Ono chooses a text, *Doubles,* which problematizes binary, essentializing constructions of race by focusing on bi- and mixed-race people to challenge images of racial purity and unpack the practice of substituting "American" for "White." Ono challenges "a rigid dialectic between 'Japanese' and 'American' " and discusses social marginalization.

■ Part IV: Narratives

Once these first three sections have explored prejudice in a largely discursive fashion, Part IV presents personal narratives. These narratives are intended as an alternative, scholarly mode of expression for the theories and concepts. Although they provide useful exemplars of the concepts, structures, and processes discussed in the first three sections, the narratives are intended here as an alternative way of knowing—a mode invested in narrativity as a way of knowing, understanding, studying, and expressing. Geertz (1988) urges us to pay more attention to the use of language in scholarly discourse. Our means of expression, he notes, are not sterile in their rhetorical effects. Drawing on the influence of Kenneth Burke, Geertz argues that style and substance both are components of effective scientific writing.

Human thought and behavior are at least partially based in narratives. Narratives are a pervasive, transcultural (White, 1980) mode of discourse through which people organize information and experiences of the world. Not only are they one of the primary means for making sense of experience (Cook-Gumperz, 1993; Fisher, 1987) and moral choices (Botvin, Schinke, Epstein, Diaz, & Botvin, 1995), but they also serve as an organizing principle for behavior (Howard, 1991; Sarbin, 1986). More than thought, narratives are a meaningful form of communicative behavior. "Much of what passes for everyday conversation among people is storytelling of one form or another" (McAdams, 1993, p. 28). Thus, narrative is an important cognitive form and communication process.

In this light, expressing knowledge or scholarship as personal narrative appears imminently reasonable. Personal narratives provide "experience-near accounts" of the phenomenon. Each narrative describes an author's experience of prejudice in his or her personal and/or professional life. These are meant to provide ethnographic and personal descriptions to present prejudice in a different medium. As Cristina González has said to me, poetry and other creative forms allow "expression of abstract understanding in a form that corresponds to its nature instead of forcing it into a linear and concrete nature of meaning." These narratives, then, are a form of scholarship in and of themselves—a form comparable to, but different from, the discursive texts that populate most academic journals and books. Thus, we would hope that they not be seen as "mere examples." Instead, they are intended as scholarly discourse in the same manner as the chapters preceding them.

The narratives that appear in this book are diverse in style and content. María Cristina González, in Chapter 12, mixes discursive text with poetry. Her narrative takes us on a journey through hierarchies to which she attributes prejudice and examines the damage to the spirit that such experience brings. Her text focuses us on the human tendency to prejudge and shows us how pervasive this tendency truly is. Through her poems and discursive text, she shows us how competition and hierarchy become "naturalized" (i.e., treated as the natural order of the world). The poems, in particular, show us the distancing and demeaning ways in which humans treat each other based on perceived differences.

Victor Villanueva, in Chapter 13, talks to the struggle with lack of acceptance—a struggle with the assumptions laid on his very existence. His narrative shows us how even "compliments" or "positive" evaluations place a burden when they are offered in a prejudiced context and shows how hard it is for those struggling against prejudice in oppressed and mainstream groups. Actions naively intended as compliments can add to the walls, darts, and obstacles faced. Villanueva also discusses the varying perceptions of his ethnicity. Is he White, Blancito, brown, or Jewish? Who defines this? Who makes this call? Is identity self-selected or ascribed? If self-selected, then does the group to which one aspires have to accept the membership application? Does the mainstream culture have the power to impose its definitions? Not too long ago, segments of the U.S. population were dismayed at news stories reporting a trend among adolescents, some of whom were prepubescent, to claim bisexuality. Others were troubled by "Black" youths claiming Latino identities, by "Chinese" American youths claiming Blackness, and so on. Were these young people "confused" about their identities or merely making a postmodern claim to indeterminancy? Who is to decide? Who is the arbiter? If a "White heterosexual" youth claims to be a bisexual Black, then are we to hate him or her?

Laura Tohe's poems document the struggles of American Indians in a mainstream culture that neither supports nor accepts this stream of diversity. Her poem, "The Names," in Chapter 14 rang a particularly responsive chord with my family history and its stories. My mother went to school in postwar Brooklyn, New York, as a young, Jewish, first-generation American with a Yiddish name that can be transliterated to "Mehrhul." The teacher, unable to pronounce it, renamed her "Mary." Obedient and wanting to assimilate as her family had been unable to do in "Rush-Poland" (Russia and Poland), as she called the land whose pogroms her family had fled, she accepted a name that represented a key figure in a religion (Christianity) that had been used by the Nazis and other groups in anti-Semitic oppression. Others may find that this resonates with their family histories if their surnames were modified by customs agents when their ancestors migrated to the United States.

Frederick Corey's narrative in Chapter 15 struggles with the personal drama of family acceptance for a son while explicating the insidious nature of homophobia/heterosexism, a form of prejudice that runs so deep it allows people to oppress and harm even those they love the most dearly. At the same time, his narrative suggests some universals of prejudice that transcend the spheres in his perceptions of his parents' prejudices toward certain prospective partners.

Deborah Wood Holton, in Chapter 16, provides us with a series of episodes depicting the experiences of an African American woman that show us prejudice intertwined in the most subtle of everyday experiences and allow us to experience, with her, the ongoing and exhausting struggle of one faced with prejudice on a daily basis. Holton reveals for us the energy that is expended in a social world that constantly asks for proof.

■ Part V: Interventions

It should be obvious from the discussion to this point that prejudice is a pervasive and deeply rooted problem with multiple causes and manifestations existing across different strata of society. Part of the problem is that prejudice appears to have its social-psychological basis in social categorization that develops early in life. For example, in one study (Bar-Tal, 1996), Israeli Jewish children had a concept of "Arab" by $2\frac{1}{2}$ to 3 years of age. The children develop these categories not on the basis of physical observable differences but rather on the basis of a social ontology or the folk theory of the culture. Only one third of the young children believe they can identify Arabs on the street, whereas by 9 to 12 years of age almost all say they can. Also, younger children define "Arab" in terms of violent and aggressive behaviors rather than physical traits and cannot draw or recognize pictures of Arabs. Physical descriptors do not appear until 9 to 12 years of age. These images are developed from parents, peers, media, and interactions. It appears that prejudice is like other developmental processes, with older children and adolescents making greater distinctions based on ethnicity and race than do younger children (Hartup, 1983). However, in another study, Aboud and Doyle

(1996) find that children's racial attitudes are not strongly related to their mothers' or friends' attitudes. Thus, it appears that the development of prejudice may be grounded in a cultural ideology or narrative in which a variety of factors play socializing roles. This means that intervention at one point in the system will not alter the prevailing prejudicial cultural narratives.

Part V addresses interventions designed to deal with prejudice at the individual, organizational, and educational levels. I originally asked the authors to address "solutions" but quickly became aware that this implied a permanent and positive outcome— the elimination of prejudice. It seems clear that such a state is unrealistically idealistic. Instead, we need to think in terms of interventions, responses, and so on. This section, of course, only begins to address the issues of successful intervention. Resources such as Ponterotto and Pedersen's (1993) book and the *Teaching Tolerance* series put out by the Southern Poverty Law Center can provide help in developing interventions. But it is clear that, like most societal problems, prejudice must be addressed across different layers and through multiple tactics and strategies.

Part V begins with Flavio Marsiglia and Michael Hecht examining personal and interpersonal interventions in Chapter 17. We start by noting the role of boundaries and boundary crossing as a key dimension to prejudice. We also note the role of narratives in creating and maintaining the boundaries that separate people and inhibit boundary crossing. Realists moderate our goals while seeking movement toward appreciation, not tolerance.

Marsiglia and Hecht view prejudice as the consequence and explanation of oppression and, as a result, believe that liberation must be central to prejudice. We review research describing individual liberatory actions—how individuals can confront prejudice in their everyday lives.

While stressing that prejudice has an internal logic of its own and operates on both conscious and unconscious levels, Marsiglia and Hecht discuss the contact hypothesis and multiculturalism. We start by discussing obstacles to interventions including the fact that people insulate themselves from information that challenges their existing beliefs and tend to be more favorable toward individual members of a category than they are toward the entire category. It also is difficult to create the type of contact needed to reduce prejudice in the "real world" with long-standing intergroup hostility and, in any case, stereotypes that are very stable. In fact, research shows that frequent contact may even hamper relations. Finally, people often do not generalize from the individual to the group, and there are, of course, structural impediments to change. Next, the chapter describes conditions under which contact can facilitate positive relationships including equal status relationships, cooperation and interdependence, supportive climates, opportunities for personal relationships, opportunities for self-revealing interactions, and egalitarian norms. Under these conditions, exposure to heterogeneous members of the out-group may reduce prejudice. Finally, a number of theories of contact are reviewed including the following:

- Common in-group identity model, which posits that effective contact occurs when members' perceptions of two separate groups ("us" and "them") becomes one inclusive category ("we") through creation of a superordinate identification
- Personalization model, which posits that contact will be effective if it consists of highly personalized rather than category-based interaction
- Distinct social identity model, which argues that positive, group-based contact is needed and that intergroup contact should be cooperative and pleasant with group membership salient (groups should be given distinct but complementary roles to play in a common task)
- Theory of optimal distinctiveness, which posits that contact is effective when it balances the need for inclusion or belonging with the need for exclusion or uniqueness and achieves an equilibrium

Following this presentation, we present two models for shaping interventions based on the contact hypothesis and its extensions. However, we also question the effectiveness of contact and multiculturalism. The chapter instead offers cosmopolitanism, an approach in which differences are appreciated and multiple realities are embraced. The chapter concludes with specific suggestions including self-awareness, language strategies, concerns about access to organizations and institutions, political action, and the role of education. We call on the helping professions to participate in this process and challenge us to seek a world in which appreciation is the norm.

Chapter 18, focusing on organizational solutions, is contributed by Sheryl Lindsley, extending her thinking about organizations as a context for prejudice presented in Chapter 10. Lindsley argues that diversity training programs are designed to reduce treatment discrimination (i.e., differential treatment of groups) and to value diversity for its own sake. She notes the prevalence of corporations already engaged in this process.

Lindsley then describes steps for developing training programs:

- Gain top management support through a solid rationale based on reducing costs (e.g., lawsuits, turnover), improving productivity, and expanding markets.
- Conduct a needs assessment through a variety of research methods to specify the issues.
- Develop a clear conceptualization of the problem. Too often, programs target sensitizing European American males by teaching them about other groups. This is problematic because it often winds up reinforcing stereotypes or encouraging overaccommodation, which is perceived as condescending.
- Address multiple layers including interpersonal discrimination, achievement barriers, and organizational systems. Lindsley notes that separating diversity from other training marginalizes it and minimizes its effectiveness.
- Develop short- and long-term objectives because true change is slow at best.

The chapter concludes with case studies of successful diversity training.

Gale Young examines the educational system as a site for intervention in Chapter 19. Young uses a "virtual discussion" format that brings together experts in the field. These experts were asked to express their opinions about educational interventions, and their responses are organized into a discussion by Young. Other experts are injected into the discussion through their published works. This discussion was then fed back to the contributors for editing and additional comments. This iterative process was carried out until a chapter with consensual agreement was derived.

The chapter has a number of important points to make. As a frame of reference, a sense of pessimism pervades the views as the discussants describe the pervasiveness of the problem. There seems to be a sense that solutions exist that can be effective if the desire for them to be so is there. The discussants question this desire. However, the discussants also note the importance of opposition, no matter how limited in focus, so that prejudice can be confronted and solutions can emerge.

The final intervention chapter is contributed by Stephanie Brzuzy, who discusses policy issues in Chapter 20. Brzuzy explains that public policy can be a solution or can reinforce prejudice, providing historical examples of slavery laws, women's rights, and immigrant and gay/lesbian rights. Brzuzy provides voting rights as an exemplar of policy that has done both. Initially, laws restricted voting to White males. Laws slowly were passed that opened the vote to Black men, to women, and, finally in 1940, to Native Americans. However, policies such as poll taxes, literacy tests, and intimidation were used to counter this movement, and it took federal legislation to create an atmosphere in which the vote was open to all citizens.

Brzuzy then examines the Americans with Disability Act (ADA) as an exemplar of policy designed as a solution and examines the Defense of Marriage Act (DOMA) as one designed to reinforce prejudice. The ADA has opened up access to public places and services. Its impact has been on a number of levels including decreased interpersonal isolation and increased availability of jobs. The DOMA, on the other hand, limited the opportunities available to gays and lesbians.

Finally, Brzuzy lays out a primer on public policy. She suggests a response on multiple levels including national, state, and local governments. To achieve public policy requires education and awareness, organization and coalition building, influence on policymakers, and passage of legislation. Maintaining policy intervention requires educating the public about benefits, monitoring enforcement, and attending to both the spirit and the letter of the law. The chapter ends with a call to use our power to affect policy.

■ Part VI: Conclusion

Finally, it was the editor's job to construct a "conclusion" to this book. I include quotations around the word because cultural knowledge must be a process, and the meanings of these thoughts will evolve over time. I do call for greater focus on the stance of *appreciation* and the *interpenetrations* among layers to complement our understanding of prejudice. In addition, I believe that our theories must be careful not to recreate the prejudicial and discriminatory systems they study and not to treat difference as bad. But because I wish to keep the discussion open-ended, I decided to write an (in)conclusion, which allows the chapters to largely speak for themselves and makes no attempt to "unproblematize" their ideas and intersections. I hope that the patterns and trends I have pointed out in this introduction, as well as the use of the layered perspective as a common language, provide a thread for the reader.

2 Tolerance/Intolerance

A Multidisciplinary View of Prejudice

John R. Baldwin

It is difficult to locate the world at the end of the 20th century in terms of tolerance and intolerance. On the one hand, we would hope that tolerance is increasing and that people would be living together in more harmony. The fall of the Berlin Wall, the warming of the cold war, and the eminent possibility of a Mideast peace suggest that this may be the case. On the other hand, hate crimes are increasing in various corners of the world, new and old ethnic conflicts come and go, and new instances of violence emerge. Headlines of the past 2 years tell the tale: civil uprising in Chiapas, Mexico; strife between Catholic and Protestant Irish; and ongoing tensions between Hutus and Tutsis, Iraqis and Kurds, and Serbs and Croats. In the United States, headlines at the writing of this chapter talk of the Women's World Caucus in China, racism and racial divides in the O. J. Simpson trial, political debates over the inclusion or exclusion of "foreigners," and so on. Issues of racism, sexism, and classism are anything but diminished at our juncture in time.

The demand for an understanding of tolerance and intolerance seems to be at an all-time high. The world is multipolar (Boggs, 1990); religious groups, political entities, and racial/ethnic groups strive together to cocreate the future of America and the world. Demographic diversity in workplaces and academic institutions, in many cultures around the world, is now accepted as a given. But the presence of diversity among members does not guarantee acceptance of people, cultures, voices, and experiences. Instead, continued or even increasing intolerance often is the reality. What maintains these practices of intolerance that require so much energy and lead to so much negativity? Intolerance is a difficult thing to understand. It is hard to grasp, for example, all of the intricacies of the situation in the Balkans and the resulting intolerances. Religious beliefs, ethnic heritage, and desire for land and resources collide to weave a web that seems impossible to untangle. Around the world, people murder in the name of gods of peace; people exclude in the name of justice and establish hierarchy in the name of equality. Even greater difficulty is encountered when one tries to get a single, general understanding of intolerance that will apply to all situations in the world.

■ "Theorizing" Prejudice

Many scholars try to do just that—find a way in which to explain all intolerance that is or that was. This attempt runs into at least two problems, as I see it. First, such attempts are framed by the writers' own perspectives and experiences (including academic training). Someone might look at ageism in the United States and chalk it up to "ignorance" based on the speakers, books, and media with which one has experience. However, this would not take into account many of the other facets of "age" in the country. Academic perspectives often run into the same "point-of-view" problems as do everyday explanations of prejudice. They rarely are synthetic. Instead, they separate from other perspectives or explanations of the same intolerance. They practice exclusion in the service of the study of exclusion/inclusion.

A possible start to understanding the broader picture of prejudice is to look at how different people try to explain it and to seek a way in which to integrate the various perspectives. This chapter describes some of the approaches scholars take to explain intolerance. Each group of scholars looks at the world from a particular perspective, focusing on specific influences on intolerance. This does not mean that scholars do not consider influences outside of their respective perspectives; it only means that each of us tends to work within our own area of focus. Because I believe that intolerances differ from one another and across culture and time (Baldwin & Hecht, 1995), it would seem that a given situation might be better explained by one perspective or another—or by a combination or intersection of certain perspectives. Intolerance of a certain group, such as race or gender, might be understood in a general framework but also should be looked at in its own specific cultural and historical context (see Hecht and Baldwin's chapter in this volume [Chapter 3]).

The primary reason for considering the multiple roots of intolerance is so that more holistic explanations can be derived that lead to more effective solutions. One can scarcely hope to solve a problem without first understanding its nature and nuances. These explanations and understandings must of necessity deal with the complexity and contradictory nature of the problem. Fragmentary explanations leading to isolated and limited solutions may be doomed to failure as they are inserted into the system. For example, it is possible that "political correctness" has made the United States a more tolerable place for members of oppressed minorities to live. The focus on politically correct (PC) language may have helped curb open expressions of intolerance (see one of Lindsley's chapters in this volume [Chapter 10]). However, the rise in hate crimes through the 1980s and into the 1990s ("FBI," 1993; Terkel, 1992) and the overtness of other forms of intolerance (e.g., toward immigrants) may suggest that intolerance itself has not changed and that only the form in which it is expressed has changed. Addressing it may require structural changes in institutions such as education, the media, and the courts; social changes such as PC language; and individual changes as well. Examining the multiple roots of prejudice can yield a more complete understanding of the problem and enable more effective solutions. Thus, this chapter has the dual purpose of understanding and action/practice. This practical focus reveals an underlying value to our research. Whereas some scholars hold that research should be "value free," I suggest that all research—even that which claims to be value free—is laden with values (Bernstein, 1976; Lincoln & Guba, 1985). Some values are worthwhile in research. Thus, I embrace the value of tolerance as one that should guide our lives and our research.

■ Approaches to Understanding Intolerance

In the past several decades, many authors have made attempts at explaining intolerance. This section considers four of these that may not be the only approaches but are central to our knowledge and interpretation of the area. I have adopted an alphabetical order of the perspectives so as not to "center" on any one approach. Specifically, I look at four perspectives or groups of theories: evolutionary theories, group-level theories, individual-level theories, and message-based (rhetorical/critical) theories.

■ Evolutionary Perspectives (the sociobiological approach)

One set of explanations of prejudice suggests that, regardless of social or personal influences, intolerance is innate or at least has a biological basis. The evolutionary approach suggests that there are innate biological factors that drive intolerance. This basic biological premise is played out in various ways. Some suggest that character dispositions, intelligence, and other traits are biologically specific to race or gender (e.g., Herrnstein & Murray, 1994) and that, as a result, there supposedly are real reasons for making discriminations due to "group belongingness."

Other evolutionary theorists explain intolerance itself through heredity. One group is concerned about how biological being or physiology (e.g., genetics, structure of the brain) influences behavior. These people would be concerned about some basic mechanism in the brain, for example, that leads people to fear difference (Sperber, 1994). Others are concerned with the evolutionary value of prejudice or tolerance. These people would argue that those who fear, separate from, mistrust, or mistreat other groups do so based on instincts common to all humans and to other animal species (Reynolds, Falger, & Vine, 1987). Both positions are based on biology causing/affecting behavior. The first position is more concerned with the biological structures, whereas the second looks at the evolutionary processes by which these structures are selected. In either case, genetic characteristics or instinctual traits are in some way influenced by environment or socialization (Stepan, 1991). Thus, some call this the *sociobiological approach*.[4]

Genetics as a Basis for Exclusion

Many of the oldest explanations of intolerance are based on the claim that the target is actually the source of intolerance. Throughout time, people have held that the reason they are intolerant toward some group (e.g., Barbarians, Gentiles, Heathens) is because there is something in that group meritorious of mistreatment. Such explanations found a new so-called justification with the advancement of modern science. In the late 1800s and early 1900s, a scientific philosophy known as eugenics swept through Nazi Germany, Europe, and the United States. In Europe, Francois Bernier, Carolus Linnaeus, Georges Louis Leclerc, Pieter Camper, Johann Kaspar Lavater, and Franz Joseph Gall laid the foundations for scientific racism (West, 1982, pp. 55-59). Eugenics, the concept of breeding humans to achieve greater (racial) purity and quality, soon spread in various forms from Europe to the United States (Glass, 1986) and Latin America (Martínez-Echazábel, 1988; Stepan, 1991). For example, in Latin America, eugenics led to attempts at "racial health" through selective immigration, forced sterilization of women, and so on (Stepan, 1991). In Mexico, José Vasconcelos turned the conclusions of eugenics upside down by insisting on a *spiritual* (as opposed to a *biological*) eugenics. Although this synergistic concept of the *raza cósmica* may have given those of mixed racial heritage a better national self-image, it led to a "depreciation of the Indian as an acceptable part of the national fabric. . . . It admitted them as long as they adapted to modernity and adopted the rationalism and materialism of the Mexican state" (Stepan, 1991, p. 150).[5]

Genetics continue to be used as the basis of some scientific theory. Franklin (1991) details a 1988 memorandum to AT&T and a 1990 *New York Times* article in which some professors urged that African Americans' IQ scores, lower for supposed "racially" based genetic reasons, make them less capable of business or academic posts that have increased "intellectual demands" (p. 43). (I should note that strong challenges stand against Eurocentric IQ measures [Allport, 1954/1979; Gould, 1981].) More recently, *The Bell Curve* (Herrnstein & Murray, 1994) suggests that racial differences are due to genetics, and Begley (1995) recounts scientific discoveries of the different processing in the brain by women and men. Where do these differences come from? Cowley (1995) suggests that "the nature-nurture dichotomy is itself an illusion. As many scholars are now realizing, everything we associate with 'nurture' is at some level a product of our biology" (p. 52). At the same time, our biology is shaped by our environment. These conclusions suggest a fine line between eugenics, which used genetics as a basis for exclusion, and genetic science in general. Glass (1986) is quick to point out that many geneticists have strongly opposed eugenics.

Prejudice as an Inherited Trait

Evolutionary theory is related to genetics, as it sees social behavior in terms of inherited traits (although the focus is more on evolution than on genetics). Purported commonalities between humans and other animals lead evolutionary theorists to explain the psychological and social roots of intolerance in terms of biological evolution (Reynolds et al., 1987). This approach is based on the premise that evolutionary drive leads species to attempt to better adapt to their environments and preserve their groups (Ross, 1991; Vine, 1987). Evolutionary theorists propose that "communication strategies that have provided a survival advantage" will be "naturally selected" (Trost & Kenrick, 1993, p. 121).

For some evolutionary theorists, the strongest subconscious human striving is for the propagation of the species or group, which is done through "inclusive fitness, meaning the survival of their genes, either through their own reproduction or through the survival of close relatives with whom they have many genes in common" (Ross, 1991, p. 169). Self-propagation supposedly occurs through fear of strangers, conformity enforcement, antipredator aggression, or enforcement of group solidarity (van der Dennen, 1987). Many evolutionary theorists believe that these traits are inherited to help propagate the race (Vine, 1987). Thus, the evolutionary perspective finds easy application in intergroup relations (Reynolds, 1987).

Several of the authors in Reynolds et al.'s (1987) edited volume discuss ethnocentrism specifically. Van der Dennen (1987) reviews several past theories of ethnocentrism from various disciplines and then compares them with fear of strangers, animal aggression, conformity reinforcement, antipredator aggression, "safety-valve" outlets for hostility, rejection of deviants, group differentiation, and scapegoating. One element van der Dennen does not see acknowledged in these theories is fear; that is, "fear of the stranger and what the stranger incorporates: the strange, the unknown, the out-of-control, the potential chaos, the potential evil, the potential impurity, contamination and pollution, the potential threat and danger" (p. 43). Just like many of the preceding traits, fear is found in all animal species and likely comes from their evolutionary pasts. Allen (1993) proposes that "humans . . . have an innate fear and hostility to strangers" and that "strangerfear is the mysterious mechanism that creates in- and out-groups" (p. 2). Allen notes,

> Freed from the necessity of proving innate strangerfear in man and beast, it is now possible to demonstrate how much of modern conflict is caused by that innate hostility to strangers. The very diversity of the proof and the many different cultural contexts within which the proof is found actually cancels out culture as a source of hostility to strangers, as cultural influence working in one direction in one society is negated by a different cultural influence working in the opposite direction in another society. When all cultural influences are cancelled out, there is nothing left but [that] the influence that the consistent hostility to strangers we see in diverse modern societies has an innate cause. (p. 87)

Allen does not leave us to cultural proofs alone. He spends the first half of his book comparing human behavior to that of rhesus monkeys, chickens, quails, wasps, cockroaches, and so on to establish that fear of strangers exists across all species and is therefore biological. He goes on to use the fear of strangers to explain national disputes (between Israel and Palestine, Libya and Chad, Japan and Korea, and Iran and other Arab states) and religious conflict in India. Even prejudices within countries, such as the Japanese disdain for the Burakumin ("social rejects and pariahs who work at unclean and despised occupations such as animal slaughter, waste removal, and disposal of the dead" [p. 125]) and interethnic relations in general are explained through Allen's concept of "strangerfear."

Besides fear, another drive that may underlie intolerance is a human need for belonging and self-/social identity (Ross, 1991). Ross (1991) argues that selective inclusion (i.e., "kin selection") explanations of ethnocentrism are limited. *Cultural* evolution, and not simply *biological* evolution, must be considered. Two main aspects of this social evolution are sociality and self-/social identity. Regarding *sociality,* Ross suggests,

> Because so much of human existence has been spent in small communities in which neighbors were also kin, the high cooperation in small groups can be just as plausibly attributed to an evolved in-group bias favoring those with whom one has strong interpersonal relationships as it can be to biological relatedness. (p. 176)

Liking, affiliation, and belongingness, apart from biological links, can lead to exclusion of out-group members. This relates directly to *self-/social identity*; humans are highly social beings and possess a "strong evolved predisposition to develop a conscious sense of an individual and a social self" (p. 172). Ross cites studies that show a consistent preference for in-group members with tendencies to exaggerate group differences and to be antagonistic toward other groups.

Ross's (1991) own research of 90 "preindustrial societies" finds that whereas the level of conflict is determined by psychocultural causes, which targets are chosen is based on social-structural considerations. Thus, one cannot say that sociobiologists neglect the influences of culture. Dunbar (1987) suggests that "in all likelihood, the genetic basis for ethnocentrism, as with much human behaviour, is quite weak" (p. 56). Culture, as well as evolution, plays a role in determining the targets and forms of ethnocentrism:

> Xenophobia and ethnocentrism as extreme forms of this search for identity cannot be attributed to man's biology. . . . Their very existence is a result of man's attempts towards understanding the world, and his strong affective need to delimit a cosmos of conspecifics with whom he can share interpretations of his socially constructed world. (Meyer, 1987, p. 93)

A fear of strangers or need for group identification might be inborn. This also might be true of certain forms of deviant or out-group rejection. But the exact nature of the rejection and the definition and importance of the groups are left up to cultural determinations.

Van der Dennen (1987) adds something beyond mere culture: the power of symbols. He quotes von Bertalanffy as saying, "The most pernicious phenomena of aggression, transcending self-preservation and self-destruction, are based upon a characteristic feature of man above the biological level, namely his capability of creating symbolic universes in thought, language, and behavior" (quoted on p. 38). Van der Dennen goes on to summarize the "maliciousness of ideological conflicts" that characterize human intolerance:

The most extensive, quixotic, and disgusting violence is justified with the invocation of a utopian ideology, a paradise myth, a superiority doctrine, an eschatological or millenarian ideal state, or other highly abstract political/ethical categories, metaphysical values, and quasi-metaphysical mental monstrosities. . . . Ideological conflicts are so malicious and venomous because they are totalitarian in pretense. The collision of two different ideologies (social cosmologies, *Weltanschauungen,* symbolic universes, or definitions of reality) will have a dramatic course because the other worldview constitutes a threat by the mere fact of demonstrating that one's own worldview is not inevitable and absolute, but a more or less arbitrary construction; that our vision of reality is largely fictional: a collective delusional system, a social myth. And nothing is more terrifying and threatening to the ego than the prospect of chaos. (p. 39)

Self-protection, then, may not refer only to one's gene pool but also to one's cosmic worldview, one's symbol system, or one's language. This view could help explain many intolerances, such as prejudice between the French- and English-speaking Québéqois in Canada, intolerance between the Blanco and Colorado political parties in Colombia, and the struggle between pro-choice and pro-life forces in the United States. Self-protective traits explain xenophobia and international relations (Falger, 1987), race relations (Reynolds, 1987), and social prejudices in general (Flohr, 1987).

Analysis

The evolutionary perspective is appealing in that it looks across levels of reality. It is not as simple as it first appears. Branches of the theory do not limit their explanation to saying that all prejudice is inborn; rather, they consider the role of biology along with psychological, sociological, linguistic, and environmental influences and their interrelationships. Evolutionary theorists provide a plausible explanation for why intolerance is found in every society, with different views as to what (innately) lies at the root of this intolerance, yet allow for contextual differences. Finally, this perspective considers history. It allows one to look at how intolerance(s) might change over time, as in social evolution.

At the same time, the evolutionary perspective has had strong critics. Answering charges that sociobiologists are genetic determinists, many of this school respond that, because of behavioral flexibility and advanced cognitive processes, sociobiology would not *intend* to predict individual behavior (Dunbar, 1987; Reynolds et al., 1987) but instead is a probabilistic science. Some argue that these social aspects could not be inherited and that their inclusion leaves the theory without any specificity; that is, there is really no need, with considerations such as power and sociality, to resort to biological accounts. Furthermore, whereas many evolutionary theorists argue against genetic determinism, opponents charge that such determinism is inevitably implied by the theory. David Theo Goldberg (personal communication, April 2, 1993) holds that

the attempt of some to distance sociobiology from biological determinism on grounds of lack of predictability is disingenuous, to say the least. Explanations can be more or less deterministic, and behavioral predictability is but one marker—one giveaway of the commitment to sociobiology. The putative undertaking to explain xenophobia, "race relations" . . . and prejudice in sociobiological terms ends up suggesting/imputing their inevitability, and so the explanation tends to [provide a] "justification" of the phenomenon's occurrence.

Regarding the "sociobiological implication . . . that racial exclusion is understandably universal in both the temporal and spatial sense," Goldberg (1990) suggests that a commitment to such an assumption "implies rational commitment to racist beliefs" (p. 344). Others oppose what they see to be sociobiology's harmful political implications. Barker (1981), for example, suggests that van den Berghe, along with other sociobiologists, frames prejudice in terms that seem to justify it as "genetically programmed in us" (p. 97). As such, Barker suggests, evolutionary theory could in fact give reasons for intolerance to continue. He argues that this is what was done in Britain during their conservative swing. Such a critique could be extended beyond the racism/ethnicity sphere to suggest that (a) "real" differences found between the brains of different groups (e.g., men and women) might be used as a rationalization for intolerance and that (b) inasmuch as these or other groups are perceived as "different" or motivate fear, one could use an evolutionary explanation to accept our fears of others simply as "natural."[6] Van den Berghe (1986) argues in response that scientific investigation, and not whether a theory is politically acceptable or emotionally desirable, should guide research: "According to this view, the search for truth has priority over all other objectives" (quoted in Mason, 1986, p. 12).

Besides the possible justification an evolutionary perspective provides for intolerance, it also could be questioned why the authors consider only the advantages of exclusionary drives such as fear, separation, and prejudice. We know that "hybrid vigor," or the mixing of difference, produces a more robust and successful biological entity. Mixed breeds are more resistant to disease. If the goal is survival of the gene pool, then it would be an evolutionary advantage to overcome difference and interbreed. Furthermore, because conflict is everywhere and many conflicts (e.g., armed conflict) actually destroy one's gene pool (or one's family, business, or country), it seems that conflict is *counterproductive* and eventually would, through natural selection, be eliminated. Fear of difference, I argue, also is highly dysfunctional for the human species. Although there may be some hereditary drives to avoid things seen as different, inasmuch as many evolutionary theorists see *adaptability* as an inherited trait, it seems we would adapt in a modern world, where difference should become increasingly less threatening. Without this consideration, some evolutionary perspectives become locked in a very distant past.

We would argue, with some evolutionary theorists, that biology is one factor in a person's intellectual, social, or physical capacity but that it is only one factor. It becomes filtered through culture and life-script/individual experience. The strength, form, and target of intolerance will vary from culture to culture and from person to person. There may, at the same time, be some underlying element that characterizes all intolerances. The early work of van den Berghe (1967)[7] suggests that ethnocentrism is universal even though certain forms of intolerance may not be. A biological or instinctual component of prejudice does not preclude solutions to address it. Instincts for inclusion could be used to create in-groups that include members of both "us" and "them" (Ross, 1991). I am perhaps idealistic in hoping that humanity someday will become the in-group (Allport, 1954/1979). The trick, at this point, will be to prevent the formation of some new out-group (e.g., Martians, Klingons) from becoming the object of our hatred.

■ Group-Level and Structural Approaches

One of the debates surrounding various intolerances is who can have a particular intolerance. Can either men or women be sexist, people of any race be racist, and so on as reflected in the popular press? Or, can only members of the dominant group (the one holding the most power) be ageist, classist, racist, sexist, and so on (Byrd, 1993)?[8] This issue points out how even the definition of an intolerance depends in part on the academic window through which one looks. Someone interested in a group-level approach would focus on the power relations involved that hold an intolerance such as heterosexism in place (see Nakayama's chapter in this volume [Chapter 6]), on the glass ceilings and sexual harassment in industry (see one of Lindsley's chapters in this volume [Chapter 10]), and on other forms of institutionalized prejudice. As some of the evolutionary theorists suggest, prejudice is influenced by more than biological or psychological factors. For example, even if we accept that fear and contempt are at the root of all intolerance, these are influenced by the presence of competing goals. Such goals often concern allocation of resources among groups. As soon as relationships among groups as social entities become a concern in the understanding of intolerance, we are considering group or structural issues.

Aronson (1992) summarizes one structural perspective on prejudice, emphasizing political and economic competition: "According to this view, given that resources are limited, the dominant group might attempt to exploit a minority group in order to gain some material advantage" (p. 112). Thus, prejudice is likely to increase or at least be sustained when there is conflict over mutually exclusive goals and societal tensions (e.g., economic crisis). Such a view could easily be seen in the late 20th-century United States debate over affirmative action policies. Aronson notes,

> Prejudice has existed between Anglo and Mexican-American migrant workers as a function of a limited number of jobs, between Arabs and Israelis over disputed territory, and between Northerners and Southerners over the abolition of slavery. The economic advantages of discrimination are all too clear when one looks at the success certain craft unions have had, over the years, in denying membership to women and members of ethnic minorities, thus keeping them out of the relatively high-paying occupations the unions control. (pp. 112-113)

There are other types of group-level explanations besides allocation of resources.[9] Mirandé (1985), for example, proposes that much conflict between Mexican Americans and European Americans results from the latter's "internal colonization" of the former.

Parillo (1980) details different ethnic groups that have immigrated to America and their degree of assimilation as well as conflicts among the different groups at each stage of U.S. history. Allport (1954/1979) notes that intolerance occurs when a controlling group does not allow a group without political control to either assimilate (the "melting pot") or maintain its own culture ("pluralism"). Forbes (1985) finds that conformity, not ego weakness, is the principal explanatory factor in ethnocentrism between Canadian French- and English-speaking high school students. Smooha (1987) explains Jewish-Arab intolerance in Israel in terms of perceived threat of the out-group (Jews toward Arabs) and anger over unequal treatment in terms of education, housing, and other resources (Arabs toward Jews).

Whether one is looking strictly at allocation of resources or is considering the movement of people groups, the economy, politics, institutions, or other factors, it often is beneficial to go beyond a "shopping list" of factors. For this reason, some sociologists propose theoretical frameworks that can be useful in the study of intolerance. For example, *what* are the resources over which groups struggle. Are they only land and the means of production, or do they include cultural and political power? Given that *groups* compete for a variety of resources, it is no wonder that the discussion of prejudice, as with other racial, gender, and class issues, frequently turns political.

Whereas sociologists seek explanations of causes of and influences on prejudice, political scientists, legal scholars, and philosophers of prejudice debate issues such as freedom of intolerant speech and allocation of resources (e.g., affirmative action, preferential admission policies, immigration policies, legal definition of marriage, accessibility of industries to people with different physical abilities). Philosophers discuss the very "goodness" or "badness" of tolerance. I see several approaches, primarily stemming from sociology, that might address interests of any of these "disciplines"[10]: the group competition approach, Marxist approaches, Weberian approaches, and moral exclusion. I borrow much of the following from Banton (1987) and from Omi and Winant (1986), who discuss racism; however, I broaden the application to other forms of prejudice.

Group Competition Approach

Omi and Winant (1986) discuss how one of the earliest sociological approaches to race was the *ethnicity* approach, based on the work of Robert E. Park and the Chicago School of Sociology, who searched for the structural variables that "held back" certain ethnic groups (e.g., Polish immigrants in Chicago) from assimilation (and, thus, from perceived progress). Their explanation considers size and density of groups, cultural patterns and mores, type of immigration, and other factors mentioned previously—basically, differences in group movements, cultures, and resources. I see Banton's (1987) discussion of "race as nation" in this category. Some writers treat races as nations in that they frame race as a type of universal entity; one's Blackness or "Chicanoness" becomes the most important identity. For example, Asante (1987) suggests that elements of African culture underlie African-descended people's experience wherever they may be found. Omi and Winant (1986) focus on the "racial formation" of the United States, a country divided at every level by race. For these writers, racial divisions seem more important even than class or gender divisions.

The group-based approach also applies to other types of intolerance. The view would suggest that it is not merely competition for resources but rather our belonging to certain groups that divides us. Thus, some feminists feel that the primary structure of importance in the United States is division (and hierarchy) by gender—that the United States is divided at every level in terms of the sociological grouping of gender, with males favored at every level.[11] For example, Schwichtenberg (1989b) sees "feminism" as "a set of political practices exposing the patriarchal/capitalist subordination of women" (p. 291). She sees feminism as a struggle to free women from existing for the desire of men. Women, as a group, must struggle for resources such as power over self-identification against the norms of a society. Knowles and Mercer (1992) suggest that "feminists have in common a recognition of themselves as a *social category* separating them from and placing them in opposition to other [social categories]" (p. 105, emphasis added). They suggest that Black feminists (e.g., Collins, 1990; hooks, 1984) see themselves as distinct from White feminists over several core issues such as reproduction, the role and status of the family, and the issue of patriarchy.

In the same vein, some look at antiforeigner intolerance as simply a matter of group belonging. By moving the groups around and changing the density or the economic situation, the intolerance might change. For example, much has been written on a notion called the *contact* hypothesis. This is the notion that under certain conditions, contact between group members will result in a more favorable feeling toward people one sees as belonging to an out-group (Amir, 1969). For example, several studies of interracial friendships in school systems in the United States and Africa (e.g., Hallinan & Williams, 1989; D. Wilson & Lavelle, 1990) find that changes in structural factors such as group composition and teaching method are related to increased numbers of interracial friendships among students. Jackman and Crane (1986) challenge the notion that intolerance is based on ignorance and that prejudice will melt away if ignorance is dispelled. They find that even if positive attitudes among students develop toward members of disempowered groups, these attitudes may not be accompanied by a desire to help those groups gain more power. This suggests that simple "groupness" is not enough to explain intolerance. In some cases, desire for group power or control of some resource is at stake. What holds these perspectives together is that each frames groups in terms of their competition with each other. Some theorists specify the exact nature of the competition or the resource over which groups compete. I now turn to two such perspectives: Marxist and Weberian explanations.

Marxist Approaches

Strict Marxism looks at intolerance in terms of the means and relations of production. Marx held that social reality (e.g., religion, culture, family relations, education) is based on the most important aspect of one's daily life—work. If one were able to own one's own tools and implements of production (i.e., "mode of production"), then one could have a complete and fulfilled life. But in a capitalistic system, the owners took over the spinning wheels, the sewing machines, and the factory equipment. This gave them economic power over the workers, which in turn "alienated" them from the products of their own hands (see "Capital" in Tucker, 1978; Smith & Evans, 1982). The owners sought to keep themselves in power through dominating the workers, maintaining a cheap labor supply, and so on (i.e., "relations of production"). Workers sell their labor for a price but end up not owning the means of production and, thus, not having any power. The relations and means of labor were the "base" on which all the rest of society ("superstructure") rested. Family, religion, education, and culture all would seek to keep those relations and means in place unless they were overthrown (see "Communist Manifesto," "Economic and Philosophical Manuscripts of 1844," and "Grundrisse" in Tucker, 1978).[12]

Marxist theory has been applied to various forms of intolerance, but the arguments share a common core: The owners of production do what they must do to keep control of production. Race, for example, is either invented or appropriated by the owners of production to keep labor cheap. By one explanation, race is used to create the idea that there are subordinate classes (including foreigners), and systems are implemented to keep those workers subordinate (Miles, 1989). By this logic, U.S. farm owners would want to hire illegal immigrants, using the threat of expulsion to keep wages low. Greenberg (1980) calls this use of capitalist development to promote cheap labor "uneven development theory" and uses it to explain intergroup tensions in Alabama (United States), South Africa, Northern Ireland, and Palestine/Israel. In another application of Marxist theory, owners in South Africa might deliberately focus on race so that White workers would abuse Black workers; divided, the workers would have less power to revolt. White workers or union members might propagate racial exclusion to protect their own moderate wages.

Marxism can be used to describe other intolerances as well. White males are seen to dictate the structures of labor (e.g., who is hired, who manages, what the policies are) and are the dominant force in media, politics, education, and religion. This gives them power to shape (intentionally or not) the notions of family, sexuality, and business leadership—indeed, the whole culture—in such a way that women are maintained in a subordinate role with less choice over their bodies and less influence over society. Thus, Knowles and Mercer (1992) propose, "Capitalism, colonialism and patriarchal social systems are frequently identified as producing inherent race and gender inequalities which, in various ways, serve the needs of the systems they perpetuate" (p. 110).

The essence of the Marxist explanation is that intolerance is an issue of *class conflict.* In the sense of "vulgar Marxism" (the most deterministic of varieties, not even held by Marx himself), either the notions of difference or the practices of a society (discarding of the elderly and disenfranchising foreigners or persons with disabilities) exist to keep the economic elite in place. Debates rage as to whether racism, sexism, and other forms of intolerance are strictly or primarily influenced by social class concerns (Miles, 1989; W. Wilson, 1978), by group membership, or by some combination of the two (Franklin, 1991). Some see traditional Marxism as simplistic in that most of the explanation is in terms of economics. However, as Solomos (1986) and Wolpe (1986) point out, there is a wide array of Marxist perspectives regarding the determination of the economic sphere. Some forms of intolerance, such as that based on religion or sexual orientation, may not be best explained in economic terms, but that does not mean that a less deterministic Marxist approach would not be useful. Perhaps the strength in this approach is in the theories that grow out from it—critical theory (discussed later in this chapter) and Weberian theory.

Weberian Approach

Weber based his sociology on Marx and yet made some fundamental modifications (Gerth & Mills, 1946). "Racial thought" is, for Weber, an outgrowth of capitalism. However, market forces, not labor forces, underlie social structure. Different groups, according to Weber, seek to control the availability of certain goods and services to other groups. This is because *prestige* or honor, not merely social class, is at work: "In contrast to the purely economically determined 'class situation,' I wish to designate as 'status situation' every typical moment of the life-fate of men that is determined by a specific, positive or negative, social estimation of *honor*" ("Wirtschaft und Gesell-schaft" in Gerth & Mills, 1946, pp. 186-187, emphases in original). In times of economic fluctuation, class conflict drives society, but when the classes stabilize, it is the attempt to maintain a "way of life" that dominates. In this sense, a dominant class might seek to make certain aspects of life (e.g., media, education, fine art) available only to those of the favored group. This explanation alone, however, oversimplifies Weber. He also addresses the way in which a group tries to maintain its standard as the norm in a society—as the "way of life" with the most prestige—as other groups attempt to gain prestige for their ways of life.

Rex (1980, 1986) applies Weber's thought to race relations. He proposes that there are more classes than just the owners and workers. There also are service providers and the like. There are factors besides class that affect the location of the various races in a society. Van den Berghe (1967) also reflects a Weberian train of thought. By comparing racism in Mexico, Brazil, the United States, and South Africa, he concludes that racism is formed or expressed in different ways in patriarchal societies as opposed to competi-tive societies. He specifically looks at social processes and social pluralism and their effects on racism. Weber, like Marx, provides many applications beyond the sphere of race; in fact, it may have more useful applications in some of those spheres of intolerance in which the victims of the intolerance are not necessarily marginalized economically. Some ethnic groups, gays, elderly, and others may receive (or show) more prejudice as an outgrowth of the struggle over a group's cultural status in society rather than over strictly economic issues. For example, Nakayama (Chapter 6) suggests that homophobia and heterosexism cannot be understood in the same frameworks and with the same intensity as can other "isms." Rakow and Wackwitz (Chapter 5) see sexism in terms of "power arrangements created and perpetuated by men that keeps women subordinated to men through harassment, the threat of violence, and economic dependence." Rakow and Wackwitz see racism and sexism as "interlocking systems," noting, for example, the treatment of Native American women. The different forms of intolerance interact, compounding each other. This view is consistent with explanations, such as Franklin's (1991), that account for overlapping influences on prejudice.

In these examples, we see that there is more than one type of power over which groups struggle. Baker (1983) argues,

> Power is the primary determinant of group relations. Racial and ethnic groups, whether in dominant, subordinate, or equal positions, mobilize their group resources and strive for control over the major political, economic, and social structures of society, for it is within these structures that most policy decisions, including the allocation or reallocation of power, privilege, and resources, are determined. (p. 25)

Power struggles occur primarily on economic and political grounds, Baker suggests, especially in decisions over structure (e.g., access to incorporation within education, employment) and cultural policy (e.g., multiculturalism, "national" culture/language debates). Baker and others apply power concerns not only to race but also to gender. Structural and cultural power also might be present in struggles, say, between two ethnic groups of the same race (e.g., Bosnia and Herzegovina) or between opposing political ideologies (e.g., Hungary in 1956 [Szemere, 1992]). Vying groups in a political structure, different departments in an organization (e.g., management and labor, sales and production), universities within a state—all might struggle for power, be that power over representation, cultural power, economic power, structural power, or some other type of power.

Moral Exclusion

In 1990, the *Journal of Social Issues* (*JSI*) dedicated an entire issue to moral exclusion. The contributing articles are difficult to place in the framework of this chapter because they cross traditional lines of "causes of prejudice." The unifying notion of these chapters seems to be the effects of intolerance on groups (thus, I include it as a subsection of the group-based theories). *Moral exclusion* is defined as a double standard that occurs "when individuals or groups are perceived as outside the boundary in which moral values, rules, and considerations of fairness apply" (Opotow, 1990, p. 1). Opotow (1987) finds that three attitude clusters tend to be associated with moral *inclusion*: (a) the belief that a common standard of fairness applies to both in- and out-groups, (b) the willingness to share community resources with others, and (c) the willingness to make personal sacrifices so that others can have the same well-being as oneself. By contrast, unequal standards of fairness, a desire to maintain an imbalance of resources, and an attitude that serves oneself or one's group would lead to exclusion. Exclusion may vary in form from slavery or torture to simple failure to recognize the suffering of others groups. Victims may be "people who are slaves, children, women, aged, Black, Jewish, mentally retarded, physically handicapped, and insane" (Opotow, 1990, p. 3).

Theorists look at moral exclusion through different lenses—psychological, evolutionary, linguistic, sociological, and so on. The common thread is a focus on exclusionary behaviors. Some writers explain moral exclusion in terms of perceptions of in-groups (e.g., moral, virtuous, peaceful) and out-groups (e.g., evil, savage), such as Opotow's (1990) survey mentioned previously. She holds that members of the out-group are seen as disconnected from the individual. Deutch (1990) adds an evolutionary tone: Humans have an instinctual drive to accept that which is favorable and to avoid that which is unknown or perceived as harmful. One's own group is "good" and other groups are "bad." However, "there will be little need for hatred if children have been helped to develop an integrated view of themselves, with sufficient confidence in their good aspects to be able to have a constructive orientation to their own shortcomings" (p. 23). Several of the writers in the *JSI* special issue echo the idea that victims of intolerance (enemies) and ways of expressing intolerance both may change with time, place, and political and historical circumstances.

Bar-Tal (1990) suggests a strong link between moral exclusion and language. He proposes that although the specifics of exclusion vary, the underlying process involves fear or contempt that leads to delegitimization—the "categorization of a group or groups into extremely negative social categories that are excluded from the realm of acceptable norms and/or values" (p. 65). Delegitimization occurs first through words. Bar-Tal sees five categories of delegitimizing talk including *dehumanization* (animals, subhuman race, demons, Satan), *trait characterization* (possessing extremely negative traits such as "aggressors"), *outcasting* (using terms that would make them outcasts in a society [murderers, psychopaths, maniacs]), *use of political labels* with negative tones (fascists, Communists), and *group comparison* (comparing the group with some group that is perceived negatively such as the Huns, Nazis, or Vandals). Delegitimization, if taken far enough, can lead to physical action—beating, looting, concentration camps, genocide, or war.

Bar-Tal (1990) then articulates two models of exclusion or delegitimization: a conflict model and an ethnocentric model. The *conflict* model shows how competing goals (or means to reach goals) lead to conflicts that, in turn, lead to threat and delegitimization of the other group. Bar-Tal proposes that "when a group perceives that the negating goal(s) of an out-group is (are) far-reaching, especially unjustified, and threatening to the basic goals of the in-group, the in-group uses delegitimization to explain the conflict" (p. 67). Groups might believe that their cohesion, their ways of life, or their national borders are threatened. Threat perception then is accompanied by feelings of stress, fear, uncertainty, and vulnerability. Bar-Tal applies this model to explain American-Soviet relations during the cold war. Delegitimization can lead to a self-justified violence against the other group. Bar-Tal sees the Palestinian-Israeli conflict as an example of this version of the model. A second model, the *ethnocentric* model, begins not with threatened goals but rather with the feeling that one's group is superior, leading to acceptance of the in-group but rejection of the out-group. Delegitimization comes into play when such devaluing is accompanied by fear and/or contempt such as the historic relations between Europeans and American Indians.

Analysis

I see two strengths to the group-level or structural approach. First, these theories help explain complex phenomena. Baker (1983) elaborates *several* bases of and influences on structural and cultural power in his study of Canada, the United States, Australia, New Zealand, South Africa, and Rhodesia. For us, this gives a fuller understanding of some intolerances than does a simple economic approach. Explanations of prejudice that are framed solely in terms of abuse or exploitation of workers by the elite (which, as I have noted, are increasingly rare explanations) ignore the complex intricacies of various forms of intolerance such as those intolerances toward people of nondominant groups (e.g., Jewish, African American, gay) who are *among* the owners of production. Second, if we can recognize the structural- or group-based factors of prejudice, then we can seek to change them at a macro level. If there are macro-level differences, then efforts aimed only at psychological, individual-level change may not address them. Looking at sociological and structural factors allows for group mobilization to reduce conflict or at least to reduce outward expressions of intolerance (Banton, 1985). Intolerance is allowed to become an issue in politics with practical changes being implemented at systems levels.

The weaknesses of strictly group-level approaches are that they often ignore the role of language in prejudice or obscure differences among individuals (different people even in the same situation may have largely different degrees of tolerance for out-group members). Many of these approaches offer only one lens through which to view the prejudice, be it economics, power, or some other lens. An approach that includes both politics *and* discourse might make more sense of the "tools of political intimidation and conflict resolution" that resulted in the genocide of 1 million Armenians at the beginning of the 20th century (Zoryan Institute, 1993, p. 86) or in the "massacre and murderous butchery" of the U.S. military against the Philippines in the Philippine War in which "racism, paternalism, and talk of money . . . mingle[d] with talk of destiny and civilization" (cited in Gioseffi, 1993, pp. 100-101). But in these cases, although many of the soldiers may have been following orders under compulsion, we cannot assume that all had the same amount of intolerance. In the same way, where a society overall might be prejudiced toward a group, group-level explanations do not clarify why so many people value that same group.

As we have seen, not all group-level approaches fall under these critiques. Several authors include both group- and individual-level explanations and also include the language and communication elements (e.g., Bar-Tal, 1990). For example, in discussing ageism, Palmore (1990) cites both causes and solutions at the individual, social, and cultural levels. Whereas a group-level approach offers explanation and practice, infusing this approach with individual and/or linguistic concepts might go even further. We often have seen structural changes (e.g., required diversity courses) that seem to make superficial change, making life more tolerable for victims of prejudice but leaving a great many individuals unchanged.

■ Individual-Level Approaches
(social-psychological theories)

It is perhaps because of the individual factor that many theorists have sought to explain prejudice in terms of concepts inside the heads of individuals. Allport

(1954/1979) sees the various preceding factors as having an ultimate influence on the psyche and cognition of the prejudiced person. But at the core, it is individual-level thought and need that leads to prejudice. Stephan (1985) suggests, "The level of analysis of a social-psychological inquiry into intergroup relations is the individual and his or her relationships with social groups" (p. 599) rather than institutional or cultural level. Individual-level analyses have been approached in a number of ways. Ehrlich (1973) discusses both the *growth and nature of stereotypes* (a cognitive process) and the *role of child-rearing practices* on self- and other-attitudes. Stereotypes are seen as generalized attitudes (usually discussed as negative) that are associated with the categories, or organizing principles, in our heads. These attitudes have "supporting mechanisms," specifically "all of the objects in an individual's environment that contribute to the maintenance of that attitude" (p. 136). These mechanisms include family, personal contact, media, and other influences on the categories we hold and the feelings those have for us. Allport (1954/1979) also differentiated two approaches to prejudice. One is focused on how people experience and categorize reality; Allport called this the *phenomenological* approach, but I call it the *cognitive* approach.[13] Another focus is derived from developmental psychology and looks at specific *emotional functions* such as relieving guilt or releasing frustration. I continue this distinction even as I recognize that the two ideas blend together and are closely related.

Cognitive Approach

Stephan (1985) provides the following summary of the cognitive approach:

> The cognitive approach . . . encompasses the organization of knowledge about groups into higher-level cognitive structures such as schemata, scripts, and prototypes, as well as providing new insights into the operation of expectancies and biased perceptions of intergroup behavior. It is also useful in understanding the affective complexity of intergroup cognitions as reflected in theories stressing ambivalence towards groups. (p. 600)

Stephan emphasizes structures such as role schemata and the way in which we perceive, store, and recall information (e.g., selective attention, retention). This is especially pertinent to the perception of out-groups. For example, if an out-group member performs the same positive behavior as an in-group member, then we are likely to not perceive it at all or to rationalize either the person or the behavior as not typical of his or her group. Allport (1954/1979) sees categorization as necessary to daily functioning in that categories help people react quickly to incoming stimuli. Unfortunately, categories are not always based on logical reasoning and may be based on one's negative personal experience (or that of parents or that represented in media or society). Allport discusses how we categorize people into in-groups (us) and out-groups (them) and how the words we use to describe people shape the ways in which we see them. Ehrlich (1973) proposes that higher cognitive ability is related to reduced prejudice. Both authors suggest that rigidity in category formation, overgeneralization, dichotomization (either/or categories), need for structure (and intolerance of ambiguity), desire for concrete (rather than abstract) thinking, and other thought processes are associated with intolerance.[14]

As one example of such an approach, some suggest that racism—and we might extend this to other forms of prejudice—is inherently irrational. First, stereotypes do not make sense in that they are based on "irrational categories" (Goldberg, 1990, p. 321). People who are racist engage in the "fundamental attribution error" of assigning more meaning to a person's racial membership than to considering social or environmental influences on a person's behavior. Second, prejudiced people have inconsistencies between their attitudes and behaviors. Goldberg, however, argues that racism "is not inherently irrational on logical grounds" (p. 331). It neither need be based on irrational categories nor involve attitude-behavior discrepancy. Furthermore, to the charge that racist exclusion is not cost-effective, Goldberg argues that in many cases it has been. Instead, he claims, we must object to racism (and other forms of unjustifiable exclusion) on *normative* (moral and political) grounds rather than on the notion that racists are irrational.

Closely tied to categories, Allport (1954/1979) suggests, are the thoughts we have associated with them. He calls these overgeneralizations about group members *stereotypes*. Stephan (1985) suggests that such overgeneralizations interfere in the processes of encoding, storing, and retrieving. For example, if we *expect* to see men as having more status or being more assertive, then that is what we are likely to see, even if a woman in a given situation has just as much or more status than the man. If we record stimuli that contradict our stereotypes, then we will be less likely to recall that information to draw future conclusions. Research suggests, however, that the process is complicated.[15] For example, one study found that subjects viewing a picture of an Asian-descended woman would draw on different stereotypes if she were using chopsticks as opposed to brushing her hair (Macrae, Bodenhausen, & Milne, 1995). The authors of the study suggest that "it may . . . be the conjunction of social categories that is crucial in these cases, rather than a differential emphasis on age, gender, or ethnicity used singularly" (p. 404), a notion that supports the layered perspective we present in this book.

Researchers have tried in various ways to explain *why* and *how* stereotypes function. A traditional explanation for why people use stereotypes is that they are simply easier than processing individual information about each person we meet (Allport, 1954/1979), a notion supported through ongoing research (Macrae, Milne, & Bodenhausen, 1994). Other experimental research finds that people who have a higher need for structure are more likely to use gender role stereotypes in their thought processing (Neuberg & Newson, 1993). Jussim, Coleman, and Lerch (1987) overview three main theories that try to explain how stereotypes function and provide data in support of each. The *complexity-extremity* approach suggests that people have more categories for people of their own groups and see other groups as less complex. The *assumed characteristics* theory suggests that "stereotypes inform us of important background characteristics of group members" (p. 537), although these stereotypes can be influenced by receiving background information on the targets. The *expectancy violation* theory shows that when expectations are violated by an out-group member, evaluations are perceived more extremely; that is, positive violations are seen more positively than are those for in-group members, and negative violations are seen more negatively than are those for in-group members.

A vast literature has been written on the variables that influence stereotypes. Some of this discusses the connection of stereotypes to prejudice. Devine (1989) suggests that there is a tension between those who see stereotypes and prejudice as related and those who believe that "stereotypes are functional for the individual, allowing rationalization of his or her prejudice against a group" (p. 5). Her research supports this latter view. She finds that people are aware of stereotypes of certain groups (e.g., Blacks-Whites) but that those who monitor the stereotypes can reduce their influence on evaluation of others' behaviors. However, Macrae, Bodenhausen, Milne, and Jetten (1994) find that people who suppress their stereotypes are more likely than those who do not to have those stereotypes later "rebound" to influence their judgments. Hepburn and Locksley (1983) find no difference between people's perceptions of how much their stereotypes affect their judgments of certain groups (e.g., Blacks-Whites, males-females, Chinese-Caucasians, overweight-underweight, unattractive-beautiful) and "objective" measures of such an effect. They also argue that people are not aware of whether or not their stereotypes are influencing their judgments. Biernat and Manis (1994) suggest that objective measures of stereotypes, in which stereotypes can be measured by using tangible things such as income or height, are more stable (less likely to shift) than subjective attitudes measured on a Likert scale. The danger of these stereotypes, as Neuberg points out, is that "we form the people we interact with and create our own realities" (cited in Olson, 1993, p. 7). The way in which we treat the others often influences them to act in the way we expect, something Neuberg (1991) and others have referred to as *self-fulfilling* prophecy.

Tajfel (1978b, 1981a, 1982) and J. Turner (1987) expand on the perceptual base of prejudice in their *social identity* theory. They note that we tend to perceive others in a combination of group- and individual-based terms. When we see another person primarily as a member of some group to which we do not belong (an out-group), the communication is more heavily intergroup. When we react to each other in terms of personal characteristics (similarities, differences, traits), the behavior is more inter-personal. The more we see someone as a member of a group rather than as an individual, the more likely stereotypes and prejudice will occur. This is similar to Miller and Steinberg's (1975) view of person perception in which we first make predictions about others based on larger demographic aspects of their person (e.g., gender, race), then based on the sociological groupings to which they belong (e.g., organizational membership), and then based on our own personal knowledge of them as individuals. Tajfel (1981a) suggests that our self-identity is tied up with the groups to which we belong; we categorize ourselves and compare ourselves to other groups to make our group look better (Tajfel, 1978b). Thus, perception of group identities can lead to intergroup hostility (Tajfel & Turner, 1979).

Related to social identity theory, others developed *ethnolinguistic identity* theory (Gallois, Franklyn-Stokes, Giles, & Coupland, 1988; Gallois, Giles, Jones, Cargile, & Ota, 1995; Giles, Bourhis, & Taylor, 1977; Giles & Coupland, 1991). This theory focuses on how or whether one changes speech patterns when interacting with someone perceived to be of another group, with language being one of the primary markers of group belongingness. Individuals tend to verbally and nonverbally mark their speech (e.g., use of slang and vocabulary, gestures, accent, discourse style) to maintain linguistic distinctiveness when their group identity is stronger (i.e., more vitality). Less vital groups tend to lose their linguistic distinctiveness and assimilate. In addition, communicators use in-group/out-group status to determine whether to converge or diverge in communicative style. Strength of group identity, power, group solidarity, out-group contact, whether communicators define the interaction in intergroup terms, and other factors have been shown to influence divergence and convergence.

Many have focused on how one's perception of one's own and other's cultural identities affects the communication process. For example, Collier (1988) concludes,

> Blacks seem to employ different rules, [and] role prescriptions differ, in that Blacks note cultural role prescriptions with Whites. Where professional and individual role prescriptions were emphasized in conversations among Blacks, cultural and gender prescriptions were noted by Blacks in conversations with Whites. (p. 133)

She also finds that Whites emphasized politeness more with other Whites and emphasized content, expression, and relational climate more frequently in their conversations with other groups. Hecht, Larkey, and Johnson (1992) find that African Americans and European Americans perceive different issues as important to interethnic communication. Braithwaite (1994) finds that people with disabilities often cognitively and communicatively reframe their disability, their culture, and their selves: "How one redefines oneself, then, from normal or able-bodied to disabled, is a process of redefinition of self. . . . During the redefinition process, individuals come to terms with both positive and negative ramifications of disability" (p. 151). Reframing helps people cope with a disability and with prejudice on the part of the dominant culture. This literature, then, suggests that perceived differences in identity can be important in both explaining and addressing prejudice.

Cognitive theories of group perception are helpful in that they show the interacting roles of language, past experience, and categories. This group of theories helps explain how there can be different racisms for different people. In Brazil, there can be many racial categories (although, in this "racial democracy," most want to label themselves as some shade of White [Nogueira, 1985]). In Jamaica, there are three categories; in England, there are primarily two (Hall, 1992). In each nation, the perception of those groups by members of both in- and out-groups can change with time. At the same time, many cognitive approaches do not address issues of power and domination; individual psychology; or interactive, relational, and social structures except as they are represented within cognition. Because these approaches tend to focus on cognitive structure and processes, other factors often are subordinated (i.e., examining an individual's perception of power rather than power hierarchies and ideology).

Developmental Approach

In addition to cognitive structures, Allport (1954/1979) suggests that personal needs and "functions" affect the way in which people perceive members of a particular out-group. Needs for a sense of superiority, for structure, for authority, and so on might be used to explain intolerances among those of different races, ethnicities, nationalities, social classes, political beliefs, or religions. In this subsection, I focus on these other individual-level approaches.

World War II and its aftermath gave impetus to a set of scholars who explained intolerance primarily in terms of personal psychology. The "Berkeley Group" produced the book, *The Authoritarian Personality* (Adorno, Frenkel-Brunswick, Levinson, & Sanford, 1950/1982). It traces the development of a scale for intolerance from earlier scales on anti-Semitism (the A-S scale [Levinson, 1950/1982a]) and ethnocentrism (the E scale [Levinson, 1950/1982b]). The resulting F scale (for fascism) explains intolerance in terms of conventionalism, authoritarian submission, superstition, preoccupation with dominance/submission, and projection of one's own negative traits on other groups (Sanford, Adorno, Frenkel-Brunswick, & Levinson, 1950/1982). Whereas the E scale focused on attitudes, the F scale dwelled more on beliefs supposed to reflect these attitudes.

Allport (1954/1979) and Sherif (1966) conceive of intolerance and group conflict in much the same way. Allport (1954/1979) proposes that nationalism and overgeneralizing the virtues of one's own culture ("love-prejudice") can easily lead to exclusion of the other culture. He defines prejudice as a dislike or avoidance of others who are perceived as having the characteristics of a group. Whereas some prejudice is merely based on conforming to social norms, Allport centers his discussion on feelings of insecurity, guilt, frustration, need for structure, and other psychological roots. Rokeach's (1960) D scale (for dogmatism) asks questions concerning uncertainty about the future, the isolation of humans, self-adequacy and inadequacy, paranoid outlook on life, authoritarianism, and intolerance. The D scale surveys both left and right opinionation.[16] Aronson (1992) lists four "causes of prejudice," three of which are individual-level ones: the *scapegoat* theory (in which we vent our frustrations on some out-group), the *prejudiced personality* (rigid and authoritarian, based on Adorno et al. [1950/1982] and Allport [1954/1979]), and *prejudice through conformity* (in which we are simply following the patterns around us).

Within the psychological needs approach, some authors focus on specific needs or psychological structures. Brewer and Campbell (1976), for example, look at *ethnocentrism* as expressed among tribes in Eastern Africa. They cite Sumner's definition:

> *Ethnocentrism* is the technical name for this view of things in which one's own group is the center of everything and all others are scaled and rated with reference to it. . . . Each group nourishes its own pride and vanity, boasts itself superior, exalts its own divinities, and looks with contempt on outsiders. Each group thinks its own folkways the only right ones, and if it observes that other groups have other folkways, these excite its scorn. (p. 2)

Brewer and Campbell also augment Sumner's definition to suggest that ethnocentrism can refer to "the individual tendency to endorse hostile statements about a variety of out-groups" (p. 4). They provide a detailed study of various social and psychological variables that are related to intergroup intolerance among the African tribes. Among the social variables are degree of similarity among groups, distance among groups, sizes of groups, and social-economic advancement (modernization). Psychological variables include self-group regard, emotion tied to out-group stereotypes, and differences in attributions toward own and other groups.[17]

Others do not see these attitudes as unidirectional. Katz, Wackenhut, and Glass (1986) explain attitudes toward those who are stigmatized (e.g., Whites' attitudes toward Blacks, able-bodied people's attitudes toward people with disabilities) through the lens of *ambivalence*. Their research reports that "dominant attitudes of prejudice against Blacks and sympathy for the handicapped are often accompanied by feelings of an opposite kind, that is, of sympathy for Blacks and aversion toward the handicapped" (p. 103). Whatever the response in such a situation, the actor will feel conflicting positive and negative feelings. The authors suggest that ambivalence tends to lead to behavioral instability, which, in its worst instances, may lead toward negative responses toward the people of the stigmatized group.

Analysis

Two of the strengths of the cognitive and behavioral approaches are the breadth of their application and the commonsense connections between the two. First, cognitive processes (e.g., intergroup differentiation) have been used to analyze a variety of prejudices such as those based on status group differences, gender communication, and factory-workforce relations (see references cited in Tajfel, 1978a). Furthermore, they have been applied to national political conflicts in Northern Ireland, Italy, Indonesia, Finland, and Britain (see references cited in Tajfel, 1982). In the sense that stereotypes represent the cognitive approach, the application is even broader, including stereotypes of the elderly (Palmore, 1990), gays (Byrd, 1993), conservatives, and so on. As noted previously, the psychological needs approach has been applied just as broadly.

Second, the cognitive and behavioral theories fit well together. For example, Bethlehem (1985) lists the following as his first principle of ethnic prejudice (which principles he feels also could apply to other forms of intolerance): "There are two interacting types of prejudice: one is based on personality structure and needs, and the other is based on misinformation—some of it culturally based—and the need to keep cognitive load light" (p. 136). This perspective, as Bethlehem lays it out, accounts for the varying influences of complexity of thought, formal education, group competition, amount of information about the other groups, and so on. Certain needs (e.g., need for structure) lend themselves easily to a relationship with cognitive variables (e.g., number and rigidity of categories).

In all of these instances, intolerance is seen to be rooted at the level of individual desires and cognitive structures, although at times the influence of group-level variables is considered. Whereas the structures of society (e.g., economic situations, status differences, immigration patterns) are seen as affecting the psychology of individuals, Allport (1954/1979) "maintains that prejudice is ultimately a problem of personality formation and development; no two cases are the same" (p. 41). This serves as both a strength and a weakness of the approach. It is valuable to note that every individual is different, and an approach to reducing prejudice (e.g., mandatory cultural-diversity classes) may increase the prejudice of some and decrease that of others. However, as Allport himself notes, these deeper motives provide only half of the picture, with the other half provided by conformity to group norms (group-level analysis). The heavy focus of much of this literature on factors of authoritarianism, unhealthy relationships with parents, and so on may lead to the same justification for the maintenance of one's prejudice as does the evolutionary perspective. (Indeed, the evolutionary perspective could be used to explain some of what is seen as psychological.)

Some would argue that the psychological approach also has maintained that all individuals have a common psyche. Gaines and Reed (1994, 1995) argue that W. E. B. DuBois offers an alternative to Allportian psychology. DuBois's "underground" approach is social-historical and proposes that African American psychology has a sense of "dividedness and duality" that are "not merely additions to, or specific variations of, some general structure of personality and identification, but historically unique patterns that emerged because of historically unique circumstances" (Gaines & Reed, 1995, p. 99). Certainly, many psychologists of different groups suggest that the psychology of minority groups in the United States must be understood in terms of "the interaction between individual personality characteristics and the social and environmental influences that help to form and shape the individual personality" (White & Parham, 1990, p. 44), especially when those influences oppose one's identity.

If we are going to consider intolerance, we must go beyond just the internal workings of the prejudiced mind and also be able to look at prejudice as an environmental influence on the psyche of those who are victims of the prejudice. Unfortunately, many psychological approaches downplay societal and other factors that may account for or influence much of intolerant behavior. The focus of such theories privileges an individualistic worldview at the expense of more collectivistic perspectives; this Eurocentric bias is particularly debilitating in the study of cultural diversity.

■ Message-Based Approaches
(linguistic/rhetorical/discourse/critical)

Linguistic and critical approaches relate to several of the previous areas. In terms of moral exclusion, Bar-Tal's (1990) consideration of forms of verbal delegitimization could be framed as rhetorical. Zur (1991), taking primarily a psychological view of enmity (especially between nations), discusses how negative qualities are "attributed to or projected onto the enemy" (p. 352). This projection, however, quickly moves from the minds of people to the symbols they create. Rhetorical studies have long been concerned with the use of language to maximize the freedom allowed to a group of people. In the early days of Greece, citizens were expected to have "the ability to speak, to listen critically to the arguments of others, and to utter appropriate responses"

(Golden, Berquist, & Coleman, 1989, p. 7). Along with settling law cases, rhetoric was used to address governments seen to be oppressive and to urge war against neighbors. Later writers such as Habermas and Foucault considered power as it is gained and held through discourse. Rhetorical studies, then, look at messages as texts, broadly defined to include interpersonal messages, media messages, and so on.[18] Growing out of rhetorical studies and literary criticism comes critical theory. However, it should be noted that not all rhetoricians are critical theorists. I look at both in turn, including linguistic and discursive work under rhetoric.

Rhetorical and Discourse Studies in General

If rhetoric analyzes messages, then both the breadth of types of messages and the approaches to analyze them are astounding.[19] Zur (1991) illustrates some of the types of messages rhetorical studies might analyze:

> *War propaganda* is a system which encourages [intergroup] enmity through explicit means (posters, leaflets, etc.) or implicit means (misinformation, disinformation, and lies). Enmity is propagated through different media: visual images (popular movies, visual arts), the written word (literature, newspapers, magazines), the spoken word (radio, everyday language), music (popular songs, military jingles), and other art forms. (p. 351, emphasis in original)

Within the rhetorical tradition, scholars look at different aspects of intolerance through different lenses. Some look at how certain groups express intolerance. For example, Zur (1991) and Bar-Tal (1990) make reference to the verbal (rhetorical) way in which groups picture ("construct") enemies. Starosta (1984) notes that "cultures, because they succeed in allowing their adherents to survive in a difficult world, are self-promoting" (p. 229). Part of this self-promotion, Starosta suggests, is the use of rhetoric to cast other cultures and their ways of life as *externalities* (external to one's own culture) that are "normally taken to be the 'incorrect' " (p. 231).

Rhetorical research can be used in various ways to study intergroup communication, one of which is to look at "terministic screens." Burke (1966) suggests that "the nature of our terms (or terministic screens) affects the nature of our observations in the sense that the terms direct the attention to one field or another" (p. 46). Individuals or groups use terms to interpret the behaviors and realities of others. Burke would suggest that if we refer to women with names that belittle them or treat them as dependent and childlike, then these words (as well as words we use to describe characteristics or behaviors) filter the way in which we see women. It is astonishing to realize that Burke (1967) first achieved widespread public notoriety by predicting Hitler's extreme level of intolerance and actions toward Jews, homosexuals, and other groups from his use of language. Burke's analysis of the campaign shows that he intended his approach to be used for tolerance:

> Our job, then, our anti-Hitler battle, is to find all available ways of making the
> Hitlerite distortions of religion [the way Hitler distorted religion to serve his
> purposes] in order that politicians of his kind in America be unable to perform a
> similar swindle. The desire for [national] unity is genuine and admirable. . . . But
> this unity, if attained on a deceptive basis . . ., is no unity at all. (pp. 219-220)

I hope the leaders of our time heed Burke's warnings better than did those of his own.

Like Burke, who applies his theories to written or verbal messages, others have
focused on both media and interpersonal discourse. *Discourse* includes every aspect of
spoken language such that discourse analysts might look at topics of conversation,
structures of sentences, rambling conversations, jokes, and so on (Scollon & Scollon,
1995). Perhaps one of the better known discourse analysts in the area of intolerance is
Teun A. van Dijk. In one study (van Dijk, 1984), he conducts nondirected interviews
of Whites in Holland about minorities, analyzing (among other things) the content of
stories, argumentation, and semantic strategies the participants used. He finds, for
example, that participants tend to express racism in more subtle, rather than overt,
fashion and seek to find ways in which to give their racial attitudes "plausibility, if not
respectability" (p. 156). In other places (van Dijk, 1987, 1993), he looks again at stories
but also at media, educational discourse, and political discourse to find the same
structures of racism present there.

Other writers look at the signs produced by certain groups in response to exclusion
of various sorts. Scheibel (1994) analyzes the graffiti at a film school and finds that one
of the many functions graffiti serves is to "portray faculty members as objects to be
feared and loathed" (p. 11). Bushnell (1990) finds similar themes in the graffiti of
Muscovite subculture: "As argot, the graffiti express[es] a cultural program and distance[s] the subculture from adult society" (p. 216). Graffiti serves to "underscore
[teenagers'] alienation from the society they terrified. Their language created a barrier
between them and the adult world" (p. 237). Both in the descriptions and allusions to
the adult world and in references to other interest groups (e.g., sports clubs, gangs), a
key element in the graffiti is "the language of the ideological and cultural enemy"
(p. 240).

Sedano's (1980) rhetorical analysis of Chicano poetry reveals the use of devices to
instill and reinforce ethnic pride and to communicate a positive image to mainstream
culture. These poems describe the effectiveness and success of Chicanos and Chicanas
to counter stereotypical images. They also emphasize language and oral tradition to
combat assimilationist pressures on language, identity, and social etiquette. Hecht,
Ribeau, and Sedano (1990) follow up on this analysis to describe problematic elements
in interethnic communication. These rhetorical analyses uncover issues of stereotyping
and acceptance that are countered by providing countertypes (examples that are
inconsistent with the stereotype) and positive images of nonassimilated Chicanos
(images of "Indianness," multilingual language, recognition of a unique history) and
by using reversal strategies (examples that take an apparent stereotype and probe to find
inner strength, undiscovered potential, and other evidence of positivity). González
(1990) finds a tension in the poetry of Ohio Latinos. He suggests that the writers express

both a sense of being "other"—of not belonging—and a desire to be included. As these examples show, rhetorical approaches uncover the social realities of groups, specifically shedding light on how these groups use words to frame themselves and out-groups. This demonstrates the usefulness of rhetoric for understanding various types of intolerance.

Critical Theory and Cultural Studies

Rhetorical studies might look at intolerance from a variety of perspectives such as thematic analysis. Critical theory (CT) and cultural studies (CS) add specific emphases: power relations and historical contextualization. CT, however, should not be seen as just linguistic or discourse research. Kellner (1989) summarizes CT in the following way:

> Critical theory is informed by multidisciplinary research, combined with the attempt to construct a systematic, comprehensive social theory that can confront the key social and political problems of the day. The work of the critical theorists provides criticisms and alternatives to traditional, or mainstream, social theory, philosophy, and science, together with a critique of a full range of ideologies from mass culture to religion. (p. 1)

CT tends to view all social science as inherently political and believes that it is appropriate to conduct science with an ideal in mind (implying a critique of the current systems). Many versions of CT are "motivated by an interest in relating theory to politics and an interest in the emancipation of those who are oppressed and dominated" (p. 1), which makes it very germane to a discussion of prejudice. According to Kellner (1989), CT had its beginnings in Marxism, through the works of Max Horkheimer, Theodor Adorno, and the Frankfurt School. In 1950, writers from this school penned *The Authoritarian Personality* (Adorno et al., 1950/1982). CT has borrowed from structuralists, such as Lévi-Strauss and Lacan, and has incorporated elements of linguistics, postmodernism, and Marxism. It currently spans fields from political science to architecture. From these roots have grown fields such as CS, some branches of feminism, and queer theory, all of which look in some way at prejudice and exclusion.

Power is a dominant theme in CT/CS research. The main focus is to instigate social change at either an individual or a structural level (Burrel & Morgan, 1979). The main areas of change involve power relations, either in the forms of equalizing power structures (e.g., race, class, gender) or *empowering* individuals to resist the messages and structures of a dominant society.

CS can be seen as branching off from CT, largely over the issue of *culture* and the focus of study. Horkheimer and Adorno, with their emphasis on structural Marxism, scorned mass culture as a way of soothing and distracting the masses, of making culture a commodity to be bought and sold in a capitalist system. Other theorists felt that popular (mass-produced) culture (e.g., romance novels, popular radio and television programs)—not the "high culture" of drama, opera, and painting—should be the focus of research. The popular forms, it was argued, represented where most people lived (Kellner, 1989).

CT and CS writers have looked at intolerance in various ways. One school of thought, the *structuralists,* follows the writings of Gramsci (1957/1983) and Althusser (1971). Gramsci (1957/1983), writing largely from the Italian prisons of Mussolini during the 1940s, complicated the notion of power by arguing that dominance, or *hegemony,* does not occur in only one area (e.g., economics) but rather in several areas or *terrains* (sites of struggle). Groups strive for cultural dominance as well as for dominance in the media, family structure, and culture. Gramsci suggests that all sides in a struggle for hegemony have some sort of power. Althusser (1971) brings the focus on power to include the notion of *ideology,* which Hall (1981a) later defines as "those images, concepts, and premises which provide the frameworks through which we represent, interpret, understand, and 'make sense' of some aspect of social existence" (p. 31). Althusser (1971) distinguishes between the *repressive state apparatuses* (courts, police, laws) and the *state ideological apparatuses* (educational system, family structure, religion), proposing that "no class can hold state power over a long period without at the same time exercising its hegemony over and in the state ideological apparatuses" (p. 139). Althusser suggests that the various spheres of a society (e.g., the economy, religion) are "relatively autonomous" but that "in the last instance" class is the determining factor.

CS writers have leaned heavily on these writers, suggesting (among other things) that (a) ideologies are social, not individual (thus, there can be an ideology of prejudice toward the elderly at a *societal* level); (b) various groups in a given society strive for power on different terrains, and prejudice between groups can exist in those different terrains (offering a "nonreductive" or less deterministic Marxist view of society); (c) ideologies (including prejudice) can be propagated through various ideological *systems* (e.g., educational, religious, economic, social) (Hall, 1986); (d) ideologies, including prejudice and the behaviors or terms that express it, take place in different "semantic zones" of history but "leave the traces of their connections long after the social relations to which they referred have disappeared" (Hall, 1985, p. 111); and (e) an ideology of prejudice works independently of, but connected to, other "spheres" in a given society such as economics, law, or politics (these points are synthesized from Hall, 1985, 1986). This theoretical lens could be used to look at various types of intolerance in which sides are struggling for control over a specific domain. An example would be the pro-life/pro-choice debate. Through media, lobbying, interpersonal debate, picketing, and so on, two sides seek to define terms, promote values, and influence politics. At any point in the struggle, either side could express intolerance—verbally or physically—toward the other side. This approach is called *structuralist* because it focuses on the various structures in a given society and on power relations between them.

Some structuralists take what is called the "linguistic turn." Following Lévi-Strauss (1963) and Lacan (1977), they focus on the meanings of words (e.g., man, woman, American, Black, Oriental, Jew, Christian) and how those meanings are "reproduced." Kristeva (1990), for example, looks at how various pamphlets by Celine during the 1930s and 1940s paint Jews as the "exemplar . . . of all hatred, of all desire" (p. 176).

Tracing the concept of the "stranger" through various philosophers, Kristeva (1991) discusses the "disquieting strangeness" that one encounters when meeting someone who is different. Gilman (1990) analyzes Victorian London representations of Jack the Ripper, described as an Eastern Jew. Stepan (1991) points out how science, although it has a degree of objectivity, is "a highly social activity and is not sealed off from the values of the society in which it is practiced" (p. 9). At times, she notes, science has had a role in maintaining arbitrary racial categories; these are *not* "preexisting, discrete, biological entities but social-political categories or perceptions created through scientific work and the social relations of power" (p. 104). Furthermore, science established a hierarchical order of superiority of races that is part of the historical baggage of racial intolerance today. In many other ways, media, individuals, and social institutions maintain the existence either of intolerances or of images that individuals use to justify their intolerances. For example, in Chapter 11 of this volume, Ono analyzes a documentary titled *Doubles* about bi- and multiracial relations in the United States. He suggests that the documentary "reinscribes racist representations" through a rigid split between what is Japanese and what is American, and it legitimates what Ono calls the postwar "colonization" of Japan. Furthermore, it promotes the English language and "Americanness" as tools to success for interracial relationships, interpreting the meanings of the informants of the video only as they fit into this "narrative logic."

Omi and Winant's (1986) notion that America is fundamentally "racialized"—divided at its very being and at every level by race—could be applied to other identities and intersections as well. Two such applications are feminism and queer theory.[20] *Feminism* addresses issues of gender identity (e.g., the social creation of what it means to be male or female) and gender politics/oppression, especially from the perspective of women. For many, feminism represents the attempt to provide "liberation" for women, including things such as the breakdown of the "dichotomy between masculine and feminine" (Marcuse, 1974, p. 281) and the liberation of feminine desire. Schwichtenberg (1989a) applies feminism directly to CS, noting,

> British feminist cultural studies is concerned with the enabling and constraining aspects of popular representations, particularly how certain "feminine" forms (such as fashion, soap operas, teen magazines, and dance) are used by girls [or women] in the construction of feminine cultural identity. (p. 204)

CS and other forms of feminism seek to resist ideologies and structures that oppress women in a variety of ways. Rakow and Wackwitz (Chapter 5) present feminism as "antisexism" and discuss how it can be used for resistance. Schwichtenberg (1989b) argues that the whole rhetorical creation and recreation of what is "beautiful" for women in the United States serves two ends: masculine pleasure (patriarchy) and corporate profit (capitalism).[21] She demonstrates this through a rhetorical analysis of the beauty craze of the 1970s, "Farrah Fawcett hair," pointing out that "hairstyle, as woman's 'renatured,' resignified body part, represents, in microcosm, the larger work undertaken by culture that uses woman's physiology to identify her with nature and thus a lower cultural order" (p. 299). Other feminists, as noted elsewhere in this chapter, look at the intersection of race and gender. For example, Wallace (1992) feels that some Black men preempt the voice of Black women by trying to establish literary canons of African American women. Collins (1990) discusses how race, gender, and social class are "articulated" in regard to African American women. Images of African American women as mammies, matriarchs, welfare mothers, and so on work against the freedom of African American women, both sexually and economically. She suggests that this domination is not only perpetrated by the White community but also reproduced through the structures and representations in the Black community. Rakow and Wackwitz (Chapter 5) detail images and meanings surrounding native women and men in the minds of Whites—meanings that subordinate natives and "justify White domination as a superior belief system," an analysis that parallels Tajima's (1989) analysis of images of Asian women as "passive figures who exist to serve men, especially as love interests for White men (Lotus Blossoms) or as partners in crime with men of their own kind (Dragon Ladies)" (p. 309).

Another application of CT to a particular identity occurs in *queer theory*. Warner (1992) suggests that queer theory is more than just an attempt to counter heterosexual thought. Its purpose is to "define itself against the normal . . . and normal includes normal business in the academy." Specifically, it seeks to "mess up the desexualized spaces of the academy, exude some rut, reimagine the publics from and for which academic intellectuals write, dress, and perform" (p. 18). Warner (1991) sees queer theory making great advances in showing the pervasiveness of the struggles of gays and lesbians in contemporary culture. Like Omi and Winant (1986), he sees the oppression of gays and lesbians at every level of society and in "a wide range of institutions and ideology" (p. 5). Hammonds (1992) considers the social construction of the "other" in the discussion of AIDS. Specifically, Hammonds suggests, dominant culture (e.g., media, textbooks) socially construct what is meant by *disease* and *sexuality* in such a way that excludes people with AIDS. However, she notes, this exclusion also is racialized with people of color, specifically women of color, being represented in a certain way. Finally, Nakayama (Chapter 6) suggests that gays are oppressed by both the words and the silence ("the love that dare not speak its name") of the heterosexual community.

In all of these notions, certain concepts are central. First is the notion of a *verbal discourse* or *construction,* through media or interpersonal communication, that places people in certain positions within a society. Part of this placement is "othering": creating a sense that members of another group are somehow different from one's own, the basis of moral exclusion discussed previously. For example, Collins (1990) states, "Maintaining images of Black women as the Other provides ideological justification for race, gender, and class oppression" (p. 68). Rothenberg (1992) suggests, "The construction of difference is central to racism, sexism, and other forms of oppressive ideologies" (p. 47). *Difference,* be it conceived in racial, cultural, religious, or some other terms, is at the heart of intolerance.

Such differences become *essentialized*; that is, a group is discussed as if it had an "ultimate essence that transcends historical and cultural boundaries" (Brah, 1992, p. 126). Schwichtenberg (1989b) suggests that ideas or objects (e.g., women, beauty) are treated as if they were solid and fixed (essentialized) through contextualizing them within a linguistic framework. Phenomena are placed in verbal dichotomies such as that between nature and culture. Things discussed ("articulated") as cultural are seen as more likely to change than are those seen as natural. Thus, as Hall (1981a) suggests, one of the main ways in which ideology is propagated as "fixed" is by making ideas seem natural or traditional. As such, any deviation or suggested change is viewed as unnatural or deviant.

This introduces another key notion: *ideology*. Ideology is not language, but certain terms such as "democracy," "freedom," and, by extension, "normal," "American," and so on can be placed in certain locations in different sets of ideas (discourses). Ideology precedes us; it is our environment. Cultural and interpersonal communication creates and passes on (produces and reproduces) ideology so that, unless it is brought to our awareness, it is difficult to escape. Words are given meaning by their placement in the sets of ideas in which they are discussed. For example, gender and class are *articulated* (or discussed and displayed) differently, as are religion and nationality. This implies, for example, that gender and class (or religion and nationality) are independent phenomena. These articulations sometimes intertwine so that people will perceive and relate to women of different social classes (or women and men of the same social class) differently. Or, we might articulate or represent a certain nationality with a certain religion (e.g., America as a Christian nation). The structuralist school, especially with its linguistic turn, opens up for us the possibility that notions such as *race, gender, class, elderly,* or *disability* are fluctuating, influenced by the contexts of the messages that surround them. If a given connection between ideas is oppressive, then groups or individuals can challenge those meanings and offer messages and texts that socially redefine the terms in less oppressive ways.

The structuralist school is not the only CT/CS approach to intolerance. Other writers reflect what is known as *postmodernism*. This school of thought places less emphasis on center and structure. Rosenau (1992) summarizes the postmodern approach(es) as follows:

> In its most *extreme* formulations, postmodernism is revolutionary; it goes to the very core of what constitutes social science and radically dismisses it. In its more *moderate* proclamations, postmodernism encourages substantive redefinition and innovation. Postmodernism proposes to set itself up outside the modern paradigm, not to judge modernity by its own criteria but rather to contemplate and deconstruct it. (pp. 4-5, emphases in original)

Postmodernism rejects much of advanced Western civilization such as industrialization, liberal democracy, and the detached neutrality of social science. In the end, "the postmodern goal is not to formulate an alternative set of assumptions but to register the impossibility of establishing any such underpinning for knowledge" (p. 6). It promotes a *de-centered* view of both society and science. At the societal level, it places multiple "voices" side by side rather than in dominant and subordinate cultural positions. In science, it deemphasizes direct causality and universal laws as means of predicting human behavior. As such, postmodernists favor "readings" over "observations" and favor "interpretations" over "findings" (p. 8).

In some cases, these readings take a *text-centered* approach. Authors look at the words or pictures used in a text (e.g., photographic representations of Oliver North [Turner, 1990]) to find underlying meanings. From the postmodern stance, meanings need not be consistent. Postmodernists tend to take concepts seen in past research as "unified" or "consistent" and to show its inconsistencies and tensions, a notion some refer to as *problematizing*. Some things that have been problematized are the very notions of nationality, gender roles, disability, and so on. Because these things no longer are seen to have a set "reality," various views of what it means to be a man or a woman, for example, can be offered and can compete against one another for acceptance. Some writers seek to uncover contradictory meanings in a concept (e.g., social class) or a text (e.g., the latest popular film) by breaking apart a text and finding its underlying meanings (deconstruction). Some of these meanings might be framed in terms of opposition to or support of a centered power structure, and some meanings might simply show the contradictory character of human nature. As an example of deconstruction, Meeks and Courtaway (1995) analyze the movie *Philadelphia*. On the surface, they suggest, the movie seeks to break down stereotypes about people with AIDS; however, beneath the surface, AIDS still is connected rhetorically with homosexuality, and the movie still reproduces gay stereotypes. Other scholars focus on how cultural artifacts or texts are consumed, looking at the multiple, competing meanings receivers give to a text (polysemy) (Turner, 1990). As an example of this, Nakayama and Peñaloza (1993) compare how White students and students of color perceive different issues in Madonna videos. Students of color often see the video *Borderline* as a commentary on interethnic relations, whereas Whites tend to see it as a love story.

Analysis

CT as a whole seeks to be holistic or nonreductionistic; it looks at things in their complexity, often taking into account their historical and social contexts. This goal gives it an advantage over many other approaches that look at only one level of social reality. Much of CT focuses on the way in which social reality is constructed with words or symbols (e.g., through media). The multidisciplinarity this engenders constitutes one of the main strengths of the approach. The approach is able to account for the historical and contextual specificity of different intolerances and also considers the role of language and popular culture in maintaining prejudice.[22] Many critical theorists have taken useful concepts from Marxism but abandoned many of its more theoretically restrictive ideas (McRobbie, 1992) that add breadth to the types of explanations CT can offer. Perhaps its most important strength in terms of prejudice is the practicality of CT and CS. CT and CS conceptualize phenomena as changing, unstable, and contested, and this viewpoint can encourage the problematizing of the social world. Counter to many theories that assume an underlying stability while studying "process," CT/CS theories (especially those with tinges of postmodernism) work from an assumption that diversity is required in both theory and method. As a result, the approaches are better able to deal with the changing nature of reality and, in fact, to work in the instigation of that change.

I perceive five main limitations in the CT/CS approach. First, many recent critical studies rely entirely on rhetorical approaches, leaving aside or even disdaining empirical or ethnographic approaches. This, despite the goals of holism, is a limiting lens. Second, although the "neo-Marxism" of many critical theorists has long abandoned strict theories of dominance by the elite, some still follow the Marxists in the a priori assumption that power is at work in all expressions of intolerance and always is one of the primary concerns. The imposition of power, while exposing possible explanations of intolerance, also may distort what is observed. Third, these studies allow for an analysis of disempowered groups but to date have said little about intolerance of the disempowered toward the empowered. The critical element is that it criticizes oppressive forces; the tendency is for the object of criticism to be, a priori, conservative or mainstream ideology. Only with modifications to past practice could CT be used to focus on intolerance held by homeless people, feminists, gays, and so on. A fourth weakness is derived from the methodological stance of some critical theorists. By choosing to study social processes from the role of critic, these critical theorists set themselves *apart* or at a distance from the observed. These critical theorists are academicians and scholars typically occupying a different social class than most of the people about whom they comment. They become potentially subject to the same charge of objectivism levied against positivists, that is, that there is a separation between the observed and the observer. Despite arguing that phenomena are socially constructed and contested, many critical theorists do not engage those whose worlds they study in dialogue about their existence. The rise of critical ethnography (Conquergood, 1991) attempts to address this problem. Finally, despite its claim to be multidisciplinary, historically contextual, and practical, much of the theory has lost its political edge (Bennett, 1992), grown institutionalized (Hall, 1992), ignored history (Steedman, 1992), and exported British or American theory without modification to other contexts (Morris, 1992; Turner, 1992).

■ Conclusion

At first glance, the multidisciplinary discussion of the roots of prejudice seems purely academic. However, the discussion is very practical in two regards. First, when it comes to discussing issues of intolerance, we often talk past each other. An understanding of the possible roots and definitions of intolerance would help us understand each other better. Recently, I was leading a discussion on racial issues and the question arose as to whether Blacks could be racist in the United States. The general consensus of the group, which was well read in multicultural studies and training, was that Blacks could not be racist; because racism is tied to institutional power, Blacks did not have the power base to be racist, and, by similar reasoning, women did not have the power to be sexist, and so on. If a group of Blacks beat up a White solely because he or she was White (or if a woman sexually harassed a man), then it would not be racism (sexism) because the power structure did not back up the Blacks (woman). If a group of Whites beat up a Black (or if a man sexually harassed a woman), then it would be racist (sexist). Some in the group disagreed. They felt that racism occurs anytime people were discriminated against based on race. The difficulty in understanding here seems to be one of definition. Specifically, for some, intolerance is seen at an institutional level and is defined by power relations; for others, it is located at an individual level and is defined by types of cognitions or behaviors. If such a distinction could be made, then individual forms of intolerance (e.g., racism, sexism) could be practiced by anyone, but institutional forms could be practiced only by those in power. Looking across definitions helps us examine more important issues.

It is in these important issues, such as the underlying causes of intolerance, that the second application comes. It is possible, as some suggest, that most of our attempts at reducing intolerance have fizzled and failed because they address symptoms rather than problems. If that is the case, then what is the problem that should be addressed? Allport (1954/1979) suggests that ignorance is one of the main causes of prejudice. Increased knowledge about another group will reduce stereotypes and strengthen our ability to categorize more accurately and better understand the behavior of others. Contact with members of other groups is a key to reducing ignorance (and therefore intolerance), as seen in the literature on intergroup contact (e.g., Amir, 1969). However, as noted previously, simply informing ourselves—simply having more contact—does not reduce our desire to maintain power over other groups (Jackman & Crane, 1986).

For other scholars, desire for group power, rather than ignorance, is the base of intolerance. Toward this end, van den Berghe (1967) suggests that "the roots of 'racial' problems go much deeper than individual prejudices. . . . Racial discrimination cannot be permanently and effectively abolished without more fundamental political and economic reforms" (p. 130). But what forms should those societal-level reforms take? The answer again depends on the author. Some favor a system that increases the possibilities of disempowered groups to participate (Ezorsky, 1991). Rabushka (1974), however, proposes that "the perfectly competitive market" (p. 97) or a "voluntary exchange in free markets" (p. 69) will keep racial conflicts to a minimum. Yet, he suggests that he cannot separate these from police enforcement, level and availability of formal education, and so on.

It is not my point here to enter into a full debate of political and individual interventions; these are addressed more completely in Section 5 of this volume. Rather, I want to suggest that any understanding of intolerance must be broad based and multifaceted. Each of the approaches discussed in this chapter has something to add to the discussion. A full understanding of intolerance—and the implementation of solid solutions—requires that we consider the various influences. The problem of intolerance must be attacked at many levels and in many ways. What is needed is a perspective that brings together the various levels at which intolerance can exist, the various types of intolerance, and the various ways of looking at intolerance. The next chapter outlines one such perspective.

3 Layers and Holograms:

A New Look at Prejudice

Michael L. Hecht
John R. Baldwin

> Our almost universal tendency to fragment the world and ignore the
> dynamic interconnectedness of all things is responsible for many of our
> problems, not only in science but in our lives and our society as well. . . .
> We believe we can deal with various problems in our society, such as
> crime, poverty, and drug addiction, without addressing the problems in
> our society as a whole, and so on. (Talbot, 1991, p. 49)

Just at a point where it seems we should have made headway toward intergroup
tolerance both at the national and world levels,[23] sources from many corners suggest
that intolerance and hatred are on the rise. For example, the incidence of hate crimes
increased in Los Angeles County by 31% between 1991 and 1992 (Nakagawa, 1993).
In 1992 alone, there were 4,558 hate crimes reported in the United States and 2,000 in
Germany ("FBI," 1993) including crimes against people of various ethnic groups, gay
males, and so on. Just as Israel and Palestine move toward peace, Yitzak Rabin is
assassinated. As peace seems near in the Balkans, it is likely that conflict will flare
someplace else; in fact, *U.S. News & World Report* lists 39 areas around the world that
were engaged in armed conflict in 1988 (Barnes, Chesnoff, Carter, Rosenberg, &
Trimble, 1988). What is characteristic about intergroup conflict—be it armed with
nuclear weapons or with media symbols, words, and subtle nonverbal behaviors—is
that it is *complex*. Conflicts often have deep roots in history as well as ongoing

contemporary circumstances that propel them forward and make them increasingly difficult to disentangle.

Many writers have attempted to explain intolerance in the press and popular books as well as in academic scholarship. In Chapter 2, we saw how a number of theoretical approaches from a variety of academic disciplines approach the issue of intolerance. Allport (1954/1979), for example, looks at how intolerance (prejudice) is developed as one grows up and how it is structured in the mind of the prejudiced person. Allport also notes the value of other approaches such as historical, contextual, and sociological ones:

> As a rule most "theories" are advanced by their authors to call attention to some one important causal factor, without implying that no other factors are operating. Usually an author selects for emphasis one [area]; he [sic] then develops his ideas concerning certain forces that operate within this approach to create prejudice. (pp. 207-208)

The difficulty is that any given theory operates from only one standpoint and, as a result, addresses only one portion of the difficult puzzle of intolerance. Talbot (1991), in the quote that introduces this chapter, urges a more holistic approach—one that looks at the entire picture and the interconnectedness of the parts. He notes our tendency to treat only parts—to disconnect reality—in the way in which we extract portions of the earth without considering the effects on the environment or treat only parts of the body without being concerned with the whole. In the same way, any solution aimed at reducing intolerance (or any theory about intolerance) must admit the complexity of the issue. As such, a perspective that allows the combination of methodologies and theoretical (and "metatheoretical") points of view is needed.[24]

We recently presented a perspective that attempts to show the complexity of intolerance and to demonstrate how the various approaches can inform each other (Baldwin & Hecht, 1995). This theory, an ongoing development from the communication theory of identity developed by Hecht (Hecht, 1993; Hecht, Collier, & Ribeau, 1993), proposes that intolerance can exist at various levels and be expressed in different ways. One of the main points of the theory is its departure from the notion of Allport (1954/1979) and others that prejudice was a unitized thing—a "generalized prejudice"—that, as a psychological structure, exists and is expressed the same way toward various targets. Instead, we argue that although there may be an underlying, global, or unifying construction of prejudice, there also are various intolerances; even ethnic intolerance can be expressed differently toward one group than toward another. With this chapter, however, we turn back on our own theory, reconsidering some of the notions as well as expanding and building on the original framework. We first present the basics of the theory—the layered perspective—and then suggest some revisions (a holographically layered approach). We want to state clearly that this is intended to be *a possible approach* to the study of intolerance. It is meant as a tool to allow dialogue between disciplines and theories, not as an end-all theory to replace or exclude other approaches.

■ The Layered Perspective on Prejudice

Before we present the specifics of the layered perspective, it would be good to discuss a few of the notions that inform us as we write this theory (called *sensitizing constructs* in Hecht et al., 1993, p. 22; see also Denzin, 1978, and Giddens, 1984). Hecht (1993) introduces the concept as follows:

> Layering implies that there are alternative ways of knowing that are continually juxtaposed and played off each other and/or blended together. There are many vehicles at our disposal for experiencing our social world. These include the experiential realms of thought or cognition, physiology, behavior, emotion, and spirituality. Just because there are inconsistencies between theories grounded in each realm does not mean that the theories are not useful individually or cannot be combined in creative ways. (pp. 76-77)

It is this multimethod, multiview focus that we see as the first advantage of layering as a possible metaphor for theory and research. Layering can refer to the use (either separately or at the same time) of various methodologies and various ways of seeing science. Not only could methods be layered, but so too can understandings of reality and of human nature. Scholars traditionally have focused on one theoretical approach at the expense of others, sometimes admitting that "quarrels among them are unprofitable" (Allport, 1954/1979, p. 207). Some disciplines have "invested great energy in separating these realms in the name of theoretical consistency and [have] continually privileged the cognitive and behavioral worlds" (Hecht, 1993, p. 77). Scholars have long noted that those who look at the various levels "rarely consult with one another" (Chaffee & Berger, 1987, p. 143). Ironically, exclusion and othering in scholarly dialogue reconstruct the prejudicial social relations it studies, setting up in-group/out-group, hierarchical power relations, stereotyping, and so on among the scientific and humanistic disciplines and approaches. Layering suggests that scholars in these areas consider other ideas, such as emotion and spirituality (but not necessarily by treating these rationally). At the same time, researchers who traditionally have focused on subjective perspectives also might let their ideas be informed by more objectivist ideas.[25] In this sense, theoretical and metatheoretical concepts can be seen as layered without recreating the very exclusionary and hierarchical processes they study.

The layered perspective joins a growing chorus of theorists arguing for multiple standpoints or perspectives. Giddens (1984), for example, tries to integrate deterministic structural functionalism with interpretivism in structuration theory. Giddens attempts this layering by casting structures as *recursive*—created, recreated, and expressed by the actions of agents whose actions are, in a sense, constrained by the structure rules and resources.

At the same time, layering reflects the multiple levels of meaning that given events have and how they are structured. For example, any given action of intolerance can be understood in its immediate context. But it also occurs in a context of past social structures, symbols, the psychological processes of the individuals involved, and the current social, economic, and political structures. These are layered with each other in consistent and contradictory ways, like covers and sheets on a bed, or through and between each other, like chocolate ribbons in vanilla ice cream, tides in an ocean, or oil and vinegar in an emulsion. Any interaction places a layer on the interactants' own personal experiences—confirming or challenging (or both) past notions and beliefs as well as preparing the context for future interactions. The actions of individuals add to the collective experience of intolerance. This may happen through the mere passing on of categories and experiences of tolerance/intolerance or through specific interactions that change social structures or are reproduced as symbols consumed by a large number of people (e.g., in a news broadcast or a situation comedy). These interactions become a layer of context for future interactants as they meet one another. Thus, social reality itself can be seen as reclusively layered (Giddens, 1984).

Finally, intolerances themselves can be layered. This notion comes from the philosophers of race who note that different intolerances compound each other. For example, Schwichtenberg (1989b) sees American constructions of beauty as oppressing women in terms of both economics and gender as they benefit "patriarchy" and the capitalist enterprise. Collins (1990) notes, regarding African American women, that images of mammies, matriarchs, promiscuous women, and so on

> form a nexus of elite White male interpretations of Black female sexuality and fertility. Moreover, by meshing smoothly with systems of race, class, and gender oppression, they provide effective ideological justifications for racial oppression, the politics of gender subordination, and the economic exploitation inherent in capitalist economies. (p. 78)

In the first case, gender and class oppression are layered on one another. In the latter, Collins notes additional layers traversing these two: Racism, sexism, and class oppression all overlap in this instance with the result that various intolerances can be seen as layered or synergistically tied together.

The layered perspective on prejudice attempts to build on the analysis of moral exclusion and to integrate previous approaches by using the construct of layering. Layering implies that the world exists on multiple levels and must be accessed through multiple perspectives on each level as well as the juxtaposition of levels on and between each other. Tolerance is not just a characteristic of the individual or of social structures but rather is a characteristic of each and their interrelationships. The implications of this are at least twofold. First, because structures change with history and circumstances, tolerances should be conceived not as static things that are single-faceted or one-way but rather as things that vary and change in structure, expression, and target. Tolerances must be considered within their cultural, historical, and symbolic milieus. Second, in addition to understanding the symbols and systems that shape intolerance, it also is necessary to see how people use, reinvent, or counter those influences as they process information, categorize people, or form group-based attitudes as well as to understand the role of prejudice in communities.

After the publication of the 1995 version of the perspective, our colleagues have challenged us to continue thought on this perspective.[26] In particular, questions were raised about the metaphor of layering. Some saw layers as linear, static, unidimensional, and separate. Although we intended layering to communicate a variety of connections, the image many perceived was of sheets of paper stacked one on top of another. At best, layering seemed to express intersecting streets—still a flat, static, and largely separate vision. From conversations with Cristina González, we explored the metaphor of holographic layering as a means of communicating a more dynamic, holistic, synthetic image. In exploring this new metaphor, we call on Talbot's (1991) holographic theory, using his description of holographic images and the insights it offers without placing our theory within his holographic theory.

■ Holographic Layering: A Reconsideration

Talbot (1991) elaborates a new way of seeing the world and the universe—that of a hologram. This view, he suggests, has not "achieved the status of a model or theory in the strictest sense of these terms" (p. 7) but rather is a sort of metaphor or analogy, a vehicle for explaining reality. Talbot's book focuses specifically on physical (e.g., universe, brain, mind, body) and metaphysical (e.g., out-of-body experiences, déjà vu, psychic healings) realities. However, we see applications of the holographic metaphor to the social world as well. We use this strictly as a metaphor in this chapter because we are not, at this point, adopting Talbot's holographic explanation completely; we are borrowing from it what makes sense of the world of prejudice and (in)tolerance.

The holographic metaphor is based on the principal notion that the world/universe is like a *hologram*. The hologram is a picture. It is produced, according to Talbot (1991), when a

> single laser light is split into two separate beams. The first beam is bounced off the object to be photographed. . . . Then the second beam is allowed to collide with the reflected light of the first, and the resulting interference pattern is recorded on film. (p. 15)

The interference is from the waves of the laser beam crossing each other in the film, which leads to one of the main principles of holography (the study of the holographic view of the world): *All reality is made up of wave particles and their interferences.*[27] Although a full explanation is beyond the scope of this chapter, the general principle is that things such as light, electrons, and even mind and spirit are, in fact, simultaneously wave motions and particles.[28] These have complex natures in that they move in waves until one tries to observe them. The only way in which to observe them is to stop them for an instant, in which they become particles. Furthermore, the holograph is enacted in intersections; it exists only due to the intersections of the wave particles. These intersection patterns are called *interference patterns* in the physical vocabulary of holographic theory.

The holographic photograph suggests two important principles for this chapter. The first is that of *multidimensionality.* What is interesting about a holographic picture is that one can turn it to look at all sides of the thing photographed, say an apple. If the holograph is projected into a tube, then one can actually walk around it to see all sides of the apple. The view "determines" what one sees; the angle of the light entering the holograph combines with the holograph to reveal an image. A different image is associated with each viewing angle. This is important to us because it seems that any "one-dimensional look" at prejudice is not enough. Prejudices are complicated, multi-dimensional things. A multidisciplinary, multilayered holographic perspective allows us to see the thing from different angles. It is the interference between these perspectives, where explanations cross and rub against one another, that reveals the most about prejudice. (In this, we realize that we are borrowing somewhat loosely from the holographic explanation.)

The second principle is *holism:*

> If a piece of holographic film containing the image of an apple is cut in half and then illuminated by a laser, each half will still be found to contain the entire image of the apple! Even if the halves are divided again and then again, an entire apple can still be reconstructed from each small portion of the film (although the images will get hazier as the portions get smaller). (Talbot, 1991, p. 16)

Holism is applied to the study of prejudice in many ways. Types of intolerance (e.g., sexism, ageism, racism) permeate all aspects of society and are reflected through various expressions and at multiple levels. For example, ageism not only is the notion of stereotyping the elderly but also involves the construction of a *way of thinking* (which takes power away from the elderly to give it to a younger group) and a *way of interacting* with elderly individuals. Ageism permeates decision making, politics, distribution of economic resources, and so on. Stereotypes reinforce a system that discredits and disenfranchises the elderly, and government structures (i.e., laws and policies) further support this hierarchical structure.

Sexism serves as another example. Sexism includes a host of definitional debates and other power struggles. For example, what are the "proper" or "allowable" roles for males and females in a society? What are the appropriate ways of treating people of a given biological sex (sexually, professionally, or interpersonally), and who defines those? But sexism is more than just a verbal-symbolic ideology. It involves the ways in which one group behaves toward another group (e.g., the normative allowing of violence or date rape), historical relationships, hierarchy, and so on.

Ageism or sexism is found in a society both in the repressive state apparatus (e.g., laws, courts, views of criminality) and in the ideological state apparatus (e.g., textbooks, MTV commercials, family structures and definitions) (Althusser, 1971); in other words, it is found in multiple terrains (Gramsci, 1957/1983). The battle occurs on various sites of struggle as the elderly vie for control (over their own lives, over public policy, over self-definition) in education, in the courts, in media, and in the family. Omi and Winant (1986) make the same point about racism, suggesting that the United States is a fundamentally racialized society, that is, that racial distinction (and racism) exists at every level of the American fabric—as we would say, in every piece of the hologram. Furthermore, the processes of ageism and sexism are reflected in racist and heterosexist practices. According to the holographic metaphor, one could look in any one area of a society (just as at any piece of a holographic film) and get a glimpse of many prejudices.

The holographic metaphor leads us to several conclusions about layers of prejudice. First, *a given intolerance, even though culturally and historically defined, will have a commonality with other intolerances;* that is, discrimination toward those with specific physical (dis)abilities will occur in the United States just as in Mexico or Pakistan. In one sense, each intolerance will be different (i.e., different "ableisms" just as there are different "racisms"). However, each of these will have some common root, and by looking at one piece of the hologram (e.g., treatment of the differently abled in Pakistan), we will see shadows of the same picture as it appears in other places and times. One might, for example, see an image of how people with certain disabilities are different from what is constituted as the norm or how they are perceived to cause an inconvenience. From there, the actual treatments and stereotypes might differ from place to place and from time to time. The application of the layered perspective to a specific time and space requires one to generate localized approaches and methods.

Second, *a given intolerance, at a given time and place, can be seen at various levels of the society in which it is found.* As in the previous examples of ageism and sexism, one should be able to look at any piece of the puzzle and get some sort of picture of the whole puzzle. This is not to deny that there are contradictions in a society, just as there are contradictions within individuals. A given society might show appreciation and inclusion of differently abled people while at the same time showing intolerance and exclusion. However, just like the hologram, in both of these main points, the smaller the piece of the film[29] we observe, the fuzzier the picture. To get a better picture of a given intolerance (e.g., ageism), we should observe more and more, as well as larger and larger, pieces together (e.g., move locations or terrains of society, cross-cultural, or cross-epoch studies).

Third, *intolerances may share some common components;* that is, if one were to look at the underlying structure of one intolerance (in a given society at a given point in time), one also may see a picture of other intolerances in that society at that point of time and of other intolerances in other societies at other points of time. This notion argues for a continued study of intolerance in and of itself, of a generalized theory of prejudice. With this, the holographic metaphor has brought us full circle from our earlier critique of Allport's (1954/1979) generalized notion of prejudice (Baldwin & Hecht, 1994, 1995). We would now conclude that any given intolerance contains a picture of any other intolerance. Studying ethnocentrism in the Netherlands will tell us something about ancient intertribal conflict in Middle America as well as something about anti-Catholic rhetoric in 19th-century Ireland.

We are not saying, however, exactly the same thing as Allport (1954/1979) says with his generalized notion of prejudice. Our conception of the framework of intolerance is broader. Allport focuses on how someone who had anti-Catholic attitudes also would likely have anti-Communist attitudes and so on. He focuses on the psychological level of prejudice. Others propose models that begin to cut across layers. For example,

Bar-Tal (1990) proposes various models of ethnocentrism. An element in each of these is a mental and verbal dehumanizing or delegitimization of the other group. He proposes a finite number of categories of delegitimizing speech to analyze intolerance across cultures, and he illustrates this through multiple examples around the world—from U.S.-Russia cold war relations, to the United States' Black-White conflicts, to the Arab-Israeli conflict. A key to these models is that a person sees the other group as repulsive and threatening (as a group) and then grows to have a different moral standard by which to treat that group (moral exclusion) (Opotow, 1990). Zur (1987, 1991) has a similar perspective on war. Zur (1987) delineates several types of war that he defines more broadly to include various types of intergroup conflict. He visualizes war as a Rorschach of culture or what we might consider to be a hologram of a culture; that is, the types and dynamics of war are cultural (not biological) and "simultaneously reflec[t] individual and shared values" within a culture (p. 127). Central in his notion of war and hatred is the need to dehumanize the enemy. This same process, Zur (1991) notes, can be seen in so-called ethnic wars (Serbs-Croats, Czechs-Slovaks), in religious wars (Protestants-Catholics, Muslims-Christians), in national wars (Iran-Iraq, Arab-Israeli), and even in ethnic/race wars (Black-White). Once an enemy is dehumanized, various psychological processes set in—"either/or" thinking (us-them), differences in how one makes attributions of characteristics, and so on.

What seems inherent in the discussions of both Bar-Tal and Zur is the idea that conflicts have more than just a psychological element. One could look at language usage, at political maneuverings, at communication, and so on and see the elements of dehumanization and prejudice. We are suggesting that the core or framework of prejudice is broader than intergroup perception and psychology; it is multilevel and multidimensional.[30] There are psychological, social, linguistic, political, historical, and economic elements to most intolerances. Dehumanization, both as a psychological concept and as a social practice, might be one of the things at the core, as might power struggles. On the surface, the notion of dehumanization might not seem to apply as readily to more subtle or covert "wars" of intolerance such as sexism or homophobia. Yet, even in these, there may be a sort of dehumanizing. For example, for males to mistreat females (e.g., using them specifically for sexual purposes, treating them as less than equal) could be dehumanizing—treating women as if they were a different "species" with lesser rights, abilities, and so on. It is just this dehumanization that various chapters in this book discuss, from Asante on racism (Chapter 4), to Nakayama on homophobia (Chapter 6), to the narratives of González (Chapter 12), Tohe (Chapter 14), and Holton (Chapter 16).

Even though there might be an element or, better, a framework of interconnected elements that supports any intolerance, all intolerances are not identical. In our exten-sion of the holographic metaphor, this would exemplify our fourth point, that *each angle (prejudice) reveals a different (although interconnected) picture.* We would continue to hold that, although there may be some underlying generalized prejudice, there also are different racisms, different sexisms, and different classisms. Van der Dennen (1987) makes this point. On the one hand, he sees similar roots to all intolerance (many of which, he suggests, may have biological roots and be similar to intolerance in other animal species):

> Ubiquitously evident in all forms of collective intolerance . . . is an expressed desire by leaders and/or members to protect and promote the uniformity, conformity, [and] "purity" of the groups by denouncing or acting intolerantly towards individuals or groups perceived—simply because, in some sense defined as critical, they are different—as threats to the well-being and integrity of the intolerant collectivity. (p. 40)

Yet, he sees human intolerance as distinctly different because it involves the creation and use of symbolic worlds: "The ultimate justification and legitimation of collective violence invokes complex ideological, symbolic constructions, superordinate goals, spiritual values, high moral principles, and the most noble, virtuous, righteous, self-transcendent and altruistic motives" (p. 38).

Although Allport's (1954/1979) notion of generalized prejudice receives some support from Bierly (1985), whose research is consistent with the notion that "prejudice is a generalized attitude encompassing the quite distinct outgroups of Blacks, women, and homosexuals" (p. 197), and from Ray and Lovejoy (1986), who also find a generalized prejudice toward the different out-groups of Australia, this conclusion is not supported by other research. A number of studies have reported only low to moderate relationships among the "isms" (Fernald, 1995; Ficarrotto, 1990; Henley & Pincus, 1978). A recent meta-analysis finds different types of prejudices (Schütz & Six, 1996), and this is consistent with our factor-analytic study of the spheres (Baldwin & Hecht, 1994). Young-Bruehl (1996) argues that the different spheres of prejudice such as racism, anti-Semitism, sexism, and homophobia have different internal (il)logics. Not only do these spheres differ within a culture, but, because ideologies, political biases, historical imperatives, enemies, and friends change, so do the finer details of intolerance. Thus, van der Dennen (1987), with several other evolutionary theorists, argues that any intolerance must be understood in its own historical, cultural context.

Fifth, we conclude that *our understanding of prejudice is maximized by examining the interference patterns—intersections, interpenetrations, connections, interactions— between and among the various approaches to prejudice, types of prejudice, and terrains of prejudice.* To understand homophobia, we need both empiricist media effect studies and critical analyses of representations of sex. We need to look at how individuals understand their own sexual orientations and at how society deals with these orientations. We need to understand how sexual orientation, ethnicity, and religion intersect. We need to look across domains, eras, and perspectives to see holographically.

Before moving on to further delineate the holographic layered perspective, we should note further criticism of our metaphor. González suggests that these images— layering and holograph—do not mix well. (We might say that they do not layer well; others might say that they war with each other.) The holograph suggests holism with elements as part of a whole rather than separate. Layers, on the other hand, suggest linearity and separation. Whereas the holographic metaphor connotes synthesis, community, and togetherness, layering stresses the connections, intersections, and contact between and among the various layers. We argue that the dynamic tension between the conceptions is a positive force. Too often, we honor the stabilizing and clarifying parts of our understanding, elevating it over the destabilizing and problematizing. Having contradictory metaphors and images creates movement from the stable to the unstable and back.

González offers an image of these forces that talks to the holographic nature of layering. She describes a body of water with waves washing sediment up on the shores. The sediment builds up in layers until disturbed; a larger wave splashes up, and an emulsion of sediment and water is created. The sediment relayers itself until the next wave. González draws parallels to life's experiences. We layer new experiences on the old and in so doing reorder our experience of the past, present, and future. The gentler waves of experience relayer more subtly with more extreme experiences associated with more revolutionary movement.

With this understanding of the basic notion of holographic layering, we now seek to provide an organizational structure to the layers. We propose four constructs to delineate and sensitize us to the layers of cultural tolerance: stances, spheres, levels of analysis, and types of understanding.[31]

■ Stances

There is a tendency to see prejudice in dichotomous terms (prejudice/not prejudice), just as the prejudicial individual tends to see only two sides (Black-White, good-bad). To avoid recreating these prejudicial structures and to better describe prejudice, we feel that the notion of attitudes toward diversity needs to be problematized or complicated. This is the concept we refer to as *stances*. Stances can be defined as the *level or type of acceptance of an out-group or of a person in that out-group based on group membership*. Regarding this and future definitions, we should note that out-group is perceptual; that is, in- and out-groups are socially created and are personally and communally perceived and enacted (a point we return to under the "levels of analysis" section later).

There are several ways in which to see stances, depending on how one sees social reality. These begin, of course, with the two-sided notion of tolerance/intolerance. This is a more traditional way of seeing (in)tolerance and one that is encapsulated in much ongoing research. For example, a common genre of writing today is about "tolerance of diversity." Byrd (1993) uses the phrase "tolerance for human diversity," as do many other writers. A perhaps superficial reading of these authors would suggest that either one is tolerant of those who are diverse or one is prejudiced.

At a slightly higher level of complexity, one could have different *categories* or *levels* of intolerance. Baldwin and Hecht (1995) originally proposed three such stances. *Intolerance* would refer to prejudice of any sort, defined according to Allport (1954/1979) as "an avertive or hostile attitude toward a person who belongs to a group, simply because he [or she] belongs to that group and is therefore presumed to have the objectionable qualities ascribed to the group" (p. 7). *Tolerance* was defined, following Staub (1990), as the application of the same moral principles and rules, caring and empathy, and feeling of connections to human beings of other perceived gro_ps. Tolerance also can be seen in an ideology of "difference blindness," which seeks to treat people as individuals and to eliminate group-based criteria for the social structure. We argued, however, that tolerance did not reflect a positive stance. At best, it reflects a neutrality. More recently, Goldberg (1997) argues that tolerance is actually a negative because it always is enacted out of a power position that demeans through condescension and makes prejudice and discrimination acceptable. Holton's narrative in this volume (Chapter 16) personalizes the negative feelings of being "tolerated."

The third level, *appreciation,* was conceptualized after Bennett (1986a, 1986b), where we not only allow or even adapt some behaviors of people from other cultures/perceived groups but also integrate some of them into our being. Goldberg (1997) uses terms such as *respect, sensitivity, engagement, recognition,* and *solidarity* to reflect this stance; that is, whereas the traditional notion of intolerance remained much the same as the notion of prejudice, tolerance was complicated to include putting up with/allowing to exist/treating with respect some other group (tolerance) and actually learning, respecting, imaging, and benefiting from that group (appreciation). However, even these definitions contain some contradiction, as intolerance is defined in terms of attitudes and the other two are described in terms of behaviors. In accordance with our notion of levels of analysis, we would need to consider the possibility that, according to one's definition of a certain type of intolerance (e.g., "race," [Baldwin, 1994, 1996a, 1996b, 1996c]), intolerance might be expressed or not expressed, attitude or behavior, and individual or group level. Thus, for each of these three definitions, it might be more useful to adopt a notion similar to the one Goldberg (1993) uses for racism—that appreciation/tolerance/intolerance can be based either on intent or on the actual result of one's actions and that they can be individual attitudes or reflected through group-level practices, norms, and laws.

At a next level of complication, one might see a continuum of tolerance-appreciation. Bennett (1986a, 1986b) presents such a continuum with his notion of *ethnorelativism.* He describes six actual levels, three of which are ethnocentric and three of which are ethnorelativistic. These present a range of attitudes or stances, from denying the very existence or humanity of another group to incorporating aspects of the group's worldview into one's own. At the highest level, we try to take the best of both or several cultures or groups. This is similar to Kim's (1984) suggestion that in science, as well as in our personal lives, we take aspects of both Eastern and Western perspectives to become more whole individuals (or, we might add, group participants). It also is similar to Harris and Moran's (1987) notion of synergy, in which a multinational corporation benefits most by incorporating diverse perspectives.

Categories or continua are not always distinctly different approaches. They can be used together. For example, although Bennett (1986a, 1986b) describes what could be a continuum, it is, in fact, divided into six categories, much like Baldwin and Hecht's (1995) three categories described previously. Furthermore, those three are divided into two overarching categories—one good and one bad. Thus, the continuum is categorized and then dichotomized. At the same time, other authors who seek to measure intolerance (e.g., Adorno, Frenkel-Brunswick, Levinson, & Sanford, 1950/1982; Baldwin & Hecht,

1994; Byrd, 1991; McConahay, 1986; Noel, 1992) often discuss it as if it were two-sided, but by allowing someone to have a score anywhere on the scale, it becomes an appreciation-intolerance continuum. It seems arbitrary to decide that someone slightly above the average on such a scale should be categorized as intolerant and that someone only slightly below the average should be seen as tolerant.

At the same time, even a continuum might be an oversimplification. On the one hand, some scholars suggest that intolerance/tolerance form a sort of *dialectic* or dynamic between polarities. Gudykunst and Kim (1992), for example, suggest that one might be both tolerant and intolerant at the same time. How this might be the case is best understood if we can draw a distinction between one's attitudes and one's actions. If stances can be cognitive, emotional, and/or behavioral, then it would be possible for one's thoughts and one's behaviors (or one's emotions and one's thoughts) to be in imperfect agreement. Thus Merton (1957) can discuss the "non-prejudiced discrimina-tor"—one who expresses prejudice due to social pressure but has not internalized prejudiced beliefs. Even more appropriate, in today's dialogue, one can enforce a code or speak in a certain way that is oppressive, even if that person is generally tolerant. In such a case, one explanation is that the person is subconsciously intolerant, with the behavior showing the true feelings/attitudes. The other possibility is that the person is merely uninformed and is not aware of how his or her actions are, in fact, intolerant. In environments that some have called "politically correct," it could be very likely for someone to express tolerance while holding intolerant attitudes (Brislin, 1991) or to express tolerance in relationships while opposing structural changes that would bring equality between groups (Jackman & Crane, 1986).

There also can be polarities at the same layer or level of experience. It is easy to imagine a person enacting a series of behaviors, some of which are intolerant and some appreciative. A deeper polarity can exist within the consciousness of individuals and cultures that "accept the person" but not who the person is (e.g., accepting gay people but rejecting homosexuality) and for people who wish they were not prejudiced but believe that certain stereotypes are true. It is interesting to note that Devine's (1989) research suggests that we all know the stereotypes and that even tolerant people often must deliberately suppress them and fail to do so on occasion.

All of this points to the notion of dialectics or dilemmas. Baxter (1990) and others apply the notion of dialectic to communication in general. For example, independence and autonomy no longer are treated as opposites; rather, they are treated as two sides of a coin, both always (and necessarily) present in a relationship. In the same sense, Billig et al. (1988)[32] discuss two dialectics of racial prejudice which may apply more generally to other prejudices as well. The first is where one feels both sympathy and contempt for another, or attraction and revulsion, at the same time. The second dialectic, inherited from the Enlightenment, is a drive both toward rationality and toward hierarchy. The drive toward rationality makes us want to be appreciative, as modern science and logic suggest that all people are equal. The drive toward hierarchy makes us want to still see our group as better than other perceived groups, much in the notion of social identity theory (Tajfel, 1978b; Tajfel & Turner, 1979). These two dialectics make sense if we can see the stances of (in)tolerance as behavioral, cognitive, spiritual, and/or emotional. The first (attraction-repulsion) is a dialectic within a stance at a given location (attitude) or possibly between thought and emotion. The latter (rationality-hierarchy) is a dialectic that seems to cross behavior and thought/emotion; that is, one feels superior but acts as if all people are equal. It is this dialect that seems to lead to complicated forms of intolerance such as "new racism" (Barker, 1990), "modern racism" (McConahay, 1986), "subtle racism" (van Dijk, 1984, 1987), and "symbolic racism" (Sears, 1988). We might add additional dialectics, borrowing from Baxter's (1990) notion of relationships, such as inclusion/autonomy. Just as inclusive movements arise (e.g., the North American Free Trade Agreement, European Economic Community economic agreements, the notion of "world community"), so do regionalism and nationalism expressed as excluding others. All of these oppositional notions of racism could easily be applied to other types of intolerance such as sexism and ethnocentrism.

Dialectics traditionally have been thought of as binary (having two polarities). However, the notions of oppositionality, paradox, contrast, polarity, and so on do not require restriction to such contrasts. Ono, in Chapter 11 of this volume, argues against binary contrasts as reconstructing the existing system and hierarchy, as do Altman and Nakayama (1991) in their discussion of race. We agree that dialectics do not have to be thought of as oppositions between two elements. However, it is difficult to discuss these more complex layers using present language models.

The final complicating notion in regard to stances is that of the *postmodern self.* The essence of postmodern thought is an opposition to structure, to hierarchy, to the linear thought of the Enlightenment, to clearly defined boundaries between academic disciplines, and among notions such as cognitive, emotional, and behavioral (Rosenau, 1992). Best and Kellner (1991) summarize, "Postmodern theory . . . rejects modern assumptions of social coherence and notions of causality in favour of multiplicity, plurality, fragmentation, and indeterminacy" (p. 4).

In short, postmodernism problematizes rather than clarifies and destabilizes rather than stabilizes. From this perspective, ethnicities, cultures, relationships, and selves are not simply "out there" but rather are fluctuating, changing, divergent, and often fractured. For example, some suggest that ethnicity, long a grounds for intolerance, is seen as shifting and changing in expression and salience from situation to situation (Clément & Noels, 1992). Some suggest that, as selves, we have multiple identities (e.g., race, gender, role) that compete for attention and that ebb and flow (Collier & Thomas, 1988; Hecht, 1993; Weinreich, 1986). Our selves are not merely our own but rather are a collage or mosaic layering of the voices we have heard throughout our lives. Selves are "contingent, forming and reforming within diverse relationships and circumstance" (Wood & Duck, 1995, pp. 8-9) and are a result of the multiple intersecting voices that have made us (Sampson, 1989).[33] As such, in the truly postmodern sense, it should not surprise us that we are full of ambivalences, paradoxes, and contradictions. According to the notion of the postmodern self, it would not even be worthwhile to look for consistencies. Thus, it is highly possible that one's given stance, even if only considered in one location such as attitude, is fluctuating. Different stances of a group or an individual can fully be expected to be self-contradictory. One might easily be intolerant in some ways but tolerant in others, as Gudykunst and Kim (1992) suggest.

In our application of postmodern principles through a layered lens, we would argue that we must seek to understand *both* stabilities and instabilities and *both* consistencies and inconsistences.

As an example of stances, one could analyze the level and nature of (in)tolerance between rival social groups at a high school (e.g., the "preps" and the "skaters"). How have these differences been constructed historically and socially, and what stances are reflected in the individuals and communities toward each other? A study might begin with a look at individuals' stances, their structure or nature (attitudes, beliefs, feelings/schema, prototypes, scripts), and the ways in which they are expressed. Why are some skaters intolerant of preps but not others? How is (in)tolerance characterized? What is the nature of the stereotypes, attitudes, and exclusions of one group toward another? What are the histories of the rivalry? Have they been institutionalized in the school structure through clubs, teams, and even classroom assignments? How and when does appreciation or tolerance manifest itself? Those addressing intolerance through intervention would need to fit their solutions into the cultural, historical framework of the particular school, with its own history between groups, and into the social worlds of the actors and their communication practices.

■ Spheres

One of the key ways in which intolerance might vary within an individual or a group is that one's stance might be different toward one type of group than another or toward one group of experiences or another. This brings us to the notion of spheres. Spheres can be defined as *group-based identities or clusters of experiences on which (in)tolerance is based.* Byrd (1993), for example, discusses intolerances based on sex, race, sexual orientation, age, and physical/mental diversity. Tajfel (1978b) and Tajfel and Turner (1979) propose that we see ourselves largely in terms of the groups to which we belong and in opposition or contrast to those to which we do not belong. We first categorize people into groups, then seek to compare the groups to which we belong to those of others, hoping to see our own groups as superior. In his notion of social identification theory, Tajfel (1981a) proposes that when we see another person in terms of his or her group membership, we treat that person and make predictions based on group characteristics rather than on individual characteristics (for another discussion of this distinction, see Miller & Steinberg, 1975). Other writers suggest that because we tend to belong to several groups, we have multiple group identities (Hecht et al., 1993) that wax and wane in importance to us (Clément & Noels, 1992; Collier, 1991; Weinreich, 1986). Because group membership is something that is gained and maintained through communication (Collier & Thomas, 1988; Davies & Harré, 1989), it seems logical that persons negotiate multiple identities in discourse. Those groups can include not only those mentioned previously (e.g., race, age) but also things such as political affiliation, church/religious membership, gang/social group membership, and occupation.

From the social-psychological perspective, much of intergroup (in)tolerance is based on group membership. The way in which we perceive information about others, retrieve stored memories (often distorting the "facts"), and pay attention to certain information (known by some as selective attention, selective perception, or selective retention) is greatly influenced by the way in which our minds place people around us into boxes or categories (Stephan, 1985). Because there are many different types of boxes into which we have been socialized to place people, it would only make sense that intergroup intolerance can exist in any set of those categories, that is, that there can be different spheres of (in)tolerance. However, as Baldwin mentions in this volume (Chapter 2), one does not need to see intergroup difficulties from only a psychological perspective. "Natural" group divisions, based on geography, religion, and so on (Allport, 1954/1979) are present in the social world before we are born. Groups based on any type of distinction may vie for resources, power, and economic control. Thus, in South Africa, there can be a struggle to end race-based domination; in Zaire, there can be conflict between tribal or ethnic divisions[34]; and in the United States, there can be a conflict over the "glass ceiling," with women seeking a stronger role in the control of resources and power in the organizational world. Furthermore, media, rhetorical messages, and so on work to produce and reproduce the categories through which we perceive the social world.

Our original thinking was based on this notion of group-based intolerance. We recently completed two studies examining a measure of (in)tolerance that has led us to question this assumption. Based on the literature we just reviewed, we conceptualized the spheres as group based (e.g., heterosexism, sexism, ageism, racism). We have reason to believe that at least one of these intolerances, racism, contains its own diversity. For example, Appiah (1990), Goldberg (1990), and Outlaw (1990) suggest that there are different racisms because race is perceived differently from culture to culture and from point to point in time within a given culture.

Continuing research suggests that even in the United States, different individuals have many different perceptions of what constitutes both race and racism (Baldwin, 1995, 1996b). The first of our two studies seemed to support this conclusion. Here we found that when one measures European Americans' attitudes toward a specific racial group, a clear factor emerges under confirmatory factor analysis; however, when race is left vague (i.e., a general racism scale), people answer the items inconsistently. However, in the second study, when we tried to examine racisms toward two groups (African Americans and Mexican Americans) as well as a general racism scale, the scales did not exhibit adequate measurement properties under the criteria of confirmatory factor analysis.

However, when we conducted an exploratory factor analysis across the two group-specific racisms, *functional* factors emerged across the groups (nonromantic relationships, romantic relationships, political issues) that mirrored McConahay's (1986) findings. The analyses of the racism scales suggest that there are functional properties to this type of prejudice that transcend specific groups. We had assumed that racial prejudice would be group based, and for some it might be. However, across our sample of European Americans and when considering African Americans and Mexican Americans, prejudice seemed to be organized around political and relational (romantic and nonromantic) issues. Thus, it is the underlying structure of racism, not the target, that seems to provide the best explanation for this type of intolerance, contradicting our original notion (Baldwin & Hecht, 1995) and that of others (e.g., Goldberg, 1990).

Perhaps these functional properties tap into the core element of this sphere and the discursive practices of applying these core elements, expressed through stereotypes, discrimination, exclusion, boundaries, and other forms are established through social interaction and are manifested in social structures. We do not know whether these findings will hold up if other ethnic/racial groups are included as targets or raters, in other historical periods, or to other intolerances. In fact, scales created for heterosexism, religious tolerance, ableism, sexism, and ageism performed adequately as independent measures.

Regardless of how one defines the spheres (i.e., group based, functional, or both), each tolerance can be considered distinct. Although Allport (1954/1979) argues for a generalized tendency to prejudice, it has seemed to us that people may be tolerant toward someone in one area (e.g., gender), appreciative of diversity in another (e.g., age), and intolerant in a third (e.g., disabilities). Even many of the scholars who find evidence for some generalized notion of prejudice still suggest that there is "hardly enough [evidence] to allow us to treat prejudice as a unitary phenomenon. . . . There is ample room for different types of prejudice to have different correlates" (Bierly, 1985, p. 564).

Having noted this diversity among the spheres, we pause to contradict ourselves and suggest that there also may be an underlying construct called prejudice and an underlying racism among the various ethnic/race-based prejudices. Think of this transcendent prejudice as a ribbon drifting through the individual but connected/intersecting layers of specific stances. Visualize a common thread in the woven mosaic that also includes identifiable, individual spheres (and spheres within spheres), with these spheres bleeding into one another. For those conversant in the language of factor analysis, think of the underlying or transcendent prejudice as a second-order factor or a communality across factors that inhibits convergence.

Baldwin and Hecht (1995) make several main points regarding the spheres. First, as noted previously, *a given sphere of intolerance (e.g., sexism) may be seen differently from one culture to another or at different points in time in a given culture.* (In)tolerance is not simply monolithic or "out there"; it is socially constructed and shaped through individual and mediated communication. Although there might be some underlying, individual consistency based on personality, other social influences (e.g., group level, media, economic) may destabilize intolerances that shift and fluctuate, just as a society's given "enemies" shift and change from time to time.

Second, due to the possible differences in self-categorization and perception of the categories, *someone can be (in)tolerant toward one group but not another.* Societies, too, can select certain groups for tolerance and others for intolerance.

Third, *different intolerances can overlap and compound one another* (some would say "be articulated" together). This is not a new notion. Many women of color (e.g., Collins, 1990) suggest that Black, Indian, or Asian women are oppressed in terms of gender relations, racial relations, and socioeconomic relations; that is, oppression and intolerance as expressed toward women of color are different from both those toward White women and those toward men of color.

Finally, *(in)tolerance can be two-way or multiway.* There is some debate as to whether, for example, Blacks can be racist or women can be sexist. Those who define racism and sexism in terms of power would say that they cannot be. Later, we offer a possible middle ground for this dialogue. For now, however, we suggest that, regardless of how one labels the intolerance of a traditionally oppressed group toward the oppressor group (whether one uses *racism* or *sexism* or some other term), and regardless of the historical justification for suspicion and mistrust, there still can be intolerance by generally oppressed groups. This is a difficult issue because we do not wish to blame the oppression on the oppressed; we return to it in the "levels of analysis" section.

To return to our high school example, preps may be somewhat intolerant of skaters (generally or individually), yet they might have a greater intolerance for "jocks" and be appreciative of the "intellectuals." Because the meanings of class, ethnicity, gender, and other items often overlap and are confused (conflated), research should first be done to clarify how each identity is articulated (What does it mean to be a prep, both to those who identify with the group and to those who do not?) and second to understand how different identities overlap or intertwine (e.g., prep, gender, class). Part of this research might be ethnographic or phenomenological in nature, as such research should provide a deep understanding of the identities in question or the experience of being a victim of intolerance. An understanding of the overlapping constructions also might reveal the factors of why, in a given context, expressions of intolerance vary or why a group (or an individual) might be more tolerant of some groups than others.

A description of spheres of intolerance should help us understand those areas in which greater intolerance is expressed; this will allow for an increased focus of our interventions in those areas. For example, in Brazil, socioeconomic status might be a greater divider among people than is color of skin, although the latter also is important (Dzidzienyo, 1979). Also, understanding the particular intolerances toward particular groups will help in developing programs to deal with specific problems rather than "general" prejudice reduction approaches. Although the latter still should be used, the former may be more helpful. The comparative advantages of both approaches would form still a new area of future research.

Finally, spheres of tolerance can be used to forge improved intergroup relations. If the tolerated or appreciated identities can be highlighted or foregrounded, this may problematize intolerance among individuals. The strategy might even be helpful at a group level but does not address structural and economic issues.

■ Levels of Analysis

The stances and spheres exist on a number of *levels of analysis.* The levels of analysis are the location in the social world where events happen and the terms under which those events should be studied and discussed. Young-Bruehl (1996) criticizes studies of prejudice for their focus on the cognitive level. At present, we can distinguish at least four levels: individual, interaction, relationship, and community (Hecht, 1993). This is based on recommendations by and debates among various authors who have tried to find the "best" way in which to look at social reality (e.g., Capella, 1987; Chaffee & Berger, 1987). For example, some argue that the individual is the locus of social action (Hewes & Planalp, 1987; Triandis et al., 1984). Our system is more in keeping with those who wish to understand the social world across and among various levels. Giddens (1984) argues that we must understand social actions across levels of analysis by looking at both the community and interaction, and Morgan (1986) argues for understandings on the levels of the individual, relationship, and social network. Kenny (1988a, 1988b) provides statistical techniques for assessing the individual and social contributions, and hierarchical regression has been used to account for different levels of analysis. Maluso (1995) distinguishes among institutional, collective, and interpersonal racism, and Lott (1995) discusses interindividual and institutional sexism. For example, Babrow (1995) proposes that we understand how problematic situations are dealt with through examining individual psychological processes, interactions, and collective responses. Our question, then, is, On what levels is a given intolerance experienced by people in their everyday lives?

At the *individual* level, one would look for (in)tolerance as a given person experiences it, either as a prejudiced person or as a target of prejudice. This is the level at which one might look at how individuals think about or process their social world (cognition). For example, what makes certain people generally intolerant of others who are different—either in any way or in certain ways? We also must consider feelings about prejudice and groups, spiritual experiences, and values.

Other scholars suggest that either apart from (Montgomery, 1986) or in combination with the individual perspective (Fitzpatrick & Indvik, 1986), we must look at the *dyadic* level of communication. Because "identities are enacted in social interaction through communication" (Hecht, 1993, p. 79), it makes sense that (in)tolerance also can exist and be shaped through communication between individuals. For example, as one person consciously or subconsciously expresses a certain identity in a conversation, another person's self-perceived identity may become salient to that person and intolerance may surface. Or, through the sharing of interpersonal messages, people may persuade or reinforce one another to greater tolerance or intolerance. As Giddens (1984) notes, structures such as prejudicial relationships are instantiated through interaction.

Some authors suggest examining the social world at the *relational* level. These authors hold that relationships are not merely a sum of interpersonal messages; rather, they have their own processes and issues such as role negotiation, power relationships, and participants' views of the relationship (Duck & Sants, 1983). Hecht (1993) describes the relational frame:

> The relationship frame has three levels. First, people define themselves in terms of others and shape their social behavior to those around them. The self that emerges (i.e., who one is) is influenced by who one is with. Second, people define themselves in terms of their relationships, gaining a sense of self through relationships with others such as marital partners, occupations, and friendship.

Third, relationships, themselves, take on identities and the dyad becomes an entity. A dating couple establishes an identity as a couple which aligns it within the larger group. (p. 80, citations deleted)

This is to suggest that (in)tolerance will express itself differently when it comes to relationships. Allport (1954/1979) suggests that if one develops an intimate relationship with someone of a disliked group, then the person's view of the group might change (or the prejudicial person might simply "re-fence" to make an exception for the liked individual). Counseling psychologists suggest that stereotypes can continue to be a problem even in intimate intercultural relationships (Falicov, 1986; Markoff, 1977; Romano, 1988). It may be that certain types and characteristics of relationships give people more resilience against intolerance from those outside the couple, or perhaps one develops greater intolerance toward a group when one perceives a threat toward someone with whom he or she has a relationship (e.g., family, partner). At any rate, it seems that relationship and (in)tolerance may blend in unusual ways that have not yet been discovered through research.

A fourth frame, the *communal* level, includes (in)tolerant images, structures, and actions of a group of people (Hecht, 1993). In Hecht's (1993) original discussion, this frame referred to identity, especially things such as rituals, rules, laws, and so on that bonded a group together, based on the notion of collective memory (Middleton & Edwards, 1990; Philipsen, 1989). In regard to (in)tolerance, we would broaden this somewhat. There are certain rituals that, through the ways in which they are celebrated, foster (in)tolerance. A cultural festival might raise acceptance of groups besides one's own yet, in a dialectical fashion, might at the same time create a stereotypical image of the other cultures that some see as a sort of intolerance. Or, it might trivialize or folklorize (Nascimento, 1978) a marginalized group, giving token acceptance of food and holidays. This also can co-opt a group's culture and can create a false image that the culture's deeper aspects are valued. A nationalistic festival, a group initiation rite, a religious or social holiday, or a convention might foster intolerance toward other groups through in-group/out-group comparisons. Social norms are passed down both subtly and overtly. In addition to norms, laws, and rituals, McLeod and Blumler (1987) suggest that, although one must define and measure a social phenomenon wherever it occurs (at the appropriate "level of abstraction"), there also is a need to consider larger level influences. These would include power relationships, mass media influences, and other "institutional sectors in the social system" (p. 277). Semiotic research, they note, has begun to look at the relationship between cultural forms and social identities, which, we have argued, are a main ingredient in the consideration of intolerance.[35]

One of the key issues, when it comes to the levels of analysis, is the *relationship of the levels to one another.* Some might argue that individuals are prejudiced, whereas groups are not. However, there seems to be a sort of collective memory of groups that may contain the elements leading to individual prejudice, and many individual-level scholars include the influence of mediated images (i.e., television and other images). We call this mutual influence *interpenetration* (Giddens, 1984). Hecht (1993) suggests, regarding identity frames (or levels), that they "are not isolated from each other. Instead they may be examined two at a time, three at a time, or all four at a time" (p. 80). One of the main intents of the holographically layered perspective is to suggest that fruitful information regarding (in)tolerance can be looked at by seeing how things at one level might be linearly and nonlinearly related to things at another level.[36] The mere complexity of all of the different relationships led us to frame our notions as a *perspective* rather than as a *theory* much the way in which Giddens (1984) casts structuration as a metatheory. Various theories might be developed about different sets of relationships at different levels. For example, Gudykunst's (1995) anxiety-uncertainty management theory looks at how communally held value systems (e.g., collectivism vs. individualism) might influence one's individual level of uncertainty or anxiety when interacting with someone who one perceived as being from a different group or culture. The communication accommodation theory of Gallois and colleagues (Gallois, Franklyn-Stokes, Giles, & Coupland, 1988; Gallois, Giles, Jones, Cargile, & Ota, 1995) points to how individual factors, situational factors (e.g., perceived threat, norms for a given situation), and group-level factors (e.g., empowerment, linguistic vitality) influence how one communicates in an intergroup encounter. Cultivation theory (Gerbner & Gross, 1976; Gerbner, Gross, Morgan, & Signorielli, 1986) looks at how media images influence one's perception of reality; television "cultivates a symbolic structure, which is then used by viewers to interpret everyday reality" (Hughes, 1980, p. 288).

The interpenetration of the individual and communal levels can be clearly seen in our assumptions about race. Race has been used as a social category throughout this chapter and throughout the book. How many of us realize that in using this category we have accepted the communal racialization of society? As Ono notes in his media chapter in this volume (Chapter 11), starting with the assumption of racial categorization does not problematize this practice but rather inscribes it. Thus, the individual practice of using racial categories inscribes and recreates the communal hierarchical practice.[37]

The second main issue that is uncovered through a look at the connections (interpenetration) among the spheres is *the very definition of various intolerances.* As noted previously, different people define each form of intolerance in different ways. This is to say that a given word, such as "classism," does not simply have a unified meaning. The meanings of words are "sites of struggle"; people (as members of groups) argue over their definitions. Thus, some see words such as "racism" as having a power component (Baldwin, 1995). Both individuals and groups may seek to define such words so that they, themselves, lie outside of them. Others define such words from their own perspectives (i.e., from their own level). Thus, it would make sense for Allport (1954/1979), as noted previously, to define prejudice as "an attitude" (p. 7) because he tends to look at the individual level and would see intolerance first at the individual level. Other scholars see racism and sexism as things that can be held only by a group in power. For example, Byrd (1993) relates "racism to power and prejudice" (p. 134). This is a definition we have heard frequently in studies of multiculturalism, and at one level the definition makes sense: Only a group that has institutionalized power in a society can fully implement intolerance toward another group; that is, only the group in power can make intolerant expression a norm or even a law.[38] On the other hand, this leaves us without good words to describe the situation when a member of an oppressed group harasses or harms someone from an empowered group simply because he or she is a member of the empowered group. It also generalizes the power of the mainstream group and imposes it on all of its individual members, essentializing the characteristics of the empowered group. Are all White males empowered? Are all wealthy White males empowered in every relationship or situation? We do not think so. As a result, we believe that it might be useful to see whether intolerance in a given sphere can exist at different levels. The power plus intolerance equation certainly would hold true at the communal level. For example, in U.S. society, generally only men have the power (so far) to institutionalize sexist practices. However, at an individual or a relational level, women still can make hiring decisions based on sex or can even sexually harass a male.

This is not intended to minimize intolerance experienced by different groups. For example, even if Whites in the United States experience what they define as racism (Baldwin, 1995), the weight, frequency, and social meaning of such experiences might not be at all comparable with the experiences of a person of color. For the latter, unequal treatment may be something that is experienced with great frequency or magnitude, something that is even expected on a daily basis. However, by considering (in)tolerance to exist at various levels, we have a vehicle through which to look at all types and directions of intolerance, whatever we decide to call them in the end.

In sum, we are concerned with the thoughts, interpretations, feelings, and behaviors of individuals; the interactions and relationships among people; and the structures and collective memories of communities. Thus, one can understand individuals' stances on the spheres of tolerance, how people interact about spheres and stances or across boundaries (intersphere/stance communication or interacting with someone from a different sphere or stance), what types of personal and professional relationships exist within and across spheres and stances, and how communities of spheres and stances are organized. We can also understand how these various levels connect with each other. For example, how is a person's stance on gender related to interactions with individuals of a different gender or with communities that have different stances on gender?

At an individual level, how do two preps with different stances on jocks interact, particularly regarding issues related to those jocks? How will it affect the dynamics of an organization if two individuals who interact frequently are intolerant but in different spheres (e.g., sex and race)? What are the dynamics of interaction or relational development of people who have intolerance toward each other's groups? Is there a dialectical tension between group intolerance and individual appreciation? At an organizational level, how might (in)tolerance be shown in hiring practices? How can a community or an organization reproduce (in)tolerance through discourse, ritual, media, and other community-based behaviors? How might individuals or groups be concerned with helping victims of intolerance find strategies of resistance—ways in which to reinterpret messages or symbols in a positive light or to reduce or cope with tolerance?

■ Types of Understanding

This brings us to our final point, the different *types of understanding* of the stances, spheres, and levels. These types of understanding include "different ways of seeing the world (ontology), human nature, and knowledge (epistemology) as well as different ways of looking at social reality (methodologies) (Baldwin & Hecht, 1995, pp. 75-76). As noted previously, some might look at intra-individual factors; others might look at group-based influences, the use of symbols in media, speeches, novels, and so on; still others might look at how each of these items affects the expression of intolerance, which strategies can be used to confront it, or how stances, spheres, and frames affect interactions or relationships. Burrel and Morgan (1979) suggest that there is a range of different ways in which to see the world, from the view that reality is outside of us and able to be fully discovered (objective) to the notion that each person perceives "reality" in a different way (subjective), with many points in between. Scholars tend to treat these either as dichotomies (e.g., objective vs. subjective paradigms) or as a continuum (from very objective to very subjective). They also suggest that theories differ along a change regulation dimension, setting up a four-quadrant system. What we are suggesting is that the notion of social research must be complicated to better understand prejudice. Social reality might not be best represented by any one point on a continuum; rather, various levels of objectivity and change are involved.

Our call for multiple perspectives joins a growing chorus moving away from the disciplinary wars (Martin & Frost, 1996) and away from the belief in the incompatibility of competing paradigms (Gioia & Pitre, 1990; Weaver & Gioia, 1994) to a belief in multiple perspectives. Monge (1996), for example, calls for multiple ways of knowing in response to globalization. We share with this movement the belief that "meshing" different theories (Gioia & Pitre, 1990) or moving to an overarching and higher level of abstraction (Martin & Frost, 1996) allows one to see a more complete picture and provides deeper understandings. Gioia and Pitre (1990) offer suggestions for accomplishing this. They suggest that the boundaries or borders between paradigms be seen as "fuzzy" or transition zones. These cites provide areas of overlap, a technique they refer to as "metatriangularization," borrowing the methodological metaphor and extending it to the use of multiple theories focused on the same domain (e.g., the study of structure). This technique is reflected in the work of Hecht (1978), who meshed a variety of theoretical perspectives in conceptualizing communication satisfaction and used multiple methods in developing his ideas on this topic (e.g., interviews, open-ended questionnaires, surveys, critical analyses of poetry, media representations), and in Giddens' (1984) structuration perspective, which seeks to merge the determinism of structural approaches with interpretivism.

We diverge, however, from some aspects of these discussion. First, we do not choose to elevate a single paradigm and treat it as metatheoretical (postmodernism in the case of Martin & Frost, 1996; structuration in the case of Weaver & Gioia, 1994). Many theories claim this metatheoretical stance, and using a single perspective, no matter how synthetic, imposes a single set of assumptions and ideology. The stability provided by a single, overarching metatheory will be useful in examining certain angles of the holograph but will ignore others. Inevitably, the emerging hegemony will be destabilized, and this is fruitful. Second, we do not agree that belief in the incommensurability of theories (à la Kuhn, 1970) necessarily compromises multiperspectivism. This is only the case if we assume the need for commensurability and consistency within a framework. Although this is one approach to multiperspectivism, it is not the only one. We can assume that dialectical contradictions are not necessarily things to be eliminated. These contradictions represent the influence patterns that give holography its richness. Instead, these patterns and contradictions are, at times, the content of our endeavors. Thus, the tensions, if they exist, between subjectivism and objectivism and between stability and change are not to be eliminated or explained away but rather to be embraced. When Hecht (1993) looked at the fuzzy boundaries between cognitive (e.g., expectation fulfillment) and behavioral approaches, he developed a new perspective on communication satisfaction that has guided research across three U.S. ethnic groups. When Hecht, Ribeau, and Sedano (1990) juxtaposed a qualitative, empirical method- ology (content analysis of responses to open-ended questionnaires) with a critical one (rhetorical analysis of poetry), the emerging patterns were richer than either was separately. We believe in a range of approaches to multiple ways of understanding, from the use of two or more separate perspectives in a metatriangulation to the synthesis of perspectives into higher order perspectives.

At the surface level, we are suggesting that, if there are many aspects to the complex puzzle of a given (in)tolerance, we must allow ourselves to look at it in different ways. Our notion of layering implies multiple means for accessing stances, spheres, levels, and understandings. Methodologically, we may use self-report inventories, interviews, critical and rhetorical analyses of artifacts, ethnographic descriptions, and other tech- niques separately or in combination to understand these diverse phenomena. There is frequent confusion between ways of doing research and ways of seeing the world. Many students think, for example, that objective research requires an analysis that includes counting or statistics (quantitative). However, research tools, or methodologies, are not bound by a given way of seeing the world. Ethnography, for example, can be subjective (Lincoln & Guba, 1985), critical (Clough, 1992; Conquergood, 1991), or even seen as "naive realism" (Hammersley, 1992).

In some cases, it is not even the "question that dictates the methodology" (an adage in many circles); rather, all questions can be answered with more than one methodology. This is a sort of extension of the notion of methodological triangulation (Denzin, 1978). For example, qualitative research (e.g., ethnography, rhetorical analysis, focus groups, in-depth interviews, open-ended questionnaires) can be used to derive notions, catego- ries, or theories that can later be validated quantitatively. Others might turn this order on its head, using qualitative methods such as member checks to "validate" quantitative research. We see qualitative and quantitative research as informing one another. Each produces information that is worthwhile, that helps us to understand reality and realities as well as truth and truths (Bernstein, 1976). The various research methods might be used simultaneously.

Some would argue that this begs questions of a fundamental deeper level: those of *ontology* (what is real or what reality should be observed) and *epistemology* (what constitutes knowledge or how is knowledge accumulated) in research. However, layer- ing also applies to these terms. Burrel and Morgan (1979) treat ontological perspectives, or the nature of reality, as a continuum. At one end are researchers who see reality as "out there"—external to the observer (and thus, if we all remove our biases, we will see the same reality). At the other end are those who see reality as internal (subjective or within the observer). Still others occupy spaces somewhere in between. Another possibility is that various types of realities exist. Collier and Thomas (1988) propose that there are individual realities but that, through communication, groups of people come to hold realities on which they can agree. These realities exist between persons (or "subjects") and are thus *intersubjective.* Kim (1984) discusses two different views of reality and research: the "holistic-contextual-qualitative" and the "analytic-reductionistic-quantitative" views (pp. 24-25). She states,

> The nomothetic ideal of universal measurement and the fact of individuality may not necessarily be considered a conflict so long as the ideal does not claim exclusivity in studying human-social phenomena. As far as reality goes, it presents itself as having universalities (regularities, commonalities, consistencies, similarities) as well as individualities (irregularities, individual uniqueness, inconsistencies, differences). (p. 27)

It is not clear if, by individualities, she is referring to individual differences still caused by external factors or to the fact that individuals construct and perceive their realities differently. Whatever the meaning, the point remains that reality, rather than being only subjective or objective, could be both at the same time in different ways.

In the holographic layering metaphor, we would say, then, that there are different levels or layers of reality—the reality we perceive as individuals, the reality we co-create through communication (the communal reality), and the reality that is external to us and acts on us. These are not a continuum but operate at the same time and in polarities with one another. They are much like a *dialectic* in which seemingly opposite poles actually work in tandem; however, rather than there being only subjective or objective (dichotomous) poles, there are multiple ontologies. We believe that although individual ways of understanding are useful by themselves, there is much to be learned by holographically layering these views, whether through dialectic juxtaposition, synthesis, transcendence, fuzzy border, metatriangularization, or some other technique. We do not accept the superordinate value of consistency, stability, and parsimony but rather look to the movement between chaos and order (Gleick, 1987).

Ethnicities (Altman & Nakayama, 1991; Hecht, 1993), views on racial politics (Baldwin, 1994), power and tolerance structures (Baldwin & Hecht, 1995), and theoretical/methodological stances often have "three or more stances in opposition" (Hecht, 1993, p. 76). A dialectical (or "polylectical" to show more than just two viewpoints [Baldwin, 1994]) may exist at every level of thinking and communicating: "Contradictions . . . may be thought of at the theoretical level (two or more theories as polarities), at the concept or process level (two or more communication processes as polarities), and at the methodological level (two or more methods as polarities)" (Hecht, 1993, p. 76). In the notion of holographic layering, one would not expect to find one end of a polarity, one point on a continuum, or one aspect of a many-sided issue as the "only" or "best" answer. Rather, several aspects existing and coexisting at once maximize understanding. It is the connections, intersections, interferences, and interpretations that excite. Thus, theory, methodology, and the everyday world have elements of both subjectivity and objectivity; human nature is at the same time influenced and voluntary.

In the same sense, in the *epistemological* sense (how we know what we know), there are different ways of knowing and different things that can be known with different certainty. In some cases, enough people from a group might share a given reality for it to be "generalizable." In some cases, factors outside of individuals (e.g., economic forces, historical situations) or beyond the awareness of individuals (e.g., self-esteem, rigidity of personality, ethnocentrism) may influence them in ways that can be "known" by studying random samples. At the same time, people with the same circumstances might still respond in different ways. This is very similar to the systems theory concepts of *equifinality,* where systems (e.g., families, relationships) can reach the same end point by different means, or *equipotentiality,* where systems can start at the same point and end up at different end points. This suggests that even generalizable findings must be tempered by an understanding of the factors including the perceptions, strategies, and choices of specific individuals. In this sense, there are different types of knowledge that can be important.

The holographic layered perspective, thus, stands as a new approach to prejudice. It seeks to bring different voices together (e.g., disciplinary, methodological) to try to understand and find ways in which to reduce intolerance. It is clearly value driven and makes no apology for that. We now provide an example of its application to the case of race and racism in Brazil. Although this book has a U.S. focus, we provide this example not only to show how the perspective may be applied but also to suggest its application outside of this cultural frame.

■ Example: The Construction of Race and Racism in Brazil

In past work, Baldwin has had an interest in race relations in Brazil, examining some of the key aspects of intolerance as it appears in different "locations" in that country (Baldwin, 1993, 1994, 1996a, 1996c). Brazil provides an interesting example for our perspective. On the one hand, many in Brazil, from the government to famous authors such as Jorge Amado (Dzidzienyo, 1979), have promoted the country as a true "racial democracy." Indeed, Gilberto Freyre, whose writings on the slave plantations (Freyre, 1944/1964) promoted a flurry of research on both indigenous peoples and African-descended peoples, saw Brazil as the *model* racial society. He used this notion to later promote the concept of *Luso-Tropicalismo,* a theory suggesting that Portugal had done such a good job in colonizing Brazil that it should be allowed to continue its colonial rule over Angola in the late 1960s (Teboul & Correia, 1985). Even many modern historians hold this view of Portugal's positive influence on Brazil. Burns (1980) suggests that "Brazil probably has less racial tension and less racial prejudice than any other multiracial society, past or present. The races mix freely in public places. Interracial marriage is reasonably common" (pp. 195-196).

On the other hand, many writers have risen to challenge this interpretation (i.e., the whole definition of the history of race in Brazil and of the current racial situation as a "site of struggle"). These writers cite various areas of Brazilian society as having entrenched racial divisions in them. Nascimento (1978) sees oppression at the individual level in sayings that float around much like proverbs. One common saying, Nascimento notes, is the following:

> White women are for marrying.
> Black women are for working.
> Mulatto women are for fornicating. (p. 62)[39]

Such sayings, attitudes against interracial marriage (even with mulattos [Nascimento, 1978]), and the vast array of names people have used to not call themselves "Black" (Nogueira, 1985) suggest that there may be race prejudice in some form, at least at the individual level. But that such sayings would be "floating around" as part of the "collective memory" might suggest that the individual and communal layers are interpenetrated.

At the dyadic level, there may not be much overt racism (by U.S. common definitions). However, Paim (1988) and others give many instances of how even upper socioeconomic status Blacks were forced to ride service elevators because they were assumed to be maids or service workers (which also suggests stereotypes and/or prejudice at the individual level). Da Matta (1979) explains that at the relational level, Blacks and Whites may mix in the streets but not in the homes or in personal relations. Thus, many modes of interpersonal speech, such as the common Brazilian saying, "Você sabe com quem está falando?" [Don't you know to whom you're speaking?], are not used by inferiors to superiors or by Blacks to Whites.

At the communal level, da Matta (1979) suggests that there is no need for formal de jure segregation in Brazil because all of it is done informally with hidden de facto rules. He details the reinforcement of racial structures through the rituals of Carnaval and through heroes and myths of the Brazilian culture. In education, authors propose that Blacks (and indigenous peoples) are misrepresented in history books that are "folk-loricized" (Nascimento, 1978) or treated as a folkloric anachronism (Moreira Bispo, 1986). Except for those authors who write in a White style or find some way of mitigating or obscuring their Blackness (Haberly, 1983), the Brazilian literary canon excludes Blacks (Moreira Bispo, 1986). At the level of law enforcement, Paim (1988) cites statements found on the wall of the Police Academy of São Paulo: "Blacks, by definition and by nature, are marginal"; "If a Black man is standing, he is suspect; if he is running, he is guilty" (p. 6).

At the government level, racial discussion was silenced through censorship during the 1960s as the authoritarian government "tenaciously defended their image of Brazil as a racial democracy" (Skidmore, 1985, p. 15). Scholars who studied race relations were banned from the universities and deprived of their rights as citizens (Dzidzienyo, 1979; González, 1985). Presidential address (Vargas, n.d.) and congressional decree, even up to the constitutional level (Mitchell, 1984), encouraged the process of *Whitening,* a process of slow moving from a mulatto nation to a White nation through genetic control (eugenics), especially via immigration control (Stepan, 1991). The government actively intervened to "un-Blacken" samba and Carnaval to make them implements for the public image of Brazil and to monitor the African Brazilian religions as a measure of national interest (Levine, 1984). During the 1960s, the government took steps to publicly define Brazilian culture, including the positions of the various racial/cultural elements, through both censorship and promotion of a national image (Ortiz, 1985). Recent studies of media suggest that Blacks are grossly underrepresented in magazine advertisements (Hasenbalg, 1982) and television (Leslie, 1992) to the point where many glamour magazines have refused to include any Black models (Paim, 1988).

This extended example demonstrates the utility of the holographically layered perspective. First, it could safely be said, following Rex (1986) and van den Berghe (1967), that racism in Brazil is different from that in the United States, South Africa, or some other locations (although we might disagree with those authors on the nature of the differences). This supports the notion of different racisms. At the same time, in Brazil the position and representation of Blacks are different from those of indigenous peoples, and Black women are treated differently than Black men; mulatto women have still a different representation, one that is continued in some rock music today (Baldwin, 1994). This suggests different spheres. At the same time, we can see some form of racial intolerance at various levels—individual, interactive, relational, and communal, with the latter including things such as discrimination in the workplace, the governmental role, social relations and norms, and media and textbook representations. Scholars have looked at these in different ways, from surveys to demographic analyses, to media content analyses, to anthropological ethnographies. Yet, the different types of studies and the different levels of analysis seem to have some core element in common. It is here, perhaps, that the holographic metaphor best serves us. One scholar might look at samba lyrics, another might look at representation in Congress, another might look at socioeconomic indicators and educational levels, another might analyze literature, and still another might look at political documents and forces. But what is seen in each is a microcosm of the whole; just as in a hologram, the more pieces of the film we assemble, the clearer the image becomes.

■ Conclusion

According to van der Dennen (1987), it is the human use of symbols that shapes and defines the final nature of prejudice. It is the human ability to define and describe enemies—to create them ideologically as different. Thus, it is not so much that two groups are different (e.g., gay-straight, male-female, old-young) but rather the fact that humans have the capacity to describe and define the groups as different that leads to intolerance. Intolerance has, inherently, a communication element. As such, we believe, intolerance can be changed toward appreciation. Any such change will come about through communication. Just as the problem has an inherent communicative component, so too must the solution. At the same time, any solution must involve more than simply communication. Solutions must aim at the individual, dyadic, relational, and communal levels. They must focus on media, on government, on social structure, on discourse and communicative styles, on thought patterns, and on psychological processes in various combinations.

A first step is a better understanding of the dynamics of prejudice. This chapter has sought to provide one way of looking at intolerance. First, we addressed the whole notion of the realms of tolerance, intolerance, and appreciation (stances) as well as how these can exist in complex patterns. So long as tolerance and intolerance name the ends of the continuum, research will be restricted in its utility because tolerance is, at best, a neutral stance and, at worst, precludes full appreciation and respect. Introduction of the concept of appreciation or Goldberg's (1997) concepts of respect, sensitivity, and engagement extend the work to discover how these are created and expressed. What leads people to appreciation? How is appreciation expressed?

Second, we mentioned the spheres of intolerance and the "isms" such as sexism, heterosexism, and ageism. These often overlap, intersect, interpenetrate, and compound each other. Focusing on more than one sphere at a time is an important challenge to research and practice.

Third, we mentioned how (in)tolerance can exist within individuals, between communication partners, in relationships, and in various places in society as a whole; that is, a given intolerance, or intolerance in general, permeates society at every aspect of its fabric.

Finally, to understand and address this permeation, we must be willing to look at the social world in different ways and with different methods. Each piece of the puzzle is important because each provides a sort of holographic image of the rest. The more pieces of the image we can observe, the better our understanding will be of intolerance as a whole and of the different intolerances as they exist in particular societies. We also learn through the processes of interpenetration and interference—how the layers intersect, their dynamic tensions, and their transcendent coalescence. The next step is to further refine theories within this perspective.

This is not intended as the final word on the subject, or as the final perspective, but is merely another step in a perspective that awaits revision from other scholars. A simultaneous step, one that cannot wait for perfect understanding, is to move from theory to social action. Even as we begin to understand intolerance, we must continue to research, at the various levels and interactions between levels, how to reduce it. As Talbot (1991) proposes of the holographic view of the world, we must see things as interrelated to be able to address them correctly: "We believe we can deal with various problems in our society, such as crime, poverty, and drug addiction, without addressing the problems in our society as a whole" (p. 49). But we cannot. We must first see the problems, or the intolerances, as interconnected. Then we must go on to deal with them.

PART II Spheres of Prejudice

4 Identifying Racist Language

Linguistic Acts and Signs

Molefi Kete Asante

As we enter the turn of the century and the next millennium, we have appropriately turned our attention to questions of diversity, pluralism, difference, *differance,* ethnicity, gender, and cultural location as never before (Bruner, 1990; Spillers, 1991; Wiegman, 1995). Ethnic, racial, and cultural consciousness have flooded the plains of our social life. We are victims of the new awareness. This has led some individuals to proclaim that there is a new tribalization. This is, of course, an exaggeration, but it does suggest apprehension, alarm, and fear. The rise of hostility, aggressive language, and epithets has produced a rush for explanation.

The breakdown of what had been thought by some to be the monolithic Soviet empire, the spread of democratic principles to the various regions of the world, the reemergence of national sentiments, and the discovery of long-silenced voices in heterogeneous societies such as ours have sparked a new debate. Nothing in this litany of social and intellectual transformation, however, can be considered signifying the end of history. Indeed, it represents the promise of a new beginning in which more people are armed with the knowledge necessary to make contributions from their various cultural perspectives. The attempt to maintain the cultural hegemony of one group has failed. The essential elements surrounding the debate have to do with the questions of society, culture, and speech.

■ Contexting the Communication

The contextualization of speech is itself a political act. By that, I mean that whenever one categorizes society in an effort to make concepts functional, one makes a choice among possibilities. Making a choice among possibilities creates cleavages that benefit some to the disadvantage of others (Asante, 1987). One knows the appropriateness of the benefits by the consequences to the society.

My aim is modest. I seek to provide a framework for examining racist language in any society. The United States is not alone in the world as a multiethnic and multicultural society. Quite frankly, the modern state is most often comprised of many nationalities, ethnicities, and cultures. Take Germany, for instance, and we see that what appears to be a rather homogeneous society is really comprised of many ethnic groups. Germans are the dominant and most popular group. However, the fact that Turks, Greeks, Italians, and Yugoslavians have come to Germany to work as *Geistarbeiter* during the past 25 years has made it a much more heterogeneous society than before World War II (Blackshire-Belay, 1994).

I intend to demonstrate that offensive speech, a form of racist language, finds its source in the structure of knowledge in a society. A society that is structured along racial lines will produce offensive racist arguments. Racism is intertwined in the most intricate patterns of our conversation and language. By analyzing discriminatory discourse, one area of offensive language, suggestions might be made for responses to other forms of offensive speech, for example, sexist and homophobic speech. By providing cross-cultural examples of racist language, I seek to demonstrate how language might function to undermine national unity in a pluralistic society.

First, it is important to know what the racist believes because what I believe often is the source of what I say. The genesis of the normative structures that reproduce racist discourse lies in the appropriation of certain values and opinions about society. This is similar to the way in which Schutte (1995) understands the White South African's response to Blacks (p. 177). Schutte emphasizes this when he writes,

> The terms of reference used for Blacks in the third person set them apart as a separate and lower category of being. Regardless of age, males are referred to as *boy* or *garden boy;* females are *girl* or *maid.* These terms indicate their minor status. This is also true of the Afrikaans equivalent *jong, tuinjong,* or *booi,* and for a woman, *meid.* (p. 184)

(*Booi* is related to "boy" and never is used for a White person. In Dutch, *meid* simply means "a young woman." It also is never used to refer to a White in South Africa. In fact, it is a great insult for a White male to be called a *meid,* meaning "lowest coward.") Thus, the construction of the social framework dictates the nature of the discourse that is possible. This is referred to as rhetorical encapsulation in *The Afrocentric Idea* (Asante, 1987) because it is precisely the interracial communication problem that occurred in the United States until the advent of the era of agency among African Americans. Encased in a historical conceptual framework created by Whites, African Americans often took on this conceptualization as reality. Dialogue was within this framework, as were rhetoric and interpersonal interactions. Self-definition was denied to the African American community, and victimization was forced on individuals by the institution of the social framework that had been constructed. There could be only one-way communication. The White person was the authoritative voice, and the Black person was the subjected receiver. Although the United States never invented 300 different types of derogatory terminology that existed in South Africa, it did make the limited number of negative words serve a multiplicity of purposes in social, political, and economic spheres.

In the United States, the communication of racism is fundamentally the communication of Whiteness as status property. On the other hand, Blackness in its reference not so much to color as to former state of enslavement communicates a lack of status. This is why color alone does not account for the historical racial discrimination against African Americans. A Black person may be genetically more akin to Europeans in color than to the general genetic pool of Africans and yet be discriminated against in the American society. On the other hand, people from other regions of the world with no history of being enslaved in the United States may be darker than African Americans and not be victims of the same discriminatory behavior. So, the problem is not so much one of color as it is one of historical relationships based on values granted to racial categories. One participates in the economy of racist communication by exchanging the value of Whiteness for privilege in relationship to African people in any social setting. The confusion that exists among some Africans who have bought into the conceptual system is largely related to the fact that they often believe that looking like, acting like, and trying to impress Whites by quoting White authors or showing that they are into White society are directly related to the value of Whiteness as property. Although it is true that Whites may affirm Blacks who are more "like" them, they do not necessarily demonstrate any less acceptance of Whiteness as privilege status. Implications for communication are complex.

Although a White person may not communicate racism in the presence of a Black person, such communication may occur in the presence of Whites. Or, communication of racism might be condemned within a White group but nevertheless be supported in one's private communication with family or intimate friends. One of the lessons learned about the communication of racism from the Mark Fuhrman tapes during the O. J. Simpson trial is that racist communicators recognize that racism is socially unacceptable in major segments of the larger society but are willing to engage in racist language when in closed or private settings. This means that the incidents of the communication of racism in our society probably are far greater than what is experienced in the public arena.

Communication of racism may take the form of the dissemination of symbols and acts or speech itself as a form of racist penetration. Take the introduction of negative images of African Americans into political campaigns. Even apart from the narratives, the symbols themselves are the instruments of racist enthymemes or commonplace arguments where Whites know automatically the meanings of the symbols as they relate to social and political issues. For the masses of people, this form of racist communication has to be explicit. Other methods include statements that end with inferences to be drawn by the audience. They most often are in the category of the hypothetical "What if . . ." or "If such happens, then. . . ." Seldom is the predicate completed in an obvious fashion. Taken together with the symbolic expressions of racism, these acts signify a great deal about each other.

Others highlight similar speech acts in the communication of prejudice. Van Dijk (1987), for example, sought to demonstrate how indirect forms of prejudice are promoted through both direct and indirect measures. In the case of direct expression of prejudice, he sees topics such as Africans as lazy, Chinese as sneaky, and Mexicans as criminals as typical of the racist communicator who speaks out of stereotypical prejudices. However, the less direct expression is to be found in arguments that have the potential of raising questions of race such as affirmative action, the "Million Man March," reverse racism, immigration, English as the official language of the United States, and welfare. In the same vein, Hecht, Ribeau, and Alberts (1989), Pettigrew (1985), and Zatz (1987) arrive at similar conclusions about the nature of prejudice and communication in different social venues and under certain conditions.

In addition to these types of communication, direct racist speech is a more pernicious form of offensive speech. Offensive speech is deliberate public or private language intended to ridicule, pose a threat, or belittle a person or persons because of cultural or racial origin, religious practice, political beliefs, or sexual orientation. Use of such language usually is intended to create discomfort in the person or persons to whom the language is directed. It may reflect gross insensitivity to cultural difference. As such, it is responsible for verbal and often physical conflicts because all conflicts are based in opposing views of reality, and the use of language to express belief or opinion is one indication that the person has accepted a certain belief about others.

■ Manifesting Racist Language

As a phenomenon of language, racism initially is manifest in terms of what people say about others and how they justify their personal attitudes and actions. Despite the impact of numerous rhetorical studies, the development in this century of semantics as a field of inquiry, and the current emphasis in some circles on intercultural interactions, the nature of racist language remains relatively unexplored. Social scientists in all fields are more inclined to study general effects of communication rather than to concentrate on racist language as a part of our national discourse.

W. E. B. DuBois, one of the most prolific scholars of the 20th century, wrote in his book, *The Souls of Black Folk,* that "the problem of the twentieth century is the problem of the color line" (DuBois, 1903/1969, p. 1). But he did not go further to describe the obvious manifestations of that problem in terms of the language people would use. DuBois may not have understood the full implications of his statement in terms of its subtle unfolding in offensive language, although there is no question that he understood what it meant from the standpoint of overt actions against African Americans. If DuBois were alive today, he might well discuss the implications of ethnicity and nationality for the 21st century because many of the ideas and attitudes that gave rise to racist language in the early part of this century are still with us. Of course, he would be faced with the same conceptual confusion that I face. Race, ethnicity, and culture often are used interchangeably in ways that add to the complexity of understanding the communication of racism. Certainly, to say the "communication of racism" is neither to say the "communication of culture" nor to say the "communication of ethnicity." The latter two expressions are devoid of any idea of evil. Indeed, even to say the "communication of race" is not the same as to say the "communication of racism." Racism carries with it some unwanted baggage that hampers effectively, that is, whole communication where the communicators view each other as wholly human (Essed, 1991).

■ Race and American Speech

Race functions as a fundamental cognitive category in personal relationships in the American society, and symbols constitute the primary reference points for those relationships. Racism derives from the conceptual framework that valorizes a particular race above another. Consequently, there exists what is appropriately called a symbology of racism in which specific signs or motifs (e.g., swastika, Confederate flag) that fuel the transcultural and transethnic interactions in society manifest racist orientations. Founded on a special monoethnicism and monoculturalism, the symbology becomes monoracial as well. An assertive Eurocentrism, not the natural presentation of a cultural view but the imposition of Europe as universal, is the carrier of this symbology in the United States, although other racial-cultural groups occupy this hegemonic place in other heterogeneous societies.

The presence of sizable African, Native American, and Latino populations in the United States from the inception of the country created, inter alia, a need for the dominant White group to distinguish itself from the other groups. In the case of the African population, this distinction relied on color and conditions of servitude. Alongside this pattern of discrimination were linguistic terms and concepts used as epithets and derogations. The origin of this pattern may be seen in the ignorance of these other cultures.

If I examine how this worked in the case of Africans, I see that African cultural and ethnic differences were neither recorded nor considered important in making distinctions; any African was Black, and any Black was a Negro, and Negroes had no cultural heritage. To recognize Africans as Asante, Yoruba, Ibo, Ibibio, Hausa, Mandingo, Fulani, Wolof, Serere, Kikongo, Fante, and so on would have meant ascribing history, cosmologies, and indeed humanity to those who were enslaved. Without humanity, Africans could be called the worst epithets thinkable by White Americans.

There is therefore the sense in which the history of Africans in America relates to the evolution of racist language among White Americans. Because the Africans who arrived as indentured servants and later were used as slaves spoke various languages, the social climate for linguistic intrigue was richly textured with strands of sophistry. Many Whites found this a design for the use of the most subtle, sophisticated form of discriminatory discourse, made more debased by the play on variation in skin color among Africans as well as perceived ethnic temperaments. Thus, Mandingo people were treated one way and Asante another based on what were perceived to be temperamental differences. The literature of slavery is abundant with stories of slave owners indicating preference for certain Africans because of perceived value based on difference traits, real or imagined (Bennett, 1984).

■ The Nature of Racist Language

Racist language, as a special category of offensive language, may be protected by a society that establishes a hierarchical language system dependent on domination of numerically smaller ethnic groups. This is not to say that members of smaller ethnic groups cannot and do not participate in offensive language themselves, just that the conditions for acceptance of offensive language are much broader within the larger group. There are three characteristics for a condition of hierarchical language. The first is the control over the rhetorical and discourse territory through *definitions.* The second is the establishment of a self-perpetuating *rite de passage.* The third is the *stifling of opposing discourse.* The metaphor works for language as well as for control over people; the process is essentially the same.

Redefining conversational ground so that the original meaning is ambiguous or lost is one method of creating hierarchical discourse. What is meant by *redefining conversational ground* is the simplification of a complex situation or the complication of a simple situation. These are the instances in which the protectors of hegemony introduce disinformation or extraneous issues into public conversation. In this way, established powers undercut the oppressed and manipulate the communication patterns among races, sexes, and classes. The self-perpetuating *rite de passage* in which "truth" is reserved for those who have been initiated by some certifying word serves to create hierarchy as well. The certifying word might be a series of verbal commitments to offensive language, much like street gang members voicing their commitments to use certain common expressions to show how tough they really are. This was the world of the South African *Bruderband* or the American Ku Klux Klan. Indeed, the Ku Klux Klan finds its authority on the certifying *ku-klos,* the Greek word for circle, establishing antiquity as well as commitment to rituals of offense.

The third form of assault is the stifling of opposing discourse. In its most offensive form, apart from the words spoken to induce discomfort themselves, the hierarchy establishes itself by denouncing all opposing views. The aim of the racist is to invalidate the other by attacking the character of the other or by denouncing the ideas brought by the other. One invalidates the other's existence by claiming either in the verbal assertion or in action that the person is nonhuman. It is this dehumanization of the other that introduces the most dangerous aspect of racist communication.

The maker of offensive speech operates from a perceived hierarchy that appropriates a pedestal from which to offend. Such a viewpoint, to realize its objective, must control discourse territory, support certain symbolic rituals, and attack ideas that might be defensive. Thus, a teacher might say that her children were "acting like a bunch of wild Indians." Now, this is clearly offensive to many people, but the teacher might perceive herself to be in a position of hierarchy to make such a statement. She would not have thought to say "wild vandals" or "wild vikings." "Wild Indians" carried for her the type of offense she was trying to convey. To some of her colleagues, this may not have been offensive because they partake of the same general cultural bias. Expressions such as "gypped" or "jewed" are equally as offensive to Rom, Jews, or others who detest racist language yet often are heard in some segments of the society. However, in a multiethnic and multicultural society, such language is inherently offensive to the quality of the social contract we hold with each other. Even more, there is something inherently unethical in the use of other people as an example of generalized depravity or negative behavior (Cose, 1993).

This is explicitly a layered reality in which personal relations that yield interpersonal interactions and conversations can be seen to reflect the larger, broader communal understandings and acceptances of racism. Thus, one can speak of the society as being racist or the government as being racist and mean essentially that the collective wills of the individuals who establish the policy have created a racist environment.

English, like any growing language, acquires proverbs, adages, and sayings that become a part of the common repository of public discourse. The sayings reflect the major architectonics of social relations. In a major university, a White professor, frustrated over the stubbornness of an issue in a faculty meeting, rose to say that the solution was "like finding a nigger in a woodstack." He later apologized to the "African Americans" present in the meeting because he immediately saw from their reactions that it was offensive speech. Obviously, it had not become offensive within his own value system, and he did not recognize the potential offense to others at the meeting.

The fabric of any complex modern society is a cultural quiltwork with the characters of the people being revealed in daily interactions by choices of asides, nuances, figures, and adages. In a race-conscious society, intercultural group solidarity becomes a value in maintaining the structure of human relations. Yet, I see in our behavior symbols the full extent of values on language. Characteristics of the society that are defined by economic, educational, or technological issues can be negatively modified by racist discourse. During the late 1960s, Bobby Seale and Eldridge Cleaver used to say that certain "profanities of speech" were not obscene but rather that the Vietnam War was obscene, cops shooting innocent people in the streets was obscene, and children going to school without breakfast was obscene. This was social discourse operating in the same way as racial discourse often had operated. In other words, the White person who says to the African American detective seeking to search her apartment, "You can look inside any room; I ain't got nothing to steal anyway," is using the predictable pattern of discourse related to values and beliefs about African Americans.

■ Offensive Speech Acts

I have identified speech acts that indicate offensive racial discourse as *matters of course, matters of fact,* and *matters of opinion.* These speech act categories might be referred to as indicator acts because they serve to indicate the possibility of racist discourse and at the same time are parts of our belief systems. Such acts identify racist and discriminatory language in significant ways that interrelate with values and behavior. Because language also is sermonic, one can examine the concept of an indicator act as a signal that certain behaviors and values are about to be expressed or are being expressed. These most often are declarative statements inasmuch as they state aggressive positions.

The *matter-of-course* statement assumes that something is of a natural or logical occurrence, that is, in the nature of events and situations. Thus, when a White person says to another, "But you know, that's the way their metabolism moves, slower than ours," he or she is expressing a matter-of-course position. The use of a code such as "you know" assumes that the listener shares in the same general value construct as the speaker. There are a number of variations on this theme, for example, "Given their ineptitude, I understand how they could develop such a project" or "What can you expect of them?" The introductory codes are no guarantee that the discourse would be racist, but they do guarantee that the expressions contain offensive assumptions. Matter-of-course statements often include crude racial slurs or expressions used to dehumanize others because of their racial origins.

The *matter-of-fact* statement is literal and prosaic. This statement usually is given rather straightforwardly as a fact. The offending speaker believes his or her own discourse because he or she never has explored the information in an objective manner. Therefore, in the United States, the matter-of-fact statement is the forte of the true racist individual. This is a person who sees reality from the standpoint of major distortions of reality. Language of the matter-of-fact variety demonstrates the ideology of prejudice in a clear fashion because the speaker is sure that his or her information on the genitalia of Blacks, the biology of Blacks, the rhythm of Blacks, the character of Jews, the habits of Jews, the smell of Chinese, the mind of Chinese, and so on has something to do with intelligence, ability, morality, and God. The elements of this type of speech act might appear novel but in fact frequently are incorrect, inadequate as biological explanations, and extremely prosaic. This is the purview of those who use the untested information of others as evidence. Statements having to do with innate qualities of race most frequently are matter-of-fact acts. This is the hardcore area for offensive speech acts.

The *matter-of-opinion* statements are prefaced by introductory remarks signifying debatable propositions. Whenever a speaker begins a discourse, "I believe that Black people . . . ," "I think it is true that you people . . . ," or simply "Don't you believe that you would be better off with . . . ," the speaker is using the matter-of-opinion statement. To make propositions with the capacity to arouse debate without considering the nature of the prejudices that cause such utterances is to complicate the process of human communication. Among other such statements are the following: "I don't have anything against your kind . . . ," "What you people should do is follow the pattern of the Whites who were poor," "To get ahead in this society, you people will have to work hard," "My parents were not racists, but they just did not want to live next to Mexicans, Puerto Ricans, or Blacks," and so on. Matter-of-opinion statements almost always are made in the presence of the person to be offended, which means that the offense is personal and direct. These statements epitomize the one-sided predisposition and its use as an indicator of offensive speech.

This predisposition to racist indicators is built into the symbol structure of our conversational paradigms. Because it is impossible to conceive of that which is not a combination of what is present within our worldview, users of the language often are limited in their ability to be open to multicultural and multiethnic realities. The language contains references that cannot stand the strain of additional definitions. Therefore, the old "flesh-colored" crayons and adhesive bandages had to go because they could not accommodate a multiracial society.

In discussing offensive speech in this manner, I am suggesting a theoretical framework for examining discreet discriminatory acts in American speech. Therefore, I intended to capture the universe of discourse that contains offensive racial speech. Culture patterns, speech acts, and behaviors change and are modified in several ways. A person sometimes changes his or her language under duress; for example, "If you call me 'kike' again, I will retaliate physically" might be enough to cause someone to change behaviors. A person sometimes changes because he or she has been informed that his or her perceptions are incorrect; this is education. At other times, a person may need an environmental or circumstantial change to modify the use of discriminatory discourse. At any rate, American speech is modifiable and expandable.

■ Structuring Knowledge

There is a fundamental proposition at the basis of my discussion: Racism cannot get into language unless someone puts it there. Offensive speech is created by people. I have an essential problem because human intervention is responsible for language and racism as well as for racist communication. It is useful to modify whatever belief I have had about the presence of racism in language if I had ever assumed its presence without human intervention. There is no racism without people, and there is no communication of racism without the intervention of the human brain. Even the laws of a society, its institutions and monuments, dictionaries, and encyclopedias are the products of people and therefore are fundamentally influenced in a layered way by human ideology.

Racist communication is an integral part of the American experience. The idea that racism was "as American as apple pie" gained sufficient credibility during the 1960s, and many African Americans and other ethnic groups believed it was the root of the society's problems. This may have been an overstatement, but it suggested that the nature of communication and speech as a part of communication was afflicted by this ever pernicious virus of racism.

What is language except a regularized code, containing lexical and syntactical elements, accepted by a common community of speakers? In American English, I have all of the generalized and generalizable assumptions of the society. They are profoundly racist because of the nature of the society I have inherited. Although I make a difference in this society by constant attempts to evolve a new rapprochement with others, I still am left with the old, staid, decrepit system that has given me so many reasons for pause.

The structure of knowledge is itself the principal problem because it generates the subproblems in terms of racist language. A recent theoretical movement, Afrocentricity, argues that society requires us to question the imposition of the Eurocentric view of the world as universal. The reason it was necessary to argue that position was because for 500 years we have lived in a make-believe world where Europeans conquered other people and then wrote the histories of the people as well as the histories of the conquests.

So, whether I speak of Native American peoples or Africans, the problem of being historically peripheralized is real. Certain elements were necessary in such histories, which became the guiding myths of many generations of Europeans in Europe and the Americas. With these myths, everything is tainted.

The child who goes to school in the United States gets the programming on the very first day when he or she learns about the Founding Fathers of the nation. There are sexist problems here, too. The racist problems inhere in the structure of the knowledge. The child is told that these White men came and created such a wonderful civilization. Already the idea floats around that this was the most marvelous thing to happen in history. The little African American, Mexican American, or Native American boy or girl sitting there filled with his or her own historical consciousness, however fragmented from his or her home, wonders deep in the soul: How could such an experiment that enslaved his or her ancestors be as wonderful as the teacher makes it out to be? The White child, already at this tender age, receives the essential dichotomy between Whites and other ethnic groups that will go with the child the rest of his or her life unless there are some interventions. Nevertheless, all children complete that grade and go through the rest of their educations with the same dichotomous structure operating so that in the final analysis, I find both of them believing that Europe is universal and that nothing really happened anywhere else.

There is nothing elusive about the multicultural realities of the United States. Those who would trivialize multiculturalism either do not know what it purports or believe in the maintenance of the hegemonic structure that imposes European interests as universal on all other cultural and ethnic groups. Terms such as "PC fluff," "reverse racism," and "revisionist history" are meant to thwart any correction of the mainline positions on events and personalities of history. A segment of the population believes that any change from a Eurocentric perspective on history is damaging to the self-image of Whites. But of course, this can only be correct if the self-image depends on a racialist interpretation of history and ignores the self-images of other groups.

Exclusive systems use language to support the racialist structure. Therefore, when I say that American English has acquired so many words, expressions, and sentiments of racism because of the conquest of the past 500 years, I mean that almost every major book and most major authors of the 18th and 19th centuries contained misinformation and racist sentiments based on this structure of knowledge that is rooted in the traditions of conquest. But alas, even into the 20th century I see this situation emerging in the strangest of places—in schools of education, in university presses, and in college classrooms. Thus, areas of scholarship and research also are affected by the same appropriation of achievements to White conquest. One realm of continuing conflict is, for example, over the ethnicity of the ancient Egyptians.

The late African scholar Cheikh Anta Diop wrote *The African Origin of Civilization* as an attempt to combat the forces of racism in the structuring of knowledge (Diop, 1974). It was his intention to begin at the beginning, that is, to examine how the European scholars had interpreted the oldest African civilization, ancient Egypt, and then to seek a restoration of the historical consciousness of Africans. Following the work of Diop, a host of African scholars, most importantly Theophile Obenga of

Congo-Brazzaville, wrote books examining the structure of the racist dogmas that underpin the symbols of racism. The British scholar and Cornell University professor Martin Bernal wrote *Black Athena,* which was published in an effort to uncover the Afro-Asiatic foundations of Greek civilization (Bernal, 1987). Bernal's thesis is that the past 500 years of European conquest has meant the emergence of an Aryan thesis to oppose the ancient model of world history, particularly as it relates to the anteriority of African and Asian civilizations to European ones. Indeed, the fact that most of the books published by university presses begin all discussions of theater, art, poetry, philosophy, communication, and political science with the Greeks instead of with the people of Kemet is indicative of the problem. Aeschylus, Sophocles, Plato, Socrates, Aristotle, and Solon came after the Africans and were students of the Africans. Rather than begin at the beginning, all discussions of knowledge in Europe and America begin in Greece. One does not have a problem with Greece as the beginning of European knowledge; the problem is that it is not the beginning of knowledge. Indeed, as Diop (1979) says, Egypt is to the rest of Africa as Greece is to the rest of Europe. However, the difference is that Egypt is the mother of Greece. Bernal (1987) goes so far as to say that the name of Athens itself is an African name. Of course, I know that Herodotus (1987) says that nearly all the names of the Greek gods came from Africa (Book 2, Paragraph 50).

Without an understanding that before there was Isocrates, Socrates, Plato, and Aristotle there was Kagemni, Seti, Ptahhotep, and Khun-anup, the earliest philosophers known in the world, one never can appreciate the depth of the racism in the language (Asante & Abarry, 1996). Even if I cleaned up the language today and the structure of knowledge remained or our conception of the origin of knowledge remained, offensive racist language would be regenerated just as soon as I eliminated the current offending words and expressions. New forms would be developed. This is not to say that change is unthinkable. New social information must provide us with new opportunities for change.

Racist communication is insinuated into society in four significant ways: (a) historical distortions, (b) eliminating agency, (c) creating illusions, and (d) using pejoratives. Almost all racist communication makes use of historical distortions, that is, telling a narrative that does not include all of the facts of time and place. A second type of racist communication is through the technique of eliminating agency by groups such as Africans, Asians, Latinos, or Native Americans in any endeavor that involves knowledge, science, adventure, or intellectual activity. Eliminating African or Asian agency, for example, is one way in which to take away the idea that Africans or Asians have civilizations, cultures, or even humanity. A third way uses the creation of illusions, making statements that have no obvious basis in fact but nevertheless are projected as fact. For example, "Africans did not write" is just such a projection. Last is the use of pejoratives to define people. Whether these terms are current in the language of racists is not the issue; they minimize the human status of individuals and therefore become racist.

From the point of view of American English, it is necessary to be vigilant, not just against the offensive speech found in the general American lexicon—not just for matter-of-course, matter-of-fact, and matter-of-opinion statements—but also in the common sentiment and expression of ideas. In the end, this is the more fundamental problem and the one I have the least opportunity to truly affect unless I also work to eliminate racism itself.

5 Communication of Sexism

Lana F. Rakow
Laura A. Wackwitz

S *exism* is a term that came into the everyday vocabularies of people in the United States during the 1960s and 1970s with the resurgence of the women's movement, building on the inroads made by the civil rights movement and drawing parallels with racism. During the 1990s, although the word continues to be used to refer to specific acts or behaviors that denigrate women, it may seem dated in the context of sophisticated feminist scholarship that has focused attention on gender and difference. If used to identify and name a belief system about gender that is based on the subordination of women to men, however, the term *sexism* becomes a powerful concept that helps explain sexist norms, values, attitudes, and behavior.

This chapter uses the latter conception of sexism to interrogate the layered ways in which sexism is communicated to create and maintain its status as a primary belief system in the dominant culture. The first section discusses (a) the difference between sexism and feminism as counterposing frameworks, (b) different interpretations of the origin of gender and the origin of sexism, and (c) the interactive nature of gender within and between different cultural groups in a racist society. The second section explores the ways in which sexism is accomplished and policed through communication at three primary levels: language, interaction, and representation. The chapter concludes with a discussion of proposed and attempted strategies for changing the sexist meaning system and an evaluation of the possibilities for success of different strategies.

■ Sexism as Belief System

Identifying sexism as a belief system requires the recognition that gender itself is a belief system; that is, gender is a web of socially constructed meanings that differentiate humans on the basis of perceived physical, social, and psychological characteristics. Dominant Western perspectives currently allow for exactly two genders; however, because gender is a belief system, gender differentiation can assume many forms throughout history and across cultures. Sexism, therefore, is only one of the many possible ideological meaning systems about gender. Others might include an egalitarian conception of gender in which all genders are treated equally, a multigendered perspective in which more than two genders are recognized and cultivated, or a genderless formation in which gender becomes a meaningless category.

Feminism stands in contrast to sexism as an alternate, or oppositional, meaning system. Those who take up feminism reject the subordination of women and work against sexism to create and promote new beliefs. Beyond these commonalities, feminists differ in their approaches to the study, critique, and eradication of sexism. Feminist scholarship has enabled people to be more systematic in their understanding of different interpretations of the origins of systems of difference and of sexism as a particular system of difference.

■ Theories of Difference and Dominance

Those who adhere to a sexist belief system about gender also differ in their beliefs about the origins of difference. Three commonly identified sources used to justify sexism, not necessarily exclusive of each other, are religion, biology, and social scientific reasoning.

Religious Justification

Religion traditionally has played a strong role in prescribing and justifying gender differences that subordinate women. Those who use religion to support a sexist worldview point to the "natural order of things" as presented by holy texts or the teachings of prophets and priests. Sexist religious beliefs may ascribe a natural sinfulness to women or, at the least, a subordinated role for women in a hierarchical arrangement (see Bullough, Shelton, & Slavin, 1988; Christ, 1992; Christ & Plaskow, 1979; Daly, 1968, 1973, 1978; Millett, 1970; Starhawk, 1987, 1988; Tannahill, 1992). In such a system, men tend to be placed closer to a god or to be specifically ordained by a god to serve as master or head in the earthly microcosm of the heavenly order. Even where women may be presumed to have more natural piety than men—a result of the late 19th-century "cult of true womanhood"—women's status in relation to men and to god remains unchanged. Religious teachings are likely to prescribe appropriate dress, behavior, and spheres of activity and influence for women as a means of enforcing and reinforcing the gender hierarchy.

Biological Justification

Biological justifications for both difference and dominance are widespread in Western cultures. Biological constructs are, in fact, the primary explanations for gender throughout Western cultures, even among those who attempt to reject or diminish the centrality of a sexist belief system. Given the Western reliance on the explanatory power of "scientific," "empirical," or "rational" exploration, it is not surprising that biology has attained such a prominent role in the construction and explanation of gender (see Haraway, 1981). Whether one adheres to a creationist or an evolutionist belief in the origin and order of the universe, the outcome of each of these beliefs has contributed to the design and institution of a hierarchical gender system. This astonishing similarity indicates that the two belief systems may be complementary rather than oppositional, despite the accusations against each other made by adherents to each.

Biological principles are used to assert essential and immutable differences among humans on the basis of their primary and secondary sex characteristics. Even where there has been an acceptance of the role of culture in shaping a gender system, most people—even some feminists—continue to believe in the foundational nature of a biological differentiation of sex. For most people, the differences are obvious and are related to reproduction, physical characteristics, and sexual activity. Physicians and scientists, however, have had to deal with the complexity of these issues in a way that laypeople have not, leading to shifting notions over time of what constitutes the essential defining characteristics of male and female. Neither physical nor genetic characteristics provide fail-safe methods of biological differentiation. Babies can be born with ambiguous or multiple organs and/or genitalia that can be surgically altered to provide a better "fit" between their gender identities and their physical characteristics. Likewise, genetic testing, although it has been seen to be a better indicator of one's "true" gender identity, reveals variations in chromosomes that negate the possibility of assigning humans into two entirely distinct sexual categories (Kessler & McKenna, 1978; Wackwitz, 1996a). Both physical and genetic criteria are, at base, human constructs—ways of ordering the biological and social world. The categories "male" and "female" are assigned to individuals at or prior to birth based on human-cultural interpretations of physical and genetic characteristics (Butler, 1990; Wackwitz, 1996b).

Despite the difficulty of locating the "essential" defining biological characteristics that differentiate male and female humans, biological explanations are part of people's "commonsense" knowledge. Laypersons often assume that men are stronger and more aggressive than women and that women are naturally weaker, more emotional, and better designed for the care and nurturing of infants and children. Indeed, a sexist belief system that is informed by biological assumptions may promote the assumption that men are naturally superior to women and therefore are naturally dominant over them. In this way, biological reasoning is commonly used to justify gender-specific spheres of activity and standards for behavior that privilege men over women. Some examples include excusing men's violence against women, advocating men's roles as natural political and military leaders, and dismissing men's encounters with multiple sexual partners as "natural" while judging women by a standard of monogamy.

Social Scientific Justification

The justifications for gender differences and a sexist gender system by religious and scientific authorities have been supported by the social sciences. Although the social sciences may not have had the same type of widespread influence on the belief systems of most people in Western cultures, they have had great influence in academic circles and further serve to justify and perpetuate the sexist belief systems promulgated by science and religion. The functionalist explanation of social order, for example, grew out of the biological sciences and subsequently was legitimated in the social sciences by Parsons (1954, 1966) during the middle decades of the 20th century. Other social theories (including Marxism and psychoanalysis) have been sexist, but functionalism serves as an exemplar form because of its recent widespread acceptance in diverse fields such as sociology, psychology, rhetoric, and media studies. Functionalism justified a sexist gender system on the basis of the functionality of separate women's and men's "roles" for the preservation of the social order. On the issue of sex role segregation, a functionalist argument might proceed as follows. The sexes are segregated by biological "function." Women's bodies function to bear and nurse children. Women, therefore, serve the social order by fulfilling their biological role and staying at home to raise and nurture human young. Women, due to their essential biological function as mothers, must be protected by men (who are naturally stronger) to ensure propagation of the species, thus requiring that they comprise a protected class. Women, therefore, must not be placed at risk and should not participate in activities such as military combat or physical exertion. In addition, because women are more nurturing by nature, they best serve the social order by performing relationship maintenance tasks in the home and the workplace as caretakers, wives, nurses, and kindergarten teachers.

In this and other scenarios, the social order takes on an autonomous status apart from human creation and agency. Social arrangements that lead to the maintenance of the social order are, by definition, appropriate and justifiable. As this example illustrates, functionalism served to justify a sexist gender arrangement that confined women to a sphere of home and family. Today, although Parsonian functionalism has passed its prime, some social scientists continue to explore its utility and adaptation for contemporary theory (see, e.g., Johnson, 1993; Stewart, Smith, & Denton, 1994).

■ Feminist Perspectives

Although religion, biology, and social theory have been used to justify the origins of a sexist gender arrangement, feminists have identified several different, although not necessarily incompatible, explanations of sexism itself. Feminist psychoanalysis has looked to the psychological construction of humans that has made sexism part of our unconscious sexual identity. During the late 1970s, Nancy Chodorow brought psychoanalysis back to the table after its rejection by feminists because of its oppressive use in justifying a damaging definition of a healthy woman's psyche. Chodorow (1978) demonstrates a deep connection between the nuclear family itself and the unconscious production of masculine and feminine personalities. She argues that male children who are raised in a traditional nuclear family—one in which the mother is the primary or sole nurturer and caretaker—grow to reject the woman as a means of self-identification and acceptance into the male world. In the workplace, these grown children enact dominance over the women they have learned to reject, thereby perpetuating gender stratification. Women, after experiencing this domination and rejection, turn to child-bearing and child rearing as a means of personal fulfillment, thus perpetuating the cycle. With its continued development since Chodorow, feminist psychoanalysis has provided, without resorting to an essentialist argument that difference and dominance are inherent, a means for understanding how male domination has become part of our identity structures. As Williams (1993) summarizes, "The structure of the traditional, Western nuclear family creates asymmetrical needs and dispositions in men and women that contribute to the reproduction of unequal and essentially oppressive relationships" (pp. 146-147).

These relationships are carried into the marketplace through defined sex roles in terms of the expenditure and earning of capital. Marxist and socialist feminists have looked, therefore, to the capitalistic economic system to explain divisions of labor between groups of people and the devaluing of women's paid and unpaid productive and reproductive contributions to society. Although economic theories traditionally have lacked explanations of gender inequality, many scholars have revisioned Marxism and socialism from a feminist perspective. Shelton and Agger (1993), for example, argue that although "orthodox Marxism" (p. 40) is sexist and inadequate to explain gender inequities, a feminist revisioning of Marxism yields valuable insights into the relationship between the subordination of women and their place within the economic system. They conclude,

> Women's subordinated position in the labor market, and their labor in the household, means that their rate of exploitation is higher than men's. That is, women perform more labor for which they are not remunerated, thus producing more surplus value than men. This clearly benefits capital and is therefore understandable in terms of the logic of capitalism. (p. 39)

Shelton and Agger further argue that such an economic interpretation has greater explanatory power than do models that posit *patriarchy* as the cause and center of women's oppression.

Radical feminists, on the other hand, embrace the concept of patriarchy as a description of a sexist social order. They define patriarchy as a system of power arrangements created and perpetuated by men that keeps women subordinated to men through harassment, the threat of violence, and economic dependence. This definition wrests the term from the hands of social scientists who had used "patriarchy" to refer to a theory of natural existence of a family headed by a male, with paternity and inheritance rights essential to the maintenance of the patriarchal family (Coward, 1983). Instead, radical feminists turned this antiquated definition on its head by making the male-dominated family problematic and by asserting the role of male-defined sexuality as central to women's oppression. This sexuality is linked to violence or the threat of violence, both real and symbolic, against women (Dworkin, 1981; MacKinnon, 1984, 1989, 1993).

Women's subordination—relational, occupational, and sexual—is supported and enforced by the U.S. system of law and its emphasis on the dichotomy between public (political) and private (nonpolitical) spheres (MacKinnon, 1987). Taub and Schneider (1993) expose two facets of the U.S. legal system that are especially damaging to the status of women, demonstrating that the law (a) "has furthered male dominance by explicitly excluding women from the public sphere and by refusing to regulate the domestic sphere to which they are thus confined" and (b) "has legitimized sex discrimination through the articulation of an ideology that justifies differential treatment on the basis of perceived differences between men and women" (p. 9). Court procedures and specialized language limit access to and critique of the law from anyone outside the trained legal arena, thereby helping to solidify the public/private distinction within the legal system.

Closed and troublesome discourses and representations comprise a realm of inquiry commonly investigated by cultural and postmodern feminists. Beginning with the creation of difference in language, early feminist work in this direction identified "woman" as a discursive category that exists only in language. Cowie (1978), for example, argues that a meaning system that justifies sexism must precede institutionalized sexist actions. Specifically, Cowie corrects anthropologist Lévi-Strauss's (1963) articulation of the development of cultural patterns. As she notes, Lévi-Strauss claims that culture is made possible by the natural human capacity for structuring relationships between elements. Culture begins with the primal structuring relationship in which men exchange women, creating kinship structure. Cowie's refutation of this assertion illustrates the difficulties inherent in social scientific reasonings that ascribe autonomy to the social order and, in the process, deny human agency. It also illustrates the way in which Cowie and other feminists are able to problematize language and other systems of representation and their relation to social reality.

■ Racism and Sexism as Interlocking Systems

Although feminists have made headway in explicating the possible sources of sexist belief systems, they have had more trouble explaining the relationship between sexism and other oppressive belief systems such as racism (hooks, 1981, 1984). This is perhaps largely because of the overwhelming presence of White women in the feminist movement and in feminist scholarship in the academy. Making the task more difficult are the multiple and sometimes contradictory layers of meaning between and among cultural groups. Racism, like sexism, has at its foundation the differentiation of humans based on cultural assumptions. How can one understand racism and sexism together?

When some cultural groups, which may or may not have sexist belief systems, are subordinated to a dominant, racist, and sexist cultural group (as is the case in the United States), racism and sexism become interlocking belief systems that explain and justify the devaluation of all women and of men who do not belong to the dominant cultural group. Women in the dominant cultural group must contend with the sexist belief system of that group while benefiting from its racist belief system. Women and men of subordinated cultural groups must contend with two belief systems about gender and race—their own and that of the dominant cultural group.

The experience of Native Americans as a cultural group conquered and dominated by European Americans provides an example of the interlocking facets of racism and sexism and their consequences for the original belief system of the group. Of course, the various tribes of original Americans had a very different conceptualization of themselves than did those who subscribed to the racist belief system that characterized them as uncivilized savages and consequently justified White domination of native peoples. Even the categorization of the diversity of tribal groups under the general rubric of "Indians" or "Native Americans" was a result of their forced subordination to the meaning system of the dominant group. Now they must struggle to recreate a belief system that provides a viable way of life in a context not of their making while fighting to change the negative and false belief system perpetuated by the dominant culture.

The belief system about gender was one important aspect of the native worldview that underwent a serious change as a result of European domination and disruption of native tribes' original ways of life. As a result of European intervention and sexism, native tribes lost their own gender systems, including those that Allen (1986) identifies as "gynocratic" or woman-centered, for a sexist one (p. 2). In fact, Allen argues,

> The physical and cultural genocide of American Indian tribes is and was mostly about patriarchal fear of gynocracy. . . .
>
> The colonizers saw (and rightly) that as long as women held unquestioned power of such magnitude, attempts at total conquest of the continents were bound to fail. . . . The invaders have exerted every effort to remove Indian women from every position of authority, to obliterate all records pertaining to gynocratic social systems, and to ensure that no American and few American Indians would remember that gynocracy was the primary social order of Indian America prior to 1800. (p. 3)

As a result, Native American women must now challenge the sexist belief system within their own tribes as well as the sexism and racism of the dominant culture.

Racism by a sexist cultural group results in women and men of subordinate groups being held to their subordinated positions by differing meanings that grow out of the sexism of the dominant group. In the case of Native Americans, native women are held to their subordinated positions in the dominant culture by specific sexist meanings that identify native women as squaws or princesses (Allen, 1983). Identification as squaws denigrates and falsifies their position in early native culture and thereby justifies White domination as a superior belief system about women. Likewise, identification as princesses establishes native women's more natural alliance with White culture and with White men and thereby justifies their assistance to Whites (or betrayal, depending on a European or a native viewpoint), as exemplified by the White mythic tales of Pocahontas and Sacagawea. Native men are identified as either noble or brutal savages, the first portrayal useful to a White quest for noncommercial values and the second useful again to justify White domination by "proving" White superiority.

In a similar way, women and men of other major but subordinated U.S. cultural groups—African Americans, Asian Americans, and Latinos—are assigned different meanings that reflect both the racism and the sexism of the dominant group while also affecting the gender system within each group as it encounters the dominant gender belief system. In this way, racism and sexism can be seen as interlocking systems, with meanings about gender different for the women and men of each cultural group but always in relationship to dominant meanings about gender that demonstrate White men's superiority over all women and all members of nondominant racial groups and White women's superiority over women of color.

■ Maintenance of a Sexist Belief System

Having shown how sexism functions as a belief system within and between cultural groups, we now turn to a more explicit discussion of sexism and its relationship to communication. It should be clear by now that because a gender system is a meaning system, gender is a product of communication. Sexism, as a particular belief system about gender, determines the specifics of the meaning system and requires a comprehensive maintenance or policing system for it to be carried out. This maintenance system depends on the communication of sexism through three dominant mechanisms: (a) sexism in the form and content of language, (b) sexism in the social accomplishment of gender, and (c) sexism in systems of representation.

■ Sexism Communicated in Language

The English language (as well as many other languages that are not discussed here) encodes a sexist belief system into its structure, content, and usage. During the past several decades, feminist communication scholars have identified both the ways in which women's devaluation occurs in language and the ways in which such sexism is maintained and policed by language "authorities" (Daly, 1978; Rich, 1979; Spender, 1980; Thorne, Kramarae, & Henley, 1983).

Among the most obvious features of the language that embody sexism is the pseudogeneric masculine, which uses references to men as supposedly encompassing both women and men. Feminists traced the origins of this practice to grammarians and other language authority figures over the past several centuries, which moved the language away from truly generic human references to one in which "man" could stand for women and men because the masculine gender was assumed to be the primary and most important gender (MacKay, 1983; Martyna, 1983; Thorne et al., 1983). In a similar way, feminist scholars identified the sheer volume of derogatory words in English for women with a lack of counterpart words for men (Mills, 1993; Thorne et al., 1983). They pointed out naming practices, such as the custom of women taking up the first and last names of their husbands when they marry (Stannard, 1977), and the unequal courtesy titles of "Mr.," "Mrs.," and "Miss" (Thorne et al., 1983).

Because language is seen by most feminist scholars not as a reflection (true or arbitrary) of a stable, external reality but rather as the ongoing enactment of reality through its categories, changing the sexism of English has been seen as a critical intervention in the continuing production of a sexist society. Consequently, great efforts were made during the 1970s and 1980s to challenge those sites at which language content and practice is prescribed and reproduced—dictionaries, publishing houses, news media stylebooks, grammar texts, composition courses, and so on. The tremendous resistance they encountered demonstrates the high stakes involved with changing the gender system.

■ Sexism Communicated in Interaction

The primary manner in which people experience a gender system is in their own lived experience as cultural actors with gendered identities who take part in gendered interactions. This primacy of the lived experience of gender has led some feminist scholars to describe gender as an accomplishment or as a verb (Rakow, 1986). In other words, gender is something we do, not something we are. Articulating gender in this way contradicts the biological and sociological notion of gender as a factual and essential core of our physical and cultural being.

Despite what physicians and scientists might say about the role of hormones, chromosomes, or genitals in the determination of one's gender, in everyday experience people determine each other's gender and convey their own in an elaborate yet mostly unconscious acting out of our gender system. In a sexist system, this requires women to participate in their own subordination in a routine, pervasive, and systematic way (Frye, 1983).

The accomplishment of a sexist gender system depends on the bifurcation of individuals into the two separate and distinct categories of "male" and "female." Because of the great variation in human physical characteristics, this categorization may require extensive physical and material alterations. These alterations may include surgery (to adjust genitals or to emphasize or deemphasize certain secondary sexual characteristics such as breasts or hips), removal of body or facial hair, hormonal therapy (to bring secondary sexual characteristics into line with gender-specific cultural expectations for males and females), diet and exercise (to change and emphasize a masculine or feminine body shape), facial cosmetics, haircuts and hair styles, and clothing selection and adornment.

A lifetime of reproducing the accoutrements of our assigned genders may affect our muscular structures and nervous systems to such an extent that, as Frye (1983) observes, gender actually has become biological. By carrying out the physical requirements of our genders—how we walk, carry and present ourselves, fit into space (men are allowed to take up more space with their bodies [Wex, 1979]), eat, and use our bodies—we have created the two physical genders we believed to exist in the first place. In our daily interactions with others, we perpetuate and accentuate the differences in a gender-marking and -announcing system that provides us with the "appropriate" scripts for interaction with the appropriate gender.

These interactions between women and men reproduce sexism through the power that men may exert by using their accepted speaking style and content. Tendencies in differences between women's and men's speaking styles are documented convincingly by feminist scholars (e.g., Bate, 1988; Gilligan, 1982; Tannen, 1990; Treichler & Kramarae, 1983). Women's and men's different social positions often result in styles described for women as more relational and dialogic and for men as more competitive and monologic (Treichler & Kramarae, 1983). Speech and interactional differences, however, usually are considered to be natural reflections of the inherent differences between women and men rather than seeing that gender *results from* the differences required of women and men as enacted and reflected in communication.

Some of the mechanisms by which interactions reproduce sexism include men's use of interruptions, their control of topics and of "the floor," and their sexual harassment of women. Fishman's (1983) work with married couples, for example, reveals how men can control conversation by refusing to acknowledge conversational opening gambits by women, whereas women may be far more likely to support men's attempts to start particular conversational topics. Others observe that men tend to talk more and to control the flow and direction of conversation through interruptions (Spender, 1980). Harassment of women on the street and in the workplace is an effective mechanism for restricting women's physical movements and economic success and independence, keeping them in their place both literally and figuratively (Kramarae, 1992). Because harassment carries the threat of physical violence or other repercussions, it reinforces the common wisdom that women need men to protect them from other men while, ironically, women generally are in greater danger from the men with whom they live than they are from strangers (Finn, 1996).

Women, conversely, tend to carry out their gendered assignments by providing the support work for others in interaction, providing verbal and nonverbal encouragement, asking questions to continue the speaker's conversation, responding to opening gambits by others, returning to points made by earlier speakers, and attempting to bring others into the conversation (DeFrancisco, 1991).

■ Sexism Communicated in Systems of Representation

From the realization by scholars such as Coward (1983) that "woman" is a sign in a system of representation rather than a direct reference to a preexisting fact of human existence, other feminist scholars have looked anew at the troubling representations of women in mass media and other forms of popular culture. As early as the publication of Friedan's (1963) *The Feminine Mystique,* feminist activists were identifying the role of the mass media in representing negative and unhealthy images of women in advertising, television entertainment, magazines, and the news media. These images were systematically documented to demonstrate that all women (as well as men of color) are vastly underrepresented in certain media forms (e.g., news), whereas White women are vastly overrepresented in others (e.g., advertising). These images have shown consistent patterns of representation—White women as homemakers or sex objects, Black women as maids or wanton sexual animals, Native American women as princesses or squaws, Asian women as "dragon ladies" or exotic and submissive sexual objects, and Latinas as suffering mother figures or cantina girls.

Theoretical work by feminist scholars on the notion of representation problematized the commonsense understanding of these images. Rather than inaccurately reflecting "reality," as early feminists charged, these representations, from this new theoretical position, are understood as a social construction referring only to other social constructions or signs. In other words, reality is itself a social construction such that media texts are representations only of other representations, not of the "real." The images represent the symbolic exchange of women in a discursive system of difference, an exchange that takes place and to which we are held accountable both outside of and within the screen or text.

An example of this symbolic exchange can be seen in television news, which most people view as an official representation of reality—selected, biased, or inaccurate as some may believe it to be, but, nonetheless, based in and on reality. On the other hand, news more usefully can be seen as a masculine narrative that refers to other narratives rather than the "real" that transcends human meaning.

A study of women as sources used on network television news (Rakow & Kranich, 1991) summarizes women's ritualized role within this masculine narrative, demonstrating the manner in which "woman" functions as a sign in discourse. In the news stories studied, women do not speak as women as part of public debate about an issue. Instead, women function as signs in several ways. First, they are used to illustrate the private consequences of public events and actions. The women are not used in the news stories as sources of information as men are; rather, they are used as evidence supporting interpretations of the problems. Second, the women speak to issues only as representatives of organizations or institutions, often apparently chosen because of their functions as signs (e.g., a woman physician from AT&T's health affairs department explaining its policy of transferring pregnant women out of jobs dealing with hazardous chemicals). Third, in the few stories in which women might speak *for* women, they have to signify as "feminists," particular and unusual types of women. Fourth, only White women are used to signify as women, retaining the clarity of its meaning and demonstrating the interlocking nature of racism and sexism (Whiteness as a mark of "real" women and men). Fifth, women's attempts to challenge the social order are carefully contained by demonstrating disagreements among women as if the issues are conflicting personalities or women's inability to get along with each other (e.g., stories about pornography).

■ Strategies for Change

It already should be apparent that feminists—scholars and activists—have been at work trying to change both the sexist meaning system and the specific communication processes that produce and maintain sexism. They have worked for language change by documenting the pervasiveness and influence of sexism in language form, content, and usage; they have raised awareness within the public and media industries about sexist language; and they have challenged certain practices such as the use of naming practices and courtesy titles. Sexual harassment has been labeled and successfully identified as a legitimate cause for women's legal action. Differences in women's and men's talk have been put on the public agenda with the widespread popularity of books such as Tannen's (1990) *You Just Don't Understand.* Representations of women in media texts and other forms of popular culture have been problematized. Pornography, for example, has received widespread social attention during the past two decades. Advertisers have been subjected to intense public pressure for their representation of women as housewives and sex objects. The television industry has been subjected to pressure to present entertainment other than soap operas that appeals to different types of women.

How successful have these strategies been? The answer is mixed. Faludi (1991), in her book *Backlash,* documents the extensive efforts by the news media to curb and reverse the progress feminists made in challenging sexism, illustrating the powerful mechanisms by which sexism is maintained and efforts to change it are policed. Even without the serious backsliding that has occurred with the media declaration of "post-feminism," the changes that were seen, particularly in representations of women, could not be clearly identified as improvements. The move by advertisers, for example, to represent "the new woman" as a "superwoman" could hardly be classified as a significant improvement for women or a significant change in a sexist belief system. Advertisers now seem to feel no compunction about moving back to older, more traditional representations of women as caring mothers and wives, reflective of a cultural nostalgia for a time period when meanings were stable and clearly defined. Representations of boys and girls in advertising and the appeal of toy and clothing manufacturers are back to a more rigid gender division.

Language change seems to have reached a peak, and sexist usage is returning. The public discussion over the pseudogeneric masculine, over courtesy titles and naming practices for married women, and over changes in male-oriented words (e.g., fireman, garbageman) has passed. Although efforts at change have not been reversed completely, these types of sexist language can be used publicly without compunction.

Although the public and legal foci on sexual harassment has problematized men's speech in the workplace in a dramatic and important way, the other ways in which men's talk is problematic for women and reinforces a sexist gender system seem unchanged. The public interest in women's and men's talk has failed to take into account the power differential between women and men, resulting in little understanding of the need for men to change their style of interaction with women if women's social place is to be reinvented.

If the changes that have been fought for so long and hard by feminists can be co-opted and reversed so easily, then how can a successful intervention in the communication of sexism take place?

Feminist interventions as described previously need to continue, indeed, need to be revived and pressed again more vigorously. Complementing these actions must be a strong educational push through women's studies and ethnic studies with a particular focus on communication. Although women's studies has attained a relatively solid foothold in the academy—reaching many students and having, we can hope, a long-term effect that may not yet be noticeable—women's studies in communication have had less impact. Changing the sexist gender system will require that people become aware of the nature of gender as a social construction, a difficult intellectual task for most people given the ideological hold that biology and religion have on their understanding of gender. Arguments against biological and religious determinism are met with resistance, disbelief, even hostility. Consequently, our educational campaign must be systematic and comprehensive at the undergraduate level, leading students through a developmental process of awareness about the social construction of culture and human difference.

6 Communication of Heterosexism

Thomas K. Nakayama

All at once they started yelling "faggot" and "fucking faggot. . . . " One of them missed me with a beer can. . . . College and my literary education agreed that I should see myself as a random conjunction of life's possibilities, certainly an enviable, luxurious point of view. But it's hard to draw on that as a model when four men are chasing you down the street. What life will that model sustain, and when aren't we being chased? . . . And what I resolved was this: that I would gear my writing to tell you about incidents like the one at Sanchez and Day, to put them to you as real questions that need answers. (Glück, 1982, pp. 1, 3-4)

I want to begin this chapter by underscoring the problematic nature of the terms *homophobia* and *heterosexism*. Both terms subsume a vast range of communication practices from physical violence, to invisibility and silencing, to institutionalized marginalization. Grammatically, homophobia and heterosexism are not parallel to *racism* and *sexism*. The range of meanings and their force are not captured by the similar terms.

There is, of course, no easy way in which to describe the myriad relations, connections, lines of movement between homophobia and heterosexism, and communication. The complexities become apparent when we recognize the myriad ways that heterosexism is embedded in social structures and the seemingly infinite modes of communicating heterosexual superiority. Hecht's (1993) model of layered identity is helpful as a metaphor for thinking about identity, but to explore the complexities of communication and homophobia/heterosexism we need to extend his metaphor. In this chapter, then, I offer a discussion of heterosexism to help the reader understand one aspect of the communication of prejudice by framing my discussion within the schizophrenia model of dynamic plateaus of Deleuze and Guattari (1987). These dynamic moving levels of meaning offer a clear, radical, dynamic approach to understanding the changing rhetorics of homophobia and heterosexism.

Yet, I sense that these discussions about the communication of homophobia and heterosexism belie the realities of living within a heterosexist society. To shed meager light on the everydayness of trying to forge a life within a heteronormative society, I am inserting news fragments that underscore the ways in which the sexual order is maintained. For example, the violence against gays and lesbians is illustrated by this item from the *Southern Voice*:

> Chad Wheeler Clifton, 24, was arrested and charged with malicious harassment after a lesbian couple and a gay man were attacked, the *Seattle Gay News* reported.
>
> According to charges filed by the King County prosecutors office, Clifton approached a lesbian couple and asked why they were holding hands. The women told him it was none of his business and began to walk away.
>
> The court record says Clifton then "ran up behind" the women and said, "Why be with her when you can be with me? I'll stick my dick in you," at which point the women threatened to "kick him in the balls."
>
> Clifton then allegedly shoved one of them in the face, calling her a "stupid dyke," the document said.
>
> A fight ensued. A gay man, who witnessed the fight, intervened. As he tried to pull the two apart, Clifton allegedly attacked the gay man and punched him in the face, knocking some of his teeth out. During the assault, Clifton said, "Faggot, do you want some of this?" . . .
>
> The report says Clifton waived his right to remain silent and excitedly told the police that he was "just a farm boy from Kansas" and didn't "care for the fags, dykes, and queers" he saw. ("He's Not in Kansas Anymore," 1995, pp. 52-53)

Much as this chapter is bracketed by homophobia and heterosexism, so too are all of our lives in the ways in which we act, communicate our sexualities, and live our lives every day.

■ Homophobia/Heterosexism

Although there are various ways of construing "homophobia and "heterosexism," it is useful to start with basic definitions that lay the groundwork for discussion. One useful conceptualization of heterosexism comes from Jung and Smith (1993):

> *Heterosexism* is a reasoned system of bias regarding sexual orientation. It denotes prejudice in favor of heterosexual people and connotes prejudice against bisexual and, especially, homosexual people. . . . Heterosexism is not grounded primarily in emotional fears, hatreds, or other visceral responses to homosexuality. Instead it is rooted in a largely cognitive constellation of beliefs about human sexuality. (p. 13)

By contrast, homophobia often is seen as operating out of emotional fear, hatred, and anger. Of course, the two forms of intolerance and prejudice often stem from similar ideological positions.

Blumenfeld (1992) makes the important observation that "within lesbian, gay, bisexual, and transgender communities, a debate is currently under way over the merits of the term 'homophobia' " (pp. 14-15). For him, heterosexism is "defined as both the belief that heterosexuality is or should be the only acceptable sexual orientation and the fear and hatred of those who love and sexually desire those of the same sex" (p. 15).

I am hesitant to invoke "homophobia" because it tends to bow too neatly to reduction to individual psychic motives (cf. Gentaz, 1994). As Fernald (1995) discusses homophobia, we can see its connection to irrational motive drives, yet the use of this term has been important in shifting attention away from the causes of sexual orientation to antigay bias. Morin and Garfinkle (1981) note more directly that "as an individual psychic dynamic, . . . the term homophobia is used to describe a specific phobic condition rather than a generalized cultural attitude" (p. 119). By situating prejudice within the individual psyche, do we ignore the larger structural and cultural configurations of heteronormativity? Do we overlook the systemic means of instantiating heterosexuality or of preserving the heterosexual order?

> Unfortunately, homophobia is not confined to the moral cesspool that is the Republican campaign headquarters. Instead, it is the stuff of American culture, audible in the schoolyards and in the bars, on television and at any open-mike comedy club.
>
> Somehow, people still think it is not only acceptable but also funny to ridicule lesbians and gay men.
>
> But it is a short path from ridicule to discrimination. . . . It is an even shorter path from discrimination to violence, and gays and lesbians are with appalling frequency the victims of hate crimes. (Rothschild, 1992, p. A9)

Rather than emphasizing psychic motives, "heterosexism" stresses the larger ideological character of heteronormativity. At some level, must one believe in heterosexuality to engage in heterosexism? But is not heterosexuality[40] yet another ideological fiction (Katz, 1995)? The invention of heterosexuality as a social and political identity underscores the power of heterosexism. It is a foundation for social institutions and social practices, from the military to weddings. Sexuality, of course, is never so easy. In our desire to categorize and understand the world in manageable ways, we have bought into a fictive identity that has ramifications across the entire social order.

Many other terms have been discussed to describe the phenomenon of antigay beliefs, attitudes, and behaviors. Yet, at this time, the term *heterosexism* seems to capture the larger social phenomenon of bias against nonheterosexual orientations. Many layers of communicative and cultural practices are enacted across the social spectrum to reinforce heteronormativity. One such practice, at the personal and interpersonal layer, is antigay humor. As noted by Friskopp and Silverstein (1995):

> Outside of the military and some "family values" companies, few organizations enshrine discrimination in their operating principles. But many tolerate a hostile atmosphere toward gay people, an atmosphere often created by antigay jokes. Because so few companies have made it clear that such jokes are not permissible, both gay professionals and sympathetic heterosexuals are at times unsure of the best way to respond when they become the unwitting audience. (Friskopp & Silverstein, 1995, p. 42)

At the communal or institutional layer, we have legislation which inscribes "heterosexism" as described in the following report:

> The New Hampshire state motto is "Live free or die." Gays and lesbians there may be hoping that nobody takes the tag too literally since the state senate voted 13-10 on April 21 to defeat a bill that would have prevented discrimination on the basis of sexual orientation in housing, employment, and public accommodations. ("No Room at the Inn," 1994, p. 15)

■ Under Siege

We are bombarded by messages that tell us how to regulate our communicative behavior and to support the supremacy of heterosexuality if not in action, then in communication. Negotiating the minefields of social relations requires attentiveness at all times.

The ideology of heterosexual supremacy and the system are intertwined in ways that escape codification. The quickly shifting sands erase all discursive foundations to take a stand:

> When we say majority, we are referring not to a greater relative quantity but to the determination of a state or standards in relation to which larger quantities, as well as the samples, can be said to be minoritarian. . . . Majority implies a state of domination, not the reverse. (Deleuze & Guattari, 1987, p. 291)

The domination of the heteronormativity ideology does not require correlation to the everyday lived sexual practices.

Sexuality is replete with confusion over labels, and this makes the entire communication process problematic. Bawer (1994) recognizes the difficulty in communicating: "Certainly a lot of confusion has arisen from the fact that many of us use the same words to mean different things. Take *gay* and *homosexual*" (p. 80, emphases in original).

Although Bawer rejects *queer,* there is a range of other labels that further complicate the discussion, from queer to omnisexual and beyond.

Fierce debates about labels and discourse within the gay and lesbian communities underscore the intense scrutiny and importance of language use. Discussions over *queer,* for example, highlight the contested character of labeling and the ways in which these labels might be read by those outside the gay and lesbian communities. Yet, the term queer also is a political choice and a defiant identity (cf. Slagle, 1995; Warner, 1991, 1992). Despite these debates, heteronormativity is resecured in innumerable ways through communication practices.

The sexual order is maintained to resecure heterosexual privilege. After all, heterosexuality means nothing without an "other"; it is a position of domination only in relation to that which is not hetero—that which is "other." The ways in which discursive practices reinscribe heteronormativity are neither simple to expose nor simple to analyze. In part, the silencing of same-sex realities makes the understanding of communication of heteronormativity more complex.

■ The Love That Dare Not Speak Its Name

The "love that dare not speak its name" reflects the silencing of same-sex realities and the imposition of heteronormativity. Boswell (1994) observes that the silencing of homosexual acts serves powerful rhetorical ends:

> Few, if any, other major cultures have made homosexuality—either as a general classification of acts according to gender or an "orientation"—the primary and singular moral taboo it has long been in Western society; "the sin that cannot be named," "the unmentionable vice," "the love that dare not speak its name." Those who have never had occasion to question this extraordinary prejudice, especially if they personally entertain reservations about homosexual acts, may have difficulty apprehending how remarkable this degree of revulsion actually is. Murder, matricide, child molesting, incest, cannibalism, genocide, even deicide are *mentionable;* why are a few disapproved sexual acts that injure no one so much more horrible than these? Because they are worse? (p. xxiii)

The silence that surrounds nonheterosexuality feeds heteronormativity in powerful ways.

We often are told that we should "hide" or silence our many sexual identities to survive, conform to, and unwittingly support heteronormativity. In upholding the antigay ballot initiative in Cincinnati, Ohio, the judge declared, "Those persons having a homosexual 'orientation' simply do not, as such, comprise an identifiable class. Many homosexuals successfully conceal their orientation" (Krupansky, 1995, p. 20). We learn how to conform to heteronormativity regardless of how we identify our sexual identities.

This silence, however, is not contained to the level of the individual. Many of its more important implications extend to the social arena. For example, many states have laws, protections, and programs regarding domestic violence. In Arizona, these laws are specifically written for opposite-sex relations. By law and by definition, "domestic

violence" refers exclusively to heterosexual relationships. None of the existing programs or protections in place are for use by Arizonans in nonheterosexual relationships.
A similar situation exists in Virginia where:

> Virginia Attorney General James S. Gilmore, in a little-noticed action, issued a
> legal opinion last year declaring that partners of same-sex couples who encounter
> domestic violence cannot seek legal redress in the state's domestic relations
> court. The effect of Gilmore's ruling surfaced in late July 1995 when a judge
> dismissed a petition filed by a gay man seeking a restraining order against his
> former lover. Judge Stephen Rideout told the man who filed the petition, Ellis
> Early, that he felt the petition had merit, but he was bound by Gilmore's 1994
> opinion. ("Virginia Is Not for Gay Lovers," 1995, p. 5)

It is not as if lesbian and gay relationships never experience spousal abuse. Yet, the
ways in which the laws, protections, and programs are specifically designed for
exclusive use by and for heterosexuals so as to make heterosexuality function despite
its clear (dys)functional moments, reinscribe heteronormativity.

In what ways do other discussions exclude same-sex interactions and reinscribe the
centrality of heteronormativity? In what ways are "date rape" discussions and programs
specifically designed for and about heterosexual interactions? Is heterosexuality a
"lifestyle choice"? What would it mean to say that these victimized women "chose"
this lifestyle, as we have so often heard when tragedies happen to those perceived to be
gays and lesbians?

Discussions about marriage, divorce, alimony, romance novels, filing joint tax
returns, adultery, and more all are about heterosupremacy and heteronormativity. This
extends to immigration. As noted in *10 Percent*:

> While a heterosexual citizen can petition the United States Immigration and
> Naturalization Service (INS) to obtain a green card for his or her noncitizen
> spouse, the INS refuses to recognize the relationships of lesbian and gay
> Americans for purposes of immigration. (Vaillancourt, 1994b, p. 54)

The assemblage of heterosexuality is rigid but dynamic; it claims the center and
leaves distorting spaces for the margins. Yet, heterosexuality must continually recon-
figure itself within changing family structures, divorce, and working parents so that the
center is never stable.

The insidious character of heteronormativity must be recognized to understand how
heterosexism and homophobia are communicated. It is not simply a matter of calling
someone a "fag" or a "dyke." The ideology of heterosexual superiority infests itself in
all levels of communicative practices.

The silencing of nonheterosexuality bends our reality so that we no longer can think
of heterosexuality as "straight." The forces of heterosexism have been mustered to
wreak many types of havoc throughout history. Yet, heterosexism insists on silencing

these connections to keep heterosexuality from becoming "bent." Monette (1994) points out,

> I've learned in my adult life that the will to silence the truth is always and everywhere as strong as the truth itself. So it is a necessary fight we will always be in: those of us who struggle to understand our common truths, and those who try to erase them. The first Nazi book burning, I would have you remember, was of a gay and lesbian archive. (p. 118)

The intertwined ideologies of heterosexism and Nazism often are silenced in social communicative practices.

■ Communicating Sexualities

When nonheterosexual realities are communicated, the space that has been carved out by decades of resistance to heteronormativity is not a neutral space. The invocation of stereotypes is overwhelming. There is little room to maneuver. People often view gays/lesbians/queers as engaging in particular activities that are unacceptable within a heteronormative framework. Brummett (1979) explains that this emphasis on the "act" rather than on the politics and identities involved is closely aligned to an antigay ideological position.

The communication about homosexuality tends to invoke that communicative practice, the practice of referring to gays and (sometimes) lesbians as homosexuals engaging in "homosexual acts." The problem with the term *homosexual* is that it places exclusive identification on sexual activities. What does it mean to identify people solely in relation to their sexual activities? In what ways does this communicative practice reinforce heterosexual privilege? How would this communicative practice look different if heterosexuality were similarly identified? How would spousal hiring look if identified as heterosexual spousal hiring? The celebrations of heterosexual showers, weddings, marriages, and anniversaries? In many ways, these communicative and cultural practices, so inscribed in everyday life, continue to exclude and marginalize those who do not identify as and communicate to others that they are heterosexual. Other gay discourse provides more aggressive and assertive moves to create space as in the following quotes:

> "I used to just live behind a closed door, thinking that none of this hatred out there would ever affect me," he says. "But now I've woken up. Now I see that the only way you can change things is to fight. I'll never be the same again." (Jerry Hon, quoted in Boulard, 1994a, p. 38)

and,

> I think coming out is the most important political decision a person can make in life. One of the things our enemies hate so much about us is that we're happy, because they've always thought it's a grim, ugly choice that makes your life

miserable. But we have proven to ourselves that we are capable of great joy and dignity and good work by being out. (Paul Monette, quoted in Vaillancourt, 1994a, p. 75)

The space for reconfiguring the discourse about sexualities is narrowly defined and under the reign of heteronormativity. However we may feel about that default position, Kirk and Madsen (1989) argue, at the outset of their shopping list of problematic, gay-political communication,

> Like it or not, what straights think of our behavior affects our lives. If we have difficulty convincing them not to hate and oppress us for something as harmless as the physical love of members of our own sex, it's going to be a whole lot harder to get them to swallow gay misbehavior that almost anyone, of any sexual persuasion, would find harmful, reprehensible, and contemptible. For our own good, we have no choice but to *look* good. (p. 279)

Kirk and Madsen's (1989) emphasis on looking good not only incorporates and claims many of the behaviors (e.g., public sex) of heterosexist ideology toward gays/queers but also reinscribes the nastiest stereotypes. The easy acceptance of heterosexist definitions and stereotypes is reflected in their own discourse, but a discourse that has little ground to maneuver: "We're *not* fighting for the right to suck and fuck in full public view, with as many one-minute stands as we can possibly line up end to end, until our mouths and anuses are sore and we're all dying of syphilis and AIDS" (p. 380).

Perhaps Kirk and Madsen (1989) feel so boxed into the tiny discursive space for same-sex discussions that they feel compelled to use antigay stereotypes in an attempt to dispel them. Their own attacks on nonheterosexuals rely on heterosexist stereotypes equating *queer* with male sexuality—with particular activities and drives—and reinforcing a "you deserve it" mentality regarding diseases. Sexual identity and sexual activities are not so easily equated except in facile discursive practices.

All of us must question the spaces that are left for us to communicate about and rearticulate nonheterosexualities. The resistance to opening up these spaces is enormous, as there are many layers and stratifications that embed heteronormativity and fuel the flames of heterosexism. Challenging these sedimentations is not easy, but viewing them in this way opens up new possibilities. In her chapter in this volume on public policy solutions, Brzuzy (Chapter 20) argues that the new policies encourage new ways of considering prejudice. But policies alone will not change attitudes and beliefs. Taking a multilayered approach to these issues is necessary. Fernald's (1995) focus on interpersonal heterosexism is helpful in understanding the interpersonal layer that reinforces heteronormativity. Corey's personal narrative in this volume (Chapter 15) focuses on the family and the ways in which it layers yet another structuring force in heteronormativity. Must "family" be built on heterosexual foundations? The layers of television, film, friends, families, coworkers, corporations, educational institutions, governmental institutions, religious institutions, and more all serve to create enormous discursive barriers that defy any simplistic solution. The history of heterosexism is so embedded in our culture that a challenge to heterosexism (e.g., same-sex marriages) often is seen as a challenge to Western civilization. This perceived threat is evidenced in the following newspaper accounts of the discussion of same-sex marriage:

> Saying its enactment would weaken marriage as an institution, California Governor Pete Wilson vetoed a bill September 11 that would have extended limited official recognition to same-sex and unmarried heterosexual couples. ("Institutional Bias," 1994, p. 15)
> Homosexuals have no right to ask Americans to sacrifice their moral principles or the future of their families under the uncivil cover of "civilrights" (Herrod, 1993, p.A18).

Although there are no facile solutions, we can begin to work toward challenging and defying heterosexism by intervening at various layers in different ways. These layers of heterosexism are not simply embedded within individual identities but rather organize the entire social order. No one tactic will serve to upend all the layers; we must be sensitive to the ways in which each layer must be challenged and reconfigured within a broader shared vision of a nonheterosexist society.

■ Toward Conclusion

> At once I was tired of my past and where it led me—a boring melancholy that trained me to be good at death. I exhausted my possibilities and nothing new started up; I could see why people kill themselves. (Glück, 1985, p. 6)

I began this chapter with a quote from Glück, and it is to his words that I return. His pessimism, however often we return to this sentiment, is but a temporary respite from the relentless heterosexism that is embedded in every level and institution. The social changes that have been won are met with increasing resistance in many different forms and in many different places.

The first step toward understanding heterosexism is to recognize the ways in which it is firmly instantiated in all aspects of our society, from its social institutions to its social practices. All of us must challenge the presumptions and restrictions of heterosexuality whenever we can.

Heterosexism is a prejudicial communication practice that condemns all of those who defy the (hetero)sexual order to the margins (e.g., beatings, harassment, exclusion). But we must not forget that this communication practice is not invoked by individuals alone; it is powerfully buttressed by social institutions that not only allow it but also encourage it.

I wish to let Monette (1994) have the last word, even if there never can be a "last word," as he expresses hope and encouragement:

Nevertheless, even if all my fears prove true, I have to do this thing. Have to hope. That the custody wars will go the other way, reason winning out over bigotry, so that gay and lesbian families aren't at risk of being scattered. . . . That the desperate queer adolescents will survive the suicidal years and rise like the phoenix from the ashes of self-hatred. That the closets will at last disgorge their prisoners into the light. That we as a tribe will come together to heal the earth with a passion equal to the death squads of our fundamentalist foes. And that those who come after never forget those of us who died of AIDS—who took care of one another and, even when our strength had dwindled to a fevered shadow, still fought the implacable agents of our dispensability. (p. 255)

7 Communication of Classism

Dreama G. Moon
Garry L. Rolison

If hard work were the sole determinant of your ability to support yourself and your family, surely we'd have a different outcome for many in our society. We also, however, believe in luck and, on closer examination, it certainly is quite a coincidence that the "unlucky" come from certain race, gender, and class backgrounds. In order to perpetuate racist, sexist, and classist outcomes, we also have to believe that the current economic distribution is unchangeable, has always existed, and probably exists in this form throughout the known universe (i.e., it's "natural"). (Langston, 1992, p. 112)

*C*lass has had a long and storied history in the social sciences. Most social scientists trace the first sophisticated uses of the term to Marx and Weber. This lineage has continued. Class in contemporary social theory is mostly informed by the work of Erik Olin Wright and J. H. Goldthorpe (Crompton, 1993). Predictably, the debate between the two is whether class is best defined within a reconstructed Marxian class framework or a modified Weberian one. We have some objection to both of these positions because, like the Langston quote with which we start this chapter suggests, both posit the economic as being definitive of class. We hope to show that class includes much more than this because it is becoming increasingly clear that class itself is an appropriated signifier in contemporary American political discourse that has increasingly less to do with the solely economic. Consider, for example, it was ironic that, during debate about the 1995 budget, the Republican party accused Democrats of trying to start "class warfare" while wishing that the American public would ignore the class basis of its own proposals—a strategy that worked, for the most part, because the American public accepted the implicit Republican definition of class as the poor. In short, class was a concept that had nothing to do with Republicans as the middle classes; rather, it was simply a code for the poor.

In this chapter, we follow Hall (1981b) and Bourdieu (1979/1984) in departing from the primacy of the economic to suggest that the cultural also is constitutive of class. In particular, we suggest that styles of consumption come to define and communicate class and further posit that the roots of classism are partially to be found in the contestation, communication, and evaluation of what we call "class-culture commodities." Although this frame is akin to Jameson's (1984) analysis of culture in the postmodern era, we extend it to suggest that cultural commodities inculcate and reproduce class relations of domination. Following Hall (1981b), they become a modality through which class and class relations are lived and through which class domination and the reproduction of class inequality (which, for the purposes of this chapter, we term "classism") is manifested.

In what follows, we offer selected reads of how class and classism are constructed in and through the communicative process at the semiotic level. In particular, we explore how the cultures of the poor and working class are discounted through the manipulation, production, and reproduction of symbols within discourses of proxemics and fashion as well as in public policy and other sites of class conflict. Throughout the chapter, we follow the lead of Hecht and Baldwin (Chapter 3 in this volume) in focusing on stance, sphere, level of analysis, and levels of understanding in our analysis. With respect to stance, we focus our attention on class intolerance, paying particular attention to middle class antipathy to the expressed cultural messages of the poor and working class. Although our level of analysis is macroscopic for the most part, we use interviews and personal narratives to identify micro-level class positions from which to speak and make use of textual analysis to add further meaning and understanding to both class and classism. In short, we take as ontological and epistemological privilege a rhetorical/discursive method to provide multitextured meaning and levels of understanding within the sphere of class domination and inequality as they come to be expressed in the contemporary moment.

We broadly conceive the communicative process to be the production, interpretation, and exchange of messages. Messages in this view are comprised of symbols of various types. This broad definition suggests that the communicative process includes not only spoken language but nonverbal codes as well. By the latter, we mean not only gestures but also messages produced through disparate phenomena such as style of dress, home decoration, and the tattooing of bodies. We take the further position that both verbal and nonverbal messages in the process of their production, interpretation, and exchange are implicated in the social (i.e., the social dynamics of power, status, and inequality). These assumptions frame our analysis as we consider the import of class, class culture, and classism in postmodernity.

For purposes of analysis, we add to the preceding assumptions Lash's (1990) observation that there have been three interrelated cultural changes that have marked the postmodern era. First is the creation of working class culture from peasant culture. Second is the creation of a popular culture from folk culture. Third, and most important for our purposes, is the "commodification of the culture of nonelite groups" (p. 51) by dominant groups. Lash indicates that this cultural commodification (i.e., making into a commodity) has been of a different order from the commodification of other goods because of the involvement of image and spectacle in its creation, a change viewed as coterminous with postmodernity (p. 52). In short, we use Lash's trajectory of cultural movement to further frame our discussion of class and classism. In broad strokes, we suggest that the shifts from both peasant and folk culture to working class and popular culture reflects a shift from the rural to the urban that devalues the artifacts of rural existence and associates them with the poor. We then indicate, in concrete analysis, how these artifacts are in turn appropriated and redefined to connote class and status inferiority of the poor in the realms of proxemics and fashion. From these concrete examples, the chapter moves to consider more abstractly how class and classism work at the discursive level. We begin our analysis with a brief discussion of class and proxemics as a prelude to a more detailed discussion of class and fashion.

■ Proxemics and Classism

Hall (1966) provides the classic definition of proxemics as the "interrelated observations and theories of man's [sic] use of space as a specialized elaboration of culture" (p. 1). By this, Hall means the ways in which space is socially structured to communicate messages. On this view, geographical location and what is placed there communicate both culture and the social. In this section, we are concerned with a very specific example of how geographical space communicates classism—the trailer park. Our concern is to show how the appropriation of the trailer park by the middle class both communicates class positionality and classism among the middle class and the poor. We do this by examining the narrative of one middle class resident who lives between the edges of a trailer park and a semiotically constructed mobile home community.

■ The Trailer Park

The trailer park has connoted a certain class position in U.S. society. Specifically, the trailer park has been a site of class location figuratively and literally in American popular culture; it has been both the symbolic and literal home of the White poor. Yet, this reading is ahistorical in that it fails to take into account the transformations of signification that both the trailer park and the trailer have taken in U.S. society. Indeed, in a reversal of Baudrilliard, we argue that the trailer of the rural South has come to stand in the postmodern moment as a signifier that has exploded (rather than imploded) with class- infused signifiers. For example, what once was considered a mark of wealth in poor rural communities—a trailer home—has become in the urban context negatively devalued ("White trash" live in trailer parks) even as it has been reappropriated by the middle classes (e.g., mobile home, recreational vehicle) as a desired commodity and a mark of prestige.

As it happens, the mother of one of the authors lives in a "mobile home community," which is distinguished from the "trailer park down the street" both in terms of physical territory and social prestige. More to the point, the park down the street does not have well-tended lawns and flowers, and the trailers are "old single-width models." In addition, the trailer park's residents do not have much space inside or out. By contrast, the mobile home community is characterized by well-tended lawns, flowers, porches, and newer double-width mobile home models complete with carports.

Socially, the residents of the community are White middle class, whereas the occupants of the park are "White trash." In sum, class position of the trailer park is communicated through its difference in comparison to the mobile home community. This difference is formalized in the rules that come to structure the "appearance" of the mobile home community. As that author's mother says, "Poor people live there who don't give a shit. They don't have any rules; anybody can move into there." By contrast, to live in her mobile home community, one has to be retired. "They have rules about who can live here. Anybody can move in anywhere else, but they have rules about who can live here." Indeed, "the rules" that structure the living space of the mobile home community give the community its distinctly middle class content. For example, the residents cannot litter or have any type of equipment setting outside on the lawn, a distinct contrast to the popular image of the trailer park as "a hole that is dirty and run down" portrayed in media.

We end our example of the trailer park/mobile home community dichotomy by noting that this use of difference in space is rather ubiquitous in the urban environment. Housing projects in center cities are similarly class infused as symbols of the poor in contrast to urban high-rise apartments. Briefly, the poor live in the dangerous "projects" while the middle class reside in security terrace apartments, clotheslines adorn the balconies of the projects while tiger lilies adorn those of the middle class, and so on. In one site, the projects, we automatically know where the poor of questionable taste live; in the other, the garden-terraced apartments, the more genteel, cultured, and urbane middle class reside. Moreover, as the number of home-owner associations, condominium associations, and so on attest, the middle class attempts to protect their space from the encroachment of the poor by the use of cultural criteria, standards of taste, and rules of adornment. In the next section, we consider how the body is used to accomplish this same class distancing through fashion.

■ Fashion and Classism

More so than the use and acquisition of space, fashion appears abstractly to be a more individuated choice; we assume no fashion police or good taste in clothing associations. In other words, fashion is assumed to represent individual tastes and choices, not necessarily group phenomena with social boundaries that are produced and reproduced. As such, fashion may appear to be fluid with respect to class. We hope to show that this view is limited in that it does not recognize how class structures individual tastes and how, through fashion's representation of class domination and class inequality, these tastes become inscribed with meanings of class; literally through putting on different clothes, we put on (or off) class markers. We examine this process through a personal biography cognizant of the intersections among race, gender, region, and class positioning in the structuring of fashion tastes and personal identity.

As a teenager growing up in a small town in the hills of West Virginia, one of the authors used *Glamour* Magazine as part of her informal education about (White) womanhood. To the young girl, raised by a single mother who earned her livelihood as a waitress, the images of beautiful, well-dressed women projected a way of living far from her grasp. On one level, the teenager understood that these images were not for women like her, but on another, the images whispered that transcendence was possible if she was willing to pay the price.

One of the regular features to which the girl paid close attention was a section titled "do's and don'ts." The reason she found this section particularly fascinating was that it featured photographs of "real" women, those who looked like her and the women with whom she interacted—women who were ordinary, overweight, interestingly dressed, and so on. In the feature, these women are presented and their fashion choices are evaluated and commented on by *Glamour* fashion "experts." As a young girl, she eagerly scanned this page looking for the telltale signs of "difference"—black hose worn with white shoes, too-tight clothing, white pumps worn after Labor Day, and so on. The girl was overwhelmed with the sheer number of rules that one was supposed to absorb to become a "do" and often experienced a sense of shame because the women in her life were, as likely as not, violators of them. Importantly, the teenager did not question the authority of these so-called experts to set the terms of acceptability for either herself or the women she knew. This questioning came much later.

Probably more than any other class group, the middle class must work hard to achieve and maintain class position. The work of the middle class involves the creation and recreation of a lifestyle that is recognizably middle class, as the trailer park example given earlier makes clear. This is tricky business because the signs of "middle classness" are easily appropriated and assimilated by members of the working class (Ehrenreich, 1989). Because the signs of middle classness often are adopted by the lower classes who desire to "move up" (at least in appearance), "class cues" must constantly be invented and reinvented. One function performed by "women's" fashion and beauty magazines is to keep middle class women abreast of exactly what constitutes a middle class lifestyle at any given moment. The frantic nature of this endeavor is evident in women's magazines such as *Glamour.*

One of the recurrent themes in androcentric and classist discourse has been the sexualization of female images, often women of color or poor or working class White women (Collins, 1995; Ehrenreich, 1989). Such objectifying images, we argue, are reflected in the "don'ts" portrayed in *Glamour*'s "do's & don'ts" feature. In addition, we argue that the strategy of "do-ing and don't-ing" women should itself be understood as a *practice* of subordination in that it involves actively constructing women's bodies in particular ways for our viewing pleasure.

Glamour "experts" objectify women of color and/or working-class White women by representing them in submissive and often humiliating positions designed to highlight their perceived deficiencies. This is accomplished through presenting full-length frontal shots of "do's" juxtaposed to partial and/or rear shots of "don'ts," which encourages a reading of "don'ts" as objects rather than as subjects. The visual effects of these representations are further made explicit through the copy that employs language with sexual overtones and informs us how to "read" the women presented. "Don'ts" frequently are photographed in compromising positions that are then interpreted in an implicitly sexual manner within the copy. In short, the photographs often are shot in such a manner as to direct the reader's attention to a particular part of the body of the "don't," which is then made the focus of comment.

For example, a January 1980 photo portrays a "don't" from the neck down—in short, decapitated—to focus the reader's attention on the parts of her body under discussion. The photographer has caught this woman in a common predicament of "static cling," wherein her dress has ridden up her thighs and apparently has become "stuck" to her breast and stomach areas. The accompanying copy proclaims, "Don't become overexposed. A clingy rayon knit reveals all that's beneath it." The subject of knit arises again in the September 1997 issue of *Glamour,* this time in the context of sweaters. Here a pair of white breasts are put on display and held up for comment. The reader is informed, "When the ribbing expands to accommodate your curves, it's a sign to get a bigger sweater or forego the body-clinging fashion." Following the knit-breast-derriere theme, in a January 1988 column, another headless "don't" appears wearing a close-fitting knit dress and is positioned by the camera so that the reader may have an unobstructed view of the curves of her body profile. She is admonished, "Don't dress to fill. This 'sprayed-on' dress is simply too sexy for 9 to 5."

In the August 1996 issue, hip-huggers are the topic at hand. This provides, of course, opportunity and justification for examination and comment on women's derrieres. In this issue, the "do" is a very thin woman of color, shown facing the camera in a total body shot, whereas the "don'ts" are represented by one set of white breasts, two white derrieres, and one brown stomach. One photo portrays a shot of a woman's derriere whose underwear is showing. The copy offers the following suggestion: "If the panties show, they're too high or the hip-huggers are too low. In either case, change the panties." Another "don't" wearing bike shorts is warned, "Mind those panty lines!" "Belly overhang" and the issue of exposed breasts are the subjects of the conversations regarding the remaining two "don'ts." Thus, under the guise of "helpful advice," the objectification of women's bodies works to advance the continuous fragmentation of "don't" women, encouraging a view of working class White women and women of color as "body parts," juxtaposed to the subjectivity granted to class-privileged White women.

In tracing the adjectives used to describe "do's" who meet with *Glamour* experts' approval, the appropriate presentation of "woman" is one who performs as lean, simple, chic, and classic. Other female bodies—those with curves and substance—seem to be offensive to the tastes of *Glamour* experts. This taste in presentation, although presented as universal and unquestioned, is, of course, racially and class situated. Matters of taste, according to Ehrenreich (1989), are in fact matters of class preferences and, we would argue, also matters of racial or cultural preference rather than universal norms of femininity (Bourdieu, 1979/1984). In *Class: A Guide Through the American Status System,* Fussell (1979) notes that one's body size is an advertisement of one's social standing. Within the United States, "thinness" often is taken to signify class privilege as well as the various meanings circulated about that privilege. He observes that an elite look requires American women to be

> thin, with a hairstyle dating back 18 or 20 years or so (the classiest women wear their hair for a lifetime in exactly the style they affected in college). They wear superbly fitting dresses and expensive but always understated shoes and hand-bags, with very little jewelry. (p. 54)

Thus, by affecting a lean, classic, understated look, "don'ts" are able to fit themselves into the confines of bourgeois notions of womanhood. Of course, this bourgeois notion of womanhood also is racialized. As a study with young junior high school girls found, White girls learn at an early age that being slender or even thin is considered desirable, whereas other racial communities often conceptualize the desirable female body as more substantial—one with full hips and large thighs (Ingrassia, 1995). For instance, when women of color appear in *Glamour,* they do so more frequently as "don'ts." When a woman of color is presented as a "do," she most often conforms to bourgeois notions of White femininity. In the four examples of "do" women of color that we located, the women's bodies conformed to the boyish figure preferred by White bourgeois standards. As one caption noted with approval, "no clutter, no bulges, no fuss."

Women of color and working class White women argue that the concept of "woman" is not an innocent one (Anzaldua, 1990; Collins, 1991; hooks, 1984; Spelman, 1988; Zandy, 1990), that such constructions are not produced by chance but rather are produced from positions of racial and class interest. All too frequently, "woman" signifies certain racial and social class positions seldom made explicit. Feminists of color (Anzaldua, 1990; Collins, 1991; hooks, 1984) point out that to be a woman in the United States is to be a White woman and, as Zandy (1990) notes, a particular type of White woman, one who is class privileged. These ideological fictions work to construct a fictional female subject who is implicitly White and middle class.

As hooks (1992) argues, it is only when one imagines "woman" in the abstract—sans race, class, and so on—that woman becomes "fiction or fantasy." *Glamour*'s version of sisterhood works to *denaturalize* difference— racial, class, sexuality—and to normalize a particular cultural construction of "woman," one who is White, middle class, and presumably heterosexual. In short, White bourgeois representations of "woman" are taken as "natural" or given, thus obfuscating the reality that this view of woman is but one cultural construction among many available.

■ How Class Works

In this section, we are concerned with explicating the ways in which classism may be said to operate both within and across various communicative levels. Three interrelated working principles are central to our discussion: *hypervisibility, alter-ideology,* and *unidirectionality.*

■ Presence as Absence: Hypervisibility

Institutionalized classism functions to make lower valenced class groups *invisible,*[41] and thus unworthy of recognition (e.g., "nonpersons" such as janitors and maids), or *hypervisible* and marked as symbols of ridicule (e.g., "rednecks," poor "White trash"), disdain (e.g., welfare recipients), and/or fear (e.g., the underclass, gangs). Rather than a dichotomy, invisibility and hypervisibility are simply inverted strategies of the same type in that they objectify dominated class subjects. In other words, they are strategies that allow the treatment of certain class subjects as "persons of no consequence" (Folb, 1994). This impulse can be observed in strategies as diverse as current welfare reform policies that destroy class-disprivileged families in the name of a class-privileged interpretation of "family values," discourses on the "culture of poverty" that blame the travails of the poor on some innate inability or inferiority, and cultural commentary such as that offered by stand-up comedian Jeff Foxworthy, who informs his audience, "If your wife is also your sister, you just might be a redneck."

Often working in tandem with hypervisibility, class stereotypes are exploited in ways that would (and should) enrage us if they were racial or gender stereotypes. Ehrenreich (1989) observes,

> While ideas about gender, and even race, have moved, however haltingly, in the direction of greater tolerance and inclusivity, ideas about class remain mired in prejudice and mythology. "Enlightened" people, who might flinch at a racial slur, have no trouble in listing the character defects of an ill-defined "underclass," defects which routinely include ignorance, promiscuity, and sloth. There is, if anything, even less inhibition about caricaturing the White or "ethnic" working class: Its tastes are "tacky"; its habits [are] unhealthful; and its views are hopelessly bigoted and parochial. (p. 7)

■ Alter-Ideology and Difference

Like other forms of difference, class difference is marked in relation to those socially and structurally situated below. We find Therborn's (1980) notion of *ego-* and *alter-ideologies* a useful starting point here. Therborn suggests that these are "class-specific *core themes* of discourses that vary enormously in concrete forms and degree of elaboration" (p. 79, emphasis in original), classifying *ego-ideologies* as those core themes that identify *who we are* and alter-ideologies as those that define *who we are not.* Therborn notes,

> From the standpoint of the constitution of class struggle subjects, the crucial aspect of the alter-ideology is, in the case of the exploiting classes, the rationale for their domination of other classes, [while] in the case of the exploited classes, it is the basis for their resistance to the exploiters. (p. 61)

Therborn refers to the ongoing contestation and struggle around the notion of *naming,* or the names imposed on one's group by dominant groups versus the names taken on in opposition by those dominated. As McKerrow (1989) points out, "It is not so much as how I see myself as how I see the other" that is at issue (p. 95). Thus, what we call ourselves and others as well as how these other groups are described plays a role in establishing and maintaining hierarchical, valenced relationships. But it is not just self-definitional, particularly when a group has less power than others. What a group is called and how it is described by other groups, particularly those in power, plays an important role in social relations. These external definitions not only influence how a group is treated but often also are internalized. This process plays itself out in a number of ways. First, we can attribute a dysfunctional culture to low-valenced groups. Second, we can personalize the "failings" of group members. Third, based on the personal responsibility for their condition, we can attribute dependence to the group. Finally, we can blame the group for the failings of society as a whole.

One such class-specific alter-ideology is the culture of poverty, a collective (dis)order of the poor said to explain their continued poverty. Ehrenreich (1989) outlines some of the characteristics of this (dis)order:

> The "culture" of the poor was (and still is) thought to be defined by two related traits: "present-time orientation" and an insufficiently developed "deferred gratification pattern" . . . the very opposite of the traits which the middle class liked to ascribe to itself (self-discipline, strong superego, ability to plan ahead to meet self-imposed goals). (p. 50)

Not surprisingly, interventions into the culture of poverty have been cultural for the most part rather than economic. The problem becomes, as Ehrenreich (1989) points out, one of making "the lower class more normal—that is, not less poor but less present-oriented" (p. 54). Poverty itself, then, is not the issue because "lower-class forms of all problems are at bottom a single problem: the existence of an outlook and style of life which [are] radically present-oriented" (Banfield, 1968, p. 53). Thus, poverty is constructed as a mere symptom in the "real" problem—some intrinsic lack located within the lower class.

In one of the first fully articulated arguments against the poor, Harvard urbanologist Edward C. Banfield, in his 1968 book *The Unheavenly City* (in an analysis echoed by Murray, 1984, almost two decades later), alternately offers and then rejects a number of "solutions" to the "cultural" problem of poverty including psychotherapy (will not work because the poor are too inarticulate to benefit from it), removal of lower class children from their parents for sale or adoption (some parents might have a problem with this), and institutionalization (unfeasible because being poor is not a crime). Although written some time ago, the impulse behind Banfield's suggestions is apparent in current discourses and government policies regarding the poor. For instance, one of the more popular discourses put forth by right-wing politicians is the so-called empowerment of the poor. As Herman (1996) explains, "The poor have been enslaved by the liberals, who lured them into dependency on government handouts from which they cannot extricate themselves without the help of compassionate politicians" (p. 10). Thus, in the interests of "Christian charity," the "slaves" must be released and be allowed "free" choice. One such act of "emancipation" is New Jersey's Right to Choose Act, which forces "former slaves" of welfare into a labor market woefully unprepared to incorporate them. Another favorite discursive ploy of the right is the rhetoric of "family values" (i.e., patriarchal family values). Consider Wisconsin's W-2 welfare reform plan, which requires mothers of children 12 weeks old or over to work (outside the home) and also sets a 5-year lifetime cap on benefits. Clearly, the poor's "right to choose" is limited to those choices sanctioned by the "welfare abolitionists" who would free them from their chattel status, alternatives that do not include the choice of staying home with one's children or the creation of jobs that pay living wages.

Another popular alter-ideology of the lower classes deals with *racial intolerance* (Ehrenreich, 1989). The working class has long been a scapegoat for class-privileged Whites' less enlightened attitudes about racial others. Even when confronted with evidence to the contrary, scholars and others will simply reassert their class-based prejudices. For instance, in *Fear of Falling,* Ehrenreich (1989) reports a 1966 study on occupational mobility and racial tolerance that found that "the higher one's class of origin or class of destination, the more likely that one prefers to exclude Negroes from one's neighborhood." She notes that the authors of the study simply refused to seriously contemplate that "such an unflattering finding could be true" (p. 113). A remark made by a self-identified White, middle-class woman in an interview with one of the authors is revealing: "People are racist in every class; maybe the middle class just have the social grace to keep it to themselves." Her comment reflects the observation of Wellman (1993), who suggests that the middle class is "trained to *verbalize* tolerance" (p. 51, emphasis in original).

When the intolerance myth is publicly breached, discourses of individualism are likely to be invoked as an explanatory device. Consider two incidents of assault on three Japanese college students by three White male teenagers in Lewiston, Idaho, that occurred in early 1997. In one case, two Japanese students taking an evening stroll were accosted by a carload of White teenagers hurling obscenities. Two of the White males got out of the car and attacked one of the students, breaking her nose. In another incident less than a week later, another White male was foiled in his attempt to assault three other Japanese students. In what was described as a "frustrated tone of voice," an interviewed police officer offered the following description of the suspects: "They were nice looking, athletic. They're not skinheads or gang members and come from *middle-class* families. One of the guys had his girlfriend driving him around in a nice vehicle. It wasn't a piece of junk" (Lin, 1996, p. 1, emphasis added).

When read in relation to the entreaty made by Sharon Taylor, director of the Intensive English Institute at Lewis and Clark State College that the Japanese students attended, the officer's comment takes another meaning. Taylor comments, "I hope that our community doesn't get treated too badly just because a few disturbed and immature young people have done something wrong" (Lin, 1996, p. 1). It appears that whereas social extremist types such as skinheads and gang members are expected to engage in this type of racist and violent behavior, when such behavior is enacted by nice, athletic, well-to-do, middle class White boys, they must be "disturbed" and "immature," thus unrepresentative of middle class Whites. In this way, Whites and the middle class are allowed to function as individuals, whereas the behavior of slaves, skinheads, and gang members is inscribed at the group level.

■ Unidirectionality: Marking Difference

Next we consider the *direction* in which classism can be said to function. We hold that whereas members of any class culture may express *class prejudice* (i.e., in the form of personal attitudes), *classism* is a top-down practice made possible by class privilege (i.e., unearned advantage and conferred dominance) and power. This claim is supported by the ways in which difference tends to be marked in general. For instance, recall that alter-ideologies always express who we are not. This marking of who we are not tends to work unidirectionally in the sense that dominant classes tend to mark class difference in relation to those classes situated below. In short, difference always is marked *against* those with whom one fears being conflated. This marking of difference carries an evaluative component in that who we are is conceived as superior to who we are not.

One of the authors noted this impulse in her dissertation work on White women and social class. The women interviewed tended to mark their own class (who we are) in relation to those situated below (who we are not), and the alter-ideologies that they constructed about these lower class cultures were remarkably similar. The lower classes routinely were described by these women as rednecked, uneducated, racist, unmotivated, sexist, loud, and unable to delay gratification (which, of course, they were not). The following excerpt by one White woman who identified herself as "middle class" stands as an example:

[In thinking about the working class,] I see people sitting around in a bar, drinking, watching television, and laughing and carrying on loudly. . . . And then a middle class environment is more of a cocktail lounge. Maybe the television is on, but it's quieter—it's the news as opposed to a sports event—and people are drinking something other than beer, maybe wine . . . and they're sitting around discussing things. Upper class people might be in their drawing rooms, sipping fine Port . . . and talking about something intellectual—art or literature or something like that. (raw data from Dreama Moon, 1997)

Note that as she proceeds in her descriptions *up* the class hierarchy, the descriptions become more favorable.

In her analysis of relations between the working and middle classes, Ehrenreich (1989) also notes this unidirectional effect:

For working-class people, relations with the middle class are usually a one-way dialogue. From above come commands, diagnoses, instructions, judgments, definitions—even, through the media, suggestions as to how to think, feel, spend money, and relax. Ideas seldom flow "upward" to the middle class, because there are simply no structures to channel the upward flow of thought from class to class. (p. 139)

Ehrenreich's remarks highlight the unidirectionality of communication between class cultures and the ability of those situated above to make judgments about those situated below. One of the middle class White women interviewed in the previously mentioned study notes this same tendency when she observes, "Being in the middle class doesn't have to do at all with defining who you are as a person; it's the other, being in the other. Being in the other end [of the class spectrum] is more defining of a person" (raw data from Dreama Moon, 1997).

But more than the personal expression of negative evaluation of those located below, dominant classes are able to *act on* these unfavorable judgments in the form of implementing informal and formal policies against nondominant classes. The *structural* advantage inherent in class privilege must be kept in mind. For instance, an article in *U.S. News and World Report* (Collins, 1994) titled "America Cranks It Up" attributes the increased productivity of U.S. manufacturing concerns to the leeway that U.S. companies have in using *layoffs* as a way of cutting costs. In a similar vein, *CBS Reports* aired a program on August 8, 1996, titled "Who's Getting Rich and Why Aren't You?" that profiled a number of U.S. chief executive officers (CEOs) who are amassing tremendous personal fortunes by increasing company profits via downsizing (otherwise known as *firing workers*). The CEOs interviewed (all were White males) spoke of the "reality" that "service to the company" (i.e., shareholders) often entailed the sacrifice of workers. As Al Dunlap, the CEO of Scott, put it: "I didn't apologize for being poor, and I damned sure am not going to apologize for being successful." One of Dunlap's first moves when he took over at Scott was to fire 11,000 workers.

In sum, class can be said to operate in terms of three interrelated dimensions: by rendering nondominant class subjects as invisible or as hypervisible, by perpetuating alter-ideological discourses about nondominant class groups, and by marking difference unidirectionally. These functions are, in turn, produced and reproduced in various forms of communication. In the following section, we explore the links among class, classism, and communication.

■ Communication and the Reproduction of Class Relations

Explicitly, we address the link between communication and social class, specifically how communication works in the production and expression of class, classism, and class privilege. In *Problems in Materialism and Culture,* Williams (1980b) theorizes communication as both a *product* and a *means* of social production. He further argues that this understanding of communication is blocked by several ideological positions, one of which is the distinction made between "natural" and "technological" means of communication. The former, Williams notes, is characterized as "ordinary, everyday language" in "face-to-face" situations, whereas the latter is grouped around mechanical and electronic communication devices and subsumed under the rubric of "mass communication" (p. 51). Williams cautions us against viewing mass communication as reproductive of social relations while excluding the ordinary and natural. In short, he maintains that the everyday means of communication (i.e., cultural practices) are both productive of social relations and produced by them. Thus, we conceptualize verbal and nonverbal communication to be a primary means through which culture is expressed and patterns of interaction are shaped. Hence, culture and cultural change are deeply implicated in the communicative process in both constitutive and reactive ways.

We argue that as culture changes, so does the communicative process, and it is through the communicative process that culture (i.e., both practices and structures) is contested, negotiated, and subsequently changed. In short, we view the relationship between communication and culture dialectically. The manner in which we have conceptualized class has at least two implications for communication research. One, it is clear that standard ways of assessing and understanding identities often used in communication inquiry are not particularly effective to the study of social class. So-called "checklist" approaches to cultural identity already have been called into question (e.g., González, Houston, & Chen, 1994; Jackman & Jackman, 1983; Larkey, Hecht, & Martin, 1993; Nakayama, 1994a), and we will not repeat those arguments here. We can offer a simple illustration noted in one of the present authors' dissertation project. A group of women were asked to indicate their "checklist" class identity on a demographic form and also were asked during an interview to identity the social class to which they felt they belonged. *Almost without exception, the women's checklist identity did not match the one articulated in the interview.* In short, although the women were able to recognize and check the social class into which *others* (i.e., society) would slot them, the class identity indicated did not reflect the richness of their personal accounts of "felt" class membership. In fact, for a number of them, using the checklist identity would have been completely misleading because they did not see themselves as members of those class cultures and did not participate in them as members (Moon, 1997).

Another concern is the treatment of classism primarily as a form of prejudice that is equated with false consciousness (Wellman, 1993). This position suggests two things: that classism is primarily an *attitude* rather than an expression of *unequal structural relations* and that tolerant, unprejudiced worldviews are characteristically American (Wellman, 1993). The treatment of classism as prejudicial attitudes encourages us to focus on *ideas* to the exclusion of the consideration of the *interests* attached to structural positions, the benefits that are incurred by some positions and not others, and the institutional arrangements that shore up and reinscribe unequal class relations. In short, we are apt to ignore the important connection between everyday cultural practices and structural arrangements.

In addition, by focusing on classism as false consciousness, we participate in dominant hegemonic discourse, which suggests that egalitarianism is a shared American value and that prejudice is seen as a *deviation* from American ideals (Wellman, 1993). This line of reasoning suggests that once individuals' faulty assumptions about others are corrected, they no longer will maintain prejudicial beliefs. Again, this approach deflects attention from social arrangements that produce and reproduce unequal class relations and reflects an untested and, we would argue, a historically unsupported assumption about the order of U.S. society. We argue that investigations of social class, classism, and class privilege need to be closely tied to analyses of structural arrangements and/or social discourses about class.

■ Conclusion

In this chapter, we have argued that the critical analysis of social class and classism is a project that needs to be addressed. We laid out the ways in which we believe it is useful to conceptualize class and related concepts such as classism and class privilege, and we suggested three working principles that are useful in thinking about how class and classism work at a variety of levels. In addition, we articulated the relationship of communication and class, arguing that communication may usefully be seen in a trilateral manner: as *productive* (i.e., a means of reproducing unequal class relations), as *product* (i.e., cultural practices), and as *critique* (i.e., a means of challenging unequal relations).

We end by calling for a renewed vigor with respect to the discovery of the processes through which classism is communicated within a variety of contexts. We attempted to show how lived experiences at both the micro and macro levels come to express class antipathy. We tried to show how this process is implicated in postmodernity and chose two areas of social interaction in which one might not ordinarily expect to study an attitudinal process such as class antipathy. In short, we took two fields of nonverbal communication—proxemics and fashion—to show how they are discursively structured to reflect classism and then offered a discursive analysis of how classism is implicated in more encompassing discourses. We hope that such an unorthodox approach makes the case for what we feel is the centrality and potential that class analysis has for the study of communication.

8 Communication of Ageism

Angie Williams
Howard Giles

Negative attitudes toward, and prejudice against, those who are elderly—ageism—has been identified as a pervasive problem in Western societies (Butler, 1987) and often is likened to sexism and racism. Palmore (1990) identifies ageism as the third great "ism" of our century, defining it as "prejudice or discrimination against or in favor of an age group" (p. 4). Butler (1987) defines ageism as

> a process of systematic stereotyping of and discrimination against people because they are old, just as racism and sexism accomplish this for skin color and gender. Old people are categorized as senile in thought and manner, old fashioned in morality and skills. . . . Ageism allows the younger generations to see older people as different from themselves, thus they subtly cease to identify with their elders as human beings. (pp. 22-23)

Bytheway and Johnson (1990) claim that this definition has been a crucial determinant not only of the scope of gerontological inquiry but also of political policies. In their analysis of the definition, Bytheway and Johnson point out that those who are young, middle-aged, and so on are excluded from this definition (Itzin, 1986). Ageism toward young people will be discussed, but, for the most part, research in recent years has been concerned with forms of ageism directed toward *older* people (usually those over 65 years of age).

The recent flurry of research and theoretical interest in the relationships between aging and communication (e.g., Hummert, Wiemann, & Nussbaum, 1994; Nussbaum & Coupland, 1995) has documented the fact that, at least in Western societies, older people often are communicated to in an ageist fashion (for a discussion of the history and components of ageism, see Radford, 1987), often due to the negative stereotypes we hold of older people, that is, as unhealthy, weak, verbose, and cognitively deficient (Braithwaite, 1986). Palmore (1990) lists a number of negative characteristics that typically are associated with older people: ill health and illness, asexuality and impotency, ugliness or unattractiveness, cognitive and mental decline, uselessness, depression, isolation and loneliness, and poverty. Despite the poverty characterization, in recent years older people increasingly have been seen as having more than their fair share of the nation's wealth. For example, a number of recent news media reports cast elders in the role of "greedy geezers," taking all the benefits of medicare and social security and leaving nothing behind for those who are younger (Coombes & Holladay, 1995).

In the American media, older people have been characterized as "invisible"; in some genres such as quiz shows and Saturday morning cartoons, they have no appearances (Dail, 1988; Davis & Kubey, 1982). Elderly women on television, apart from soap operas, are particularly negatively portrayed as "past it," whereas elderly men are portrayed either as authority figures or as rather villainous (Bell, 1992). Shaner (1995) alerts us to the fact that older men and women often may be portrayed very differently in motion pictures as well. Her comparative analysis of *Grumpy Old Men* and *Widow's Peak* points out that older adults of both sexes are portrayed as "busybodies" but that the women are overwhelmingly more nosy than the men. The men are portrayed as much more active and healthy, both physically and mentally, and also are portrayed as sexual. Although this research was exploratory and preliminary given that it draws on only two movies, it may well be worthwhile to turn our attention to the issues underlined here, that is, the interaction between ageism and sexism. Indeed, other evidence also suggests that there seems to be a double standard such that women are negatively stereotyped at a younger age than are men (Hummert, Garstka, & Shaner, 1995).

Overall, one report estimates that some 82% of U.S. media portrayals of the elderly are stereotypical (Gerbner, Gross, Signorielli, & Morgan, 1980). Those elderly who are "heavy viewers" (and therefore potentially most cognizant of their age group not being represented adequately) suffer most in terms of lowered self-esteem compared to those who are "light viewers" (e.g., Passuth & Cook, 1985). Harwood and Giles (1992) argue that even the supposedly anti-ageist television program *The Golden Girls,* rather than dispelling ageist assumptions, inadvertently could have perpetuated them.

When talked about, older people suffer the indignity of having numerous ageist adjectives such as "biddy" and "codger" levied against them (Nuessel, 1993), an inherent feature of the literature for some years (Berman & Sobkowska-Ashcroft, 1986) as well as of social scientific writing (Schaie, 1993). Covey (1988) conducted a historical survey of words used to describe old people that frequently were negative and focused on *decline* and *disability*. Contemporary older people do not like to be called *old* (Barbato & Feezel, 1987) and thus seek to distance themselves from the negative associations reflecting the decline in the status of the old. Nuessel (1982) identifies a large lexicon of ageist words that are used routinely in everyday language. Indeed, the following examples of ageist colloquialisms listed by Palmore (1990) lend weight to this argument: *coot, crone, geezer, hag, old buzzard, old crock, old duffer, old fogey, old maid, old-fangled, old-fashioned,* and *over the hill.*

Such terms sometimes are used explicitly to insult, but often we let these terms "pass" in conversation, and they frequently are used to tease or for humorous effect. For example, in 1995, a British newspaper reported a dispute between the English rugby captain and the executive board of the then English Rugby Union. At one point, the captain referred to the latter as "old farts." Much discussion revolved around the competencies of the management and the legitimacy of the captain's public statement, but no attention ever was afforded the ageist rhetoric itself. Likewise, humorous cartoons that portray ageist sentiments rarely are condemned for their discriminatory social meanings; they are not questioned in the same way as we might challenge derogatory images of women or ethnic minorities. Nuessel (1982) also points out that there are few positive age-specific terms used to refer to the elderly and that this is particulary so for older women, who suffer the indignity of the double jeopardy of ageism and sexism. Along with Oyer and Oyer (1976), Nuessel (1982) calls for a new vocabulary to eliminate ageism from language, although it is doubtful whether changing the words themselves will help to completely eradicate ageist sentiment. Comparatively, attempts to reduce and reform sexist language have produced rather mixed results (Prentice, 1994).

Because of such pervasive images and language forms, older people often are not spoken to as though they are individuals with distinctive idiosyncratic qualities. Rather, they are addressed in a depersonalized (often patronizing) manner as members of a negatively valenced social category (i.e., as "elderly"). Particularly for those who are socially and cognitively alert, this can be very demeaning (see Harwood, Giles, & Ryan, 1995, for an intergroup perspective on intergenerational communication). Ageist communication behavior has been noted in a number of applied settings including caring (Ashburn & Gordon, 1981) and medical (Adelman, Greene, Charon, & Friedman, 1990) ones. For example, in medical settings, studies by Greene, Adelman, Charon, and Hoffman (1986) and Greene, Adelman, Charon, and Friedman (1989) show that, compared to young patients, physicians address elderly patients with less respect, engagement, and patience; give them less detailed information; and support and ask fewer open-ended questions. This occurred despite the fact that there were no differences in patient behaviors and severity of illness was controlled. Physicians also were less likely to respond to a topic raised by the elderly.

An early review of the literature by Coupland and Coupland (1990) maintains that much current research on elderly language and communication is "age decremental" in orientation; that is, elderly people are documented as having deficient communicative and sociolinguistic competencies. Gerontology itself has been criticized for an ageist focus on decrements such as in linguistic competence (Estes & Binney, 1979). Psycholinguistic experiments have documented a litany of relative deficits, such as a decline in working memory, making it harder for older people to understand and use more complex linguistic structures (Kemper, Kynette, & Norman, 1992). In addition, older people are typified as talking slower (Stewart & Ryan, 1982), using their grammar in a less sophisticated way (Emry, 1986), being verbose (Gold, Arbuckle, & Andres, 1994), and being overly concerned with their ages and painful life events (Coupland, Coupland, & Giles, 1991). Academia does not stand outside society as scientists, gerontologists, and so on draw on available images, understandings, and stereotypes to formulate questions, design studies, and weave interpretations around a framework of assumptions (Giddens, 1984). This is not to say that this is malevolent in intent or that older people are passive victims; in fact, certain older people unwittingly collude themselves in promoting dependence. We would not deny that some of the forgoing deficits can be interpreted and understood in more functionally advantageous ways for older people, and positive aspects of "elderspeak" have been reported (e.g., Kemper et al., 1992).

However, the fact remains that older people have been investigated in ways that support wider social views, and they are communicated with in stereotypic ways that can be uncomplimentary at best. Although we have evidence that there are some facets of elder communication that are appreciated, in the main, elder communicators are the subject of considerable intolerance in the West as well as in the East (Williams et al., 1997). In this chapter, we review intolerant perceptions of older (and younger) communicators as well as manifestations of communicative intolerance toward older (and younger) adults. We also explore a range of responses to, and management of, elder ageism and what routes, if any, might promote change.

■ Perceptions of Older Communicators

A number of experimental studies have taken advantage of the fact that listeners can fairly accurately attribute age to a speaker from voice cues alone (Hollien, 1987; Ryan & Capadano, 1978). This is because typically older voices have certain qualities such as lower pitch and tone and increased breathiness that are easily distinguishable. However, interestingly, Mulac and Giles (1996) show that the perceptual age of an older person's voice can be quite independent of both that person's chronological age and his or her subjective or psychological age. In other words, one can feel "young" yet be heard to sound "old." Not surprisingly perhaps, the older the perceptual age of the voice, the more frailty and vulnerability are attributed to the speaker. Studies surely will be undertaken in due course to assess which cues—physiognomic (Hummert, 1994), vocal, verbal, dress—and which combinations of cues lead to heightened or lowered levels of social intolerance.

Ryan and Laurie (1990) considered the ways in which a speaker's adult age and messages with varying levels of effectiveness might interact to affect judgments of that speaker. Age interacts with message effectiveness such that an effective message results in more positive evaluations for the younger speaker but not for the older speaker. Furthermore, the older speaker giving a message with a white noise background was rated as the least competent target. As the authors point out, this suggests that the older speaker, in comparison to the younger one, received more blame for the poor quality recording and less credit for the effective message.

Two studies show that ageism is inherent in other decoding practices. In the original study (as well as the follow-up), the speaker was a male actor (in his mid-30s) whose professional viability depended on his ability to change his voice to produce different authentic age- and class-related voices (guises). This is an accomplishment he achieved many times on national television. In the first study, the speaker produced a number of different versions of the same (neutral) 320-word passage in which he was heard talking about his car, supposedly during an interview. Although the content of the passage was the same, he systematically varied several features of his speech—*speech rate* (fast vs. medium vs. slow), *accent* (standard British vs. nonstandard Northwest English), and *voice quality* (elderly vs. young adult) (Giles, Coupland, Henwood, Harriman, & Coupland, 1990; Giles, Henwood, Coupland, Harriman, & Coupland, 1992). The different combinations of these features resulted in 12 versions of the passage so that although the speaker sounded different in each version, he was in fact the same speaker in every case. Thus, any differences in judgments of the speaker resulted not from idiosyncratic qualities of different speakers but rather from the systematic variations in speech rate, accent, and voice age.

Young adult listener judges from South Wales, Great Britain, rated 1 of these 12 versions of the passage on speaker personality traits. Manipulation checks substantiated that the speaker's guises were perceived as intended and that when "elderly" he was judged to be 62 years old. Predictably, the guises using standard accents were upgraded on status and downgraded on benevolence and integrity (Ryan & Giles, 1982). The older guises were considered more aged (i.e., frail, old-fashioned) and more vulnerable (i.e., weak, insecure) with the most vulnerable voice being the slow, nonstandard, older voice. Although the use of fast speech and a standard accent by an older speaker reduced perceived vulnerability, he was nonetheless seen as asocial and egocentric. Moreover, this guise was rated as the least benevolent of the older age variants. Thus, regardless of the other cues present, the older voice always was associated with some negative characteristics. Unlike most others working in this domain, the researchers also gathered open-ended qualitative information by asking participants to give reasons for their particular ratings of the speaker and by asking them to explain why the speaker had made certain statements. Findings from this aspect of the research showed that the combination of old age and nonstandard speech produced responses that drew heavily on assumptions about both old age and relative disadvantage. The researchers found that listeners had different interpretations of extracts from the text, such as the speaker saying "I didn't know what to think," depending on the speaker's age; hence, this statement was more likely to be attributed to the speaker's being "confused" if elderly (and recall he was perceived as being only in his early 60s) but to his "wishing to withhold judgment given the complexity of issues at hand" if he was young. When asked why they rated the speaker the way they did despite the fact that he said exactly the same thing in each condition, listeners described the standard young speaker as "arrogant and pompous", the nonstandard young speaker as "trying to impress" or "using the words of others," the standard elderly speaker as "egocentric, living in the past, and talking of trivia," and the nonstandard elderly speaker as "stupid and losing his grip." When invited to substantiate these accounts by recourse to pinpointing textual information, respondents very often highlighted exactly the same utterances to justify their very disparate claims. These open-ended data clearly indicate that respondents were actively interpreting what they had heard and tailoring information to fit schemata prompted by age and class (as indicated by standard and nonstandard speech) variables.

Building on this foundation, a follow-up study employed the same speaker varying the same speech qualities but with different message content (Giles, Henwood, et al., 1992). Again, the speaker was talking about his car, but this time in the context of an interview following a car crash (no personal injury involved). The speaker's competence was held in question, and the responsibility for the crash was kept uncertain. In addition, respondents were given a questionnaire asking them, among other things, to list their thoughts and feelings when the speaker was talking. Other measures included textual interpretation items (e.g., "Was the speaker aware of damage?" and "Was the speaker to blame?") and a passage recognition questionnaire administered 2 days later. Results of listener judges' interpretations of the text revealed potent age effects in that the younger speaker was perceived to be more aware of the damage caused by the accident than was the older speaker. The older speaker was denigrated as doddery, vague, and rambling; was seen as being more upset and weak; and was commented on less than was the younger speaker, who was seen as stronger. A couple of days later, information spoken by the younger speaker was remembered more accurately than was the same information spoken by the older speaker.

These studies demonstrate that speech markers such as accent, rate, and age separately, and in combination, can act as sociolinguistic triggers. In other words, as soon as such markers are heard, listeners call on relevant cognitive stereotypes or schemata and use them for interpreting and understanding what has been said. Such biasing often means that older people's communicative behaviors are negatively evaluated, actively processed in a stereotypical manner, and recalled less effectively than are the comparable behaviors of younger people (see also Ryan & Johnston, 1987).

■ Formulating What to Say to Elders

It stands to reason that if respondents are using schema-driven processing in interpreting the behavior of others, then they also would use such strategies when seeking information from others. Carver and de la Garza (1984) had two groups of students read the same brief five-line description of an automobile accident involving either an older (84-year-old) or a younger (22-year-old) male driver-protagonist—the impetus, as it happens, for the stimulus messages in the studies described previously. Respondents were presented with a list of nine empirically derived questions that could be posed to the protagonist. These questions were to be rank-ordered by the respondents in terms of their perceived importance in assigning responsibility for the accident. As predicted, age labels induced stereotypical information seeking. Specifically, the *elderly* label (referring to the 84-year-old) led to differential patterns of information seeking concerning the physical, mental, and sensory inadequacies of the driver; conversely, and also concordant with stereotypes, the *young* label (referring to the 22-year-old driver) led to questions concerning speeding and alcohol consumption.

A later study conducted in Britain extended this design to include 77-, 66-, and 55-year-olds as well as the original 84- and 22-year-old targets (Franklyn-Stokes, Harriman, Giles, & Coupland, 1988). As age of target increased, the importance of questions about health, physical condition, quickness of reaction, and mental competence also increased linearly. In other words, such questions were thought least important for the youngest target and most important for the oldest target. The reverse pattern occurred for questions concerning alcohol consumption in that these were more frequently asked of young targets and tailed off linearly as the targets' ages increased.

In a follow-up study conducted in New Zealand (Ng, Moody, & Giles, 1991), the target ages were extended to cover the life span from 16 to 91 years (in 10-year age bands). Again, health and competence information was sought more frequently from older speakers, whereas speeding and alcohol information was perceived as more relevant for younger targets. However, rather than a steady linear trend as in the previous study, the importance of health and competence information seeking was observed to increase most sharply at 31 and 81 years of age. As in the previous study, information seeking based on speeding and alcohol was considered less important for older targets. In this case, therefore, not only was information seeking ageist, but information seeking that seemed to rely on a decremental perception of growing older was present for middle-aged targets, increasing dramatically with a target in his very early 30s. Of course, the attributions of criminal behavior (in this case, drunken driving) to the young person also can be seen as ageist and can be linked to stereotypical perceptions of young people as irresponsible and reckless.

Ageist information seeking, therefore, affects all age categories. That young (and older) adults have beliefs that allow them to formulate what to say to each other has been amply demonstrated by an experimental examination of how young adults might address older people when requesting different types of assistance (Dillard, Henwood, Giles, Coupland, & Coupland, 1990). This research tapped into the prodigious area of inquiry known as compliance gaining (Miller, 1983).

Working from the premise that older adults are stereotyped as less effective communicators than their younger counterparts, this study attempted to tease apart two potentially stereotypical views of older communication (Brewer, Dull, & Lui, 1981). One view proposes that older people are labeled as "weak and feeble," and thus their influence strategies would tend to be characterized as gentle and polite. The opposing view of "egocentric" and "abrasive" older people suggests stronger, more directly assertive strategies. Dillard et al. (1990) examined these two views while manipulating the legitimacy of the request made. Young adults completed a questionnaire designed to investigate how people set about persuading someone else to do something for them. They were asked to imagine themselves as either a "typical 20-year-old" or a "typical 70-year-old" and to ask a particular favor of either a 20-year-old or a 70-year-old. In addition, participants were told that they should either feel justified (legitimate request) or unjustified (illegitimate request) in asking the favor because they had or had not granted a similar favor about a week before. Respondents were first asked to write down what they would say and then to check off from a list which strategies they thought they might use. Although the results did not succinctly confirm either stereotype, young respondents believed that older actors in general were willing to exert more pressure than were their younger counterparts. They construed older people to be more direct with young targets than with their peers and to be more forceful and aggressive in their compliance-gaining attempts. This could reflect construals of older persons as authority figures who may use age status alone as justification for exerting pressure to comply.

The respondents in this study were hypothesizing about strategies that might be used in a way that allowed access to young people's perceptions of older persons' strategies. Obviously, these types of studies need to be replicated in an interactional context from both generations' perspectives before any hard-and-fast conclusions can be extracted. Nevertheless, the fact that age had an effect on the type of strategy used in the study indicates some profitable directions for future research in this area and underscores the vital role stereotypes often can play in mediating actual communication. Whatever the strategies used in compliance gaining, they are sure to be influenced by interactants' beliefs about what may be the most effective forms of talk (Giles, Coupland, & Wiemann, 1992).

■ Beliefs About Language Skills

A number of recent studies have used the Language in Adulthood (LIA) Scale to investigate perceptions about older adults' language and communication abilities, particularly their receptive and expressive language abilities. In an initial study, Ryan, Kwong See, Maneer, and Trovato (1992) asked a group of young (mean age 26.4 years) and elderly (mean age 72.9 years) adults to provide assessments of their own language abilities as well as those of either a typical 25-year-old or a typical 75-year-old. As expected, when judging their *own* language skills, the older adults reported more language problems than did the younger adults. However, three supposedly age-positive items (sincerity, vocabulary size, and storytelling skill) did not reveal the expected advantage for older adults, even though these are identified in gerontological studies as skills that increase with age. Only one reached significance (vocabulary size), and the difference favored the *younger* respondents rather than the older ones.

Furthermore, results indicated that *typical* 75-year-old targets generally were seen by those in both age groups as experiencing more problems in receptive and expressive language performance than were *typical* 25-year-old targets. Receptive problems included difficulty hearing and keeping track of topics, and expressive problems included word finding ("tip of the tongue" phenomenon). Typical elderly (75-year-old) targets were rated as more skilled than typical younger (25-year-old) targets on only two of the supposed pro-age items: sincerity in speaking and storytelling ability, both expressive language skills. Not unrelatedly, Ryan and Kwong See (1993) revealed that adults' predictions about their own and others' memory performance at different ages showed the expectation of significant decline from young adulthood, to middle age, to older adulthood.

These investigations demonstrate that both older and younger people expect older adults in general to experience more communication difficulty than do young adults. However, if we hold multiple stereotypical perceptions of elders and older adults that can be split into various positive and negative substereotypes, perhaps positive sub-stereotypes can accrue some gains for elders.

A recent study by Hummert, Garstka, and Shaner (1995) used the LIA Scale to assess beliefs of young, middle-aged, and elderly participants about their own communication skills and those of four elderly targets. Traits used to characterize the targets corre-sponded to two positive (Golden Ager, John Wayne Conservative) and two negative (Despondent, Shrew/Curmudgeon) stereotypes[42] (see Hummert, Garstka, Shaner, & Strahm, 1994). Overall, the Golden Ager was viewed most positively and the Despon-dent most negatively. Participants of all ages believed that the number of communication problems in hearing and memory would be lower for the Golden Ager and the John Wayne Conservative than for the Despondent and the Shrew/Curmudgeon. It should be noted that this was true even though the traits of the two negative targets gave no indication of memory or hearing difficulties. In addition, perceptions of age-related increases in word recognition and storytelling skills favored the positive targets over the negative ones. Thus, although generalized negative views of elders can be shown to be powerful stimulants of negative evaluations (Harwood & Williams, in press), beliefs about the communication competence of elderly individuals often result from their being categorized as a particular type of elderly person—an issue we revisit later.

Therefore, studies that examine voice decoding, attributions, and beliefs about age groups demonstrate that people rely on ageist stereotypes to interpret what others say as well as to formulate what to say to others. It is important to realize that respondents typically go well beyond the information provided in such studies, and this reveals an extensive use of socially shared assumptions about older and younger people. This typically enables respondents to extend negative information and to infer other negative traits and consequences from it. Finally, it is important to note that elders themselves downgrade older people, as demonstrated by the LIA Scale survey.

■ Underaccommodative Intergenerational Talk

When younger people are asked to characterize intergenerational talk, they frequently describe older people's communication in ways that can be labeled as *underaccommo-dation*. Underaccommodation has been defined (Coupland, Coupland, Giles, & Hen-wood, 1988) as occurring when some style or quality of talk is perceived to be underplayed relative to the needs or wishes of at least one interactant. Coupland, Coupland, Giles, and Henwood (1990) invited young women (30-40 years of age) to view and discuss videotaped snippets of intergenerational conversations between 30- to 40-year-old and 70- to 80-year-old women. In these discussions, the older women's talk (which often included disclosures of painful life events) was described quite negatively by younger women as interrupting, inattentive, rather self-centered, and even egocentric—as underaccommodative. The young women also described a sense of powerlessness when involved in such conversations in that they felt unable to control topics and develop themes. On a more positive note, some of these younger women seemed to take a sympathetic and benevolent stance, characterizing the older speakers as rather harmless, sweet, and deserving, a reaction we discuss further later. In other studies as well, young people have evaluated older women speakers as more "out of it" and inflexible than young women speakers (Ryan & Capadano, 1978).

Recently, we investigated young evaluations and characterizations of intergenerational talk. Williams and Giles (1996) content analyzed younger people's written accounts of satisfying and dissatisfying conversations with older people. Satisfying conversations were characterized by a cluster of positive dimensions including elder supportiveness, sensitivity, narrative skill, and positive emotion, and often the partner was seen as different from "other old people." By contrast, three quarters of the reports of dissatisfying conversations were characterized as "underaccommodative" (when the older partner was described as inattentive, not listening, interrupting, and dominating the conversation with their own agendas). In addition, these conversations were characterized by restricted communication, young people felt obligated to be polite, certain censured topics and forms of talk and emotions were negative, and young people felt negatively stereotyped. Despite this very clear positive versus negative pattern, there were indications that both types of conversations were ageist in some sense because stereotyping of older partners was equally frequent in both satisfying and dissatisfying conversations, although it was more benign in satisfying instances and more outrightly negative and prejudiced in dissatisfying encounters. Interestingly, the blame for dissatisfying encounters was placed primarily on the shoulders of older conversational partners, and young people's own suggested improvements for such conversations often involved more older persons' accommodation to the young persons' needs.

This same research study suggested that those young people who saw the conversation in intergroup age-salient terms (those young people who self-reportedly perceived age as salient and themselves and the older person as typical of their respective age groups [Hewstone & Brown, 1986a]) tended to rate the conversations more negatively than did those for whom intergroup salience was low (Williams & Giles, 1996). These results raise the possibility that those people who tend to perceive intergenerational conversations in such ways are predisposed to evaluate them more negatively.

Older people, therefore, are reportedly underaccommodative to young people's conversational needs. In a complementary fashion, young people's talk to elderly can be characterized as overaccommodative. Overaccommodation is defined by Coupland et al. (1988) as a miscommunicative process in which at least one participant perceives a speaker to go beyond a sociolinguistic style judged necessary for attuned talk. Thus, in many cases perhaps, under- and overaccommodation go hand in hand in carving out the topography of intergenerational conversations. It seems logical that among a variety of reactions to perceived underaccommodation, young people often may overcompensate, responding by overaccommodating.

■ Overaccommodative Intergenerational Talk

In fact, it is not uncommon for older people to be the recipients of patronizing and overaccommodative talk from young adults—also labeled "elderspeak" (Cohen & Faulkner, 1986) and "baby talk"—and this is perhaps the most widely researched aspect of interactional ageism. Patronization can be defined as talk that is ideationally simpler, slower, and more childlike in intonation (for a review, see Ryan, Hummert, & Boich, 1995) and is attributed as patronizing by the recipient (Ytsma & Giles, in press). Caporeal (1981) and Caporeal and Culbertson (1986) were among the first to document patronizing speech directed from young to elderly interlocutors. They described an extreme form of patronization to institutionalized elderly people irrespective of their functional ability labeled "secondary baby talk" (see also Kemper, 1994). In addition, older people often are susceptible to inappropriate forms of address (Wood & Ryan, 1991) and overly familiar nonverbals such as frequent touching (Lancely, 1985).

A series of experimental studies have been aimed at teasing apart some of the processes of patronizing or overaccommodating talk to the elderly. Although patronizing talk is not limited to the intergenerational context (and is apparent in other intergroup contexts such as in talk to persons with disabilities [e.g., Fox & Giles, 1996]), it is a feature worthy of considerable attention for a number of reasons. First, it is interesting in that it can potentially occur "bidirectionally"; young people can patronize the elderly, and the elderly can patronize the young. Second, patronizing talk seems to carry with it considerable implications for the power relations of the individuals (and groups) involved. In other words, it is a type of talk that we feel may reflect, more immediately than others, the societal relations underlying the minutiae of interaction (Ng & Bradac, 1993). In addition, because these modifications are not necessarily based on realistic needs of the individuals (although sometimes such talk is helpful [Kemper, 1994] and appreciated [Ryan & Cole, 1990]), many socially and cognitively active elders view such acts as communicating a lack of respect that undermines their self-esteem and dignity. Third, we also have observed that when negative images associated with age are made salient to older individuals (e.g., by overaccommodating to them, by making visible a magazine attending to age decrements), they will look, move, sound, think, talk, and account "older" compared to controls—a self-stereotyping phenomenon (Turner, Hogg, Oakes, Reicher, & Wetherell, 1987) that we have termed "instant aging." Hence, in line with attribution principles and the self-fulfilling hypothesis, hearing different people in various contexts inform an individual (indirectly by overaccommodations or through societal images) that he or she is "over the hill" ultimately will induce many a recipient to accept this as reality.

Following the procedures of Ryan, Bourhis, and Knops (1991), Giles, Fox, and Smith (1993) used a vignette of a middle-aged nurse talking with an elderly nursing home resident and found uniformly more negative evaluations of the nurse when she used patronizing talk (e.g., "Be a good girl," "Poor dear") compared to when she used a more neutral style. For example, she was perceived as less respectful, less considerate, less competent, and less benevolent in the former condition. The resident herself was perceived as more frustrated and helpless in the patronizing condition. Data also were interpreted as showing that elderly respondents were more sensitive to the characteristics of the individual receiving the patronization than were younger respondents. When the nurse spoke patronizingly, older (but not younger) respondents rated the resident as less competent, more weak, and less alert. At one level, this implies that older adults—and especially older women (Viledot & Giles, in press)—incorporate contextual cues in their evaluations of particular episodes of talk, whereas younger individuals appear less inclined to do so. However, it also suggests that elderly persons may be more willing to denigrate their peers on dimensions of competence as a result of the particular types of talk directed toward them. The results of a follow-up investigation with elderly respondents (reported in the same study) indicated that many of them claimed to have been patronized themselves (albeit, interestingly, to a lesser extent than they believed others of their own age to be patronized) and that it made them extremely irritated.

Harwood, Giles, Ryan, Fox, and Williams (1993) extended this research in two ways. First, they examined patronizing talk from the young to the elderly and from the elderly to the young within a single design. Second, they were interested in various response strategies to patronizing talk, not least with a view to formulating recommendations for appropriate strategies to ward off unwanted patronization. Previous work in this domain has portrayed the elderly target as a (behaviorally) passive recipient of patronization and, hence, possibly as colluding with the patronizing behavior (see also Edwards & Noller, 1993; Ryan, Meredith, & Shantz, 1994).

We wished to confront the dilemmas and management problems associated with being the recipient of ageism (in this case, patronization), and our design included conditions in which the recipient of it was either "accepting" or "assertive." Results showed that patronizing the elderly was viewed as negatively as was patronizing the young and that, predictably, intergenerational communication was judged as far more satisfactory when patronizing talk was not present. Assertive responses from the patronized person led to evaluations of her as higher status, more controlling, and less nurturing than when she provided a neutral response. That said, a recent study by Ryan, Kennaley, Pratt, and Shumovich (1996) showed that rather than accruing any socio-evaluational gains, the older person who provided a directly assertive response to being the recipient of ageism was rated as least competent and polite. Further research along these lines would do well to distinguish between verbal aggression (in which case evaluations would be less favorable) and argumentation (which seems to accrue more favorable evaluations) (Infante & Rancer, 1996).

■ Tolerance and Accommodative Processes

Processes of overcompensation or psychological overaccommodation to perceived stereotypes may be strongly connected to patronizing speech directed toward older people. Whereas some negative stereotypes may result in extreme prejudice, explicit ageism, or even verbal abuse, others may lead to more positively motivated outcomes such as patronization. We must deal with a range of stereotypes, ageisms, and ageist talk. Kalish (1979) identifies a form of ageism he titles "new ageism" that he claims is an outgrowth of Butler's writings (e.g., Butler, 1987) in which elderly people as a group are seen as weak and ineffective but "appreciated" as worthy and deserving. For example, a study of physicians' attitudes toward their older patients (Revenson, 1989) showed that although negative age stereotypes were less prevalent than expected, there was evidence that rather than harboring explicitly negative attitudes, physicians who treated elderly patients drew on compassionate stereotypes. Of course, this may be an important aspect of good care, but it also may reinforce assumptions that older people are a homogeneous group of weak and needy persons and thereby may assist in masking the heterogeneity of the older population.

This tendency may not be restricted to physicians and those working within a medical or caring context. In a study that used a hypothetical vignette, Williams (1996) found that college students upgraded an underaccommodative (i.e., not listening and interrupting) target woman when she was portrayed as 70 as compared to 25 years old. These young people were prepared to excuse such negative communications from an older person as somewhat expected due to her age. Open-ended responses to this study indicated that young people were working with a sympathetic or compassionate stereotype of the older person, one that emphasized the norm of toleration out of respect and "understanding" given her age—a form of positive age discrimination. Thus, rather than outright negatively ageist attitudes toward elders, many people may feel positively disposed to certain elders based on sympathy or compassion (see also Scheier, Carver, Schulz, Glass, & Katz, 1978).

Whereas some forms of patronization may be motivated by stereotypes that appeal to our sympathy and understanding, others have a more positive valence. Recent research has identified a number of "positive" stereotypes of older people. As alluded to previously, Hummert and colleagues (e.g., Hummert, 1990; Hummert et al., 1994), through a number of studies, have investigated both positive and negative stereotypes of older people. This research has identified four predominantly negative stereotypes (Severely Impaired, Despondent, Shrew/Curmudgeon, Recluse) and three positive stereotypes (Perfect Grandparent, Golden Ager, John Wayne Conservative) of older people held by young, middle-aged, and older persons. Moreover, experimental studies (e.g., Hummert et al., 1994) indicate that unfavorable evaluations of older targets follow activation of negative stereotypes; accordingly, positive stereotype activation stimulates correspondingly positive evaluations. Recent research by Hummert and colleagues has indicated that when young respondents think they are addressing a more negative stereotypical target older person (e.g., Despondent), they are more likely to modify their speech in ways that can be described as patronizing (Hummert, Shaner, Henry, & Garstka, 1995).

Although activation of negative stereotypes may lead to age-adapted speech, activation of positive stereotypes of older people by young people would more often result in "normal adult speech" (Hummert, 1994). In actuality, whether a "normal adult speech" register can be identified as a result even of positive stereotyping has not yet been fully explored. Evidence from interethnic studies suggests that some people object to being addressed as members of a social category even when it is positively motivated (Hecht, Ribeau, & Alberts, 1989). In addition, positive stereotyping often may be socially debilitating for older people, for example, when older women are expected to play the role of the "kindly grandmother." It seems that the best stereotypical image that older people can hope to achieve is that of "Golden Ager." Thus, although more favorable images of elderly people and their activities are emerging, whether or not this signals a change in the status of older people in our society is perhaps a moot issue, as we highlight later.

In sum, it is clear that the ways in which older people are talked to, and talked about, in Western societies are age discriminatory. Indeed, future work may well show that some older people—perhaps those who endorse a psychologically younger age than their objective chronology would attest—may engage in some of the very same ageist and intolerant attitudes and communicative behaviors we have just documented. Research and theory in the burgeoning area of communication and aging has not taken on an explicit ageism stance (but see Coupland & Coupland, 1993). Rather, scholars have concerned themselves with constructs such as intergenerational predicaments, dilemmas, and miscommunications and have not investigated, in any direct sense, when, how, and why communication is expressly ageist and when it is interpreted and labeled by recipients as such.

■ Managing Ageism

Many older people appear to accept ageism, and this is inscribed into the passive responses to patronization in many of our vignette studies as well as being an implicit component of our diagrammatic and theoretical attempts to model such processes (e.g., Harwood et al., 1993). Of course, we recognize that there is a variety of ways of coping with ageism, all of which have far wider implications than the often localized context of their enactment suggests.

Observational research has documented older people not only accommodating or accepting ageism but also as unwitting co-conspirators in its realization. Coupland and Coupland's (1993) study of medical discourse reveals that some elderly patients appropriated ageist and stereotypical images to resist health-related behavioral changes (e.g., giving up smoking). Although this appears to serve individuals' localized conversational and other needs, reliance on such notions is at the same time "self-disenfranchising" (Coupland & Coupland, 1993).

In other instances, older people may be construed as accepting ageism but of creatively turning it to their advantage to protect and enhance self-esteem as a member of a denigrated group. Comparison of self-as-individual to peers who are not doing so well is an example of this (for examples, see Coupland et al., 1991). Relatedly, more rigorous and explicit distancing from negatively viewed subgroups is another method of enhancing self-esteem or protecting oneself from the face-threatening aspects of a negative social identity. In this case, an older person may categorize himself or herself as a member of a more positive subgroup as compared to "other older people" or "frail" older people. We have recognized these strategic possibilities in our interview data when elders explicitly deny that they are the type of person who elicits discriminatory communication such as patronizing speech from younger people, although other, more frail peers may do so (Giles et al., 1993).

Of course, strategic conversational avoidance of unwanted social comparisons, topic switching, dominating the conversation, and so on (for an explication of these in the context of communication conflict, see Sillars, Coletti, Parry, & Rogers, 1982) can look like underaccommodation. But more confrontational and communicatively divergent strategies also are an option (Sillars et al., 1982). One of these that we have studied directly is assertive responses to being patronized, and evaluations of such have been modeled in our experimental studies as we have already discussed. There surely are others. For example, one of our elderly informants described how she coped with what she felt to be inappropriate use of her first name by a family doctor by pointedly using his first name. This suggests that some form of matching or "mirroring" may be used to signal dissatisfaction. There probably is a variety of other strategies that deserve more systematic investigation.

Health professionals, carers, and others concerned with the welfare of the elderly also attempt to refute ageism by engaging "discourses of anti-ageism" (increasingly, they are encouraged to do so by training regimens) but do so in the face of a minefield of threats to their own and elderly persons' face concerns (Coupland & Coupland, 1993). It is this minefield of contradictory concerns that Coupland and Coupland (1993) suggest often leads doctors to "acquiesce to ageist remarks or offer bland non-committal responses" (p. 293), although some are prepared to challenge ageism and attempt to manage the conflict that it engenders. Even attempts to tackle ageist talk sometimes backfired because stereotypes often are produced to refute ageism but are reified by their production (Henwood, Giles, Coupland, & Coupland, 1993).

Thus far, we have discussed problems involved in managing ageism in an interaction at the individual level and some individual-level responses to such ageism. Dealing with and attempting to eradicate age discrimination can occur, of course, at other levels, for example, at a group or community level. Undoubtedly, social change is a very slow and nonlinear process that can be observed at all levels of analysis and instigated through a number of different agents such as the media, interpersonal contact, pressure groups (e.g., American Association of Retired Persons [AARP]), political policy, and so on. Moreover, it should be noted that change in one part of a social system may have far-reaching, often unintended consequences in another (Giddens, 1984).

The identification, naming, and salience of an issue must be one of the first steps toward social change (Devine & Monteith, 1993). Intergroup and social identity theorists (e.g., Tajfel & Turner, 1986) have outlined a number of routes for social change for ethnic and other groups. If we can draw comparisons among age-, ethnic-, and other category-based processes (see Harwood et al., 1995), then this theoretical perspective may prove useful in analyzing the changing status of age in society as well as the ways in which this is communicated.

Tajfel and Turner's (1986) routes for change provide a central role to a group's awareness of cognitive alternatives to the status quo as a prerequisite to change strategies. For group members to begin to change their social status, at least three questions might be considered. First, we must ask whether individuals are aware of their group's negative identity or low status vis-à-vis other groups. Second, we must ask whether individuals envision alternatives to their current identity status. Third, to determine whether or not a group strategy is likely, we must ask whether and how strongly individuals self- identify as group members. In other words, for individuals to engage in group-based strategies for social change, they must be aware of, and attach value to, a social identity.

In recent years, books and articles propounding an awareness that older people constitute a denigrated or oppressed group have begun to emerge (e.g., Bytheway, 1995). But this awareness is most prevalent among academics and professionals concerned with aging (e.g., Coupland & Coupland, 1990). There seems to be far less awareness among the lay public (evident in the proliferation of things such as unchecked ageist jokes and birthday cards), although it has to be acknowledged that grassroots pressure groups such as the AARP are trying to raise group-based awareness much as feminists did for women during the 1950s and 1960s. Incidentally, and again on the issue of commonalities between intolerances, a recent interview study of ours with Ellen B. Ryan showed community-living, active, older people denied that they were patronized or treated differently due to their ages but agreed that other older people were (see also Giles et al., 1993). Although we are only beginning to appreciate the complexity of the matter, it is important to investigate and theorize about how people ease along the age continuum from young adulthood, to middle age, to elderliness (to name but a few junctures) and how they are eased along it (sometimes resistantly) by the way in which others communicate with them. Developmental adaptation, and ultimately a positive personal identity, is likely to be achieved through being exposed to more enlightened values and interactional stances by younger people (Taylor, 1992). Naturally, we are tempted to see parallels between denial that one is treated in an ageist fashion and early studies of children's denial of racial group membership (Milner, 1983).

Of course, denial that one is a member of a denigrated social group is an important individual and group device for maintaining self-esteem. A number of writers have commented on the denial of aging and older people's— especially women's—strategies for looking young, from using hair dye and cosmetics all the way to surgery (Sontag, 1978). Indeed, Western advertising media very commonly market "age-defying" and "age-correcting" products that in effect promise social mobility or the "passing" of women from being "old" back to being "young"—fighting back "the ravages of time" or signs that they belong to an undesired and stigmatized out-group. Aging in Western media is not promoted as a process in which one can mature gracefully and positively. Rather, valued attributes of particular older people are heralded as rarities or even exceptions (perhaps thereby to be discounted [Hewstone, 1989]); witness catch phrases such as "Still provocative at . . . ," "Still creative at . . . ," "Life is still fun at . . . ," or "Still attractive at. . . ." Some ads also draw explicit attention to the itemized physiognomic features, and hence criteria, for what is to be considered physical aging (and demise).

But it is when individuals identify with a denigrated group and attempt to change the status of it that they may engage in group-based strategies for change. Intergroup theorists suggest that a social group will attempt to bring about a change with respect to its position vis-à-vis other more favored groups when it perceives the status quo as illegitimate but stable (Tajfel & Turner, 1986). In this case, "social creativity" may be the preferred strategy in which the image of the group is redefined in more positive ways, painful in-group/out-group comparisons are avoided, attributed group values are changed in a more positive direction, or new dimensions are used to make in-group/out-group comparisons.

As with the case of racism and sexism, negatively valenced perceptions of a group may be reinterpreted and represented positively by charismatic spokespersons (e.g., Martin Luther King, Germaine Greer). Notably recently, feminists such as Greer (1991), Friedan (1993), and Sontag (1978) have taken up the cause of ageism, especially with reference to aging women, but we have yet to hear slogans such as "Gray is beautiful" or "Gray Pride" from older folks themselves (apart from within very common advertising that is explicitly, and shamelessly, aimed at the presumed large, prosperous elderly market). We can recognize some of the themes of in-group redefinition, avoidance of painful comparisons, and so on in the following quotation from Friedan (1993). In this excerpt, she urges older people to stop the quest for youth and to embark on a new venture, effectively to redefine (more positively) who they are:

> The problem is not how we can stay young forever, personally . . . the problem is, first of all, how to break through the cocoon of our illusory youth and risk a new stage of life, where there are no prescribed role models to follow, no guideposts, no rigid rules of visible rewards, to step out into the true existential unknown of these new years of life now open to us, and *to find our own terms for living it.* (p. 33, emphasis added)

In parallel, a recent birthday card asks on the outside, "D'you know how the well-adjusted age?" and says on the inside, "Neither do I!" We suggest that such sentiments capture a sense of a vacuum here for older people; negative images are so ubiquitous, and positive ones are so confining. What is old age, what are its positive attributes beyond ageist ones, how can old age attributes be redefined more positively without mimicking youth, and what does well-adjusted old age look like? How can we creatively reinterpret images of aging without denying the very real (health and life quality) challenges that some older people face?

According to intergroup theory, if group members perceive the status quo as illegitimate and unstable, then they may begin to confront perceived injustices by engaging in processes of social competition; however, the risk of out-group or dominant group retaliation here is high. Social competition is a more confrontational strategy in which groups actively resist their subordinate status and may campaign for social justice or compete for resources. We have witnessed some of these processes with racism and feminism as pressure groups have campaigned for social justice and won legislative victories for racial and sexual equality. Some of Palmore's (1990) calls for action against ageism can be characterized in terms of social competition. Among his many suggestions are resisting ageist language and jokes, writing letters of complaint to advertisers, boycotting ageist consumer products, and using the power of the ballot. In spite of the fact that both the Gray Panthers and AARP have tried to campaign on behalf of both younger and older people, their activities often have been reinterpreted as self-interest at the expense of younger generations. For example, electronic and print media commonly express fears that the swelling ranks of the elderly will burden younger generations by sending social security and medicare costs spiraling out of control. In this light, elders' efforts to protect medicare and other services for the aged are interpreted as selfish; in media sound bite terms, they are "greedy geezers" (Coombes & Holladay, 1995). Not only does this further feed negative stereotypes, but it sets the stage for intergenerational conflict by putting age groups in competition for economic and social resources, and we already have noted pockets of backlash from pressure groups advocating youth interests (e.g., Nelson & Cowan, 1994). In this respect, the media and researchers have spoken of intergenerational conflict over resources, especially health care and social security. Of course, conflict is the ultimate social competition strategy.

■ Stereotyping and Ageism Toward the Young

Older people are not the only group who suffer discrimination on grounds of their chronological ages. Young people also are subject to many similar linguistic and communicative stigmatizations as those who are old. For example, in earlier sections, we briefly considered derogatory terms used to describe older people. Can we recognize similar themes when we examine terms used to describe the young? The proportion of derogatory terms for the young compared to those for the old may reflect the relative balance of power and especially a shared social perception that being young is a preferred state. However, there are a few considerations that we would like to discuss. As a starting point, we would suggest that stereotypes of young people tend to rest on images of inexperience, eagerness to impress, irresponsibility, and laziness. For example, many terms for the young refer in a derogatory way to immaturity and naïveté— *whippersnapper, babe-in-arms, babysnatching, young rake,* and the denigration intended in referring to a person as a *child* when he or she is not.

We do not have to look too far to provide a more specific example. In the U.S. media particularly, there has been a vast amount of recent press concerned with the current generation of young people (i.e., those born anywhere between 1961 and 1981). The labels for the generation, some of which are positive and some of which are negative, are worth considering here. For example, a popular label for this generation, "X" (taken from a popular novel by Coupland, 1990), has been used to represent the "facelessness" and aimlessness of a generation whose members have no distinct identity, causes, ambitions, and so on. *Time* Magazine is credited with the first use of a more positive label, "twentysomethings" (Ladd, 1993), and Howe and Strauss (1993) coined the term "The thirteenth generation."

On their own, these labels sound relatively neutral, but many media reports also have included some very negative trait characterizations of the generation characterizing them as "losers," "slackers," and "whingers and whiners" who are dependent on their parents. In fact, a close examination of popular press reports shows that negative characterizations of the generation are ubiquitous and are lined up against younger people's attempts to debunk them. This is evident by the negative redefinitions given to the labels themselves; for example, the term twentysomething often has been rephrased as "twentynothing." Recent articles in *Newsweek* Magazine cite *Advertising*

Age as referring to the generation as "that cynical, purple-haired blob watching TV" (Quinn, 1994, p. 67) and a *Washington Post* headline as declaring "The Boring Twenties: Grow Up, Crybabies, You're America's Luckiest Generation" (Giles, 1994, p. 63). Along the same lines, *New Republic* columnist Michael Kinsley writes, "These kids today, they're soft. They don't know how good they have it. Not only did they never have to fight a war . . . they never had to dodge one" (quoted in Giles, 1994, p. 63). Of course, self-claimed representatives of Generation X argue that it is the out-group (i.e., "baby boomers") who perpetuate such images, which often are cast contrastively with notions of baby boomer demographic vitality, economic security, and generational imperialism (Williams, Coupland, Sparks, & Folwell, 1997). At present, there is little research concerned with ageist attitudes toward young people and youth subculture, but this may prove to be an important and interesting direction for future research.

Just as with ageism toward the old, the effects of ageism toward the young can be observed through all our social institutions, education, law, health care, and so on. No less so in government, for example, early attempts to undermine the Clinton administration may have involved raising public fears by expressing doubts about a young presidency and young people inappropriately taking over the corridors of power. Readers will perhaps remember media references to "kids" in the White House who listened to rock and roll on their boom boxes, presumably in between policy meetings. Writing in *The New Republic,* Shalit (1994) acknowledges that "social critics have denounced the Clinton youth corps as a brood of ill-mannered bumblers" (p. 24). According to this article, Oliver North had "declared war" on an administration replete with "twentysomething staffers with an earring and an ax to grind" (p. 24), and writer Stephanie Mansfield of *G.Q.* Magazine is said to have "warned of the perils of government policy being formulated . . . by propeller-beanied adolescents who were stringing macaroni necklaces during the last Democratic regime" (quoted on p. 24).

Even a brief and informal examination of our cultural artifacts reveals ageism toward the young. Although this could be dismissed by some as unsystematic and "nonscientific," our experimental studies have begun to reveal similar themes. For example, patronization may not be a one-way intergenerational street, although it often is portrayed as such in the literature. Giles and Williams (1994) examine young people's reactions to patronizing talk from older adults to younger adults. Undergraduates reported that they too were the recipients of patronizing speech and that this annoyed them. Furthermore, a distinct typology emerged from a content analysis of their open-ended descriptions of elder patronization. In a following study, an independent set of undergraduate participants were presented with two examples of each of the patronization types and were asked to make similarity judgments of each combination. Analyses showed that they cognitively represented the different types of patronizing speech on three primary dimensions: *nonlistening* (e.g., "The elderly don't listen to what I have to say"), *disapproving* (e.g., "You're all party animals"), and *overparenting* (e.g., "When you get older, you will see this was best").

A further study used these three different patronizing dimensions for social evaluation in a vignette alongside a nonpatronizing (control) variety. Patronizing of any of the types by a 70-year-old or by a 40-year-old was seen very negatively by young adults, but a hierarchy of judgments did emerge depending on the question posed. Stereotypical disapproving was considered by judges to convey the most negative intent, but nonlistening was considered the most difficult to manage communicatively, with overparenting considered the least offensive of the three. Different causal attributions were afforded patronizing targets when they were middle-aged rather than elderly (e.g., age envy was, interestingly, associated far more with the 40-year-old than with the 70-year-old).

The parallels between young-to-elder patronization and elder-to-young patronization may extend beyond the labels. Some form of wide-ranging accommodative practices may be operating such that a form of discriminatory talk in one direction is matched by a similar (although not identical) type of talk in the other direction. This form of competitive, yet complementary, counterattuning (when one does not attune oneself to the conversational needs of one's partner) could reflect matching or mirroring strategies by which individuals of different age groups express dissatisfaction with their interlocutors through the use of strategies similar to those that annoy them. Such tendencies also have been noted in studies of interpersonal (Sillars, Wilmot, & Hocker, 1993) and intergenerational conflict (Bergstrom & Williams, 1996). Indeed, it would be interesting to see whether those who experienced being patronized most as children and young adults are precisely those who model this behavior later in life and overaccommodate to the young. Furthermore, certain parents and adults make explicit intergroup boundaries in their talk to children (e.g., "It's grown-ups' time now," "That's an adult word,"), and again, maybe those who are socialized early into seeing the life span predominantly in these terms could, in cyclical fashion, be those who later linguistically discriminate against the young.

■ Epilogue

Ageism, therefore, is a life-span issue, although clearly it may be more salient and pertinent at some points of the life span than at others. As Itzin (1986) so succinctly puts it, "The chronology of aging becomes the hierarchy of ageism . . . putting limits and constraints on experience, expectations, relationships, and opportunities" (p. 114). Social historians have shown that over the past 100 years or so, constructions of the life span have become more sharply boundaried. One example that frequently is given is the fairly recent evolution of the notion of childhood as a discrete life stage. Drawing boundaries around various life stages and making them special and distinct also tends to overemphasize life stages as distinct from each other with chronological age marking out who belongs in which age groups. Thus, we have childhood, adolescence, young adulthood, middle age, and old age; and the members of these age groups may tend to be seen in terms of the stereotypes of what is expected at each stage. Recent research has shown that the ways in which young individuals perceptually characterize the life span into discernible units is enormously variable and undergirded by the myriad life concerns with schooling, career, family, and so on (Giles & Harwood, 1997).

Ageism is produced and reproduced at all levels of society (individual, dyadic, and community). By way of example, consider two age groups (adolescents and the old) who can be characterized as disenfranchised, marginalized, and problematized. A glance through books and journals concerned with adolescent development seems to show an overwhelmingly prevalent view of this period of life in terms of its problems: drug abuse, unwanted pregnancy, alienation, and antisocial behavior. Likewise, gerontologists have been criticized for their focus on the problems of aging. At a community level of analysis, both groups can be seen as on the margins of the labor force; adolescents are entering, and older people are leaving. Legislation excludes from employment those who are too young, and those who are considered too old are encouraged to retire (Franklin & Franklin, 1990). Relatedly, members of both age groups may be considered incompetent and therefore unsuitable for certain tasks by virtue of their chronological ages.

The point of this discussion is not to advocate child labor or the abolition of retirement but rather to call attention to some of the ways in which a categorical view of the life span is legitimated. At the level of the community, this may be reinforced by legislation and long-held social practices. At the level of interaction, it is achieved in talk between young people and older people; at the level of the individual, it is a cognitive schema that guides what is appropriate for interacting with others.

Giddens' (1984) structuration theory seeks to liberate us from focusing on one level of analysis. He shows that, for example, community-level features of a social system are resources available for use in interaction that in turn reinforce and reproduce the status quo. Importantly, such features are at the same time enabling and constraining, and they may have unintended consequences. Thus, as a result of the creation of a distinct period called "childhood" during the industrial revolution, children's lives have become much improved. But by marking out life phases in this way, we open the door to other processes that are constraining. Discrete life phases lead to categorization, which leads to differential treatment of individuals based on their assumed characteristics. This becomes ageist when the differential treatment is based on overgeneralizations and is applied carte blanche to all individuals irrespective of their needs, wishes, and so on.

There are different but interconnected ageisms. In the spirit of Baldwin and Hecht (1995; see also Hecht & Baldwin's chapter in this volume [Chapter 3]), we would characterize a continuum of tolerance toward older people. There are underlying ambivalences toward age, especially old age, and these ambivalent feelings are held by young and old alike and are related to different degrees of tolerance. Our studies with young students show that they report feeling fear, anxiety, and even disgust as well as compassion and sympathy for elderly people. Even when intergenerational interactions are reportedly satisfying for younger people, they often report mixed emotions (Williams & Giles, 1996). Thus, there is a number of different stances or levels of tolerance that we can identify from research concerned with perceptions of age. At the negative end of a tolerance scale, Levin and Levin (1980) coin the term "gerontophobia" to indicate extremely negative perceptions of older people—this combined avoidance and denial with disgust, revulsion, and extreme dislike of the elderly. Relatedly, extreme prejudice can come about as a result of perceived competition for social resources. The recent debates pitting the old and young as competing for declining social security coffers, medicare, and so on feed into such prejudices.

There is another form of ageism also based on negative views of old age but combined with a glimmer of positivity in the form of compassion. Kalish (1979) terms this "new ageism," in which elderly people as a group are seen as weak, ineffective, and needy but also as worthy and deserving. Kalish's comments are directed at those in caring professions, especially gerontology, but new ageism almost certainly is a predominant stance among the wider population. Of all forms of tolerance, this may be the most likely to lead to patronization, and much patronizing speech research assumes that this underlies motives for patronization (Harwood & Giles, 1996).

Next on the scale, we would identify forms of positive ageism that are, nevertheless, based on stereotypes. Such stereotypes are comprised of a cluster of traits and behaviors that are expected from certain older people. A rather typical example is the image of a kindly elderly lady or the grandmother type (Hummert, 1994). The stereotype is female, kindly, selfless, benevolent, and often also slightly naive or behind the times, but in an endearing way. Although the stereotype may be fairly positive, the ageism that accompanies it is very questionable, combining both ageism and sexism to limit individuals' options and possibilities. Deviations from this role (or any other) may be responded to with distaste and pressure to conform.

Finally, the positive end of the continuum would afford older people their individuality and would value them as who they are and appreciate the experience of development through aging. As indicated previously, these tolerances can be related to stereotypical subtypes and competing motivations in intergenerational talk.

There is scope for change. Individuals and groups taking action at all levels—community, group, family, interindividual, and so on—can bring about change. In the Baldwin and Hecht scheme, the in-group "appreciation" of out-group communities and their communicators—and in our case the mutual appreciation of younger and older people—is an ideal state to achieve. How we arrive there, however, is another question and for the most part depends on interventions at all levels.

We have discussed some community and group interventions. At the dyadic level, some speculative thoughts for intervention could be invoked from recent research in psychocardiology. Researchers at the Institute of HeartMath (IHM) in Boulder Creek, California, have been exploring ways of managing everyday stress. Their experimental work (e.g., Rein, Atkinson, & McCraty, 1995; McCraty, Atkinson, Tiller, Rein, & Watkins, 1995) shows that "positive heart-powered emotions such as care, love, and appreciation increase immune antibodies and balance heart rhythms" (Jordan, 1995, p. 41) and has favorable implications in brain/cognitive activity and behavior. By contrast, experiencing frustration, anger, and anxiety can create the opposite immunological and cardiological reactions. Although this work is focused on interpersonal relationships, note that affective responses such as anxiety often are associated, at the intergroup level, when in-group members encounter out-groups (Dijker, 1987; Gudykunst, 1995; Stephan & Stephan, 1985). Intergenerational communication, as we already have argued, often is fraught with dissatisfaction, negative stereotypical expectations, and counterattuned talk. Indeed, the IHM, coincidentally, also invokes the construct "appreciation," in which therapeutic procedures (called "freeze-frame") are used to enhance interindividual contact; perhaps this can be adapted at the intergenerational domain as well as at other intergroup domains.

Transforming their recommendations (Jordan, 1995, p. 41) for our purposes, we could propose the following:

    a. Be aware of negative feelings (should they exist) when encountering (ideally before conversing with) a member of the other age group.

    b. Attempt to eradicate these emotions by shifting the focus from negative thought patterns about the group to positive emotions ("the power of the heart") for 10 seconds.

    c. Recall a positive reaction with someone of that age (which could be yourself when younger in one case) and appreciate that experience.

    d. With this affective refocusing allowing for more cognitive balance, consider how the encounter (or the disturbing issue at hand) could be construed, or even attributed, more efficiently. For instance, rather than focusing on the motive for one being the recipient of patronizing talk as due to negative stereotypes, one could reattribute it to a nurturing and overly protective motivation (and, hence, not as patronizing at all [Ytsma & Giles, in press]), assuming that, in many instances, this is the motivation.

This should not be construed as furnishing ready-made excuses or diverting responsibility from those who would be ageist or, indeed, to place responsibility for repair on the shoulders of the victim; outright negative and discriminatory ageism should be forcefully challenged. Rather, the aim is to help the recipient transcend the encounter and place him or her in a better emotional state to accommodatively educate the perpetrator about the negative intergroup dynamics and social harm that are being generated there.

It is interesting that the IHM argues that appreciation can be discharged and accommodated by both interactional partners. In other words, it has transactive potential in social interaction. Given that positive stereotypes (e.g., wisdom, experience) are associated with elderly people and others (e.g., activity, strength) are associated with younger people—and in ways that have much cross-cultural currency (Harwood et al., 1997)—there are affective resources on which both age groups can call. Such (straightforward) affective-cognitive strategies might well promote better attuned intergenerational talk and, thereby, make some modest contribution to the reduction of ageist discourse at the interactional, and ultimately social, level.

We suggest that formulating an explicit model of communicative ageism might be premature at this stage in the intellectual process, and this is especially so when so many models have emerged recently. In other words, it might be more useful to elaborate current theories, such as various revisions of the communicative predicament (e.g., Harwood et al., 1993) and age stereotype activation (Hummert, 1994) models, to take into account the constructs and attending processes of ageist attributions and motives, intolerance, tolerance, and appreciation in a manner that acknowledges that age discrimination occurs throughout the life span and at multiple levels of analysis. Indeed, such a move offsets a danger in separating ageism vacuously away from sexism, racism, heterosexism, and so on. When and why an older woman, for instance, is the victim of one or more of these over the others are fascinating questions. When and why she might prefer to select one over another to account for ambiguous or distasteful communications directed toward her is a companion quest.

What is more clear is some of the applied agendas that follow as a consequence of the forgoing. First, we need to educate young people very early in school about the life-span adventure and pitfalls. Although "let the young be young" is a very liberal and laudable appeal, it seems important to socialize young people away from ageism and their unwitting collusions in sustaining the same. Life skills in high school ought to include a life-span component that will better prepare young people to understand that ageism is apparent at all ages (as perpetrator and recipient) and that it has intense intergroup dynamics (Harwood et al., 1995). Second, and more generally, young and old people alike need to be more alert to ageism and depersonalizations and need to strategize how to manage their variable forms in interaction and through media literacy. Ryan, Meredith, and Orange's (1995) "communication enhancement model" is a fine discussion of the ways in which members of one age group ought to assess the *individual* competencies and needs of members of the other and resist homogenizing, often disrespectfully and illogically, the out-group. In addition, we need to promote a genuinely age-sensitive media in tandem. Third, and relatedly, we need to empower life-span education and its values. Currently, education seems to be the prerequisite of certain age groups but, rather, should be the normal diet of all ages. Indeed, involving older people in our research seems a fundamental necessity if we are to avoid ageist assumptions and biased designs of our own (Glendenning, 1995). Fourth, we need to better support older persons in a changing, arguably more violent society, and in ways that do not foster vulnerability and fear. Communication research to date has focused on potentially short-term harmful effects of age discrimination—as opposed to ageist abuse (Braithwaite, Lynd-Stevenson, & Pigram, 1993)—in an empirically controlled manner and for obvious reasons. Alarming data do exist, however, suggesting that elder abuse can be far more pernicious and direct than any of that outlined here (Baumhover & Beall, 1996; Pillemer & Finkelhor, 1989). Finally, we need to consider carefully ways in which to bring younger and older people into contact with each other. Mere communication will not suffice and, indeed, can backfire and make matters even worse. In parallel, we need to specify what our goals are for contact programs and implement them according to the needs of appropriate representatives of both parties (Fox & Giles, 1993).

We end with our starting point. Ageism as a form of intolerance is a contemporary problem that has only just begun to be widely realized outside the gerontology field and senior care industry. We argue that, alongside the other "isms," it also receives its impact through and is shaped in turn by communication. If aging is not to be feared, and if ageism is not to be an indelible marker throughout our lives, then we need to blot up its stains immediately by researching and theorizing about why it comes about

(Branco & Williamson, 1982), what its variable forms are at different levels, how it is communicatively managed to various good effects, and how it can be overcome in concert with other manifestations of social discrimination.

■ Acknowledgments

We are grateful to Philip Smith and Sharon Lloyd (recent participants at the IHM) for bringing the research, practice, and materials of this group to our attention as well as to Michael Hecht for his support, patience, and helpful detailed feedback on an earlier draft of this chapter.

PART III Contexts of Prejudice

9

Communicating Prejudice in Personal Relationships

Stanley O. Gaines, Jr.
Julie Chalfin
Mary Kim
Patrick Taing

In this chapter, we examine the ways in which individuals communicate prejudice—in particular, negative thoughts and feelings directed toward members of one or more out-groups—directly toward relationship partners *when those partners also are members of the out-group(s) in question.* To understand the potential impact of communicating prejudice from one relationship partner toward another within the relationship process, we draw on communication accommodation theory (Giles & Powesland, 1975), ethnolinguistic identity theory (Giles, 1978), and the layered perspective (Baldwin & Hecht, 1995; see also Hecht & Baldwin's chapter in this volume [Chapter 3]) that serves as a unifying framework for the present book. We begin, however, by exploring the processes by which attraction between two persons initially develops and evolves into a close or personal relationship.

According to Kelley (1986), "Close relationships are ones in which persons affect each other frequently, strongly, in diverse ways, and over considerable periods of time" (p. 11; see also Kelley et al., 1983). Some of the major tasks to be accomplished during the process of relationship development, then, are that (a) Individuals must progress from interacting occasionally to interacting quite often, (b) individuals must progress from having negligible impact on each other to having considerable impact on each other, (c) individuals must progress from interacting in a narrow band of settings to interacting in a wide array of settings, and (d) individuals must progress from interacting over a period of minutes, hours, or days to interacting over a period of weeks, months, or years. To the extent that two individuals succeed at one or more of these tasks, the resulting relationship between them may be regarded as personal or close.

As the literature on long-distance and e-mail relationships attests (Lea & Spears, 1995; Rohlfing, 1995), partners conceivably can maintain long-term personal relationships without necessarily interacting face-to-face on a daily basis. However, the level of disposable income required to maintain long-term personal relationships via certain forms of mediated communication (e.g., telephone, Internet) may make potential long-term relationships impractical to all except middle or upper class individuals. Similarly, the issue of variety of settings might be more relevant to the relationships of middle class individuals (who often interact with friends in multiple settings such as each other's homes) than to the relationships of working class individuals (who often interact with friends in a specific setting such as a pub [Allan, 1989; see also Moon & Rolison's chapter in this volume [Chapter 7]). Thus, assumptions that individuals simply need to be creative to maintain relationships across long distances, or that relationships can become close or personal only after individuals interact across a wide variety of contexts, may be socioeconomically bound.

As Levinger and Snoek (1972) point out, *attraction* serves as the emotional glue that binds relationship partners together. Levinger and Snoek define attraction as "one person's [positive] attitude [or feeling] toward another" (p. 3), as experienced in socioemotional states such as liking, loving, satisfaction, affection, and respect. Furthermore, as Byrne's paradigm of research suggests (e.g., Smith, Byrne, & Fielding, 1995), attraction generally is facilitated by the degree to which two individuals are similar to one another. Studies of similarity and attraction typically focus on personality characteristics such as motives, traits, and attitudes (Berger & Calabrese, 1975; Dodd, 1991; Levinger & Snoek, 1972). However, in this chapter, we emphasize relationship partners' (dis)similarity regarding socially defined group memberships (sites for the "spheres of prejudice," as described by Hecht & Baldwin in this volume [Chapter 3], along the relationship layer or level of analysis), as reflected in communication patterns in general and expressions of prejudice in particular.

■ Spheres of Influence as Reflected in Personal Relationship Processes

Baldwin and Hecht (1995) define the *relationship level of analysis* in their layered perspective on communicating prejudice as "the negotiation of identity as communication partners develop relationships, especially as a relationship gains its own identities or as certain relational roles (e.g., marital, employment, friendship) interact with personal identities" (p. 74). At first glance, the domain of personal relationships might seem antithetical to the study of the communication of prejudice. After all, most social scientists and laypersons alike probably view personal relationships—at least those that are voluntary in nature—as necessarily entailing equity (Canary & Stafford, 1994; Roloff & Cloven, 1994), if not equality (Brown, 1986; Zorn, 1995).

In turn, as Allport (1954/1979) observes, equal status contact between interactants is much more likely to foster the communication of tolerance and appreciation than it is to foster the communication of intolerance or prejudice (Gudykunst, 1994; Taylor & Katz, 1987). Clearly, however, individuals often communicate sexism (Henley & Kramarae, 1991; see also Rakow & Wackwitz's chapter in this volume [Chapter 5]), racism (Rosenblatt, Karis, & Powell, 1995; see also Asante's chapter in this volume [Chapter 4]), heterosexism (Stronmen, 1990; see also Nakayama's chapter in this volume [Chapter 6]), classism (Gordon, 1978; see also Moon & Rolison's chapter in this volume [Chapter 7]), ageism (Coupland, Nussbaum, & Coupland, 1991; see also Williams & Giles' chapter in this volume [Chapter 8]), and religious dogmatism (Crohn, 1995) toward relationship partners who also happen to be members of stigmatized out-groups. Levinger and Snoek (1972) contend that similarity in terms of demographic characteristics (e.g., ethnicity, age, socioeconomic class, religious denomination) seems to be extremely important in determining whether two individuals will meet each other, let alone find each other attractive (Levinger & Rands, 1985).

In turn, these and other demographic constructs make up the *spheres of influence* that Baldwin and Hecht (1995) describe in their layered perspective of (in)tolerance(s). Of course, several spheres of (in)tolerance(s) may be manifested within personal relationships in general. Nevertheless, certain spheres of (in)tolerance(s) might be more prominent in certain types of relationships than in others. When personal relationships involve individuals whose respective in-groups historically have been depicted within a given society as "at war" or "at odds" (reflected linguistically in terms such as "battle of the sexes," "race riots," and "holy wars" [see Hecht & Baldwin's chapter in this volume [Chapter 3]), we might expect that intolerance will surface from time to time, especially when relationship partners are engaged in conflict. What might otherwise be interpreted by relationship partners as strictly *interpersonal* conflict when their in-group memberships overlap perfectly well may be interpreted instead as *intergroup* conflict when their in-group memberships fail to overlap along the spheres that historically have been deemed important in the society in question.

For example, *sexism* may be evident in a variety of male-female relationships and may make it difficult, but not impossible, for women and men to sustain long-lasting, platonic relationships (Fehr, 1996; Gaines, 1994; Ickes, 1993; Tannen, 1990). *Racism* may be evident in a variety of relationships between Anglos and persons of color[43]; romantic relationships and subsequent family relationships often are discouraged by various social agents (particularly the families of would-be interracial romantic partners [Essed, 1991; Porterfield, 1978; Rosenblatt et al., 1995]). *Heterosexism* may be evident in a variety of straight-gay relationships and, by definition, precludes romantic relationships between members of the two groups (unless bisexual individuals are counted as "gay"). *Classism* may be evident in a variety of affluent-poor relationships and makes it hard for individuals who come from two different socioeconomic groups to form long-lasting friendships or romantic relationships. *Ageism* may be evident in a variety of relationships between middle-aged persons and non-middle-aged persons and largely precludes friendships and romantic relationships. Finally, *religious dogmatism* may be evident in a variety of Christian/non-Christian relationships[44] and makes it difficult for individuals from two different religious backgrounds to form marital and family relationships (although religion may not be as salient as a relationship barrier in the United States during the 1990s as it was during the 1950s [Melnick, 1988; Miller, 1983]).

One might ask whether it really is that hard for individuals from different socially defined groups to establish and maintain enduring, satisfying relationships. For instance, with regard to male-female friendships, partners often say that their gender differences either do not matter (e.g., "He's just one of the girls to me," "I don't think of her as a female") or can be an important source of insight (e.g., "It's nice to learn about the other sex's thoughts on this topic") (Reeder, 1996). Whether the respective partners, especially those partners whose in-group (e.g., gender) is privileged in a given society, actually view their relationships as equal in status may be open to question (Fehr, 1996). To the extent that both relationship partners acknowledge the persistent status inequities accrued to their respective group memberships in the larger society (e.g., in cross-sex friendships in which both male and female partners embrace feminist views; see Rakow & Wackwitz's chapter in this volume [Chapter 5]), it might not be difficult for partners to develop mutually satisfying relationships. Such partners might be said to adopt the stance of tolerance or appreciation (Baldwin & Hecht, 1995; see also Hecht & Baldwin's chapter in this volume [Chapter 3]). To the extent that one or both partners refuse to acknowledge present-day status inequalities (e.g., men who complain that women are trying too hard to "be like men"), however, relationship conflict along the spheres of prejudice (Baldwin & Hecht, 1995; see also Hecht & Baldwin's chapter in this volume [Chapter 3]) is likely to ensue.

With the exception of sexism (e.g., Huston & Ashmore, 1986; Spence, Deaux, & Helmreich, 1985), theories and research within the field of personal relationships rarely deal with the spheres (i.e., social- or group-based identities on which tolerance/intolerance is based [Baldwin & Hecht, 1995, p. 69]) mentioned previously. Part of the problem is that personal relationships typically are depicted as islands unto themselves, unperturbed by waves of real-world influences. In addition, even personal relationship researchers frequently use the *individual,* rather than the couple or pair, as the unit of analysis (Berscheid, 1986), thus making it virtually impossible to determine how societal stereotypes are communicated by individuals to their relationship partners. Furthermore, the very nature of personal relationships may stymie researchers' efforts at identifying discernible patterns of communicating prejudice. After all, close, intimate relationships tend to be idiosyncratic (Baxter & Wilmot, 1983; Bell, Buerkel-Rothfuss, & Gore, 1987; Knapp, Ellis, & Williams, 1980), with interactants creating their own "cultures" using specific rules for interaction (Dodd, 1991; Duck, 1994; Wood, 1982) and using individual, personal, or psychological information rather than intergroup or sociological information (Miller & Steinberg, 1975). Perhaps it should not be surprising, therefore, that the field of personal relationships has offered relatively few insights into the verbal and nonverbal manifestation of prejudice (Giles & Franklyn-Stokes, 1989).

Part of what makes the study of communicating prejudice in personal relationships interesting is the uniqueness of the forms of prejudice that might be manifested. For example, in one scene from the motion picture *Jungle Fever,* Flipper (a married African American man) tells his lover Angie (a single Italian American woman) that they will never have children together because he does not want any "half-White babies." Although Flipper has not overtly said to Angie that he is prejudiced against White people, Angie tells Flipper that such a remark sounds just as racist as the far more overt statements that her father makes every day regarding Black people. Another example comes from an episode of the television series *Thirtysomething,* in which an inter-religious married couple (Michael, who is Jewish, and Hope, who is Protestant) quarrel over whether to celebrate Christmas or Hanukkah with their young daughter during mid- to late December. At one point, Hope criticizes Michael for insisting on celebrating Hanukkah when he fails to practice his Judaism on a daily basis; for a moment, Michael and the television audience are left to wonder whether Hope is really criticizing Michael for being Jewish. In these examples, heterosexual romantic partners' conflicts over how to raise children, and whether to have children in the first place, give rise to speech acts that easily could be interpreted as covertly communicating prejudice.

By examining the processes by which prejudice is communicated in personal relationships, we will be in a better position to identify continuities in the communication of prejudice at additional levels of analysis that might otherwise seem disjointed or unrelated (Baldwin & Hecht, 1995; see also Hecht & Baldwin's chapter in this volume [Chapter 3]). For example, according to Sullivan's (1953) interpersonal theory of personality, individual differences in tendencies toward communicating or not communicating prejudice cannot be understood apart from a sociopsychological context; that is, to understand individuals' communication of prejudice, we must examine the relationship contexts (e.g., family relationships, friendships) in which individuals are especially likely (or unlikely) to convey prejudice. Furthermore, according to Mead's (1934) symbolic interactionist theory (cf. O'Keefe & Delia, 1982), relationship partners' communication of prejudice toward each other cannot be understood apart from a sociocultural context; that is, if we are to understand relationship partners' communication of prejudice toward each other, then we must examine the predominant norms and values emphasized by the cultures and societies of which relationship partners are members. By studying the communication of prejudice at the relationship level, then, we succeed in constructing a conceptual bridge between individual-level (i.e., purely psychological) and society-level (i.e., purely sociological) aspects of the communication of prejudice (Baldwin & Hecht, 1995).

■ Intergroup and Interpersonal Aspects of Relationship Development

Personal relationships involving two persons differing along multiple-group dimensions can be understood in terms of the intergroup salience as well as the interpersonal salience perceived by the relationship partners. According to Gudykunst (1986), close or personal relationships are likely to be high in interpersonal salience but low in intergroup salience. Furthermore, when relationships cross along multiple-group lines (and, hence, involve persons with multiple-group memberships), the salience of any single membership decreases (Giles & Johnson, 1987). In turn, the development of such relationships can lead to higher personalization and differentiation among relationship partners (i.e., partners increasingly are seen as unique individuals rather than as members of social groups [Levinger & Snoek, 1972]).

The societal barriers that prevent intergroup relationships from becoming interpersonal are numerous and compelling. Especially with regard to romantic relationships that cross taboo lines (e.g., ethnicity), many of the barriers formerly were (and, to some extent, still are) institutionalized. Lampe (1982) explains how, despite the espousal of freedom and equality as cherished values in the United States, mate selection inevitably is influenced by centuries-old customs and myths:

> Presently in the United States, marriage is based on the ideal of romantic love and, therefore, the most commonly accepted reason for dating would appear to be emotional attraction. At the same time, however, it has been found that propinquity, especially residential and occupational, is an important variable in mate selection. . . . Thus, it appears that the development of emotional attraction is generally dependent upon nearness. Since there is still a great deal of physical and social separation between racial or ethnic groups, many members of each group have but limited or highly structured contact with members of the other ethnic groups. This situation may result in at least two possible negative responses as regards interethnic dating: [A] lack of interethnic dating due to lack of opportunity and/or a lack of desire to interdate due to lack of knowledge and/or understanding. A further consequence may be perception of exogamous marriage as being especially divorce-prone and, therefore, a refusal to even consider such dating and possible marriage. (p. 116)

Even in ostensibly integrated settings (which typically were segregated White settings in the past but which have been desegregated by Blacks and other persons of color more recently), social norms often dictate that individuals "stick to their own kind." Given the variety of obstacles that make it difficult for friendship or romance to develop between individuals across group lines, it is a wonder that some pairs persist at all (Gaines & Ickes, 1997). To attain a better grasp of the subtle manner in which individuals frequently communicate prejudice to their relationship partners, let us turn to a communication theory that, appropriately enough, is based in part on social-psychological research on interpersonal attraction (Berscheid, 1985; Giles, Mulac, Bradac, & Johnson, 1987; Giles & Powesland, 1975).

The *communication accommodation theory* developed by Giles and his colleagues (e.g., Gallois, Franklyn-Stokes, Giles, & Coupland, 1988; Giles & Coupland, 1991; Giles, Coupland, & Coupland, 1991; Giles et al., 1987; Giles & Powesland, 1975) posits that during the course of interaction, individuals frequently try to adjust their own communicative behaviors so as to become increasingly similar to that of other persons with whom they are engaged in conversation (Duck, 1992; Hecht, Collier, & Ribeau, 1993).[45]

To the extent that individuals have successfully modified their manner of speech to be more congruent with that of their relationship partners, individuals may be said to engage in *convergent* communication. By contrast, to the extent that individuals somehow have failed in their efforts at making their patterns of communication increasingly congruent with that of their partners—or have chosen not to do so—individuals may be said to engage in *divergent* communication. In turn, divergent communication may be separated into *underaccommodation* (e.g., failure to change one's own behavior in the face of discrepancies between the behavior of oneself and the behavior of one's interaction partner) and *overaccommodation* processes (e.g., sometimes "trying too hard," for example, bringing up "gay topics" to gays).

According to Gallois et al.'s (1988) theory of communication accommodation, members of subordinate *and* dominant groups "are likely to be initially oriented in intergroup encounters to defining the situation as low in intergroup salience and high in interpersonal salience" (Gudykunst & Nishida, 1989, p. 27) under the following conditions: Members of subordinate *and* dominant groups (a) belong to many other social categories, (b) identify moderately with their ethnic group, (c) do not feel that their ethnic in-group is threatened, and (d) see their group as having soft and open boundaries; that is, members of the subordinate group see their group as having low vitality, whereas members of the dominant group see their group as having high vitality. Communication accommodation theory thus suggests that partners in interethnic/intercultural relationships ideally should attempt to view themselves and each other in a multifaceted rather than stereotyped manner. Case studies of intercultural married couples in therapy lend empirical support to communication accommodation theory. According to Falicov (1986), intercultural partners who adopt such a *balanced view* of their similarities and differences (i.e., view themselves as neither wholly similar nor wholly dissimilar but instead take both similarities and differences into account) are likely to interact in a way that respects partners' unique cultural heritages while simultaneously establishing a basis for mutuality in experiencing and expressing love.

Gallois et al.'s (1988) theory of communication accommodation indicates that differences between relationship partners' ethnicities—which, in turn, are composed of elements such as race, language, religion, and nationality (Gaines, 1995)—may have a stronger impact on the communication of prejudice than do within-couple differences along other dimensions (e.g., gender, age). We hasten to add that differences regarding certain aspects of ethnicity may be especially consequential (Gaines & Ickes, 1997). As DuBois (1903/1969) correctly anticipated, race has played a singular role in setting the course for interpersonal and intergroup conflicts in the United States and elsewhere throughout the 20th century. Also, as Allport (1954/1979) observed during the 1950s, the increasing significance of race has been accompanied by a decreasing significance of religious denomination in 20th-century America. Therefore, ethnicity—and, more precisely, socially constructed race—represents one aspect of individuals' roles and personalities that is likely to trigger a number of stereotyped thoughts, feelings, and behavior among relationship partners (Gaines & Reed, 1994, 1995).

Under what conditions will an individual *refrain* from communicating prejudice to his or her relationship partner? According to communication accommodation theory, one is unlikely to communicate (a) sexism if the partner is of the same gender as oneself, (b) racism if the partner is of the same ethnicity as oneself, (c) heterosexism if the partner is of the same sexual preference as oneself, (d) classism if the partner is of the same socioeconomic status as oneself, (e) ageism if the partner is of the same age cohort as oneself, or (f) religious dogmatism if the partner is of the same religious faith as oneself. Moving beyond communication accommodation theory per se, we also might expect that if the communication of prejudice is primarily an institutional (rather than an individual) phenomenon as sometimes is assumed (see Baldwin's chapter in this volume [Chapter 2]), then one would be less likely to communicate prejudice toward members of socially privileged groups than toward members of socially oppressed groups. Hence, in the United States, one would be less likely to communicate (a) sexism toward a male partner than toward a female partner, (b) racism toward an Anglo partner than toward an African American or Latino/Latina partner, (c) heterosexism toward a "straight" partner than toward a gay or lesbian partner, (d) classism toward an upper class or middle class partner than toward a working class or lower class partner, (e) ageism toward a middle-aged partner than toward a juvenile or elderly partner, or (f) religious intolerance toward a Protestant partner than toward a Jewish or Catholic partner. This latter set of predictions depends in part on the assumption that not only do members of socially advantaged groups internalize negative stereotypes regarding stigmatized out-groups, but also many members of stigmatized groups internalize negative stereotypes regarding their own in-groups (Allport, 1954/1979).

From the preceding predictions, what are the profiles of the most likely and least likely targets of prejudice in personal relationships? Among the *least likely* to have prejudice communicated to them from relationship partners, we might include males, Anglos, heterosexuals, affluent persons, middle-aged persons, and Protestants. Among the *most likely* to have prejudice communicated to them from relationship partners, we might include females, persons of color, gay males, lesbians, bisexuals, poor people, young and elderly people, and non-Protestants. Imagine the potential communication problems to be faced, then, in a platonic relationship involving John (a Baptist, middle-aged, affluent, straight, White male) and Mary (a Catholic, "twentysomething," poor, Black lesbian). Even if the would-be friends met at a political rally and discovered, through their conversation, that they shared similar views on social issues such as abortion, affirmative action, gun control, and the death penalty, it might be difficult for John to avoid making a remark about one or more of the stigmatized out-groups to which Mary belongs that she sees as disparaging unless John has stopped to consider all of the ways in which he is socially advantaged *and* all of the ways in which Mary is socially disadvantaged (van Dijk, 1993). Conversely, if John (like Mary) adopts a stance of tolerance or appreciation (Baldwin & Hecht, 1995; see also Hecht & Baldwin's chapter in this volume [Chapter 3]), then he might be less likely to behave in ways that some have termed "politically incorrect," not because he is attempting to appease some ill-defined group of "thought police" but rather because he genuinely rejects appeals to prejudice.

Assuming that strangers are more likely than personal relationship partners to communicate prejudice to target persons, what are likely to be the daily social-psychological experiences of individuals who occupy various social strata? We might imagine that neither strangers nor relationship partners are likely to communicate prejudice to the chief executive officer of a major international corporation. Strangers, but not necessarily relationship partners, are likely to communicate prejudice to the waitperson at a small cafe. Finally, both strangers and relationship partners are likely to communicate prejudice to an unemployed street person. Thus, in many respects, frequency of communicating prejudice depends on the target person's status as well as on the social context, and even close relationship partners may inadvertently resort to using verbal and nonverbal cues to distance themselves from those individuals who are stigmatized in one form or another (Frable, 1993; Frable, Blackstone, & Scherbaum, 1990; Gaines & Ickes, 1997; Goffman, 1963).

■ Power Differentials and the Asymmetrical Communication of Prejudice in Personal Relationships

It seems that for every epithet directed by members of an in-group toward members of an out-group, a corresponding epithet is directed by members of the out-group toward members of the in-group. These complementary (as opposed to complimentary) epithets potentially may be used as verbal weapons, as "nouns that cut slices" (Allport, 1954/1979) and that help cement ties among in-group members and foster in-group/out-group bias. However, the epithet hurled by a member of a socially devalued out-group toward a member of a socially valued in-group might not have quite the same impact as does the epithet volleyed by a member of a socially valued in-group toward a member of a socially devalued out-group. Because the power differential inherent in many personal relationships (e.g., male-female, older-younger, White-Black, straight-gay) mirrors inequities within the larger society as well as the sheer frequency with which one hears these terms, perhaps it is not surprising that partners from devalued out-groups may consciously refrain from using an epithet toward partners from valued in-groups; or, even worse, they may internalize the complementary epithet and apply it to other members of the devalued group. (For a discussion of racist language in American discourse, see Asante's chapter in this volume [Chapter 4]).

In the United States (at least since the modern-day civil rights and women's rights eras), much of the institutional support for overt manifestations of power differentials in personal relationships has been dismantled (Spence et al., 1985). The southern double standard, whereby White men could rape Black women with impunity but Black men could be lynched for *allegedly* looking White women in their eyes (Allport, 1954/1979; Hernton, 1965/1988; Penn, Gaines, & Phillips, 1993), has fallen by the wayside in recent years. Marital rape, which formerly was viewed as a contradiction in terms, increasingly has been granted legitimacy as a punishable offense in at least a few states. Nevertheless, many (if not most) of the more covert forms of power differentials in personal relationships have gone unchallenged.

Regarding the communication of prejudice, the fact that Blacks and women are more likely to change their patterns of interaction to suit those of Whites and men than vice versa can be interpreted as a sign of persistent power differentials in personal relationships (Giles & Coupland, 1991; Tannen, 1986, 1990). "Deadbeat dads" still are relatively successful at avoiding their financial commitments (and thus overburdening their estranged or former wives) where children are involved. Feminists have long maintained that the balance of power must shift in the bedroom as well as in the boardroom (French, 1985) for power differentials involving partners from unequal status groups to be eradicated and, hence, for the communication of prejudice in personal relationships to be lessened.

■ Communication Processes Manifested in Relationship Development: A Hypothetical Example

For one person to become attracted to another, according to the relationship development model proposed by Levinger and Snoek (1972), the two individuals must progress from the level of *zero contact* (i.e., complete lack of relatedness between the two persons) to the level of *awareness* (i.e., one person forms positive impressions of the other). No actual interaction is required for the relationship-in-the-making to progress from zero contact to awareness (via a process termed *approach*). However, for the other person to become attracted as well, the two individuals must progress from the level of awareness to the level of *surface contact* (i.e., the two persons form initial attitudes toward each other). Some amount of overt interaction between the two individuals must occur if the relationship is to reach this level (via a process termed *affiliation*). Finally, for the relationship to become personal or close, the two individuals must achieve *mutuality* (i.e., a state in which "each person's actions and attitudes are markedly influenced by the other person's actions, views, and experiences in the relationship" [p. 5]). Except perhaps for cases involving "love at first sight," prolonged interaction between the two individuals must occur if the relationship partners are to reach this stage (via a process termed *attachment*).

A hypothetical example will allow us to illustrate the processes of approach, affiliation, and attachment in the development of personal relationships. Suppose that an academic department at a large state university is under pressure from administrators and students alike to diversify its faculty. Most of the members of the department are middle-aged, White, Anglo-Saxon Protestant men with tenure who, at least on principle, are not opposed to the prospect of hiring a tenure-track faculty member who can claim membership in one or more underrepresented groups. Sensing an opportunity to add a new faculty line (thus easing the problems of overcrowded classrooms that have begun to plague the department), the department chair, who happens to be a 48-year-old White Episcopalian male, seizes the moment and persuades his colleagues and the academic dean to begin a nationwide search for candidates for a tenure-track "diversity" position.

Suppose that the search commences, a short list is constructed, and three candidates are interviewed. One of the candidates, who happens to be a 27-year-old Puerto Rican Catholic female, looks quite good on paper and is established quickly as the department chair's favorite. Up to this point, we have seen the emerging relationship between the candidate (whom we will call Guadalupe) and the department chair (whom we will call Frederick) progress from zero contact to awareness by virtue of Frederick's securing approval to advertise for a national search, receiving Guadalupe's promising vita (along with the vitae of 100 other candidates), and then leaving a message for Guadalupe to set up an interview. Once Frederick calls Guadalupe and leaves a message on her answering machine to call him back, we can assert that Frederick has *approached* Guadalupe.

Suppose that Guadalupe then returns Frederick's call and agrees to be flown in for an interview. When they first meet, Frederick knows much more about Guadalupe than Guadalupe does about Frederick; Guadalupe races through her interview schedule and has a difficult time matching names with faces, let alone forming any definite impressions of Frederick or of the other department members. However, after Guadalupe and two other candidates are interviewed, Frederick successfully lobbies the department and the academic dean to offer the position to Guadalupe. Frederick then calls Guadalupe and offers her the job; a flattered and exuberant Guadalupe accepts the offer. Frederick confides to Guadalupe that she had been his choice from the beginning, and Guadalupe thanks Frederick for his role in ensuring that she would be hired.

At this point, the relationship has progressed from awareness to surface contact by virtue of Guadalupe's agreeing to be interviewed and then being hired by Frederick on behalf of the department. By the end of the phone conversation, Guadalupe feels warmly toward Frederick, and Frederick's initial positive feelings toward Guadalupe are magnified. Therefore, we can now say that *affiliation* has developed between Guadalupe and Frederick.

By the end of her frenzied first semester as a faculty member, Guadalupe (known to her friends as Lupe) is busy trying to finish paperwork and finds that the last page of a survey for new faculty members is missing. Lupe exclaims, *"Ay Carramba!"* (i.e., "Dammit!") and puts her elbows on her desk (and her head in her hands) for a moment. The department chair, Frederick (known to his friends as Rick), walks by Lupe's office, hears her exclamation, and peeks into Lupe's office just as she starts to stare up at the ceiling. Rick playfully responds, *"Que palabras tan malas!"* (i.e., "Such bad words!"), at which point Lupe first looks puzzled but then starts to laugh.[46]

"I didn't know that you spoke Spanish," Lupe says to Rick. Rick then enters Lupe's office and explains matter-of-factly, "I lived in Madrid a long time ago and became a pretty good Spanish speaker." Lupe then glances downward at her work. Noticing how preoccupied Lupe is with her paperwork, Rick says, "You know, sometimes it's just good to get away from that bureaucratic paper-pushing and take a break. I was about to go to the new pub across the street. Would you like to join me?" Lupe first looks startled, then responds, "Sure. I've been curious about that new pub, but I've avoided going there by myself. I'll be right with you."

By now, the relationship between Lupe and Rick has progressed from surface contact to mutuality. Lupe has turned to Rick on many occasions during the semester for advice while making the adjustment from graduate student to faculty member. In turn, Rick has offered advice to Lupe on many occasions without being asked. Now, Rick has affirmed Lupe's use of her native Spanish by attempting to communicate with her in that language; in Giles' (1978) terms, Rick has attempted to achieve *ethnolinguistic convergence* with Lupe in the language in which she is an expert. Consequently, the positive feelings between Lupe and Rick are strengthened further as the two prepare to go out for a drink. Thus, we can now say that *attachment* has developed between Lupe and Rick.

■ An Apparent Paradox: Attraction Over Prejudice in Cross-Group Personal Relationships

The perceptive reader may have noticed the apparent paradox that we have created in the forgoing example. In terms of demographic characteristics, Lupe and Rick hardly could be more different. According to mainstream social-psychological perspectives on *in-group/out-group bias* (i.e., the tendency for individuals to view members of their in-group as more heterogeneous and as having more desirable qualities than they view members of out-groups [Allport, 1954/1979; Duckitt, 1994; Stephan, 1985]), the fact that Lupe and Rick do not share the same ethnicity, gender, age, or religion should provide numerous opportunities for mutual misunderstanding, not mutual liking. According to the layered perspective (Baldwin & Hecht, 1995; see also Hecht & Baldwin's chapter in this volume [Chapter 3]), even if Lupe's membership in various socially disadvantaged groups (e.g., Latinos, women, youths, Catholics) makes her relatively accepting and tolerant of individual and group differences, Rick's membership in various socially advantaged groups (e.g., Anglos, men, middle-aged people, Protestants) should make it difficult (if not impossible) for Rick to avoid displaying sexism, racism, ageism, or religious intolerance toward Lupe.

Here we have an example in which the feelings experienced by Lupe and Rick toward each other are not of the negative variety that we might expect if prejudice were to prevail but rather of the positive variety that we might expect if attraction were to prevail. How would social-psychological theories relevant to intergroup relations account for such a relationship? A personal relationship between two such demographically dissimilar individuals seems to contradict the rules of relationship development posited by *mate selection theory* (Kerckhoff & Davis, 1962), in which individuals are presumed to be outside each other's "field of eligibles" as potential relationship partners unless they share external (i.e., demographic) characteristics and remain unlikely to become relationship partners unless they also share internal (i.e., psychological) characteristics. The relationship between Lupe and Rick also seems to contradict *social identity theory* (Tajfel, 1979), which posits that individuals' self-esteem is bolstered largely by identifying with members of in-groups and derogating members of out-groups. Finally, *contact theory* (Allport, 1954/1979; Johnson & Hendrix, 1985) would predict that because the relationship between Lupe and Rick inherently involves two individuals who have unequal status within the department (i.e., Rick is Lupe's boss), the relationship is destined to be formal rather than informal, distant rather than close.

From the literature on communication and attraction, it is clear that convergence tends to enhance attraction, whereas divergence tends to inhibit attraction (although those intergroup relationships that develop into acquaintanceships are stronger in initial attraction than are intragroup relationships [Gudykunst & Ting-Toomey, 1988]). According to communication accommodation theory (discussed earlier in this chapter), we would expect divergence in communication between two individuals to the extent that (a) the situation in which the individuals find themselves is intergroup, (b) group vitality is strong, and (c) people wish to dissociate from the other group. According to *ethnolinguistic identity theory* (Gudykunst & Ting-Toomey, 1988), we would expect divergence in communication between two individuals to the extent that (a) the individuals see language use as important to group membership, (b) the individuals see boundaries between the groups as hard and closed, and (c) the individuals perceive high group vitality (e.g., via status, numbers, or institutional support). Finally, according to *uncertainty reduction theory* (Berger & Calabrese, 1975), the hypothetical relationship between Lupe and Rick should minimize rather than maximize each individual's probability of predicting each other's behavior and of responding appropriately to each other's behavior. How, then, can we explain the existence of a personal relationship such as that between Lupe and Rick?

■ Resolving the Paradox: Emphasizing Similarities, Deemphasizing Differences

Perhaps one method of resolving the apparent paradox created by the relationship between Lupe and Rick would be to focus on the similarities instead of the differences between them. First, let us reevaluate the social-psychological perspectives on personal relationships. From the standpoint of mate selection theory, this might mean focusing on the similarities in socioeconomic status (an external characteristic) and intellectual development (an internal characteristic) between Lupe and Rick. Assuming that both Lupe and Rick are members of the upper middle class and of the intellectual elite, these similarities might be sufficient to facilitate liking between them (Gordon, 1978). From the standpoint of social identity theory, the fact that both Lupe and Rick are professors (as opposed to, say, undergraduate students) might in itself promote solidarity and liking between them. Finally, from the standpoint of contact theory, the fact that Lupe and Rick are experts in the same academic field might confer a certain degree of equality on the two of them (especially if they specialize in the same research topics).

In terms of theories from the field of communication studies, communication accommodation theory might allow us to understand the relationship between Lupe and Rick if we find that both of them tend to be active in approaching persons from ethnic/racial backgrounds different from their own (or, at the very least, tend not to be active in avoiding persons from ethnic/racial out-groups). Ethnolinguistic identity theory might allow us to comprehend the relationship between Lupe and Rick to the extent that the two of them can converse in both Spanish and English. Finally, uncertainty reduction theory might allow us to fathom the relationship between Lupe and Rick to the extent that they use the jargon of their shared academic subdiscipline in a variety of settings (e.g., office chats, pub conversations, conference paper sessions).

Of course, in attempting to reinterpret the hypothetical relationship between Lupe and Rick according to the aforementioned theoretical perspectives from social psychology and communication studies, we run the risk of making it impossible to disconfirm any of the theories. Our intention is not to create a foolproof theory of relationship development that could "explain" any conceivable personal relationship. Instead, we simply wish to point out that many personal relationships involving persons with seemingly dissimilar demographic characteristics might not be as dissimilar as they appear at first. As clinical studies of intercultural marriages attest, focusing on both their similarities and their differences allows relationship partners to resist the temptation to view each other through stereotyped lenses (Falicov, 1986).

■ Applying the Layered Perspective to the Study of Prejudice as Communicated in Personal Relationships

Throughout this book, the layered perspective (Baldwin & Hecht, 1995; see also Hecht & Baldwin's chapter in this volume [Chapter 3]) has been employed in examining the communication of prejudice in a number of social contexts. We believe that the layered perspective is particularly useful for understanding the potential impact of covert and overt prejudice on intergroup relationship development processes. If at least one potential relationship partner is *intolerant* of persons from one or more out-groups, then the fledgling relationship is unlikely to progress beyond the awareness stage; that is, the approach process may occur, but affiliation is unlikely to occur (Brislin, 1986). If at least one potential relationship partner is *tolerant* (but not appreciative) of intergroup differences, then the fledgling relationship is unlikely to progress beyond the surface contact stage; that is, the affiliation process may occur, but attachment is unlikely to occur. By contrast, if both potential relationship partners are *appreciative* of intergroup differences (or, perhaps, if differences are not perceived as existing in the first place), then the fledgling relationship may well progress to mutuality; that is, attachment is likely to occur (Romano, 1988).

In *The Nature of Prejudice,* Allport (1954/1979) concludes that equal status contact between African Americans and Anglos would be achieved with greatest ease within the realm of employment and with greatest difficulty within the realm of romantic relationships (following Myrdal, 1944). More than 40 years after the publication of Allport's classic, it is evident that equal status between Blacks and Whites en masse still has not occurred, even within the employment sector (National Research Council, 1989). Nevertheless, several studies of the benefits of equal status contact (e.g., Gaertner, Dovidio, Mann, Murrell, & Pomare, 1990; Hallinan & Williams, 1989; Jackman & Crane, 1986; Johnson, Johnson, Tiffany, & Zaidman, 1984; Riordan & Ruggiero, 1980; Schofield, 1979) offer hope for agents of social change. Furthermore, the prospect of genuine appreciation for intergroup differences—an important extension beyond Allport's (1954/1979) tolerant-intolerant dichotomy—suggests that the layered perspective (Baldwin & Hecht, 1995) can aid relationship theorists in challenging social-scientific and lay stereotypes concerning the ostensibly inevitable decline of relationships involving persons who are dissimilar in gender, ethnicity, age, religious orientation, sexual orientation, or socioeconomic class (Ting-Toomey, 1986).

Interestingly, the literature on interethnic/interracial romantic relationships often exaggerates the spectrum of intergroup differences between partners. For example, although interracial relationship partners frequently are presumed to occur across class lines (Rogler, 1989), historically most such relationships actually occur between persons from the same socioeconomic class (Merton, 1973). In addition, although interracial relationship partners often are presumed to embrace dissimilar cultural values (e.g., Maretzki, 1977), a recent study of interethnic/interracial romantic relationships (Gaines et al., 1996) indicates that partners typically share several cultural values (e.g., individualism, collectivism, familism, romanticism). In fact, among both men and women in interethnic/interracial relationships, the degree to which individuals embraced romanticism (i.e., an orientation toward the welfare of one's romantic relationship) was a significant positive predictor of individuals' communication of affection and respect to each other (see also Lampe, 1982; Romano, 1988).

■ Relationship Cultures and the Communication of Prejudice

Taken together, the layered perspective on communicating prejudice (Baldwin & Hecht, 1995) and the model of relationship development (Levinger & Snoek, 1972) suggest that for approach, affiliation, and attachment processes to occur in personal relationships involving persons who are not of the same gender, ethnicity, age, religious orientation, socioeconomic class, or sexual orientation, partners ideally should appreciate intergroup differences. By the same token, partners should be able to appreciate the similarities that may become apparent only after prolonged interaction; for example, during the course of conversation, a Latina might learn that an Anglo male whom she met recently had spent most of his life in a barrio not unlike the one in which she grew up. Finally, at some point during relationship development, partners ideally should progress from viewing each other in terms of role constraints to viewing each other as unique individuals. Wood's (1982) conceptualization of *relational cultures* (also termed *relationship cultures*) may be particularly useful in understanding exactly how partners in personal relationships transcend roles imposed by society:

> Definitive of intimacy is relational culture, a privately transacted system of understandings that coordinate attitudes, actions, and identities of participants in a relationship. . . .
>
> Like any culture, a relational culture consists not of objective things and cognitions, but rather of the interpretive orientation to them. It is the forms and definitions of experience that people have in mind, their models for perceiving and acting, the worldview imagined together which two individuals agree to believe in. The privately transacted definitions and orientations that comprise a relational culture become anchors for individual judgment and activity beyond the bond itself.
>
> Relational culture is fundamentally a product of communication; that is, it arises out of communication, is maintained and altered in communication, and is dissolved in communication. It serves as the nucleus of a relationship by providing to partners a shared universe of discourse and definition in matters deemed important by the partners. (p. 76)

According to Wood (1982), as relationship partners learn more about each other and reveal more about themselves over time, the partners develop a shared history that belongs to the two of them and to no one else. One technique by which relationship partners achieve their shared sense of uniqueness is by the use of relationship-specific language (e.g., terms of endearment). Empirical studies of relationship cultures (e.g., Baxter, 1987; Oring, 1984) indicate that the use of relationship-specific language is common among friendships and among romantic relationships. The construction of relationship cultures may be crucial for the long-term survival of interethnic/interracial romantic relationships, in which partners often must fend off verbal and psychological attacks from strangers, acquaintances, and even friends and family (Fontaine & Dorch, 1980; Porterfield, 1978; Rosenblatt et al., 1995).

Wood's (1982) analysis of relationship cultures helps explain why romanticism was more strongly reflected in individuals' affectionate and respectful behaviors toward their partners in Gaines et al.'s (1996) study of interethnic/interracial dating and marital relationships. Perhaps romanticism is reflected in individuals' relationship-specific language, which in turn serves to communicate affection and respect between the partners (Baxter & Wilmot, 1983; Bell et al., 1987). Furthermore, romanticism may be reflected in individuals' joint creation of a relational identity that transcends other identities (e.g., ethnic, gender). In any event, the concept of relationship cultures also may aid in explaining how relationships that at first are defined primarily by their intergroup nature are *redefined* primarily by their interpersonal nature (Brown, Altman, & Werner, 1992; Montgomery, 1992; Stephen, 1992)—an essential step if attraction, rather than prejudice, is to prevail.

■ (Re)Creating the Paradox: Discredited and Discreditable Identities

As Duck (1994) observes, relationship cultures are important contexts in which individuals can try out possible selves without fear of rejection from partners. However, in some instances, the question is not whether individuals are free to work toward stabilizing their identities but rather whether individuals feel that they are free to reveal potentially stigmatizing aspects of themselves before their partners' eyes. As Goffman (1963) notes, *discreditable* aspects of individuals' identities (e.g., socioeconomic status, sexual orientation) may threaten the nature of the relationships that individuals have painstakingly constructed, especially if those individuals also are marked from the outset by *discredited* characteristics (e.g., gender, ethnicity) (Gardner, 1991).

To make the aforementioned arguments more concrete, let us return to our hypothetical example of Lupe and Rick. So far, we have deliberately left the nature of the relationship between Lupe and Rick rather vague, using the catch-all term *colleague* to describe their relationship (Knapp et al., 1980). In the time since we last saw them, Lupe and Rick have gone to the new campus pub and have had two drinks apiece. Both Lupe and Rick feel comfortable in their interaction. Lupe asks Rick, "When I saw you at school this evening, you said that you had learned Spanish in Madrid. Did you go there as part of a study abroad program, or maybe on a backpack tour of Europe?" Rick grins and responds, "No, nothing as exciting as all that. When I was growing up, my family owned a second home in Madrid, and we used to spend our summers there. The times I spent there were pretty boring, actually. Probably the one good thing about the whole experience was that it gave me the opportunity to learn Castillian Spanish, not the bastardized Spanish that you hear in the New World."

Although Rick does not immediately realize it, he has betrayed his classist leanings to Lupe (see Moon & Rolison's chapter in this volume [Chapter 7]). Rick normally does not have to confront this potentially unsavory aspect of his personality given that virtually everyone in his social circle comes from the same upper middle class stratum. In "polite" (i.e., nonconfrontational) conversation, Rick and his cohorts typically do not even challenge each other when they slip into snobbish patterns of speech or behavior; they are "fair weather liberals" at best and "timid bigots" at worst, in the words of Gudykunst and Kim (1984). However, Lupe is the first member of *su familia* (i.e., both her immediate and extended family) to attend college, let alone graduate school. Despite her current level of relative affluence, Lupe's background is strictly lower working class. Although Lupe does not want to embarrass either Rick or herself, her momentarily stunned expression alerts Rick to his faux pas (Berger, 1986).

At this juncture, both Lupe and Rick must begin to renegotiate their identities. Lupe is rightfully proud of her accomplishments but becomes somewhat defensive at the hint of a put-down just because she did not grow up with a silver spoon in her mouth. Indeed, Lupe probably has grown accustomed to both intentional and unintentional slights and has learned over time that attributing such negative feedback to out-group members' prejudice is quite functional (Crocker, Voelkl, Testa, & Major, 1991). Moreover, the fact that Rick is her boss, rather than her equal in status (Zorn, 1995), may make Lupe hesitant about confronting Rick regarding the connotations of his remark. For his part, Rick wants to see himself as a champion of the oppressed but becomes defensive at the hint that his own snobbery can make him look like a hypocrite. What then follows is one of those interpersonal interludes in which both parties struggle to find a mutually interesting yet nonthreatening topic.

Although he might believe that he is safe in assuming that Lupe is Catholic, Rick is careful not to place further strain on the interaction. Rick therefore jokes, "Okay, so you're Puerto Rican and you speak Spanish. Would I be a totally insensitive clod to ask you if you're Catholic as well?" This line elicits an unrestrained laugh from Lupe, which brings enormous relief to Rick. Lupe says, "Yeah, you guessed right on that one. I'm what they call a cradle Catholic. Or, at least that's what I was raised to be. How about you?" Rick responds, "I'm Episcopalian, but you might have guessed *that* from my occasional upper crust snootiness." Both Lupe and Rick enjoy a good laugh.

Just when all seems to be well, Rick inadvertently puts Lupe on guard again. Ever since Lupe came out to interview several months ago, Rick has wanted to find out whether Lupe was romantically attached. Of course, it would have been illegal for him to have asked during her interview, and even now it really would not be a good idea for him to ask because he is her boss. Nevertheless, Rick is so eager to know whether their relationship might advance further that he says, ever so gingerly, "You mentioned that you didn't want to come here by yourself. Does your husband or boyfriend work odd hours that keep you two from going out for happy hour?" Lupe begins to fidget, thus prompting Rick to add, "I'm sorry, that question was way out of line. You don't have to answer that if you don't want to. Gosh, I'd better get some coffee quick, with twice the sugar and twice the caffeine!"

Lupe looks down at the table and responds, "No, I don't really mind. It's just that I don't have a husband or a boyfriend." Rick then interjects, "Sure. You've been here only a few months, and anyhow, with the long hours that you work at school . . ." Lupe sighs and says, "No, it's not that. I hope I don't get fired or anything for telling you this, but . . . I'm a lesbian. Part of the reason that I say I was *raised* a Catholic is that once the nuns found out during my junior high school days, they almost had me excommunicated. I don't really identify much with the Church anymore. I'm a Catholic in name only." Lupe knows that she is taking a huge chance by self-disclosing such socially discreditable information (see Nakayama's chapter in this volume [Chapter 6]). However, given that she and Rick apparently entered the conversation with dramatically divergent expectations and concerns based in part on their differing group memberships (Hecht, Larkey, & Johnson, 1992), Lupe feels that she has no other choice if their expectations are to converge.

Fortunately for Lupe, Rick is quite supportive. He apologizes and says, "Why don't we start over. My name's Dr. Foot-in-Mouth; what's yours?" The two of them laugh almost uncontrollably, and their budding friendship is strengthened by their mutual disclosures. Notice, however, that it was not the readily identified differences between Lupe and Rick that almost derailed their relationship. From the day they met, Lupe and Rick were aware that they did not belong to the same gender, ethnicity, or age cohort. Even though their different religious orientations were not visibly apparent, it was not hard for Rick to guess that Lupe was Catholic or for Lupe to guess that Rick was Protestant (although not necessarily Episcopalian); simple base rates would have led them to predict as much (Falicov, 1986). Instead, Lupe's discomfort during the interaction stemmed more from her uncertainty—magnified by Rick's initial comments—as to how Rick would react to her membership in two *discreditable* or "invisible" groups (i.e., product of working class, lesbian [see Baldwin's chapter in this volume [Chapter 2]) than from her membership in the *discredited* or visible group of Latinas/Latinos (Goffman, 1963).

■ Taking Stock: Strategies for Establishing, Maintaining, and Repairing Out-Group Relationships

As the preceding example illustrates, even in those out-group relationships marked by genuine attachment and by appreciation of intergroup differences, individuals sometimes behave in a way that partners interpret as communicating prejudice. The influence that we invoked was the *discreditable* status of partners' identities (Goffman, 1963). However, our more general point is that in personal relationships involving persons whose memberships in one or more socially defined groups do not overlap, partners must exercise some degree of vigilance regarding what they say and what they do, lest they run the risk of placing their relationship in jeopardy. We make this point not to provoke discussion over the merits or demerits of "political correctness" (see Baldwin's chapter in this volume [Chapter 2]) but rather to underscore the enormous conscious effort required for relationship partners to avoid taking the stance of outsiders (Gaines & Ickes, 1997) and thus rendering each other less than unique.

It would be interesting if we could follow the fictitious relationship between Rick and Lupe over time and find out how many communication "gaffes" Rick could make before Lupe decides that she simply must confront him, regardless of the fact that Rick conceivably could make or break her career (Zorn, 1995)—or, conversely, how many interactions it would take for Rick to become so adept at "repair" or communication improvement strategies (e.g., corrective maintenance, preventive maintenance) (Dindia, 1994) that such previously uncomfortable interactions begin to recede into memory. We also might consider the extent to which Lupe's ability to take Rick's apparent motives into account helps minimize the conflict between them (Burleson & Samter, 1994) and whether, for some members of socially stigmatized groups, a single negative encounter with a relatively advantaged person such as Rick would be sufficient to render the relationship-in-progress null and void (Andersen, 1993). Finally, it would be intriguing to see whether Rick and Lupe ultimately "incorporate each other into themselves" (Aron & Aron, 1986) such that Rick begins to embrace Lupe's disdain for academic elitism (van Dijk, 1993) while Lupe begins to embrace Rick's passion for making their department the most intellectually and culturally diverse in the nation.

So far, we have depicted relationship conflict between members of mutually exclusive out-groups primarily as resulting from socially advantaged group members' lack of interpersonal skills and as resolved primarily by socially advantaged group members' ability to learn from their negative interactions with socially oppressed group members. But to what extent does this particular pattern of communication breakdown and repair characterize real-life relationships involving members from different social backgrounds? In the following section, we examine the onset and resolution of conflict in a sampled conversation involving two upper middle class male intellectuals who are members of ethnic minorities—one who belongs to a group stigmatized on the basis of race (Cornel West) and one who belongs to a group stigmatized on the basis of religion (Michael Lerner).

■ A Real-Life Example: Cornel West, Michael Lerner, and the Communication of Prejudice in Black-Jewish Friendships

Much of the intellectual discourse regarding conflict and cooperation between African Americans and Jewish persons casts Black-Jewish relations as analogous to family squabbles (Berman, 1994). If one assumes that the family squabbles in mind are among siblings (i.e., brothers and sisters), then it follows that Black-Jewish relations would be perceived as relatively egalitarian in nature. However, if the family squabbles in mind are between parents and offspring, then Black-Jewish relations no longer would appear to be egalitarian but rather would represent static, unyielding power differentials (possibly with the Jewish person cast as parent and the Black person cast as child).

Therefore, likening Black-Jewish relations to family squabbles might emphasize the degree to which intergroup behavior ultimately is manifested in interpersonal behavior but does not guarantee that interactions between members of the two groups will be characterized by mutual affection or respect (Foa & Foa, 1974).

By the same token, one might wonder why intellectual discourse on Black-Jewish relations consistently invokes the analogy of family relations but so seldom uses ongoing personal relationships as the contexts within which they explicitly or implicitly communicate prejudice to each other. An intriguing exception is *Jews and Blacks: Let the Healing Begin* (Lerner & West, 1995). In that book, Lerner and West not only attempt to represent their own respective constituencies but also consider the ways in which disagreements, agreements, and compromises regarding particular attitudes affect their own friendship. Thus, the relationship between Lerner and West no longer is *analogous to* but rather is *illustrative of* the more abstract construct of intergroup relations.

Even though Lerner and West (1995) both are regarded as progressive intellectuals, their views sometimes clash tremendously. For example, on the issue of affirmative action, Lerner favors payment of reparations to African Americans (having been enslaved for centuries) rather than continuing to promote affirmative action. By contrast, West favors uprooting abuses of existing affirmative action programs but not doing away entirely with such programs. In another example, Lerner asks why Blacks as a group are not more thankful toward Jewish persons for having joined their struggle, whereas West asks why Jewish persons as a group are not more willing to admit that they benefit disproportionately from the current social structure. Despite their differences of opinion, Lerner and West display a remarkable tenacity for maintaining mutually high levels of affection and respect for each other, even as they disagree on issues such as the potential impact of Louis Farrakhan on the future of Black-Jewish relations:

> [West:] You'll have to show how Farrakhan, whose fundamental commitment is against White supremacy, is going to join forces with White fascists whose fundamental commitment is the promotion of White supremacy.
>
> [Lerner:] A central part of Farrakhan's current policies are based on the notion that Blacks should build up their own capitalist institutions. He might be able to work out a deal with some section of the American ruling elite that says, "You join us in suppressing freedom of speech, and we'll give you a cut to the Black capitalist institutions that you support, that you've been saying are the key to success for the Black world."
>
> [West:] White fascists who are dedicated to White supremacy will give the money to Farrakhan?
>
> [Lerner:] Because he's not challenging White supremacy. That's the point.
>
> [West:] You see, that's where we disagree. We're not talking about challenges, we're talking about what his fundamental commitment is.
>
> [Lerner:] I detect in much of your reaction to our fear of anti-Semitism a tone that suggests that Jews are overreacting. I think it is sometimes hard for Black progressives to take Jewish fears of Black anti-Semitism seriously. So let me

paint another picture of how the impact of Black anti-Semitism might spread, a picture suggested by my son Akiba.

[West:] Akiba, he's a good brother, and he's sharp. How is he doing?

[Lerner:] He's wonderful. He still talks about how wonderful it was to be with you a year and a half ago when you spent a week living with us in our house in Berkeley while we were working on the first draft of this dialogue, and how much he enjoyed the discussions with you about Jewish history and Black history. After graduating from college, he has made *aliyah* and is now living in Israel.

Akiba told me the following: One of the things that is going on in White culture, given the absence of any White protest organization, any major forum for expression for White alienation, is that White kids in high school are more and more listening to rap music, including music with anti-Semitic themes. Just as in the late fifties it was Black music that entered the White mainstream and created a space for a certain amount of rebellion, that same phenomenon is happening today. White youth today are the major consumers of rap. (pp. 206-207)

Notice that, just as their conversation seems to have stalled amid different subjective interpretations of the same objective reality (i.e., whether Farrakhan is anti-Semitic), Lerner's initial remark about his son Akiba prompts West to ask for more information about Akiba's current living situation. This line of conversation subsequently leads Lerner to elaborate on his son and also to defuse what had begun to resemble a rhetorical free-for-all.

At least over the short term, the preceding example of conflict resolution may be viewed as functional in the sense that it allows Lerner and West to continue to communicate in spite of their differences of opinion. However, over the long term, repeated use of this "changing the subject" strategy might be *dysfunctional* if it exacerbates simmering, unresolved tensions between the relationship partners in question (Hecht, 1984). As intellectuals, Lerner and West might believe that no matter how strongly they disagree, they must avoid "losing their cool" while engaged in a task-oriented, rational, and ostensibly noncompetitive conversation (Roloff & Cloven, 1994). But if keeping their cool means failing to gain closure on any particular subject, the two intellectuals may wind up overestimating their degree of convergence or divergence on that and related subjects. Such failures to understand each other's perspective could result in strained future interactions and, eventually, relational damage that cannot be repaired in spite of both partners' desire to maintain their relationship (Dindia, 1994).

From the preceding passage, one might construe the relationship between Lerner and West (1995) as one in which Lerner is trying to identify those African Americans who do or do not merit legitimization by the African American community. To the extent that West views Lerner as adopting the stance of the superior White male (see Asante's chapter in this volume [Chapter 4]), West might conclude that Lerner's dislike for Farrakhan is at least partially motivated by Lerner's own subtly communicated racism. Alternatively, one might construe the relationship between Lerner and West as one in which West is trying to identify those public figures who are or are not in a position to impose anti-Semitic prejudice and discrimination on Jewish persons in the United States and abroad. To the extent that Lerner views West as adopting the stance of the superior Protestant (Allport, 1954/1979), Lerner might conclude that West's defense of Farrakhan is at least partially motivated by West's own subtly communicated religious intolerance. Finally, one might construe the interaction as typical of equal status persons (Allport, 1954/1979), both of whom abhor anti-Semitic language in Farrakhan's speeches but simply disagree as to other aspects of Farrakhan's impact on interethnic relations between African Americans and Jewish persons.

All in all, the dialogue established between Lerner and West (1995) arose out of a shared hope that they not only were willing to try and fill a noticeable void in contemporary Black-Jewish discourse but also were willing to put their own developing relationship on display as a possible model for other African Americans and Jewish persons who might wish to cross the "color line" (DuBois, 1903/1969)—as well as religious lines—and develop friendships but are reluctant to do so. Viewed in this context, Lerner and West may have unwittingly communicated prejudice to each other during the course of their dialogue, or at least interpreted each other's comments as communicating prejudice, but they also may have made one of the most sincere intellectual efforts to transcend their (and our) own cultural and ethnic boundaries since novelist James Baldwin and anthropologist Margaret Mead published *A Rap on Race* more than a quarter century ago (Baldwin & Mead, 1971).

■ Directions for Future Research

As we have seen, the communication of prejudice in personal relationships represents an intriguing line of inquiry that draws on the layered perspective of cultural (in)tolerance(s) developed by Baldwin and Hecht (1995). We have examined an array of spheres of communication of prejudice (i.e., sexism, racism, heterosexism, classism, ageism, and religious dogmatism) informed by one level of analysis (i.e., the relationship level) and bridged existing gaps between other levels of analysis (e.g., individual, societal). By no means, however, have we exhausted the possibilities regarding the ways in which prejudice is communicated in personal relationships.

One promising area of research is that of cultural value orientations and cultural hegemony (e.g., Ramirez, 1983; Spence & Helmreich, 1978; White & Parham, 1990). To the extent that the "we values" held by various socially disadvantaged groups (e.g., women, persons of color, gays and lesbians, young and old people, poor and working class persons, Catholics and Jewish persons) are implicitly or explicitly adopted by relationship partners who come from more socially advantaged backgrounds (e.g., men, Anglos, heterosexuals, baby boomers, middle and upper class persons, Protestants), the communication of prejudice is likely to decrease. However, to the extent that the "me values" held by socially advantaged persons are allowed to hold sway against the we values held by socially disadvantaged persons, the communication of prejudice—primarily by the higher status person toward the lower status person—is likely to remain constant or even accelerate.

Another possible area of inquiry regarding the communication of prejudice in personal relationships has enjoyed a long tradition within personality and social psychology. Individual differences in authoritarianism, which has been associated with multiple spheres of (in)tolerance(s) (Allport, 1954/1979; Baldwin & Hecht, 1995; see also Hecht & Baldwin's chapter in this volume [Chapter 3]; Christie, 1991; Snyder & Ickes, 1985), seldom have been used in predicting verbal or nonverbal communication specifically at the relationship level of analysis. Even though the sociopolitical climate has changed dramatically since the original World War II era research on authoritarianism was conducted, perhaps the trait of authoritarianism will allow researchers to explain variance in the communication of prejudice in personal relationships beyond that explained by the demographic variables that have been the primary focus of the present chapter.

Yet another interesting line of inquiry would be the communication of prejudice in out-group relationships that are both physically and socioemotionally intimate. Both the hypothetical and real-life examples that we provided in this chapter have covered the relatively safe terrain of friendship. Within popular culture, however, it is clear that interethnic romance, *not* interethnic friendship, represents the biggest out-group taboo (Gaines & Ickes, 1997). How do partners in interethnic romantic relationships resolve conflict? How are "love ways" (Marston & Hecht, 1994) communicated, especially when prejudice is communicated simultaneously, in these relationships? Communication patterns among interethnic couples often are depicted as inherently dysfunctional (for exceptions, see Porterfield, 1978; Rosenblatt et al., 1995). More examples of actual conversations among interethnic couples are needed.

Finally, prejudice is not communicated solely in out-group relationships. Even in in-group relationships between members of the same ostracized group (e.g., elderly persons, persons with lower socioeconomic status), partners may invoke negative societal stereotypes when communicating with each other, particularly when the partners are angry at each other. For example, an 82-year-old husband might refer spitefully to his 80-year-old wife as an "old battle-ax", or a woman on welfare might criticize her unemployed live-in boyfriend as a "no-count, shiftless bum." Such speech acts may signify self-hatred (Allport, 1954/1979) and deserve increased attention from personal relationship scholars.

■ Conclusion

Throughout this chapter, we have seen that the relationship level of analyses (Baldwin & Hecht, 1995; see also Hecht & Baldwin's chapter in this volume [Chapter 3]) offers unique insights into the contexts in which individuals may communicate prejudice. We touched on several spheres of prejudice such as sexism (see Rakow & Wackwitz's chapter in this volume [Chapter 5]), racism (see Asante's chapter in this volume [Chapter 4]), heterosexism (see Nakayama's chapter in this volume [Chapter 6]), and classism (see Moon & Rolison's chapter in this volume [Chapter 7]). Obviously, an exhaustive treatment of communicating prejudice on personal relationships could occupy an entire volume. Our goal in this chapter was more modest—specifically, to illustrate some of the ways in which communication processes involving persons from different social backgrounds may reflect one or more of the spheres of prejudice, often concurrently.

Although we focused on linguistic convergence as an overt example of appreciation/tolerance in personal relationships involving partners from different socially defined groups, communication theorists and researchers also might find it useful to consider *paralinguistic* forms of convergence in relationship partners' behavior (Gallois et al., 1988). For example, a gay Black male who absorbs Black feminist literature so thoroughly that he can recite entire passages from the works of Zora Neale Hurston or Audre Lorde with the greatest of ease still may incur the wrath of even his closest Black lesbian friend if he tells her, "I know just where you're coming from," in a condescending tone of voice. Understandably, the Black lesbian friend might respond, "No, you *don't* know just where I'm coming from! You've been privileged by your maleness all your life. How can you presume to know all of the ways that I have been treated as less than human?" In such an example, the gay Black male's recital of Black feminist literature might be interpreted not as linguistic accommodation but rather as paralinguistic *over*accommodation. If two friends or two lovers are from different groups, then it might be difficult for them to convey their appreciation for each other successfully unless both the tone and the content of their speech acts express socioemotional acceptance (Foa & Foa, 1974).

In conclusion, we wish to stress that research on personal relationships in general has been limited primarily to individual-level, rather than relationship-level, data (Berscheid, 1986). Given that theories specifically regarding relationship development have not been tested adequately among dyads or couples, it is not surprising that theories of the communication of prejudice similarly have not received their due in research on personal relationships. We hope that this chapter will encourage enterprising researchers to examine the relationship level of analysis as a largely unexplored terrain for understanding processes of communicating prejudice within interpersonal or social contexts.

■ Acknowledgments

The authors are indebted to Michael Hecht and Norma Rodriguez for their constructive comments on earlier versions of this chapter. This chapter was completed while the first author was a visiting scholar at the University of North Carolina at Chapel Hill, supported by a postdoctoral fellowship from the Ford Foundation and by institutional funds from Pomona College.

10 Communicating Prejudice in Organizations

Sheryl L. Lindsley

> If we are to achieve a richer culture, rich in contrasting values, we must recognize the whole gamut of human potentialities, and so weave a less arbitrary social fabric, one in which each diverse human gift will find a fitting place. (Mead, 1935, p. 322)

Americans face major challenges in recognizing "the whole gamut of human potentialities" because cultural diversity, rather than similarity, is a predominant characteristic of many organizations today. Currently, more than half of the workforce in the United States is composed of women, minorities, or recent immigrants (Kavanagh & Kennedy, 1992). These groups are expected to compose the majority of the net new entrants into the U.S. workforce in the near future. By the year 2000, it is estimated that only 15% of the new hires in the U.S. workforce will be European American males (Johnston & Packer, 1987). Other demographic trends relating to birthrates affect diversity in the workforce as well. Importantly, the estimated 76 million "baby boomers" (born between 1946 and 1964) are hitting their fifth decade now (Solomon, 1995). Based on these figures, projections show that within 20 years more than a third of all workers will be 50 years of age or older (Thornburg, 1995). In this rapidly changing environment, intergroup (in)tolerance influences both worker satisfaction and productivity.

The concept of "tolerance" is problematized in organizations by difficulties in achieving intergroup understandings, remedying historical inequalities, and alleviating discrimination. Although people of every cultural background have contributed to the economic prosperity of the United States, our historical foundations reflect inequality among people of different sexes, races, ethnicities, ages, and sexual orientations.

Although scholars assert that most Westerners embrace the ideal of equality, their behaviors are not always reflective of these cherished values (e.g., Ponterotto & Pedersen, 1993; van Dijk, 1990). Both economic statistics (e.g., U.S. Bureau of the Census, 1994) and social science research reflect continued disparities in income, status, and treatment among diverse groups (e.g., Albeda, 1986; King, 1992). The outcomes of intergroup prejudice are argued to affect both the victims and victimizers (those who oppress out-group members) negatively (Bowser & Hunt, 1981). In organizations, manifestations of prejudice negatively affect intergroup processes and goal outcomes, resulting in higher turnover, lawsuits, conflict, and poor performance (Fernandez, 1974, 1981; Kanter, 1977; Pettigrew & Martin, 1987).

On the other hand, organizational programs supporting equality across pluralistic groups have been found to result in substantial rewards including expanded employee potential (Simonsen & Wells, 1994); enhanced intergroup processes and public relations as well as decreased complaints, turnover, and lawsuits (McEnrue, 1993; Roberts, 1994; Rynes & Rosen, 1994); improved product and service quality (Anfuso, 1995; Filipczak, 1992; Jones, 1983; McEnrue, 1993); and, ultimately, higher bottom-line productivity (McEnrue, 1993; Roberts, 1994). Thus, in creating an equal opportunity climate, not only are people empowered to maximize their personal potential, but organizations may capitalize on the richness of diverse human experiences (e.g., Griesemer, 1980). In reviewing the negative effects of prejudice and the positive benefits of supporting diversity, one must wonder why good people who appreciate the ideal of equality often are caught in murky debates about what types of policies and procedures should be developed to guide organizational interaction. Intergroup relationships today are permeated with antagonistic debates revolving around equal employment opportunity (EEO) laws and affirmative action programs (AAPs) (Katz & Proshansky, 1987; Kluegel & Smith, 1983).

The enormous complexity of problems revolving around the enactment of "prejudice" in organizational settings must be viewed through a holistic lens. In this chapter, problems are described through layers that reflect the historical, mass-mediated, and behavioral underpinnings of discrimination. Hecht and Baldwin's layered perspective (Chapter 3 in this volume) is used as a descriptive framework in examining how each of these analytical layers interpenetrate and mutually influence one another. Prejudice, or degrees of (in)tolerance, may influence many types of organizational-intergroup relationships, for example, between union and nonunion members, administrative and service personnel, and managers and workers. However, the predominant focus of this chapter is on the spheres of intergroup relations between members of differing gender, racial, ethnic, age, and sexual orientation groups. In examining the interpenetrated layers of issues that influence intergroup relations, a clearer path for enhancing positive organizational-intergroup relationships is illuminated.

■ Historical Economic Trends

Theory suggests that knowledge of historical-economic contexts increases our understanding of intergroup prejudices (Allport, 1954/1979). In addition, conditions of real or perceived conflicting goals or competition between groups have been shown to increase intergroup hostilities (Rabbie & Horwitz, 1969; Tzeng & Jackson, 1994) and negative outgroup stereotyping (Sherif, 1979). Therefore, this discussion highlights economic trends over the past three decades and links these to the increasing intergroup conflicts surrounding EEO laws, AAPs, and other workplace diversity issues. It is important to understand, first, the role and function of EEO programs; second, the economic progress under these programs; and third, the significant national economic trends that have escalated intergroup tensions.

■ Roles and Functions of Equal Employment Opportunity Programs

The Equal Employment Opportunity Commission (EEOC) was created by Title VII of the Civil Rights Act of 1964. This legislation emerged in response to social movements during the 1950s and 1960s that brought about public support for basic human rights issues. The EEOC's current responsibilities include eliminating "discrimination based on race, color, religion, sex, national origin, disability, or age in hiring, promoting, firing, setting wages, testing, training, apprenticeships, and all other conditions of employment" (U.S. Bureau of the Census, 1994, p. 556). Executive Order 11375 in 1968 by President Johnson set goals and timetables for federal contractors to establish AAPs to increase the representation in education and in the workplace of available and qualified women, minorities, and other historically marginalized groups (Public Agenda Foundation, 1990, p. 23).

Current debate over EEO laws and AAPs is centered within claims of ongoing discrimination by members of EEO-designated groups as well as discrimination by nondesignated groups (Kenworthy & Edsall, 1991; Martin, 1994; Sherman, Smith, & Sherman, 1983). Those who feel programs such as affirmative action also result in discrimination based on group identity would argue that any form of discrimination is wrong; if it is wrong to discriminate against women and people of color, then it also is wrong to discriminate against European American males. In addition, they would argue that two wrongs do not make a right. Opponents to affirmative action often perceive programs as substituting group-based criteria (e.g., gender, race) for merit-based criteria (e.g., education, experience) (Loden & Rosener, 1991). This is seen as undermining meritocracy values, whereby those individuals who have the best credentials receive the best opportunities based on individual merit. This leads to an additional problem when women and minorities working in companies with active AAPs are suspected of being hired for reasons other than their qualifications and are, therefore, viewed as incompetent. Current political trends to either eliminate or modify EEO laws and AAPs often are based on assumptions that we have remedied past inequalities and no longer need government policies to eliminate group-based discrimination in organizational settings (Kluegel, 1985; Pech, 1995).

Over the past few decades, lawsuits have challenged the application of these laws (Foner & Garranty, 1991). In the first landmark case dealing with affirmative action, *Bakke v. University of California* (1978), the use of rigid quotas was struck down as unconstitutional, but the use of race was supported as meriting "some attention" in considering university admissions criteria. In other words, race alone could not be a determining factor in admissions but could be taken into consideration along with other merit criteria (Foner & Garranty, 1991). In a more recent decision, the U.S. Supreme Court let stand a federal appeals court ruling that struck down the University of Texas law school's 1992 AAP to raise enrollment figures of African Americans and Mexican Americans (Freedman, 1996). The federal appeals court in this case had decided that the "law school has presented no compelling justification" to allow it to use "substantial racial preferences in its admissions program" ("Text of Appeals Court's Opinion," 1996, p. A28). However, at this time, the U.S. Supreme Court did not overturn the *Bakke* decision. Thus, affirmative action mandates have been challenged by difficulties in establishing clear and constitutionally supported policies. The thrust of this program and subsequent court rulings, however, allows preferential consideration for members of historically marginalized groups, but only for those who are *qualified*. Thus, there is no burden for organizations to hire unqualified applicants, but debate often is stimulated around organizational policies that reinforce preferential treatment, applying differing standards for EEO-designated groups than for non-EEO-protected groups.

■ Economic Progress Under Equal Employment Opportunity

The Johnson administration passed these bills to ensure that the guarantees of civil rights legislation would be matched by results. Therefore, it is essential to examine the types of results that have been achieved over the past three decades. Trends in decreasing ethnic/racial and gender inequality show some progress, although they do not reflect a steady improvement. Carlson's (1992) longitudinal analysis of "occupational inequality" found that the most significant declines in both gender and racial inequalities occurred during the period 1960 to 1980, the two decades in which the EEO laws were most actively reinforced (Smith & Welch, 1984). However, Carlson's (1992) analysis shows that these trends toward improvement significantly declined during the 1980s when the Reagan administration decreased funding for EEOC enforcement of antidiscrimination policies. In fact, by 1987, a U.S. General Accounting Office (1988) audit of the performance of EEOC district offices found that "many were closing 40% to 80% of their cases without proper, if any, investigation" (p. 58). Therefore, the figures reflect that EEO was most effective when there was strong federal government economic support and reinforcement for policies. Trends in decreasing inequality faltered when this backing declined.

Highlights of key economic indicators and research on opportunity, stability, job segregation, income, and status levels illuminate the types of changes that have and have not occurred. Research reflects that women have increased both job opportunities

TABLE 10.1   Mean Annual Income, by Highest Degree Earned: 1990

	High School Graduate	Bachelor's Degree	Master's Degree	Professional Occupation
Sex				
Males	22,236	38,820	44,976	76,404
Females	11,316	20,376	31,368	36,840
Race[a]				
White	16,860	30,624	38,976	67,332
Black	12,108	24,024	33,432	n/a
Hispanic[b]	13,104	22,740	34,080	n/a

SOURCE: U.S. Bureau of the Census.
a. Other racial groups are not included in this report.
b. Hispanics may be of any race and therefore are listed separately.

and "stability" in terms of more days worked per year (Uri & Mixon, 1991). However, gender segregation by job type has not been significantly affected (Albeda, 1986; King, 1992; Sokoloff, 1988). According to government figures, at every level of education, males continue to earn higher salaries than do females, and European Americans earn more than do other ethnic/racial groups (see Table 10.1). In addition, controlling for education levels, statistics reflect the negative components of "double discrimination" with economic well-being for women of color adversely affected by both race and gender prejudices in the workplace. Among single female heads of families, reported average earnings for 1993 were $21,580 for European American women, $18,356 for Hispanic women, and $17,368 for African American women (U.S. Bureau of the Census, 1994). Although some could argue that perhaps inequality relates to differing qualifications, this argument is not supported by research. For example, studies comparing the earnings of male and female MBAs find that after controlling for seniority, industry, job performance, and other factors, females still earned less than their male counterparts (Cox & Harquail, 1991; Olson & Frieze, 1987). This research clearly demonstrates that although advances have been made in terms of opportunities, no parity has been achieved among gender, ethnic, and racial groups in terms of economic well-being.

In addition to comparative income statistics, other research highlights workplace inequalities. Males, as a group, enjoy both greater access to opportunities and higher status within corporations than do females (King, 1992). In addition, European American males occupy 91.7% of top management and 88.1% of director positions in organizations (Galen, 1994). Even in "pink-collar" professions (e.g., librarianship, nursing, elementary school teaching, social work), managers and administrators are predominantly male (Williams, 1992). The higher status of European American males in organizational structures has been linked to both "glass walls" and "glass ceilings" that often form barriers to women's and ethnic minorities' status advancement in corporations (Freeman, 1990; U.S. Congress, 1991). These metaphors are used to refer to "invisible barriers" that keep individuals from equal opportunity. Glass walls occur when individuals are positioned in segregated jobs, and glass ceilings exist when individuals are placed in jobs that have limited opportunity for vertical mobility (U.S. Congress, 1991). For example, women who are relegated to jobs that require traditionally feminine skills (e.g., clerical roles, counseling, human relations) are in positions that do not typically include a career ladder in which doing well at this level allows advancement to another ("Study Says," 1992, p. B2; see also Holton's chapter in this volume [Chapter 16]). In addition, prejudice results in other types of role constraints for non-White ethnics. For instance, in the journalism industry, studies of African American and Latino/Latina American news reporters find that these reporters often are pigeonholed into reporting on only ethnic/racial community events (Shafer, 1993; Sunoo, 1994). In each of these examples, both sex and race prejudices result in placement of individuals in jobs that include a narrow range of role responsibilities, precluding individuals from demonstrating their full potentialities and moving up in an organization. Therefore, the impact of government legislation has resulted in increased integration of the workplace, although opportunities often are limited. In light of the lack of parity in job types, income, and organizational status, these reports indicate that additional actions are required to break down barriers to equality.

■ Economic Trends Escalating Intergroup Tensions

Over the past three decades in which women and ethnic/racial minority groups have experienced both increased opportunities and barriers to advancement, simultaneous upheavals in the national economy have occurred. These trends significantly affect the majority of our national workforce, with heightened competition for fewer jobs influencing intergroup tensions. These changes include growth in the potential workforce accompanied by the movement of U.S. manufacturing plants to foreign countries (Wilson, 1992), post-cold war defense system and military layoffs, and corporate downsizing. During the 1980s, the potential workforce grew by 19.4 million, while the number of manufacturing jobs shrank by 1.8 million (Bartlett & Steele, 1992). In addition, thousands of jobs in the aerospace and defense industry were eliminated including 2,500 at TRW Inc. and 5,000 at Allied Signal Inc. Finally, recent corporate downsizing in the private sector includes 20,000 layoffs at International Business Machines Corporation (IBM), 8,000 layoffs at GTE Corporation, and 4,000 layoffs at Westinghouse Electric (Bartlett & Steele, 1992). Downsizing continued in 1993, as illustrated by the substantial reduction in labor forces of more than 16 large multinational corporations ("Few Jobs," 1995). These patterns negatively affect job opportunities for blue- and white-collar workers, middle level managers, and professionals.

Although members of many groups are affected by the changes in our society, there is evidence that some groups are more negatively affected than are others. The phenomenon of corporate downsizing has been linked to a dramatic increase in the number of age bias claims filed over the past few years. In 1992 alone, there were 19,264 age bias complaints filed with the EEOC, representing 27% of total EEO claims (EEOC, 1994). As corporations seek to shrink their overhead, the older employees who have the most experience often are the highest paid and are reported to be among the most vulnerable targets (Wilcox, 1992). In addition, stereotypes about older workers (e.g., they have a lower capacity to learn new methods and jobs than do younger workers; see also Williams & Giles' chapter in this volume [Chapter 8]) may affect their perceived expendability, even though these beliefs are inaccurate. For most people, learning abilities do not diminish until 70 years of age (Kauffman, 1987). Thus, age affects the relative impact of economic changes among American workers. In addition, race remains a substantive issue that affects differential group experiences. For example, whereas the 1990 unemployment rate for European Americans was 6%, it was more than double (12.9%) for African Americans (U.S. Bureau of the Census, 1994). These findings indicate that there are significant issues that must be addressed in striving for inclusiveness and prosperity in both public and private organizations. It is evident that patterns of experiences are differentiated along group identity lines. One way of understanding their persistence is to examine social identity theory.

■ Interpretation of Intergroup Relationships

Tajfel's (1978b, 1981a, 1982) and Turner's (1987) research on social identity theory establishes the human tendency to label and contrast self and others in terms of individual and social identities. These tendencies also form the basis for interpreting and evaluating human behaviors on either individual- or group-based norms. In this changing economic climate, characterized by an increasing influx of women and non-White ethnics into the labor force as well as by decreasing opportunities, individuals' interpretations and evaluations of these issues are influenced by social categorization. Do individuals identify with a common label (e.g., it is an issue of Americans faced with economic challenges)? Do individuals identify with organizational status groups (e.g., it is an issue of conflicting needs of management and workers)? Do individuals identify with diverse gender, ethnic, racial, and age groups and see out-group members as barriers to satisfying outcomes (e.g., it is a problem of men competing with women, European Americans competing with non-White ethnics, youths competing with older workers)? Each of these different ways of interpreting workplace issues affects ways of addressing solutions. However, it also is apparent that this economic environment has resulted in increased intergroup disparities and divisiveness. It is in these types of contexts that intergroup hostilities are accelerated when group members scapegoat other groups for shrinking opportunities (Allport, 1954/1979) rather than striving to cooperate in achieving mutually beneficial outcomes. A closer examination of the way in which historical economic trends over the past three decades affect intergroup relationships may be related to mass-mediated constructions of these issues.

■ Mass-Mediated Construction of Images

Within an environment characterized by changing economic conditions, it is critical to understand the role of mass media news coverage to "mold popular perceptions by transforming and shaping the meanings of social phenomena and thus construct social reality" (Fernandez & Pedroza, 1981, p. 6). Public opinion and issue saliency regarding a particular news item often are shaped by the amount and type of coverage it receives (Behr & Iyengar, 1985). I highlight the ways in which mass media construe intergroup work relationships through (a) metaphorically constructing workplace integration as "war," (b) trivializing social movements and tolerance, and (c) stigmatizing historically disenfranchised groups. Mass-mediated constructions influence organizational policies and procedures, interpersonal relationships within the organizations, and intergroup interaction.

■ Workplace Integration as "War"

Analysis of news coverage of national social issues has found that media often generalize group characteristics, emphasize differences between groups, and concentrate on conflict (Gans, 1980). Both the civil rights and women's movements have been brought into the homes of millions of Americans through a lens focused on conflicts between militants and moderates (Gans, 1980). Although Gans's (1980) research findings center around news stories during the 1960s and 1970s, current media coverage reflects a similar conflict focus, and the conceptual implications are relevant to interpreting media constructions of reality today. In shaping stories around "the races" and "the sexes" and giving voice to spokespersons who represent bipolar positions, entertaining "stories" are created. Ignored are the visions articulated by moderates within and between groups. In addition, coverage often is superficial, minimizing holistic coverage of economic trends and neglecting commonalties between members of diverse groups as well as positive outcomes manifested in inclusive organizational policies.

Intergroup divisiveness may be exacerbated by news coverage relating to EEO and AAP issues, framing integration, equality, and pluralism as threatening to the social order. Threats are enhanced by mass-mediated communication that frames intergroup work relations through images of war. Negative images are encapsulated in news headlines such as the following:

- "Does Affirmative Action Mean, 'No White Men Need Apply'? The Battle Over Race and Gender Preferences" (1995)
- "De-escalating the Gender War" (Leo, 1994, p. 24)
- "'White, Male, and Worried': White men still dominate corporate America. But in companies with aggressive diversity programs, they are beginning to feel angry and resentful. What should companies do?" (Galen, 1994, p. 50)
- "Tonight the Battle of the Sexes declares a new war zone in: The Gender Wars" (1994)

The war-and-conflict imagery is obvious in the headlines. Even Faludi's (1991) review of gender inequality in the United States relies on fear appeals generated through militaristic rhetoric: "Backlash: The Undeclared War Against American Women." Through focusing on and exaggerating intergroup differences, groups are construed as diametrically opposed to one another. Media constructions of workplace integration through images of war reinforce fears in all groups and often highlight European American males as "losing ground" in this metaphorical battle.

By drawing out and focusing attention on gender and racial "wars," media images reinforce the belief that European American males' economic hardships result from workplace integration. An emphasis on intergroup conflicts diverts attention from ecological consideration of economic trends that are the effects of offshore movement of industries, shrinking military expenditures, and corporate downsizing. Thus, a focus on in-group/out-group differentiation between the sexes and races misrepresents economic issues that have negatively affected all groups due to corporate goals for enhancing efficiency and increasing profitability. In addition, coverage of discrimination against European American males that generalizes and exaggerates race and sex differences suggests to audiences that only historically disenfranchised groups are beneficiaries of EEO policies. This ignores the fact that 27% of EEO complaints currently are based on age discrimination that includes European American males. Instead of framing workplace trends within a holistic view that considers multiple factors affecting workplace issues, news analysis exacerbates intergroup tensions through reductionistic analyses of processes and outcomes from EEO laws and AAPs.

In a pluralistic society in which multiple interdependencies inextricably bind us to one another, envisioning equality as disruptive to the social order is neither morally nor practically sound. Reductionistic mass-mediated constructions in which groups are pitted against one another deflect attention from holistic consideration of economic trends as well as the needs of diverse groups. Our common concerns, as well as those unique to diverse groups, will be best addressed by capitalizing on the creativity and richness of human resources available in pluralistic organizations.

■ Trivializing Social Movements and Tolerance

In the mass-mediated construction of the 1960s feminist movements and 1980s-1990s "politically correct" tolerance issues, images trivialize the actual experiences of inequality by drawing attention to the "sign" and neglecting what the sign "signifies." For example, early media coverage of feminist activities were couched in ostracism and ridicule, bringing to center stage images of "bra burners" (Tuchman, 1978). Attention to the image of bra burning negated the importance of what bra burning signified: What was the meaning of this act? In actuality, very few women were burning bras; however, media trivialization and exaggeration of the importance of the sign deflected from consideration women's experiences of restricted roles and opportunities.

Similarly, over the past two decades, there has been increasing media devotion to attacking political correctness while simultaneously minimizing people's actual experiences of intolerance (Calabrese & Lenart, 1992; Tuchman, 1978). When media attack politically correct (PC) language (e.g., chairpeople, congresspersons, ombudspersons), they "make a story" by extending the implications of tolerance to the level of the absurd. After all, there is not much of a story in a simple act of civility (e.g., using the term *congressperson*). Entertainment demands conflict between oppositional forces. Thus, the concepts of "tolerance" and "appreciation" are perverted by the media through humorous characterizations of those who need glasses as "optically impaired," short people as "vertically impaired," senior citizens as "chronologically advanced," and those who commit civil atrocities as "kindness impaired" (e.g., Garner, 1994). Media coverage confuses the sign with what it signifies, effectively diffusing the importance of the latter. Calabrese and Lenart's (1992) review of media coverage of "P.C." suggests that the "term should be buried, as it has been emptied of meaning through over-use and distortion" (p. 33). In addition, through media manipulation of images surrounding P.C. issues, an interesting role reversal emerges: Those who are members of traditionally privileged groups are construed as "victims" of academic liberals who are mandating impositions on individuals' freedom of speech. Thus, tolerance is artfully construed as an attack on basic human rights and, in particular, on the rights of the most powerful members of our society. The actual effects of intolerance on targeted groups are lost in the margins of this media discourse, and White males are cast as the victims. Thus, mass-mediated constructs juxtapose intolerance as more desirable than tolerance because it liberates people from this absurd imposition. As in the media coverage that construes EEO and AAP issues as war, PC language is framed as threatening to social order because it undermines our basic constitutional rights for freedom of expression. Overlapping and interpenetrating mediated images implicitly uphold the virtues of an inequitable status quo in appealing to the maintenance of order in societal and organizational structures.

■ Stigmatizing Disenfranchised Groups

Affirmative action often has resulted in stigmatizing women and diverse ethnic groups, based on an assumption that they are evaluated with a lower set of criteria than that which is applied to other groups (Waters, 1991). This belief permeates intergroup interactions in organizations (Waters, 1992). If individuals assume that members of these groups are hired and promoted based solely on group memberships rather than on qualifications, then one also may assume that an individual member of such a group who is promoted is incompetent. Therefore, it is important to understand the roots of prejudices that assume that members of EEO-designated groups are inherently deficient. Research findings show that mass media portrayals of EEO-designated groups influence both attitudes toward inequality and interactive behaviors in the workplace. For example, findings show that a positive relationship exists between the amount of television news watched and support for structural-racial inequality (Allen & Kuo, 1991). Beliefs supporting racial inequality may be influenced by the underrepresentation and stereotyping of African Americans, Hispanic Americans, and Asian Americans in the media (see Asante's chapter in this volume [Chapter 4]; Berg, 1990; Faber, O'Guinn, & Meyer, 1987; Greenberg, 1983; Johnson, 1991; Thomas, 1994). In addition, media constructions of women in roles of diminishment and subjugation (Dohrmann, 1975; Lichter, Lichter, & Rothman, 1986; see also Rakow & Wackwitz's chapter in this volume [Chapter 5]) reinforce negative stereotypes that influence organizational roles, competency evaluations, and sexual harassment behaviors (Bargh & Raymond, 1995; Fiske & Glick, 1995; Garlick, Dixon, & Allen, 1992; Kanter, 1977). In addition, studies of portrayals of older people on television indicate that they often are shown as lacking common sense, eccentric, and prone to failure (Arnoff, 1974; Gerbner et al., 1977; see also Williams & Giles' chapter in this volume [Chapter 8]), none of which reflect characteristics of a competent employee. Finally, mass-mediated and social constructions of people with disabilities (Stevens, 1989), homosexuals (Reiter, 1991; see also Nakayama's chapter in this volume [Chapter 6]), and career women (Japp, 1991) in terms of deficit models may negatively affect inclusion, equality, and respect in organizational contexts.

In reviewing the ways in which mass-mediated images metaphorically construct workplace integration as war, trivialize social movements, and stigmatize EEO-protected groups, a vision of social disorder is perpetuated that encourages media consumers to embrace the order of the inequitable status quo. The reductionistic view that all of the problems that European American males experience in the workplace stem from increased opportunities of women and diverse ethnics (all of whom are unqualified based on their group memberships) calls on European American males to "circle their wagons" metaphorically in protection against out-groups who are threatening not only their livelihoods but, more important, quality in goods and services (because members of stigmatized groups cannot achieve competent ends). Although the image overstates and simplifies the message, it captures the tenor of mass-mediated images of diversity, and this reinforces public support for discrimination against members of traditionally disenfranchised groups regardless of individual characteristics and merit. In addition, the trivialization of tolerance complements the need for status quo order, reinforcing a mediated vision that we have rectified inequalities of the past and that all that remain are trivial PC language issues that do not merit serious consideration.

■ Organizational Enactment of Prejudice

Mass-mediated images that sensationalize workplace integration through war rhetoric, trivialize the communication of tolerance, and impose negative identities on specific subgroups may be viewed as contributing to intergroup prejudice in organizations. Media influence public attitudes toward diversity policies and also create and reinforce stereotyped group identities. To gain a broader understanding of both the scope of prejudice and the way in which it is expressed, this section first examines the spheres in which prejudice is reportedly manifested, showing its impact in both private and public organizations. Second, it analyzes overlapping and interpenetrating layers of issues that affect prejudiced beliefs, attitudes, and behaviors. Third, it provides examples of the ways in which people perceive that prejudice is communicated. This multilayered analysis lays a foundation for understanding organizational remedies for prejudice (see one of Lindsley's chapters in this volume [Chapter 18]).

■ Organizational Spheres

Research shows that discrimination is reported in a variety of spheres across diverse types of public and private organizational contexts. These include gender, class, and ethnic discrimination among hospital employees (Gowen, 1991); gender and race discrimination in law enforcement (Martin, 1994) and the military (St. Pierre, 1991); race discrimination in public relations (Zerbinos & Clanton, 1993), journalism (Shafer, 1993), construction industries (Feagin & Imani, 1994), and the military (Smither & Houston, 1991); gender discrimination in multiple contexts (Houston & Kramarae, 1991) including sports (Theberge, 1993), the Job Corps (Quadragno & Fobes, 1995), and toward female MBAs (Murrell, Olson, & Hanson Frieze, 1995); age discrimination in multiple contexts (Wilcox, 1992); and sexual orientation (Taylor & Raeburn, 1995) and racial discrimination in university settings (Hendrix, 1995). Whereas enactment of prejudice may involve some types of behaviors that are context specific, the next subsection helps to illuminate processes that influence the enactment of prejudice across multiple organizational contexts.

■ Interpenetrating Layers

Whereas preexisting attitudes regarding affirmative action and stereotyped images of specific groups influence intergroup (in)tolerance, additional factors mediate prejudiced beliefs and behaviors in organizations. These include (a) individual characteristics (e.g., preexisting attitudes, previous contact), (b) organizational factors (e.g., organizational climate, in-group/out-group ratios), (c) intrapersonal processes (e.g., perceptions, evaluations, attributions), and (d) interpersonal communication (e.g., treatment discrimination).

Based on Amir's (1969) contact hypothesis, previous studies have investigated the extent to which contact influences individual prejudices. Whereas contact acts to mediate stereotypes under conditions of equality (see Baldwin's chapter in this volume [Chapter 2]) in organizations, status inequality often exists between men and women and between European Americans and non-White ethnics. Since the 1960s, however, government policies reinforcing school integration have, in some cases, created the types of contexts in which prejudice is reduced. For example, recent research shows that European American adults who had attended integrated schools and lived in integrated residential areas as children held significantly less anti-Black stereotypes and prejudice than did those who had not (Wood & Sonleitner, 1996). In other words, positive interracial interaction in childhood had long-lasting effects on European Americans' beliefs as adults. Although these are substantive outcomes, it should not be seen as a panacea in light of recent reports that suggest that attempts to integrate schools have resulted in limited success (Kunen, 1996). Nevertheless, it is likely that experiences of positive interracial contact in childhood influence adult attitudes and behaviors in interracial interaction in organizations.

In addition, factors such as organizational climate affect workplace discrimination. Adler (1980) argues that organizational diversity climate may take one of three different forms: dominance, compromise, or synergy. In a cultural dominance model that neither recognizes nor tolerates diversity, individuals are expected to conform to dominant members' rules and norms for behaving. A cultural compromise model emphasizes the similarities among cultural groups, and these provide the core for organizational policies and practices while minimizing or ignoring differences among groups. Finally, in a cultural synergy model that is based on transcending individual, cultural, and organizational characteristics, cultural diversity is used as a resource in designing and developing the organization. These differing approaches are evident in the ways in which organizations address diversity. The extent to which organizations emphasize either conformity, compromise, or synergy is addressed in organizational solutions to prejudice (see one of Lindsley's chapters in this volume [Chapter 18]).

Finally, other organizational characteristics such as the proportions of members of differing groups both affect and reflect intergroup relationships and stereotyping. Researchers have found that the greater the discrepancy in size between two (or more) groups in a setting, the more attention that is paid to perceived group characteristics rather than individual uniqueness (Kanter, 1977; Turner, 1985). In organizations, individuals may be tokenized when they are few in number or are alone ("solo"). In these cases, there often is a tendency for exaggeration of intergroup differences (Fernandez, 1974). Of course, it is difficult to determine the order of cause and effect. In other words, stereotyped beliefs may lead organizations to hire a few "tokens" to meet EEO requirements or to showcase their "tolerance," and stereotypes are reified when organizational actors perceive that the tokens' behaviors are typical of all members of their group or perhaps reward only those behaviors that reinforce stereotyped identities.

Overgeneralizing in-group/out-group distinctions affects intrapersonal-perceptual and interactional-behavioral processes in a number of other ways that significantly affect workplace experiences (Allison & Herlocker, 1994). Because individuals may either consciously or unconsciously communicate prejudice (van Dijk, 1990), awareness of these processes is critical in considering remedies. First, individuals have a tendency to perceive members of their own group as heterogeneous and members of out-groups as relatively homogeneous. This results in acting on rigid, oversimplified, and overexaggerated stereotypes toward out-group members (Allison & Messick, 1985). Second, members of one's in-group often are evaluated more positively than are members of out-groups (Wilder, 1986). Third, causal attributions for behaviors of in-group versus out-group members differ significantly. Success of in-group members may be attributed to internal factors (e.g., intelligence, hard work), whereas achievements of out-group members often are attributed to external factors (e.g., good fortune, unearned privilege). On the other hand, in "failure" situations, attributions often are reversed; failure of in-group members may be ascribed to external factors (e.g., misfortune), and failure of out-group members may be ascribed to internal factors (e.g., traits such as race or gender) (Deaux & Emswiller, 1974). Therefore, a range of factors influence the extent to which prejudice is enacted in organizations. Individual characteristics (e.g., attitudes, previous contact), as well as the organizational climate (conformity, compromise, synergy) and organizational diversity (in-group/out-group ratios), may reflect and affect intrapersonal dynamics (perception, evaluation, and attribution processes). In addition, each of these levels may be seen as interpenetrating the other; for example, degrees of individual (in)tolerance influence the organizational climate, and climates of (in)tolerance influence individual perceptions and interactions. In addition, the proportion of in-group/out-group members may be a reflection of organizational (in)tolerance and also influence individuals' perceptions of and behaviors toward others.

Knowledge of both individual and organizational factors influencing (in)tolerance sets the stage for understanding the next layer—the ways in which (in)tolerance is manifested in interpersonal communication processes. The multiple ways in which prejudice is manifested in organizational contexts is referred to as *treatment discrimination,* meaning that distinctive organizational subgroups receive fewer rewards, resources, or opportunities (Greenhaus, Parasuraman, & Wormley, 1990). In developing a Workplace Prejudice/Discrimination Inventory, James, Lovato, and Cropanzano (1994) identify seven dimensions of treatment discrimination: negative evaluation of out-group members, social isolation, lack of access to information, negative race-linked and gender-linked behaviors, inequity in allocation of rewards and promotions, intolerance for out-group values and behavioral norms, and antilocution (verbal expressions of prejudice). Other research suggests the need to include the additional overlapping dimensions of sexual harassment (Murrell et al., 1995), physical threats (Taylor & Raeburn, 1995), and initial positioning of out-group members within organizational structures (Haberfeld, 1992). In addition, discriminatory treatment of individuals based on presumed characteristics associated with group membership must be viewed holistically as symbolically negating individual identities and alternative group identities.

■ Communicating Prejudice

The ways in which treatment discrimination affects members of differing groups varies across organizational roles and contexts. This subsection provides some examples to help enrich understanding of the ways in which prejudice is communicated. These illustrations are especially useful in facilitating awareness of the range of ways in which prejudice is manifested from overt forms of antilocution and avoidance to intolerance for group norms and negation of individual or group identities. Although not exhaustive, it highlights people's personal perceptions as a way of giving voice to the affective and cognitive experiences of prejudice in differing types of contexts. Examination of the ways in which intolerance is communicated suggests ways of improving the communication of tolerance and valuing diversity.

Social Isolation

Women or minority group members often may be excluded from important social interaction in the workplace. This may be manifested in differing forms ranging from exclusion in discussions about job-related information either within the organizational walls or in other informal gatherings (e.g., business lunches or dinners, organizational golf tournaments or other company-sponsored events). In the law enforcement arena, social isolation results in particularly devastating effects. African American female law enforcement officers report double discrimination when they fail to receive support from either European American and African American males who have sex prejudices or European American males and females who have race prejudices (Martin, 1994). Their accounts explain the types of behaviors that reflect this problem:

> Males didn't want to work with females, and at times I was the only female or Black on the shift, so I had to do a lot to prove myself. I was at the precinct 10 days before I knew I had a partner 'cause (the men) called in sick and I was put in the station. The other White guys called the man who was assigned to work with me the 11th day and told him to call in sick. . . . He came in anyway. (p. 390)

These types of discriminatory behaviors reflect the social isolation that minority group members often experience on the job that undermine both job satisfaction and role effectiveness. In law enforcement, failure to obtain support also can result in physical threats given that patrol officers rely heavily on each other for physical backup in dangerous situations. Thus, attitudes affecting (in)tolerance have multiple types of detrimental outcomes in this context. Other African American female officers report similar types of prejudices, as exemplified by the following account:

> My first day on the North Side, the assignment officer looked up and said, "Oh shit, another fucking female." That's the way you were treated by a lot of the men. The sergeant called me in and said the training officer doesn't want to ride with you but I've given him a direct order to work with you. (Martin, 1994, p. 390)

These female officers' perceptions indicate that specific antilocution both reflects and reinforces other types of discriminatory behaviors. Intolerance in this case occurs because people fail to communicate respect and support for others who have multilayered and interpenetrated identities—as unique individuals, African Americans, females, and law enforcement officers.

Intolerance for Group Norms

Interethnic interaction often results in problematic communication due to actual differences in ethnic norms that govern communication styles. A great range of diversity exists in both African American and European American ethnic experience in the United States, and research has identified some differences in communication styles with, for example, African American patterns reflecting greater emotional expressivity and direct assertiveness than European American patterns (Hecht, Collier, & Ribeau, 1993; Kochman, 1981). Of course, not all African Americans conform to these styles, and many African Americans learn to code switch, adapting European American norms in European American-dominated contexts in response to perceived pressure to conform. Some argue that pressure to conform stylistically represses ethnic identity. One African American manager explained it this way:

Many of us are more spontaneous and expressive than some of our White counterparts, especially if we've grown up in a mostly segregated northern city. We're not afraid of verbal conflict. We like to debate openly and to challenge ideas. But if we have an animated argument on an issue, we are seen as hostile or aggressive or as having an "attitude." It's as if everyone is comfortable with us only when we are passive. (Blank & Slipp, 1994, p. 24)

Thus, ethnic differences in African American and European American styles of communicating can result in outcomes in which members of each group misunderstand the other (Kochman, 1981). African Americans may perceive European Americans' relatively indirect forms of assertiveness and less emotionally expressive styles as meaning that Whites are not very open to debate and do not care very much about issues. By contrast, European Americans may misinterpret African American styles as being too aggressive and emotional.

Differences in ethnic styles also are confounded by stereotypes that serve as filters for interpreting communicative behaviors. For example, to the extent that non-African Americans are influenced by mass-mediated depictions of African American males as being violent, misinterpretations of assertiveness are exacerbated. An African American who "likes to debate openly" may be misconstrued as a dangerous individual. In addition, some accounts suggest that stereotypes influence European Americans to evaluate African American assertiveness negatively and European American assertiveness positively, even when the communicative behaviors are similar (e.g., Blank & Slipp, 1994; McCall, 1994). Therefore, stereotypes may create a double bind for African Americans in organizational communication. They understand that dominant European American male cultural norms often require assertive communication to achieve personal and organizational goals. However, when they enact these norms, they may be perceived as threatening (Blank & Slipp, 1994; McCall, 1994). Understanding how negative stereotypes affect attribution and evaluation processes is essential in creating the type of organizational climate that enhances professional growth for all employees. In addition, recognizing diverse ethnic communication styles can help to eliminate misunderstandings and promote tolerance.

Negating Individual Identity

Individual identity is negated when individuals are stereotyped and characteristics are attributed to them based solely on group membership. Stereotypes often result in a negatively imposed identity. For instance, people with disabilities often are stigmatized or treated as though they are deficient in all ways (Coleman & DePaulo, 1991). This experience is captured in the story of a female worker with a spinal injury that requires her to use a wheelchair:

I am not a wheelchair. Yet some people treat me as if that is the only important factor about me and somehow define me as a "defective person." I am a skilled accountant, with ten years of experience; I am a wife and a mother. I come from the South. I love music. My friends tell me I have a good sense of humor. All of these describe who I am. On the other hand, as it is for virtually everyone who must use a wheelchair, accessibility is an important issue for me, yet people often totally ignore this factor when planning a meeting or selecting my work site. And then they wonder why it is difficult for me to do my work. It seems as if people either think of me only as a person in a wheelchair or totally ignore the fact that I do have special needs. (Blank & Slipp, 1994, p. 11)

This example not only evokes an understanding of the way in which multifaceted individual identities may be negated through overgeneralizing characteristics of people with disabilities but also recognizes the appropriateness of attention to specific needs or experiences of people who belong to this group (e.g., physical access to workplace). In other words, a recognition of both individual uniqueness and accommodation for specific group needs is necessary in promoting tolerance in the workplace.

European American males also experience a negation of individual identity in organization contexts when members of that group are stereotyped as being powerful and privileged. In reality, many White males say they often feel powerless and vulnerable (Blank & Slipp, 1994). There are several explanations for differing perspectives on White male privilege. First, McIntosh (1988) has argued that majority group members often are unaware of their advantages. The flip side of prejudice against minority group members is privilege for the majority group. This results in a positive bias associated with majority group membership that has tangible effects but is "invisible" to the extent that it is outside of one's conscious level of awareness. For instance, European American males are able to take jobs with affirmative action employers without having coworkers suspect that their positions were obtained based on race rather than qualifications. European Americans also have greater freedom in thinking over options for social, political, or professional activities without having to ask whether a person of their race would be accepted in the situation (McIntosh, 1988). A lack of understanding about how privilege is conferred in multiple contexts is reinforced when European Americans have limited involvement with members of other racial/ethnic groups. Cox's (1993) study of European American male managers' interethnic experiences finds that most had rarely or never participated in educational or social experiences in which non-Whites represented more than 15% of those present. This means that European Americans with limited interethnic contact lack personal experience in understanding minority group experiences. Second, individual European American males may not feel "privileged and powerful" due to actual within-group variation ranging from individual characteristics to education and class level as well as the changing conditions in the American workplace discussed earlier (e.g., downsizing, offshore movement of industries). In fact, there is a growing White underclass consisting of an estimated 2.5 million people who feel substantially alienated from achieving "the American dream" (e.g., see Moon & Rolison's chapter in this volume [Chapter 7]; Whitman, Friedman, Linn, Doremus, & Hetter, 1994). The frustration that White males experience in being labeled as uniformly "privileged" is captured in one engineer's statement:

I hear all this talk from women and Blacks about how White men have all the power in our society, and I wonder who they're talking about. I know it's not me. I'm holding onto my job by my fingernails. There's a tremendous amount of competition—from other White men, and also from women and minorities. I always feel I'm at the mercy of the top guys who run the organizations. Maybe the CEOs and the top execs, who are mostly White men, have the power, but not White guys on my level. (Blank & Slipp, 1994, p. 174)

Negative stereotypes of all European American males as being powerful, racist, sexist, and/or heterosexist are reflected in antilocution, commonly referred to as "White male bashing." Many European American males feel that this type of intolerance currently is in vogue, that a double standard exists whereby it is appropriate to engage in verbal attacks against White males but not against members of other groups (Blank & Slipp, 1994). In addition, stereotyping all European American males as supporting inequality exacerbates ingroup-outgroup dichotomies and enhances resistance to change (Mobley & Payne, 1992). Finally, characterizing all White males as uniformly privileged fails to recognize heterogeneity in individual experiences. One man expressed his experience the following way:

I went to a small Catholic college in upstate New York, and I feel as if I can never compete in my corporate bank setting, despite my MBA from a local city college. I'm third-generation Irish German, from a working-class background, and I probably feel as estranged from the "establishment" Ivy Leaguers as most of the women and Blacks do. In fact, some of the Black male Columbia law graduates or MBAs seem to have more in common with the top guys than I do, yet there is that idea that all White guys have it made.

The preceding example illustrates how individual experience and identity are negated in stereotyping European American males. It highlights Ferdman's (1995) argument that although group differences are significant, researchers need to pay more attention to within-group variation and multiple group memberships. Specifically, research, theory, and practice need to focus on furthering understanding of the intersections of multiple group identities (e.g., race, gender, class, education, religion) and the ways in which these interpenetrate individual experience and socially constructed identities. In addition, problems with White male bashing pinpoint the need for identifying effective strategies for communicating about inequality between groups in ways that lead to satisfying outcomes. It is important to recognize that scapegoating all members of a particular group for organizational inequalities devalues individual experiences. In examining approaches to diversity, both individual and group experiences need to be understood. Communication needs to reflect an awareness of problems attendant with stereotyping, recognition of individual and group experiences, and a willingness to address commonalties and differences in creating climates in which personal and organizational goals may be realized.

■ Conclusions

This overview of prejudice in organizations integrates historical economic trends, mass-mediated images of intergroup relations, and research identifying treatment discrimination to gain a holistic perspective. It is evident that solutions to ongoing inequality in organizations must incorporate ecological-level considerations. Although advances in integration of the workforce have been achieved, intergroup parity has not. The most significant advances in decreasing inequality have occurred with federal legislative support including reinforcement of sanctions for discrimination. Mass-mediated images that sensationalize gender and racial/ethnic relations through war rhetoric, trivialize social interaction that promotes tolerance, and minimize coverage of multifaceted economic trends must be recognized as escalating unproductive intergroup divisiveness. Research highlighting income, status, and job type inequalities as well as ongoing treatment discrimination stand in stark contrast to public opinion reports that inequality for historically disenfranchised groups has been eliminated.

Research shows that treatment discrimination is manifested in numerous ways across a variety of contexts. These spheres include both public and private organizations. Multilayered analysis reveals the ways in which individual, organizational, intrapersonal, and interpersonal factors are related to prejudice in organizations. Illustrations of some of the ways in which prejudice is communicated in organizations help in understanding ways in which to improve tolerance and appreciation among diverse work groups.

11 Communicating Prejudice in the Media

Upending Racial Categories in *Doubles*

Kent A. Ono

A lthough it is impossible to predict with precision where and how often people of color are going to appear in mainstream U.S. media, I have noticed that there are certain times when we show up en masse, such as in news coverage of the Million Man March. This media presence may be evidence to some that we now live in a "post"-racist, "post"-civil rights world, implying that society has successfully progressed beyond racism. I would borrow Balibar's (1991) term "neo-racism" to say, however, that what appears as a sign of a post-racist society to some may actually be evidence of a new form of racism, one that makes things appear better when they really are not. Thus, it may be possible to assume that, at least for some viewers, the many spots of African and African American athletes during the coverage of the 1996 Summer Olympics held in Atlanta, Georgia, signaled the end of racial oppression in the United States and a renewed national commitment to racial equality. Because of the strong presence of images of African and African American people during the Million Man March and the Olympics, among other places, some viewers may conclude that African Americans, as a group, "have made it" or that media now discriminate more against European Americans than they do against African Americans.

In a "post"-liberation society in which stories circulate about European Americans (men, for the most part) losing jobs and people of color getting them (e.g., in the film *Falling Down*), racism (not to mention sexism, colonization, and poverty), as Gray (1995) argues, simply may appear to have gone away or never to have existed in the first place. However, despite the relative presence of racial images and absence of racial oppression discourse in contemporary popular culture, as Asante argues in his chapter in this volume (Chapter 4), lingering systems of race and racial hierarchies continue in part through language in academic, political, and social institutions including media.

To challenge oppression meaningfully, I believe we will have to engage in coordinated efforts for social change that, together, dismantle the theoretical and practical bulwark on which racism and other prejudices continue to rely for their cultural authority. This entails examining taken-for-granted assumptions about race and the systems in which those assumptions are communicated and put into play. Specifically, in this chapter I examine media representations (visual and aural discourses) to discuss racial prejudice in the larger society. Even more specifically, within this context I examine representations of bi- and multiracial people.[47] Criticism of objects about bi- and multiracial people may provide a model for scholarship that crosses what Hecht and Baldwin, in their chapter in this volume (Chapter 3), call interconnecting, overlapping, and crisscrossing "layers" of social experience, providing a context for a discussion that has the potential to incite critical thinking about, if not elimination of, categorical understandings of prejudice. In short, categorical thinking about race accepts the premise that the existence of racial categories is logical, and because it is logical, it is necessary; it is one of the goals of this chapter to argue otherwise.

This chapter supports this argument by examining how one documentary video, *Doubles: Japan and America's Intercultural Children* (Life, 1995), deconstructs one representation of bi- and multiracial peoples while replacing it with another.[48] *Doubles* resists portraying bi- and multiracial people as "tragic mulatto" figures, figures that Gaines (1988) and Orbe and Strother (1996) argue appear as mixed-up, confused, afflicted, pathological, and traumatized people in mainstream U.S. films and television. Instead, *Doubles* highlights positive aspects of bi- and multiracial people by portraying them as subjects "on the cutting edge of where the world is headed," as Tino Ramirez, one of the subjects of the video, says. But although *Doubles* begins to fill an important gap simply by representing bi- and multiracial peoples, challenging negative historical stereotypes and condemning the rhetoric of racial purity, its own rhetorical appeal relies heavily on aspects of that same discourse, preventing the video from successfully challenging the very grounds on which race and racial relations currently depend. Overall, this study of *Doubles* finds that media representations themselves may effectively divert attention away from contemporary social issues and solutions to social problems, even while addressing and contesting other problematic aspects of social life.[49]

This documentary is part of what could be called a subgenre of Asian Pacific American independent (non-Hollywood-financed) media productions (Leong, 1991): films and videos about bi- and mixed-race people and their identities. Several additional films and videos address Asian Pacific bi- and multiracial identities as a part of their overall narratives (e.g., *Afterbirth* [Hwang, 1982]; *En Ryo Identity* [Berges, 1990]; *Quiet Passages* [Herbison & Schultz, 1990]), but other films and videos address it as a substantive, if not central, aspect of their content (e.g., *Banana Split* [Fulbeck, 1990]; *Juxta* [Yamazaki, 1989]; *Mixed Blood* [Soe, 1992]; *None of the Above* [Wilson, 1992]; *Do 2 Halves Really Make a Whole?* [Chono-Helsley, 1993]). Other films, often marketed and distributed as bi- and multiracial texts, are really about interracial experiences of people who live within a country other than their country of origin or heritage (e.g., *I'm British, But . . .* [BFI & Channel 4, 1989]; *Maceo* [Esaki & Kato,

1993]; *The Story of Vinh* [Tsuno, 1991]). Bi- and multiracial productions address gender, race, and sexuality issues at the same time that they explicate bi- and multiracial identities. For example, *Juxta* examines the complex issues of women's friendship and racism by Japanese parents of bi- and multiracial children against bi- and multiracial children with African American identities, *Mixed Blood* focuses on interracial relationships between bi- and multiracial Asian Pacific Americans and Asian Pacific Americans, and *None of the Above* strives to provide a social context in which bi- and multiracial people can come together.[50]

In this chapter, I study *Doubles* to call attention to the complex way in which race is discussed in a single text. This is not to suggest that analyses of multiple texts are not important; nor is it to suggest close textual analysis is the most important method of media criticism. It simply means that closely studying one text can help illustrate complex narrative and representational processes that shed light on larger cultural issues such as mixed-racial identity, race, and prejudice. Moreover, extended close textual analysis of *Doubles* provides the opportunity to explain the video's own unique features as well as aspects of the genre of bi- and multiracial media.

Before describing the video, analyzing it, and commenting on its role in mediating issues surrounding race generally, I discuss three theoretical issues to frame this study. The first of these entails studying both mainstream and independent, culturally specific productions. To deconstruct images of a post-racist society, attention to what I call emergent media—usually independent media products without wide distribution made by, for, and about disenfranchised groups—is necessary.[51] Criticism of emergent media texts challenges an academic predilection for studying canonical, nationalist, or dominant texts and helps articulate methods and theories that further contextualize the vernacular communities that undergird the larger society (Ono & Sloop, 1995). Furthermore, criticism of emergent media begins a public dialogue about issues relevant to marginalized peoples that may perhaps stimulate further conversation and social action within localized communities. Through careful, critical examinations of media objects by, for, and about underrepresented peoples, strategies for countering seemingly endless streams of colonizing media representations are suggested. Such a focus potentially yields strategies not available in dominant texts, strategies that the dominant systems of production might find threatening (for good reason).

Currently, most critical media scholarship about marginalized groups examines mainstream media messages. For instance, Cloud (1996) encourages critics to

> continue to attend to the most persuasive, most popular, and most widely available dominant culture narratives and icons in order to understand and critique—not to reify, as Ono and Sloop fear—the continuing force of racism, sexism, and class-based exploitation in our society. (p. 131)

The need to criticize "dominant culture narratives" cannot be overestimated, and it is important to continue to do so, as I suggest elsewhere (e.g., Buescher & Ono, 1996; Ono & Sloop, 1995). Criticism of dominant cultural narratives certainly provides for resistant interpretations, potentially radical readings that not only can undermine dominant ideologies and disrupt oppressive hegemonic relations but also can perhaps lead to social activism that challenges the very system by which problematic discourse circulates and power is applied. Analysis of dominant cultural narratives illuminates structures, exposes power below the threshold of common recognition, and, by so doing, ultimately encourages a radical, transformational politics to form.[52]

However, too little critical attention has been paid to media products created by members of marginalized communities about issues germane to "border" existences—life experiences considered tangential, minor, marginal, or simply not mainstream.[53] Furthermore, attention only to dominant popular culture deemphasizes the significance of cultural products in marginalized communities. For example, media products that overtly challenge and resist dominant conceptions of race and race relations are grossly underanalyzed in academic literature, let alone represented in popular culture itself.[54] A text that appears within a mainstream cultural context as a critique might appear within a marginalized cultural context as support for the status quo. For many reasons, then, it is important for us to examine emergent media. In praising "globalizing" technological innovations such as cyberspace for having the potential to democratize societies (e.g., Kellner, 1995), scholars frequently overlook emergent media cultures altogether. Thus, they overlook texts that educate people about cultural groups and bring people together for coalition building and social activism. By focusing on texts distributed through well-defined corporate channels rather than on texts that circulate primarily within smaller communities, scholars may indirectly call attention to these texts as worth consuming, thus de-centering emergent media and centering products of transnational corporations.

The second theoretical issue I raise relates to the role criticism has and has not played in dismantling oppressive racial systems. Many studies of media and race have been done in the past quarter century.[55] Most have studied stereotypes, positive and negative representations, media pedagogy, audiences, and uses and gratifications. More recent scholarship on race and media within a cultural studies context is critical of both academic and cultural practices.[56] However, within media research on race generally, to study representations of race, scholars first have had to presuppose the existence of race as a legitimate social category. To do this, researchers often have relied on past understandings of what race means. Although there is a lot of research *about* race, very little research aims at altering its prima facie existence as a social category, thus problematizing its taken-for-granted meanings, associations, and usages.

For example, in her powerful critique of media depictions of African American male athletes, Wonsek (1992) begins her study by defining race and racism in terms of "Black" and "White"—a pervasive approach in studies of race in media. Thus, she suggests that race relations in the United States are primarily about color relations between Blacks and Whites, not about structural racism (i.e., racism perpetuated as a common practice in institutions because no antiracist policy has been put into place to alter what is otherwise considered appropriate behavior), racism by or against other marginalized groups (e.g., racism by Asian Pacific Americans against Mexican Americans), or U.S. politics against people of color internationally (e.g., U.S. politics with regard to China, Japan, Korea, and Vietnam). Wonsek's study is compelling and successfully protests racism, but even in the process of doing so, the very definition of race as a relationship between Black and White tends to reify—take as a matter of fact—a common understanding of race as a binary issue. Race relations between two groups is a subset of social relations generally, which means that the responsibility for racial antagonism is a social one that pertains to multiple racial and ethnic groups. Popular memory of racism in the United States tends to revolve around the experience of the enslavement of African Americans by European Americans; in fact, much of the story of the United States as a nation tends to revolve around and through this narrative. In the process, focusing on Black and White relations exclusively may divert attention away from studying, for instance, colonialist racism against Native Americans, inner family racism within interracial families, racial identities of bi- and multiracial Native American college basketball players, and institutional violence against Native American women falsely imprisoned for crimes they did not commit (Ross, 1994). Obviously, no essay can address all representations of race or account for all of the nuances of language, but in Wonsek's essay (arguably as within most essays on race) the search for prejudice to negate its ever-present and ever-changing effects necessitates the reproduction of part of the very system of relations under critique to fulfill the requirements of criticism. Part of the goal of criticism, as it tends to be practiced, is to identify this commonsense notion of what race is by naming, categorizing, and documenting it, rather than to pose the question of whether or not we should assume a commonsense definition of race as a practice in the first place.

Problematizing meanings entails disrupting the typical uses of terms to make easy reflex associations more difficult. By asking the question, "What is the relationship between our a priori understanding of race and the way in which race functions in specific texts?," problematization of those meanings may be possible. For example, a friend of mine recently asked whether or not biracial African American/Asian Americans resented assumptions made by others that they were African American (only); that is, any racial group, club, or organization might count biracial and multiracial people as "one of them" without asking how a person self-identifies. Without evidence to the contrary (and sometimes even with it), people assign single racial categories to those with bi- and multiracial experiences. This suggests that people make a priori assumptions about group affiliation based on looks, name, address, and family and then act on those assumptions. From this example, I would suggest that criticism ought to (a) continue to illuminate reified hegemonic processes in all of their various forms and (b) end dependence on the system of racial ordering by theorizing the potential for the irrelevance of criticism itself as a negative response to an affirmative racial system.

The third and final theoretical issue I address before discussing the video directly has to do with the persistence of racism in contemporary society and how a focus on representations of bi- and multiracial peoples might be necessary to upend that racism. In several typical examples that meet Asante's criteria for "racist language" (see Asante's chapter in this volume [Chapter 4]), nation substitutes for the "preferred" and "deferred" race, for example, when "American" stands for "White" (e.g., when someone asks "What race are you?" and a European American person responds, "I'm American"), when a non-Asian American person greets a Korean American person by saying, "I really like Chinese food," or when a non-Asian American person greets an Indonesian American person by asking, "Where are you from?" and when the person says, "I was born in Chicago and so were my grandparents," the person says, "No, really, where are you from?" There is a saturation point when a particular term becomes popular and acceptable enough to be used to describe particular members of groups. Hence, race becomes reified and people begin to feel comfortable using a term such as "Latino" to describe members of a particular social group.

We, as critics, should be aware of the power our own representations have and the potential effects they can have on others. Critical media communication scholarship itself contributes to the social production of knowledge about race. Spickard (1992) suggests that, rather than employing prior notions of cultural citizenship as a basis for choosing social relationships, "we ought to pay attention to the things that characterize groups and hold them together, to the content of group identity and activity, to patterns and means of inclusiveness and belonging" (p. 21). One way (but not the only way) in which to do this is to study representations of bi- and multiracial peoples to focus on identities not yet fully categorized and not yet fully mediated (i.e., identities in the process of becoming fully mediated identities, or dynamic identities), where the pressure to produce a fixed racial origin can be questioned and where the use of language to define identity still feels awkward. In this way, the very topic of research problematizes assumptions about race and racial groupings rather than starting with the a priori categorizations that a racist culture provides. In this context, contestation of the very grounds of race can be conducted.

Root (1992) argues that a focus on "racially mixed persons challenges long-held notions about the biological, moral, and social meaning of race" (p. 3). She argues that the study of mixed-race people allows scholars to "reexamine our construction of race and the hierarchical social order it supports" (p. 3). She defines bi- and multiracial peoples as constructed in between, or squeezed between, two categories (pp. 4-5). Rather than view mixed-race people as moving "back and forth between color lines" (p. 6), for purposes of ease societies have tended to suppress anything other than already-present racial categories largely to benefit those in power (p. 5). Thus, regardless of genetic makeup or other signifiers of racial origin, groups have tended to pressure people with "one drop" of racialized blood into embodying the racial category assigned by the dominant racist society. For example, although Spickard (1992) speaks specifically about African Americans in his essay, all people of color were held to the " 'one-drop rule': One drop of Black blood made one an African American" (p. 16). To contest this disciplining of people of color, "we will need to perform several social, political, and psychological 'surgeries' to remove the deeply embedded, insidious, pseudo-scientific construct of race from our social structure" (Root, 1992, p. 9).[57] Thus, this analysis focuses on constructions of bi- and multiracial peoples—peoples not fully understood, and thus in the process of being constituted, within popular culture.[58]

■ Doubles

Doubles addresses the events just after World War II, specifically the immigration of "war brides"—spouses of U.S. military personnel stationed in Japan—and their bi- and multiracial as well as bi- and multicultural children. The 59-minute video intercuts 50-year-old archival footage from before, during, and after World War II as the voice-over narrator tells us that this population is part of our "global" future. The subjects of the video are children of U.S. military personnel stationed in Japan during the war and Japanese women who became their lovers (and, in this video, usually their wives). Whereas each mother is both from Japan and ethnically Japanese, the U.S. father's racial identity is variable (e.g., African American, Native American, Japanese American, Latino, Caucasian, biracial, multiracial). Overall, the video argues that despite hardships resulting from their racial "differences," these children ultimately gained a sense of identity and pride that helps them survive successfully within racist U.S. and Japanese societies.

Technically, the documentary combines a male voice-over narration, interviews in Japanese and English, subtitles, music (primarily jazz), and archive film and video images. Throughout the video, archival film clips and photographs are intercut with contemporary video images. Cinematic strategies include dissolves in and dissolves out of black-and-white and color visual images, montages, sound matches with moving and nonmoving visual images, talking heads, and slow zooms in and slow zooms out toward still and moving images. Interviewees tell both good and bad aspects of bi- and multiracial identity, but the video uses editing and narrative development to ensure that each story ends happily.

Before the title appears, the video narrates the story of children living in Japan who were abandoned by their U.S. fathers who left Japan after the war. These children explain in interviews how they were forced to fend for themselves. One woman describes her trauma of being called "half-breed." She says, "I believe I am Japanese, but people don't see me as one." The video conveys the tragic nature of her story in two ways: by close-up long takes of her crying on camera and by filming her speaking only in the language of the people who deny the woman her Japanese identity. Before the title appears, the prelude ends with a montage of bi- and multiracial people (most are smiling) who are the subjects of the rest of the video.

The next section explains the purpose of the documentary and expands on U.S. military occupation of Japan, men's and women's relationships, and the tragic lives of orphaned Japanese children. Interviewees describe how Japanese people, especially children, appreciated and liked U.S. servicemen. One Japanese expert, Kasumi Kitabatake, explains how children asked soldiers for chocolate, after which we see archival clips showing soldiers giving children food and gifts. The editing here implies, because of Kitabatake's mature age today, that he could have been one of the thankful children during that time. Through editing, he no longer is an expert of Japanese history like his three male Caucasian expert counterparts in the video; rather, he is a possible subject of the documentary. One could justifiably imagine him to have been one of the thankful children pictured.

Aside from a brief segment on interracial couples arriving in the United States from Japan, the rest of the video depicts interviews with bi- and multiracial children (most of whom are now adults) and describes their lives. In the following order, interviewees tell stories about how their parents met, interracial cuisine, their struggles with and against assimilation, concentration camp experiences, racism in Japan and the United States, experiences in Hawai'i, and the future. Ultimately, however, all of the stories about racial strife end as courageous stories of achievement, solidarity, fortune, good-will, accomplishment, and happiness. One interview subject, Margo, describes the shift from strife to happiness:

> On the one hand, I felt kind of alienated in the community at large. Within this kind of subcommunity of interracial Japanese and U.S. households, there was a very strong sense of community, and I remember having parties, birthday parties, Japanese celebrations, you know, U.S. Thanksgiving, those kinds of things going on pretty regularly, and I think that gave me a place that I otherwise wouldn't have had.

In another story, Curtiss Rooks suggests that his life was made more meaningful by his "intercultural" lifestyle. He says, "I didn't like chitlins, at least not cooked in traditional sauce, so my mom made a teriyaki sauce with soy sauce and sugar, and I would eat teriyaki chitlins. Might sound gross to other folks, but I loved it." Whereas this segment primarily features humorous stories about their parents' first dates and their own experiences eating intercultural cuisine, after telling her story about her mother cooking "blood" bread and sausage for her Finnish American father, Amy Hill (who the video never tells us is a professional comedienne who played the grandmother on the recent television show *All-American Girl*) claims her mother is happier living in the United States than she would have been had she stayed in Japan. She says, "My mother really adjusted a lot, but even in the hardships that she met with in Deadwood, she said it was way easier than her life as a woman in Japan, so she never looked back."

The next segment addresses issues of assimilation and the uncertain future of these now adult bi- and multiracial children. Yet, uncertainty becomes a virtue even in one of the most painful stories of the video, during which a biracial mother, after her son's birth, allows hospital officials to describe her son's race as "Caucasian" (despite her own refusal to be categorized as singly "White Caucasian female") by insisting that both Caucasian and Japanese be listed on her son's birth certificate as the mother's race. Later, she tells a story about how, after her son once told her he was an "undercover Japanese," she asked him why and he replied, "I'm Japanese but nobody knows it." Although she is, by inference, one of the people he thinks does not understand his Japanese identity, the video juxtaposes her voice-over as she tells this story about the invisibility of his Japanese identity with a slow zoom into a picture of a young, blond, green-eyed boy dressed in Japanese clothes, making visible, and thus highlighting, both his Caucasian physical appearance and his hidden Japanese culture.

Following this segment, the video briefly acknowledges bi- and multiracial U.S. and Japanese children not born to parents who met during the U.S. occupation of Japan. It narrates the story of bi- and multiracial progeny of U.S.-Japan relations prior to World War II. One story leaves out key details about an intercultural relationship that produced two sets of bi- and multicultural families, one in the United States and one in Japan (neither family knowing of the other). It ends with each family discovering the other and being happier for it. In another story, we learn that one man with U.S. citizenship who lived in Japan went in search of his Caucasian father who was living in the United States, only to be trapped in the United States just as Japanese Americans were incarcerated in concentration camps in 1942. He later renounced his U.S. citizenship in protest after being told both to enlist in the U.S. military and to go to a concentration camp.

Having established that these children were born before, during, or immediately after World War II, the next segment of the video focuses on their childhood experiences, specifically about the difficulties children had socializing with others. Tokiwa Taft tells a story about having difficulty fitting in both in Japan and in the United States. She says she tried "to be more like them [Japanese] so they would accept me." She tells a story about how she and her brother were watching television with their father and, when they saw African American people, they "pointed to the TV and started laughing" and called them foreigners in Japanese. Their father was, as she says, "kind of in shock, I think, at that point because my brother and I didn't realize we too were African American, and that was a trait in us, so he kind of panicked." Although she also would encounter difficulty adjusting to U.S. culture, she and her family moved back to the United States to find their "other half." Moreover, the still photo separating the story of her life in Japan from the story of her life in the United States shows her smiling, possibly inferring that her move to the United States ultimately was good for her.

Velina Hasu Houston tells a story about how kids told her to "go home. Why don't you go back to your own country?" But her story also has a happy ending. As a result of that experience, Houston's father, using a neapolitan ice cream metaphor, teaches her that she was like a chocolate stripe (her African American father), a vanilla stripe (her Japanese mother), and a strawberry stripe (his Blackfoot Indian mother). As Houston recalls, after mixing the three different scoops of ice cream together, "He said, 'Now that's you. . . . Now, can you take that mixture and put it back into the three stripes?' "

As the video builds toward its conclusion, the next segment focuses on intercultural children living in Hawai'i who, for the most part, say they experience little oppression and feel at home there. Even Ramirez's tragic story of his parents' strained relationship and his Japanese mother's subsequent suicide ends on a happy note. As a result of his mixed-race experiences, Ramirez says (with uncharacteristic optimism within the context of his comments in the video so far) that he sees himself, as I quoted earlier in this chapter, "on the cutting edge of where the world is headed."

The final segment consists of a series of interviews with bi- and multiracial people who believe "double"—rather than "half"—describes their racial identities and experiences best. As Scott Watanabe says,

I'm not gonna let people identify who I am. If they want to see me one way, then that's their problem. If Black people let other people identify who they were, then we would still be seeing Stepin Fetchit on television. If Chinese people and other Asians just allowed people to identify them as Charlie Chan or Hop Sing from *Bonanza,* then we'd still be seeing those things in the media and in popular culture, and to an extent we still do. But different ethnicities are making the point that we will define ourselves, this is a privilege we keep for ourselves, and while you may have different ideas about us, only *we* can tell *you* who *we* are.

The video ends with a montage of pictures of the intercultural subjects of the documentary and with the voice-over narrator saying, "The future will be determined by the children, and these intercultural children could be the ambassadors that help shape and lead the global community of the future."

■ Analysis

Although *Doubles* interrupts a long-standing history of tragic stories about bi- and mixed-race peoples and affirms the value of "double" cultural experiences, it nonetheless reinscribes problematic aspects of race through the maintenance of what JanMohamed (1986) calls a "Manichean allegory"—what I argue here is a rigid binary between "Japanese" and "American" that depends on a history of dialectical distinctions between races. In the video, two nations come together to produce children with double experiences; thus, the video maintains the autonomy of nations and equates nation with culture.

Furthermore, the video reconstructs the ideal of an American national identity as uniquely able and willing to accept bi- and multiracial people. It indirectly legitimates U.S. military practices and colonization of Japan by framing the U.S. military occupation of Japan as "help" and by suggesting that bi- and multiracial children living in Japan were, for the most part, sad about who they were, whereas those in the United States were predominantly happy. Moreover, as the video suggests through the voice of Hill, racism in the United States against her Japanese mother could not match the discrimination that women feel in Japan. The video suggests, indirectly and directly, that the English language and U.S. culture are two of the optimal ingredients for the successful lives of the parents and children the film portrays. For instance, although she also says she experienced difficulty fitting into U.S. society, the video focuses primarily on Taft's story about moving to the United States after laughing and pointing at images of African Americans on television. In these examples, preferences for one nation over another are reinscribed, and even though this may not be the overall intention of the video, it nonetheless promotes a U.S. nationalist perspective through its depiction of bi- and multiracial people adjusting more successfully to the United States than to Japan.

The video also fails to address the complex identities of multiracial and multicultural people. For instance, the video places Houston—who identifies as African American, Native American, and Japanese American—within the video's dominant framework of doubles without, for instance, creating an alternative video called *Triples* or, perhaps ideally, ceasing to count altogether. I make this claim based on the way in which her interview and her story about neapolitan ice cream resist the video's positioning of her identity within a binary framework. The video downplays her hybridity, her pastiche of racial and cultural experiences (Ono & Sloop, 1995) in favor of a focus on doubles—people born of parents from the United States and Japan. By disciplining the subject back into the mold of the double, the video ultimately sacrifices cultural and racial differences and normalizes them within the mainstream social process of the dualistic Manichean allegory that rests on an economic, nationalist, military, and couplist ideological system.

As a result of this reinscription, the video rarely portrays interviewees as having lives beyond their roles as informants to the video or identities beyond racial and ethnic ones. This is an ethnographic issue. The people as they appear in the video are not people living lives; rather, they are subjects living essentialized identities within the terms and roles that the film creates.[59] Houston's testimony, for instance, reveals the fact that she has written a play, *Tea* (Houston, 1988), about interracial families.[60] The video, however, fails to acknowledge her extramural life as a playwright, one who speaks directly about bi-, multi-, and interracial identities and therefore whose insight on the very concept of "double" would have enhanced the subject matter of the video had her life outside the video been addressed. Ironically, she cannot break out of the role created for her by the video to become the playwright she is (also) in real life or to argue against the assumption that her identity is in any way relevant to a video called *Doubles*. Similarly, although Rooks tells a story that reveals his identity as an associate dean of students, the video does not pursue his sense of how his hybrid identity might intersect with his philosophical beliefs about academic life. In addition, Hill's extra-filmic life as a television actor does not figure into the video's content. Houston's and Rooks's brief references to their professional identities demonstrate how important these successful professionals are to the video's production yet how secondary their subjectivities truly are, whereas Hill's professional life is undisclosed altogether.

Parents crossing racial boundaries do not speak in this video except through the children's third-person perspectives. For instance, we find out about tensions between Ramirez's mother and father from Ramirez himself, about Taft's father moving the family to the United States from Taft herself, and about Watanabe's Caucasian adoptive parents from Watanabe himself. Overall, through third-person storytelling, the video sublimates family tensions, pain, anxiety, and estrangement to produce empathy, laughter, and celebration and thus to conclude on a positive note, as if the bi- and multiracial interviewees, themselves, are responsible for resolving any family problems. This positive note becomes particularly problematic when we begin to realize that much of the history of "miscegenation" in this country was the effect of colonizers, White men who often raped women of color (Davis, 1983). Born in harsh conditions, children of cross-racial rapes and those who grew up before civil rights in predominantly Caucasian environments, for example, had various difficulties surrounding race and mixed-race heritage not addressed by this video. The video never talks about incest, divorce, rape, crime, or any other troubling family-related issues, whether directly experienced by the subjects of the video or not. After the March 10, 1996, San Francisco public premiere screening of *Doubles,* a woman in the audience commented that the film did not address her pre-civil rights experience growing up in an isolated part of Colorado where she experienced "not being accepted by the Black community or the Asian community or the White community and then seeing that division within the family." In response, the director of *Doubles,* Regge Life, who identified himself as singly African American, said he did not want to portray people of color as victims because one of the major problems with contemporary documentaries is their portrayal of clear-cut victims from whom media encourage audience members to distance themselves. He gave an example of something he chose to leave out of the video: part of an interview with Houston in which she tells a traumatic story about being stopped in her own neighborhood by African American girls, who then called her a "chink" and threw rocks at her. Life said the movie "came to a complete halt" as a result of that traumatic story, which meant he had to make an artistic decision to edit it out altogether.

The fact that the video never stops; that it appears "seamless" and "smooth"; that it dissolves in and out of visual images cleanly; that it masks filmic borders of separation; that it flows neatly from history, to dating, to marriages, to births, to immigration, to overcoming obstacles, and finally to the celebration of the term "doubles" as a term that evokes the proud sense of being able, finally, to affirm one's own lived identity perpetuates an unproblematic binary racial system that continues to haunt attempts toward more egalitarian vocabularies for social change. Perhaps also to prevent the video from halting, parents, in particular, do not suffer from their own "internalized racism." Because we never see them other than in archival images, the video's subjects rarely discuss them in anything but positive terms; we never see parents struggle to come to terms with racism in themselves and its effects on others. This absence may imply, because they chose to marry out of their own race and have interracial children, that, as a result of this decision, they are immune from the larger social structure that produces, contains, and maintains racism. They teach their children resistant values to the larger system rather than reproducing the racist values in the family. Hence, the domestic family (without messy issues of sexuality, gender and gender confusion, and class) is the site for reform, the locus of therapeutic success, and the protective bulwark against the larger society's racial pressures. From this perspective, this video plays a role in articulating part of the larger public rhetoric about "family values" and a return to the family as a site for economic and psychological success (Gray, 1995; White, 1992).

Indeed, "doubles," as defined by the video, really represents a successful therapeutic experience in which parents highlight the beneficial aspects of a dual cultural and racial identity without difficulty and their children act as receptacles of this matter-of-fact ideology and, more often than not, perform this identity easily in defiance of a racist society.[61] The subjects of the video have little difficulty accomplishing this idealized state of being. In fact, aside from occasional racist epithets and actions of others, especially in Japan, these informants do not struggle with identity; they already have successfully integrated duality and multiplicity into their lives.

In a sense, by presenting a positive stereotype of doubles, the video sets up an expectation that will be applied to less "successful" people in the same way as positive stereotypes generally limit the activities of group members to whom they refer. For bi- and multiracial children who do not adapt, do not call themselves "double," fail to succeed, have continuing emotional and psychological difficulties, leave their families, do not get proper help, or do not have a larger vision of themselves as part of a group of bi- and multiracial people and as members of both of their parents' racial groups, the video ultimately implies that these children and their families have somehow failed and therefore are not deserving of media attention.

■ Conclusion

The goal of this chapter has been to address the representation of race within media through an analysis of *Doubles*. Through this analysis, we can begin to see that although alternative media such as *Doubles* allow for the possibility of challenges to racist representations, the reinscription of "double" as opposed to "half" identities contained in this video tends to continue problematic aspects of the history of representations and to avoid more complex issues surrounding racial prejudice, social injustice, and social identities generally.

Moreover, the issue of bi- and multiracial identities, although examined in the video, does not necessarily produce more radical possibilities that imply resistance to racist cultures. Instead, the video produces an unproblematic therapeutic rhetoric that relies on the successful domestic family, the unproblematic pedagogy of the parents, and the success of the individual in overcoming obstacles within a U.S. nationalist context. The video suggests that problems experienced by bi- and multiracial people can and should be overcome if people have good, understanding, and racially aware families. They should not attribute any problems or lack of success to this aspect of their lives given that others have shown they can succeed.

In fact, it is possible to see this video as part of the larger post-racist rhetoric of contemporary culture. By emphasizing the success of the individual and not addressing present social relations and institutions in which people of color continue to suffer, the video may facilitate the view that nothing more needs to be done and that the difficult hurdle of successful cross-racial relations has been overcome. By stressing success, post-racist rhetoric may play a significant role in the success of legislative attacks on affirmative action programs, anti-immigrant legislation, and attacks on the welfare system; it implies that the social problems in society have been solved.

It is important to point out that many of the points of criticism made in this chapter could easily be made of most media products in the United States and that many more critiques could be made of products distributed through dominant channels with big budgets. Documentaries generally tend to objectify subjects, to eliminate or blur lines between images, and to tell linear narratives with less than adequate historical context.

White (1992) shows that contemporary television is therapeutic overall; hence, in contemporary culture, television uses a therapeutic rhetoric to maintain its viewership. Moreover, media represent race through binaries generally, as Cloud (1992) argues about *Spencer: For Hire.* Finally, NBC's recent coverage of the 1996 Summer Olympics in Atlanta reminds us just how nationalist television can be.

Even within the subgenre of Asian Pacific American films and videos on bi- and multiracial peoples, *Doubles* explores, with subtlety, the Hawai'ian context, whereas others do not. Even the compelling film *None of the Above,* like *Doubles,* uses a title that refers to and perpetuates racial categories even as it challenges them. It would be virtually impossible to unpack all racist, sexist, classist, ageist assumptions in our cultural worlds and then to produce a text that successfully challenges all of them at once.

We should not forget that there is a very long history of dominant (and some local) texts that have helped bring us the media representations we have now. Thus, this chapter is not meant to hold *Doubles* somehow singly responsible for being able to portray more liberatory images, nor is it meant to suggest that *Doubles* is any more faulty than most media at addressing issues of social relevance. It is not meant to encourage people to view *Doubles* negatively, nor is it meant to discourage people from viewing it at all. And it is not meant to indict people who gain confidence from watching the video.

Rather, this essay is meant to encourage people to take a critical, self-reflective, and scrutinizing view of all mediated products and perhaps not to fall into viewing patterns of suspended disbelief. This chapter is meant to be an example of how we can examine media representations of bi- and multiracial people to challenge the larger system of race and racial categories. Although this essay does not itself solve all of the problems, it does begin a conversation about how to continue to work to do so.

The educational value of *Doubles* dismantles standard definitions of race that argue for an understanding that race is pure, that it is easily observable, that it is unproblematic, and that we should continue to use it. Because this chapter is part of a conversation with *Doubles,* pedagogically, I hope they work together to create a discourse that challenges more problematic conceptions of race generally.

I consider it worthwhile to restate that criticism should attempt to upend the structure that provides for criticism in the first place. As a method, media criticism could seek to upend categories even as it uses categories, provisionally, as a means of deconstructing other ones. Now that this chapter on bi- and multiracial representations is written, further research should challenge the system of race constructed here. Thus, studies of bi- and multiracial representations in media should be encouraged so as to move society toward a more critical analysis of the sedimented structures of racial relations. This chapter argued that such a project must be forever wary not to reinscribe the very structure of binary race relations that both the criticism and the representations of bi- and multiracial people may intend to challenge. In this chapter, I tried to engage this wariness in relation to the concept of "double" as represented in this one video, and I tried to resist settling on one understanding of what it means to be bi- or multiracial. Although *Doubles* does much to acknowledge the existence of people who do not fit into one racial category, it falls short of challenging the existence of racial categories altogether. In my criticism, I tried both to describe and to challenge the representation of race in media products and in scholarly practice. Further studies of racial identities that confront the very complicated system of racism and the larger system of marginality are needed. This study could be paired with similar studies examining representations of homophobia, sexism, or classism and the cultural and social elements that make the work of upending them more difficult. Together, perhaps, such studies have the potential to challenge prejudice generally by theorizing the possible absence of it in productive and ultimately transgressive ways.

■ Acknowledgments

I thank Sarah Projansky and Hoa Giang for their helpful readings of this chapter and for helping me locate materials relevant to the essay.

PART IV Personal Narratives

12 Abandoning the Sacred Hierarchy

Disempowering Hegemony Through Surrender to Spirit

María Cristina González

Untitled

Triggered by the sound
us them you me right wrong
of words familiar
we see difference
anger surging within
as the memories return
times oppressed
times accused
go there in our minds once more
to this place
this way
this prejudice.

When the word "prejudice" is spoken, our typical U.S. context creates automatic images and senses of its meanings for us. More often than not, these meanings have to do with race or ethnicity. The word has become practically synonymous with discrimination, and it often is the trigger for discussions as emotion laden and impossible as those around the topics of abortion, politics, or religion.

This is unfortunate, because by allowing the popular connotations to predominate our use of the word, we are unwittingly led off the path to deep reflection and the resulting levels of understanding that serious and nonpredetermined thought can nurture. All we really have to do to demonstrate the nature of such a process is examine the realm of political campaigns and the powerful use of sound bites and image association.

Once a popular connotation can be solidified in a people, it is difficult to halt the processes of attribution and meaning that are set in motion by the use of a symbol tied to particular associations. "The Sixties," "Watergate," "politically correct," "family values," "affirmative action"—each symbol carries with it a whole package of meanings and their consequent and companion decisions, actions, and predispositions. We need not have direct experience or deep knowledge about what we think if the packaged meaning is powerfully set in our minds.

This meaning process works in effect by using the human predisposition to prejudge when someone determines that he or she "knows" something to be true or right, correct or moral, accurate or fact. When this happens, the ability to engage in new thought is severely crippled and dialogue is all but extinguished. So, I begin this narrative on issues of prejudice and the hegemony of oppression rooted in prejudice by framing my ideas within a conceptualization of prejudice that is based not on experiences of racial or ethnic discrimination but rather on the nature of the processes by which we come to prejudge the aspects of our social experience, including each other.

To arrive at my perspective of prejudice, I have processed my own experience of "street" prejudice, including the familiar racial and ethnic discriminatory practices and systematic oppression in social institutions. I also have used the approaches based in social scientific research that focus on prejudice as a form of judgment rooted in ignorance and absence of supporting data. I reject neither of these views; rather, I have incorporated their truths into an approach that attempts to explain the "hows" and "whys" of these practices and tendencies.

Furthermore, I see the tragedy of prejudice not in socioeconomic or political terms but rather in spiritual terms. The ultimate victim of prejudice toward human beings is the human spirit, and I use examples of rational, material, and emotional experience to inform this position. My basic starting premise is that human beings are innately spiritual beings in a human form whose primary purpose in life is to find expression— not survive, profit, succeed, or win. The emphasis on material experience as the focus of the prices of prejudice co-opts the central injury that enables the crippling of human beings, distorting beliefs to the point of belief that material experience is the ultimate determinant of the quality of human life.

Would It Be Alright?

Would it be alright
would it be okay
if we drove Cadillacs
had personal secretaries
waved gold cards
carried cellular telephones?
Would it be alright
would it be okay
if our cupboards were never bare

our closets full of clothes
water flowing freely
lights burning brightly
from power that will never
be turned off?
Would it be alright
would it be okay
if we got into the right schools
got invited to the right meetings
had little letters behind our names
offices, big desks
job titles with a flair?
Would it be alright
would it be okay
if you never heard my voice
never knew my soul
never saw the face
behind the mask?

Prejudice is rooted in our human tendency to limit and delimit human potential through forms of organization. In particular, I believe this occurs with organization that implies a hierarchical ordering of experience. In our sociocultural experience, we are most familiar with hierarchical forms of organization that carry with them implicit assumptions about status as well as relative significance and importance by nature of positioning or place.

When such a form of organization becomes the taken-for-granted experience of human life, the assumptions of hierarchy are carried over into the ways in which all things are viewed and processed. Authority and power have their source in hierarchical positioning, and human spirits longing for expression eventually will strive for these attributes. A hierarchical form of organization limits the realms and scopes of authority and power by placement, privileging the few. Competition for key positions becomes a "natural" outcome, and decisions and actions are based on the ordering of experience and data according to the assumptions of hierarchical organization.

This form of organization, which has been the basis of human social experience for much of our world for thousands of years, creates the unquestioned belief that it is natural for one thing or one person to be "better" or "higher" (more powerful, more correct, etc.) than another. It is correspondingly, then, also natural for things to be "wrong" (lower, weaker, inferior, etc.). The experience of prejudice, I believe, evolves from the use of this human construction of organic structure for social interaction. We become inherently capable of prejudging, and in fact are required to prejudge, the value of elements of our experience when provided with cues that have been linked to hierarchically positioned meanings. We are required to practice prejudice.

Therefore, if the little girl who paid 10 cents to rent a basket at a local swimming pool was dark-skinned with little black braids and big almond-shaped eyes, these attributes could be used to position her values, status, and attributes within a socially established hierarchy as a dirty little Mexican who had to pay twice to be given the same privilege as the Anglo children whose attributes positioned them more favorably on the hierarchy.

Innocence

Giggles rise through the air
in the way they do
whenever children are gathered
in playgrounds
or backyards
swimming pools
or urban water hydrant fountains
indiscernible shrieks of delight
Get those damned
niggers
spics
wops
white trash
chinks
redskinned little savages
out of the street
I don't want my kids
anywhere near them,
ya hear?

But as I have said earlier, prejudice is not just about the experience of discrimination based on race or ethnicity. If in fact it is organically based, then it will be endemic in our experience of socially organized life. As a woman with a hunger to understand the communication between human spirits, and with a passion for the divinely endowed ability to express myself, I wish to demonstrate how I see prejudice at the root of all forms of socially constrained expression and systematic silencing within a hierarchically based society.

Hegemony

You sounded
so much
like
them
But you
look
so much
like
us

The bruises
on my throat
look remarkably
like imprints
of my own hands.

When a people truly believe it is natural that some should "have" while others "do"
that one should rule while another simply follows, it is easy to see how systematic
oppression of whole peoples could be legitimated and even glorified as the work of
God in some instances. The process by which persons who are hierarchically defined
as appropriate recipients of oppression become the agents of this very oppression is
commonly encompassed by the term "hegemony." A condition of hegemony exists, for
example, when a people defend their state of oppression as natural by citing the
hierarchical assumptions of their society as supporting evidence.

Wake Up!

Like a sleeping giant
coming out from under his blanket
—or hers
the world around us
is roaring violently
as we turn on the lights
it never feels good
to be faced
with brightness—
LIGHT!
when we've been
asleep
eyes closed
in a dream state
politically correct dream state
And then those cute little people
from your dreams
are suddenly in your real world
running around while you try
to stay in bed
covered by your hierarchical blanket
quilted patterns of control
those cute little multicolored
singing dancing multilingual people
are tugging at your covers
pulling up the shades
turning on the light
and screaming that

it's time to get up
time to WAKE UP
open your eyes, face the world
Your eyes will get used to it
yes they will
ours have
your eyes will get used to the light
but you're gonna have to keep them
Open.

Oppression per se is not possible within a hierarchical worldview; it is invisible. Oppression can be "viewed" only by persons who, for a moment or slice of experience, transcend the constraints of hierarchy and the oppressive actions rooted in an assumed logic of prejudice. If a person (or a group of persons) is able to maintain this level of transcendent awareness, then that person is a great threat to the experience of reality for those around him or her.

In this sense, much postmodernist discourse is extremely threatening to traditional academic thinkers. Persons who question the way in which knowledge has been organized, how history has been ordered, or how someone has more claim to authentic knowledge threaten the privilege of those who have benefited from the power and authority legitimized by the existing structuring of knowledge. It is difficult even for the postmodernist to be true to his or her philosophies if he or she exists within the academy.

In a spirit of true cooperation, in walks hegemony. Hegemony operates as a mechanism for the maintenance of oppressive hierarchical organization of experience. It can do so insidiously well because it uses the faces of the multitudes as its masks. Hegemony is like a possessive spirit that occupies the self of a human being, using the resilient attributes of a beautiful natural being to serve the base purposes of the dominating ideological forces and structures. Hegemony is a master of illusion, drawing one's learned thought processes into an argument rationalizing domination and oppression.

I'd like to present some hypothetical examples. First, imagine the transcendent direction of the ideas of many postmodern visionaries. Let's imagine her for this example as a member of the academy of higher education. If her ideas can be harnessed by a segment of her identity that is linked to hierarchical thinking, then we will likely witness the emergence of intellectual elitism. She becomes the postmodernist "judge" of scholarship and a reproductive agent of the apparatuses of the very structures that she likely questioned and deconstructed. The liberating lexicons and grammars of postmodernist thought become the nooses by which innocent bystanders are hanged— often graduate students who naively believed that this "school of thought" would somehow free them.

Let's take another example. Imagine a Roman Catholic man who discovers an experience of Christ that transcends the structures of the Church through his relationship with a Protestant woman. Hegemony rears its ugly face when aspects of his hierarchically organized spiritual experiences begin to challenge his sense of security or validation, moving him to abandon his plans to marry her if she will not become a Catholic. He will find comfort in his ability to participate in the sacraments with a clean conscience, defining his transcendent erasure of denominational boundaries as a momentary experience of spiritual backsliding. The intuitive sense that he would not have in fact been "sinning" to marry "out of the Church" is rapidly defined as worldly rationalism. The reality of many groups of non-Catholics who experience joy-filled Christianity without obedience to the Vatican is framed either as the error of humans who believe in the possibility to experience God democratically or, more superciliously, as something that must be piously respected in the spirit of ecumenicism touted by Vatican II.

This hegemonic process, by which the internalized values of oppressive hierarchical organization can be triggered to prevent, reverse, or punish deviation from hierarchical reasoning, is necessarily supported through the existence of individuals who aid its success. We all have the potential to be these individuals, these hegemonic "police." As agents, they are members of hierarchically oppressed groups; however, because of certain attributes, they can function as police for the maintenance of the oppressive structures and statuses. We can arrest deviation from hierarchically based prejudice and can apprehend transcendent experience to stifle its liberating potential simply by calling on them.

These undercover hegemonic cops often are leaders who are surfacely unrecognizable from other oppressed individuals. In fact, at times they speak explicitly to create imagery of counterhegemony.

She Says "Sí Sí"

Feigning the nos
and empowered argument
of feminists who court her
she says "sí, sí"
to power whose authority is naught.
She has a penis, we quipped
she has a penis
and it has affected her mind
confusing power with protrusions
she protrudes in angles
sharpened by avarice
wears the mask of a woman
over the mask of a man
raping her sisters
and fucking her soul
betraying her compadres
by confirming their illusions
with illusionary thrusts
She has a penis, you know
I wonder if she knows it's limp.

Hierarchy creates status, often through use of group affiliations as the basis for inclusion at various ranks or in esteemed positions. It is precisely the in-group status that enables this dynamic that I somewhat facetiously call "hegemonic policing." The face of an "insider" provides the trustworthiness that make the hegemonic police so powerful.

The hegemonic police are the individuals who work to guarantee that persons such as the elitist postmodern scholar and the orthodox heartbroken Catholic never see their contradictions. They are the ardent enemies of the transcendent visionary, the liberated mystics, and voices of radical rebels; to the police, these strident voices are "going about things the wrong way. You have to work within the system."

Working within the system is a radically different enterprise from a liberated, unattached recognition of the need for structures in order to act (what I call "working the system" as opposed to working within it). Working within the system is to believe it is real. Working within the system is to believe that one's role is one's identity. Our hegemonic police strive to create the impression that they are working the system when in fact they *are* the system. They enjoy benefits from their oppression and are afraid of the struggle for liberation if it puts their hierarchically gained privilege at risk.

Untitled

I'd like to say
my people have suffered
my people are suffering
my people want justice
but first . . .
what's in it for me?
I'd like to feel important
Could I have a token throne?
Cinderella feminist
Macho castrati
Slaves in the kitchen
Indians around the fort
These are
my brothers
my sisters
my friends.

The hegemonic police often enjoy legitimized position authority. They are the tokenized senior scholars of ethnic studies whose work essentializes their group to the delight of the hierarchy and who gained their status through novelty. The power of the hierarchical appeal cannot be quenched even in light of their own very real and intense experiences of oppression throughout their careers. They have identified success as the attainment of status within the hierarchy. In many instances, it has become their definition of who they are.

The hegemonic police will systematically use symbols and language of affiliation with their fellow members of the categorically oppressed group. They might, for example, use the language of activism, thereby confusing fellow oppressed into assuming that they are truly counterhierarchical, counterhegemonic agents. If this succeeds, then they can control the implementation of radical action or prevent it, thereby ensuring that the status quo never is truly threatened.

The hegemonic police are the feminists who live an apparently "correct" lifestyle to "look" like feminists but who at every turn support patriarchal hierarchy when given an opportunity to challenge it in deed and not just cosmetically. The hegemonic police are the New Age spiritual gurus who redefine balance and harmony to include their socioeconomic skyrocketing at the expense of the truly spiritually suffering. A skillful camouflaging of capitalistic hierarchies and conservative spiritual rationales allows for the creation of spiritual elite. Or, a philosophy such as reincarnation can be adopted to justify a system of religious belief that creates caste systems or avoids intervention in the lives of the oppressed who surround those who have been "born into" more fortunate lives. Everyone who buys in and justifies action according to the rationales wears a badge.

The hegemonic police are those individuals who function as if they have realized that without becoming members of the police, they would be hierarchically impoverished and disempowered along with their fellow category of others. As such, these police cling vehemently to their affiliation with their group as evidence that success is universally possible within the hierarchy, *even for us*. They are the Clarence Thomases, the Linda Chávezes, the Richard Rodríguezes. They are the plastic medicine men and women who profit from the stereotyping, appropriation, and distortion of their people's spirituality. They are the "oreos," the "apples," and the "coconuts" who cloak themselves in traditional indigenous clothing and give their children traditional names while teaching hierarchical prejudice in the home with regard to socioeconomic status and images of success.

Privilege

I can represent you from my chair
stay outside there in the cold
while I drink tea and discuss your plight
engage in liberal nostalgia
of when I was like you
or when I knew you
but give up my chair?
oh no!
it is too comfortable
it's mine
I earned it
by being one of you.

The hegemonic police are the people on Wall Street and Pennsylvania Avenue who turn children and nature, as well as family and intimacy, into commodities. The hegemonic police are the persons striving to save higher education by calling students "customers" and an education a "product."

The hegemonic police will use what is most sacred to the oppressed and will twist it to serve the hierarchy. Because they are in positions of leadership, they can influence the attitudes, beliefs, and behaviors of their fellow group. Native Americans will believe they should not speak up because it is their tradition to be "silent." Struggling Catholics will provide money to pay the Vatican because it is their spiritual duty, whereas its walls and coffers are lined with treasures gained at the expense of the lives and cultures of whole civilizations. African Americans will alter their physical appearances to appear more "White" and will glorify celebrities who exemplify these images. Children are led to believe that their athletic shoes must cost $150, and parents will believe their ability to provide and care for their children means that they must buy those shoes.

No One Is a Victim

No one is a victim
not in this game
equal opportunity for all
with a slight of hand
a slick tongue
illusion
we can all join in the fun
sharpening our minds
on the whetstones of our labor
until their edges cut
the connection
to our souls.

I began by stating that we are spiritual beings longing for expression in these human bodies. It is my belief that if the solutions to the problems of hegemony and prejudice are simply political, intellectual, or violent, then we never will see liberation.

The reason for "fighting" oppression cannot simply be to gain access to the hierarchy. This in itself supports a belief in the hierarchy and activates a hegemonic process, creating perhaps unwitting hegemonic police in the process. What better way to arrest one's liberation than to do so in the name of one's cause? Hegemony is an elliptical dance of death in which the dancers wear masks that look as if they are wearing none at all and in which the steps appear to be everyday strolling. Unless the spirit of the process—its inherent contradictions—can be transcended through appeal to a greater unity, the pleasures of life soon become specious.

The problem of prejudice cannot be seen foremost as material without distorting its nature and playing in to the hands of the mechanisms in our society of utilitarian and capitalistic thought that have defined material wealth as the prime indicator of hierarchical authority or power. Oppression and categorical prejudice keep individuals from the possibility of a free attainment of their potential that would not require hierarchical determination of success.

Illusion

Butterfly trapped in a glass cylinder
crystal walls encasing its beauty
frenzied flapping of its wings
impossible to fly through the invisible
but the ends are open. . . .

Only a spiritual solution can offer the necessary transcendence for persons to truly see and believe that even the materially comfortable are oppressed and in need of liberation. Only a spiritual solution can provide the consolation to frightened White men losing authority or to persons trapped by religious belief systems that have taught them that to honor their god-given abilities to question or feel free means that they have somehow sinned and strayed off the path. Only a spiritual solution can nurture a violent and frightened husband who batters his wife through the pain necessary to relinquish his hierarchical belief system and truly love. Only a spiritual solution can free the wife from believing she is a victim.

Maslow's Error

Nothing can remove
the incessant cry
it isn't about food
not about esteem
not about friends
or actualizing
Maslow had it wrong
everyone has the right to be free
even the hungry.

Prejudice functions because we have bought into the illusion that our value is externally determined. As humans, our lives always will depend on social constructions for our material survival and organization. But to believe that these constructions are real and are the source of our power or authority, strips us from our spiritual nature. We maintain illusions to survive materially, but they are not necessary in any particular form for us to be fulfilled human beings. It is the rigidity in faithful adherence to belief in our constructions that enables hierarchy. To be free of prejudice will require that all we hold sacred be abandoned.

Breakthrough

Echoes
in my spirit
oh God, free me of God

I can not fight for my right
to be in your place
if there truly is
no place
can not argue
who is more deserving
if the system itself
is flawed
can not make claims even
for holiness
if in truth
we are all holy.

To adopt a deconstructionist agenda without acknowledging the liberation of the spirit endangers us to the reconstruction of new illusions that also block the spirit with their emphasis on material, emotional, or rational experience. The spirit offers us the ability to enter into paradox and not feel trapped because we enter into a place where there are no walls. The spirit invites us to be faced with what we see as difference and experience similarity. It offers the strength to rebuild our organizations, to surrender our hierarchical authority and power, and to cease identifying with the illusive constructions around which human experience revolves. The spirit infuses us with the courage to take the leaps of faith outside of the imaginary boxes. It provides the breath for the voice that utters the words regarded foolish by those secure in illusion but recognized as divinely inspired by mystics and the suffering in our world. Prejudice silences this voice.

La Lavandera

You say I've shared our dirty laundry
that the neighbors across the road will talk
make it look like we're all bad
when in fact it's they who are evil.
I've seen a man of God believe he was righteous
when he beat his child for speaking truth
seen the rich and mighty
trapped within their privileged pain
felt the idols crumbling
beneath the pressure of their fame
It is our envy in delusion
makes us think we suffer more
It is our fear the lies might be true
that prevents us from leaping from our cliffs.

13 Scenes From an Individual of Color

On Individuals and Individualism

Victor Villanueva, Jr.

"High School Dropout to Ph.D.," the newspaper supplement said. That headline said a lot. It said too much. It said so much that it didn't say it quite right. It didn't tell of driving around town, trying to find a used tire because a new one was economically out of reach. It didn't say that this had happened just the day before the Horatio Alger headline. That headline didn't tell of Sunday mornings skulking about at the local Safeway store at 6 a.m., trying not to be seen with food stamps in line, the college professor without excessive—without any—credit, full-time, riding the tenure stream, still qualified for food stamps. No mention of moonlighting as a cook in a greasy spoon. "High School Dropout to Ph.D."; that's nice. "High School Dropout to Ph.D. Still Faces Discrimination"; that would have been the story better told, the story about the individual who picked himself up by the bootstraps, and the story about the systemic forces still to be contended with.[62]

The problem with a focus on individualism and the individual's ability to pick himself or herself up by the bootstraps is that individualism does not allow us to see larger systemic forces at work. There are systemic forces that subsume race, gender, and class but keep us focused on them. There are larger systemic forces at work that affect all of us and thereby give all of us reason to acknowledge our individual capabilities and our allegiances to particular groups but also to acknowledge our common need to confront the fragmentation that is a part of the postmodern era and to realize, recognize, and perhaps begin to loosen the concentration of time, space, and money that determines the nexus of power.

To say that racism is a handy construct that allows us to avoid thinking in more global terms (even more global than the global nature of racism) is not to say that the problem that is race, class, or gender discrimination is not real or significant. For that matter, I don't discuss the global in what follows. I provide some scenes that reflect recent manifestations of racism, the racism in which "nigger" or "spic" isn't heard much but in which such matters continue nonetheless.[63] Racial slurs or the lack thereof notwithstanding, we know that racism is real. It is everywhere for us to see. We can see that ghettos are growing larger, not smaller, not slowly getting better, not the steady progress ideology that is part of the same liberalism that believes that all choice is individual choice, that fates have captains and destinies have masters. We can see racism as more entrenched than ever, a condition that arises whenever there are larger economic problems.

There is no avoiding the economy, no matter how much we try. We can see the gap between the rich and the poor continuing to widen, the rich needing the poor to keep whatever riches they have, and the divisions among races, genders, and classes necessary to the present world economy.[64] We can see the ghetto dwellers growing desperate, their beginning to believe less and less that there is hope even for the next generation coming.[65] Crackheads crack heads, zip guns become uzies, and gangs take on a corporate quality—national gang networks with corporate headquarters in Los Angeles. So, their problems become everyone's problems in one sense or another as we make adjustments over matters that we should not have to make adjustments over, and the resentments rise against those races and ethnicities that traditionally have peopled those ghettos—resentment over the expenses incurred by poverty (in a number of ways), over the lack of safety of our neighborhoods, over the care and upbringing of our children. And "they" get the brunt of it, the traditional blame of victims for the manifestations of victimage, when we are—all of us—the victims of the postmodern condition.

That postmodern condition: For us in America, it is that time after whatever was halcyon about the 1950s, the realization that whatever comforts there might have been in the post-World War II/pre-Vietnam conflict era were historical flukes not likely to return—the changes in time, space, and money. Concern over family, the loss of the community as a social entity, and the need for two earners to have what had once been provided by one wage earner are not racial or ethnic problems. Flextime, split shifts, and part-time are not matters of choice but rather matters of economic necessity, disallowing a cohesive, day-to-day family. And the family is necessarily small because one can ill afford the time, the space, or the cost of the larger family. The academic, for instance, may not punch clocks, but home hours are spent more on grading papers, performing research, or publishing than on tending to the family. We don't punch clocks; clocks punch us. Extended families are extended throughout the globe as market forces, more than anything else, fling the various nuclei of what once had been the extended family hither and yon. So, time for community is lost. And time with community is lost.

So, we find ourselves in constant motion, working away time, and vying for space. These are the elements of the postmodern condition. And we share in it, all of us, although the postmodern condition is writ larger for some of us, with each group having its own peculiar historical, cultural, political, and economic conditions. I can claim family, the academy, Newyorquino (a New York brand of Puerto Rican), and American. In all that, I can only really know and tell about one man of color's conditions. There are experiences that I no doubt have in common with others of color, experiences that those not of color never will be able to understand fully. By the same token, I can never know fully the experiences of the White or middle class. We need to cling to our various collectivities—Puerto Rican, Latino, of color, academic, American—and they need not be mutually exclusive if we consider them critically and if we accept that we carry contradictions.

So here, some thoughts of one Newyorquino, long ago removed from the New York of his birth, removed from the Williamsburgh district of Brooklyn and Brooklyn's Bed-Stuy. Here, some thoughts and scenes of one becoming increasingly aware of the pervasiveness of racism. In all this is the hope that we recognize that we share in a common insanity—sexism, racism, and the class system. And in all this is maybe a collective sense of how any of this is allowed to continue and in coming to know, coming better to consider, ways in which to help us all.

■ Opening Scenes: Coming to Know Racism

The Puerto Rican boy looks at the experiences of the African American and says, "That's racism. They can't escape their skin. No one will let them." Mami always did carry on about his good hair, curl but no kink, his *naríz fino,* a Roman nose, she used to say. *Blancit* on the block. Steven Figueroa looked Asian somehow. Enchi (enchilada) looked more Mexican. The others looked mulatto or Black. He's the White kid, *el blancito,* among the browns and Blacks of Brooklyn's Williamsburgh and Bedford-Stuyvesant.

A long time later, a beard and long hair. The hair is not intended as a political statement, only as a response to too many years of "Get a haircut" and "Shave again," a response to dress codes in school and to 7 years in the army. Standing by a hamburger stand in the American Midwest, someone speaks to him in a decidedly foreign tongue. Turns out to be Farsi. He must look Iranian. Trying to enter the All American Crafts Fair in the heart of America, the man behind the ticket counter asks whether he is Indian (from India). He must look Indian. Sitting in a bus in Seattle, a Japanese-looking fellow handing out fliers for a Christian radio station says, "Jesus loves you, my little Jewish friend." He must look Jewish. The White kid in Brooklyn ain't just White elsewhere. He's some sort of ethnic.

Shakespeare saw Othello as Black. Americans wouldn't. But if Othello were to walk American streets today, he still wouldn't be White. Othello the Moor, *el morro.* There's a U.S. army base in Puerto Rico called *el Morro. El Blancito,* the White one in Brooklyn, not White elsewhere, is more the Moor than the Puerto Rican Taino Indian or the West African Black, apparently, a hint of some ancient Islamic strain, maybe, or the descendant of the Safardic Jews of Spain. Spain housed so many, the mixes unique to Europe, made even stranger when transplanted to the Caribbean, grafted to West Africans from the slave trade and the people native to America.

"This is my son, Fidel," says his dad. Fidel, the bearded White guy who would not be quite White in a Seattle bus, at a Kansas City crafts fair, or at a suburban hamburger stand. There are other Caribbean Latinos who look like him, some famous (or infamous). He's just not typical of the stereotypical, not one to look at and say, "You 'Portorican'?" So many subtleties to the absurdities of racism.

"Congratulations on your book," says a coworker. The department's brag sheet had announced his receiving a contract, a book on language, rhetoric, and teaching from the perspective of a person of color. But the colleague couldn't just leave it at congratulations: "Still, I have a hard time seeing you as someone of color." My guess is that he meant that as a compliment, likely having something to do with competence. The colleague must see "color" as brown and Black and not quite as able. With competence, the moorish hue goes undetected.

I didn't always see myself as a person of color. Nor did I question my competence back then, although the more the awareness of color, the greater the insecurity as I grew older. But in those early years, I was *el blancito,* after all. I could see myself as poor, the working class. And there is a connection between class and color, some overlap. But "color," back then, meant shades of brown, the coffee-and-cream color of Osbardo, the deep, deep, nearly Black brown of *Tío Tito.* It hadn't occurred to me that the Puerto Rican would somehow not be White, not be White although lighter in skin color. My father's childhood friend, Archibál Sydney Radcliffe, is Anglo-named, blue-eyed, and blond-haired. White? Likely not. He's a many-generationed Puerto Rican, monolingual in Spanish. If not White, a spic. No speak English; no speak; speak; spic (with a Latinate *i* at first)—a racial slur derived from a linguistic problem. Language also is race in America. Spanish is color.

Yet, color didn't really strike me—not really—til college, as I attempted to move within the class system and as more of America's cultural heritage, seen through literature and rhetoric, became clear. W. E. B. DuBois told me of the souls of Black folks and the degree to which education does not transcend racism. Faulkner introduced me to the octoroon, who for all his success, for not being seen as Black elsewhere, could not transcend a Black genetic line. Of course, the Puerto Rican is colored—what with *el morro,* the West African, and Columbus's Indians; what with my grandmother, Mama Pina, looking stereotypically like the American Indian; what with my brown-skinned, curly-haired sister, my brown daughter, and my Spanish surname. Octorican.

He sees himself as essentially of the same race as the majority, and he knows that sometimes they see him that way too, so he wonders how it is that what he hears, sees, and feels, and never seems able to escape, is racism nevertheless.

He looks at the experiences of the Mexican immigrant and says, "That's ethnocentrism. They're Mexican; they're immigrants." His dad would tell of coworkers who would ask whether he had been in the Portorican army. "I was in the American army," he'd say. "We're American citizens from birth. We're citizens." His dad would tell of Operation Bootstrap, Governor Muñoz Marín's Puerto Rican prosperity program. Corporations such as Pfizer prosper, tourism does well, and the Atlantic fleet does well, while the majority of the Puerto Rican people have the honor of ranking second in the nation for poverty and for food stamp allotment, second only to American Indians. The Indian reservations: colonies within the United States. Puerto Rico: a U.S. possession, a colony. Both have the inordinate economic dependence of neocolonialism. Texas,

Utah, Arizona, New Mexico, and Colorado: colonies once. And California. Not immigrants, yet not equal to other citizens.

The colonized. "You Spanish?" "Where you from?" "What's your national origin?" "What's your ethnic heritage?" Folks are quick to tell of their German or their Irish. They search for roots. Their roots never are exposed. No one seems to see their roots. Seems like everyone sees his. He doesn't think to ask them roots questions in the same way that they're compelled to ask him, and he doesn't see that they ask each other as a matter of course.

A manuscript in the mail: "Would you please review this bibliography of Mexican American literature?" He enjoys the literature well enough, enjoys Galarza, Anaya, and others. But he knows more of Chaucer, Milton, and Yeats than of Puerto Rican writers such as Piri Thomas, Tato Laviera, and Nicolasa Mohr. He knows Mexicans less. He has been stereotyped again: Hispanic, a monolith, all the same in everything; all know one another, and all read the same things. He doesn't even teach literature as a matter of course, ethnic or otherwise.

I teach rhetoric, matters of language and mind, language and the world, matters of persuasion, ways with discourse, especially ways with written discourse—in English. I know next to nothing about bilingual education from a professional perspective. I teach and study the Greeks and the Romans and their influence on contemporary English discourse—American discourse. I study and talk about modern rhetoricians such as Kenneth Burke or Wayne Booth, postmodern French cultural critics who speak in essentially rhetorical terms such as Foucault or Derrida. I am professionally distanced from the Latino in many ways. Not even the Brazilian pedagogical theorist so influential to my thinking, Paulo Freire, quite qualifies as Latino to me insofar as I have come to know of him through non-Latino channels and insofar as his Brazilian Portuguese is more foreign to me than is Greek. I probably have learned more about the history and political economy of Mexico and Latin America from my non-Latina wife.

I never have stopped trying to assimilate. And I have succeeded in all the traditional ways—the planet's highest college degree in the language of the dominant and a job reproducing those ways. Yet, complete assimilation is denied—the Hispanic English professor. One can't get more culturally assimilated and still remain an other. But there is a historical precedent in this: The Athenian colonized were compelled to assimilate but nevertheless were denied full participation in the polis. America's people of color historically are of the colony—Latinos and American Indians, the special colonial state that is slavery.[66] People of color carry the colony wherever we go. Internal colonialism: a political economy, an ideology, a psychology.[67]

And so he recognizes that despite the cultural differences between Puerto Ricans and the mainstream, he sees himself as essentially of the same culture as the majority—even the transmitter of the majority culture—and as no immigrant. So, he wonders how it is that what he hears, sees, and feels and never seems able to escape is ethnocentrism nevertheless.

He looks at the experiences of the African American speaker of Black English, the Spanish-speaking Mexican American, Puerto Rican, or other Latino, and says, "That's xenophobia; they lack sophisticated speaking skills in the language of the majority." Then he remembers having spoken Spanish and Black English and the standard required of the school—seems like always—and he wonders how it is that he got sorted outside the mainstream, relegated to a vocational high school, a high school dropout. He is racially White, despite the subtle hue, a native-born citizen and lifetime resident of the continental United States, a quick study in linguistic code switching, a Ph.D. in the language and the literary traditions of the majority, a reproducer of those traditions. And still an other. And he realizes that there is more to racism, ethnocentricity, and language than is apparent, that there are long established systemic forces at play that maintain bigotry, systemic forces that can even make bigots of those who are appalled by bigotry.

He has made it by the bootstraps: general equivalency diploma (GED) to Ph.D. An American success story. But he knows that for most like him, the bootstraps break before the boots are on, that too many have no boots. So, he tries to grasp at concepts such as colonialism, ideology, and hegemony and the ways in which they are imbricated with language; he tries to figure this out.

How a GED? I accept some blame, individual responsibility. I remember giving up. But systemic forces, surely—matters of colonialism, old-fashioned and neo and internal; matters of race, culture, and class and their manifestations in speech. Then how a Ph.D.? There always are some who get through. Some must get through, a matter of ideological credibility in the land of opportunity, the workings of hegemony. But getting through does not equate with equity.

This isn't to imply that the Ph.D. was just a gift, a giveaway to prove that those of color can get through. I worked hard. I still work hard. In the beginning, in college, getting that Ph.D. was a matter of individual will, greater maturity and motivation—and the bliss of ignorance, not always recognizing the critical but nevertheless knowing, in some sense, that there is the systemic. A direct contradiction, I know. Yet, no less true. There were greater forces, I knew, not just bootstraps. Yet, there was the will and the compromises, the bending to ways counter to my cultural ways, denying the color, attempting a racelessness, living with the knot within for declaring a "not without," declaring "not other" and knowing better. I may not have known what I was getting into, but I knew I was getting into something not intended for the likes of me.

There are always the contradictions.

Containing contradictions is difficult, sometimes crazy making, a mutual affirmation and denial. I am an American academic of color. Fully an academic. I imagine what I would do if I were among the truly wealthy—lottery fantasies. I imagine that after seeing the world, I would settle down to reading and writing, learning and teaching, likely about politics and language— academics. Yet, fellow academics are foreign to me in many ways, and I think they always will be, that I always somehow will be an outlander. I often feel alone professionally. But I just as often feel a member of a professional community—a community that extends beyond the university that employs me, a community that includes all English-language teachers. Contradictions.

And now there is the contradiction that comes from being the academic success of color, a representation of possibility for who speaks of obstacles.

■ Another Scene: A Decade Into the Profession

The associate professor of color, publishing on things concerning color, somewhat known in his field. Others of color breaking into the business seek him out, more for support than for advice. But he's taken by that opening scene to *The Godfather,* where Marlon Brando almost overplays the patriarch yet somehow different from *el patrón. Patrón:* Porfírio Díaz addressing the peons as his children. Patriarch: honorable (even if just as pejorative when it comes to gender). The professor of color likes the dialogue in the movie, a manner reflecting another language, another culture ("You must let others drink from the well," comes the line, so different from "I want my cut"). The professor of color likes seeing other ways with language, although within the standard dialect of the dominant language. When face-to-face with others of color, he believes he can speak in a manner different from his ways with White folks, having to explain less, able to slip into a more comfortable language—"colorful." So, he is compelled to advise, even as he continues to try to figure this thing out himself, this thing so indefensible yet so pervasive, this racism, a racism that so often has nothing to do with race, race itself a social construct.

He warns against complacency. Racism lurks in the halls, rises up the ivory tower.

A meeting of the Composition Committee. An outspoken senior professor speaks with impatience about the experimental curriculum designed with minority retention in mind: "We're wasting our time here. I haven't passed a Navajo student in 15 years!" He misses the implication. He's a good man, really, the voice of morality at faculty meetings.

Another meeting, more discussion on the experimental retention curriculum. Another longtime faculty member, soon to retire. He worries aloud that all this attention to minorities threatens to cause us to ignore the more important university minority: the top 10%. And he, too, is affable, likable, one who would never think to make the faculty member of color feel like the other. Not conscious of the systemic racism, they remain unconscious of their own, Professor V, the would-be Godfather tells the new breed of color.

Abandoning the Godfather pose, Professor V leans forward to tell those junior professionals of color not to believe that they are somehow "less than" when their attempts to address those things that concern us fall on deaf ears or, worse, when their attempts elicit pious, seemingly rational rejections. He tells another story.

It was an attempt to publish an article that would explore the connection between racism in America and colonialism. Along the way within the essay, a caution against taking the term "postcolonialism" literally given America's contemporary colonial holdings—Puerto Rico, the U.S. Virgin Islands, islands in the Pacific—and given the United States' unprecedented neocolonial power (even over economically superior nations, a contradiction that is nevertheless real), not to take postcolonialism too literally given the underlying assimilationist assumptions of current literacy instruction in English. He writes. Along the way, something on the complexities of invoking hybridity to define the once colonized. Along the way, Frantz Fanon on such matters. The associate editor of the journal to which the article had been submitted responds: wonderful voice, great breadth, but a danger of essentializing (although I'd argue that some things might get at essences), especially in resurrecting Fanon. Funny word to invoke—resurrecting. Seems like we're continually resurrecting, although no Lazarus among those with countersystemic voices. The essay told of Aristotle and Cicero: no concern of essentializing, no concern about resurrections. "Can't use it" is the bottom line. Don't bother revising. Sorry. So, without revision, the manuscript goes to a British editor. Easy acceptance (although indeed in need of rigorous revision).

And the senior professor of color warns of the too easy acceptance, warns of at least the insecurity that comes with too easy acceptance, the fear that strikes the professional of color that tokenism, not competence, has again won sway. They look at him. And there is something in their look that renders the Godfather fantasy foolish. They appreciate his advice and seem grateful for his care, for his presence, but they smile that smile that says, "Those were the old days." And he tries to tell them that he lives the old days every day. The old days remain.

■ Scene: An Awakening

She had won a special award: recognition of the young scholar of color at a national convention, no older than one of his children, surely. She speaks, a beautifully presented story of the hardships suffered by her mother and other members of the family. She's followed by a White researcher who tells of her naturalistic observations of one classroom. The ethnographer finds Latinas docile, the victims of machismo, the machismo so clear in the Latinos in her study. The scholar of color objects, says these are just stereotypes. Machismo for the Latino is not the same as it is for the Anglo—still a disservice to women, but a different disservice. She goes on to say that the Latina is hardly the cowed and the beaten, as a rule, even when confronted with the worst-case sexist Latino. Discussion devolves into name calling. The young scholar of color spits out an epithet (now hurled at the entire audience), storms out of the meeting, leaving the audience in stunned silence. She's in tears. She thought such things ended with her mother's generation, not now, not among scholars.

There is something to the Latina scholar of color's not knowing. It comes from racism's grand scope, from its pervasiveness, from its being within the order of things, from a too easy acceptance that everything always is getting better, that the bad days died with the sacrifice of Martin Luther King, Jr.

■ Scene: Administrative Liberalism

A memo on mentoring the professional of color and the woman faculty member. The opening section ends in a statement, typed in boldface, commanding that initial efforts at a universitywide mentoring program be focused on women faculty and faculty of color. The preamble is cursory: Mentoring has a long history, and there shall be a mentoring program, with initial efforts aimed at women faculty and faculty of color. So, what's wrong with that?

Without some sort of preamble, it is too easy to see a kind of social Darwinism at play, helping the unfortunates who can't help themselves, the good ol' boys' burden. In a conversation with his bosses, the department's chair and the college's dean, the one faculty of color not on a joint appointment with ethnic studies, the only associate professor of color he knows in the college (of color, not immigrant, and of the colony, not the old country), voices his concern about the mentoring memo. He says that he appreciates the good intentions of the memo but that something must be added that makes explicit a recognition of systemic forces. The chair, a woman, listens, seems to understand. The dean says he already had seen the problem, would have all references to women faculty and people of color removed from the memo, to be replaced with "underrepresented groups."

And Professor V wonders at the power of hegemony as rhetorical. Language can be used to obscure the systemic and render the systemic harmless. I think of colleges of education in universities, I think of English departments, and I think of departments of ethnic studies. English departments and schools of education tend to be well represented when it comes to women, but that—the question of representation—does not negate the political, ideological problems that women must nevertheless face. English departments and schools of education become almost microcosms of America's particular brand of apartheid, in which women are strong in number without correlative political strength. Presence without power.

There is a familiar saying (euphemistically) that a person of color must strive twice as hard to get as far as a White person. In universities, this too often is more than a historical truism. It ends up institutionalized: joint appointments, too often the situation of people of color, housed in the departments of their disciplines and housed in departments of ethnic studies. People of color are very well represented in departments of ethnic studies. Representation becomes a reflection of a racist system that ghettoizes cultural concerns, that assumes "color" equates with ethnic studies, that still has severe underrepresentation in the departments to which they are joined beside ethnic studies. And given the need for camaraderie, ethnic studies departments pretty much ensure that the ethnic studies folks never will really become part of the foreign-ness of their home departments. In the name of representation comes discrimination, separate but equal. Euphemisms serve to disguise (the newest for White folk: Euro- or European American, which does not include Latinos or Latinas, who can claim Spain, although some would rather not—Spain, still a part of Europe, no matter how unique its history on the continent).

■ Some Closing Scenes: Again Looking Back

A long dinner table at a fancy Italian restaurant in New York. Some of Victor's fellow graduate students are seated there. Some of his heroes are seated there too, those he had read. One of his heroes tells of the need for more work on basic writers, college students who are not quite ready for college writing, most often people of color and people from poverty. A fine sensibility. Then some glasses of wine later, the same hero tells of being bilked by a Portorican boy during the most recent New York City blackout. "Clever, the things these Portoricans will do for a buck." The hero seems genuinely charmed by the incident. The comment is completely innocuous. The hero seems not to hear his own stereotyping, seems not to understand, or be troubled by, the economic and racial conditions that make for clever Portorican hustlers. And in his stereotyping, the hero had not seen Victor as a Portorican, wouldn't have thought about it, likely, given that Portoricans are not rhetoricians or compositionists. In the 19 years since Victor first entered the university, the 10 years active as a professional, he has yet to meet another Puerto Rican professor of rhetoric and composition.

The chair of a national organization on composition studies, an African American woman that year, gives Professor V a call. She calls to warn him that his candidacy for a committee position has been questioned—to her—on the grounds that the seven-seat committee already has three minorities on it. The committee threatened to have representation rather than tokenism. The committee's charge is to review and comment on manuscripts submitted for publication. He reads like never before, more careful than ever before, at pains to demonstrate his thorough understanding of rhetoric, composition, literacy, philosophy—his competence despite his color.

A discussion at the microphones of an open meeting at a professional conference. At issue is divestiture of investments in South Africa. There is an argument that the organization cannot know with certainty which investments are indirectly linked to South Africa. The African American constituency is irate and insistent. Another hero turns to him and asks, "Do you know what they're so upset about?" Victor is struck dumb. It should be obvious— apartheid. Divestiture does take place, but only after heated debate.

Another conference, another debate. Yet another hero takes the microphone. The hero advises the voting body to act cautiously, says that the organization has taken precipitous actions in times past because it has been unwilling to confront a certain small but very vocal constituency—a thinly veiled reference to the African American membership.

A local hiring committee for a new department chair. Only a handful of the applicants appear to be of color. One makes the final cut, a Latino, minimally qualified, but affirmative action must be appeased. Prior to the telephone interview, a member of the committee cautions the rest of the committee, says something like, "We've got to keep an eye out for these people. They've gotten so much handed to them that they might not know their own limitations."

Victor has a private conversation with a boss. Victor talks of the insecurity that comes with the realization that tokenism is rampant. He has seen committee decisions on the basis of a person's race or ethnicity with little regard to abilities. He knows that one reason he sits on so many committees is because the system is not yet working, that there is too limited a racial or ethnic pool from which to draw. He is glad to take part, figures he has something to offer, realizes that tokenism does serve a purpose to persons of color, the foot in the door, the possibility for opening the door wide for others of color to enter, the possibility for true equity sometime in the future, as the majority learns that people of color are in many ways, especially professionally, no different from Whites—equally committed, equally concerned, equally competent, equal at worst. But he never can be sure, not really, of his own competence, can never be sure if the laurels proffered are more honorary than earned for the kid of color. The assurance comes back: "Look, we got the best of both worlds. We filled our quota and got somebody really good to boot." He hears that color was the first consideration.

There never seems to be an end to such scenes.

The graduate student speaks to the senior professor of color's wife about the struggle in renting out the family house (while the senior professor still can't afford his first family home), speaks of how frightening all of this is, the fright at the prospective renter coming to the door: a Black woman, wearing lots of earrings, toting a bunch of children. What's a struggling property owner to do?

None of these scenes is intended to call any individuals, organizations, or institutions racist. I believe that all are fundamentally concerned with bettering conditions for people of color and from poverty. It is how a book like this can exist, how this book can even promise to be a market for a publishing company—how it could carry enough interest to hold the possibility of profit for the publishing house. The scenes serve to demonstrate how deeply embedded racism is systemically. I have offered these scenes to suggest the limitations of liberalism, the ideology that has at its base the belief that change is an individual concern, a matter of pulling one's self up by the bootstraps, that all that is needed is to provide the conditions that will facilitate the pull. This is individualism. This is liberalism. It is America's dominant ideology.

Liberalism as an ideology, more than as a political affiliation, is pervasive and extreme. It has taken a radical dimension, a point in which collectivities of any sort must perforce become secondary, the needs of the one surpassing the needs of any other one. The liberal ideology of individualism allows for the unchecked continuance of the bootstrap sensibility. It allows for things such as English-only legislation, laws to force individuals to pick themselves up by their bootstraps, laws that don't recognize the ways of language acquisition. It allows for the confusion between immigrant and minority, an ahistorical perspective that doesn't make for seeing how long some groups have been without boots, the argument that two generations and all will be well when more than two generations have come and gone for African Americans, for Puerto Ricans, citizens since World War I (and a colony for longer), have come and gone for those Mexican Americans who never crossed a border to become part of the United States. Even when some within those groups manage to put on boots, the boots are not of the same quality as others' boots, the legacy of internal colonialism. For all that, there is, I believe, a collective possibility in America's democratic ideals. But such ideals are too easily countered by the ideology of liberalism, countered by economic forces, countered by the current hegemony. Individuals do need encouragement, but that encouragement needs to be balanced by a recognition of, and a change in, the conditions that affect all of us.

14 A Contextual Statement Surrounding Three Poems of Prejudice

Laura Tohe

I want to make it clear that this narrative is written from the perspective of a Diné woman. We call ourselves "The People," although we also are referred to as Navajo, Native American, or American Indian by the rest of the world. I am not speaking for the Hopi, Chippewa, Pawnee, urban Indians, or terminated Indians. They have their unique experiences to tell, although we share similar experiences with U.S. colonialism and capitalism. My contribution to this collection focuses on three of my poems that illustrate personal experience in the communication of prejudice. My intent is not to provide a literary critique of my own work. Instead, my objective is to offer a context for three of my poems that speak to the communication of prejudice from my viewpoint as a Native American tribal person. A contextual framework is important to understand the historical, cultural, and contemporary elements of these works, as it is to understand Native American literature. My narrative focuses primarily on the historical and the personal elements in these poems.

"The Names" arises from my experience when I attended government boarding schools on and off the reservation. In "Conversations in Passing," resistance is met with violence. The final poem, "Little Sister," focuses on a young woman stereotyped by the media but whose honor is redeemed by her brother and by the natural world.

The Names

Lou Hon, Suzie, Cherry, Doughnut, Woody, Wabbit, Jackie, Rena Mae,
   Zonnie, Sena, Verna, Grace, Seline, Carilene

"Virginia Spears," the Algebra teacher calls roll.
(Her name is Speans,)
And Virgie winces and raises her hand.
"Here." Soft voice.
>She never corrects the teachers.

"Leonard T-sosie."
(His name is Tsosie.) Silent first letter as in ptomaine,
>Ptolemy.
Silent as in never asking questions.
Another hand from the back goes up. No voice.
"Mary Lou Yazzy. Are you related to Thomas Yazzy?"
Yazzie is a common Navajo name, like Smith or Jones.
She rhymes it with jazzy and snazzy
Mary Lou with puzzled expression. "No."
"Oh, I thought you might be. He's quiet, too."
I start to tense up because I'm next
with my name that sticks out
like her sensible black high-heeled lace-ups
clap, clap, clap down the hall
"Laura Toe."
And I start to sink,
to dread hearing it on the bus tossed around
>like kids playing keep away.

Suddenly we are immigrants,
>waiting for the names to obliterate the past.
Tohe, from T'ohii, meaning Towards Water.
Tsosie. Ts'ohsi, means Slender.
And Yazzie, from Yazhi, meaning Beloved Little One/Son.
The teacher closes the book and
we are little checkmarks besides our names.

Roanhorse, Fasthorse, Bluehorse, Yellowhorse, Begay, Deswod, Nilwod, Chee,'
Atsidi, Tapahonso, Haabaah, Hastiin Neez

The world in which I grew up already had been shaped by colonialism. In 1864, the Diné, who had resisted westward expansion, had been forcibly driven from their homelands by Colonel Kit Carson and his troops to Fort Sumner, New Mexico, sometimes referred to as Bosque Redondo or what the Diné call *Hweeldi,* "the place of extreme hardship and devastation" or the "Long Walk of the Navajos." In 1868, after the Diné were released from captivity, my ancestors returned to their homelands in what is now known as Arizona, New Mexico, and southern Utah. After 4 years of starvation and near extinction at Hweeldi, the Diné signed a treaty with the U.S. government. One condition of this treaty stipulated that the Diné would send their children to government schools. At the time, they were unaware that they had agreed to assimilation.

The federal government's assimilation policy intended for Indian children to "become like the White man." "Kill the Indian, save the man" was the philosophy behind establishing the off-reservation boarding schools. When Richard Henry Pratt addressed a Baptist convention in 1883, he used the metaphor of baptism by drowning to illustrate how assimilation would take place: "In Indian civilization, I am a Baptist . . . because I believe in immersing the Indians in our civilization and when we get them under holding them there until they are thoroughly soaked" (Pratt, 1964, p. xv). Pratt was brigadier general of the U.S. army when he made this genocidal statement. In 1879, he established one of the first off-reservation Indian schools, Carlisle Institute at Carlisle, Pennsylvania. As a military man, he modeled this school after the rigorous military institutions of his time. His intent was to remove Indian children from their families and from their rich cultural life to enable assimilation to take place. Pratt and others who ascribed to this idea advocated the forced removal of Indian children from their families. They asserted that replacing Indian culture with White values, Christianity, and White education would make the Indian over into White men with dark skin and dark hair. They believed that punishing Indian children for speaking their native language would hasten the assimilation process. Later, Pratt's belief in forced assimilation became instrumental in shaping the federal government's policy toward all Indian people.

Throughout the early years of forced assimilation, Indian children were taken to boarding schools great distances away from their families and homelands through coercion and even were kidnapped at times. Then the government agents proceeded to cut the children's long hair into a blunt across-the-forehead-and-neck style. The Diné believe that hair represents rain, which ensures growth and nourishment for the people and the land. Cutting the children's hair was akin to cutting away the possibility for new life to grow. Assimilation into mainstream society began with changing the external appearance of Indian children. Internally, colonialism instilled a sense of inferiority or shame in being Indian. Take away our language and we were at a loss in understanding the world except through the language of the colonizer, and even then we still are clumsy with this language.

One of the most devastating policies of assimilation forbade Indian children to express themselves in their native language. The forced assimilation policy remained in effect when I entered first grade at the government school at Crystal Day School in Crystal, New Mexico, during the late 1950s. In first grade, most of my classmates knew little or no English. The teachers, acting as agents of the government, physically punished us or shamed us in front of our classmates if we spoke our native language in the classroom. We were made to stand in the corners of the classroom or in the hallways, were called derogatory names, and felt the sting of a ruler on our hands if we spoke one word of Diné. Such punishment is antithetical to traditional Diné teaching and child-rearing practices. We learned to keep quiet and to seek refuge in the back rows of the classroom. Because we were forbidden to speak our native language, younger generations of Indian people didn't learn to speak their language. This policy has resulted in the loss of some native languages and has put some languages in danger of extinction. Ironically, during World War II, the Diné language was used successfully as a secret code to transmit sensitive military information. A group of young Diné Marines called the "Navajo Code Talkers" devised and used the Navajo language to foil the Japanese and German armies, who were never able to break the code. Only recently did the U.S. government recognize these veterans for their role in the war effort.

To further promote assimilation, the agents changed the names of the children. They often assigned names arbitrarily, depending on the agent's preference. A Diné child might receive the surname of the White trading post owner or perhaps a favorite name of the agent. For example, when working at the Public Health Hospital in Gallup, New Mexico, I came across the chart of an elderly woman named Mae West. Perhaps she had received her name during West's Hollywood reign. By the late 1950s, when assimilation already had been enforced for 75 years, my classmates arrived at school with names such as Juanita, Stella, Rena, Nellie, and Ella. None of the girls had "Bah" attached to her English name, even though it is part of every traditional Diné female name and translates to "woman of warriors." In comparison to our English names, our Diné names held greater meaning.

Names given by Indian people are given with purpose and much meaning, and in some tribes name-giving is accompanied by a special ceremony for the individual. The Diné often give a name because of a characteristic or circumstance of an individual. Therefore, a name is special and reflects the identity of an individual. In fact, a traditional name belongs to the individual, and permission must be asked of the owner to give it to another family member. Names carry such an important meaning that the dead take their names with them. Moreover, it is believed that harm could come to an individual if one's name were used with malicious intent. Therefore, caution was taken to ensure that one did not give out his or her name carelessly. In boarding school, we used to joke that our ears would dry up and fall off if we pronounced our own names, including our American names. One's name is taken as seriously as it is in African American culture. "Calling outa one's name" is to insult or hurl an accusation and carries serious repercussions. "She come talkin' bout I stole her ring. I don't appreciate nobody callin' me outa my name (i.e., implying that she's a thief)" (quoted in Smitherman, 1994, p. 75). Hence, because a name could be used with malicious intent, it had to be guarded against evil-doers or troublemakers. On the other hand, the use of pet names and nicknames also was a common practice in the Indian school.

The Diné are notorious for giving themselves and others nicknames. Among the more colorful nicknames at the boarding school were "Doughnut," "Lou Hon," and "Wabbit." A boy who always wore his collar buttoned at the neck was nicknamed "Collar." A jilted girl dubbed her jilter "Bonehead." A young White man who quickly turned red in the sun was named "Red Man" by his Diné in-laws. "Baby Moon" designated a CB radio user. The origin of some of these names leaves one wondering (e.g., Doughnut, Lou Hon).

By the time I reached ninth grade, I attended an off-reservation government school where I lived at the boarding school and attended public school. In "The Names," the poem refers to the White ninth-grade algebra teacher and others like her who didn't understand the cultural background of their Indian students. Our teachers assumed that all the students with the surnames Begay and Yazzie were related when in fact they were as common as Jones and Smith. Our algebra teacher mispronounced our Navajo surnames every time she took roll. Tsosie became "T-so-see" because the teacher didn't know that the *T* was silent as the *p* is in ptomaine and Ptolemy. My Diné surname is connected with water but usually was mispronounced as "toe."

Not all the Diné names were replaced with European names. Some retained their names such as Tsosie, Tohe, Tapahonso, and Chee, to name a few. In other cases, the English equivalents were given, as in Silversmith and Laughing. Tillman Hadley, an elderly man, recalls how he acquired the name Hadley. His grandfather was a medicine man or singer, an *Hataalii,* whose name the White people had trouble pronouncing.

> It was from his Navajo name, *Hataalii,* that we were called. At that time the Anglos had difficulty pronouncing Navajo. They would pronounce just part of a word sometimes, or they couldn't say it right; so, they called me Hadley, and that is the way I have been called to this day. (Hadley, 1977, p. 285)

Unfortunately, Hadley does not recall how he acquired the name Tillman.

Before my first day at Crystal Boarding School on the Navajo reservation, I didn't know I had an American name. I always had been called by my Diné name that my aunt had given me when I was an infant. On my first day of school, I was armed with my new pencil that I couldn't wait to sharpen. My older brothers had begun school with American names, and therefore I must have thought that I needed an American name too. Somehow I must have equated having an American name with having a presence in the non-Indian world, and therefore I needed an American name, I needed a colonized name. Within the hour before I began first grade, my mother finally revealed that my name was Laura.

When we entered school, our surnames were multinational—Diné, Irish, German, English, and Italian, even though most of the contact we had with non-Indian people was with the few teachers, missionaries, and trading post owner who lived and worked within my mostly Navajo community of Crystal. And like the early immigrants debarking at Ellis Island, we too were treated like immigrants in our own land in a country that didn't recognize our individuality, our uniqueness, or our names. Our names had been changed to suit mainstream culture.

Like the silent *T* in Tsosie, we sat quietly in school because we had been silenced from the first day we ever stepped into the classroom. If we didn't run away from the schools, as many did (sometimes with perilous consequences), we found that not calling attention to ourselves by sitting in the back row of the classrooms created a safety zone for us. We had been silenced; government boarding schools had taught us well. Perhaps we even used our invisibility when we wanted to avoid interaction with the mainstream world. Our native voices were suppressed, and we learned not to ask questions when we didn't understand the learning material; partly our traditional belief prevents us from questioning our elders, but we also learned that speaking could bring dire consequences. Eventually, our silencing fed activism and resistance.

The government's policy, "Manifest Destiny," had nearly wiped out Indian populations and taken away tribal lands during earlier centuries. Violent confrontations between police and Indian people breed in the streets and jails of Indian country. Growing up in a country that had failed the indigenous people led two young Diné men to resort to desperate measures to call attention to the plight of native people. In 1974, during the Wounded Knee takeover in South Dakota by the American Indian Movement, Larry Casuse and Robert Nakaidine, both students at the University of New Mexico, drove to Gallup, New Mexico, and kidnapped the mayor and marched him at gunpoint to a sporting goods store, where they held him hostage. A shootout with the police resulted in Casuse's death. The mayor and Nakaidine were unharmed. The local newspaper, the *Gallup Independent,* reported that Casuse's death resulted from a self-inflicted gunshot wound. Casuse and Nakaidine, like many young native people, had become frustrated and disgusted with the treatment of Indian people. After nearly 500 years of cultural genocide, the time had come to take action. The time had come to show the world how Indian people felt. Indian voices protesting past and present injustices dominated much of the news in 1974.

conversations in passing

two university vans!
man, if that wasn't letting
all the animals out of the zoo
we were on our way to seattle for the niea
when we got to brigham city
it was wake up man!
got any brothers or sisters or cousins in intermountain?
we need a place to crash
it was party all the way!
i mean make-out city pow-wow all night
49 to the max! and snagging!
that was some trip
that was when larry was still alive you remember larry
larry casuse?
he kidnapped the mayor of gallup him and bob
held him hostage
right there at that sporting goods store on highway 66
you know that main street where all the tourists
pass through on their way to california

that's the street where all the winos get picked up
and put in jail

sheeeit! what they call pc
protective custody
they put my brother in there all the time
i'm telling you
that ain't no protective custody
three times they beat him up
once they broke his arm
and cracked a rib
wouldn't even take him to the hospital

damn! you know he used to be in special forces
went to nam even
guess he tried to use that fightin' stuff he learned
but there were too many cops sticks and feet

when he came back from nam all he could do was drink
now he spends a lot of time in and out
of the va hospital
he ain't getting any better
nobody knows what to do for him anymore

so like i was telling you about larry
he had this crazy idea that he could stop the system
so he and bob took the mayor out of city hall
and marched him at gunpoint down to the
sporting goods store
said he was gonna show the world what a false person he was
that's what he called him false person
see larry found out this mayor guy was just appointed
to the board of regents
not only that he was also part owner of the navajo inn
that liquor store just outside the rez near window rock
that place where probably hundreds of skins got wiped out
    in the bushes on the roads in the ditch
    helpless kids crying and clinging
    to their moms' skirts
    dads' gone astray on the weekend
    teenagers out to party then getting into wrecks
    grandmas and grandpas that never made it home

talk about massacre that place was another sand creek
only this time the killers came in liquid form

larry never had a chance
during the shoot-out
larry got killed
of course the police said it was self-inflicted
i mean they run the whole town, most of it anyway

so it's been ten years now since that ordeal
maybe we'll survive the streets of that town

Mayor Munoz recently had been appointed to the New Mexico Board of Regents. Munoz also was part-owner of the Navajo Inn, a liquor store that stood just outside the Diné reservation a mile from Window Rock, Arizona, the capital of the Navajo Nation. Because tribal law prohibits liquor sales on the reservation, this establishment provided easy access to alcohol. It also became a dangerous place to drive by, particularly in the evenings and on weekends. Numerous fatal car accidents occurred near the Navajo Inn. Motorists occasionally struck men, women, and children as they crossed or stood along the highway near this liquor store. Teenage drinking in the area increased dramatically. Stories still abound today about the ghosts that hitchhike near the Navajo Inn, and one is cautioned not to pick up hitchhikers near this killing place.

Having grown up on the Diné reservation, Casuse was familiar with the social problems caused by drinking and alcoholism. Casuse was a young man who was tired of waiting for things to change; he wanted to take action to expose the injustices inflicted on native people. When he and Nakaidine kidnapped the mayor, it was reported that he wanted to show the world what a "false person" the mayor was. Not only was Munoz part-owner of a liquor store that contributed to the fatalities of Indian people, but he also was the mayor of a city that had the largest number of drinking establishments per capita of any town or city in the United States. Border towns, such as Gallup, located near Indian reservations often are the most intolerant of Indian people, as is Gordon, Nebraska; Farmington, New Mexico; and Flagstaff, Arizona, to name a few. In these towns, Indian people experience the most blatant forms of racial intolerance. Casuse's death symbolized that resistance could end the promise of a young Indian man.

Casuse did not die in vain. Hundreds of native people from all over the country attended his funeral in Gallup. The funeral procession became a prelude to a later protest march that wound through downtown Gallup. Many more supporters from all over the country attended this protest march. News media from around the world covered this historic event.

Through the news media, the world witnessed what was going on in the hearts and minds of Indian people in Indian country. For the first time, I saw my Diné elders verbalizing in our own language the kinds of indignity they received in a town they had helped to support economically for decades: being waited on last or ignored by clerks, paying higher than average interest rates on vehicles and other major purchases, exploitation of Indian people's lack of understanding of business dealings, grocery stores that refused to load groceries for the elderly and handicapped, and so on. As a result of the call to consciousness issued by Casuse and Nakaidine, the local Indian people called for a boycott of the services and businesses in Gallup. The bold act of two young men made Indian people realize that their relationship to Gallup was based on economics and exploitation. Indian people had been supporting Gallup businesses since the town was founded. Committees and coalitions were organized to advocate better treatment and services on behalf of Indian people who shopped in Gallup. Because of the pressure exerted by the protests and by a group of student activists, Munoz was removed from the Board of Regents, the Navajo Inn was closed and demolished, and the news media exposed the plethora of bars in Gallup. Although changes came about through social activism, many Indian people did not survive the streets of the border towns and the ensuing alcoholism. These casualties remain unsung.

Michelle LaMere, a young Winnebago woman, was unheard of until an article about her death appeared in the *Omaha World Herald* in July 1984. She had been the victim of a hit-and-run crime in Omaha, Nebraska. Soon afterward, Frank LaMere, her brother, issued a statement in response to how the *Omaha World Herald* reporter had portrayed the death of his sister. LaMere protested that his sister had been portrayed as a "streetwise woman" who had met her death through alcohol abuse. This kind of portrayal is insensitive and dangerous to Indian people because it reinforces the stereotypical image of Indian people as drunks. Although she led a troubled life, Michelle LaMere did not deserve to be characterized as anything less than a victim of foul play. During the mid-1980s, after the social protests had quieted down and mainstream media once again ignored Indian news unless a scandal, political confrontation, or other unsavory story broke out, Michelle LaMere's story served only to reinforce the negative stereotype of Indian people. By refuting the newspaper portrayal of his sister, Frank LaMere responded in the traditional manner of the Winnebago people: He defended his sister's honor. He spoke of her as having suffered personal losses during her young life and said she had a family who loved her.

When this article first appeared, I clipped it out without having a reason to save it. After all, I didn't know Michelle LaMere or her brother. I didn't even know any Winnebago people. Several years later, I attended the "Restoring the Hoop" conference in Lincoln, Nebraska, where Frank LaMere was one of the invited speakers. He directed some of his comments toward the death of his sister. On the day of her funeral, it had rained and she had been borne away by the rain that fell after her burial. It was a fitting end to her short life because of the tribal belief that when it rains after a burial, the spirit has moved on to its proper destination in a good way. It was then that I wrote the following poem about her and how her brother and the rain had defended and saved a young Winnebago woman's honor. Indeed, she was connected not only to her family but to the natural world as well.

Little Sister (for Frank LaMere)

I was the youngest of nine children. The morning they found me, the
    mulberries
had already given away their young fruit. And summer was a smooth, slender,
dark woman dancing to the center of the drum. My grandfathers' voices still
    rise

above the rolling hills along the Niobrara where my people dance.

But my voice was invisible against the onslaught. Their words lie. They create
divisions, arrange my life in numbers, add and subtract me, and put me into
    neat
boxes for storage.

My life unraveled early alone in a large city where I followed shadows and
    chased
the jagged promise of empty bottles. There I thought I heard my father's voice
softly calling me "baby, baby, you're my baby" when my mother first
    unwrapped me, a newborn present, a young heartbeat to strengthen the
    drum.

In the blossoming light the earth goes on gathering the dripping fruit of
    mulberries in her outstretched arms along the Niobrara. In the season
    of gathering mulberries
I danced the fury of buffalo and dreamed the slender, dark woman and my
    brother
singing, singing in the voice of praise:

Little sister, little sister,
        tasted her life again
    in the spiraling dance of thunder beings,
            and buffalo
        and was borne away in the
                        thunderclouds
            and the rain that
            fell and fell
            afterwards.

As a Native American woman and a writer, I cannot ignore the destructive effects
that colonialism and capitalism have had on Indian people and the natural world. These
poems depict the personal and historical aspects of my life as I have witnessed it. I write
these poems, which are essentially stories, because they are truth, at least my truth.
When I write about these injustices, I take the responsibility to claim who I am; to claim
my voice; to claim my heritage, my people, and my history. Through writing, I begin
to decolonize myself.

The stories that Indian people have to tell about the "settling" of this country are not
about creating a new identity, escaping an oppressive European government, having
access to land ownership, or espousing the ideology of individualism. The truth that
Indian people know about America and prejudice is not printed in the history books that
our children read in school but rather in the stories that Indian people know and are

beginning to write. Despite how the U.S. government treated Indian people, have always been patriotic citizens of a country that took young Indian men to fight in wars in foreign countries. My father was a young man of 16 years when he illegally joined the Marines to fight in World War II. He returned having been given the Purple Heart, but he carried the horrors and scars of war for the rest of his life. Like my father, Indian people carry the scars of a country divided by prejudice—race, class, and gender—and how it continues to be communicated in subtle and overt ways. My father never spoke of the war in which he fought, but I write of these things with the intent that we can begin to move toward new possibilities. We've had more than 500 years to tell us what divides and pulls us apart, but we don't dialogue about what connects and restores our humanity. It's time we did.

■ Acknowledgment

"Little Sister" was first published in *Nebraska English Journal* in 1994 (Vol. 39, No. 2, p. 101).

15 Blessed Are the Mysteries

Frederick C. Corey

The nuns at Our Lady Queen of Martyrs would answer any complex or baffling question by saying, piously and authoritatively, "It's a mystery." I was cynical even at the age of 6 years. I scoffed. Yet, at the age of 33, when my lover was dying, the map of my Irish Catholic upbringing guided me and, to my surprise, provided comfort. I found myself praying to statues of the Blessed Virgin. I prayed Kim into his death with the Hail Mary, and I still find solace in the beatitudes. This from a person who would tell you he is not at all religious. I out myself, then, not only as a gay man but also as a Catholic, and I turn to the narrative as a way of unraveling the mysteries.

> *Blessed are the poor in spirit,*
> *For theirs is the kingdom of heaven.*[68]

Kim and I first became a couple in 1987, at a Christmas party. I was busy chasing a tall, dark, cute guy named Joe. I had been chasing Joe since the summer, and he was giving me just enough incentive to keep on chasing, even though I knew this chase was futile.

A former student of mine was having a big Christmas party, and there were two parts to this party. The first was on a motor home; everyone was to board this motor home and tour the Christmas lights in Paradise Valley, a swank suburb of Phoenix. I passed on this part. I had visions of a newspaper headline:

> Gay Bash Crash
> 20 Homosexuals in Motor Home Collision
> University Professor Involved

But the party following the tour sounded like fun, and besides, I knew that Joe would be there. I arrived just before midnight. Joe immediately brought me out to his car to give me my Christmas present, a beautiful sweater from I. Magnin. I've always received my best Christmas presents from my Jewish friends. It's a mystery.

"Joe," I asked, "are we ever going to get together?"

"No," he said. That simple. I went back into the house, and Steve told me that there were two people interested in me. I forget who the first was, but the second was Kim. I had met Kim before, and we were friends, but being hell-bent on Joe, I never considered dating him. Suddenly, however, I was available, and I looked into his green eyes—contact lenses—and fell in love. Boom. Bells. We were together that night, and I never felt so comfortable with anyone, so at ease, so willing to touch and explore another human body. It was the first time I ever had slept—as in sleep—with a man, and I felt like a child, a silly, happy child. Everything was warm and safe, like a leather bomber jacket with an old lining and well-placed shoulder pads. No, like a man who believes for the very first time in his life he really could love another human being. We were together that night and every subsequent night. I abandoned my apartment and moved into his, and a year later we moved into our house in Scottsdale. For the first time in my life, I was happy.

> *Blessed are they who mourn,*
> *For they will be comforted.*

The day of doom was Wednesday, December 18, 1990. Kim had to go in for another test of some sort, and because his mother was in town, she would take him. I could spend the day at the office getting ready for the final exams I would be giving on Thursday. I was relieved; I had read every magazine in every doctor's office in Scottsdale, and this would give Betty something useful to do.

I talked to Kim in the early afternoon; we did not say much. But then, around 5:30, he called me from the doctor's office. He had to go to the hospital right away. I remember only three words—liver, bone, and cancer. I stopped thinking.

I went home and went into the bathroom, where I started to pack an overnight bag—hair dryer, gel, bathrobe, hair spray, and wrinkle cream. I heard the front door open. Kim entered the bedroom and closed the door behind him. He was wearing a purple mock neck from the Gap, a pair of faded inverse silhouette Levi blue jeans, London Fog black loafers, a black belt, and white socks. He said to me in a voice that could not have been more clear, more precise, more terrified: "I have cancer."

He started to cry. As I held him, I knew everything was changed. I began living on two simultaneous planes: the first, the *survivor,* the task master, he who packs an overnight bag, remembers the toothpaste, and extra toothbrush, a list of phone numbers, and the insurance card; the second, the *knower,* the sad one, he who now discovers everything will not be okay, will not be good, will not work out, no matter how much planning, trying, manipulating, or hoping, no matter how good things may seem, life is a tragedy punctuated by a few pleasant moments. From that moment forward, I never again would want life entirely.

> *Blessed are the meek,*
> *For they will inherit the land.*

We often seem to wonder whether our parents know we're gay. Mothers always know, as the saying goes, but they never really know until you tell them.

Kim's parents did not know. Betty and John spent winters in Arizona. The problem with his parents was that we never knew when they were coming (or when they were leaving). The cold would settle into North Dakota, and one day John would wake up and say, "Today we go." Betty, the dutiful wife, would pack the car, and then, a week later, they'd call from somewhere just outside of Phoenix. Our only way of knowing when they were coming was to call North Dakota, and if there was no answer for several days in a row, then we could assume they were somewhere between Mount Rushmore and the Grand Canyon.

The first year we lived in our house, Betty and John stayed 9 weeks. They stayed in what was conceptually my room, otherwise called the cabin because of the dark wood and the four-poster bed. We straightened up the house, putting all of the blatantly gay stuff out of the way, but Kim and I still acted like a couple, wore the same clothes, wore matching wedding rings, and, of course, still slept together.

Betty told everyone, "The boys are bunking up."

Both Betty and John were feeling a little ill that year, so they never left the house. For 9 weeks, John never got out of his bathrobe, and Betty coughed a lot. John is mostly deaf, too. The television had to be on high volume. Both Betty and John liked to watch the weather channel. From 6 in the morning until 7 at night.

Betty, a hardened Swedish woman with a bad perm, wanted to stay out of the way. "Oh, don't mind me, I'll just be over here." And then she'd bump her head on the cupboards. John liked to walk around in his bathrobe, taking 3-inch steps, making some sound that was halfway between a grumble and a moan.

"Next year," I said, "they rent an apartment."

Kim's family became a part of my life. During the crisp, warm Arizona winters, the whole house was filled with his family. There was John, of course, with his colostomy, and Betty, who left the door open when she used the bathroom, and then there was Craig, Kim's perfect brother. Craig lived in Minneapolis with his pert wife, Michelle. Everything about Craig was, as Kim would have me believe, perfect; he had the ideal job, was the president of his fraternity, lived in an adorable house, was loved by his father, and had Michelle.

After a long day of golf, we would sit around and play parlor games, usually *Pictionary,* and I would listen to stories about Oakes, North Dakota. By and large, the stories were ruined by Betty's determination to recall names and dates. "Do you remember the time," Kim once said, "we all went to Carrington for that family reunion?" The whole room broke out laughing, and I looked forward to a story that provided some insight into my lover's history. As though on cue, Betty thought out loud, "Now let's see, that was in '65, or no, it was '64, and we were on our way to Kitty's house, no, it must have been '66 because Kitty was in Fargo during '64. Or were we on our way to Ginny's place? That's it, we were going to Ginny's, not Kitty's, and it was in '65 because I had that old Ford that we sold by '66. Yes, it was '66, and we were going to Ginny's—"

"We sold that Ford in '63," John interrupted Betty. Betty glared at John. He lowered his face and mumbled something completely inaudible, a language lost in the archives of his jowls.

"I'm not talking about that Ford," Betty screamed. "I know we sold that Ford in '63. I'm talking about the Falcon, the one we were taking to Kitty's in '64 for the reunion. The kids are trying to tell a story, and you—" She paused. "I mean Ginny's in '65. Now you've got me confused, you old fart."

"Falcon's not a Ford. Chrysler. It's a Chrysler," John fumed. The shouting match was ready to go into full gear.

Craig, the great mediator, saved the day. "No, Dad, Falcon's a Ford. Anyone want a beer?"

The only story that survived interruption was the saga of Caesar, the family dog. Betty told this story, and John loved hearing it. Caesar was a Cocker Spaniel with big, floppy ears, and Caesar could not get enough of John. Everywhere John went, Caesar went, whether it was to the back yard for simple chores, to the golf course, or to the grocery store. John loved Caesar, and the boys did too, especially Craig, Betty assured us. At this point in the story, Craig stopped Betty and said, "Oh, mom, you don't need to tell this story. Everyone's heard it a million times." Kim opened another beer, and Betty proceeded with the story. Caesar died in the middle of winter from kidney failure, and they would have to wait until the spring thaw to give Caesar a proper burial. Poor Caesar's corpse, then, lay in a plastic bag behind the garage, but the thought of this frozen corpse was too much for Craig, who, one blustery morning, packed the remains and carried them out to Oakes Country Club. After tremendous effort and with the aid of an ice pick, Craig dug a grave for Caesar on the golf course and left a marker:

Here Is Caesar

John wept silently as the story was told, the wound still fresh, while Craig blushed, and Kim was relieved when the story was over. Kim never did like Caesar, but John, who a year after Kim's death would shoot himself on the fairway of the very course on which Caesar was buried, had an affinity with the dog.

John was ornery, and he mumbled everything except racist remarks. Those seemed to come out clear as a bell. During that first long visit, we were having a conversation of sorts, and he asked me a question, and in the question he used a derogatory word to describe African Americans. I said, and I spoke loudly because he was, after all, largely deaf, "That is not a word I use, so I won't be able to answer your question." Kim, who was in one of the back rooms, dashed into the living room to run interference.

When Kim was in the hospital, John would be driving down the street and would see someone, and this someone inevitably was someone Mexican, and John would say, "Why couldn't *he* have cancer? Why does it have to be Kim?" And I never could convince him that Dr. Gonzalez was not Black. For John, not White was Black.

John himself was quite dark. He was French, and he tanned very well. This fact was noted on his license plate. Customized: NIG. I could conclude only that Kim's family was informed more by their geography than by their religion or ethnicity, that they were a simple people, not malicious, mean in effect but not in spirit. North Dakota is a landscape that I do not know. Nor do I know whether a simple people can be held accountable for absorbing the attitudes of their territory, for reproducing hate they do not recognize, or for homophobia that stems from an absence of vocabulary. I do not know whether suicide is an escape from pain, guilt, or terror. I do not know what constitutes sin. I do know that I admired Kim's escape from the tyranny of simplicity.

Blessed are they who hunger and thirst for righteousness,
For they will be satisfied.

When I first met Kim, he wore a wedding band on the ring finger of his right hand. I knew the ring was from his old boyfriend. Kim continued to wear his ring, and one day we were in bed, just talking, and I asked him why: "Because you still love him?"

"No," he said.

"Well, then, why do you wear the ring?"

"Because I believe in relationships."

"Let me try that ring on." It was a perfect fit, and I was admiring it on my hand. I went into the bathroom to see how it looked in the mirror. While I was in the bathroom, I had a clever idea. I took the ring off my finger and slipped it into my pocket. A few minutes later, I went back into the bedroom, opened the closet, and got a wire shirt hanger. When he asked me what I was doing with a hanger, I said, "Oh, nothing."

Back in the bathroom, I jiggled the hanger down the drain, and I waited. I jiggled a little louder. A few seconds later, he came running into the bathroom and looked at me.

"I can get it," I said. "I'm sure it's down here somewhere."

Suddenly, Kim, who could barely change a light bulb, was underneath the sink pulling the entire plumbing apart. He had the entire drain dismantled. Pipes everywhere. I was dumfounded.

"Kim," I said, and when he turned around I showed him the ring. I held the ring in my hand and told him that I would wear the ring because I too believe in relationships.

On our first anniversary, I bought him a matching wedding ring. The rings became a symbol of our commitment to each other, our comedy, and our love. When Kim died, Betty wanted his ring. She recognized it as one of his most precious possessions. I had removed his ring upon his death and slipped it alongside the ring on my finger. Kim's brother, seeing the dual desire for the ring, asked me to find a solution. I went to the store, purchased a duplicate ring, scuffed it up, and gave it to Craig to give to his mother. In her presence, while the faux ring dangled from a gold chain around her neck, I hid the real ring in my pocket. The lie seemed right, even kind.

Blessed are the merciful,
For they will be shown mercy.

On December 24, 1990, I woke up early. 5:30. It was too early to go to the hospital—Kim usually woke up around 8:30—so I decided to write a letter to my parents and tell them everything. They did not know Kim was sick. They did not know Kim. They did not even know I am gay. I sat at my desk, watching the sun rise, and I wrote the following:

Dear Mother and Dad,

The man I am living with has cancer, and it appears to be terminal. This has affected my life greatly.

Kim and I are devoted to each other. We are partners and lovers. We have been together for 3 years, and 2 years ago we knew that our commitment to each other was permanent. We will spend the rest of our lives together.

I have never had the courage or strength to tell you about me. Deep inside I've always known, but I chose not to mention it. I know that you do not understand or accept homosexuality, and I am not asking you to understand or accept it now, but I am asking you to be aware of the fact that I am gay.

Kim's cancer does not appear to be related to AIDS, but the hospital is running some tests to be sure. One of the doctors seems to think it is related, and though I think he is wrong, I suppose it is necessary to leave it as an option.

In either case, the prognosis is not good. The cancer is in the liver and the bones, and there appears to be a tumor. The tests show that the primary source is not in the bone, but beyond that, the tests reveal little. They are going to conduct a biopsy on the rib today and start chemotherapy and/or radiation on Wednesday.

I have never known such grief. For 4 years, I have been an emotional support volunteer for people with AIDS—I have held the hands of people who are dying, I've been company to people who have just heard they've had positive test results, I've had a "client" for 3+ years, and I've picked mothers up at the airport to take them to the hospital. I never knew it felt like this.

We have a strong support system. We have many, many friends; Kim's family is coming down from North Dakota (his parents are here already); and my employer is extremely supportive. Given the situation, everything will work out.

I'm sorry I never had the strength or courage to tell you about Kim. I have wanted to tell you. I've called with scripts written out ready to be read over the phone. I wanted to tell you while we were in Paris. I wanted to fly in to Detroit with Kim so that you could meet him.

I never wanted to write you a letter, because this gives me no opportunity to talk it through with you.

Rosemary [my sister] knows Kim, and she knows he's been sick, but she does not know about the cancer. Patrick [my brother] has never met Kim, but he knows about him, and I think he knows Kim is sick. John [my oldest brother] knows about me, but not about Kim, and Tom [my youngest brother] knows I'm gay (although we've never talked about it), and Bob [I have four brothers] does not know anything about me or [about] me and Kim.

I do not know what else to say, except that I am sad and I am afraid of the new year.

Fred.

As I finished the letter, the phone rang. I went into the bedroom, picked up the receiver, said hello, and I heard Kim on the other end of the line, screeching. I screeched back. We sat on the phone for 5 minutes of eternity, screeching, until finally he told me what I already knew. The doctors said there was nothing they could do; he would be dead within a year.

I drove to the hospital and we sat together, silently.

He asked me to tell Betty and John. I called them and told them that this would be a good time to come down to the hospital, and when they arrived I brought them into a little waiting room. We all sat down, and I held John's hands as I said, loudly, "Today, it's okay to cry."

They knew exactly what I meant.

We all went back into the room, and I said I was going for a walk to let them talk, and when I returned Kim was upset with me. They did not have that much to talk about. "What took you so long?"

The doctor then came into the room and said we could go home—for the holidays. What the hell. We packed up his stuff, called everyone, and said, "It's Christmas Eve, we're going home, come on over." The house was full, of course, everyone smoking away, and I begged Kim not to have a cigarette, but as Cindy said that evening, "Oh, what difference does it make?" What the hell.

My grades were due on the 26th, and I had not even started grading yet, so my best friend from graduate school, Cindy, had come up from Tucson to help me grade. We spent 4 hours grading, stopped at a dumpy diner—Jerry's on Scottsdale Road—and then went home. Bonnie, David, and Eddie were there, but Kim was in the emergency room.

Cindy went back to Tucson, and I went to the hospital. Dennis and Theresa were there, moving Kim on and off the X-ray table. He couldn't walk or even stand; maybe he fractured his leg, but no, it was only the cancer moving through the bones.

Dennis and Theresa took Kim home, and I went to fill a prescription for Dilaudid, a type of morphine.

Here it was, 12:30 between Christmas Eve and Christmas Day, and the pharmacist said to me, "I've been in this business for 33 years, and this is only the third time I've filled this prescription. Your friend must be in some kind of pain."

When I got home, they still were trying to carry Kim into the bed. Throughout the night, I knelt at his side with a straw in my mouth, washing morphine down his throat, trying to ease the pain.

Blessed are the clean of heart,
For they will see God.

I did very well in college, getting mostly A's and B's. I got one C. A sociology course: Human Sexuality. That was my third clue.

Learning about the facts of life was my second clue. 1968. I was in the kitchen. Faith, my mother, was cooking over the gas stove, and I was walking past her when she said, without even looking at me, "Honey, I want to talk to you about something."

I leaned against the Frigidaire, its whiteness dulled by years of scouring with steel wool. "What about?" I asked.

"In class tomorrow, you will be learning about something, and I want to talk to you first." I stood in my mother's kitchen, looking at the floor. "The penis," she said, "gets hard and enters the vagina." Everything was phrased in terms of husband and wife, mother and father, marriage and women, women and children, and when my mother finished the technical details, she launched into a celebration of her uterus.

I was dizzy from the details, and I leaned against the refrigerator thinking, "If this is what we do for birth, I wonder what we do for death." Could the penis enter the vagina again? Could the penis attack the vagina in reverse? Could you determine your own death by having a penis enter—? I would have to ask my older brother.

I knew my mother was coming to a close when her tone of voice changed. "When unmarried people do this in the back seat of a car, it's called 'fucking.' Nice people don't even use the word."

My first clue was falling madly in love with one of the lifeguards at the Beverly Hills Athletic Club. I was 6 years old, too young to drive, but I knew I wanted to see him in the back seat of a Ford. I may never see God.

Blessed are the peacemakers,
For they will be called children of God.

I had no idea how my parents would respond to the letter I wrote on Christmas Eve. Given the circumstances, I did not place their response high on my list of things to worry about, but I did need to deal with the "parent problem" in a quick and efficient way.

My brother, Pat, had been trying to reach me by phone, and when I would arrive home from the hospital I would find messages such as, "Call Pat immediately." I threw the notes away. A couple of days later, Pat called very early in the morning. Thinking it was Kim, I answered. "Fred," he said, "you have to talk to mom and dad." I was the best man at Pat's wedding, and during the reception my mother was in an excellent mood, holding the people at her table captive with her views on politics and the Church. "I don't want to go to Church," she said, "and hear the priest read a letter from the bishop telling us how the pope feels we should vote." She then railed on the Church's treatment of Geraldine Ferraro, on how, based on the single issue of abortion, we were to vote for Ronald Reagan. "Sexism," she said. "Nothing but sexism. The Church does not respect women. Never has. This has got to change." I liked my mother when I heard her talk like that, and I credit my ability to think independently to her, but I was deeply hurt when she concluded her views with, "Only one thing I agree with the pope on, and that's the question of homosexuality."

She then turned to my brother, Bob, and asked him what he thought about the question, and I wondered why she was asking Bob. As though to garner support, she asked my most conservative brother, the one who said he likes his house but hates the neighbors, "especially," he said, "those two queers down the street."

"I don't understand it," Bob said, "and I think it's sick."

My father looked uncomfortable, and I wondered what he was thinking. I wondered if what I heard was true, that he once said he'd rather his son were dead than gay.

"Well, everyone has rights," I offered the conversation, trying not to go too far out on a limb.

"I support rights," my mother responded, "but that doesn't mean I want two lesbians living down the street."

"I agree with that," my father said. "Besides, I am sure they would not want to live in a family neighborhood." I was silent, in need of a drink, confused, and angry at myself. I was a 30-year-old college professor who could not tell his own parents that the right of the individual to live and love is more important than society's right to have everything fit into neat little boxes, who could not point out the parallels between their position on gay people and others' positions on African Americans. My parents taught their children the horrors of racism and protected themselves from anti-Catholic attitudes by associating only with Catholics, and they could not see beyond their insularity. Yet, I could not instruct, could not say, "I am your family, and I might want to live in a family neighborhood." I felt small in my silence.

My letter, then, did not bring terrifying news of Kim's cancer but instead brought the shocking news that I am gay.

My parents wanted to talk. About what, I did not know, but I sure as hell did not want to talk about being gay while Kim was in the hospital dying, and I told this to Pat, who became furious. "They are your parents," he shouted from Philadelphia. "Do you really think they don't love you?" I could use the support of my family, I thought, and deep down I wanted my mother to fly to Phoenix to be with me and to meet Kim. I was to call my parents at 12:00 noon Phoenix time.

At 11:30, I left the hospital and went home to make the call, and at 12:00 sharp, when their phone rang, both my mother and father answered, one on the upstairs line and the other downstairs. "We love you very much," my mother said before saying hello or asking whether it was me, and my father echoed her. I wept. They went on to talk about the terror of cancer, as both of their mothers had died wicked deaths of cancer, and after we talked for about 30 minutes I returned to the hospital and told Kim that the conversation went very well. He was relieved, even a little envious. "My parents might even come out," I said, after my parents' trip to their chalet at Higgins Lake, after their visit with Pat in Philadelphia, and after Rosemary's baby is born. He was not too thrilled about their pending visit.

The next day, I received the following letter from my mother:

Dear Fred,

I love you very much, Fred, not only because you are my son, which is a very good reason, but because you are a very sensitive, caring person. So often after a telephone conversation, I have realized we only talked about me and my concerns, not you and yours. . . .

I will never understand or approve of your orientation, but I do love you. You will have to exercise some understanding and acceptance of me, too. . . .

I read the letter but did not show it to dad. I will wait for the right opportunity.

The dying of one we care for is always heart-wrenching. I held my mother's hand and prayed her out with the last part of the Ave Maria. "Holy Mary, Mother of God, pray for us sinners now and at the hour of our death. Amen." John L's [her youngest brother] accidental death was harder because we never said goodbye. Unresolved differences were forever unresolved. I do believe in God, His Blessed Mother, and in prayer. In fact, tomorrow will find me at the monastery praying. There is a beautiful poem by Francis Thompson entitled "The Hound of Heaven" which might comfort you. It ends with, "All that I did take from you, I took not for your harms, but just that you might seek it in my arms." (God is speaking.)

I love you, Fred.

Mother.

When I was chasing Joe, I imagined telling my mother about my being gay in the context of that relationship. Mother, I would say, I have good news, and I have news we need to talk about. Not being one who enjoys that type of game, she would say, "Oh, well, what is it?"

"The good news is I'm in love. Very much in love."

"And what do we need to talk about?"

"Mother," I would say, "mother, he's Jewish."

In many ways, my mother's letter typified her deep reliance on religion, literature, and family secrets. I was taken aback at her acceptance of my offer to let her not "understand or approve" of my being gay, but I did set myself up for that, so I must learn to live with it. I do not, however, need to live with denial. The day after I received her first letter, I received a second, and as I read I became irritated:

I forgot to thank you for the beautiful sweater. I have a Pendleton Manson plaid skirt it will go beautifully with, also a navy skirt and a white. I wore your last year's sweater to a Moose Milk brunch today. I found a purple skirt and blouse that just picks up one of the embroidered flowers in the sweater, and it looks very sharp. I have worn that sweater a lot this fall and winter, and it always gets a compliment.

Dad has been wearing his new robe evenings. It looks very snug and warm. . . .

I hope everything is a little better, Fred. I hope some of Kim's pain is alleviated and that he is able to find some comfort. He is so young to be facing this.

I love you, Fred. You are in my thoughts and prayers.

Love,

Mother

P.S.   Did you like your sweaters. You may be able to get black buttons at a sewing store.

I had not yet opened the package under the Christmas tree, so I did not know whether I liked the sweaters. She did not put a question mark after her question. Deeply, she may have known the question was irrelevant. Her inquiry may have been a valiant attempt to get things back to normal.

A few weeks after Kim died, my parents came out west. They were going to visit my father's brother in Las Vegas, and they were going to Palm Springs, and they wanted to come to Phoenix. I was still in a state of shock, and I assumed that they wanted to be with me, console me, and support me. I wanted them to stay in my house, but they opted for a hotel, and on their first evening in town I stopped by after teaching my night class. I knocked on their hotel room door, and my father answered. The room was filled with uncertainty.

"Well, Fred," my father said as he shook my hand. My mother came out from the bathroom, and she looked frightened. After she gave me a small kiss on the cheek, my father offered me a glass of wine, and I said no, thank you, and then I sat at the small table. My father sat across from me, and my mother sat across the room at the desk.

"How was your trip?" I asked.

"Real good," my father said.

"Everyone is fine," my mother said, assuming I would be wondering about my nieces and nephews, brothers, sisters-in-law, sister, and brother-in-law. "Andrew is walking now, and Alison is just a doll. Now Jackie looks just like Doris, just like her, not a bit like Pat." My father poured himself a little wine and pulled out a map. "Pat does not seem to like his job," my mother continued, "but we don't know exactly what he does. Government work, you know, at GE. Just like my brother Pat. Now my brother Pat is still mad he wasn't promoted to vice president, and I'm afraid the same thing will happen to our Patrick [my brother], so I tried to get him to call my Pat. He worked on the Manhattan Project, so he can keep government secrets."

My father had the map out on the table, and he was ready to trace the yellow highlight, prepared to show me their route through Pennsylvania in an effort to move the conversation away from people and toward the physical world, the tangible experiences of life. While his finger moved along the yellow line, my mother narrated: "The hills in Pennsylvania are beautiful. Very different from the Rocky Mountains, smaller,

and not so foreboding. And reddish, not brown or gray, more like the hills just outside
Ann Arbor." My father's finger moved toward Michigan, as though I did not remember
the location of Ann Arbor.

"The hills outside Ann Arbor are much smaller," he said.

"And a little greener, wouldn't you say, Jack?"

"Different soil," he said, "and the elevation would be different."

"Ann Arbor would be higher or lower?"

"Let's see, higher I'm sure, but how much? This map does not seem to have
elevations marked."

"And the soil! The Pennsylvania soil is red."

"That would be from the rock," my father said, and finally I said I was very tired.

"I bet," my mother offered, "Did you teach tonight?"

"Yes."

"Now, what are you teaching?" my father asked.

"A graduate course in performance studies."

"Oh," they both seemed to say, and there was an uncomfortable silence.

"I really should be going."

The next day, when they were at my house, we went to the master bedroom, a large
room that opens out to the pool, furnished well with a Techline bed and large bold
paintings I gave Kim on one of our anniversaries. My mother asked, "Was this Kim's
room?"

"This was *our* room," I said.

"What a beautiful pool," my father said.

I could not, under the circumstances, teach them how to deal with the subject of their
gay son's dead lover. Their world never taught them about such things, never gave them
the vocabulary, never equipped them with the critical skills necessary to reevaluate
everything they thought they knew about gay men. We stood in our bedroom, oddly,
anxious to leave.

After they left for Palm Springs, I started cleaning out drawers. I found a letter from
my mother postmarked January 7, just 5 days before Kim died. The letter was unopened.

Dear Fred,

We are going up to the chalet for a few days, then traveling to Philadelphia.
Doris wants us to stay "very long," but she will probably long to show us the
door before too long. I'll have to pick up signals. Dad and I plan to run into New
York one day. . . . Plays are so expensive in New York. I doubt whether we will
go unless it's something I have to see.

I hope things are better at your end. Keep in touch.

Love,

Mother.

I suppose it is easy for me to scoff at the note, laugh, or become angry, but ultimately I appreciate and understand the power of her denial because I too denied my sexuality. I was complicitous in constructing the "messages that tell us how to regulate our communicative behavior and to support the supremacy of heterosexuality" (see Nakayama's chapter (6) in this volume. I expended tremendous amounts of energy on anything at all except the truth. I focused on school, work, and my writing; my mother focused on travel, family, and her reading.

My father was not absent, he was just not around much. He spent most of his time at work, 50 or sometimes 60 hours a week. When he was being fatherly, he made an effort, but sometimes it was hard to distinguish between his good-natured barbs and his bad-natured barbs.

He wanted me to be adept at sports. Not good at sports, but good enough to avoid being heckled at school, and good enough not to be an embarrassment to him. He gave me lessons, structured very much like courses, on how to look like a boy. A game of catch, then, was not a leisurely pastime or a bonding between father and son but instead was an instructional unit on how to throw a baseball. Midway through the most memorable training session, I complained about the entire educational experience and asked why we had to be doing this.

"Because you throw like a girl," he said.

From inside the house, through an open window, my mother's voice shot back, "Because a girl taught him how to throw." Class was dismissed.

The following summer, he taught me how to run. I ran like a girl, he said, and I needed to learn how to hold my arms with my fists held just below my rib cage, and don't flail, he said, hold them steady. I actually enjoyed learning how to run, and when I would go over to Tim Burnside's house to play I would run a block, walk a block, and run a block, and when I ran I would be sure to hold my arms steady, and if my hands did move, then they moved like a boxer's, ready for the punch.

When I was ready to enter manhood, he taught me how to golf. I was a less than enthusiastic student. I didn't hate golfing. I just didn't like it. One day, while we were on the golf course, I said to my father, "I just don't want to learn how to golf."

He had this look of horror and hurt on his face. "But," he said, "if you don't golf, you won't have any friends." What he meant, I thought, was that I would not be successful in business, because in the world of General Motors, people who don't golf are left out of the big deals. But I was wrong, and my father was right. I needed to golf to make friends because in Phoenix, gay men golf.

In the years following Kim's death, I settled into an often uncomfortable peace with my family. The initial quest for a "return to normalcy" contributed to my ulcer. To deny my life experiences through conversations of anything except my life was to erase the essence of my world. I forced myself and others into open discussions of my life and Kim's death. My being gay no longer was a private matter of desire but rather was a public issue of relationships and honesty. I resisted constructs of normalcy at its multiple levels; to not talk about my life is to normalize oppressive silence, to talk about my relationships in terms of marriage is to privilege the vocabulary of heterosexuality, to let pass homophobic remarks is to normalize hatred, and to not call into question the very concept of "normal" is to struggle within relations of power that privilege heterosexuals. I did not want to be "tolerated." Out of this ideology grew my challenge to my mother, offered 2 years after Kim died during a visit she took without my father. We were in a restaurant at the Grand Canyon, and over the dinner salads I said, "Accept me on my terms or not at all."

"I would prefer a compromise," she said, meaning, I assumed, that she would accept my being gay but not discuss it. She was making a pitch for tolerance, a second-rate form of grudging acceptance sans appreciation.

"No," I said, and I glared. "I will not compromise. If you do not want to talk about my being gay, you will not talk to me at all. You can think of it as a divorce." The word that good Catholics fear most hit the floor and rose to fill the room. She lowered her head and said nothing.

Three days later, the phone rang all afternoon. My brother called. My sister called. My other brother called. Yet another brother called. I said the same thing to each of them, "I am serious. Accept me for who I am or not at all."

Mine are not a simple people. They are educated people born and raised in the city. They are fully capable of thinking critically and recognizing homophobia. Oppression is a concept well within their realm of comprehension. I stood firm. Two of my brothers and my sister pursued immediate lines of communication based in inquiry and honesty, and my mother has become, in her own way, something of a gay rights advocate. She interrupts homohateful discussions with the proclamation that her son is gay, she asks me whether I am dating anybody, and on one occasion she took great pride in informing the captain of a cruise ship that the stand-up comedians should not tell hateful jokes about gay people when "some of the nicest people on this ship are the gay couples." Although my father has remained silent on my being gay, his silence is not violent, and although two of my brothers and I do not talk much, their absence does not distress me. They have their lives, and I have mine. We have found a family peace, an unlikely but realistic mixture of silence, conversation, absence, honesty, and, most important, recognition of the truth.

> *Blessed are they who are persecuted for the sake of righteousness,*
> *For theirs is the kingdom of heaven.*

Trashing Catholicism has become a literary sport and an academic pastime. The Church is sexist, homophobic, anti-Semitic, patriarchal, and, in insidious ways, racist. The documentation is sufficient, and the arguments are persuasive. Yet, for all of its sins, I turn to the Church when my life falls apart. I kneel before statues of Mary for comfort, a votive gives me a feeling of transcendental permanence, and prayer becomes an involuntary reaction to crisis. The very institution that fills me with guilt and shame provides a path of recovery. I can no more escape my Catholicism than I can escape my desires.

Yet, I am not Catholic. I am not a part of the institution. I do not go to mass, I do not take communion, I resent the pope's body politics, and I live in what the institution would call "sin." I am not a recognized part of Irish Catholic culture. My people are not included in St. Patrick's Day celebrations. We are outsiders, anomalies, and living contradictions. How, as the Ancient Order of Hibernians asks, can a person be both Irish Catholic and gay? But cultural identity is more than an institution and transcends approval.

I am, in no fixed order, gay, Catholic, and Irish. Shame is my friend. I take clandestine delight in my sinful desire to love another man. Mea culpa. Not so very long ago, my mother told me, "Not meeting Kim is one of the biggest disappointments of my life, but whose fault is that?" Mea culpa. And as I write these words, my mother is in the hospital with a broken hip, her third broken bone in as many years. And her fragile bones are a surprise? She gave birth to six children. Mea maxima culpa. If, however, I am to take ownership of my faults, then I shall claim, in a conflated cultural triune, all my faults. I am guilty of finding solace in prayer and beer, although not at the same time. I am guilty of wanting to feed a room crowded with people, and when those people all are gay men, so much the better. I am guilty of talking too much, of weaving one story into another, even when those stories hurt other people. I am guilty of fighting for my rights, of resisting colonization, and of searching for liberty. I am guilty of wanting to have a family, a family of two, a man and a man, two men who would be faithful to each other, drink beer together, throw parties for their friends, talk up a storm, and fight for their liberties. I am guilty of wanting to die in peace.

16 Upsetting That Delicate Balance

Reflections on Experiential Subtleties

Deborah Wood Holton

■ I

When I was first asked to contribute to this volume, I thought that it would be a relatively simple process, for I was sure that in my life history I had come across intolerance and thought, in fact, that I had experienced it in a variety of ways. Being from the Midwest, I thought that my experiences would lend themselves to careful scrutiny. Furthermore, I have experienced the South and have a set of experiences about which I could talk. I could discuss what prejudice is not, for example, or how my mythology about prejudice was overcome and then confirmed as I left a major southern city. Now that I have embarked on this journey of exploring my encounters with prejudice, I am not so sure. Perhaps this is a condition attributable to the turbid midwestern experience, that insidious form of prejudice that always keeps the person experiencing unsure whether he or she has experienced it. I have experienced so many shades of what I would call prejudice, and have had to negotiate my way through that prejudice in so many ways, that I no longer am clear about my own definitions anymore. I question whether this means that I am more "fair-minded," taking into account what the other person may feel or think while sacrificing my own feelings—a condition that regularly sends me to the therapist's couch. Or, I wonder whether this means that I am so accustomed to the affronts of prejudice that I am numb in my feelings and cannot express them even if I wanted to, which again sends me to the couch. In any event, there is considerable time spent on the couch when the perception of prejudice is a daily or frequent experience. In the case of others less fortunate, I can only assume from their responses played out on the streets of the city, on their children, in the solitude of their own homes, or in work environments that their ways of coping with what they confront can be even more depressing and dangerous.

Here in Chicago, the news media often highlight a situation that seems charged with prejudice. Recently a postal worker, known in the office for having a low tolerance for people unlike himself, "went off" on a couple of his coworkers, sending them to the hospital with serious injuries. In my mind, prejudice reflects a serious internal malaise that is masked by this kind of destructive behavior, hence my question about what this person must be going through to prompt such expressions of hatred and intolerance. "What is his problem?" one might hear some ask as they shake their heads in disbelief. We have a tendency to try to see everything individually. I suppose that is because as Americans we are entitled to be our individual selves and have become so at the expense of community responsibility as well as humane caring behavior, that is, caring for fellow human beings. I also suppose that at the heart, prejudice always raises the following questions in the back of the mind of the beholder, if not consciously. Is that person really a human being? Is that person really someone with whom I can share thoughts and feelings, my own humanity? Is that person someone who will care about me?

As an African American woman associate professor at a Catholic university where the ideas of tolerance and individual expression are not mutually exclusive, I have encountered various situations that suggest the haze of intolerance. I say "suggest" because in the North it is this way—unclear. Intolerance on the part of a few students, and buttressing support by systemic institutional practices, must be constantly mediated and interpreted so that I, and colleagues like myself, can "keep our heads" about ourselves at all times. This is difficult, especially when a part of what it means to live in the Midwest is to fall prey to the masking, which is a shrouding of the blatant prejudice lines with the intention of keeping one off-balance and less self-assured. It takes a strong individual to be able to discern, turn, filter, rebalance, and shift the situation when confronted with prejudice and intolerance.

Writing this narrative, then, has been more difficult than I first envisioned it would be. After all, the opportunity to talk about the impact of society's "isms" on the individual, in this case myself, does not reveal itself often, nor does it solve immediate problems. On the contrary, for those who have experienced the "isms," I suspect that it makes life more difficult because such discussions upset the equilibrium, the delicate balance that allows one to function with dignity and harmony with fellow human beings in the world. This certainly has been the case for me. I know that there are those who thrive on discussions about race, gender, class, and the like, but I am not one of them. I know many, friends among them, who will run out and get the latest book describing the "ism" experiences of women and Black folk in particular. Although I have made it a point to understand history and psychosocial perspectives, I try not to feed on the dissonance that this understanding heightens for me. Having said this, I must admit that recently I was surprised to discover that I have several shelves of books that deal solely with race, gender, and class and that these books and articles span years, even decades. What surprised me the most, I think, was not that I have these books but rather that I don't need to read them anymore. Perhaps they are so much a part of my fabric that I take for granted how they have helped shape my view of things. These days, I feel that although I must engage myself in understanding these social problems so that I can communicate with my colleagues, I also know that what I read will not ultimately change my experiences; rather, it will only reinforce the negative memories of those experiences. To read about these issues on one level is to be provided with a language to discuss them with other intellectuals and academics. At the same time, I realize that over the years I had become so sensitive to certain realities that to talk about such issues, even when I knew that the conversations were nothing more than conversations designed to go nowhere, still put salt in the wounds of my psyche.

I find that I am more angry these days, and this is hard terrain. So, I speak from a place of anger. I feel the effects of racism and sexism more sharply now, and I find myself struggling to find ways in which to transform my feelings into something useful, meaningful, and essential. I am frustrated because I no longer am numb. Being numb may be a byproduct of so many assaults that the pain no longer is localized. To be numb is to be a part of the walking wounded. I get images of Civil War veterans when I think about what that means—walking wounded.

> *In this light the one leg left, the one arm remaining, eye damaged, limbs and organs maimed, torn, punctured, seared, are metaphorical images reflecting the growing national malaise. Walking wounded. Crazy in the head. Seeing with distorted vision. Hearing voices. Hearing God. Seeing God. Hearing and seeing something that goes beyond the ordinary perceptions of normal reality. A transforming experience, unarticulated. So powerful it cannot be spoken, so compelling the words gush in inaudible sounds, illogical patterns, unintelligible meaning. Or silence. Action behind eyes. A fortress of thought. Protection. Psychic protection. The severing of connection, performing the functions—containing the rage. Numb . . .. The rage of the walking wounded. Too tired to unknot the threads that make the mind tight, that squeeze the heart. Too apathetic to think anymore that anyone cares anyway. Too damaged to see hope. Too sensitive to remain open, hopeful after so many tries, so much optimism failed.*

Yes, I thought this would be straightforward, simple, and easy.

In preparation for writing this narrative, I reviewed some of the materials I had collected over the years such as Collins's (1990) *Black Feminist Thought,* James and Busia's (1993) *Theorizing Black Feminisms,* Gates's *Race, Writing and Difference* (1986) and *Reading Black, Reading Feminist* (1990), Feagin and Sikes's *Living With Racism,* Early's (1993) *Lure and Loathing,* McClain's *A Foot in Each World* (edited by Page, 1986), West's (1993) *Race Matters,* Pinderhughes' (1989) *Understanding Race, Ethnicity and Power,* Greenlee's (1990) *The Spook Who Sat by the Door,* and, of course, hooks's books such as *Yearning* (1990), *Ain't I a Woman* (1981), and *Killing Rage* (1996). Of them all, I resonated most with Leanita McClain's work, edited by Page (1986). McClain was a journalist who wrote for the *Chicago Tribune.* A Chicago native, a Black woman who grew up in the projects, McClain became a success story and role model by all accounts: a member of the *Tribune*'s editorial board (the "first Black member"); a provocative writer who wrote about Chicago, its racial divisions and tensions, but also other things such as education, family, justice, and politics; a woman who crossed class boundaries and gave back to her community. McClain committed suicide at the age of 32 years. She had a "foot in each world" and decided to step away from it all. Now, more than ever, I can relate to her insightful and powerful words—and her ultimate choice.

I was not in Chicago when she was alive. I was living my experience elsewhere. But now that I have returned, I read her editorials and see how tremendously gifted she was as a writer. She had a talent for being able to interpret and respond to what she witnessed and felt around her in a language that was simple, direct, deep, and clear. For example, McClain's (1983) article, "How Chicago Taught Me to Hate Whites" (a piece she published through *The Washington Post* because the racial intensity of Chicago during the 1983 elections made publication in the *Tribune* risky), is powerful in its depressing reflection of today's society. Here was a woman who stood by her words and made multitudes—the broad *Tribune* readership and beyond—think about themselves through those words. The price for the pressure was too much, and so she paid for speaking out with her life. Life was too painful to live with given the knowledge and vision she had. I have gotten much from McClain in preparing this narrative. She has spoken very clearly to me.

Given her words, I found myself struggling more and more with this narrative. What is my story, anyway? What makes my story unique or special? Nothing, actually. I have found, in my self-examination, nothing particularly unusual to make it stand out in the face of others' experiences. Yet, there is no doubt in my mind that because I am not unique, I can say with all candor that this is exactly what makes our "isms" so insidious. I can lose myself in the myriad complexities of intolerance and know that I am in oceans of company. I can submerge my own personal confusion that swirls and swills around me as I live with northern racism (as opposed to the more obvious yet clarifying forms found in the South) and know that I am not alone. This was, I believe, one of the reasons that made living in the South so palatable. I knew that when I encountered someone who found it difficult to accept me because of my color or gender, I could trust that this person was "clear" with me. He or she would say upfront that my kind was not welcomed, and I would be able to respond accordingly, based on my own sense of self-worth. My life was not in a constant question, and I did not have to explain myself, my motives, or my actions for speaking out for justice and understanding (as required in the North by the privileged). I could act clearly and with full voice. My northern experience is the opposite of this clarity. It is murky and snide, opaque and oblique.

This narrative comes on the heels of the O. J. Simpson trial. My words here draw from the frustrations I have felt in conversations in which I declined comment about Simpson. As one professor, a role model for me, once told me, "Just because people ask for your opinion does not mean you have to provide it. Don't let them shift your focus from your work." No more than now has this been true. I dodged banal conversations about Simpson like a Chicago Bears running back. I didn't want the distraction and couldn't afford the superficial banter. Perhaps what I experienced was a communication breakdown, but I don't think so. I have just become less willing to provide the saving word or to be the understanding soul. "Do the homework if you really want to understand, if you really want to know" is my internal reply. Meanwhile, I am learning to respect my own anger and seek means to transcend it in ways that empower me and feed me.

Because I see my life as a quest—a quest to integrate within myself, my spirit, my mind, and my body—I welcome the opportunity to speak on the experiences that have punctuated the meaning of quest. I see myself as an artist, a creative writer. By spirit, inclination, and vision, I see and feel the world with color and textures. To me, this means that the thaw from numbness requires a form of expression that can contain the gush and flow of emotion that I am experiencing. For something this painful, I cannot talk about it in purely cerebral terms. It is too deep. What follows, then, is a series of reflections. They mark points in time and draw attention to experiences, past and present. In a way, they are like editorials and perhaps reveal McClain's increasing influence on my writing as I seek a broader audience.

■ II

I am a product of the African American middle class. My parents' ability to live in decent housing on Chicago's near South Side and send their two daughters to private high school stemmed not from family wealth but rather from the access their own educations gave them to good-paying jobs. Both parents worked, and my father worked two jobs. Our family was extended to other relatives in the city and a host of friends and church members who took interest in my sister's and my well-being and educational goals. My parents, both college educated, worked hard to maintain a living. They struggled with debt as they tried, and succeeded, to keep our small two-bedroom apartment. They worked hard to shelter my sister and me from the harsh realities of urban living, an almost impossible feat in Black Chicago. We learned pride, but I also saw them "keep their place" and make the sacrifice of pride to help ensure their children better opportunities than they had. I recall clearly, and still with pain, the time I was hit in the face by an angry White boy, Jerry, who lived in our apartment complex. He was not in my class although we went to the same school, and so we had no real contact except on the playground. We all knew his name, but he never played kickball or softball with us. One day, while I was walking home with a few of my seventh-grade classmates, he walked quickly ahead of us. We were laughing and talking behind him, although not about him. Without provocation, he turned, said some foul words, and hit me in the face because I was closest to him. He stormed away while we stood stunned as I realized my glasses were broken and my nose was bloody. (As I think about it now, perhaps he thought he was being followed by a gang.) I remember going home and being cleaned up as I recounted what happened. My parents told me that they would get another pair of glasses for me. (We could not afford a spare pair, and because I was extremely nearsighted, the few days it would take to get a replacement would be particularly difficult for me). I wanted my mother to talk with Jerry's parents and make them pay for my glasses, which I knew were expensive. My mother said she would take care of it but never talked with them about Jerry's behavior or about my glasses. I never forgot that moment, for I interpreted my experience as sacrifice of my immediate well-being to the power of "power"—White, privileged, and therefore superior. After all, I was all right, wasn't I? There were no lasting bruises, and my glasses could be repaired. As if to confirm and affirm my thinking, my mother later explained that she was in Jerry's father's graduate school class at the time and that she didn't—couldn't—mention it because she needed a good grade from him, especially because it was a hard class and the professor was difficult. The professor had double power—power in the classroom and power in his caste. It was a crucial insight for me; her need to attain a grade that would help her achieve a higher level in the Chicago public school system, thus making more money to feed, clothe, and send me to private school, was greater than the need to prevent a humiliating and degrading outcome for me. I would get over it, she reasoned. But I never did. Even now, it takes great effort to stand up for myself. I am better at it now that I am older, yet I also know that rather than being able to respond to injustice swiftly and reasonably, I have to wade through rationalization after rationalization as to why I should let any humiliation, big or small, go— always thinking of the other person before myself.

■ III

I consider issues of intolerance to be complex, subtle, and dynamic all at the same time. I sometimes look at personal events to see whether there are indicators that suggest prejudice and reassess them in terms of what I might have done to deflect the blow of that particular intolerance. Life as a dodgeball game. Life as a series of fancy footwork steps on a slippery floor. Life as a constant challenge. Will I get up and face this day? These are the questions that I face and yet find that I so deftly maneuver away from them that I am hardly aware of them at all. Do I take a stand and fight this intolerance? Is every intolerance worth my energy? Is what I think happened actually what happened?

I have found that I am more kind, more tolerant, these days. I can walk down the street with someone and see something entirely different from what is seen by the person I am with. An example of this happened recently. Three people were leaving an "open house" offered by a local realty company in an affluent part of town. Two of the people seemed to be in their late 20s or early 30s and were a couple. The third person presumably was older with gray hair. All three were White. As we passed them on our way to the open house, the older man established eye contact and smiled. My companion said that the third person was unsure of us as we approached; I said I didn't think so, that the smile was genuine. Now, this is an example of how I have changed through the years. There was a time when I would have agreed with my friend and perhaps gone further to say that the man probably wondered why Black people were walking in the neighborhood in the first place. We were not particularly coded in our dress to symbolize affluence, but then neither were they. Their mere presence complicates the coding because their color gives them status and privilege that ours does not necessarily give. What has happened that I am more open to other possibilities now? Have I become the "enemy" of my people, betraying them because I am more kind as a human being? These questions raise feelings of ambivalence about my own prejudice. Here is another spin on the same thing. As of this writing, there is a conference coming to the city featuring Black writers. Will my White colleagues understand that I do not want to be with them at an all-Black conference, which is reminiscent of similar conferences I attended during the late 1960s, because I know what that coding means? Does this betray my professional relationship with them as colleagues? Does this mean that because I have an intimate understanding of the psychic cost of being there with them because they are White, I choose not to spend my life energy—on that particular day—with that kind of conflict? Is my mediation of these social-political situations an indication of my lack of courage, my feelings about group pressure, or a heightened sense of self-protection? Am I bowing to group pressure by denying myself the opportunity to bond with my colleagues, albeit White women? Does the fact that they are going to see Alice Walker make it okay for me to be with them at a predominantly Black college known for its nationalist stance? Is this my own prejudice issue staring me in the face? Is it worth thinking about at all? How deeply is my foot in each world, and at what cost?

These questions come at a time in my own life when I find myself at a crossroads. A crossroads that asks of me, "What path is the path to a happier state of well-being? What path will lead me to experiencing an inner joy all the time?" Coping with intolerance is exhaustive and can be debilitating. My responses to prejudice and mediating its potential effects affect the way in which I look at the world. The path I choose is one I must live with for a while, until another crossroads appears before me. So, who do I become to manage prejudice now? I am getting too old to respond in the ways of my youth. Back then, I might have become belligerent or cut myself off from the lessons that I could learn from that person. Is that what we are talking about—cutting ourselves off from the lessons we can learn from other human beings? Perhaps this is it. Perhaps mediating prejudice means acknowledging that there is something to be learned here. There is something important that we must overcome. In my life now, the life role that appears to be emerging is that as entities on this planet, we have a responsibility to play out what we have been given and to evolve from it. The process of evolution suggests that we do not come into the world complete and that we are not born ready to change the world. If our bodies have to go through stages of development, then why not our spiritual selves?

For me, writing on intolerance seems to be more about articulating a spiritual awareness, both by those who feel they must exercise prejudice against others as a way of confirming their own human-ness and by those who are the targets of prejudicial behavior. I do not use the term "spirituality" in a strict Christian sense, as in "turning the other cheek." What may be the appropriate response to intolerant behavior may involve a response that is quite contrary to passivity. But there is some medication needed. When prejudice arises, there is agony on the part of the target and self-satis-faction or self-importance exhibited by the person inflicting the prejudice. Remorse or regret means that the intolerant person may be ready to engage on a more spiritual level, informed perhaps by a better understanding of history and context, to do the life work that is necessary to recognize, understand, and change the prejudicial behavior. Our distrust for each other makes this difficult. Our disillusionment at the failures to change prejudice fuels our apathy. We see our nation sliding back to a time when oppression and racism were common characteristics thought essential for the national good. We see the power structure, the institutions reedifying themselves to support "the way it was."

> *Enough with all this pluralism. We were founded on the belief that only certain people were created equal, no matter what the Constitution says, and now, by God, we are going to enforce that principle to the last breath. There are too many of us out of work. Hell, I never thought I'd see the day when I'd be back in school.*

The rationalizing goes on.

hooks (1996) talks about it poignantly in her recent book, *Killing Rage.* In it, she performs surgical incisions at the joints of racism and sexism, opening up scar tissue to remove the layers of denial, of fear, of misinterpretation. She also provides a healing hopeful view. She sets out to kill rage while acknowledging the killing effect of it. Whose rage is it? Are we once yet again expected to make the steps toward harmony— while denying our own pain? Are harmony and appreciation synonyms with integration?

A comment that hooks makes in *Interview* Magazine (Sischy, 1995) about writing the book impressed me. She describes the first essay and in the process distills away the dismissal of "hypersensitivity" from a story about a friend of hers and herself on an airplane. She talks about the subtleties that reveal themselves in recapturing seemingly insignificant incidents and points out that talking about these more subtle forms of intolerance is difficult, mainly because of the tendency to trivialize the complex. Racism is not simplistic, nor is it always overt. hooks stimulated my memory with her words, and so I began thinking back to incidents in my own life that reveal this complexity for me. Like the one that hooks describes, the incidents are subtle. So subtle, in fact, that they can be explained by a denying soul that they are unique to me—that I must have done something to provoke such behavior—or that I must be leaving something out. But we are talking about truth here. As a Black woman educated at historically Black universities at the undergraduate and graduate levels and then at a Big Ten university for my doctorate, I have had the benefit of a variety of kinds of education. I know that what I am about to share is part of the knotty truth because, thanks to my education, I know the history and have seen how it repeats itself. I know because, as one who is karmically inclined to be "the first one" in certain professional endeavors, I talk with others and seek others from whom I can learn. And although I may not be consumed by "race literature," I often must look through the dirty glasses of racism and sexism, sexism and then racism again, and then classism to protect myself.

■ IV

I have been thinking about *The Spook Who Sat by the Door* (Greenlee, 1990) lately. I have been that spook for 6 years at my current place of employ. Alone, the "only one" at my rank and residence in my college until this year. This experience of being the only one is not new to me. One of many other experiences, I once was a reporter-editor for a major publishing company at a branch office in Washington, D.C. Before applying for the position, I had been told by my mentors at Howard University that if I wanted to be a writer, then an excellent way in which to sharpen my skills was to work at a publishing company. Although quite qualified and given the title of reporter-editor, I found myself typing all day. The "reporter" to whom I was, on paper at least, equal to could not let go of a part of the overwhelming number of tax court petitions she edited that were overflowing in our office. I am talking about stacks and stacks and stacks of petitions. Here I was, a graduate with honors from a major university who had served as writer in residence for 2 years for the DC Commission on the Arts, and I was not considered capable of reading a tax court petition and using the standard phrase "deduction disallowed" where appropriate. In addition, I sat at a desk directly in front of the vice president, a middle-aged White gentleman from West Virginia. I sat directly across from a genteel, white-glove-wearing, elderly White woman, who was responsible for "keeping time," among other things. To my right and forward was the front door. To my immediate right was a young White woman, and kitty-corner in the rear was a middle-aged White man from North Carolina, whom I can only describe as the "overseer"—a man so chummy with the Black receptionist and her cousin who worked the phones part-time that I could feel their sexual tension every time they came within inches of each other, so full of innuendo and double entendre that I quickly learned to stay away and feign ignorance. My supervisor was a short, pudgy Irish man who made it clear that I was a stereotype, in his view. In my early experiences during that first year, I could not go to the "executive ladies room" without being "written up" and questioned by one of the men I just mentioned. I am not talking about abusing privilege. I typed all day. My only excitement came when I decided to paint my baby fingernails and watch them flash against the typing keys. All the vice president had to do was open his door, and I had better be there.

At my first-year review, he told me that the quality of my work was good, that I adhered to the codes of the company well, but that I had a problem with time. I was late too often (didn't matter that I came in with other reporters), and I wasn't "blending." Wasn't blending. I was the only Black, one of the few women who worked at that level as a reporter-editor. The walls throughout were stark white. The desks, low without cubicles or partitions, also were white. My desk in front, in full view, was by the door. The blend for me would mean becoming what I obviously was not. To blend meant less Black, more White.

During the remaining years, I practiced the lessons learned from the literature of social change. I found my own way. I made one. Wanting to keep my job (I needed it), I conceived my own way of blending. Integration being the expectation, I quickly learned that integration was a one-way street; integration was tolerable if it meant that the minority becomes more like the majority.

I took Dunbar's (1913) poem, "We Wear the Mask," as my anthem and proceeded to masquerade. I did not clown, ape, or make jokes, but I took myself less seriously, I think. I let things roll off. I "lightened up." In retrospect, I cannot say that at that time I would consider myself "conscious" given that "consciousness" is a willful awareness of the connectedness between human beings, indeed, all life forms. I did not consciously have God in my life then. If I had, perhaps I would have responded differently. But the unwarranted suspicion, the false accusations, and the heightened weight of minor infractions were seen in bold relief by me then and were outwardly reflected as proof of my perceived unworthiness. So, I learned to wear the mask. I learned to enjoy the game of the masquerade. I acted the part. I became strategic.

Toward the end of my second year, I was given a very complex set of excise tax law publications to sort through and update based on then newly formulated laws. No one else in the office wanted the job. My supervisor did not want to do it, and having listened to my humanizing sob story that I greatly embellished from my personal truth, I convinced him that I was the one to tackle the excise tax, determined to conquer him with my humanity. My work on the excise tax publications was one of the events that allowed me to create circumstances to get around the racism in my own way. From my success with the publications, I was able to communicate directly with editors at the main office and receive instruction and criticism that challenged my thinking. This was a short-lived but useful experience. I still was typing, but after 2½ years I finally was getting work that allowed me to problem solve—to think.

The second event revolved around hiring two women reporters, one White and one Black. Both were well qualified and capable. No longer was I the "only one," although socioeconomic background and stereotypic projections did strain my relationship with my Black colleague. The office could now choose their lesser evil, me or the other Black reporter. (This curious phenomenon of having a favorite minority, a colored "pet," is popular even now.) The possibility of blending increased as the new White reporter planned events to bring the White, male-dominated reporting staff together with the increasingly female one.

Meanwhile, I continued refining my mask. During this time, I found myself needing to have my wisdom teeth removed. I went to a major university dental school because of its reputation of providing quality care at reasonable cost. An unfortunate accident occurred during surgery. A mallet to break the wisdom teeth slipped and broke my front teeth instead. It was, like the incident described by hooks, something that could have happened to anyone. How the attending physician chose to respond to me allowed me to see racism and possibly sexism at work at the individual level.

Because part of my mask at work required that I let go of my own sense of personal pain and suffering, I went back to work the day after the accident. With my mouth swollen on both sides, my front tooth missing, and in excruciating pain, I went to work. I went because I was afraid that they would think of me, in spite of my professionalism and reliability, as shiftless, lazy, and irresponsible after all. After all that I had done to try to erase the stereotype from their collective expectations, this was what I knew to be true. When I arrived, it was clear to all that I was in pain. I said nothing. Like a "good darky woman," I put the "boss men" and how they thought about me before my self-worth and self-esteem. The Black receptionist said to me in the bathroom, "Girl, you better go home and take care of yourself. There ain't that much work in the world." *Where was I under the mask? What had I become—a spook, a shadow of myself?*

Several days later, I went back to the clinic. I recall my experience with pain even now. Before my appointment I went to the cafeteria. My face swollen still, my mouth traumatized, all I could do was eat soup and sip tea. I sat alone, looking like a battered

Black woman. Hard to keep my head up under the pain. Hard to keep the tears away. Ironically, the attending physician sat at the table near me. I watched him glance and then stare at me during conversation with his colleague seated across from him. At the moment our eyes met, he turned away and soon thereafter got up and walked away. I never saw him again.

Such a little thing. Could have happened to anyone. Was it my race, my gender, or my face that looked so abused that the possibility of a smile seemed fleeting? Was it one or all of these things that prevented him from seeing me as a human being suffering because of his charges' incompetence? Yes, he was a jerk. But what kind of jerk? At the moment our eyes met, he *chose,* as hooks reveals, to remain disconnected. He chose his "own comfort" entirely complicitous in the act. His action elevated, in my case, a mistake to an expression of racism among others; looking at me, I was still inconsequential, unimportant, and invisible.

There are a lot of responses that one could have, and that I had, in trying to rationalize and understand what I was experiencing at work and living as a single woman in the city. That I was a young, upcoming "reporter cub," unfamiliar with corporate structure and therefore requiring more supervision, could be argued but does not account for what I had been told I would be doing when I was hired and what I was expected to actually do. I dressed the part, with the exception of my short, well-groomed Afro, so it could not be my appearance except for the obvious. I was blending as best I could under the circumstances. A genuinely shy person, I found that I had to rely a lot on the performance training I learned while at Howard. I was not an acting student, a playwright instead, but I, like others, had to learn the art. Those skills helped me keep the mask intact as I smiled and conversed with people who couldn't have cared less about me. No birthday parties or acknowledgments for me. No easing up on the typing with the exception of the brief excise tax assignment.

I was able to parlay an assignment at a nearby government agency during my final days, which allowed me to act like I was one of the reporting group. I knew I was being watched, followed by my supervisor and "overseer," so I was even more careful about making sure I signed out correctly and accurately. Eventually, I was able to leave with dignity; I was offered another job and took it. It was then that I learned about the office "hot seat." For *3 years,* I had sat by the door in the desk that all the other reporters occupied during their *3-month* probation periods. The hot seat was a part of the office ritual designed to see whether reporters could take the pressure and the heat.

■ V

The O. J. Simpson trial ended today. I am relieved that it is over and that Simpson can now move forward. I do not condone abuse of any kind, yet I am torn by my heightened awareness of abuse against women and by my deep understanding of what justice has meant for Black people in this society, particularly Black men. And so, I am not judging him. His peers did that. Evidence was presented. Witnesses testified. Examination after examination, cross-examination after cross-examination took place. His peers found him not guilty, and that is enough for me. I am disturbed because the media (which are a collective of "you" and "you" with very few of "me" in decision-making roles, not some monolithic, unscalable tower of authority we would like to blame) saw fit to embrace the notion that this was a racial trial and hold onto it so tightly that the fact that in this country one is "innocent until proven guilty" never could capture the seeming majority thinking. The justifiable outrage about the cruel and vicious murders was sensationally and stereotypically fused with the image of a big Black man, famous and wealthy, doing the deed. The media succeeded in raising the short hairs on the back necks of many European Americans, planting fear and justification for all the reasons why they never would have their daughters marry Black men. When D. W. Griffith sensationalized the stereotype of "big Black brute" forcing himself on the pure White (presumably) virgin in the national mind, and when that specter became the standard for the industry, people of African descent realized that the nation had descended to a new low. Justifying Jim Crow, segregation, lynchings, and murder, the film *Birth of a Nation* was a phenomenon at the beginning of the century that galvanized the minds of many against people of African descent. Now, almost 100 years later, we revisit that specter without taking into account the fact that the framing of Black men by the justice system has been in practice since slavery. (Think of all those free men and women captured illegally and sold into slavery.) Our history haunts us. We have taken only baby steps during all those years.

What disturbs me is the fact that people do not really know what "racism" is, although it has been a word volleyed back and forth, especially in reference to the Simpson case. People of African descent and other minorities of color may experience racism, but as far as being formally educated about its place in American history and its resistance to eradication is concerned, they know, generally speaking, only a little more than their Euro-brethren and -sisteren. I am, therefore, neither amazed nor amused, to paraphrase Stevie Wonder, when I hear people talking about racism without understanding the complexities of our national problem. When I hear someone talking about race, I often inquire as to the following. Did you formally take a class that looked at American history from the broad spectrum? If not, have you picked up Franklin and Moss's (1994) *From Slavery to Freedom* or Bennett's (1993) *Before the Mayflower* and read either of those texts from cover to cover? I listen to the answers in their conversations. I am not talking about Black studies. I am talking about revealing and interpreting the American landscape that includes the perspective of those "minority groups" who experienced, and still experience, the impact of White supremacy as it has flourished in this society.

I had to learn about racism, just as I am learning about sexism. My high school years were spent at a small private academy that originally was a midwestern prep school for Harvard University. I lived a relatively sheltered life. I had experiences that could have informed me about racism but did not have the benefit of theory or structure to apply the appropriate lenses to see. I used to laugh and joke along with everybody else about the future and would privately wonder about why the European and Asian kids were counseled to go to the best schools—many with grades much worse than mine—and remain puzzled by how I, as well as others like me, was lucky to get advised to go to college at all. In the end, it was our parents and friends of the family who counseled us reliably. I still remember the woman who called and called, asking that I consider going to a small junior college in northern Illinois. At the end of the 1960s, I felt that I needed to remove some variables that I only sensed affecting my future. Yet, it was not until I went to college that I really discovered what racism was. I went to Howard University in Washington, D.C., a historically Black institution of higher learning. There I realized that without the stigma of color, I, as well as other students, could achieve and ascend or fail and descend, as our individual natures inclined us to do. We were not prejudged as to whether we could do the work, make the grade, or become "somebodies." There we already were "somebodies," and to apply ourselves meant that we were following a tried-and-true path to realizing whatever dreams propelled us forward. At Howard, I learned that people are people, that there are people who live with great integrity as well as people who do not, that there are people who have talent and gifts and those who do not, that those who apply themselves can succeed and those who don't can fail. Later, when I went to Atlanta University (also a historically Black institution of higher learning) for my master's, I learned how important self-esteem is for success. I learned the value of nurturing and the value of rational, systematic inquiry. These two institutions prepared me in infinite ways in how to think, how to think about myself and others, how to find dignity in adversity, and how to survive the subtle and not so subtle blows that are bound to hit every person of color who lives in the real world.

Because I learned about racism formally, I had the benefit of tempering the impact of its terrible lessons with the realization that "still we survive, still we strive" through my engagement with professors and projects that broadened my perspectives and possibilities for self-expression. When I think about the jury in the Simpson trial, I think back to the women and men that I saw and knew at these institutions. Because of my Howard and Atlanta university experiences, I can see how those people on the jury could very well have looked at the facts as presented (not as interpreted and reinterpreted by the media with slants toward the stereotype) and found Simpson not guilty because there was reasonable doubt, surely and swiftly—in no nonsense fashion. I find disgusting the cry of "emotionalism" that went out loudly when the verdict did not go the way of the seeming majority; it suggests to me that the stereotype of Black people (and the few "others" with them) not being capable of making rational decisions, based on the facts as they were presented in the case, is getting ready to blossom along with many forms of backlash that will send all people of color reeling well into the next century. Give the jury some credit. The jurors did what they were charged to do. Enough. Let Simpson live out the rest of his life in peace. Let all of us get on with our lives and transcend this insidious, blinding disease called American racism. All it will take is courage and a healthy appetite for the truth.

PART V

Interventions

17 Personal and Interpersonal Interventions

Flavio Francisco Marsiglia
Michael L. Hecht

As we were discussing possible approaches to overcoming prejudice, Flavio Marsiglia recalled a particular effort undertaken by the Council of Christians and Jews in a large midwestern city. The project aimed at bringing together people who did not spontaneously interact with each other on a regular basis. The organizers' assumption was that by bringing people together in small discussion groups, individuals would share their fears and uneasiness about each other and prejudice would diminish. Marsiglia is not sure about the overall effectiveness of the effort. However, he remembers a comment made by a Puerto Rican woman during one of the meetings he attended. She said that eliminating prejudice was too high of an aim for that community and suggested starting by tolerating each other. His first reaction was to question such a proposal. He remembers saying, "Aren't we beyond the tolerance point?" But he gained a different perspective on the subject just a few days after that meeting, when the following incident took place. Here is Marsiglia's narrative:

I was having lunch with other Latino/a colleagues in a neighborhood restaurant. We formed a handsome bilingual and multiracial group. I had been in that restaurant before, and the food and service were always to my satisfaction. That was not the case on this particular occasion. The server was rude and no one at our table was served what he or she ordered. When the level of discomfort began to escalate, I spoke with one of the owners. She responded to my concerns by saying, "If you and your friends are not satisfied, you have the choice of not returning to our establishment." I had chosen the restaurant. I was angry and confused. Later, I gained some clarity. On previous occasions when I visited that establishment, I was part of a White-looking group. On this occasion, I was part of a multiracial group. I shared the incident with all my other friends and acquaintances, and by doing so I felt I was beginning my own small-scale boycott. The restaurant went out of business a few months later. I knew that the closure could not have been directly related to our boycott, but at some level I had kept alive the fantasy that we had helped close the doors of an establishment that fostered bigotry and hate.

The restaurant experience changed my initial reaction to the comment made by the woman at the Council of Christians and Jews meeting. Was she right about aiming just for increased tolerance? I was somehow prepared to deal with prejudice in the workplace and in other institutions, but through the described restaurant experience I learned that prejudice may appear anywhere and at any time. Was the restaurant owner just prejudiced, or was she also trying to enforce an unwritten norm given to her by her regular customers? From my previous visits to the establishment, I had thought of her as an older, gentle woman. During the incident, her facial expression changed and I saw hate in her eyes. A great distance surfaced between us, and she effectively conveyed the message that we were not welcome in her restaurant. Many years later, I still wondered how I should have responded. Was there something else I was supposed to have done or said? Was there anything we could have done to help her overcome her prejudice? The experience changed me as I suppose every experience with prejudice changes those affected by it. From those experiences with prejudice, we start to develop a map that tells us where we belong and where we may be rejected. Almost in an unconscious way, we probably start to avoid places and situations where we do not feel welcome.

The idea of boundaries appears to advance our understanding of these intricate dynamics. Marsiglia and his friends crossed some boundaries that were firmly in place separating the insiders from the outsiders. The group's presence in that forbidden space challenged the boundaries' mere existence, and they were punished for their transgression. Prejudice was explained and justified by a(n) (il)logical existing canon. Prejudice originated and later enforced and maintained a set of arbitrary and unjust boundaries. These boundary-maintaining efforts probably were passed on in that community through narratives.

We can assume, as in the restaurant example, that narratives give meaning and interpret realities for individuals included or excluded by set boundaries. The stories generated by insiders and outsiders inscribe themselves in larger narratives that provide and distribute the operative vocabularies, identifying the forbidden and determining to whom the prohibitions apply (Marsiglia & Zorita, 1996). As we look for solutions, those narratives need to be examined and challenged. The idea of accepting tolerance as the goal of our efforts to overcome prejudice presents the risk of accepting oppressive narratives as the norm. To overcome prejudice, we need to do more than tolerate each other's narratives. As we teach graduate and undergraduate cultural diversity courses, we have grown to appreciate students' tolerance toward each other; however, underneath that polite tolerance often rests baggage in the form of unspoken words and repressed narratives. In these politically correct times, we may confuse tolerance with make believe. Pretending to accept others as they are is not helping us much in our efforts to overcome prejudice. There is some evidence that people who express tolerant attitudes act in discriminating ways. This conflict between attitude and behavior needs to be explored, particularly when considering the more subtle discriminatory behaviors.

Prejudice, discrimination, and oppression appear to form some of the layers of the human experience leading to intolerance. In this chapter, we reflect on these concepts and attempt to identify some strategies to overcome prejudice at the personal and interpersonal levels.

■ Prejudice, Discrimination, and Oppression

Prejudice, from the Latin *praeiudicium,* is commonly understood as "an adverse judgment of opinion formed beforehand without knowledge of the facts" (Dell Publishing, 1994, p. 653). Prejudice can be described as a negative attitude toward an entire category of people and involves attitudes, thoughts, affect/emotions, and beliefs (Schaefer, 1996). Those attitudes create and justify social distance between people. Prejudice may or may not lead to discrimination (Merton, 1976) but alone is problematic because it robs us of part of our humanity. Prejudice coupled with misuse of power is discrimination that is even more distressing because it involves acting out one's prejudiced attitudes. These attitudes and the beliefs on which they are based are used to justify the oppression and alienation of entire groups of people. In the vignette presented in the introduction, we had an example of discrimination—a negative attitude and behavior toward a group of people based on their skin color. The example went beyond prejudice to discrimination when the intolerance was acted out through negative treatment of customers singled out based on their differences.

Prejudice appears to have a dialectical relationship with oppression and misuse of power. Those in power attempt to maintain their status quo by developing opinions without knowledge of facts or change the facts to justify their oppressive behaviors. "The oppressed are regarded as the pathology of the healthy society" (Freire, 1970/1995, p. 55). The dynamics of domination and oppression attempt to strip individuals of their own dignity. Other authors associate discrimination more strongly to situational factors than to the presence of prejudice (e.g., Duckitt, 1993). From this approach, we may say that people become prejudiced toward each other when they are competing for perceived limited resources. For example, when unemployment was high in southern California, there was a wave of anti-immigrant sentiment and actions (e.g., Proposition 186). Rather than examining the economic reasons for unemployment, those in power benefited when they distracted their constituencies by blaming those who were different from the majority. The perceived near collapse of the Californian economy was irrationally traced to immigrant workers. As a consequence, an already oppressed group became doubly marginalized by the intensification of prejudice.

If prejudice is the consequence and the explanation of oppression, then liberation needs to be a central element of any efforts to overcome prejudice. Freire (1970/1995) suggests that it is through critical and liberating dialogue, which presupposes action, that prejudice can be overcome. Following Freire's approach to action presupposes gaining more clarity on how prejudice affects people. For example, Young-Bruehl (1996), in her recent book *The Anatomy of Prejudices,* charges researchers with two fundamental shortcomings in the study of prejudice: treating all prejudices as if they were one and treating them as essentially cognitive. She argues that racism, anti-Semitism, sexism, and homophobia differ in their internal (il)logic; that is, although all expressions of prejudice are oppressive, they may differ in intensity and scope. In part, Young-Bruehl traces prejudice to the unconscious, and she recommends action and confrontation of one's oppressors as a way in which to combat prejudice. These confrontations need to bring about solutions toward lasting change. Individual and collective efforts toward overcoming prejudice need to take place within a broader framework that would guarantee their viability.

Unfortunately, most of the work on responses to discrimination focuses on the discriminator (Lalonde & Cameron, 1994), assuming a passive role for the "victim."[69] This work focuses on techniques to restructure systems or change discriminating, prejudiced, or stereotyping people. An alternative, less traveled road examines the self-liberatory action that targets of discrimination can take. Some of the major steps in reducing discrimination have emerged naturally from individual action. Rosa Parks' refusal to give up her bus seat set off political protest in the United States that changed the discriminatory practices of the Montgomery, Alabama, bus system and contributed to the civil rights movement. Fortunately, there is some research examining these individual strategies for combating prejudice. Three lines of research are relevant: Neuberg's (1994) work on stereotyping, Lalonde and Cameron's (1994) work on responses to discrimination, and Hecht and colleagues' work on communication improvement strategies (Hecht, Collier, & Ribeau, 1993; Martin, Hecht, & Larkey, 1994).

Neuberg (1994) examines actions that either encourage or discourage stereotyping. Negative stereotyping and prejudice are decreased when a potential target acts in an ingratiating fashion by trying to get the other person's positive regard. Developing friendships or being seen as credible or reliable are two such ingratiating strategies. On the other hand, when people act in a superior or intimidating style, stereotypes are more likely to be invoked. So, it would seem that going along with the other might be a good way in which to avoid stereotypes. Unfortunately, accommodating the other's interactional script (i.e., going along with the way in which the other wants to interact) tends to confirm stereotypes and is described as the "self-presentational death knell of any target wishing to be perceived as an individual distinct from the stereotyped group" (p. 124). This work suggests that a potential target avoid acting superior and intimidating while at the same time pushing for a proactive self-presentational agenda of its own—a delicate balance indeed.

Lalonde and Cameron (1994) provide a range of options, starting with preparatory actions such as talking to other people and exploring options. They describe five dimensions along which responses to discrimination can vary: active/passive, normative/non-normative, individual/collective, self-directed/system-directed, and public/private. Active responses are more likely in typical situations, whereas passive responses often are internal (e.g., reacting to stress by changing the way in which one thinks about things). The normative/non-normative dimension refers to conduct with and without support of the social system. Normative actions include self-improvement and political participation, whereas non-normative responses include actions outside the system up to and including violence. Non-normative responses are more likely in situations where there is little chance of otherwise escaping the disadvantaged position. Individual actions are more likely in an open group or when facing one-on-one or interpersonal discrimination. Collective responses occur more frequently when the group borders are not permeable (allowing movement in and out) and when facing institutional discrimination. These responses are similar to self-directed versus system-directed responses except that this category refers to the target, not the entity pursuing the change. Finally, responses may be public or private, with the latter often being the more costly.

Hecht's own work with colleagues examines problematic intergroup communication and the responses to these problems (Martin, Hecht, & Larkey, 1994). A number of problems or issues are identified in this work, including some that are clearly of an intergroup nature (e.g., negative stereotyping) and others that may be more interpersonal (e.g., authenticity, genuineness). However, the intergroup nature of this interaction suggests that they are not purely interpersonal, and the descriptions of issues (e.g., powerless, lack of acceptance) support this interpretation (Hecht, Collier, & Ribeau, 1993). While work continues, 12 responses, called communication improvement strategies, have been identified thus far: asserting a point of view, avoidance, interaction management, other orientation, inform and educate, express genuineness, confront, treat as individual or equal, internal management, be open and friendly, positive self-presentation, and language management.

These strategies can be linked to Neuberg's (1994) and Lalonde and Cameron's (1994) suggestions. For example, asserting one's point of view and interaction management are similar to Neuberg's (1994) idea of establishing one's own agenda, but assertion also includes expressing ideas and management includes the general flow of the conversation (e.g., turn taking, turn length). Avoidance is a passive strategy that comes with the belief that some people never will change. Other orientation involves expression of interest in the other and is similar to Neuberg's ideas of ingratiation. Inform and educate refers to the need to give people information where ignorance might underlie prejudice and stereotypes. Internal management is a passive strategy that we often find tied to religious teachings. Both positive self-presentation and language management (e.g., avoiding slang, using educated words) are reflected in Neuberg's ideas about presentational issues.

Our findings to date also converge. For example, we find (Martin et al., 1994) that in low-intimacy relationships (e.g., acquaintances, colleagues), active responses are more likely. Conversely, in more highly intimate relationships (e.g., close friends), responses tend to be more passive. In addition, African Americans generally use more active (assertiveness) and mutual (avoidance, other orientation) responses than do European

Americans, who use more passive individual strategies. We also find that when the situation is more clearly intergroup than interpersonal, either accommodative strategies or divergent or confrontational strategies may be used. In more clearly interpersonal situations, accommodative strategies tend to be used exclusively.

Clearly, our understanding of liberating and personally empowering actions is in its infancy. We are just beginning to understand how people can respond to prejudice in their daily lives, and we need to learn more about this important process. Fortunately, more is known about interventions on a more global level.

The democratic process appears to provide that broader framework for implementing and sustaining desired changes. However, American democracy itself has been identified as a fertile ground for prejudice. West (1993) refers to American democracy as an experiment that "took for granted the ugly conquest of Amerindians and Mexicans, the exclusion of women, the subordination of European working-class men, and the closeting of homosexuals" (p. 156). What does one do when the main tool offered by society to combat prejudice is itself an instrument of oppression? One approach to this dilemma is to search deeper and attempt to gain in our understanding of viable strategies toward change at different levels or layers. The personal level needs to be connected to the collective in some dialectical form. Different theoretical approaches to the study of prejudice can assist us in identifying some possible alternatives.

■ Theoretical Basis for Solutions

The layered perspective presented by Hecht and Baldwin in Chapter 3 challenges us to expand on the traditional conceptualization of the phenomenon. We are invited to research and understand prejudice from a multimethod and multiview approach. The authors suggest that we enrich the classical psychological dimension of prejudice with other layers such as social, linguistic, political, and economic dimensions. They underline the communication element present in prejudice. They propose that intolerance can be changed into tolerance and that tolerance can be changed into appreciation. Communication between two individuals needs to be examined and, if need be, changed. They propose to work at the individual, dyadic, relational, and communal levels.

The layered perspective provides us with a compass pregnant with possibilities and frees us from the rigidity that characterizes other narrower approaches. It is from a layered perspective that we would like to revisit our previous concern about tolerance. How do we define tolerance? Do we pretend that our differences are not there? The term *tolerance* continues to challenge us. We find the term and the attitude attached to it a bit patronizing. We hear a voice saying, "I do not like you, but I will be polite about it. Please do the same, keep your distance, and stay in your place." Starting with Allport's (1954/1979) contact theory, we review some of those layers and multiple views about overcoming prejudice.

According to Allport (1954/1979), "Prejudice is an antipathy based upon a faulty and inflexible generalization. . . . It may be directed toward a group as a whole or toward an individual because he [or she] is a member of that group" (p. 9). Prejudice, according to Allport, can be manifested through interpersonal discrimination. Interpersonal discrimination exists on a continuum, from antilocution through avoidance, exclusion, and physical attack to extermination. All these attitudes and behaviors evoke the idea of distance and hate between people. Prejudice becomes an expression of what we do not know about each other, the unexplored, the unfamiliar, the inhumanity we carry within us. The basic premise of this theory is that personal contact between members of two groups would break down negative stereotypes and reduce prejudice and discrimination. Whereas this is primarily a social-psychological theory, more recent research provides structural and relational extensions.

The contact hypothesis has stimulated a great deal of focused research. Some of this research describes the sources of resistance to change. At least seven interpersonal obstacles have been identified:

1. People insulate themselves from information that challenges their existing beliefs (Rothbart, 1996).
2. People tend to be more favorable toward an individual member of a category than they are toward the entire category (Rothbart, 1996).
3. It is difficult to create the type of contact needed to reduce prejudice in the real world with long-standing intergroup hostility (Rothbart, 1996).
4. Stereotypes are very stable and serve different functions for different people as well as multiple functions for any one individual (Snyder & Miene, 1994).
5. People often do not generalize from the individual to the group (Rothbart, 1996). This resistance may be accomplished by subtyping the group or by seeing the individual as atypical or as a nonmember. Good-fitting, typical exemplars of a stereotype are more likely to be activated by the category label than are bad-fitting, atypical, disconfirming exemplars that tend to be treated as exceptions or "nonmembers." The central paradox is that, on the one hand, the more people refute the stereotype through contact, the more the stereotype changes; on the other hand, the greater refutation weakens the association of the individual and the group and makes for less change. Contact somehow must maximize the refutation of the stereotype, but the link between the refuting individual and the group cannot be ignored. The problem is that an optimal level of disconfirmability must both disconfirm and activate a category, and these are inversely related. Five strategies suggested for overcoming this dilemma are that (a) disconfirming attributes are embedded in an otherwise typical exemplar; (b) disconfirming aspects of the exemplar can be made salient; (c) contextual variables such as social context, task demands, and linguistic usage can maintain the perceived link between exemplar and category; (d) the exemplar should be moderately disconfirming; and (e) when the disconfirming evidence is not concentrated (but is spread out over a number of members and perhaps over time), recent research suggests that the group membership of minorities has to be made salient to members of the majority culture (otherwise, they are seen as atypical, and

positive contact has no effect on prejudice (van Oudenhoven, Groenewoud, & Hewstone, 1996).

6. Emphasizing group heterogeneity will reduce prejudice (Aboud, 1993; Aboud & Doyle, 1996).

7. Even under ideal conditions, only a limited amount of change is likely (and then over a long period of time).

We can see that even when focusing only on personal and interpersonal factors, obstacles are daunting. However, research does demonstrate that under certain conditions contact does help. Surprisingly, frequent contact is not one of the conditions and may, in fact, even hamper relations (Brewer, 1986). However, contact among equal status relationships, involving cooperation and interdependence occurring in a supportive climate with egalitarian norms and opportunities for personal relationship and self-revealing interaction, has been shown to reduce prejudice (Allport, 1954/1979; Amir, 1969; Cook, 1985; Stephan & Stephan, 1996). This research also suggests that individuals or groups need to be working toward common goals where there are sufficient resources to avoid competition and institutional support is provided (Cook, 1985). Under these situations, people are motivated to form accurate impressions and to use their cognitive and behavioral resources for change (Neuberg, 1994). Other research suggests that exposure to heterogeneous members of the out-group may reduce prejudice (Aboud, 1993; Aboud & Doyle, 1996) and that promoting a more differentiated, less stereotypical view of the out-group also reduces prejudice (Aboud & Doyle, 1996).

This research has spawned a number of theories to explain this array of findings. The *common in-group identity model* (Gaertner, Dovidio, & Bachman, 1996) argues that effective contact occurs when members' perceptions of two separate groups ("us" and "them") becomes one inclusive category ("we"). A superordinate identification is created that generates a "dual" identity and refocuses attention away from the intergroup nature of contact toward a common identity. As a result, the positive feelings associated with in-group membership in this superordinate identity become generalized to what previously had been considered out-group members.

The model is based on the idea that intergroup bias is based on in-group enhancement rather than on out-group devaluation and that group formation brings in-group members closer to each other. However, people do not necessarily give up their separate group memberships when the dual identity is formed. In fact, if both subgroup and superordinate group identities stay salient, then the reduction in bias can generalize to other groups (Anastasio, 1993: Anastasio, Bachman, Gaertner, & Dovidio, 1997). One method for creating this dual identity is to assign roles within the superordinate group that crosscut the original group membership.

Studies support the viability of this approach (for a review, see Gaertner et al., 1996). The studies have established that cooperation and feeling like one group (as opposed to two groups) reduces out-group bias and makes out-group members appear closer and that these factors could be induced through group structure and task. Also, those with dual identities were more likely to see less bias and a single, superordinate group rather than subgroups. However, in a bank merger situation, dual identities were associated with more bias. So, whereas common superordinate identity decreases bias, dual identity's effects depend on the context. Where the subgroup identities are divisive or counterorganizational roles (e.g., in a merger situation), dual identities may increase bias. In addition, affective reactions mediate effects of conditions of contact on bias.

A second approach is called the *personalization model* (Brewer & Miller, 1984). This model predicts that contact will be effective if it consists of highly personalized rather than category-based interaction. The model argues that one should reduce the salience of the group membership.

The *distinct social identity model* (Hewstone & Brown, 1986b) provides a third approach. This model is closest perhaps to Allport's (1954/1979) original formulation and argues that positive, group-based contact is needed. Intergroup contact should be cooperative and pleasant with group membership salient. Groups are given distinct but complementary roles to play in a common task.

Brewer (1996) argues that to be successful, contact must balance the need for inclusion or belonging with the need for exclusion or uniqueness and achieve equilibrium. This creates an "optimal distinctiveness" that is independent of group status or evaluation by others. Brewer argues that the common in-group identity model does not satisfy the need for uniqueness, the personalization model does not satisfy the need for belonging, and although the distinct social identity model fulfills both conditions (inclusion and distinctiveness), the interdependence is unstable and equilibrium is not reached.

This critique led her to develop the *theory of optimal distinctiveness* (Brewer, 1996), which attempts to balance these three elements. The model argues for a salient superordinate category that allows for differentiation and individuation. Social structures are *not* nested hierarchies; rather, intergroup structure has crosscutting roles and social categories, and roles and social categories are functionally independent. Here subgroup identities are salient, and the individual's contributions are judged in relation to the collective goal. For example, where A and B are two groups and 1 and 2 are two roles, structure would be as follows:

$$A1 \quad A2$$
$$B1 \quad B2$$

However, there still are potential problems with these arrangements. If subgroup membership is salient (i.e., identification is high), then cooperative interaction may threaten group membership. Status differences also can cause problems. In addition, it is not clear whether both inclusion and distinctiveness are operative at all times. If they both are operative, are they dialectically or dimensionally related? How is equilibrium maintained? What are the destabilizing forces that might be useful in creating positive intergroup relationships?

Despite the remaining questions, this integrative approach seems a promising direction for intervention research combining the structural elements with the personal and interpersonal elements. We know, for example, that prejudice and discrimination may not relate in situations with clear and salient normative criteria for equitable and fair behavior but that the relationship becomes stronger in informal social interaction (Duckitt, 1993). However, if the norms exist over a long period of time, will the prejudicial attitudes and feelings change slowly to conform to the behaviors and structure? Similarly, if we change the institutional arrangements that privilege certain groups and provide them with the power to discriminate as Pettigrew (1986) suggests, will this embed lasting change in society at both the individual and structural levels, or are individual and group- level interventions needed as complements?

The structural and personal levels sometimes may impose competing demands. Van Oudenhoven et al. (1996) show that intergroup identity must be visible for contact to ameliorate prejudice. However, highlighting these identities reinforces their use as social categories and contributes to the racialization, sexualization, and so on of our thinking and intergroup relations. So, although making one's group membership salient during an interaction may help reduce intergroup bias on the individual level, it adds to the problem on the communal or societal level.

Of course, historic and economic relations would have to be considered in developing the model, and they provide a serious complication. What does "equal status" mean to members of the two groups that historically have had unequal status relationships? How recent or distal does the equalization have to be? If groups have historical enmity, how can the process begin, and what sort of developmental process can move toward the quickest resolution?

Keeping in mind these complications, it is possible to formulate a model for interventions based on the existing dynamics and the nature of the problem. This model is based on the premise that the appropriate intervention depends on the causes and levels of prejudice. Snyder and Miene (1994) argue that interventions must address the appropriate functions with different interventions designed for different functions. Following the layered approach, at the personal and interpersonal levels, prejudice and discrimination are seen as caused by four types of problems: out-group derogation, in-group enhancement, negative interdependence, and differentiation/individuation conflict. In addition, there are at least three levels for problems: individual, groups, and communities. Based on these premises, the model depicted in Table 17.1 is offered as a beginning or suggested direction. A second model might also be explored based on the types of threat enumerated by Stephan and Stephan (1996). This model is depicted in Table 17.2.

Finally, we would like to briefly address the largest scale experiment in contact school integration. Although not an unequivocal success, research suggests that integration works best when done in an elementary school structure (Grades 1-8), which emphasizes both social and academic goals, rather than a junior high school structure (Grades 7-9), which emphasizes academic goals only (Rich, Ben-Ary, Amir, & Eliassy, 1996). This work also suggests that in the case of immigrants, they should be integrated immediately into heterogeneous classrooms, providing some special tutorial work and assigning someone (e.g., a coordinator of newcomers) to be responsible for the immigrant students (Rich et al., 1996).

TABLE 17.1: A Layered Model of Prejudice Intervention

Problem	Level	Model	Solution
Out-group derogation	Individual	Decategorization/ personalization	Positive one-on-one contact without salient intergroup distinctions to improve relations with an individual member of an out-group
Out-group derogation	Group	Decategorization/ personalization	Positive one-on-one contact; intergroup distinctions to reduce out-group bias
In-group enhancement	Superordinate group	Recategorization/ common in-group/ Identity	Create superordinate identity
Negative interdependence	Subgroup	Subcategorization/ distinct social identity	Distinct but complementary roles
Differentiation/ individuation conflict	Superordinate and subgroups	Optimal distinctiveness	Crosscutting roles

TABLE 17.2: A Threat-Based Model of Prejudice Intervention

Type of Threat	Solution
Symbolic	Provide intercultural training programs that stress value similarities
Realistic	Create superordinate identity through common in-group identity model
Intergroup anxiety	Provide training about out-group's subjective culture and structure positive contact
Negative stereotypes	Foster equal status contact with people who moderately counter the stereotypes

Having posed these models and reviewed the literature, we wanted to apply these principles to situations we have experienced. We discussed situations that met some or all of the conditions for successful contact. We talked about our lives and the lives of those around us. After telling each other stories, we identified two that we wish to share. These are offered not as "tests" of the contact hypothesis but rather as a springboard for our analyses.

■ Michael Hecht's Story

Flavio, when I think about contact in my life, it reminds me of my son's exposure to gay and lesbian culture. Growing up, he knew a number of my gay and lesbian friends.

Most of these people were "out" to him, so he knew them not only as my friends and in their professional roles (most were professors) but also as members of a community. However, these people did not fulfill all of the criteria for successful contact. In particular, they did not provide equal status contact.

In college, my son joined the debate team. On his team and throughout the debate circuit, he met numerous gays and lesbians. Again, this contact was less than ideal because some of it was unequal status contact and other contact was competitive.

When my son graduated college, he began work in the television industry. This work led him to Orlando, Florida. On one show, he found himself working among a number of gay colleagues. Needing housing, he began to share an apartment with three of these coworkers. I saw in him a growing sense of acceptance and appreciation because he not only experienced the roommates as colleagues and friends but also gained entrance into their world. Whereas his exposure to my friends and gay debaters may have opened him up to these experiences, I believe it was this equal status, noncompetitive, friendly contact that led to his more appreciative understanding of gay life.

■ Flavio Marsiglia's Story

The city of Sarajevo in prewar times came to mind as we were searching for such an example. As an uninitiated visitor to that beautiful town during the mid-1980s, I found Sarajevo to be a city meeting all the criteria for successful contact. I was unaware of the latent and long repressed resentments among the different communities of Bosnia-Herzegovina. Serbs, Croats, Bosnians, Jews, Moslems, Catholics, and Orthodox Christians appeared aware of their differences and at the same time committed to share a common space and to maintain a healthy level of curiosity about each other. Just a decade after my trip, it is difficult and painful to write about Sarajevo and its former cosmopolitan charm. During the same trip, I visited the city of Mostar located just a few hours (by train) south of Sarajevo. I was taken by Mostar's beautiful Turkish bridge unifying the East and the West. Residents in both cities looked to me as though they were more than tolerating each other. History tells me otherwise; for example, the majestic Turkish bridge in Mostar, where I saw young people of all backgrounds gathering at evening time to chat, was destroyed during the war, probably by the same young people who were coexisting peacefully during my visit.

These experiences made us question the principle of coexistence and sustained contact as a comprehensive strategy to overcome prejudice. Although the contact theory of intergroup relations has provided a theoretical framework for important research efforts, it appears to be limited to a psychological understanding of the phenomenon. Contact is an important component of interventions designed to deal with individual prejudices such as the ones Michael's son felt. Contact may even play a role in structural relations such as those experienced one-on-one in an organization. However, my story points to its limitations. Contact does not take into account the historical and cultural aspects of prejudice that were present in Sarajevo. It also does not address our concerns about "tolerance" as a goal of intervention. Perhaps if we wish people to engage in politely distanced interaction and create systems of coexistence, then contact may work as a guiding principle. But if we are to commit ourselves to truly appreciate each other and our differences, then we need to search for a more encompassing principle.

Tolerance traditionally has been associated with the multicultural paradigm as a means of transcending differences between people. Influenced in part by the Frankfurt school and various French poststructuralist philosophers, multiculturalists have questioned the hegemony of Western humanism and at the same time have embraced relativist and essentialist analyses. Multiculturalism rejects Eurocentrism and at the same time nurtures itself almost exclusively from European theoretical models. Multiculturalism lacks a conception of power and, because of this, treats all symbols of difference as equally valid (Knowles, 1996). Multiculturalism is a limited strategy that often cannot recognize its own limits. Its limitations become obvious when, for example, Muslim young women are not allowed to attend French schools wearing their traditional veils. The multicultural perspective supports the expression and celebration of differences in the private sphere, but it lacks a conception of how tensions arising from these differences can be managed. President Clinton's "don't ask, don't tell" policy in treating gay men and lesbians in the military takes the ideal of private multiculturalism to its limits. The message to gays and lesbians in the military is as follows: You will be "tolerated" so long as you remain in the closet. This so-called tolerance is a far cry from acceptance of diversity in sexual orientation. Multiculturalism needs to be questioned in terms of its outcomes, not just accepted based on its rhetoric. Free self-expression, for example, does not always translate into diminishing prejudice. If the only purpose of multicultural efforts is to delineate the boundaries between people more clearly, then it probably can be interpreted as an antithesis of the contact theory instead of as a perspective that complements or furthers the scope of the contact theory.

Cosmopolitanism (from *cosmo polis,* a cosmos within a city) appears to be a good alternative to multiculturalism and a challenging expansion of the contact theory. Cosmopolitanism challenges us to become "near" and takes us a step further than multiculturalism by suggesting curiosity and proximity about differences (Feher, 1994). Instead of being color-blind, we are called on to become color-curious. In many instances, the cosmopolitan paradigm follows an ethnographic approach. Relationships are approached from an emic perspective, recognizing and accepting multiple realities (Fetterman, 1996). From the cosmopolitan perspective, differences are misrepresented just as badly when they are neutralized (i.e., taking away their relevancy) as when they are naturalized (i.e., we are part of the human family). In other words, differences are neither meant to define an inviolable territory nor meant to be reduced to a secondary particularity. Differences are understood as a source of attraction. A cosmopolitan paradigm calls for a dynamic of mutual transformation, not for a static respect of the other's integrity or for a pledge to a universal notion of humanity (Feher, 1994).

It is interesting to note that *cosmopolitan* was the adjective used frequently by the mainstream media to characterize life in Sarajevo before the onset of the war in Bosnia-Hezergovina. Sarajevo, with its cosmopolitan character, became a powerful symbol during a cruel war. The city's residents before the war had sustained contact among different people, had similar status, had sufficient resources, and had the government's support. Their experience does not negate the cosmopolitan vision but rather serves to caution the visionary to be alert to negative manifestations of differences and prejudice.

The adjective cosmopolitan also has been used in the United States to describe the traditional alliance between the African American and Jewish communities (Feher, 1994). Contemporary separatist movements have questioned this alliance and in some cases have effectively undermined the cosmopolitan aspect of this old and significant relationship.

These two examples of cosmopolitanism provide specific approaches to overcoming prejudice. Prewar Sarajevo and the traditional African and Jewish alliance in the United States are good testimonies that prejudice can be overcome. In both cases, the ability to be cosmopolitan has been challenged. We hope that both will rise again like the phoenix and continue to inspire us in our search of approaches to overcoming prejudice.

■ Some Personal and Interpersonal Ideas About Overcoming Prejudice

From the theoretical discussion, we can extract some ideas on how to deal with prejudice at the personal and interpersonal levels. Although prejudice is a learned attitude, we probably do not often identify it as such. It is part of our most basic repertoire of attitudes coined since early childhood. On the other hand, as the target of prejudice, we often have the choice of reacting to or ignoring those attitudes. In both cases, we often are paying a personal price. Tolerance again emerges as an alternative. As we review more specific strategies to deal with prejudice, tolerance becomes questioned in its honesty. From a cosmopolitan approach, the idea of curiosity pushes the boundaries of multi-culturalism and questions attitudes and beliefs. As a generator or recipient of prejudice, we may consider some of the following suggestions at the personal and interpersonal levels and at the micro-, mezzo-, and macrolayers.

1. Let us become more curious and work on knowing who we are (self) and arrive at some level of celebration of our identities. Recognizing the diversity within ourselves will better prepare us to recognize and cherish the diversity around us. When our own diversity is denied or we are excluded or oppressed because of who we are, let us speak up, organize, and mobilize.

2. Let us examine our language as an expression of our feelings and attitudes toward ourselves and others. We need to move beyond the politically correct rhetoric and attach true meaning and honesty to our words. When we feel uncomfortable with the language used by others, we need to express those feelings and articulate an explanation as well as confront, correct, and educate those using oppressive and offensive language. Let us avoid using, and stop others when using, pejorative humor.

3. Let us be sensitive about representation, access, and equity in organizations and institutions to which we belong or with which we work. Are we being inclusive? Are we being included? If we realize that we are ignoring or excluding a certain group or groups or that we are being excluded, then corrective actions are needed.

We need to start by raising awareness about the issue among peers, and then the issue needs to be raised at an organizational level. Raising a flag implies follow-up and hard work.

4. At the political level, we need to work on integrating workplaces, schools, neighborhoods, and recreation facilities. Let us support or develop structures that facilitate dialogue between people that may be sharing a common physical space for the first time (e.g., discussion groups). Let us participate in cultural/social events across cultures.

5. In the workplace and educational settings, let us provide quality training, continuing education, and other experiential opportunities to lower ignorance, fears, and defenses, and let us address issues of prejudice.

The described ideas can lead to tolerance; however, the true challenge rests on the content given to that tolerance. Embracing the diversity within us and around us becomes a permanent challenge to our honesty and humanity. This journey needs to include the personal, mezzo, and macro social and political layers. These efforts need to occur simultaneously. The former Yugoslavia example and the failure of that diversity model can be interpreted as an incomplete or partial effort. Marshall Tito and his political regime forced people to get along. Once the repressive mechanism was loosened up after his death, the so-called tolerance dissipated and gave way to tragic confrontations. Are we doing the same thing in our communities when we unidirectionally enforce political correctness? Government efforts at a macropolicy level are very much needed; however, they need to be complemented by mezzo-level efforts through community, neighborhood, corporate, church/synagogue, and school programs. At the personal level, we need to gain a sense of empowerment to effectively reject messages, resist behaviors, and question attitudes that work against a cosmopolitan society.

The helping professions have an ethical obligation to take a leadership role in these efforts. Institutions of higher education need to become better laboratories of cosmopolitanism. We all need to have opportunities to enjoy the benefits of diversity so as to become better promoters of cosmopolitanism. The benefits of diversity need to be made explicit at all levels. The more insular we become as communities and people, the more afraid we become of the unknown. Although racism, classism, xenophobia, sexism, and homophobia appear to be part of our universal human experience, all of us can and need to do more to be able to honestly call ourselves part of the human family.

18 Organizational Interventions to Prejudice

Sheryl L. Lindsley

While the demographic makeup of our national workforce is changing dramatically and U.S. organizations are increasingly involved in international interdependencies, most companies are inadequately prepared to deal with either national or international diversity (Albert, 1994; DeWine, 1994). Failures to eliminate workplace prejudice negatively affect both individual and organizational experiences and successes. Individual effects include diminished interpersonal trust, reduced motivation, negative outcomes of self-fulfilling prophecies, increased stress, and psychological damage (Cox, 1993). These individual effects, in turn, influence organizational outcomes in the areas of product/service quality, productivity/efficiency, labor turnover, and, ultimately, bottom-line productivity and goal attainment (Cox, 1993). Movement from intolerance, to tolerance, to appreciation of diversity can help organizations reap the benefits of a diverse national workforce as well as improve international experiences and successes. Thus, it is imperative not only for individual workers' personal experiences but also for sound organizational reasons to examine multiple approaches to eliminating organizational prejudice and moving toward valuing diversity.

Organizational interventions often are crafted under "diversity training" programs. These are aimed at eliminating "treatment discrimination" (see Lindsley's other chapter in the volume [Chapter 10]), which occurs when members of distinctive subgroups receive fewer rewards, resources, or opportunities (Greenhaus, Parasuraman, & Wormley, 1990) as well as valuing diversity as a way of developing better work relationships

302

and higher productivity among members of differing groups. Organizational terminology describing diversity training programs often uses the words *valuing diversity* as a way of reflecting an organizational perspective aimed at redefining cultural differences as opportunities rather than as problems to be solved (Cox, 1993). It is important to review the breadth of options available when addressing diversity because the ways in which issues are conceptualized and implemented have a significant impact on the effectiveness and scope of outcomes. This chapter overviews practitioner reports and academic research covering organizational training approaches to diversity.

■ Corporate Support for Diversity Training

Comprehensive information on the number of organizations that implement some form of "diversity" training is not available. Existing research shows that more organizations support diversity training than implement it. Organizational support is found at close to 75% ("FaxForum Results," 1994; McEnrue, 1993; Rynes & Rosen, 1994), whereas reports of actual implementation vary from 25% (McEnrue, 1993), to 32% (Rynes & Rosen, 1994), to 57% ("FaxForum Results," 1994). The number of organizations that oppose training represents approximately 25% of the populations surveyed ("FaxForum Results," 1994; McEnrue, 1993).

Corporate motivations for implementing training include the need to comply with equal employment opportunity (EEO) guidelines, the desire to enhance intergroup relations and employee productivity, and the goal of addressing humanitarian concerns for employees' well-being (Cox, 1993; "FaxForum Results," 1994; McEnrue, 1993; Rynes & Rosen, 1994). One study of New York businesses reveals that 85% of those that did training listed competitive issues and business needs as their primary motivations (Geber, Gordon, Hequet, & Picard, 1994).

Reasons given for supporting but not implementing training include lack of top management support, lack of prioritization among other organizational goals, and uncertainty or fear of outcomes (McEnrue, 1993). The uncertainty or fear revolving around program development is likely affected by mass-mediated construals of intergroup relations as "war" that perpetuate polarized visions of intergroup relationships (see Lindsley's other chapter in this volume [Chapter 10]). The schism between stated organizational support and action may relate to the recognition of tensions in the existing employee climate and fear that openly addressing attendant issues will make matters worse (McEnrue, 1993). In addition, members of higher status groups may have concerns that privileges associated with group membership will be lost (Cox, 1993; Kanter, 1977). Finally, sometimes disagreement exists among managers about whether or not to implement change or which types of approaches will produce the most desired outcomes (McEnrue, 1993). Those organizations opposed to training reportedly address diversity in other ways such as attempting to "Anglicize" employees or replacing people with technology (McEnrue, 1993). Developing an awareness of critical issues involved in implementing training may help those organizations that support diversity but are uncertain how to proceed.

■ Development of Training Programs

Practitioner experiences have shown that program development must include top management support, comprehensive needs assessment, close attention to the conceptualization of diversity, understanding spheres of focus in relation to outcomes, integrating diversity issues across a breadth of experiences, and developing short- and long-term outcome objectives.

■ Top Management Support

Top management support is one of the keys to successful intervention (McEnrue, 1993; Rynes & Rosen, 1994). When human resource managers implement programs without strong initial support, ongoing accountability for objectives is undermined. Considering that organizations initiate change predominantly to improve organizational outcomes, one of the best ways in which to garner top management support is to establish a clear business rationale for diversity initiatives (Baytos, 1992; Mueller, 1996). This can move administrators, managers, and employees from fearing differences in others to valuing them (Caudron, 1994). Mission statements can be tied to the desire to avoid negative consequences of treatment discrimination or to gain positive benefits that stem from valuing diversity. A look at the varied experiences of organizations can increase understanding of a multitude of sound business concerns for diversity programs. For example, management objectives can be tied to the avoidance of costly lawsuits. In 1988, Honda Motor Company made a $6 million settlement of a suit involving discrimination against Blacks and women in its U.S. operations (Cole & Deskins, 1988). In 1992, Shoney's set aside $105 million to compensate victims of racial discrimination after a lawsuit was filed against the company (Pulley, 1992). In 1997, Texaco Corporation agreed to a historic $176.1 million settlement with its African American employees after a race discrimination lawsuit received widespread public attention ("EEOC to Monitor Texaco," 1997).

In contrast to these negative experiences, organizations can develop rationales for training that recognize that nurturing the potential of a diverse employee workforce can help in adapting their products and services to diverse market groups. In the United States, Asians, Blacks, and Hispanics now collectively represent nearly $500 billion annually in consumer spending (Cox, 1993). Studies show that firms such as Avon Cosmetics and Gannet Company's *USA Today* have increased profitability when they have strategically developed and relied on manager and employee diversity to assist their organizations in developing marketing programs to meet the needs of diverse market groups (Cox & Blake, 1991). These are a just a few examples of diversity issues that may be explored to develop training programs that will garner top management support.

■ Comprehensive Needs Assessment

Developing a program tailored to specific organizational contexts should be based on a needs assessment of all program participants at multiple organizational levels as well as consideration of information on the current or emerging markets or consumer bases that the organization serves (Delatte & Baytos, 1993; McEnrue, 1993; Mueller, 1996). Organizational contexts influence the types of issues that need to be included in eliminating discrimination and enhancing intergroup work relationships. Therefore, training development needs to recognize managers' and employees' individual and interdependent role responsibilities, barriers to achievement, and personal and organizational goals. The needs of personnel at each level of the organization can be assessed through a variety of techniques including open- or close-ended written surveys; face-to-face, phone, or electronic mail interviews; and focus groups. It is important to ensure anonymity to those individuals who provide information so that they may feel free to disclose problems without fear of retribution. Information may be summarized and results analyzed in aggregate form to protect individuals in the organization. Based on the assessment, a customized training program can be developed to address the specific needs of a particular organization and its employees.

■ Conceptualizing Diversity

In addition to a comprehensive and contextualized needs assessment, the way in which diversity is conceptualized influences content development and outcomes efficacy. Many programs that have been aimed at "sensitizing" European American males to the issues of women or other racial/ethnic groups actually reinforce intergroup divisiveness for a number of reasons (Mobley & Payne, 1992; Solomon, 1991). First, this approach minimizes heterogeneity within groups by ignoring the complexity of individual identities and reinforcing stereotypes along gender and racial lines (Solomon, 1991). Second, this type of program is discriminatory in that it assumes that European American males need to change and members of other groups do not. This ignores the possibility that minority group members have prejudices against majority group members and that differing minority groups may hold intergroup or intragroup prejudices against each other (Foeman, 1991) that negatively affect workplace experiences (e.g., prejudice between Korean Americans and African Americans, prejudice between Mexican Americans who are recent immigrants and those whose families have lived in the United States for many generations). Third, oversensitizing White males can lead to overaccommodation, which is dysfunctional to satisfying intergroup relationships (Hecht, Collier, & Ribeau, 1993) as well as the advancement of members of historically disenfranchised groups. For example, overaccommodation is communicated when White male managers are oversolicitous, make fewer demands, or are reticent to give negative feedback to minority group members because of anxiety about offending them (Blank & Slipp, 1994; Kanter, 1977). Instead of assuming one-way accommodation and narrowly focusing categories of group identities (typically racioethnic and sex identities), experience suggests conceptualizing diversity across a spectrum of multiple-layered identities as a way of personalizing the program content to address the needs of all participants. Loden and Rosener (1991) suggest that program development should include recognition of both primary and secondary identity issues that influence employees' experiences. At the primary level are age, race, ethnicity, gender, physical abilities/qualities, and sexual/affectional orientation. The secondary level includes marital status, parental status, military experience, religious beliefs, geographic location, education, work background, and income. In dimensionalizing identity, inclusive programs address multiple issues relating to multilayered and inter-penetrated identities that affect managers' and employees' needs and experiences. Although Loden and Rosener suggest that these identities are hierarchical (e.g., age is a more important aspect of identity than is religious beliefs), affective and cognitive affiliation with a particular group identity varies among individuals and across cultures, situations, and contexts. Therefore, their model for dimensionalizing identities should be seen as one way in which identities are arranged that is not necessarily universal. Nevertheless, understanding multilayered identities can help organizations envision programs and policies that will meet the needs of a diverse workforce. For example, program development may explore policies that traditionally have discriminated against fathers by allowing family leave only for mothers (e.g., upon childbirth) and adversely affecting males' roles within families (Basow, 1992; Solomon, 1991). Increasingly, men, especially younger men, are emphasizing family as a priority in their lives. In fact, one study reveals that 75% of men would accept reductions in career advancement in exchange for more time to spend with their families ("Working Dads," 1991). Changing organizational policies to support male roles within families can be beneficial for both families and women's job advancement because females often are overburdened with familial and household responsibilities.

In summary, diversity should be conceptualized in a way that recognizes the intricacies of individual identities and experiences and facilitates inclusiveness in developing an organizational climate that values diversity. This aids organizational members in understanding not only their differences but also their commonalties in relating to one another.

■ Focusing Layers

Recognition of multiple layers at which diversity may be addressed also is critical in formulating expectations for outcomes. These layers include interpersonal inter-action, achievement barriers, and organizational systems (Johnson, 1992).

The layer of interpersonal interaction is the most common focus in organizational training ("FaxForum Reports," 1994; McEnrue, 1993; Rynes & Rosen, 1994), and content often includes group-based concerns, stereotypes, value orientations, world-views, or communication styles. Research has found that interpersonal training needs to encompass cognitive, affective, and behavioral dimensions to be effective (Hammer & Martin, 1992). Therefore, effective interpersonal approaches often rely on the use of combined techniques such as group discussions (Foeman, 1991), readings (Barnum, 1992), films (Foeman, 1991), cultural assimilators (e.g., Brislin, Cushner, Cherrie, & Yong 1986; Landis, Brislin, Swanner, Tseng, & Thomas, 1985; Landis, Day, McGrew, Thomas, & Miller, 1976), role playing (e.g., Brislin & Pedersen, 1976; Foeman, 1991; Gudykunst & Hammer, 1983), and simulations (e.g., Blohm, Hartley, & Lapinsky, 1995; Fantini, 1995; Fowler, 1994; Pedersen, 1995).

At the alternative layer of achievement barriers, individual weaknesses in organizational roles and responsibilities are targeted for job enrichment, personal development, and improved relationships (e.g., Simonsen & Wells, 1994). At this layer, structural barriers to advancement may be addressed. For example, one of the problems confronting women and minority ethnics in organizations has been glass ceilings, which are created by segregating members of these groups in jobs that have little opportunity for advancement (see Lindsley's other chapter in this volume [Chapter 10]). The limitations of these roles can be overcome by redesigning jobs, finding bridges across job assignments (e.g., between clerical, technical, and lower management jobs), identifying competencies and skills associated with differing job roles, rotating jobs, and providing employees with the training they need for advancement (Kanter, 1977).

At the largest layer of organizational systems, addressing diversity issues means promoting adherence to EEO or affirmative action program (AAP) regulations as well as a comprehensive review and modification of policies and procedures to incorporate pluralistic views (Johnson, 1992; McEnrue, 1993). Scholars argue that this macro level of organizational change is the most important for holistic change and also is the most neglected (Johnson, 1992; McEnrue, 1993). Because many organizations typically reflect a Eurocentric male value system, developing a pluralistic organizational culture involves changing institutionalized biases (Cox, 1993). Cox and Finley-Nickelson (1991) suggest that although organizational members need to share common understandings regarding core organizational values, dissipating pressure for conformity on more peripheral norms and values allows for more expression of differences in behaviors in areas where uniformity is not critical to organizational results. Therefore, task forces composed of members of differing groups can work to formulate core organizational values that are essential to meeting organizational goals and can work to eliminate prescriptive policies and procedures that are neither critical to achieving organizational goals nor reflective of valuing workforce pluralism. Traditional Eurocentric male biases may be institutionalized in a variety of ways including, but not limited to, emphasizing self-promotion in hiring and promotion interviews, maintaining a separation of work and personal/family life, reinforcing English-only monolingualism, and defining effective leadership in terms that reflect typical traits of European American males (Cox, 1993). Each of these types of biases needs to be examined to assess its negative impact on diverse organizational groups, workplace relationships, and productivity. For example, self-promoting communication styles reflect individualistic values that are common for many European American males but not necessarily for European American females or other ethnic groups who tend to have more collectivistic values. In IBM's assessment of its corporate culture, the company found that recruiting, motivating, and rewarding policies reflected strong biases for those with individualistic values (Caudron, 1994). After determining that these values were inconsistent with not only diversity objectives but also quality management initiatives, the corporation restructured policies and procedures surrounding these issues to place more emphasis on collaborative values. The dual benefits that IBM has gained from these changes help in establishing an organizational climate that not only supports values of women and minority ethnic groups but also enhances quality management processes and outcomes (Caudron, 1994).

In summary, focusing on a single layer misses issues at other levels. For example, the predominant focus of training on the layer of interpersonal relationships fails to address achievement barriers or institutionalized organizational bias. People still may perceive themselves as interacting within a context in which they have limited opportunities for personal and professional development and in which policies, procedures, or goals are inconsistent with their cultural orientations (Foeman, 1991). Therefore, diversity needs should be addressed across layers of relational training, achievement barriers, and organizational systems rather than being limited to a particular focus.

■ Integrating Training

Most diversity programs focus on enhancing intergroup relationships through "awareness" training and allow 1 day or less for training exposure (Rynes & Rosen, 1994). Separating diversity issues from other ongoing training programs and from daily organizational life undermines program efficacy. Practitioners also report that "one-shot" training increases the occurrence of "backlash" because of superficial treatment of diversity that reinforces stereotypes ("FaxForum Results," 1994). Making diversity issues an integral part of all training (e.g., orientation, customer service, decision making, marketing, management skills) helps organizational members understand that diversity is central to organizational life rather than a tangential issue. For example, research has identified benefits associated with diversity in small group processes and outcomes. Heterogeneous ethnic groups produce more feasible and effective ideas in decision processes than do homogeneous ethnic groups (Cox, 1993). In addition, heterogeneous groups produce higher quality solutions to problems than those produced by homogeneous groups because people of differing backgrounds can bring a broader range of perspectives to a given task than can those who are similar (Hoffman & Maier, 1961; McGrath, 1984; Shaw, 1981). Therefore, it makes sense for organizations to tie diversity to training on small group interaction and team processes.

In summary, it is not surprising that integrating diversity issues into the fabric of training in other aspects of organizational life has been found to be beneficial not only in decreasing discrimination but also in enhancing intergroup relations and improving organizational outcomes (Delatte & Baytos, 1993; Rynes & Rosen, 1994).

■ Program Evaluation

Developing measurable criteria for program evaluation often is neglected. The training itself often is considered an organizational goal (Johnson, 1992; McEnrue, 1993). Similar to one-shot training, using the training itself for a benchmark isolates diversity issues from ongoing organizational processes and goals and may make it harder to "sell" to upper management or other reluctant organizational members. In consideration of this training, development must include short- and long-term identifiable objectives (Johnson, 1992; McEnrue, 1993) linked to both individual employee and organizational goals (Katz, 1977). As in other phases of training, both managers and employees should be encouraged to participate in establishing goal outcomes (Katz, 1977). In addition, it is important to develop a feedback loop so that continuous monitoring of training outcomes can be used to modify and improve the program efficacy. Finally, managers and employees need to be held accountable for meeting program objectives, and a system of incentives should be established for rewarding successes (McEnrue, 1993). Understanding this need, both Xerox Corporation and Hughes Aircraft have developed bonus pay incentive programs linking managerial compensation to diversity goals (Davis, 1994). The success of these initiatives is apparent. For example, Xerox data reflect a much higher level of structural integration of women and ethnic minorities in managerial and professional positions than the average in American industry (Cox, 1993). Thus, in identifying measurable outcomes and establishing incentives for their achievement, diversity training may become better integrated within the daily processes and goals of organizational structures.

■ Conclusions and Future Directions

This chapter has examined the ways in which organizations address prejudice in the workplace through diversity training initiatives. It relied on both practitioner reports and research findings to examine actual experiences of the ways in which training approaches attempt to decrease discrimination and enhance pluralism by "capitalizing" on diversity. Organizational responses to discrimination exhibit a wide range of ways of addressing diversity. Organizations that have successfully developed diversity programs report extensive benefits. However, the majority of organizations either are ambivalent to adopting programs or have implemented training that lacks strong conceptual foundations for achieving effective outcomes.

By analyzing the strengths and limitations of differing approaches to training, important insights for more carefully crafted programs arise. Each phase of development from gaining upper management support, to constructing the initial needs assessment, to conducting the program evaluation must consider the primary pitfalls to effective training—lack of top management support, superficial conceptualization of diversity, limited layers of focus, inadequate integration with ongoing training, undefined incentives or rewards, and unclear or short-term program objectives. In addition, elements of program development should be viewed in terms of their overlapping and interpenetrating influences. For example, when diversity training is neither integrated with other training procedures nor established with measurable objectives, it is easy to see how lack of top management support may be perpetuated. Through comprehensive treatment of these issues, the multiple benefits of diversity training may be realized.

The often limited scope of organizational interventions means that sociostructural inequalities between groups will be slow in changing. Influencing ongoing changes, therefore, must embrace creative solutions that may be initiated by either employees, managers, or organizational administrators. There is a plethora of research that highlights other ways of addressing organizational diversity that provide useful insights for creative solutions. These approaches seek to enhance the psychological, emotional, or spiritual well-being; interpersonal relationships; and power status of members of traditionally disenfranchised groups through mentoring (Brooks, 1995; Dreher & Ash,

1990; Whitely, Dougherty, & Dreher, 1991), social networking, and informal or formal group alliances (Cox, 1993; Etter-Lewis, 1991; Kanter, 1977; Taylor & Raeburn, 1995).

Case studies of creative alliances abound and may serve as models for examining multiple forms of action. For example, an African American worker alliance at Caterpillar Corporation worked to identify racial barriers to employee productivity and advancement and was able to gain management support for formulating a new training program that is now mandatory for all employees (Simonsen & Wells, 1994). This alliance was able to advance the structural integration of African Americans into management positions from which they traditionally had been excluded (Simonsen & Wells, 1994). Another cooperative liaison was created by chamber of commerce members in Lafayette, Indiana, who pooled together community business and university personnel support and resources to implement a series of training workshops for organizations throughout their metropolitan area (Hanson & Fox, 1995). Innovative forms of alliances among employees, organizations, and community members have been effective in coordinating positive change.

Others have been less successful, but we must learn from their experiences as well. For example, academic professionals who created the Sociologists' Lesbian and Gay Caucus to identify and promote strategies for eliminating university discrimination and promoting equality between heterosexuals and homosexuals have experienced mixed outcomes (Taylor & Raeburn, 1995). Although successes have come in the inclusion of sexual orientation in college and university AAPs as well as the incorporation of gay and lesbian studies into college and university curricula, political activism also has taken a personal toll on caucus members in terms of increased discrimination, harassment, intimidation, devaluation of work, and exclusion from social and professional networks (Taylor & Raeburn, 1995; see also Nakayama's chapter in this volume [Chapter 6]). This type of backlash often is created when members of a traditionally disenfranchised group seek to improve their status and prestige. However, it is evident in this review of literature that basic human rights for homosexuals are not given the same consideration as those for other groups. There presently are no federal laws prohibiting discrimination based on sexual orientation. Employment protection does exist in eight states and more than 100 municipal laws as well as in the management policies of a small number of corporations (Blank & Slipp, 1994; see also Brzuzy's chapter in this volume [Chapter 20]). Therefore, further studies are needed to identify ways of eliminating treatment discrimination and promoting respect for gays and lesbians in organizational structures.

Finally, although age-related biases result in almost 30% of EEO claims, there is a dearth of literature addressing intergenerational differences between groups in organizational contexts (see Williams & Giles' chapter in this volume [Chapter 8]). As our workplace is increasingly "graying" (see Lindsley's other chapter in this volume [Chapter 10]), more attention must be focused on shared experiences of intragenerational members and the ways in which these contribute to (in)tolerance in organizations. Increasing cooperative liaisons and satisfying relationships between members of pluralistic groups who are inextricably bound through interdependency may help us in shaping inclusive organizational contexts. It is only through working to foster recognition and respect for diverse human potentiality that we may move toward a healthier and more prosperous nation for all our citizens.

19 Educational Interventions

The Lions Roar

Gale Young

If a solution were known to reduce prejudice in higher education, then well meaning and powerful agents of change would have implemented it long ago. Although all the effective multicultural course requirements, policies, practices, and daily efforts carried out by the many fine educators throughout the country are crucial and significant, they are not, I believe, permanent or comprehensive solutions. Rather, they are substantial pieces to a pervasive puzzle. The glue or interlocking notches might well be the qualities of openness, fearlessness, and perseverance found in those making the efforts.

This chapter focuses on the agents of change. I interviewed 13 professional colleagues whom I dearly respect. Working for equity and excellence in education is their highest priority, and reducing prejudice is at the forefront of their consciousness when making decisions. They are leaders both within their institutions and nationally through their scholarship and positions. All are students of ethnic, race, and gender relations; of the 13, 3 currently teach in ethnic studies with 1 serving as a chair, 1 is a librarian specializing in Chicano literature, 2 are college presidents, 4 are vice presidents (2 provosts, 1 vice president for student affairs, and 1 associate vice president for academic resources), 1 is director for faculty development, 1 is an affirmative action officer, and 1 is president of a statewide faculty union. Ethnically and racially, there are 5 African Americans, 3 Latinos/Latinas, 2 Asian Americans, and 3 European Americans. With regard to gender, 6 are men and 7 are women (5 are women of color). With regard to discipline of origin, 4 are from sociology, 3 are from communication, and 1 each is from physics, economics, political science, education, counseling, and literature. Six educational institutions are represented. I am a European American woman, codirector of the Center for the Study of Intercultural Relations on my campus, and a professor of communication.

I asked my colleagues for their "gut honest" responses (as opposed to their expert-conditioned ones) to the following two questions. What will it take to solve the problems of prejudice in education? What would a prejudice-free educational environment look like? Several follow-up questions ensued.

Each person's interview revealed such honesty, passion, despair, and perseverance that a mere summary would not do it justice. So, I decided to format this chapter as a listserv virtual conversation that does not so much solve the problems of prejudice in education as it illuminates the reality of the change agents. The many statements from each interviewee have been rearranged to simulate a discussion in which I am the facilitator. I have taken the liberty of inserting cameo appearances by notables such as James Baldwin, Chogyam Trungpa, Carlos Castaneda, and bell hooks.

With regard to methodology, I asked each person for a 15- to 30-minute interview in response to the two questions. Each interview lasted 30 to 60 minutes, with five interviews conducted in person and eight via phone. I took handwritten notes of the interviews, typed them up, and gave each participant a copy along with a draft of the essay highlighting their contributions. Participants were allowed to edit and add to their individual responses, choose pen names, and insert cameo guests' remarks. In so doing, I tried to adhere to and expand the spirit of member checking (Denzin, 1994; Van Maanen, 1988), whereby participants in a study are given the opportunity to shape the outcome of how their interviews are being used.

■ Learning to Listen to the Lions Roar

Be forewarned that the following responses are filled with despair. It is the similarity and depth of their despair, coupled with the realization that the respondents are highly knowledgeable about prejudice and daily use their power to try to diminish it, that makes their statements so significant. Moreover, most of the respondents are recipients of the very prejudice they seek to reduce. They are the lions. In the African tradition, it is said that the story of the hunt always is told differently by the lion. In the Tibetan tradition, "The lion's roar is depicted by lions looking in the four directions" (Trungpa, 1973). This image symbolizes openness and fearlessness, a willingness to see and understand the depth and texture of the experiences and emotions from all perspectives without trying to gloss over or patch up what may seem like unreasonable problems (p. 68).

The conversation follows three themes: exposing and examining the despair and hopelessness of solving the problems of prejudice in higher education, articulating a vision beyond hope, and making daily decisions.

■ Exposing and Examining Despair and Hopelessness

Question: What will it take to solve the problems of prejudice in education?

T: Deep in my gut, I don't think it is solvable.

N: There isn't a hope in hell of doing it in secondary schools because segrega-
         tion is so fierce.

Jo: My first reaction is that it can't happen. I am so dry on this. I fight for this
         every day and yet I feel like it can't happen.

RC: I don't think it can be solved. I am feeling very pessimistic.

Jy: This is a hard place for me. Because of my counseling background, I want
         to believe people can change, but the institutional force is so ingrained that
         it is hard to move. We can make progress, but not in my lifetime. I feel
         frustrated, concerned, and helpless.

F: It's a tough question, bigger than all of us.

A: You'll never solve it. Human nature will always be prejudiced, and our only
         hope is to make it better.

S: I think it is impossible. I'm extremely discouraged because I am tired of
         always having to explain and educate. I'm not into fantasy.

Spirit: The status quo and the power structure are too strong. I am in the belly of
         the beast. I'm not real optimistic.

CA: I don't allow myself to think about a vision because it is so depressing.
         We've been at it for so many years, and new forms of racism and hate emerge
         everywhere. You no more get a handle on it, and then more sophisticated
         and hateful ways emerge. I feel overwhelmed and depressed.

B: We are dealing with a myth or contradiction: that you can educate people
         and their prejudices will be modified. That's true for some people but not
         enough people. The problem is that we spin our wheels educating about
         prejudice. It's not going to make a bit of difference. What is it going to take?
         Not education. If what we are doing is changing now, we are not going to
         see it in our lifetimes and it makes me mad.

Uhuru (Kiswahili for freedom): The sad news is that this might be the best it gets.

[Chogyam Trungpa:] Negativity clearly seen becomes intelligence. (Trungpa,
1976, p. 73)

Gale: Let's assume the intelligence of clearly seen negativity and move even closer
         toward the hopelessness and despair, into the belly of the lion's roar.

Uhuru: Race prejudice is part of my reality. Education helps to shape and perpetuate
         that reality. Prejudice is to humans as humans are to prejudice. It is essential
         to who we are. It is not necessarily evil. The tendency to prejudge in favor
         of your group is not evil. But when we malign other groups, then we step
         over the line.

RC: You need to change the whole hierarchy. It's all White at the top. It gets
         gender mixed as you go down the ladder, but not until the bottom do you

get people of color in any significant numbers. It cannot be solved until you have a complete flip-flop.

Spirit: I am not convinced that would do it. Everything is so structured to glorify individual recognition. We are so needy and fragile as a society. Our society creates needy [people], not healthy whole people. The greater good is not considered the most important value. If satisfying our needs is always going to be the most important value, then the greater good will never prevail.

RC: The diversity issue gets co-opted. We see it all the time. Our own U.S. diversity gets co-opted as "international." Chinese Americans, for example, are considered part of the international and globalization goals. They are not international; they are in the United States. Besides that, diversity has become a code word to circumvent ethnic relations.

T: You got it. The university has taken the heart and soul of what people fought and died for in the civil rights movement and softened it, called it diversity and made a mockery of it.

A: Civil rights folks are prejudiced, too. Latinos against Blacks and Asians, etc., the very folks who should know better. I'd be willing to bet that most of the Mexican Americans and blue-collar workers I know voted for Proposition 187 [California's anti-immigrant initiative], and I bet the same for Proposition 209 [California's anti-affirmative action initiative]. We've always been a prejudiced society. I don't know any admissions officer who doesn't discriminate. The question is, on what basis do you discriminate? What sort of standard do you create?

S: It's not possible to have a prejudice-free educational environment. Education is part of the bigger environment full of "isms." What makes us even think we can have a prejudice-free educational environment? Ethnocentrism makes you feel so good about your own standard, country, etc. Out of ethnocentrism grows prejudice. If prejudice is natural, are we fooling ourselves to think there can be an environment without it? I am not feeling very encouraged after all the time we put into affirmative action and the civil rights movement.

RC: Even the liberal, White, male professors who are really nice guys say and hold such sexist and racist beliefs about women and students of color. On my campus, they were opposed to studying pay equity issues. They weren't even open to the validity of inequity of White women. The feelings of White males are so ingrained in our institution that even nice, White, liberal guys don't get it, and then they pass it on to their coworkers and children.

Jy: Everyone comes bringing their prejudices. There are those who think inclusion is a partisan issue, and the dominant criteria for excellence are the quantity and type of experiences valued by White males.

F: Prejudice is as natural to being human as being human is to prejudice. I started by confessing a gloomy view of human nature. But I do believe that human nature is perfectible but dependent on the economy of society and who owns the [means of] production. When equitable economic means are available, then prejudice is minimized. When an economic system is stratified, then prejudice is maximized.

Uhuru: We've made an art out of stratifications. This kind of conversation isn't occurring. People are not talking about investigating how humans have constructed how we have stratified ourselves. Stratification systems need to be abolished.

Spirit: Maybe yes, maybe No. Racism is more indirect and insidious. It is at the level of a finely tuned machine. The deals are now so sophisticated to disenfranchise everyone. Look, diversity is more real in business. They know they have to train these people. They see the fight over affirmative action as foolish. Affirmative action is in business's self-interest. So, eventually the economic structure may get diversified, but the individual gluttony and neediness will prevail. It could only change if the people of color who will populate the next generations can hold on to what W. E. B. DuBois called the "double consciousness." But it is unlikely. Look at all the women doctors and lawyers. They have not been able to make real changes. They are fighting a thousand-pound gorilla.

Jaye Dominguez: I've got another take. Prejudice is perpetuated when professionals in power lack skills, motivation, and responsibility. People learn prejudice from parents, school, and the media. Prejudice happens when there is a lack of access to "other." The greater experience with other is the beginning of the road to a prejudice-free educational environment.

Uhuru: But education is a very conservative and powerful institution, especially given the history of the "isms" of how powerful those strains of prejudice are. As a society, we are not willing to muster the resources to ferret out how education perpetuates racism. We think, talk, and write about it in think tanks and the academy, but as a society we are not committed enough to ferret it out.

B: How can you effect all these people, all the history and social events of prejudice? The legacy of our generation is that we believed we could effect change. Clearly, we're not going to see major change in our lifetimes.

[James Baldwin:] You know, and I know, that the country is celebrating one hundred years of freedom one hundred years too soon. We cannot be free until they are free. (Baldwin, 1963, p. 24)

Gale: James Baldwin's vision is far more optimistic than Derrick Bell's. Baldwin is at least suggesting that freedom will come. Dr. Bell, as well as most of you, have suggested that freedom from prejudice is impossible and that education is no balm. Where do we go from here?

■ Visions Beyond Hope

Gale: Derrick Bell in his book *Faces at the Bottom of the Well: The Permanence
          of Racism,* (1992) challenges us to recognize that our best efforts may fail
          and even contribute to maintaining the system's inequity and yet we have
          no other choice than to act (pp. 198-199). If we take up Bell's challenge
          and, in a sense, lick honey from the razor, then we must go beyond
          acknowledgment and actually befriend our rage, sorrow, and insight into
          the permanence of prejudice. This could mean living with the hopelessness
          of profound changes in education while simultaneously not giving up on
          ourselves, our students, our colleagues, and the institution of education. So,
          if we are going to go beyond hope, let's articulate the hope we are going
          beyond.

Question: What would a prejudice-free educational environment look
              like?

A: To start with, you'd walk into a classroom and not care about the students'
          race any more than the color of their eyes.

RC: Faculty would be leading discussions to bring out the bigotry. You can do
          it in the abstract, but it takes real practice to do it in a diverse environment.

CA: The problems of prejudice can only begin to be solved with the following
          kinds of exchanges between women and men of different races. The ability
          to see other people's reflections is the first step.

[M. S. Kimmel and M. A. Messner:] A discussion between a White woman and
Black woman revolved around the question of whether their similarities as
women were greater than their racial differences as Black and White. The White
woman asserted that the fact that they were both women bonded them in spite of
their racial differences. The Black woman disagreed.

"When you wake up in the morning and look in the mirror, what do you see?"
she asked.

"I see a woman," replied the White woman.

"That's precisely the issue," replied the Black woman. "I see a Black woman.
For me, race is visible every day because it is how I am not privileged in this
culture. Race is invisible to you, which is why our alliance will always seem
somewhat false to me."

Witnessing this exchange, Michael Kimmel was startled. When he looked in
the mirror in the morning, he saw, as he put it, "a human being: universally
generalizable. The generic person." What had been concealed—that he possessed
both race and gender—had become strikingly visible. As a White man, he was
not able to think about the ways in which gender and race had affected his
experiences. (Kimmel & Messner, 1995, p. xiv)

F: That type of dialogue, as well as all kinds of other dialogues, would be happening that aren't now—dialogues about what it means to be an ethnic American. There would be an openness and honesty of dialogue and investigation that isn't happening now with all the accusation, threat, guilt, and little dances with code words. People would be able to discern clearly and accurately what is going on in society.

CA: My ideal environment is one where everyone is who they really are unmasked. There would be true diversity at all different levels —faculty, students, and staff—and they would be interacting in an authentic way.

[M. Omi and H. Winant:] One of the first things we notice about people when we meet them (along with their sex) is their race. We utilize race to provide clues about who a person is. This fact is made painfully obvious when we encounter someone whom we cannot conveniently racially categorize—someone who is, for example, racially "mixed" or of an ethnic/racial group with which we are not familiar. Such an encounter becomes a source of discomfort and momentarily a crisis of racial meaning. Without a racial identity, one is in danger of having no identity. (Omi & Winant, 1986, p. 63)

Gale: The ethnic identity crises that individuals experience are indicative of the ethnic identity crises we are experiencing as a society. It seems to me that in many ways, the brittleness of race relations and the failure of accurate information to heal the racial wounds have brought us up against a raw and vulnerable edge as a pluralistic society. We can try to build better racial defenses and rationales to shore up our socially constructed biases and racial divisions and thus continue to perpetuate the myth that the principle of racial equality is the practice. Or, we could cultivate the courage to expose our vulnerability. Not knowing what to be to one another—what to think, do, or say in interracial interactions—is actually a rare opportunity to experience a societal version of the existential void. We could acknowledge the relevance of the emotional and intellectual confusion that prevails. We could become curious about those feelings and confusions and begin to use the classroom as a way to inquire into this state of affairs.

Uhuru: Universities could take the lead in creating the dialogue. They could create a national dialogue to discuss prejudice, discrimination, and racism. Institutions could collaborate and engage in a series of colloquia even via distance and discuss these issues. Members of Congress and state legislatures would be part of the dialogue for the purpose of formulating public policy on discrimination and prejudice. Universities could become the bully pulpit for designing national dialogue for forming public policy. The responsibility lies with education, with those who want to risk being educated, to take off blinders. We have an opportunity to re-vision public policy. Universities can do it, but they don't.

F: Public discourse now is namby-pamby. People think it is enough to think
          and speak good thoughts.

[Carlos Castaneda:] That's the flaw with words. . . . They always force us to feel
enlightened, but when we turn around to face the world they always fail us and
we end up facing the world as we always have, without enlightenment. (Castaneda, 1974, p. 32)

Gale: So, dialogue can be both the antidote and the poison.

B: When I read a poem by Maya Angelou (1994) where she states that she
          won't trust Whites until they can let Blacks take the lead (p. 47), I remember
          thinking, I wouldn't know who I am or how to respond to that type of
          environment. What keeps me going is knowing I'm in a prejudice-filled, not
          prejudice-free, environment. It would require that I go through an identity
          change. But what might it look like? It will certainly require more than just
          words. Well, first of all, students would see other communities, speak other
          languages, and be exposed to differences. Curriculum would address the
          emotions. Classes would be a kind of psychology to get them laughing and
          crying. Degrees would have to be renewed every 10 years to have students
          demonstrate their continued learning in the area of prejudice as well as any
          other area. Race would become decentralized regarding who responds to it.
          When Whites in large numbers get grossed out and outraged and act on
          prejudice, then that will mark a change. And when you have large numbers
          of Blacks outraged by reverse discrimination, then we can talk. Now we
          have race-based camps.

A: We need to take a social problem and bring all our tools to work on it in one
          place. We come from different disciplines, which brings powerful tools but
          tunnel vision. There isn't much commitment by academia to apply knowl-
          edge to social problems. We need more.

T: I couldn't agree more. In my vision, people, regardless of race and gender,
          would be represented by their willingness to participate in the centrality of
          the education. The emphasis would be on the individuals and the commu-
          nities from which they came. The promotion and tenure policies would be
          turned upside down. Professors would get tenure based on life experience.
          "Outstanding Professor Awards" would be mutually agreed on by the
          university and community that the university serves. Budgets would be
          based on how well you are serving diverse communities. Promotion would
          depend on to what extent research writings serve and tie-in to help solve
          problems of diverse communities, whether it be math or ethnic studies. Each
          professor must answer in [his or her] syllabus how this course is useful for
          dealing with the individual's, community's, and/or society's problems.

Jaye Dominguez: Let me continue spinning on this vision. Scapegoating doesn't happen when the vision is, "This school has to work for everyone." You wouldn't hear, "This school would be great if we didn't have the severely handicapped or those underprepared students." Creating a prejudice-free educational environment would be creating a healthy community. The school is viewed as a comprehensive community center with a gym, counseling welfare, mental health, and career center. In secondary education, this is called contextual or grounded learning. Educational community is defined by total inclusivity—that sense that we are all here to make this place work. Everyone participates and has a stake in the outcome. Educational units need to be bound to the community. The reward system within academia would be grounded in working in and for the community. Now we have disincentive. The departmental structure itself is not only not useful to this approach, it is destructive.

Spirit: You got it! It will take structural changes from kindergarten through doctoral programs. Institutions have to know what it means to live in multicultural America. They have to understand that education is first and foremost personal, and ethnic identity is a piece of that. Ethnic issues aren't just an add-on but are essential to the learning process. Mainstreaming doesn't work. You have to have a full array of specific courses that address specific ethnic perspectives. I want to see teachers starting with individual experiences of people and then engaging in comparative examination. We must move beyond self-righteous nationalism. Nationalism is one stage that must be gone through, but we can't stop there. We need a people of a common mind willing to struggle for humanity.

N: We would find a way to work with families and their values. Education doesn't just begin and end while at an institution. We need to do more to provide opportunities for second, third, or fourth chances—provide ways to continue the education process when life gets in the way. We have a responsibility to the community. We need to figure out a way to bring the community in to help us hire more diverse teachers. We cannot do it alone. We need the community.

S: People with all kinds of differences would have an equal opportunity to be hired, to be leaders, and to have information about their various groups disseminated and studied. In an authentic way, not clichéd, differences would be truly valued and respected. Everyone would be a part of all the workings.

N: I agree, and you wouldn't be able to guess students' majors by name, culture, race, or gender. There would be lots more mixture. Faculty and staff would look like the student body. There would be a good deal more mingling. There would be an effort made to keep alive the nature and depth of various cultures, not for the purpose of making you feel comfortable but rather for the thrill of understanding the variety of human experiences and what it can tell you about yourself, history, and humanity. You wouldn't hear such comments as "concrete thinkers from Oakland." Students would feel welcomed and as if they had something to contribute.

CA: The curriculum must go beyond the university. It must be very rich, representing all different perspectives, even those that we consider backlash or conservative viewpoints. If no one ideology dominated, we could truly entertain all perspectives. Now I feel I must concentrate on "alternative" perspectives and histories as a corrective to all the inaccurate or misleading information out there.

Jy: On the outside, you would see teams of people of all ethnicities, genders, sexual orientations, and diversity. This role modeling and imaging has to be there. Everyone is valued, and it is visibly shown. The criteria for excellence would reflect the value of inclusivity in all aspects of the university—the curriculum, the faculty, the administration, and the policies. Everything must change.

[Gordon Allport:] [Racism] may be reduced by equal status contact between majority and minority groups in the pursuit of common goals. The effect is greatly enhanced if this contact is sanctioned by institutional supports . . . and provided it is of a sort that leads to the perception of common interests and common humanity between members of the two groups. (Allport, 1954/1979, p. 281)

Spirit: Administrators would have a very important role to play in the reward system. They would create a humane, nonpatronizing pressure and presence toward ethnic studies. All academics would assure that goals and rigorous standards to be upheld for all ethnic and multicultural classes the same way they do in chemistry. Most campuses have an ethnic studies requirement but no committee to oversee it. They don't care if you are teaching basket weaving.

Uhuru: As a system, we need to reflect values of equality and power sharing. In a prejudice-free environment, we wouldn't spend much time on the ways people are deprived or injured by prejudice; we would develop a new set of values wherein relationships are governed by fundamental equality. There would be a certain amount of remediation built-in so as to guard against the re-emergence of killer forms of prejudice. We would present students with models to think beyond the capitalist political economy of individualism and money that we are born into and will die out of.

Jo: On a day-to-day basis, we would teach out of respect rather than the presumption that we have knowledge that students need. We would model respect for students. We have faculty who respect the learning process and knowledge, but they don't always respect students. They respect students who do well but not the experience of being a student. Faculty wouldn't be so arrogant as to presume that there is a right and a wrong way to look at something. We would redefine the role of faculty so that their arrogance is no longer acceptable. From job descriptions to graduate school, we would reconceptualize teaching as facilitating. Students' ability to acknowledge what they don't know would go up. What I fight for is for students to feel respected and affirmed, not denigrated. I hate seeing students belittled or hurt for asking a question. I don't want students to feel like they cannot participate or challenge the professor. I want students to play intellectually with ideas.

N: Yes, Yes! I want the students to be greedy for knowledge. Let them learn without defensiveness, and let us teach without fear. Let the teachers learn from the students.

Gale: So, what I hear from you is a revolutionary change affecting the bone marrow of everything and everyone. No one race, gender, class, or sexual orientation would dominate the hierarchy, the curriculum, the values, and the policies governing the institution. Each person's experience with his or her color, culture, gender, class, age, religion, and sexual orientation would be truly valued. Education, as DuBois reminds us, would grow out of the people being educated. The faculty would see themselves as students and learners. They would learn to be facilitators for the students. Students would learn the value of knowing, sharing, and creating their own life experiences. Moreover, academia would be a fully engaged, caring, and inclusive learning environment where students and faculty alike would engage in difficult dialogues as one of the means for cultivating wisdom through intellectual and emotional inquiry. Educational institutions would be a nexus, a bully pulpit, and a powerful force for equity and excellence in society.

Question: What will it take to get us to this vision? Is it truly beyond hope?

Jaye Dominguez: Let me say that the university has no other choice but to engage in this kind of revolutionary change. If we don't, it spells our death. Most of the education we offer now can be put on TV or the Internet. If all we do is impart knowledge and give students the space to recall their information, then students with their busy, complicated lives would rather sit at home and get educated off the Web. If all we want is the goods delivered, then technology will do it for us. But if we want something more, then the educational community must be grounded in caring. Technology can be a supplement to community, but true community cannot be only technological. We must create and maintain a caring place for students, and that means *all* students.

Jo: You're right. On the one hand, technology has forced us to become more facilitators of knowledge, and yet on the other hand, it can take us into no interaction.

CA: The racial cues we use are the basis of all kinds of prejudice, and technology is one way to erase the cues. Yet at the same time, this is so alienating.

F: I agree with Jaye; the universities have a very doubtful future. Twenty-five years from now, it will be very different. The new technology brings its own values. In and of itself, it will have no impact on increasing or reducing prejudice. It is all in how it is used.

Gale: So, if we have no other choice than to go for a revolutionary change, and if, as you say, technology may only assist and/or impede us but not free us, *will the fire next time do it?*

F: Damned if I know.

S: I don't know. I'm not into fantasy.

Uhuru: Severe and persistent struggle. People have to be willing to reinvent and revision themselves. But overall, it's not going to happen soon. No folks of color, or for that matter White folks, are creating havoc. There are no fires to which folks need to respond.

T: But there should be. What will it take? Blow it up! I'm serious. The only way to wrestle the White male domination of scarce resources is by a superior amount of force. I mean some kind of violent reaction to this obscene domination. Not how they did it in the '60s; rather, poisons in water, bombs in airplanes, a message of "If I can't come in, nobody is coming in." It is happening now with terrorism. We blame it on Islamic and right-wing groups, but if you look behind it, it's about usurping scarce resources. The White militia and people of color have similar outrages. They are just masked differently. White militias are about bringing down an unjust and corrupt system, but it is masked as racism. The government will maim and ridicule the White militias as fast as it will people of color. It is related to education. Education is the last vestige of free intellectual enterprise, and yet its very nature is to teach White boys to be White men. In order to get rid of discrimination in education, we will have to blow the place up.

Jaye Dominguez: Well, I don't know if I am ready to join your militia yet. But I do believe it will take a major threat of extinction to get folks to really change. They have to believe, "You're not needed anymore if you continue to do business as usual." No vision or leader can implement the change. It is going to take apprehension of and fear of extinction.

Jo: I am convinced more than ever of the problem, but I don't know. I don't think even the threat of extinction will do it.

Jy: Or at least a major crisis to wake up people—students refusing to come to college by depending on the technology.

F: Threat of extinction is not going to do it. That just closes people down rather than opening them up. That won't help faculty or universities change. The end result is to change society.

B: Right, but I'm at a loss as to how that's going to come down, either because I'm impatient or not confident of what I do think. We need a worldwide organization like a United Nations or an Amnesty International with solid funding and a strong organizational staff. We need a priesthood/sisterhood devoted to seeing change in society. Perhaps we could replicate the infrastructure of the Catholic Church, masons, or army that can pull international chains to make a statement and then go after something in 15 places. We need to organize thousands of people to put pressure on issues of equity and justice. It has to be multigenerational wherein a leader can die or get assassinated and the organization can keep on stepping. This organization would be able to use the world as its resource to make equity and justice real.

Gale: Prejudice in education feels like a contagious, terminal illness. Yet, like many who are in life-threatening situations, the reflex to deny, ignore, or go for the quick fix is stronger than the desire to see, feel, and know clearly. Until the volcano erupts, the bomb explodes, the worldwide equity foundation emerges, and more lions roar, how do we live and work with the persistent awareness of the permanence of prejudice in education and with a vision that truly matters?

Question: When making decisions, how do you simultaneously hold both the vision and the despair?

T: Keep trying. Keep the ball in play. As long as the ball is in play, you have a chance to win. You can't win if you don't play. We may not be winning, but at least we're not losing.

Jy: I get energized around things I can change, but it's a limited view.

Jaye Dominguez: I look to all the pilot programs and the next generation of bright shining stars out there. I hold on to hope.

R: I work in the areas where I can make some impact. I get support and sustenance from them—a center on campus, a systemwide committee, or a national network of other librarians of color in ethnic studies. I try to do work where I think I can make an impact and where my voice can be heard. On a day-to-day basis, it can be discouraging.

Jo: I am not hopeful at all. I don't think the solution is ever going to happen, so ameliorating it is the only goal I have to work for.

A: I am with you on that one. I deal with it on a daily basis—on an ad hoc micro basis—and hope it is in a nondiscriminatory way. My mother used to say, "I can't save the world, but I can damn well try to save this little piece of it." I find it very difficult to get folks to work within a grand plan. But if

I go to them and say, "Look, we have 10 students at risk, and this is what we can do," then they are more willing to work. All grand plans have exceptions which prevent action. Castaneda is right. You can discuss things to death and get no productivity. There is such a multitude of problems, just get busy and start solving some of them. We can't change the world, but we can create a bit of light where there is darkness and we can offer a tender soothing touch where is then hurt.

[bell hooks:] Much of the work I do revolves around racism and sexism, and on one hand, I want to start right where I am in the now. But on the other hand, I also have to have this vision of a future where these things are not in our lives. Do you think that's too utopian? (Chodron & hooks, 1997, p. 26)

[Pema Chodron:] . . . I give up both the hope that something is going to change and the fear that it isn't. We may long to end suffering, but somehow it paralyzes us if we're too goal-oriented. Do you see the balance there? It's like the teaching that Don Juan gave to Carlos Castaneda, where he says that you do everything with your whole heart as if nothing else matters. You do it impeccably and with your whole heart, but all the while knowing that it actually doesn't matter at all. (p. 26)

[bell hooks:] Yet it seems very hard for people to fight this racism and sexism without hope for an end to it. There is so much despair and apathy because of the feeling that we've struggled and struggled and not enough has changed. . . . I am on tour right now talking about my book about ending racism, and I hear people say things like racism doesn't exist or don't you think we've already dealt with that? And I start to feel irritable. This irritability starts mounting in me, and I notice how it collapses into sorrow. I came home the other day, and I sat down at my table and just wept because I thought, it's just too much. (p. 27)

[Pema Chodron:] Well, isn't that the point? That other people and ourselves, we're the same really, and we just get stuck in different ways. Getting stuck in any kind of self-and-other tension seems to cause pain. So if you can keep your heart and your mind open to those people, in other words, work with any tendency to close down towards them, isn't that the way the system of racism and cruelty starts to de-escalate?

The thing is, once we get into this kind of work, we are opening ourselves for all our own unresolved misery to come floating right up and block our compassion. It's difficult and challenging practice to keep your heart and mind open. It takes a lot to be a living example of unbiased mind! . . . I think it begins with the aspiration to connect with open heart, the knowledge that cultivating openness is how you want to spend the remaining moments of your life. (p. 27)

Spirit: I'll never give up. I know for certain that if one gives up, there may be some
          answers down the road that are missed, but that I could have been useful.
          I've got no choice but to stay in. I can't allow myself to slide into fatalism.
          It's presumptuous to think that those in the past or present know that all is

predetermined. I've got to believe that we might contribute something worthwhile or we might not, but we must try. The chance to get my brains beat out at this job wasn't available to me 20 years ago. I don't think it's better or worse or bad or great. But it is different, and that brings different opportunities. There is no frustration that is going to make me take myself out of the game. No amount of calling me "nigger" or making me jump hurdles is going to cause me to destroy myself or others. They might destroy me or I might die of high blood pressure, but I am going to suck it up and keep on moving, wake up every morning, focus, and move forward.

Gale: Thank you! Thank each and every one of you for your fearless honesty and your willingness to share in this venue. And with a grateful heart, I thank each of you for the inspiration and education you bestow.

20 Public Policy Interventions to Prejudice

Stephanie Brzuzy

Public policy can be a powerful tool to alleviate prejudice through the enactment and implementation of laws, rules, and regulations. At the same time, prejudice can be manifested through public policy that excludes some groups from the rights and privileges experienced or given to the majority. Thus, public policy can be either a solution to prejudice or a reinforcement of prejudice.

When a dominant group chooses to use fears and dislikes as guiding principles for the laws, rules, and regulations that govern our society, prejudice dictates our public policies. Prejudice on a national level has been used by powerful majorities throughout history to control minority groups. The most glaring example of publicly mandated policy based on prejudice in the United States came through the government-supported laws that enforced slavery and segregation of African Americans. Many more examples exist including control of women's rights and fights over the rights of gay Americans and immigrants today.

The powerful use of legislative control to reinforce prejudice requires the equally powerful force of mandated public policy to undo or dissipate the damage of legislated prejudice. Slavery came to a legal end with the passage of federal legislation through the enactment of the 14th Amendment to the U.S. Constitution, which declares,

> All persons born or naturalized in the United States, and subject to the jurisdiction thereof, are citizens of the United States and of the state wherein they reside. No state shall make or enforce any law which shall abridge the privileges or immunities of citizens of the United States; nor shall any state deprive any person

of life, liberty, or property without due process of law; nor deny to any person within its jurisdiction the equal protection of the law. (Bicentennial Productions, 1986, pp. 23-24)

With the passage of a constitutional amendment, albeit an extremely difficult task, 200 years of slavery were undone. Although the implementation and enforcement of this law took decades to ensure, through public policy, social injustice was reversed.

This chapter presents an analysis of the contradictory pressures between laws that promote prejudice and those that seek its end. The discussion begins with the issue of voting rights. The struggle to gain voting privileges demonstrates well the contradictory pressures. Next, the chapter considers a policy that attempts to ameliorate the effects of prejudice, the Americans with Disabilities Act, and then presents one that inscribes and reinforces prejudice, the Defense of Marriage Act. These discussions are used to highlight principles for creating and implementing effective public policy to combat prejudice and discrimination.

■ The Historical Tension Between Condoning Prejudice and Eradicating Prejudice Through Public Policy: The Right to Vote

The apparent contradiction between legislation that condones prejudice and legislation that eradicates it has been an ongoing tension in the struggle for guaranteed rights in this country. The history of voting rights illustrates this tension.

Originally, the right to vote was not clearly defined by the Constitution. Who was eligible to vote, and under what circumstances, was left to each state to decide. As a result, from ratification of the Constitution until the Civil War, voting was a right reserved for White men who owned property. Consequently, all women, poor men, and men of color had no voice in government and political decisions. Because public policies were developed and chosen by those who could vote, those who were excluded from the process also were excluded from most of the rights and privileges that were extended through public policy (Jansson, 1997; Trattner, 1994).

The Civil War fueled the movement to expand voting rights. In 1870, the 15th Amendment was passed, giving any male the right to vote, regardless of race: "The right of citizens of the United States to vote shall not be denied or abridged by the United States or any state on account of race, color, or previous condition of servitude" (Bicentennial Productions, 1986, p. 24). Women's groups had tried to gain inclusion of gender in the amendment but were not successful. Thus, women did not gain the right to vote through passage of the 15th Amendment. Although this public policy clearly gave the right to vote to African American men who had been slaves, the tension of continued prejudice blocked successful implementation of the law.

Local rules and regulations, particularly in the South, made it impossible for former slaves to actually vote. Because of the deeply entrenched reluctance to let go of slavery, and with it the imbedded prejudice, local laws such as poll taxes (charging citizens a tax to vote), literacy tests, and intimidation by local White officials created barriers that blocked former slaves from voting (Polenberg, 1980). The impact of these local laws and practices, in spite of the constitutional guarantee, lasted for 100 years until 1965 and the passage of the Voting Rights Act. It took the power of the federal government to both pass the law and later enforce the right to vote for African Americans.

Although women had been very instrumental in the fight to end slavery in this country and were active in supporting the 14th and 15th Amendments, their right to vote was long in coming. Although the Women Suffrage Amendment was first introduced in 1878 and was reintroduced in every congressional session until passage, it was not enacted until 1920 (Klein, 1984).

For Native Americans, the right to vote also was very slow in coming. Indian tribes were ruled as "wards of the nation" by the Supreme Court and, as such, were denied sovereign rights and citizenship (Nabakov, 1992). Although granted citizenship in 1924 as a result of service in World War I, states were slow to grant Native Americans the right to vote. Not until the 1940s were Native Americans permitted to vote in all states.

The struggle for the right to vote for people of color and women in this country demonstrates the power of public policy to both curtail and ensure rights. The exclusion of groups of people from participation in the democratic process leaves them without a voice and consequently bars them from access to opportunities and resources. Without both the power of public policy and the enforcement of these policies by federal authorities, rights cannot be guaranteed and the consequences of exclusion cannot be overturned.

■ The Power of Public Policy to Influence Prejudice

The enactment and enforcement of public policies can have a profound impact on the extent and consequences of prejudice throughout our society. Although it is very difficult to control or prescribe people's thoughts and therefore their prejudices, public policy can set a national tone and put in place the parameters of acceptable behavior. It also can open rights and privileges to previously excluded groups and can increase opportunities and resources. Thus, from a national level or layer, personal or individual behaviors and actions can be influenced, persuaded, and even regulated. The following examples demonstrate how U.S. public policy legislates behaviors that ameliorate prejudice and discrimination, create opportunities, and give access to resources. Conversely, the chapter also shows how public policy reinforces prejudice and discrimination.

■ Public Policy as Providing Opportunities

Public policy can be used to provide groups with opportunities or access that previously has been denied by society. The Americans with Disabilities Act (ADA) of 1990 (U.S. Government, 1990) is an example of federal public policy that attempts to regulate actions and increase public awareness and understanding of people with disabilities. Building on the Rehabilitation Act of 1973, which prohibits discrimination against people with disabilities only in federally funded programs, the passage of the ADA was landmark legislation for the estimated 43 million Americans with disabilities in this country. The act provides comprehensive civil rights protections for people with disabilities who historically have experienced severe social and economic inequality (West, 1991; Yellin, 1991). For example, it has been estimated that as many as 66% of all working-age people with disabilities are unemployed (Kirkpatrick, 1994). The ADA legislation acknowledges these social conditions. It states, "Historically society has tended to isolate and segregate individuals with disabilities, and, despite some improvements, such forms of discrimination against individuals with disabilities continue to be a serious and pervasive social problem" (U.S. Government, 1990, sec. 2).

Prior to the ADA, people with disabilities were denied equal access to public services and public spaces, and they lacked the opportunity to compete equally in the marketplace due to physical and attitudinal barriers by employers. These barriers denied people with disabilities access to education and employment and limited their opportunities to live independently.

The ADA was designed to ameliorate these barriers and exclusions for people with disabilities. The ADA prohibits discrimination against people with disabilities in employment, public services, public accommodations, transportation, and telecommunications (Perritt, 1990). Employers are required to make reasonable accommodations for employees with disabilities, and all public spaces must be made accessible. New buildings must meet ADA accessibility requirements, and public transportation and telecommunication services must be accessible as well. If these requirements are not met, then government sanctions are in place to monitor those who are out of compliance.

The ADA has made an impact on multiple levels. The ADA has increased public attention to the needs of people with disabilities. It has begun to eliminate isolation because access creates more opportunities for interaction, and the law mandates changes that have shifted the public's awareness to those needs. The shear magnitude of the legislation has required action on the national, state, and local levels. Changes such as installation of curb cuts, accessible parking, classroom support (e.g., note takers for students with learning disabilities), and accessible buildings all are a result of the ADA. Builders are required to learn the specifics of the ADA to ensure public access for all in buildings. It is not uncommon today to see interpreters signing at speeches, plays, and concerts as well as in the classroom.

For example, during the 1996 presidential campaign when President Clinton held a rally at Arizona State University, the speech was interpreted for hearing-impaired students. This level of sensitivity and understanding was practically nonexistent 10 years ago. Organizers were sensitized to the need through the existence of legislation outlawing discrimination and requiring access for people with hearing impairments. A total of 20,000 people attended the rally and were exposed to the needs of deaf students and citizens. These types of activities create public awareness and build both support and understanding.

Workshops have been held across the country to sensitize and inform employers of their responsibilities under the act. In compliance with the ADA, places of employment and public facilities have become more accessible and accommodating. A preliminary assessment of the impact of the ADA in 1995 found that half of all small towns in America had complied with the accessibility requirements. In addition, although still limited, employment opportunities were beginning to increase and attitudes had changed (Wolf, 1995).

The ADA also has been empowering for people with disabilities. Gregory Dougan, a man with cerebral palsy, states, "The ADA has made me feel for the first time like I'm a real American. It has given me a sense that I have federal laws as well as moral law on my side" (quoted in Wolf, 1995, p. B8).

There still is much work to be done to end discrimination and create more opportunities for people with disabilities, but the ADA as a piece of public policy has moved our nation forward in this fight. The potential to eliminate prejudice toward people with disabilities through the ADA is more powerful than any national efforts we have had to date.

■ Public Policy as Limiting Opportunities

The Defense of Marriage Act (DOMA) of 1996 (U.S. Government, 1996) is an example of public policy used to exclude a minority from the rights and privileges enjoyed by the rest of society. Through marriage, people have access to federal benefits such as social security survivors' coverage and tax laws covering spouses, are eligible to be covered by health insurance as spouses, and are ensured protections such as guaranteed survivorship rights. These privileges of marriage are extended to those who choose to be married. However, not all who choose to marry are recognized to have that right and the privileges it entails.

On September 10, 1996, Congress passed the DOMA, which Clinton signed into law. The law is short—one page—but its message is clear: Gay men and lesbians do not have the right to be legally recognized as married. Thus, gay men and lesbians do not have the same rights and privileges as do heterosexual couples.

The DOMA denies gay couples the right to federal benefits to which married people are entitled as a result of their legally sanctioned unions. In addition, it allows states to reject the legal marriage of a gay couple where such a union might be- come legal. (Although no states have done this yet, Hawaii is considering such action.) According to the law, "The word 'marriage' means only a legal union between one man and one woman as husband and wife, and the word 'spouse' refers only to a person of the opposite sex who is a husband or a wife" (U.S. Government, 1996, sec. 3).

The consequences of this law are twofold. First, this law disregards the constitutional guarantee that states will honor the acts of other states under the "full faith and credit" clause. All states historically have honored other states' marriage contracts. By allowing states to disregard the marriage licenses of other states that might in the future choose to allow gay Americans to marry, Congress has effectively said that states do not have to honor the "full faith and credit" clause of the U.S. Constitution (Article IV) for this issue. This clause guarantees that states will honor public acts, records, and proceedings from other states. Because of this position, the law may be found to be unconstitutional (Biskupic, 1996).

The second consequence is that this law is exclusionary and codifies prejudice against gay men and lesbians. The prejudice reinforced by this bill is exemplified by the comments of some of its supporters. Trent Lott, the senate majority leader, called gay marriage a "radical social agenda" imposed on the entire nation. Senator Robert C. Byrd, a West Virginia Democrat, claimed, "The drive for same-sex marriage is, in effect, an effort to make a sneak attack on society by encoding this aberrant behavior in legal form before society itself has decided it should be legal" (quoted in Schmitt, 1996, p. A11). The DOMA is an example of policy that reinforces intolerance and stereotypes. As a result, it limits access to privileges and resources for gay Americans and fuels prejudicial attitudes.

■ Public Policy as a Solution to Prejudice

For public policy to be successful in diminishing prejudice, a multidimensional approach must be instituted. Such an approach necessitates a public policy response that occurs on multiple levels or layers. It means passage and enactment of public policies on the national, state, and local levels as well as organizational and individual compliance.

The use of public policy as a solution to prejudice is best analyzed as two related components: achieving public policy and maintaining the impact of that policy. To achieve public policy, several steps must be taken: educating and making aware the public, organizing and building coalitions, developing public support, influencing policymakers, and passing legislation. However, the successful enactment of public policy is not enough. After a law is passed, there are a number of steps that must be taken to implement and maintain the impact of the policy: educating the public, enforcing the desired behavior by government officials, maintaining vigilance by concerned citizens to keep the laws in place, and paying attention to the "spirit" and the "letter" of the law.

■ Achievement of Public Policy

To gain support for passage of a public policy, it is important to develop public awareness, understanding, and support. Education that creates understanding and awareness by the public is an ongoing process for the successful passage of legislation to alleviate prejudice. The serious nature of a problem often must come to the public's attention for action to take place. Education on issues that are in need of national attention often come through dramatic events. For example, riots that occur when citizens feel victimized and oppressed in their communities can create a forum for education on the prejudice, discrimination, and social and economic inequalities that oppressed groups experience. Such was the case in the race riots during the 1960s.

Once these events have taken place, actions for change can be recommended through coalitions that come together within the community. Coalitions can press for changes in the policies of local, state, or national governments and can demand the need for more sensitivity to the residents of the community. When the public becomes aware of the problems, policymakers are forced to respond to the issues that previously were unnoticed or ignored by the majority in power. If the problems are greater than can be addressed locally, state governments may need to look at the structural inequalities that are at work. If pressure is great enough, the introduction and passage of legislation to eliminate these inequalities can be demanded. Problems that go beyond state boundaries become issues of national concern, and public support must be broad enough to press for federal legislative changes. Key political leaders must feel pressure for change. Public support on an issue can achieve that pressure.

Congressional leaders must be educated about an issue to get legislation enacted. They also must feel that their constituents are in support of passage. Influencing policymakers can be done on many levels through voting, meeting with representatives, giving testimony at hearings, lobbying, writing letters and making phone calls, running for office, organizing protests and demonstrations, gaining media attention, and getting as many people as possible involved in the effort.

Legislative remedies can be swift when a traumatic event takes place. The shooting death of a doctor who performed abortions at a clinic in Florida by an anti-abortion protester in 1993, as well as the 1994 murders of clinic workers in Boston by another protester, resulted in public outrage that moved Congress to pass legislation to protect women's access to abortion clinics. The Freedom of Access to Clinic Entrances Act was passed by the federal government in 1994. Prior to the passage of this bill, women had experienced relentless harassment and violence by protesters when they tried to use clinic services, but the public had not been sensitized enough to this issue. The education and public awareness that resulted through legislative hearings, speeches by the murdered victims' families, press conferences by political action groups who advocate women's abortion rights, and media attention moved Congress to action to remedy the oppression and to protect women's rights to access abortion clinics. The impact of the legislation has been significant. In 1993, 3,429 incidents of violence and disruption occurred at clinics around the country. By 1995, that number had decreased to 1,815 incidents. As of September 1996, less than 400 incidents had occurred (Pear, 1996).

■ Maintenance of the Impact of Public Policy

Once a public policy is passed, it is necessary to monitor the implementation and development of the actual impact of the law. A law can be enacted, but without enforcement of the desired behavior by government officials and vigilance by concerned citizens, the law can have little impact. The previous example of the history of voting rights in this country demonstrates this well. The constitutional amendment ensuring African Americans the right to vote was passed, but without any type of enforcement by the federal government or vigilance by the public, it took another 100 years for African Americans to actually get the right to vote.

After passage of a law, the federal government must put in place enforcement policies that will ensure that state and local governments comply. A law without proper enforcement through some type of serious governmental sanction is not very powerful and can have little impact. When prejudice is deep-seated and long-standing, a law without any penalty for noncompliance will not be honored.

Vigilance by concerned citizens also is crucial in the process to ensure that enforcement procedures are developed and actually used to hold liable those who do not comply. Enforcement of public policies can change over time. Groups must be prepared to take cases to the courts if enforcement of the laws wanes, and they must be prepared to seek additional legislative changes if the laws are reinterpreted by the courts.

Laws to eliminate prejudice and to ensure rights also do better when the spirit and the letter of the law are working together. In many cases, enforcement of a law requires a bare minimum of standards for behavior that must be met. For example, the ADA requires accessibility to buildings, but it does not require that every entryway be accessible. Therefore, people with physical disabilities who use wheelchairs may be able to get in and out of a building, but they may have to use an entrance that is not convenient. Instead of making one doorway accessible, which is consistent with the letter of the law, what if buildings were built to be universally accessible without steps? Ramps are just as efficient and can be used by everyone—people with baby strollers, people who use wheelchairs, people with temporary disabilities, and so on. When sentiment for the spirit of a law is strong, enforcement becomes much easier because the public's way of thinking has shifted as opposed to when people are concerned only with meeting minimum requirements. Embracing the spirit of a law can occur with continued public education and sensitization to the issues.

■ Final Thoughts

Although we have public policies that outlaw many forms of discrimination based on race, ethnicity, religion, gender, and ability, the spirit of these antidiscrimination laws has not been embraced by the dominant culture. If the spirit of antidiscrimination laws was embraced, then a great deal of oppression that exists today would be eliminated and the need for constant vigilance to ensure that these policies are enforced would be lessened.

We have great power to influence the public policy process, and we must use this avenue in our fight to eliminate prejudice whenever possible. When public policy is used to support intolerance and bigotry, we must work to eradicate its impact through reversal of such policies and through challenges in the courts. We can set a tone and shift the debate on issues by legislating changes that do not allow intolerance to prevail.

PART VI

Conclusion

21 (In)Conclusion

Michael L. Hecht

The original plan for this book called for me to provide you with a conclusion. But conclusions imply a finality, a certainty, and an ending that I do not wish to communicate. Instead, one of our major goals was to problematize, or call into question and uncertainty, our knowledge and assumptions about prejudice and its expression. In addition, the contributors to this volume were selected to represent diversity—diversity of ideas, personhood, origin, demography, and so on. In the introduction (Chapter 1), I attempted to preview some of the commonalities across chapters. Here I wish to retain the dynamics of difference—what some would call tension, but I prefer to avoid negative connotations for this element.

In keeping with this value of difference, I wish to encourage a fuller understanding of the stances. One of the conclusions I reached, in reviewing this research and the chapters throughout the book, was that little attention has been paid to the appreciation of difference. Most of our efforts have been focused on understanding prejudice and discrimination and on ameliorating their effects so that we have paid little attention to appreciation—what it is, how it is expressed, what appreciative relationships are like, what an appreciative structure would be like, and so on. We are learning a lot about prejudice and are beginning to understand how to overcome its effects, but we are not taking a positive or proactive approach toward understanding appreciation and how to create it. Although critiques of prejudice are important, they tell us little about appreciation. Similarly, although eliminating prejudice may enhance appreciation, it is more likely only to attain tolerance.

Second, it is important to examine the interpenetrations of various spheres and levels of analysis. Isolating racism from other "isms" (e.g., sexism, classism) and examining it at the interpersonal level ignores the social-historical context in which it is experienced and glosses over the important differences among gender, gender orientation, economics, and other social positions.

Finally, if difference is to be appreciated and valued, then this must be reflected in our theories and methods. Disciplinary wars mirror ethnic strife. Requiring logical consistency and commensurability of ideas is analogous to patriarchy. Elevating certain styles of expression reflects the hierarchies of class, age, and other systems. Although monomethod, monotheory understandings are useful, they should not preclude those who walk the borders or even obfuscate these divisions.

These three observations are meant to spark discussion and exploration. Rather than "in conclusion," I offer you "(in)conclusion," borrowing on the critical theory practice of bracketing to convey that, although this chapter concludes the book, it does not conclude the discussion. Academics have long treated clarity and certainty as values. In part, this is why they often privilege discursive style over narrative style. At this point, it should be clear that this book does not accept this value. So, we encourage your participation in our dialogue and in (in)concluding this book.

Notes

1. A relationship perspective looks at the relationship or dyad rather than the individual or social structure. This perspective emphasizes what goes on between *people* rather than separating the people or focusing on social structures.

2. Note that the word "among" is used to avoid emphasizing binary contrasts between two people, two groups, and so on as well as the inevitable centering of European Americans that seems to follow such binary thinking (e.g., relationships between European Americans and African Americans, between European Americans and Asian Americans). Instead, the focus is on the intergroup nature of these processes.

3. Essentialism refers to the process of reducing a person to a single identity and treating that identity as stable and a priori. For example, the editor is not *just* a male; maleness may be part of an identity that includes many other identities. Reducing the editor to his maleness strips him of his essential human qualities.

4. Because *evolutionary theory* seems to be a more current usage and subsumes those theories that consider social influence (sociobiology) as well as those that do not, I use this term from this point on to refer to these theories as a whole. Furthermore, most modern evolutionary theorists are interactionists who believe that environmental and social controls, as well as human volition, combine with evolutionary influences in a probabilistic model. My discussion focuses on the biological or evolutionary aspects of this equation.

5. I have greatly simplified the eugenics movement here. As I have done with most of the theories, I have tried to summarize. Stepan (1991) details the ongoing history of two main branches of genetics in Latin America: those who believed genetics were influenced by environment (Lamarkism) and those who felt that genetics stood independent (Mendelism). Barker (1981) outlines the differences between ethologists and sociobiologists in Britain. The depth of this debate is beyond the scope of this chapter.

6. A student of mine who was doing some research on the Ku Klux Klan, upon reading some of the sources on sociobiology, said that both types of arguments are frequent in Ku Klux Klan literature and discourse.

7. Barker (1981) and others suggest that van den Berghe changed his position from a "liberal scientist" during the 1960s to an evolutionary scientist during the 1980s.

8. Hecht and Baldwin (Chapter 3 in this volume) return to this argument in more detail.

9. For a more extended view of some of these theorists, see Moon and Rolison (Chapter 7 in this volume). In their discussion of classism, they give specific details to Weber, Marx, and postmodern theories of economically based intolerance.

10. I place "disciplines" in quotations to highlight its social constructedness. I believe that what concerns an academic discipline changes from culture to culture and from time to time in history. Furthermore, I believe that the socially constructed walls between disciplines often are barriers to our understanding of complex social realities such as prejudice.

11. For a more extended discussion of feminism and sexism, see Rakow and Wackwitz (Chapter 5 in this volume).

12. All readings of Marx are taken from Tucker's (1978) *The Marx-Engels Reader* (2nd ed.), unless otherwise noted.

13. One of the reasons for not using Allport's "phenomenological" label is that there is a school of philosophy and research, based on Shutz, Heidegger, and others, called phenomenology (Becker, 1992; Bernstein, 1976). Because it looks at reality in different ways than do cognitive psychologists, the use of the word *phenomenology* by the latter becomes confusing.

14. Social categorization processes are adaptive, basic, and efficient. Although there are individual differences in our degrees of categorization, many believe that people are "hardwired" to use these categories to make sense of our environment (Bruner, 1958; Fiske & Neuberg, 1990). We know, for example, that the social categorization process occurs automatically on perception of a target, is extremely rapid, and is not influenced by a perceiver's accuracy-driven attention (Fiske & Neuberg, 1990). Consequently, if social categorization is an innate and overlearned process, then it seems that we invariably stereotype others without intent and without responsibility (Fiske & Neuberg, 1990). This view of cognition is closely aligned with evolutionary theory, discussed earlier.

15. To even begin to tap this extensive literature is a foreboding task. I have chosen to look at some authors and research, but I realize that there are entire lines of research untapped in this brief review, and I intend no slight by this. For more information on this area, see reviews that have been written (e.g., Neuberg, 1991).

16. Forbes (1985) sees this as an improvement over the one-sided view of intolerance measured by the Berkeley Group's instruments. The direction of these instruments may well have been due to the fact that the group was asked specifically to study anti-Semitism.

17. This notion differs from ethnolinguistic identity theory (ELIT), discussed previously, in that it is really looking at individuals' attitudes toward their own and other groups. ELIT does consider attitudes but is more concerned with (a) how a group is linguistically identified (which is more focused than *ethnocentrism*) and (b) how identity is influenced by group-level variables such as the vitality of one's language in a given area. There is a great deal of overlap as well, with both approaches incorporating some elements of both individual and group levels of analyses.

18. A text is a set of signs that are woven or blended together to give meaning (Turner, 1990) and can be verbal (e.g., messages with words such as democracy, free enterprise, and liberalism) or cultural images (e.g., visual messages in print or broadcast media or in everyday life). Thus, texts might include billboards, music videos, newscasts, or clothing in addition to traditional materials such as speeches and literature. The key is that texts are meaningful.

19. As elsewhere in this chapter, I do not expect to tap the variety and depth of rhetorical theory but rather to sample *some* approaches that have application in a study of intolerance. I am here using the term *rhetoric* broadly, not in the classical sense of persuasion but rather in the sense of message or textual analysis, be those texts/messages written, oral, or visual.

20. Feminism and queer theory cannot properly be placed solely under the heading of CS. Authors in these areas rely on many different types of analysis (e.g., "Marxist cultural criticism, structuralism, psychoanalysis, deconstruction, and postmodernism" [Wallace, 1992b, p. 659]).

21. I discussed the connection she sees between beauty and capitalism earlier in the "Marxist Approaches" section. The need to include her thoughts in both cases shows the fuzzy lines between

different approaches such as Marxist/sociological and critical (Marxist)/rhetorical approaches. Rather than being a weakness, this dilemma supports my point that disciplinary walls are themselves arbitrary.

22. This is not to say that it is the *only* approach that considers language. Scholars from different areas link language and intolerance. For example, Allport (1954/1979) discusses the role of language usage in riots and lynchings, and Burke (1967) uses the metaphor of dramatism to show how Hitler used language strategies in his campaign against Jewish people. Language also is central to ethnolinguistic identity theory (Giles & Coupland, 1991).

23. The authors write as Americans in the United States. Various groups and individuals in that nation have been working on civil rights and reducing various forms of intolerance for years. However, we feel that similar trends that *should* have led to increased tolerance can be found in many other nations around the globe.

24. *Metatheory* refers to theory about theory. Specifically, it describes the assumptions and approaches different theories take to what is real, what constitutes knowledge, and so on. For more discussion, see Burrel and Morgan (1979, pp. 1-9) and Littlejohn (1989, pp. 23-29).

25. Burrel and Morgan (1979) explain the difference between objective and subjective ways of scientific thinking. The objective stance tends to see reality in the object—external to individuals. Because reality is in the object, if we remove biases, we all will see the same thing. The purpose of science is to determine the laws (generally in a cause-effect sense) that govern human nature. The subjective approach sees reality as individuals experience it and seeks, through research, to discover individual understandings. Burrel and Morgan see these perspectives as a continuum rather than as a dichotomy. They also note another continuum, that some science exists to explain, predict, and control social reality and other science exists to change social reality in terms of a predetermined stance of the way in which things *should* be. We are suggesting a layered viewpoint that treats these differences as dialectical and continuous and otherwise juxtaposed.

26. Special thanks go to Cristina González, the anonymous book reviewers, and students of COM 492 (Seminar in Communication Theory, Fall 1995, at Illinois State University) for their thoughtful comments on the 1995 versions of the theory.

27. These summary statements are our own, based on the book. They are derived from Talbot's (1991) writing but are not his directly, unless noted otherwise.

28. It is regarding the metaphysical arguments that Baldwin parts with some of the notions of holography. He holds a different view of the nature of the metaphysical, which is beyond the scope of this chapter.

29. Perhaps video would provide a better visual image than does film. Whereas film relies on multiple still images to create the appearance of motion, video uses an emulsion that may be closer to the holographic essence.

30. This is similar to what Allport (1954/1979) says when he discusses the various influences on prejudice (specifically in Chapter 13 of his book). Perhaps what is different is that we want to broaden the *focus* of what we look at to fully understand (in)tolerance and admit the possibility that there might be something besides cognition or psychological need at the "core."

31. For a greater elaboration of these along with assumptions and possible research questions that one might ask, see Baldwin and Hecht (1995).

32. Billig (1976) provides an in-depth discussion of the notion of dialectic, including its roots in Marxist theory, as it applies to social sciences.

33. Sampson (1989) goes on to suggest that a strictly "individuated manner of viewing the world and its inhabitants" (p. 17) both serves certain ways of thinking (ideologies) that "repress the fluidity and indeterminacy of the process in the name of a fixed point of origin" (p. 14) and leads to the continued repression of group over group and of individual over individual. This is because Sampson sees the individualistic and analytical way of thinking closely associated with a "nonreciprocal and hierarchical" view of the world "with certain people on top" (p. 17).

34. It is our opinion that what constitutes membership in a given social grouping (e.g., race, ethnicity) is socially constructed; that is, what it means to be White or Black, despite any purported scientific basis, changes in practice from culture to culture and from time to time. Furthermore, the very meaning of a social categorization such as "race" or "ethnicity" is socially created. Thus, a conflict that Americans might commonly define as racial or ethnic might not be seen in those terms by the society being discussed. We realize, then, that any term we use to label these different conflicts has a bit of arbitrariness. In the end, a more general term such as "intergroup" might be useful to discuss these more broadly. This is not to deny that there are certain implications of discussing things in certain categories, such as "racial" with its biological intonations (Thomas Nakayama, personal communication, September 1995), but the full differences and discussion of these differences are beyond the scope of this chapter.

35. Some might associate different levels of research with different levels of analysis. For example, social psychology has been seen largely as an individual-level approach, sociology as a macro-level or communal-level approach, semiotics as more of a linguistic approach, and so on. We hinted at this same perspective in our 1995 chapter (Baldwin & Hecht, 1995). However, we increasingly see that the various disciplines always have "bled" among various approaches. There is no simple classification of any discipline along a single level of analysis.

36. It is important to note that layering is not meant to imply discrete separate entities. That is why we imported the holographic metaphor.

37. Thanks go to T. A. Niles for continually reminding us of this point.

38. This view of "isms" (e.g., racism, classism, heterosexism) is complicated if one accepts Gramsci's (1957/1983) notion of power, that is, that all groups in a given society have some form of power, not just the "dominant" group. Still, even with this concept, groups with a larger proportion of power in a given area (terrain) would be better able to institutionalize intolerance in that area. Any translations here from the Portuguese are by John Baldwin.

40. Here I write "heterosexuality" *sous rature*—under erasure (Derrida, 1976)—to mark its ideological character and the ways in which the word does not communicate the fiction of heterosexuality. It is not as if heterosexual activities do not take place; however, the belief in heterosexuality as fixed, transhistorical, transcultural, and "natural" is clearly a fiction. Sexual activities through history and across cultures demonstrate the diversity and ideological character of sexuality.

41. By *valence,* we mean that some positions are privileged over others in hegemonic culture.

42. *Golden Ager* is a substereotype of older people as lively, adventurous, healthy, active, sociable, witty, independent, productive, successful and so on. *John Wayne Conservative* is a subtype seen as patriotic, religious, nostalgic, reminiscent, retired, conservative, emotional, mellow, determined, and proud. *Despondent* is a subtype seen as depressed, sad, hopeless, afraid, neglected, and lonely. *Shrew/Curmudgeon* is a subtype seen as complaining, ill-tempered, bitter, prejudiced, demanding, inflexible, selfish, jealous, stubborn, and nosy.

43. In addition, it is possible that racism is evident in relationships involving members of different ethnic minority groups (e.g., African American/Cuban American, African American/Japanese American, Mexican American/Chinese American).

44. Also, Protestant/non-Protestant relationships can be included in this category.

45. Note that this use of the term *accommodation* differs substantially from that typically found in research in personal relationships. For example, Rusbult, Verette, Whitney, Slovik, and Lipkus (1991) use the term *accommodation* to signify individuals' tendency to refrain from reciprocating anger that relationship partners have displayed, instead responding with pro-relationship behaviors (Giles & Coupland, 1991).

46. The authors are indebted to Norma Rodriguez for her expert advice regarding the accuracy of our Spanish usage. To the extent that any errors remain, the first author bears sole responsibility.

47. Briefly, representation refers to images, stories, and characters that stand in for everyday, lived social experiences. Media representations provide a specific site for cultural struggles where ideas, images, and beliefs are contested. Media representations are, themselves, objects of political struggle that provide a space where beliefs about society can be contested and where a power struggle over access to representation takes place (Gray, 1995). Scholars interested in issues of representation often are concerned with how representations are shown and how they affect people and communities that might have something at stake in the way in which they appear publicly.

48. *Doubles* first aired in the summer of 1995 on public broadcasting channels across the United States. Conferences across the United States have screened it, and it circulates via video distribution. Arguably, hereafter its largest audience will be biracial, multiracial, and intercultural audiences.

49. Similar points have been made in recent scholarship on media hegemony in the United States that argues that media adapt messages to the contemporary social environment to appear to be in favor of past social protests when in fact they simply reinscribe problematic, hegemonic, and oppressive relationships in the process (e.g., Cloud, 1992; Dow, 1990; Hanke, 1990).

50. All of these films and videos focus on bi- and multiracial identities as they relate to Asian Pacific issues. Hence, although they necessarily touch on issues affecting African American and Native American bi- and multiracial people, they neglect to address how these issues would change in social contexts other than Asian Pacific ones.

51. I am drawing specifically from Williams's (1980a) distinction between residual and emergent cultures. Although residual cultures are nondominant, they borrow from previous social formations (p. 40). On the other hand, emergent cultures create "new meanings and values, new practices, new significances and experiences" (p. 41). The key difference for Williams is that residual cultures can easily be incorporated into the dominant culture, whereas emergent cultures tend not to be so easily incorporated. My interest here is with the degree to which emergent media may affirm a unique discourse via their independence from Hollywood and may simultaneously support various aspects of the existing social system.

52. Indeed, studying mainstream productions may shed light on the process by which groups are marginalized. As Lindsley points out in one of her chapters in this volume (Chapter 10), mainstream media go so far as to trivialize movements for social change and stigmatize historically disenfranchised groups by, among other strategies, stereotyping and underrepresenting their power and number, which makes attempts to challenge and ultimately change social realities all the more difficult.

53. For stunning analyses of "minor" productions, see Chen (1989) and Marks (1994).

54. There are exceptions; for example, see *Unthinking Eurocentrism* (Shohat & Stam, 1994).

55. A complete account of this literature is beyond the scope of this chapter; however, a brief survey of literature relevant to this study of *Doubles* is possible. Studies generally have taken an empirical approach, focusing on issues such as (a) the history of images and stereotypes especially as they pertain to designated racial groups (e.g., Bogle, 1973, 1988; Dates & Barlow, 1990; Holte, 1984; Humphrey & Schuman, 1984; Noriega, 1992; Wilson & Gutierrez, 1985), (b) whether or not specific representations positively or negatively affect people of color (e.g., Bakerman, 1984; Brown & Campbell, 1986; Drummond, 1990; Heeter, Greenberg, & Mendelson, 1983; Morsey, 1986), (c) how media images contribute to discrimination that can be documented (e.g., Entman, 1990; Wonsek, 1992), (d) what and how media teach us about race and racial differences (e.g., Atkin, Greenberg, & McDermott, 1983; Tucker & Shah, 1992), (e) varying experiences and reactions people have while viewing media texts (e.g., Brown & Schulze, 1990; Johnson, 1984; Matabane, 1988; Nicolini, 1987), and (f) the uses to which media are put and/or pleasures derived from them through media consumption (e.g., Blosser, 1988; Gandy, Matabane, & Omachonn, 1987).

56. For example, see the following articles and books focusing on, among many other issues, alternative critical discourses (e.g., Chabram & Fregoso, 1990; Dent, 1992; Gever, Parmar, &

Greyson, 1993), critiques of Whiteness (e.g., Dyer, 1988; Nakayama, 1994b; Nakayama & Krizek, 1995; Pfeil, 1995), analyses of diasporic cultural production of people of varying heritages living and existing in cultures to which they have affiliative and resistant relationships (e.g., Mercer, 1994), analyses of culture and people exiled from their home cultures (e.g., Naficy, 1993), and a postcolonial critique by people who are living in or who have left once colonial societies (e.g., Trinh, 1989).

57. A national debate is brewing over the increasing numbers of bi- and multiracial peoples in the United States. Some organizers want to have a "multiracial" category put on the national census form in place of the "other" category. Some fear that many people would then check the multiracial category rather than, for instance, the African American or Native American category, which would significantly alter demographic statistics and perhaps decrease access to social welfare benefits.

58. Of course, this is just one type of identity that could be studied. For example, Chinese girls adopted by European American lesbian, gay, or heterosexual parents in the United States, children in foster homes, homeless children, and people in the process of having sex changes all blur the boundaries of multiple identities (including race)—at least as the present system currently understands them—and could be sites for further research.

59. Essentialized identities are those that focus on one characteristic of a person's overall character (e.g., biological) while simultaneously ignoring others in the process (e.g., social). Hence, assuming that all women are feminists would, for example, necessitate an essentialized definition of feminism to mean women's experiences as opposed to a political definition of feminism that focuses on subjective ideological commitments to the eradication of classism, sexism, homophobia, and racism; the unity of women; and the affirmation of women's lives.

60. *Tea* tells the story of five Japanese women married to U.S. military servicemen and their post-World War II experiences in Kansas, where they lived in a predominantly German and Irish American Protestant farm community.

61. Therapy is one function that television serves in contemporary society; however, therapy is also a strategy that media use in attracting and maintaining viewers. The success of daytime talk shows especially demonstrates the fact that television as therapist is a strategy that gains a viewership. See White (1992) for a fuller discussion of this argument about the therapeutic nature of television.

62. Much of this is borrowed from Harvey's (1990) *The Condition of Postmodernity,* as is his notion of the postmodern nexus of power—time, space, and money.

63. Parts of this chapter also can be found, although with minor differences, in Villanueva's (1993) *Bootstraps: From an American Academic of Color.*

64. For a review of an emerging discipline that sees race, class, and gender, among other things, as necessary to the world economic system, see Balibar and Wallerstein's (1991) *Race, Nation, Class* and Wallerstein's (1990) "World-Systems Analysis."

65. For more on this, see West's (1993) *Race Matters,* in which West defines the current state of African Americans in ghettos as "nihilism in Black America."

66. That African Americans have been victims of colonialism has been a bone of contention among historians and sociologists for some time. The argument goes that colonialism is a matter of land takeover and domination of the many by the few. Yet, Curtin (1974) argues persuasively that although not colonized in terms of the traditional definition, African Americans have suffered the same fate as the victims of traditional colonialism.

67. Although there is quite a bit of literature on the concept of internal colonialism, I am thinking here along the lines first discussed by Frantz Fanon such as *Black Skin, White Masks* (Fanon, 1967).

68. The beatitudes in this narrative are taken from the *New American Bible With Revised New Testament* (Confraternity of Christian Doctorine, 1986, Matthew, Chap. 5, Verses 3-10).

69. One exception to this is the work of Wolf (1986), who examines the legitimization of oppression by subordinate groups. She describes four interrelated parts: acknowledging the right of the ruler to dominate, subordinating responses such as obedience, continuing negotiations with the superordinates about the ground rules for the relationship, and internalizing oppression through validating subordination. Because these are not responses to reduce prejudice, they are not discussed at length here.

References

Aboud, F. E. (1993). A fifth grade program to reduce prejudice. In K. McLeod (Ed.), *Multicultural education: The state of the art* (pp. 20-27). Toronto: University of Toronto Press.

Aboud, F. E., & Doyle, E. (1996). Parental and peer influences on children's racial attitudes. *International Journal of Intercultural Relations, 20,* 371-384.

Adelman, R., Greene, M., Charon, R., & Friedman, E. (1990). Issues in physician-geriatric patient relationships. In H. Giles, N. Coupland, & J. Wiemann (Eds.), *Communication, health and the elderly: Fulbright International Colloquium 8* (pp. 126-134). Manchester, UK: Manchester University Press.

Adler, N. (1980). Cultural synergy: The management of cross-cultural organizations. In W. Burke & L. Goodstein (Eds.), *Trends and issues in O.D.: Current theory and practice* (pp. 163-184). San Diego: University Associates.

Adorno, T. W., Frenkel-Brunswick, E., Levinson, D. J., & Sanford, R. N. (1982). *The authoritarian personality* (abridged ed.). New York: Norton. (Originally published by Harper in 1950)

Albeda, R. P. (1986). Occupational segregation by race and gender, 1958-1981. *Industrial and Labor Relations Review, 39,* 404-411.

Albert, R. D. (1994). Cultural diversity and intercultural training in multinational organizations. In R. L. Wiseman & R. Shuter (Eds.), *Communicating in multinational organizations* (pp. 153-165). Thousand Oaks, CA: Sage.

Allan, G. (1989). *Friendship: Developing a sociological perspective.* London: Harvester Wheatsheaf.

Allen, D. (1993). *Fear of strangers and its consequences.* Grawn, MI: Bennington.

Allen, P. G. (1983). *Studies in American Indian literature, critical essays and course designs.* New York: Modern Language Association of America.

Allen, P. G. (1986). *The sacred hoop: Recovering the feminine in American Indian traditions.* Boston: Beacon.

Allen, R. L., & Kuo, C. (1991). Communication and beliefs about racial equality. *Discourse and Society, 2,* 259-279.

Allison, S. T., & Herlocker, C. E. (1994). Constructing impressions in diverse organizational settings. *American Behavioral Scientist, 37,* 637-652.

Allison, S. T., & Messick, D. M. (1985). The group attribution error. *Journal of Experimental Social Psychology, 21,* 563-579.

Allport, G. W. (1979). *The nature of prejudice.* Reading, MA: Addison-Wesley. (Originally published in 1954)

Althusser, L. (1971). *Lenin philosophy and other essays* (B. Brewster, Trans.). London: New Left Books.

Altman, K. E., & Nakayama, T. K. (1991). Making a critical difference: A difficult dialogue. *Journal of Communication, 41*(4), 116-128.

Amir, Y. (1969). The contact hypothesis in ethnic relations. *Psychological Bulletin, 71,* 319-342.

Anastasio, P. A. (1993). *Generalizations of positive impressions from individual to outgroup: Interpersonal vs. intergroup interactions.* Unpublished doctoral dissertation, University of Delaware.

Anastasio, P. A., Bachman, B. A., Gaertner, S. L., & Dovidio, J. F. (1997). Categorization, recategorization, and common ingroup identity. In R. Spears, P. J. Oakes, N. Ellemers, & S. A. Haslam (Eds.), *The social psychology of stereotyping and group life* (pp. 236-256). Oxford, UK: Blackwell.

Andersen, P. A. (1993). Cognitive schemata in personal relationships. In S. Duck (Ed.), *Individuals in relationships* (pp. 1-29). Newbury Park, CA: Sage.

Anderson, D. C. (1994, April 19). Boston's shame. *The Advocate,* pp. 24-25.

Anfuso, D. (1995). Diversity keeps newspaper up with the times. *Personnel Journal, 74*(7), 30-41.

Angelou, M. (1994). *The complete collected poems of Maya Angelou.* New York: Random House.

Anzaldua, G. (1990). *Making face, making soul: Haciendo caras.* San Francisco: Aunt Lute Books.

Appiah, A. (1990). "Racism" and "racisms." In D. T. Goldberg (Ed.), *Anatomy of racism* (pp. 3-17). Minneapolis: University of Minnesota Press.

Arnoff, C. (1974). Old age in prime time. *Journal of Communication, 24*(4), 86-87.

Aron, A., & Aron, E. N. (1986). *Love and the expansion of self: Understanding attraction and satisfaction.* New York: Hemisphere.

Aronson, E. (1992). Causes of prejudice. In R. M. Baird & S. E. Rosenbaum (Eds.), *Bigotry, prejudice, and racism: Definitions, causes, and solutions* (pp. 111-124). Buffalo, NY: Prometheus.

Asante, M. K. (1987). *The Afrocentric idea.* Philadelphia: Temple University Press.

Asante, M. K., & Abarry, A. S. (Eds.). (1996). *The African intellectual heritage.* Philadelphia: Temple University Press.

Ashburn, G., & Gordon, A. (1981). Features of a simplified register in speech to elderly conversationalists. *International Journal of Psycholinguistics, 8,* 7-31.

Atkin, C., Greenberg, B. S., & McDermott, S. (1983). Television and race role socialization. *Journalism Quarterly, 60,* 407-414.

Babrow, A. S. (1995). Communication and problematic integration: Milan Kundera's "Lost Letters" in The Book of Laughter and Forgetting. *Communication Monographs, 62,* 284-300.

Baker, D. (1983). *Race, ethnicity, and power: A comparative study.* London: Routledge & Kegan Paul.

Bakerman, J. (1984). Cutting both ways: Race, prejudice, and motive in Tony Hillerman's detective fiction. *Multi-ethnic Literature of the United States, 11*(3), 17-25.

Bakke v. Regents of California, 132 Cal. Rptr. 680 (S. Ct. 1978).

Baldwin, J. (1963). *The fire next time.* New York: Dial Press.

Baldwin, J. R. (1993, November). *A rose by another name: Racial democracy in Brazil.* Paper presented at the annual meeting of the Speech Communication Association, Miami, FL.

Baldwin, J. R. (1994). *European-Americans' perceptions of "race" and "racist" communication: An interpretive (and critical) study.* Unpublished dissertation, Arizona State University.

Baldwin, J. R. (1995, November). *Description, emotion, and power: Various European-American perceptions of the uses of the word "racism."* Paper presented at the annual meeting of the Speech Communication Association, San Antonio, TX.

Baldwin, J. R. (1996a, April). *Politics of race and identity in Brazil: Branqueamento and beyond.* Paper presented at the annual meeting of the Central States Communication Conference, St. Paul, MN.

Baldwin, J. R. (1996b, April). *Race: A sign of the times—European-Americans' construction of "race."* Paper presented at the annual meeting of the Central States Speech Association, St. Paul, MN.

Baldwin, J. R. (1996c, February). *Representations of Blackness: Towards a new theory of "race" in Brazil.* Paper presented at the annual meeting of the Western States Communication Association, San Jose, CA.

Baldwin, J. R., & Hecht, M. L. (1994, November). *Attitudes toward diversity: A two-sample analysis of a scale of (in)tolerance(s).* Paper presented at the annual meeting of the Speech Communication Association, New Orleans, LA.

Baldwin, J. R., & Hecht, M. L. (1995). The layered perspective of cultural (in)tolerance(s): The roots of a multidisciplinary approach. In R. Wiseman (Ed.), *Intercultural communication theory* (pp. 59-91). Thousand Oaks, CA: Sage.

Baldwin, J., & Mead, M. (1971). *A rap on race.* New York: Lippincott.

Balibar, E. (1991). Is there a "neo-racism?" In E. Balibar & I. Wallerstein (Eds.), *Race, nation, class: Ambiguous identities* (pp. 17-27). London: Verso.

Balibar, E., & Wallerstein, I. (Eds.). (1991). *Race, nation, class: Ambiguous identities.* London: Verso.

Banfield, E. C. (1968). *The unheavenly city.* Boston: Little, Brown.

Banton, M. (1985). *Promoting racial harmony.* Cambridge, UK: Cambridge University Press.

Banton, M. (1987). *Racial theories.* Cambridge, UK: Cambridge University Press.

Barbato, C. A., & Feezel, J. D. (1987). The language of aging in different age groups. *Gerontological Society of America, 27,* 527-531.

Bargh, J. A., & Raymond, P. (1995). The naive misuse of power: Nonconscious sources of sexual harassment. *Journal of Social Issues, 51,* 85-96.

Barker, M. (1981). *The new racism.* London: Junction Books.

Barker, M. (1990). Biology and the new racism. In D. T. Goldberg (Ed.), *Anatomy of racism* (pp. 18-37). Minneapolis: University of Minnesota Press.

Barnes, J., Chesnoff, R. Z., Carter, S., Rosenberg, R., & Trimble, J. (1988, August 1). Truce in troubled waters. *U.S. News & World Report,* p. 50.

Barnum, C. F. (1992, May). A novel approach to diversity. *HRMagazine, 37,* pp. 69-73.

Bar-Tal, D. (1990). Causes and consequences of delegitimization: Models of conflict and ethnocentrism. *Journal of Social Issues, 46,* 65-81.

Bar-Tal, D. (1996). Development of social categories and stereotypes in early childhood: The case of "the Arab" concept formation, stereotype and attitudes by Jewish children in Israel. *International Journal of Intercultural Relations, 20,* 341-370.

Bartlett, D. L., & Steele, J. B. (1992). *America: What went wrong?* Kansas City, MO: Andrews & McMeel.

Basow, S. A. (1992). *Gender: Stereotypes and roles* (3rd ed.). Pacific Grove, CA: Brooks/Cole.

Bate, B. (1988). *Communication and the sexes.* New York: Harper & Row.

Baumhover, L. A., & Beall, S. C. (1996). *Abuse, neglect, and exploitation of older persons.* Baltimore, MD: Health Professions Press.

Bawer, B. (1994, October 18). Confusion reigns. *The Advocate,* p. 80.

Baxter, L. A. (1987). Symbols of relationship identity in relationship cultures. *Journal of Social and Personal Relationships, 4,* 261-279.

Baxter, L. A. (1990). Dialectical contradictions in relationship development. *Journal of Social and Personal Relationships, 7,* 69-88.

Baxter, L. A., & Wilmot, W. W. (1983). Communication characteristics of relationships with differential growth rates. *Communication Monographs, 50,* 264-272.

Baytos, L. M. (1992, March). Launching successful diversity management initiatives. *HRMagazine,* pp. 91-97.

Becker, C. S. (1992). *Living and relating: An introduction to phenomenology.* Newbury Park, CA: Sage.

Begley, S. (1995, March 27). Gray matters: Science: New technologies that catch the mind in the very act of thinking show how men and women use their brains differently. *Newsweek,* pp. 48-52.

Behr, R. L., & Iyengar, S. (1985). Television news, real-world cues, and changes in the public agenda. *Public Opinion Quarterly, 49,* 38-57.

Bell, D. (1992). *Faces at the bottom of the well: The permanence of racism.* New York: HarperCollins.

Bell, J. (1992). In search of a discourse of aging: The elderly on television. *The Gerontologist, 32,* 305-311.

Bell, R. A., Buerkel-Rothfuss, N. L., & Gore, K. E. (1987). Did you bring the Yarmulke for the cabbage patch kid? The idiomatic communication of young lovers. *Human Communication Research, 14,* 47-68.

Bennett, L. (1984). *Before the Mayflower.* New York: Penguin.

Bennett, L., Jr. (1993). *Before the Mayflower: A history of Black America* (6th ed.). New York: Penguin.

Bennett, M. J. (1986a). A developmental approach to training for intercultural sensitivity. *International Journal of Intercultural Relations, 10,* 179-196.

Bennett, M. J. (1986b). Towards ethnorelativism: A developmental model of intercultural sensitivity. In M. P. Paige (Ed.), *Cross-cultural orientation: New conceptualizations and applications* (pp. 26-69). Lanham, MD: University Press of America.

Bennett, T. (1992). Putting policy into cultural studies. In L. Grossberg, C. Nelson, and P. Treichler (Eds.), *Cultural studies* (pp. 23-37). New York: Routledge.

Berg, C. R. (1990). Stereotypes in films in general and the Hispanic in particular. *Howard Journal of Communications, 2,* 286-300.

Berger, C. R. (1986). Social cognition and intergroup communication. In W. B. Gudykunst (Ed.), *Intergroup communication* (pp. 51-61). London: Arnold.

Berger, C. R., & Calabrese, R. J. (1975). Some explorations in initial interaction and beyond: Toward a developmental theory of interpersonal communication. *Human Communication Research, 1,* 99-112.

Berges, P. M. (producer). (1990). *En ryo identity* [video]. (Available from National Asian American Telecommunications Association, 346 Ninth Street, Second Floor, San Francisco, CA 94103)

Bergstrom, M., & Williams, A. (1996, May). *Intergenerational conflict: Attributions, beliefs, communication satisfaction and response tactics.* Poster presented at International Communication Association Conference, Chicago.

Berman, L., & Sobkowska-Ashcroft, I. (1986). The old in language and literature. *Language & Communication, 6,* 139-145.

Berman, P. (1994). Introduction: The other and the almost the same. In P. Berman (Ed.), *Blacks and Jews: Alliances and arguments* (pp. 1-28). New York: Delacorte.

Bernal, M. (1987). *Black Athena: The Afroasiatic roots of classical civilization.* London: Free Association Books.

Bernstein, R. (1976). *The restructuring of social and political theory.* New York: Harcourt Brace Jovanovich.

Berscheid, E. (1985). Interpersonal attraction. In G. Lindzey & E. Aronson (Eds.), *Handbook of social psychology* (3rd ed., Vol. 2, pp. 413-484). New York: Random House.

Berscheid, E. (1986). Mea culpas and lamentations: Sir Francis, Sir Isaac, and "the slow progress of soft psychology." In R. Gilmour & S. Duck (Eds.), *The emerging field of personal relationships* (pp. 267-286). Hillsdale, NJ: Lawrence Erlbaum.

Best, S., & Kellner, D. (1991). *Postmodern theory: Critical interrogations.* New York: Guilford.

Bethlehem, D. W. (1985). *A social-psychology of prejudice.* New York: St. Martin's.

BFI and Channel 4 (producers), with Chadha, G. (director). (1989). *I'm British but . . .* [video]. (Available from National Asian American Telecommunications Association, 346 Ninth Street, Second Floor, San Francisco, CA 94103)

Bicentennial Productions. (1986). *The Constitution of the United States.* Washington, DC: Author.

Bierly, M. M. (1985). Prejudice toward contemporary out-groups as a generalized attitude. *Journal of Applied Social Psychology, 15,* 189-199.

Biernat, M., & Manis, M. (1994). Shifting standards and stereotype-based judgments. *Journal of Personality and Social Psychology, 66,* 5-20.

Billig, M. (1976). *Social psychology and intergroup relations.* London: Academic Press.

Billig, M., Condor, S., Edwards, D., Gane, M., Middleton, D., & Radley, A. (1988). *Ideological dilemmas.* Newbury Park, CA: Sage.

Biskupic, J. (1996, September 9-15). Once unthinkable, now on center stage: The congressional debate over gay marriages is a sign of changing times. *The Washington Post National Weekly Edition,* p. 29.

Blackshire-Belay, C. A. (1994). *The Germanic mosaic.* Westport, CT: Greenwood.

Blank, R., & Slipp, S. (1994). *Voices of diversity: Real people talk about problems and solutions in a workplace where everyone is not alike.* New York: American Management Association.

Blohm, J. M., Hartley, C., & Lapinsky, T. (1995). Piglish: A language learning exercise. *International Journal of Intercultural Relations, 19,* 303-312.

Blosser, B. J. (1988). Ethnic differences in children's media use. *Journal of Broadcasting and Electronic Media, 32,* 453-470.

Blumenfeld, W. J. (1992). Introduction. In W. J. Blumenfeld (Ed.), *Homophobia: How we all pay the price* (pp. 1-19). Boston: Beacon.

Boggs, G. L. (1990). Beyond Eurocentrism. *Monthly Review, 41*(9), 12-18.

Bogle, D. (1973). *Toms, coons, mulattoes, mammies, and bucks: An interpretive history of Blacks in American films.* New York: Viking.

Bogle, D. (1988). *Blacks in American films and television.* New York: Garland.

Boswell, J. (1994). *Same-sex unions in premodern Europe.* New York: Villard.

Botvin, G. J., Schinke, S. P., Epstein, J. A., Diaz, T., & Botvin, E. M. (1995). Effectiveness of culturally focused and generic skills training approaches to alcohol and drug abuse prevention among minority adolescents: Two-year follow-up results. *Psychology of Addictive Behaviors, 9*(3), 183-194.

Boulard, G. (1994a, June 14). The anti-Twinkie defense. *The Advocate,* pp. 33-34, 36, 38.

Boulard, G. (1994b, November 1). If words could kill. *The Advocate,* pp. 40-43.

Bourdieu, P. (1984). *Distinction: A social critique of the judgment of taste* (R. Nice, Trans.). Cambridge, MA: Harvard University Press. (Originally published in 1979)

Bourhis, R. Y. (1994). Power, gender, and intergroup discrimination: Some minimal group experiments. In M. P. Zanna & J. M. Olson (Eds.), *Ontario Symposium on Personality and Social Psychology,* Vol. 7: *The psychology of prejudice* (pp. 171-208). Hillsdale, NJ: Lawrence Erlbaum.

Bowser, B. P., & Hunt, R. G. (Eds.). (1981). *Impacts of racism on White Americans.* Beverly Hills, CA: Sage.

Brah, A. (1992). Difference, diversity, and differentiation. In J. Donald & A. Rattansi (Eds.), *Race, culture, and difference* (pp. 126-145). London: Sage.

Braithwaite, D. (1994). Viewing persons with disabilities as a culture. In L. A. Samovar & R. E. Porter (Eds.), *Intercultural communication: A reader* (pp. 148-154). Belmont, CA: Wadsworth.

Braithwaite, V. A. (1986). Old age stereotypes: Reconciling contradictions. *Journal of Gerontology, 41,* 353-360.

Braithwaite, V., Lynd-Stevenson, R., & Pigram, D. (1993). An empirical study of ageism: From polemics to scientific utility. *Australian Psychologist, 28,* 9-15.

Branco, K. L., & Williamson, J. B. (1982). Stereotypes and the life cycle. In A. G. Miller (Ed.), *In the eye of the beholder: Contemporary issues in stereotyping* (pp. 365-410). New York: Praeger.

Brewer, M. B. (1986). The role of ethnocentrism in intergroup conflict. In S. Worchel & W. G. Austin (Eds.), *The psychology of intergroup relations* (pp. 88-102). Chicago: Nelson-Hall.

Brewer, M. B. (1994). The social psychology of prejudice: Getting it all together. In M. P. Zanna & J. M. Olson (Eds.), *Ontario Symposium on Personality and Social Psychology, Vol. 7: The psychology of prejudice* (pp. 315-330). Hillsdale, NJ: Lawrence Erlbaum.

Brewer, M. B. (1996). When contact is not enough: Social identity and intergroup cooperation. *International Journal of Intercultural Relations, 20,* 291-304.

Brewer, M. B., & Campbell, D. T. (1976). *Ethnocentrism and intergroup attitudes: East African evidence.* New York: John Wiley.

Brewer, M. B., Dull, V., & Lui, L. (1981). Perceptions of the elderly: Stereotypes as prototypes. *Journal of Personality and Social Psychology, 41,* 656-670.

Brewer, M. B., & Miller, N. (1984). Beyond the contact hypothesis: Theoretical perspectives on desegregation. In N. Miller & M. B. Brewer (Eds.), *Groups in contact: The psychology of desegregation* (pp. 281-302). New York: Academic Press.

Brislin, R. W. (1986). Prejudice and intergroup communication. In W. B. Gudykunst (Ed.), *Intergroup communication* (pp. 74-85). London: Arnold.

Brislin, R. W. (1991). Prejudice in intercultural communication. In L. A. Samovar & R. E. Porter (Eds.), *Intercultural communication: A reader* (6th ed.). Belmont, CA: Wadsworth.

Brislin, R. W., Cushner, K., Cherrie, C., & Yong, M. (1986). *Intercultural interactions: A practical guide.* Beverly Hills, CA: Sage.

Brislin, R. W., & Pedersen, P. (1976). *Cross-cultural orientation programs.* New York: Gardner.

Brooks, K. W. (1995, November). *The Black professional: An analysis of the communicative strategies used in cross-race mentoring.* Paper presented at the annual convention of the National Speech Communication Association, New Orleans, LA.

Brown, B. B., Altman, I., & Werner, C. M. (1992). Close relationships in the physical and social world: Dialectical and transactional analysis. In S. A. Deetz (Ed.), *Communication yearbook 15* (pp. 508-521). Newbury Park, CA: Sage.

Brown, J. D., & Campbell, K. (1986). Race and gender in music videos: The same beat but a different drummer. *Journal of Communication, 36*(1), 94-106.

Brown, J. D., & Schulze, L. (1990). The effects of race, gender and fandom on audience interpretations of Madonna's music videos. *Journal of Communication, 40*(2), 88-102.

Brown, R. (1986). *Social psychology* (2nd ed.). New York: Free Press.

Brown, R. J. (1988). *Group processes: Dynamics within and between groups.* New York: Blackwell.

Brummett, B. (1979). A pentadic analysis of ideologies in two gay rights controversies. *Central States Speech Journal, 30,* 250-261.

Bruner, J. S. (1958). Social psychology and perception. In E. E. Maccoby, T. M. Newcomb, & E. L. Hartley (Eds.), *Readings in social psychology* (3rd ed., pp. 85-94). New York: Holt, Rinehart & Winston.

Bruner, J. (1990). *Acts of meaning.* Cambridge, MA: Harvard University Press.

Buescher, D. T., & Ono, K. A. (1996). Civilized colonialism: *Pocahontas* as neocolonial rhetoric. *Women's Studies in Communication, 19,* 127-153.

Bull, C., & Gallagher, J. (1994, April 19). The surgeon general's cardinal sin. *The Advocate,* p. 26.

Bullough, B. L., Shelton, B., & Slavin, S. (1988). *The subordinated sex: A history of attitudes toward women.* Athens: University of Georgia Press.

Burke, K. (1966). *Language as symbolic action.* Berkeley: University of California Press.

Burke, K. (1967). *The philosophy of literary form: Studies in symbolic action* (2nd ed.). Baton Rouge: Louisiana State University Press.

Burleson, B. R., & Samter, W. (1994). A social skills approach to relationship maintenance: How individual differences in communication skills affect the achievement of relationship functions. In D. J. Canary & L. Stafford (Eds.), *Communication and relational maintenance* (pp. 61-90). San Diego: Academic Press.

Burns, E. B. (1980). *A history of Brazil* (2nd ed.). New York: Columbia University Press.

Burrel, G., & Morgan, G. (1979). *Sociological paradigms and organisational analysis.* London: Heinemann.

Bushnell, J. (1990). *Moscow graffiti: Language and subculture.* Boston: Unwin Hyman.

Butler, J. (1990). *Gender trouble: Feminism and the subversion of identity.* New York: Routledge.

Butler, R. N. (1987). *Ageism: The encyclopedia of aging.* New York: Springer.

Byrd, M. L. (1991, November). *Research note on an exploratory investigation of the concept of tolerance toward cultural diversity.* Paper presented at the annual meeting of the Speech Communication Association, Atlanta, GA.

Byrd, M. L. (1993). *The intercultural communication book.* New York: McGraw-Hill.

Bytheway, B. (1995). *Ageism.* Bristol, PA: Open University Press.

Bytheway, B., & Johnson, J. (1990). On defining ageism. *Critical Social Policy, 27,* 27-39.

Cage, M. C. (1993, March 10). Openly gay students face harassment and physical assault on some campuses. *Chronicle of Higher Education,* pp. A22-A24.

Calabrese, A., & Lenart, S. (1992). Cultural diversity and the perversion of tolerance. *Journal of Communication Inquiry, 16,* 33-44.

Calvert, C. (1997). Hate speech and its harms: A communication theory perspective. *Journal of Communication, 47*(1), 4-19.

Canary, D. J., & Stafford, L. (1994). Maintaining relationships through strategic and routine interaction. In D. J. Canary & L. Stafford (Eds.), *Communication and relational maintenance* (pp. 3-22). San Diego: Academic Press.

Capella, J. N. (1987). Interpersonal communication: Definitions and fundamental questions. In C. R. Berger & S. H. Chaffee (Eds.), *Handbook of communication science* (pp. 184-238). Newbury Park, CA: Sage.

Caporeal, L. R. (1981). The paralanguage of caregiving: Baby talk to the institutionalized aged. *Journal of Personality and Social Psychology, 40,* 876-884.

Caporeal, L. R., & Culbertson, G. H. (1986). Verbal response modes of baby talk and other speech at institutions for the aged. *Language and Communication, 6,* 99-112.

Carlson, S. (1992). Trends in race/sex occupational inequality: Conceptual and measurement issues. *Social Problems, 39,* 268-287.

Carver, C. S., & de la Garza, N. H. (1984). Schema-guided information search in stereotyping of the elderly. *Journal of Applied Social Psychology, 14,* 69-81.

Castaneda, C. (1974). *Tales of power.* New York: Simon & Schuster.

Caudron, S. (1994). Diversity ignites work terms. *Personnel Journal, 73*(9), 54-63.

Chabram, A. C., & Fregoso, R. L. (Eds.). (1990). Chicana/o cultural representations: Reframing alternative critical discourses [special issue]. *Cultural Studies, 4.*

Chaffee, S. H., & Berger, C. R. (1987). Levels of analysis: An introduction. In C. R. Berger & S. H. Chaffee (Eds.), *Handbook of communication science* (pp. 143-145). Newbury Park, CA: Sage.

Chen, K.-H. (1989). Deterritorializing "critical" studies in "mass" communication: Towards a theory of "minor" discourses. *Journal of Communication Inquiry, 13,* 43-61.

Chodorow, N. (1978). *The reproduction of mothering.* Berkeley: University of California Press.

Chodron, P., & hooks, b. (1997, March). News you can use: Pema Chodron and bell hooks talk over life and all its problems. *Shambhala Sun, 5*(4), pp. 26-31.

Chono-Helsley, M. (producer/director). (1993). *Do 2 halves really make a whole? A video by Martha Chono-Helsley and Joe Leonardi* [video]. (Available from National Asian American

Telecommunications Association, 346 Ninth Street, Second Floor, San Francisco, CA 94103)

Christ, C., & Plaskow, J. (Eds.). (1979). *Womanspirit rising.* New York: Harper & Row.

Christ, C. (1992). Feminists: Sojourners in the field of religious studies. In C. Kramarae & D. Spender (Eds.), *The knowledge explosion: Generations of feminist scholarship* (pp. 82-88). New York: Teachers College Press.

Christie, R. (1991). Authoritarianism and related constructs. In J. P. Robinson, P. R. Shaver, & L. S. Wrightsman (Eds.), *Measures of personality and social psychological attitudes* (pp. 501-571). San Diego: Academic Press.

Clément, R., & Noels, R. A. (1992). Towards a situated approach to ethnolinguistic identity: The effects of status on individual groups. *Journal of Language and Social Psychology, 11,* 203-232.

Cloud, D. L. (1992). The limits of interpretation: Ambivalence and the stereotype in *Spencer: For Hire. Critical Studies in Mass Communication, 9,* 311-324.

Cloud, D. L. (1996). Hegemony or concordance? The rhetoric of tokenism in "Oprah" Winfrey's rags-to-riches biography. *Critical Studies in Mass Communication, 13,* 115-137.

Clough, P. T. (1992). *The end(s) of ethnography: From realism to social criticism.* Newbury Park, CA: Sage.

Cohen, G., & Faulkner, D. (1986). Does "elderspeak" work? The effect of intonation and stress on comprehension and recall of spoken discourse in old age. *Language and Communication, 6,* 91-98.

Cole, R. E., & Deskins, D. R., Jr. (1988). Racial factors in site location and employment patterns of Japanese auto firms in America. *California Management Review, 31*(1), 9-22.

Coleman, L. M., & DePaulo, B. M. (1991). Uncovering the human spirit: Moving beyond disability and "missed communications." In N. Coupland, H. Giles, & J. Wiemann (Eds.), *"Miscommunication" and problematic talk* (pp. 61-84). Newbury Park, CA: Sage.

College-educated Blacks' earnings lag behind Whites'. (1991, September 20). *Tribune Newspapers,* pp. A1, A6.

Collier, M. J. (1988). A comparison of intracultural and intercultural communication among acquaintances: How intra- and intercultural competencies vary. *Communication Quarterly, 36,* 122-144.

Collier, M. J. (1991). Conflict competence within African, Mexican and Anglo American friendships. In S. Ting-Toomey & F. Korzenny (Eds.), *Cross-cultural interpersonal communication* (pp. 132-154). Newbury Park, CA: Sage.

Collier, M. J., & Thomas, M. (1988). Cultural identity in inter-cultural communication: An interpretive perspective. In Y. Y. Kim & W. B. Gudykunst (Eds.), *Theories in intercultural communication* (pp. 94-120). Newbury Park, CA: Sage.

Collins, P. H. (1990). *Black feminist thought: Knowledge, consciousness, and the politics of empowerment.* Boston: HarperCollins Academic.

Collins, P. H. (1991). *Black feminist thought.* New York: Routledge.

Collins, P. H. (1995). Symposium: On West and Fenstermaker's "Doing Difference." *Gender & Society, 9,* 491-494.

Collins, S. (1994, March 28). America cranks it up. *U.S. News and World Report,* pp. 57-60.

Collison, N.-K. (1992). Young people found pessimistic about relations between races. *Chronicle of Higher Education, 38,* A1, A32.

Color bias is ruled possible within race. (1989, May 14). *Arizona Repubic,* p. B2.

Confraternity of Christian Doctorine. (1986). *New American Bible with revised New Testament.* Washington, DC: Author.

Conquergood, D. (1991). Rethinking ethnography: Towards a critical cultural politics. *Communication Monographs, 58,* 179-194.

Cook, S. W. (1985). Experimenting on social issues: The case of school desegregation. *American Psychologist, 40,* 452-460.

Cook-Gumperz, J. (1993). The relevant text: Narrative, storytelling, and children's understanding of genre—Response to Egan. *Linguistics and Education, 5,* 149-156.

Coombes, W. T., & Holladay, S. T. (1995). The emerging political power of the elderly. In N. F. Nussbaum & J. Coupland (Eds.), *Handbook of communication and aging research* (pp. 317-343). Mahwah, NJ: Lawrence Erlbaum.

Cose, E. (1993). *The rage of a privileged class.* New York: HarperCollins.

Coupland, D. (1990). *Generation X: Tales for an accelerated culture.* New York: St. Martin's.

Coupland, J., Nussbaum, J. F., & Coupland, N. (1991). The reproduction of aging and agism in intergenerational talk. In N. Coupland, H. Giles, & J. M. Wiemann (Eds.), *"Miscommunication" and problematic talk* (pp. 85-102). Newbury Park, CA: Sage.

Coupland, N., & Coupland, J. (1990). Language and later life. In H. Giles & W. P. Robinson (Eds.), *Handbook of language and social psychology* (pp. 451-468). Chichester, UK: Wiley.

Coupland, N., & Coupland, J. (1993). Discourses of ageism and anti-ageism. *Journal of Aging Studies, 7,* 279-301.

Coupland, N., Coupland, J., & Giles, H. (1991). *Language, society, and the elderly: Discourse, identity and aging.* Oxford, UK: Blackwell.

Coupland, N., Coupland, J., Giles, H., & Henwood, K. (1988). Accommodating the elderly: Invoking and extending a theory. *Language in Society, 17,* 1-41.

Coupland, N., Coupland, J., Giles, H., & Henwood, K. (1990). Formulating age: The management of age identity in elderly talk. *Discourse Processes, 141,* 87-106.

Covey, H. C. C. (1988). Historical terminology used to represent older people. *The Gerontologist, 28,* 291-297.

Coward, R. (1983). *Patriarchal precedents: Sexuality and social relations.* London: Routledge & Kegan Paul.

Cowie, E. (1978). Woman as sign. *m/f, 1,* 49-63.

Cowley, G., with Murr, A., & Rogers, A. (1995, March 27). It's time to rethink nature and nurture: Ideas—Biology and free will aren't at odds: They're inseparable. *Newsweek,* pp. 52-54.

Cox, T. H., Jr. (1993). *Cultural diversity in organizations: Theory, research and practice.* San Francisco: Berrett-Koehler.

Cox, T. H., Jr., & Blake, S. (1991, August). Managing cultural diversity: Implications for organizational competitiveness. *The Executive,* pp. 45-56.

Cox, T. H., Jr., & Finley-Nickelson, J. (1991). Models of acculturation for intraorganizational cultural diversity. *Canadian Journal of Administrative Sciences, 8*(2), 90-100.

Cox, T. H., Jr., & Harquail, C. V. (1991). Career paths and career success in the early career stages of male and female MBAs. *Journal of Vocational Behavior, 39,* 54-75.

Crandall, C. S. (1994). Prejudice against fat people: Ideology and self-interest. *Journal of personality and social psychology, 66,* 882-894.

Crocker, J., Voelkl, K., Testa, M., & Major, B. (1991). Social stigma: The affective consequences of attributional ambiguity. *Journal of Personality and Social Psychology, 60,* 218-228.

Crohn, J. (1995). *Mixed matches: How to create successful interracial, interethnic, and interfaith relationships.* New York: Fawcett.

Crompton, R. (1993). *Class and stratification: An introduction to current debates.* Cambridge, UK: Polity.

Crosby, F., Bromley, S., & Saxe, L. (1980). Recent unobtrusive studies of Black and White discrimination and prejudice: A literature review. *Psychological Bulletin, 87,* 546-563.

Curtin, P. (1974). The Black experience of colonialism and imperialism. In S. W. Mintz (Ed.), *Slavery, colonialism, and racism* (pp. 17-29). New York: Norton.

Dail, P. W. (1988). Prime-time portrayals of older adults in the context of family life. *The Gerontologist, 28,* 700-706.

Daly, M. (1968). *The church and the second sex.* New York: Harper & Row.

Daly, M. (1973). *Beyond God the father: Toward a philosophy of women's liberation.* Boston: Beacon.

Daly, M. (1978). *Gyn/Ecology: The metaethics of radical feminism.* Boston: Beacon.

da Matta, R. (1979). *Carnavais, malandros e heróis: Para uma sociologia do dilema brasileiro* [Carnavals, rogues and heroes: Toward a sociology of the Brazilian dilemma]. Rio de Janeiro: Zahar.

Dates, J., & Barlow, W. (Eds.). (1990). *Split image: African Americans in the mass media.* Washington, DC: Howard University Press.

Davies, B., & Harré, R. (1989). Positioning: The discursive production of selves. *Journal of the Theory of Social Behavior, 20,* 43-63.

Davis, A. Y. (1983). Rape, racism and the myth of the Black rapist. In A. Y. Davis (Ed.), *Women, race and class* (pp. 172-201). New York: Vintage Books.

Davis, G. (1994). Cultural diversity and corporate America: Commitment or smokescreen? *The Black Collegian, 224,* 127-131.

Davis, R. H., & Kubey, R. W. (1982). Growing old on television and with television. In D. Pearl, L. Bouthilet, & J. Lazar (Eds.), *TV and behavior: Ten years of scientific progress and implications for the eighties* (Vol. 2, pp. 201-208). Rockville, MD: National Institute of Mental Health.

Deaux, K., & Emswiller, T. (1974). Explanations of successful performance in sex-linked tasks: What is skill for the male is luck for the female. *Journal of Personality and Social Psychology, 29,* 80-85.

DeFrancisco, V. L. (1991). The sounds of silence: How men silence women in marital relations. *Discourse & Society, 2,* 413-423.

Delatte, A. P., & Baytos, L. (1993). Eight guidelines for successful diversity training. *Training, 30,* 55-50.

Deleuze, G., & Guattari, F. (1987). *A thousand plateaus: Capitalism and schizophrenia* (B. Massumi, Trans.). Minneapolis: University of Minnesota Press.

Dell Publishing. (1994). *The American heritage dictionary.* New York: Author.

Dent, G. (Ed.). (1992). *Black popular culture.* Seattle: Bay Press.

Denzin, N. K. (1978). *The research act: A theoretical introduction to sociological methods* (2nd ed.). New York: McGraw-Hill.

Denzin, N. K. (1994). The art and politics of interpretation. In N. K. Denzin & Y. S. Lincoln (Eds.), *Handbook of qualitative research* (pp. 500-513). Thousand Oaks, CA: Sage.

Derrida, J. (1976). *Of grammatology* (G. C. Spivak, Trans.). Baltimore, MD: Johns Hopkins University Press.

Deutch, M. (1990). Psychological roots of moral exclusion. *Journal of Social Issues, 46,* 21-25.

Devine, P. G. (1989). Stereotypes and prejudice: Their automatic and controlled components. *Journal of Personality and Social Psychology, 56,* 5-18.

Devine, P. G., & Monteith, M. J. (1993). The role of discrepancy-associated affect in prejudice reduction. In D. M. Mackie & D. L. Hamilton (Eds.), *Affect, cognition and stereotyping: Interactive processes in group perception* (pp. 317-344). San Diego: Academic Press.

DeWine, S. (1994, November). *Goal setting and strategic planning in culturally diverse organizations.* Paper presented at the annual convention of the Speech Communication Association, New Orleans, LA.

Dijker, A. J. M. (1987). Emotional reactions to ethnic minorities. *European Journal of Social Psychology, 17,* 305-326.

Dillard. J., Henwood, K., Giles, H., Coupland, N., & Coupland, J. (1990). Compliance-gaining young and old: Beliefs about influence in different age groups. *Communication Reports, 3,* 84-91.

Dindia, K. (1994). A multiphasic view of relationship maintenance strategies. In D. J. Canary & L. Stafford (Eds.), *Communication and relational maintenance* (pp. 91-112). San Diego: Academic Press.

Diop, C. A. (1974). *The African origin of civilization.* New York: Lawrence Hill.

Diop, C. A. (1979). *The cultural unity of Black Africa.* Chicago: Third World Press.

Dodd, C. H. (1991). *Dynamics of intercultural communication* (3rd ed.). Dubuque, IA: William C. Brown.

Does affirmative action mean, "No White men need apply?" (1995, February 13). *U.S. News and World Report,* cover page.

Dorf, J. (1995, January/February). Border patrol. *10 Percent,* pp. 24, 26.

Dohrmann, R. (1975). A gender profile of children's educational TV. *Journal of Communication, 25,* 56-65.

Dow, B. J. (1990). Hegemony, feminist criticism and *The Mary Tyler Moore Show. Critical Studies in Mass Communication, 7,* 261-274.

Dreher, G. F., & Ash, R. A. (1990). A comparative study of mentoring among men and women in managerial, professional and technical positions. *Journal of Applied Psychology, 75,* 1-8.

Drummond, W. (1990). About face: From alliance to alienation—Blacks and the news media. *The American Enterprise, 1*(4), 22-29.

Dubin, M. (1991, December 13). A high rate of anti-Asian incidents: Human relations panel releases annual report. *Philadelphia Inquirer,* p. B9.

DuBois, W. E. B. (1969). *The souls of Black folk.* New York: Signet. (Originally published in 1903)

Duck, S. (1992). *Human relationships* (2nd ed.). London: Sage.

Duck, S. (1994). *Meaningful relationships: Talking, sense, and relating.* Thousand Oaks, CA: Sage.

Duck, S. W., & Sants, H. K. A. (1983). On the origin of the specious: Are personal relationships really interpersonal states? *Journal of Social and Clinical Psychology, 1,* 27-41.

Duckitt, J. (1993). Prejudice and behavior: A review. *Current Psychology: Research and Review, 11,* 291-307.

Duckitt, J. (1994). *The social psychology of prejudice.* Westport, CT: Praeger.

Dunbar, P. L. (1913). We wear the mask. In *The complete poems of Paul Lawrence Dunbar* (p. 71). New York: Dodd, Meade.

Dunbar, R. I. M. (1987). Sociobiological explanations and the evolution of ethnocentrism. In V. Reynolds, V. Falger, & I. Vine (Eds.), *The sociobiology of ethnocentrism: Evolutionary dimensions of xenophobia, discrimination, racism and nationalism* (pp. 48-59). London: Croom Helm.

Dworkin, A. (1981). *Pornography: Men possessing women.* New York: Putnam.

Dyer, R. (1988). White. *Screen, 29,* 44-65.

Dzidzienyo, A. (1979). The position of Blacks in Brazilian society. In A. Dzidzienyo & L. Casal (Eds.), *The position of Blacks in Brazilian and Cuban society* (Report No. 7). London: Minority Rights Group.

Early, G. (Ed.). (1993). *Lure and loathing: Essays on race, identity, and the ambivalence of assimilation.* New York: Allen Lane/Penguin.

Economic ills of U.S. strain race relations. (1991, November 30). *Arizona Republic,* p. C32.

Edwards, H., & Noller, P. (1993). Perceptions of overaccommodation used by nurses in communication with the elderly. *Journal of Language and Social Psychology, 12,* 207-223.

EEOC to monitor Texaco discrimination settlement. (1997, January 4). *The Washington Post,* p. 1.

Ehrenreich, B. (1989). *Fear of falling: The inner life of the middle class.* New York: HarperCollins.

Ehrlich, H. J. (1973). *The social psychology of prejudice: A systemic theoretical review and propositional inventory of the American social psychological study of prejudice.* New York: John Wiley.

Emry, O. B. (1986). Linguistic decrement in normal aging. *Language and Communication, 6,* 47-64.

Entman, R. M. (1990). Modern racism and the images of Blacks in local television news. *Critical Studies in Mass Communication, 7,* 332-345.

Equal Employment Opportunity Commission. (1994). *Combined annual report, fiscal years 91-92* (Document Y3.EQ2: 1/991-92). Washington, DC: Government Printing Office.

Esaki J., & Kato, A. E. (producers), with Esaki, J. (director). (1993). *Maceo: Demon drummer from East L.A.* [video]. (Available from National Asian American Telecommunications Association, 346 Ninth Street, Second Floor, San Francisco, CA 94103)

Essed, P. (1991). *Understanding everyday racism: An interdisciplinary theory.* Newbury Park, CA: Sage.

Estes, C. L., & Binney, E. A. (1979). The biomedication of aging: Dangers and dilemmas. *The Gerontologist, 29,* 587-596.

Etter-Lewis, G. (1991). Standing up and speaking out: African American women's narrative legacy. *Discourse and Society, 2,* 425-437.

Ezorsky, G. (1991). *Racism and justice: The case for affirmative action.* Ithaca, NY: Cornell University Press.

Faber, R. J., O'Guinn, T. C., & Meyer, T. P. (1987). Televised portrayals of Hispanics: A comparison of ethnic perceptions. *International Journal of Intercultural Relations, 11,* 155-169.

Falger, V. S. E. (1987). From xenophobia to xenobiosis? Biological aspects of the foundation of international relations. In V. Reynolds, V. Falger, & I. Vine (Eds.), *The sociobiology of ethnocentrism: Evolutionary dimensions of xenophobia, discrimination, racism and nationalism* (pp. 235-250). London: Croom Helm.

Falicov, C. J. (1986). Cross-cultural marriages. In N. S. Jacobson & A. S. Gurman (Eds.), *Clinical handbook of marital therapy* (pp. 429-450). New York: Guilford.

Faludi, S. (1991). *Backlash: The undeclared war against American women.* New York: Crown.

Fanon, F. (1967). *Black skin, white masks.* New York: Grove.

Fantini, A. E. (1995). Aba-Zak: A worldview exercise. *International Journal of Intercultural Relationships, 19,* 297-302.

FaxForum results. (1994, February). *Training and Development,* p. 26.

FBI: Racism cause of most hate crime. (1993, January 5). *Tempe Daily News Tribune,* p. A3.

Feagin, J. R., & Imani, N. (1994). Racial barriers to African American entrepreneurship: An exploratory study. *Social Problems, 41,* 562-584.

Feagin, J. R., & Sikes, M. P. (1994). *Living with racism: The Black middle-class experience.* Boston: Beacon.

Feher, M. (1994). The schisms of '67: On certain restructuring of the American Left, from the civil rights movement to the multiculturalist constellation. In P. Berman (Ed.), *Blacks and Jews: Alliances and arguments* (pp. 263-285). New York: Delta.

Fehr, B. (1996). *Friendship processes.* Thousand Oaks, CA: Sage.

Ferdman, B. M. (1995). Cultural identity and diversity in organizations: Bridging the gap between group differences and individual uniqueness. In M. M. Chemers, S. Oskamp, & M. A. Constanzo (Eds.), *Diversity in organizations: New perspectives for a changing workplace* (pp. 37-61). Thousand Oaks, CA: Sage.

Fernald, J. L. (1995). Interpersonal heterosexism. In B. Lott & D. Maluso (Eds.), *The social psychology of interpersonal discrimination* (pp. 80-117). New York: Guilford.

Fernandez, C., & Pedroza, L. (1981, April). *The Border Patrol and news media coverage of undocumented Mexican immigration during the 1970s: A quantitative content analysis in the sociology of knowledge.* Paper presented at the annual meeting of the National Association for Chicano Studies, Riverside, CA.

Fernandez, J. P. (1974). *Black managers in White corporations* (U.S. Department of Labor Technical Report DLMA 92-11-72-36-1). Springfield, VA: National Technical Information Service.

Fernandez, J. P. (1981). *Racism and sexism in corporate life.* Lexington, MA: Lexington Books.

Few jobs, few workers. (1995, August 12). Porterville Recorder, p. 3b.

Fetterman, D. (1996). *Ethnography: Step by step.* Thousand Oaks, CA: Sage.

Few jobs, few workers. (1995, August 12). *Porterville Recorder,* p. B3.

Ficarrotto, T. J. (1990). Racism, sexism, and erotophobia: Attitudes of heterosexuals towards homosexuals. *Journal of Homosexuality, 19,* 111-116.

Filipczak, B. (1992). 25 years of diversity at UPS (United Parcel Service of America Inc.). *Training, 29,* 42-47.

Finn, G. (1996). *Why Althusser killed his wife: Essays on discourse and violence.* Atlantic Highland, NJ: Humanities Press.

Fisher, W. (1987). *Human communication as narration: Toward a philosophy of reason, value, and action.* Columbia: University of South Carolina Press.

Fishman, P. (1983). Interaction: The work women do. In B. Thorne, C. Kramarae, & N. Henley (Eds.), *Language, gender and society* (pp. 89-102). Cambridge, MA: Newbury House.

Fiske, S. T., & Glick, P. (1995). Ambivalence and stereotypes cause sexual harassment: A theory with implications for organizational change. *Journal of Social Issues, 51,* 97-115.

Fiske, S. T., & Neuberg, S. L. (1990). A continuum of impressions formation, from category-based to individuating processes: Influences of information and motivation on attention and interpretation. In M. P. Zanna (Ed.), *Advances in experimental social psychology* (Vol. 23, pp. 1-74). New York: Academic Press.

Fitzpatrick, M. A., & Indvik, J. (1986). On alternative conceptions of relational communication. *Communication Quarterly, 34,* 19-23.

Flohr, H. (1987). Biological bases of social prejudices. In V. Reynolds, V. Falger, & I. Vine (Eds.), *The sociobiology of ethnocentrism: Evolutionary dimensions of xenophobia, discrimination, racism and nationalism* (pp. 190-207). London: Croom Helm.

Foa, U. G., & Foa, E. B. (1974). *Societal structures of the mind.* Springfield, IL: Charles C Thomas.

Foeman, A. K. (1991). Managing multiracial institutions: Goals and approaches for race-relations training. *Communication Education, 40,* 255-265.

Folb, E. A. (1994). Who's got the room at the top? Issues of dominance and nondominance in intracultural communication. In L. A. Samovar & R. E. Porter (Eds.), *Intercultural communication: A reader* (pp. 131-140). Belmont, CA. Wadsworth.

Foner, E., & Garranty, J. (Eds.). (1991). *The reader's companion to American history.* Boston: Houghton Mifflin.

Fontaine, G., & Dorch, E. (1980). Problems and benefits of close intercultural relationships. *International Journal of Intercultural Relations, 4,* 329-337.

Forbes, H. D. (1985). *Nationalism, ethnocentrism, and personality: Social science and critical theory.* Chicago: University of Chicago Press.

Fowler, S. M. (1994). Two decades of using simulation games for cross-cultural training. *Simulation & Gaming, 25,* 464-476.

Fox, S., & Giles, H. (1993). Accommodating intergenerational contact: A critique and theoretical model. *Journal of Aging Studies, 7,* 423-451.

Fox, S., & Giles, H. (1996). Interability communication: Evaluating patronizing encounters. *Journal of Language and Social Psychology, 15,* 265-290.

Frable, D. E. S. (1993). Being and feeling unique: Statistical deviance and psychological marginality. *Journal of Personality, 61,* 85-110.

Frable, D. E. S., Blackstone, T., & Scherbaum, C. (1990). Marginal and mindful: Deviants in social interactions. *Journal of Personality and Social Psychology, 59,* 140-149.

Franklin, A., & Franklin, B. (1990). Age and power. In T. Jeffs & M. Smith (Eds.), *Young people, inequality and youth work* (pp. 1-27). Hampshire, UK: Macmillan Education.

Franklin, J. H., & Moss, A. A., Jr. (1988). *From slavery to freedom* (7th ed.). New York: McGraw-Hill.

Franklin, R. S. (1991). *Shadows of race and class.* Minneapolis: University of Minnesota Press.

Franklyn-Stokes, A., Harriman, J., Giles, H., & Coupland, N. (1988). Information seeking across the lifespan. *Journal of Social Psychology, 128,* 419-421.

Freedman, D. (1996, July 7). U.S. Supreme Court's surprising decisions. *San Francisco Examiner,* p. A4.

Freeman, S. J. (1990). *Managing lives: Corporate women and social change.* Amherst: University of Massachusetts Press.

Freire, P. (1995). *Pedagogy of the oppressed* (M. Bergman Ramos, Trans.). New York: Continuum. (Originally published in 1970)

French, M. (1985). *Beyond power: On women, men, and morals.* New York: Ballantine.

Freyre, G. (1964). *The masters and the slaves: A study in the development of Brazilian civilization* (abridged ed., S. Putnam, Trans.). New York: Knopf. (Originally published in 1944)

Friedan, B. (1963). *The feminine mystique.* New York: Norton.

Friedan, B. (1993). *The fountain of age.* London: Jonathan Cape.

Friskopp, A., & Silverstein, S. (1995, July/August). Can't you take a joke? *10 Percent,* pp. 42-43.

Frye, M. (1983). *The politics of reality: Essays in feminist theory.* Trumansburg, NY: Crossing.

Fulbeck, L. K. (producer/director). (1990). *Banana split: 25 stories by Kip Fulbeck* [video]. (Available from National Asian American Telecommunications Association, 346 Ninth Street, Second Floor, San Francisco, CA 94103)

Fussell, P. (1979). *Class: A guide through the American status system.* New York: Simon & Schuster.

Gaertner, S. L., & Dovidio, J. F. (1986). The aversive form of racism. In J. F. Dovidio & S. L. Gaertner (Eds.), *Prejudice, discrimination, and racism* (pp. 61-89). Orlando, FL: Academic Press.

Gaertner, S. L., Dovidio, J. F., & Bachman, B. A. (1996). Revisiting the contact hypothesis: The induction of a common ingroup identity. *International Journal of Intercultural Relations, 20,* 271-290.

Gaertner, S. L., Dovidio, J. F., Banker, B., Rust, M. C., Nier, J., Mottola, G., & Ward, C. (in press). Does pro-Whiteness necessarily mean anti-Blackness? In M. Fine, L. Powell, I. Weis, & M. Wong (Eds.), *Off White.* London: Routledge.

Gaertner, S. L., Dovidio, J. F., Mann, J. A., Murrell, A. J., & Pomare, M. (1990). How does cooperation reduce intergroup bias? *Journal of Personality and Social Psychology, 59,* 692-704.

Gaines, J. (1988). White privilege and looking relations: Race and gender in feminist film theory. *Screen, 29,* 12-26.

Gaines, S. O., Jr. (1994). Exchange of respect-denying behaviors in male-female friendships. *Journal of Social and Personal Relationships, 11,* 5-24.

Gaines, S. O., Jr. (1995). Relationships between members of cultural minorities. In J. T. Wood & S. Duck (Eds.), *Under-studied relationships: Off the beaten track* (pp. 51-88). Thousand Oaks, CA: Sage.

Gaines, S. O., Jr., & Ickes, W. (1997). Perspectives on interracial relationships. In S. Duck (Ed.), *Handbook of personal relationships* (2nd ed., pp. 197-220). Chichester, UK: Wiley.

Gaines, S. O., Jr., & Reed, E. S. (1994). Two social psychologies of prejudice: Gordon W. Allport, W. E. B. DuBois, and the legacy of Booker T. Washington. *Journal of Black Psychology, 20,* 8-28.

Gaines, S. O., Jr., & Reed, E. S. (1995). Prejudice: From Allport to DuBois. *American Psychologist, 50,* 96-103.

Gaines, S. O., Jr., Rios, D. I., Granrose, C., Bledsoe, K., Farris, K., Page, M. S., & Garcia, B. F. (1996, January). *Romanticism and resource exchange among interethnic/interracial couples.* Paper presented at the annual meeting of the Social Psychologists in Texas, Arlington, TX.

Galen, M. (1994, January 31). White, male, and worried. *Business Week,* pp. 50-55.

Gallois, C., Franklyn-Stokes, A., Giles, H., & Coupland, N. (1988). Communication accommodation in intercultural encounters. In Y. Y. Kim & W. B. Gudykunst (Eds.), *Theories in intercultural communication* (pp. 157-185). Newbury Park, CA: Sage.

Gallois, C., Giles, H., Jones, E., Cargile, A. C., & Ota, H. (1995). Accommodating intercultural encounters: Elaborations and extensions. In R. Wiseman (Ed.), *Intercultural communication theory* (pp. 115-147). Thousand Oaks, CA: Sage.

Gandy, O. H., Matabane, P. W., & Omachonn, J. O. (1987). Media use, reliance, and active participation: Exploring student awareness of the South African conflict. *Communication Research, 14,* 644-663.

Gans, H. J. (1980). *Deciding what's news: A study of CBS Evening News, NBC Nightly News, Newsweek and Time.* New York: Vintage Books.

Gardner, C. B. (1991). Stigma and the public self: Notes on communication, self, and others. *Journal of Contemporary Ethnography, 20,* 251-262.

Gardner, R. C. (1994). Stereotypes as consensual beliefs. In M. P. Zanna & J. M. Olson (Eds.), *Ontario Symposium on Personality and Social Psychology,* Vol. 7: *The psychology of prejudice* (pp. 1-32). Hillsdale, NJ: Lawrence Erlbaum.

Garlick. B., Dixon, S. & Allen, P. (Eds.). (1992). *Stereotypes of women in power: Historical perspectives and revisionist views.* Westport, CT: Greenwood.

Garner, J. F. (1994). *Politically correct bedtime stories.* New York: Macmillan.

Gates, H. L., Jr. (Ed.). (1986). *Race, writing, and difference.* Chicago: University of Chicago Press.

Gates, H. L., Jr. (Ed.). (1990). *Reading Black, reading feminist: A critical anthology.* New York: Meridian.

Gays under fire. (1992, September 14). *Newsweek,* pp. 34-40.

Geber, B., Gordon, J., Hequet, M., & Picard, M. (1994). Diversity training pays—Doesn't it? *Training, 31,* 17-18.

Geertz, C. (1988). *Works and lives: The anthropologist as author.* Stanford, CA: Stanford University Press.

Gentaz, C. (1994). L'homophobie masculine: Préservatif psychique de la virilité? [Masculine homophobia: Psychic protector/guardian of virility?] In D. Welzer-Lang, P. Dutey, & M. Dorais (Eds.), *La peur de l'autre en soi: Du sexisme à l'homophobie* [Fear of the other in one's self: Of homophobic sexism] (pp. 199-224). Montreal: VLB Éditeur.

Gerbner, G., Gross, L., Elley, M., Jackson-Beek, M., Jeffries-Fox, S., & Signorielli, N. (1977). TV violence profile #8. *Journal of Communication, 27*(11), 171-180.

Gerbner, G., Gross, L., Morgan, M., & Signorielli, N. (1986). Living with television: The dynamics of the cultivation process. In J. Bryant & D. Zillman (Eds.), *Perspectives on media effects* (pp. 17-40). Hillsdale, NJ: Lawrence Erlbaum.

Gerbner, G., Gross, L., Signorielli, N., & Morgan, M. (1980). Aging with television: Images on television drama and conceptions of social reality. *Journal of Communication, 11,* 141-148.

Gerbner, G., & Gross, M. (1976). Living with television: The violence profile. *Journal of Communication, 26*(2), 172-199.

Gerth, H. H., & Mills, C. W. (Eds.). (1946). *From Max Weber: Essays in sociology.* New York: Oxford University Press.

Gever, M., Parmar, P., & Greyson, J. (Eds.). (1993). *Queer looks: Perspectives on lesbian and gay film and video.* New York: Routledge.

Giddens, A. (1984). *The constitution of society: Outline of the theory of structuration.* Berkeley: University of California Press.

Giles, H. (1978). Linguistic differentiation in ethnic groups. In H. Tajfel (Ed.), *Differentiation between social groups: Studies in the social psychology of intergroup relations* (pp. 361-393). London: Academic Press.

Giles, J. (1994, June 6). The myth of Generation X: Seven great lies about twentysomethings. *Newsweek,* pp. 63-72.

Giles, H., Bourhis, R., & Taylor, P. (1977). Toward a theory of language in ethnic group relations. In H. Giles (Ed.), *Language, ethnicity, and intergroup relations* (pp. 307-348). London: Academic Press.

Giles, H., & Coupland, N. (1991). *Language: Contexts and consequences.* Pacific Grove, CA: Brooks/Cole.

Giles, H., Coupland, N., & Coupland, J. (1991). Accommodation theory: Communication, contexts, and consequences. In H. Giles, N. Coupland, & J. Coupland (Eds.), *Contexts of accommodation: Developments in applied sociolinguistics* (pp. 1-68). Cambridge, UK: Cambridge University Press.

Giles, H., Coupland, N., Henwood, K., Harriman, J., & Coupland, J. (1990). The social meaning of RP: An intergenerational perspective. In S. Ramsaran (Ed.), *Studies in the pronunciation of English: A commemorative volume in honor of A. C. Gimson* (pp. 191-210). London: Routledge.

Giles, H., Coupland, N., & Wiemann, J. M. (1992). "Talk is cheap" but "My word is my bond": Beliefs about talk. In K. Bolton & H. Kwok (Eds.), *Sociolinguistics today: International perspectives* (pp. 218-243). London: Routledge.

Giles, H., & Evans, A. (1986). The power approach to intergroup hostility. *Journal of Conflict Resolution, 30,* 469-485.

Giles, H., Fox, S., & Smith, E. (1993). Patronizing the elderly: intergenerational evaluations. *Research on Language and Social Interaction, 26,* 129-149.

Giles, H., & Franklyn-Stokes, A. (1989). Communicator characteristics. In M. K. Asante & W. B. Gudykunst (Eds.), *Handbook of international and intercultural communication* (pp. 117-144). Newbury Park, CA: Sage.

Giles, H., & Harwood, J. (1997). Managing intergroup communication: Lifespan issues and consequences. In S. Eliasson & E. H. Jahr (Eds.), *Studies for Einar Haugen* (pp. 105-130). Berlin: Mouton de Gruyter.

Giles, H., Henwood, K., Coupland, N., Harriman, J., & Coupland, J. (1992). Language attitudes and cognitive mediation. *Human Communication Research, 18,* 500-527.

Giles, H., & Johnson, P. (1987). Ethnolinguistic identity theory: A social psychological approach to language maintenance. *International Journal of Social Language, 68,* 69-99.

Giles, H., Mulac, A., Bradac, J. J., & Johnson, P. (1987). Speech accommodation: The first decade and beyond. In M. McLaughlin (Ed.), *Communication yearbook 10* (pp. 13-48). Newbury Park, CA: Sage.

Giles, H., & Powesland, P. F. (1975). *Speech style and social evaluation.* London: Academic Press.

Giles, H., & Williams, A. (1994). Patronizing the young: Forms and evaluations. *International Journal of Aging and Human Development, 39,* 33-53.

Gilligan, C. (1982). *In a different voice: Psychological theory and women's development.* Cambridge, MA: Harvard University Press.

Gilman, S. (1990). "I'm down on whores": Race and gender in Victorian London. In D. T. Goldberg (Ed.), *Anatomy of racism* (pp. 146-170). Minneapolis: University of Minnesota Press.

Gioia, D. A., & Pitre, E. (1990). Multiparadigm perspectives on theory building. *Academy of Management Review, 15,* 584-602.

Gioseffi, D. (Comp.). (1993). *On prejudice: A global perspective.* New York: Anchor Books.

Glass, B. (1986). Geneticists embattled: Their stand against rampant eugenics and racism in America during the 1920s and 1930s. *Proceedings of the American Philosophical Society, 130,* 130-154.

Gleick, J. (1987). *Chaos: Making a new science.* New York: Penguin Books.

Glendenning, F. (1995). Education for older adults: Lifelong learning, empowerment, and social change. In N. F. Nussbaum & J. Coupland (Eds.), *Handbook of communication and aging research* (pp. 467-490). Mahwah, NJ: Lawrence Erlbaum.

Glück, R. (1982). *Elements of a coffee service.* San Francisco: Four Seasons Foundation.

Glück, R. (1985). *Jack the modernist.* New York: Gay Presses of New York.

Goffman, E. (1963). *Stigma: Notes on the management of spoiled identity.* Englewood Cliffs, NJ: Prentice Hall.

Gold, D. P., Arbuckle, T. Y., & Andres, D. (1994). Verbosity in older adults. In M. L. Hummert, J. M. Wiemann, & J. F. Nussbaum (Eds.), *Interpersonal communication and aging* (pp. 107-129). Thousand Oaks, CA: Sage.

Goldberg, D. T. (1990). Racism and rationality: The need for a new critique. *Philosophy of the Social Sciences, 20,* 317-350.

Goldberg, D. T. (1993). *Racist culture: Philosophy and the politics of meaning.* Oxford, UK: Blackwell.

Goldberg, D. T. (1997). The power of tolerance. In T. Kushner & S. Jones (Eds.), *On tolerance.* London: Brill.

Golden, J. L., Berquist, G. F., & Coleman, W. E. (1989). *The rhetoric of Western thought* (4th ed.). Dubuque, IA: Kendall/Hunt.

González, A. (1990). Mexican otherness in the rhetorical analysis of Mexican Americans. *Southern Communication Journal, 55,* 276-291.

González, A., Houston, M., & Chen, V. (1994). *Our voices: Essays in culture, ethnicity, and communication.* Los Angeles: Roxbury.

González, L. (1985). The unified Black movement: A new stage in Black political mobilization. In P.- M. Fontaine (Ed.), *Race, class and power in Brazil* (pp. 59-66). Los Angeles: University of California, Center for Afro-American Studies.

Gordon, M. M. (1978). *Human nature, class, and ethnicity.* New York: Oxford University Press.

Gould, S. J. (1981). *The mismeasure of man.* New York: Norton.

Gowen, S. G. (1991). Beliefs about literacy: Measuring women into silence—Hearing women into speech. *Discourse and Society, 2,* 439-450.

Gramsci, A. (1983). *The modern prince and other writings* (L. Marks, Trans.). New York: International Publishers. (Originally published in 1957)

Gray, H. (1995). *Watching race: Television and the struggle for "Blackness."* Minneapolis: University of Minnesota Press.

Greenberg, B. S. (1983). *Mexican Americans and the mass media.* Norwood, NJ: Ablex.

Greenberg, S. B. (1980). *Race and state in capitalist development.* New Haven, CT: Yale University Press.

Greene, M., Adelman, R., Charon, R., & Friedmann, E. (1989). Concordance between physicians and their older and younger patients in the primary care medical encounter. *The Gerontologist, 29,* 808-813.

Greene, M. G., Adelman, R., Charon, R., & Hoffman, S. (1986). Agism in the medical encounter: An exploratory study of the doctor-elderly patient relationship. *Language and Communication, 6,* 113-124.

Greenhaus, J. H., Parasuraman, S., & Wormley, W. M. (1990). Effects of race on organizational experiences, job performance evaluations, and career outcomes. *Academy of Management Journal, 33,* 64-86.

Greenlee, S. (1990). *The spook who sat by the door.* Detroit, MI: Wayne State University Press.

Greer, G. (1991). *The change: Women, aging and the menopause.* London: Hamish Hamilton.

Griesemer, H. A. (1980). *Racial harmony, leadership, and unit effectiveness in combat units: An exploratory assessment of causal relationships* (Research Note 84-71). Monterey, CA: U.S. Army Research Institute for the Behavioral and Social Sciences.

Gudykunst, W. B. (1986). The influence of culture variability on perceptions of communication behavior associated with relationship terms. *Human Communication Research, 13,* 147-166.

Gudykunst, W. B. (1994). *Bridging differences: Effective intergroup communication* (2nd ed.). Thousand Oaks, CA: Sage.

Gudykunst, W. B. (1995). Anxiety/uncertainty management (AUM) theory: Current status. In R. L. Wiseman (Ed.), *Intercultural communication theories* (pp. 8-58). Thousand Oaks, CA: Sage.

Gudykunst, W., & Hammer, M. (1983). Basic training design: Approaches to intercultural training. In D. Landis & R. Brislin (Eds.), *Handbook of intercultural training,* Vol. 1: *Issues in theory and design* (pp. 118-154). New York: Pergamon.

Gudykunst, W. B., & Kim, Y. Y. (1984). *Communicating with strangers: An approach to intercultural communication.* New York: Random House.

Gudykunst, W. B., & Kim, Y. Y. (1992). *Communicating with strangers: An approach to intercultural communication* (2nd ed.). New York: McGraw-Hill.

Gudykunst, W. B., & Nishida, T. (1989). Theoretical perspectives for studying intercultural communication. In M. K. Asante & W. B. Gudykunst (Eds.), *Handbook of international and intercultural communication* (pp. 17-46). Newbury Park, CA: Sage.

Gudykunst, W. B., & Ting-Toomey, S., with Chua, E. (1988). *Culture and interpersonal communication.* Newbury Park, CA: Sage.

Haberfeld, Y. (1992). Employment discrimination: An organizational model. *Academy of Management Journal, 35,* 161-181.

Haberly, D. T. (1983). *Three sad races: Racial identity and national consciousness in Brazilian literature.* Cambridge, UK: Cambridge University Press.

Hadley, T. (1977). Tillman Hadley. In B. H. Johnson (Ed.), *Stories of traditional Navajo life and culture* (pp. 285-298). Tsaile, AZ: Navajo Community College.

Hallinan, M. T., & William, R. A. (1989). Interracial friendship choices in secondary schools. *American Sociological Review, 54,* 67-78.

Hall, E.T. (1966). *The hidden dimension.* New York: Doubleday.

Hall, S. (1981a). Notes on deconstructing the popular. In R. Samuel (Ed.), *People's history and socialist theory* (pp. 227-240). London: Routledge.

Hall, S. (1981b). The whites of their eyes: Racist ideologies and the media. In G. Bridges & R. Brunt (Eds.), *Silver linings: Some strategies for the eighties* (pp. 28-52). London: Lawrence & Wishart.

Hall, S. (1985). Signification, representation, ideology: Althusser and the post-structuralist debates. *Critical Studies in Mass Communication, 2,* 91-114.

Hall, S. (1986). Gramsci's relevance for the study of race and ethnicity. *Journal of Communication Inquiry, 10*(2), 5-27.

Hall, S. (1992). Cultural studies and its theoretical legacies. In L. Grossberg, C. Nelson, & P. Treichler (Eds.), *Cultural studies* (pp. 277-294). New York: Routledge.

Hallinan, M. T., & Williams, R. A. (1989). Interracial friendship choices in secondary schools. *American Sociological Review, 54,* 67-78.

Hamilton, D. (1994, May 10). Gay men become No. 1 hate-crime targets. *Los Angeles Times,* p. B1.

Hammer, M. R., & Martin, J. N. (1992). The effects of cross-cultural training on American managers in a Japanese-American joint venture. *Journal of Applied Communication Research, 20,* 162-183.

Hammersley, M. (1992). *What's wrong with ethnography?* London: Routledge.

Hammonds, E. (1992). Race, sex, AIDS: The construction of "other." In M. L. Anderson & P. H. Collins (Eds.), *Race, class, and gender: An anthology* (pp. 329-340). Belmont, CA: Wadsworth.

Hanke, R. (1990). Hegemonic masculinity in *Thirtysomething. Critical Studies in Mass Communication, 7,* 231-248.

Hanson, J., & Fox, W. (1995, January). Communicating across cultures. *Training and Development,* pp. 56-58.

Haraway, D. J. (1981). In the beginning was the word: The genesis of biological theory. *Signs: Journal of Women in Culture and Society, 6,* 469-481.

Harris, P. R., & Moran, R. T. (1987). *Managing cultural differences: High-performance strategies for today's global managers.* Houston, TX: Gulf.

Hartup, W. W. (1983). Peer relations. In E. M. Heatherington (Ed.), *Handbook of child psychology* (4th ed., pp. 103-196). New York: John Wiley.

Harvey, D. (1990). *The condition of postmodernity: An enquiry into the origins of cultural change.* Cambridge, MA: Blackwell.

Harwood, J., & Giles, H. (1992). "Don't make me laugh": Age representations in a humorous context. *Discourse & Society, 3,* 403-436.

Harwood, J., & Giles, H. (1996). Reactions to older people being patronized: The role of response strategies and attributed thoughts. *Journal of Language and Social Psychology, 15,* 395-421.

Harwood, J., Giles, H., Ota, H., Pierson, H. D., Gallois, C., Ng, S. H., Lim, T. S., & Somera, L. (1997). Trait ratings of three age groups around the Pacific Rim. *Journal of Cross-Cultural Gerontology, 11,* 307-317.

Harwood, J., Giles, H., & Ryan, E. B. (1995). Aging, communication, and intergroup theory: Social identity and intergenerational communication. In J. Nussbaum & J. Coupland (Eds.), *Handbook of communication and aging research* (pp. 133-159). Mahwah, NJ: Lawrence Erlbaum.

Harwood, J., Giles, H., Ryan, E. B., Fox, S., & Williams, A. (1993). Patronizing young and elderly adults: Response strategies in a community setting. *Journal of Applied Communication Research, 21,* 211-226.

Harwood, J., & Williams, A. (in press). Expectations for communication with positive and negative subtypes of older adults. *International Journal of Aging and Human Development.*

Hasenbalg, C. A. (1982). O negro na publicidade [Blacks in advertisements]. In L. González & C. Hasenbalg (Eds.), *Lugar do negro* [The place of Blacks] (pp. 103-114). Rio de Janeiro: Marco Zero Limitada.

Hate groups increasing, study finds: New organizations are more militant. (1992, February 19). *Tribune Newspapers,* pp. A4, B4.

Hecht, M. L. (1978). Toward a conceptualization of interpersonal communication satisfaction. *Quarterly Journal of Speech, 64,* 47-62.

Hecht, M. L. (1984). Satisfying communication and relationship labels: Intimacy and length of relationship as perceptual frames of naturalistic conversations. *Western Journal of Speech Communication, 48,* 201-216.

Hecht, M. L. (1993). 2002: A research odyssey—Toward the development of a communication theory of identity. *Communication Monographs, 60,* 76-82.

Hecht, M. L., Collier, M. J., & Ribeau, S. A. (1993). *African American communication: Ethnic identity and cultural interpretation.* Newbury Park, CA: Sage.

Hecht, M. L., Larkey, L. K., & Johnson, J. N. (1992). African American and European American perceptions of problematic issues in interethnic communication effectiveness. *Human Communication Research, 19,* 209-236.

Hecht, M. L., Ribeau, S., & Alberts, J. K. (1989). An Afro-American perspective on interethnic communication. *Communication Monographs, 56,* 385-410.

Hecht, M. L., Ribeau, S., & Sedano, M. V. (1990). A Mexican American perspective on interethnic communication. *International Journal of Intercultural Relations, 14,* 31-55.

Heeter, C., Greenberg, B. S., & Mendelson, B. E. (1983). Cross media coverage of local Hispanic American news. *Journal of Broadcasting, 27,* 395-402.

Hemphill, E. (1990, December 26). In living color: Toms, coons, mammies, faggots and bucks. *Outweek, 78,* 32-40.

Hendrix, K. G. (1995, November). *Student perceptions of the influence of race on professor credibility.* Paper presented at the annual meeting of the Speech Communication Association, San Antonio, TX.

Henley, N. M., & Kramarae, C. (1991). Gender, power, and miscommunication. In N. Coupland, H. Giles, & J. M. Wiemann (Eds.), *"Miscommunication" and problematic talk* (pp. 18-43). Newbury Park, CA: Sage.

Henley, N. M., & Pincus, F. (1978). Interrelationship of sexist, racist, and anti-homosexual attitudes. *Psychological Reports, 42,* 83-90.

Henwood, K., Giles, H., Coupland, J., & Coupland, N. (1993). Stereotyping and affect in discourse: Interpreting the meaning of elderly, painful self-disclosure. In D. M. Mackie & D. L. Hamilton (Eds.), *Affect, cognition, and stereotyping: Interactive processes in group perception* (pp. 269-296). San Diego: Academic Press.

Hepburn, C., & Locksley, A. (1983). Subjective awareness of stereotyping: Do we know when our judgments are prejudiced? *Social Psychology Quarterly, 46,* 311-318.

Herbison, C., & Schultz, J. (producers), with DePaepe, T. (director). (1990). *Quiet passages: The Japanese-American warbride experience* [video]. (Available from National Asian American Telecommunications Association, 346 Ninth Street, Second Floor, San Francisco, CA 94103)

Herman, E. S. (1996, April). Low intensity class war. *Z Magazine,* pp. 9-12.

Hernton, C. C. (1988). *Sex and racism in America.* New York: Anchor Books. (Originally published in 1965)

Herodotus. (1987). *The history of Herodotus* (D. Greene, Trans.). Chicago: University of Chicago Press.

Herrnstein, R. J., & Murray, C. (1994). *The bell curve: Intelligence and class structure in American life.* New York: Free Press.

Herrod, C. (1993, May 6). Gay America definitely doesn't look like straight America. *Arizona Republic,* p. A18.

He's not in Kansas anymore. (1995, August 24-September 6). *Echo Magazine,* pp. 52-53.

Hewes, D. E., & Planalp, S. (1987). The individual's place in communication science. In C. R. Berger & S. H. Chaffee (Eds.), *Handbook of communication science* (pp. 146-183). Newbury Park, CA: Sage.

Hewstone, M. (1989). Changing stereotypes with disconfirming information. In D. Bar-Tal, C. F. Graumann, A. W. Kruglanski, & W. Stroebe (Eds.), *Stereotyping and prejudice: Changing conceptions* (pp. 47-72). New York: Springer-Verlag.

Hewstone, M., & Brown, R. (Eds.). (1986a). *Contact and conflict in intergroup encounters.* Oxford, UK: Blackwell.

Hewstone, M., & Brown, R. J. (1986b). Contact is not enough: An intergroup perspective on the "contact hypothesis." In M. Hewstone & R. J. Brown (Eds.), *Contact and conflict in intergroup encounters* (pp. 1-44). Oxford, UK: Basil Blackwell.

Hoffman, L. R., & Maier, N. R. F. (1961). Quality and acceptance of problem solutions by members of homogeneous and heterogeneous work groups. *Journal of Abnormal and Social Psychology, 62,* 401-407.

Hollien, H. (1987). "Old voices": What do we really know about them? *Journal of Voice, 1,* 2-17.

Holte, J. C. (1984). Unmelting images: Film, television, and ethnic stereotyping. *Multi-ethnic Languages of the United States, 11*(3), 101-108.

hooks, b. (1955). *Killing rage.* New York: Henry Holt.

hooks, b. (1981). *Ain't I a woman: Black women and feminism.* Boston: South End.

hooks, b. (1984). *Feminist theory: From margin to center.* Boston: South End.

hooks, b. (1990). *Yearning: Race, gender and cultural politics.* Boston: South End.

hooks, b. (1992). *Black looks: Race and representation.* Boston: South End.

hooks, b. (1996). *Killing rage: Ending racism.* New York: Henry Holt.

Houston, M., & Kramarae, C. (1991). Speaking from silence: methods of silencing and resistance. *Discourse and Society, 2,* 387-399.

Houston, V. H. (1988). *Tea.* New York: Theatre Communications Group.

Howard, G. S. (1991). Culture tales: A narrative approach to thinking, cross-cultural psychology, and psychotherapy. *American Psychologist, 46,* 187-197.

Howe, N., & Strauss, W. (1993). *13th generation: Abort, retry, ignore, fail?* New York: Vintage Books.

Hughes, M. (1980). The fruits of cultivation analysis: A reexamination of some effects of television watching. *Public Opinion Quarterly, 44,* 287-301.

Hummert, M. L. (1990). Multiple stereotypes of the elderly and young adults: A comparison of structure and evaluations. *Psychology and Aging, 5,* 182-193.

Hummert, M. L. (1994). Stereotypes of the elderly and patronizing speech. In M. L. Hummert, J. M. Wiemann, & J. F. Nussbaum (Eds.), *Interpersonal communication in older adulthood* (pp. 162-184). Thousand Oaks, CA: Sage.

Hummert, M. L., Garstka, T. A., & Shaner, J. L. (1995). Beliefs about language performance: Adults' perceptions about self and elderly targets. *Journal of Language and Social Psychology, 14,* 235-259.

Hummert, M. L., Garstka, T. A., Shaner, J. L., & Strahm, S. (1994). Stereotypes of the elderly held by young, middle-aged, and elderly adults. *Journals of Gerontology: Series B, Psychological Sciences, 49,* 240-249.

Hummert, M. L., Shaner, J. L., Henry, C., & Garstka T. A. (1995). *Patronizing speech to the elderly: Relationship to subject age and stereotypes.* Unpublished manuscript, University of Kansas.

Hummert, M. L., Wiemann, J. M., & Nussbaum, J. F. (Eds.). (1994). *Interpersonal communication in older adulthood.* Thousand Oaks, CA: Sage.

Humphrey, R., & Schuman, H. (1984). The portrayal of Blacks in magazine advertisements: 1950-1982. *Public Opinion Quarterly, 48,* 551-563.

Huston, T. L., & Ashmore, R. D. (1986). Women and men in personal relationships. In R. D. Ashmore & F. K. Del Boca (Eds.), *The social psychology of female-male relations: A critical analysis of central concepts* (pp. 167-210). Orlando, FL: Academic Press.

Hwang, J. (producer/director). (1982). *Afterbirth* [film]. (Available from National Asian American Telecommunications Association, 346 Ninth Street, Second Floor, San Francisco, CA 94103)

Ickes, W. (1993). Traditional gender roles: Do they make, and then break, our relationships? *Journal of Social Issues, 49,* 71-85.

Infante, D. A., & Rancer, A. S. (1996). Argumentativeness and verbal aggressiveness: A review of recent theory and research. In B. R. Burleson (Ed.), *Communication yearbook 19* (pp. 319-353). Thousand Oaks, CA: Sage.

Ingrassia, M. (1995, April 24). The body of the beholder. *Newsweek,* pp. 26-33.

Institutional bias. (1994, October 18). *The Advocate,* p. 15.

Itzin, C. (1986). Ageism awareness training: A model for group work. In C. Phillipson, M. Bernard, & P. Strang (Eds.), *Dependency and interdependency in old age: Theoretical perspectives and policy alternatives* (pp. 114-126). London: Croom Helm.

Jackman, M. R., & Crane, M. (1986). "Some of my best friends are Black . . . ": Interracial friendships and Whites' racial attitudes. *Public Opinion Quarterly, 50,* 459-486.

Jackman, M. R., & Jackman, R. W. (1983). *Class awareness in the United States.* Berkeley: University of California Press.

James, K., Lovato, C., & Cropanzano, R. (1994). Correlational and known-group comparison validation of a workplace prejudice/discrimination inventory. *Journal of Applied Social Psychology, 24,* 1573-1592.

James, S. M., & Busia, A. P. (Eds.). (1993). *Theorizing Black feminisms: The visionary pragmatism of Black women.* London: Routledge.

Jameson, F. (1984). Postmodernism or the cultural logic of late capitalism. *New Left Review, 146,* 55-93.

JanMohamed, A. R. (1986). The economy of Manichean allegory: The function of racial difference in colonialist literature. In H. L. Gates, Jr. (Ed.), *"Race," writing, and difference* (pp. 78-106). Chicago: University of Chicago Press.

Jansson, B. S. (1997). *The reluctant welfare state* (3rd ed.). Pacific Grove, CA: Brooks/Cole.

Japp, P. M. (1991). Gender and work in the 1980s: Television's working women as displaced persons. *Women's Studies in Communication, 14,* 49-74.

Johnson, D. W., Johnson, R. T., Tiffany, M., & Zaidman, B. (1984). Cross-ethnic relationships: The impact of intergroup cooperation and intergroup competition. *Journal of Educational Research, 78,* 75-79.

Johnson, E. (1984). Credibility of Black and White newscasters to a Black audience. *Journal of Broadcasting, 28,* 365-368.

Johnson, G. D., & Hendrix, L. (1985). A cross-cultural test of Collins' theory of sexual stratification. In B. C. Miller & D. H. Olson (Eds.), *Family studies review yearbook* (3rd ed., pp. 532-542). Beverly Hills, CA: Sage.

Johnson, K. A. (1991). Objective news and other myths: The poisoning of young Black minds. *Journal of Negro Education, 60,* 328-341.

Johnson, M. M. (1993). Functionalism and feminism: Is estrangement necessary? In P. England (Ed.), *Theory on gender/Femimism on theory* (pp. 115-130). New York: Aldine de Gruyter.

Johnson, R. (1992). Diversity training: Integral steps for bridging race, language, gender gaps. *Training, 29,* 801-804.

Johnston, D. (1995, June 8). Wave of bashings in Midtown. *Southern Voice,* p. 14.

Johnston, W. B., & Packer, A. H. (1987). *Workforce 2000: Work and workers for the 21st century.* Indianapolis, IN: Hudson Institute.

Jones, R. (1983). Increasing sensitivity to Black clients. *Social Casework, 64,* 419-425.

Jordan, P. (1995, September/October). Freeze-frame. *American Fitness,* pp. 40-41, 70.

Jung, P. B., & Smith, R. F. (1993). *Heterosexism: An ethical challenge.* Albany: State University of New York Press.

Jussim, L., Coleman, L. M., & Lerch, L. (1987). The nature of stereotypes: A comparison and integration of three theories. *Journal of Personality and Social Psychology, 52,* 536-546.

Kahn, A. (1984). The power war: Male response to power loss under equality. *Psychology of Women Quarterly, 8,* 234-247.

Kalish, R. (1979). The new ageism and the failure models: A polemic. *The Gerontologist, 19,* 398-402.

Kanter, R. M. (1977). *Men and women of the corporation.* New York: Basic Books.

Katz, I., & Proshansky, H. M. (1987). Rethinking affirmative action. *Journal of Social Issues, 43,* 99-104.

Katz, I., Wackenhut, J., & Glass, D. C. (1986). An ambivalence-amplification theory of behavior toward the stigmatized. In S. Worchel & W. G. Austin (Eds.), *Psychology of intergroup relations* (pp. 103-117). Chicago: Nelson-Hall.

Katz, J. (1995). *The invention of heterosexuality.* New York: Dutton.

Katz, J. H. (1977). The effects of a systematic training program on the attitudes and behaviors of White people. *International Journal of Intercultural Relations, 1,* 77-89.

Kauffman, N. (1987). Motivating the older worker. *SAM Advanced Management Journal, 52,* 43-48.

Kavanagh, K. H., & Kennedy, P. H. (1992). *Promoting cultural diversity: Strategies for health care professionals.* Newbury Park, CA: Sage.

Kelley, H. H. (1986). Personal relationships: Their nature and significance. In R. Gilmour & S. Duck (Eds.), *The emerging field of personal relationships* (pp. 3- 19). Hillsdale, NJ: Lawrence Erlbaum.

Kelley, H. H., Berscheid, E., Christensen, A., Harvey, J. H., Huston, T. L., Levinger, G., McClintock, E., Peplau, L. A., & Peterson, D. R. (1983). *Close relationships.* New York: Freeman.

Kellner, D. (1989). *Critical theory, Marxism and modernity.* Baltimore, MD: Johns Hopkins University Press.

Kellner, D. (1995). *Media culture: Cultural studies, identity, and politics between the modern and the postmodern.* New York: Routledge.

Kemper, S. (1994). "Elderspeak": Speech accommodation to older adults. *Aging and Cognition, 1,* 17-38.

Kemper, S., Kynette, D., & Norman, S. (1992). Age differences in spoken language. In R. West & J. Sinnot (Eds.), *Everyday memory and aging* (pp. 138-154). New York: Springer-Verlag.

Kenny, D. A. (1988a). What makes a relationship special? In T. Draper (Ed.), *Family variables: Conceptualization, measurement, and use* (pp. 161-178). Newbury Park, CA: Sage.

Kenny, D. A. (1988b). Interpersonal perception: A social relations analysis. *Journal of Social and Personal Relationships, 5,* 247-261.

Kenworthy, T., & Edsall, T. B. (1991, June 4). Whites see jobs on line in debate; some Chicagoans fear reverse discrimination. *The Washington Post,* p. A1.

Kerckhoff, A. C., & Davis, K. E. (1962). Value consensus and need complementarity in mate selection. *American Sociological Review, 27,* 295-303.

Kessler, S. J., & McKenna, W. (1978). *Gender: An ethnomethodological approach.* New York: John Wiley.

Kim, Y. Y. (1984). Searching for creative integration. In W. B. Gudykunst & Y. Y. Kim (Eds.), *Methods for intercultural communication research* (pp. 13-30). Beverly Hills, CA: Sage.

Kimmel, M. S., & Messner, M. A. (Eds.). (1995). *Men's lives* (3rd ed.). Boston: Allyn & Bacon.

King, M. C. (1992). Occupational segregation by race and sex, 1940-88. *Monthly Labor Review, 115,* 30-36.

Kirk, M., & Madsen, H. (1989). *After the ball: How America will conquer its hatred and fear of homosexuals in the '90s.* New York: Doubleday.

Kirkpatrick, P. (1994). Triple jeopardy: Disability, race and poverty in America. *Poverty & Race, 3*(3), 1-3.

Klein, V. (1984). The historical background. In J. Freeman (Ed.), *Women: A feminist perspective* (3rd ed., pp. 519-532). Palo Alto, CA: Mayfield.

Kluegel, J. R. (1985). If there isn't a problem, you don't need a solution: The bases of affirmative action attitudes. *American Behavioral Scientist, 28,* 761-784.

Kluegel, J. R., & Smith, E. R. (1983). Affirmative action attitudes: Effects of self-interest, racial affect, and stratification beliefs on Whites' views. *Social Forces, 61,* 797-824.

Knapp, M. L., Ellis, D. G., & Williams, B. A. (1980). Perceptions of communication behavior associated with relationship terms. *Communication Monographs, 47,* 262-278.

Knowles, C. (1996). Racism, biography, and psychiatry. In V. Amit-Talai & C. Knowles (Eds.), *Re-situating identities: The politics of race, ethnicity, and culture* (pp. 47-67). Toronto: Broadview.

Knowles, C., & Mercer, S. (1992). Feminism and anti-racism: An exploration of the political possibilities. In J. Donald & A. Rattansi (Eds.), *"Race," culture and difference* (pp. 104-125). London: Sage.

Kochman, T. (1981). *Black and White styles in conflict.* Chicago: University of Chicago Press.

Kramarae, C. (1992). Harassment and everyday life. In L. F. Rakow (Ed.), *Women making meaning* (pp. 100-120). New York: Routledge.

Kristeva, J. (1990). "Ours to Jew or die": Celine and the categories of anti-Semitism. In D. T. Goldberg (Ed.), *Anatomy of racism* (pp. 171-182). Minneapolis: University of Minnesota Press.

Kristeva, J. (1991). *Strangers to ourselves* (L. Poudier, Trans.). New York: Columbia University Press.

Krupansky, Judge. (1995, July/August). Clips. *Out,* p. 20.

Kuhn, T. S. (1970). *The structure of scientific revolutions* (2nd ed.). Chicago: University of Chicago Press.

Kunen, J. S. (1996, April 29). Back to segregation. *Time,* pp. 39-45.

Lacan, J. (1977). *Écrits: A selection* (A. Sheridan, Trans.). New York: Norton.

Ladd, E. C. (1993). The twentysomethings: "Generation myths" revisited. *The Public Perspective, 5,* 14-18.

Lalonde, R. N., & Cameron, J. E. (1994). Behavioral responses to discrimination: A focus on action. In M. P. Zanna & J. M. Olson (Eds.), *Ontario Symposium on Personality and Social Psychology,* Vol. 7: *The psychology of prejudice* (pp. 257-268). Hillsdale, NJ: Lawrence Erlbaum.

Lampe, P. E. (1982). Interethnic dating: Reasons for and against. *International Journal of Intercultural Relations, 6,* 115-126.

Lancely, A. (1985). Use of controlling language in the rehabilitation of the elderly. *Journal of Advanced Nursing, 36,* 12-29.

Landis, D., Brislin, R., Swanner, G. M., Tseng, O. C. S., & Thomas, J. A. (1985). Some effects of acculturative training: A field evaluation. *International Journal of Group Tensions, 15,* 68-91.

Landis, D., Day, H. R., McGrew, P. L., Thomas, J. A., & Miller, A. B. (1976). Can a Black "culture assimilator" increase racial understanding? *Journal of Social Sciences, 32,* 169-183.

Langston, D. (1992). Tired of playing monopoly? In M. L. Anderson & P. H. Collins (Eds.), *Race, class, and gender: An anthology* (pp. 110-120). Belmont, CA: Wadsworth.

Larkey, L. K., Hecht, M. L., & Martin, J. N. (1993). What's in a name: African American ethnic identity terms and self-determination. *Journal of Language and Social Psychology, 12,* 302-317.

Lash, S. (1990). *Sociology of postmodernism.* New York: Routledge.

Lauderback, L. (1970). *Fat power: Whatever you weigh is right.* New York: Hawthorne.

Lea, M., & Spears, R. (1995). Love at first byte? Building personal relationships over computer networks. In J. T. Wood & S. Duck (Eds.), *Under-studied relationships: Off the beaten track* (pp. 197-233). Thousand Oaks, CA: Sage.

Leo, J. (1994, April 18). De-escalating the gender war. *U.S. News and World Report,* p. 24.

Leong, R. (Ed.). (1991). *Moving the image: Independent Asian Pacific American media arts.* Los Angeles: UCLA Asian American Studies Center and Visual Communications, Southern California Asian American Studies Central.

Lerner, M., & West, C. (1995). *Jews and Blacks: Let the healing begin.* New York: Grossett/ Putnam.

Leslie, M. (1992). Representations of Blacks on prime time television in Brazil. *Howard Journal of Communications, 4,* 1-9.

Levin, J., & Levin, W. C. (1980). *Ageism: Prejudice and discrimination against the elderly.* Belmont, CA: Wadsworth.

Levine, R. M. (1984). Elite intervention in urban popular culture in modern Brazil. *Luso-Brazilian Review, 21*(2), 9-22.

Levinger, G., & Rands, M. (1985). Compatibility in marriage and other relationships. In W. Ickes (Ed.), *Compatible and incompatible relationships* (pp. 309-332). New York: Springer-Verlag.

Levinger, G., & Snoek, J. D. (1972). *Attraction in relationship: A new look at interpersonal attraction.* Morristown, NJ: General Learning Press.

Levinson, D. J. (1982a). The study of anti-Semitic ideology. In T. W. Adorno, E. Frenkel-Brunswick, D. J. Levinson, & R. N. Sanford (Eds.), *The authoritarian personality* (abridged ed., pp. 57-101). New York: Norton. (Originally published by Harper in 1950)

Levinson, D. J. (1982b). The study of ethnocentric ideology. In T. W. Adorno, E. Frenkel-Brunswick, D. J. Levinson, & R. N. Sanford (Eds.), *The authoritarian personality* (abridged ed., pp. 102-150). New York: Norton. (Originally published by Harper in 1950)

Lévi-Strauss, C. (1963). *Structural anthropology* (C. Jacobson & B. Grundfest Schoepf, Trans.). New York: Basic Books.

Lichter, R., Lichter, L. S., & Rothman, S. (1986). From Lucy to Lacey: TV's dream girls. *Public Opinion, 9,* 16-19.

Life, T. R., Jr. (producer/director). (1995). *Doubles: Japan and America's intercultural children* [video]. (Available from The Doubles Project, 957 Route 5, East Chatham, NY 12060)

Lin, S. C. (1996, March 12). Japanese students attacked at Idaho school. *Rafu Shimpo,* p. 1.

Lincoln, Y. S., & Guba, E. G. (1985). *Naturalistic inquiry.* Beverly Hills, CA: Sage.

Littlejohn, S. W. (1989). *Theories of human communication* (3rd ed.). Belmont, CA: Wadsworth.

Loden, M., & Rosener, J. B. (1991). *Workforce America! Managing employee diversity as a vital resource.* Burr Ridge, IL: Irwin.

Lott, B. (1995). Distance from women: Interpersonal sexist discrimination. In B. Lott & D. Maluso (Eds.), *The social psychology of interpersonal discrimination* (pp. 12-49). New York: Guilford.

Lott, B., & Maluso, D. (Eds.). (1995). Introduction: Framing the questions. In B. Lott & D. Maluso (Eds.), *The social psychology of interpersonal discrimination* (pp. 1-11). New York: Guilford.

Lowy, R. (1991). Yuppie racism: Race relations in the 1980s. *Journal of Black Studies, 21,* 445-464.

Macdonald, E. (1995, September). Our Schindler's list. *Out,* pp. 79-83, 122-123.

MacKay, D. G. (1983). Prescriptive grammar and the pronoun problem. In B. Thorne, C. Kramarae, & N. Henley (Eds.), *Language, gender and society* (pp. 38-53). Cambridge, MA: Newbury House.

MacKinnon, C. A. (1984). Not a moral issue. *Yale Law and Policy Review, 2,* 321-345.

MacKinnon, C. A. (1987). *Feminism unmodified: Discourses on life and law.* Cambridge, MA: Harvard University Press.

MacKinnon, C. A. (1989). Sexuality, pornography, and method: Pleasure under patriarchy. *Ethics, 99,* 314-346.

MacKinnon, C. A. (1993). Difference and dominance: On sex discrimination. In D. K. Weisberg (Ed.), *Feminist legal theory: Foundations* (pp. 276-287). Philadelphia: Temple University Press.

Macrae, C. N., Bodenhausen, G. V., & Milne, A. B. (1995). The dissection of selection in person perception: Inhibitory processes in social stereotyping. *Journal of Personality and Social Psychology, 69,* 397-407.

Macrae, C. N., Bodenhausen, G. V., Milne, A. B., & Jetten, J. (1994). Out of mind but back in sight: Stereotypes on the rebound. *Journal of Personality and Social Psychology, 67,* 808-817.

Macrae, C. N., Milne, A. B., & Bodenhausen, G. V. (1994). Stereotypes as energy-saving devices: A peek inside the cognitive toolbox. *Journal of Personality and Social Psychology, 66,* 37-47.

Maluso, D. (1995). Shaking hands with a clenched fist: Interpersonal racism. In B. Lott & D. Maluso (Eds.), *The social psychology of interpersonal discrimination* (pp. 50-79). New York: Guilford.

Marcuse, H. (1974). Marxism and feminism. *Women's Studies, 2,* 279-288.

Maretzki, T. W. (1977). Intercultural marriage: An introduction. In W. Tseng, J. F. McDermott, Jr., & T. W. Maretzki (Eds.), *Adjustment in intercultural marriage* (pp. 1-11). Honolulu: University of Hawaii Press.

Markoff, R. (1977). Intercultural marriage: Problem areas. In W. S. Tseng, J. F. McDermott, & T. W. Maretzki (Eds.), *Adjustment in intercultural marriage* (pp. 51-60). Honolulu: University of Hawaii Press.

Marks, L. U. (1994). A Deleuzian politics of hybrid cinema. *Screen, 35,* 244-264.

Marsiglia, F., & Zorita, P. (1996). Narratives as a means to support Latino/a students in higher education. *Reflections, 2*(1), 54-62.

Marston, P. J., & Hecht, M. L. (1994). Love ways: An elaboration and application to relationship maintenance. In D. J. Canary & L. Stafford (Eds.), *Communication and relational maintenance* (pp. 187-202). San Diego: Academic Press.

Martin, J., & Frost, P. (1996). The organizational culture war games: A struggle for intellectual dominance. In S. R. Clegg, C. Hardy, & W. R. Nord (Eds.), *Handbook of organization studies* (pp. 599-621). Thousand Oaks, CA: Sage.

Martin, J. M., Hecht, M. L., & Larkey, L. K. (1994). Communication improvement strategies for inter-ethnic communication: African American and Euro-American perspectives. *Communication Monographs, 61,* 236-255.

Martin, S. E. (1994). "Outsider within" the station house: The impact of race and gender on Black women police. *Social Problems, 41,* 383-400.

Martínez-Echazábel, L. (1988). Positivismo y racismo en el ensayo hispanoamericano [Positivism and racism in the Latin American essay]. *Cuadernos Americanos* (No. 9, Nueva epoca), 121-129.

Martyna, W. (1983). Beyond the he/man approach: The case for nonsexist language. In B. Thorne, C. Kramarae, & N. Henley (Eds.), *Language, gender and society* (pp. 25-37). Cambridge, MA: Newbury House.

Mason, D. (1986). Introduction: Controversies and continuities in race and ethnic relations theory. In J. Rex & D. Mason (Eds.), *Theories of race and ethnic relations* (pp. 1-19). Cambridge, UK: Cambridge University Press.

Matabane, P. W. (1988). Television and the Black audience: Cultivating moderate perspectives on racial integration. *Journal of Communication, 38*(4), 21-31.

Mathabane, M., & Page, C. (1991). Minorities' racist attitudes are a serious problem. In W. Dudley (Ed.), *Racism in America: Opposing viewpoints* (pp. 32-37). San Diego: Greenhaven.

McAdams, D. (1993). *Stories we live by: Personal myths and the making of the self.* New York: William Morrow.

McCall, N. (1994). *Makes me wanna holler: A young Black man in America.* New York: Random House.

McClain, L. (1983, July 24). How Chicago taught me to hate Whites. *The Washington Post.* (Reprinted in Page, 1986, pp. 30-38)

McConahay, J. B. (1986). Modern racism, ambivalence, and the modern racism scale. In J. S. Dovidio & S. L. Gaertner (Eds.), *Prejudice, discrimination and racism* (pp. 99-125). Orlando, FL: Academic Press.

McCraty, R., Atkinson, M., Tiller, W. A., Rein, G., & Watkins, A. D. (1995). The effects of emotions on short term power spectrum analysis of heart rate variability. *American Journal of Cardiology, 76,* 1089-1093.

McEnrue, M. (1993). Managing diversity: Los Angeles before and after the riots. *Organizational Dynamics, 21*(3), 18-29.

McGrath, J. E. (1984). *Groups: Interaction and performance.* Englewood Cliffs, NJ: Prentice Hall.

McIntosh, P. (1988). *White privilege and male privilege: A personal account of coming to see correspondence through work in women's studies* (Working Paper No. 189). Wellesley, MA: Center for Research on Women.

McKerrow, R. E. (1989). Critical rhetoric: Theory and praxis. *Communication Monographs, 56,* 91-111.

McLemee, S. (1994, November 16). Religion and the racist right. *The New York Times,* sec. 7, p. 30.

McLeod, J. M., & Blumler, J. G. (1987). The macrosocial level of communication science. In C. R. Berger & S. H. Chaffee (Eds.), *Handbook of communication science* (pp. 271-322). Newbury Park, CA: Sage.

McRobbie, A. (1992). Post-Marxism and cultural studies: A post-script. In L. Grossberg, C. Nelson, & P. Treichler (Eds.), *Cultural studies* (pp. 719-730). New York: Routledge.

Mead, G. H. (1934). *Mind, self, and society.* Chicago: University of Chicago Press.

Mead, M. (1935). *Sex and temperament in three primitive societies.* New York: William Morrow.

Means, M. (1994, June 19). Religious intolerance giving rise to "politics of hate." *Tribune Newspapers,* p. I4.

Meeks, T., & Courtaway, K. R. (1995, November). *Philadelphia: A fantasy theme analysis of polysemic meaning in a popular media depiction of gay culture.* Paper presented at the annual conference of the Speech Communication Association, San Antonio, TX.

Melnick, B. A. (1988). When love and tradition meet: Intermarriage between Jews and non-Jews in Orange County, California. *Masters Abstracts International, 27,* 61.

Mercer, K. (1994). *Welcome to the jungle: New positions in Black cultural studies.* New York: Routledge.

Merton, R. K. (1957). *Social theory and social structure.* New York: Free Press.

Merton, R. K. (1973). A theory of marital choice applied to interracial marriage. In I. R. Stuart & L. E. Abt (Eds.), *Interracial marriage: Expectations and realities* (pp. 17-35). New York: Grossman.

Merton, R. K. (1976). *Sociological ambivalence and other essays.* New York: Free Press.

Meyer, P. (1987). Ethnocentrism in human social behaviour: Some biosociological considerations. In V. Reynolds, V. Falger, & I. Vine (Eds.), *The sociobiology of ethnocentrism: Evolutionary dimensions of xenophobia, discrimination, racism and nationalism* (pp. 81-93). London: Croom Helm.

Middleton, D., & Edwards, D. (1990). *Collective remembering.* London: Sage.

Miles, R. (1989). *Racism.* London: Routledge.

Miller, A. A. (1983). An exploration of ethnicity in marriages between White Anglo Saxon Protestants and Jewish Americans. *Dissertation Abstracts International, 44*(05B), 1600.

Miller, G. R. (1983). On various ways of skinning symbolic cats: Recent research on persuasive message strategies. *Journal of Language and Social Psychology, 2,* 123-140.

Miller, G. R., & Steinberg, M. (1975). *Between people: A new analysis of interpersonal communication.* Chicago: Science Research Associates.

Millet, K. (1970). *Sexual politics.* Garden City, NY: Doubleday.

Milner, D. (1983). *Children and race.* Beverly Hills, CA: Sage.

Mills, J. (1993). *Womanwords: A dictionary of words about women.* New York: Henry Holt.

Minorities admit bias toward Anglos, each other. (1994, March 3). *Arizona Republic,* p. A14.

Mirandé, A. (1985). *The Chicano experience: An alternative perspective.* Notre Dame, IN: University of Notre Dame Press.

Mitchell, M. (1984). Race, legitimacy, and the state in Brazil. *Afrodiaspora, 4,* 109-124.

Mobley, M., & Payne, T. (1992, December). Backlash! The challenge to diversity training. *Training and Development,* pp. 45-52.

Monette, P. (1994). *Last watch of the night: Essays too personal and otherwise.* New York: Harcourt Brace.

Monge, P. (1996, November). *Communication theory for a globalizing world.* Paper presented at the annual meeting of the Speech Communication Association, San Diego.

Montgomery, B. M. (1986). A commentary on Indvik and Fitzpatrick's study of relationship defining communication. *Communication Quarterly, 34,* 14-18.

Montgomery, B. M. (1992). Communication as the interface between couples and culture. In S. A. Deetz (Ed.), *Communication yearbook 15* (pp. 475-507). Newbury Park, CA: Sage.

Moreira Bispo, D. (1986). O negro e a cultura [Blacks and culture]. In A. Ferreira dos Santos (Ed.), *Eu, negro: Discriminação racial no Brasil—Existe?* [I, Black: Racial discrimination in Brazil—Does it exist?] (pp. 46-51). São Paulo, Brazil: Edições Loyola.

Morgan, D. L. (1986). Personal relationships as an interface between social networks and social cognitions. *Journal of Social and Personal Relationships, 3,* 403-422.

Morin, S. F., & Garfinkle, E. M. (1981). Male homophobia. In J. Chesebro (Ed.), *Gayspeak: Lesbian and gay male communication* (pp. 117-129). New York: Pilgrim.

Morris, M. (1992). On the beach. In L. Grossberg, C. Nelson, & P. Treichler (Eds.), *Cultural studies* (pp. 450-478). New York: Routledge.

Morris, R. (1995, October 16-22). Across the racial divide: A new survey reveals the depths of our differences. *The Washington Post National Weekly Edition,* pp. 6-10.

Morsey, S. A. (1986). The bad, the ugly, the super-rich, and the exceptional moderate: U.S. popular images of the Arabs. *Journal of Popular Culture, 20,* 13-29.

Mueller, N. (1996, March). Workforce diversity: Wisconsin Power and Light's model diversity program. *Training and Development,* pp. 57-60.

Mulac, A., & Giles, H. (1996). "You're only as old as you sound": Chronological, contextual, psychological and perceptual parameters of elderly age attributions. *Health Communication, 8,* 199-216.

Murchison, W. (1992, January 18). Moral law: Owner's manual for the human body. *Arizona Republic,* p. A17.

Murray, C. (1984). *Losing ground: American social policy 1950-1980.* New York: Basic Books.

Murrell, A. J., Olson, J. E., & Hanson Frieze, I. (1995). Sexual harassment and gender discrimination: A longitudinal study of women managers. *Journal of Social Issues, 51,* 139-149.

Myrdal, G. (1944). *An American dilemma: The Negro problem and Negro democracy.* New York: Harper.

Nabakov, P. (Ed.). (1992). *Native American testimony: A chronicle of Indian-White relations from prophecy to the present, 1492-1992.* New York: Penguin Books.

Naficy, H. (1993). *The making of exile cultures: Iranian television in Los Angeles.* Minneapolis: University of Minnesota Press.

Nakagawa, M. (1993, March 19). Community leaders, police talk, hate crimes. *Asian Week,* p. 12.

Nakayama, T. K. (1994a). Dis/orienting identities. In A. González, M. Houston, & V. Chen (Eds.), *Our voices* (pp. 12-17). Los Angeles: Roxbury.

Nakayama, T. K. (1994b). Show/down time: "Race," gender, sexuality, and popular culture. *Critical Studies in Mass Communication, 11,* 162-179.

Nakayama, T. K., & Krizek, R. L. (1995). Whiteness: A strategic rhetoric. *Quarterly Journal of Speech, 81,* 291-309.

Nakayama, T. K., & Peñaloza, L. N. (1993). Madonna traces: Music videos through the prism of color. In C. Schwichtenberg (Ed.), *The Madonna connection: Representational politics, subculture identities, and cultural theory* (pp. 39-55). Boulder, CO: Westview.

Nascimento, A. D. (1978). *O genocídio do negro brasileiro: Processo de um racismo mascarado* [The genocide of the Black Brazilian: The process of a disguised racism]. Rio de Janeiro: Paz e Terra.

National Research Council. (1989). *A common destiny: Blacks and American society.* Washington, DC: National Academy of Sciences.

Nelson, R., & Cowan, J. (1994). *Revolution X: A survival guide for our generation.* New York: Penguin.

Neuberg, S. L. (1991). Expectancy-confirmation processes in stereotype-tinged social encounters: The moderating role of social goals. In M. Zanna & J. Olson (Eds.), *The psychology of prejudice* (pp. 103-130). Hillsdale, NJ: Lawrence Erlbaum.

Neuberg, S. L. (1994). Expectancy-confirmation processes in stereotype-tinged social encounters: The moderation of social goals. In M. P. Zanna & J. M. Olson (Eds.), *Ontario Symposium on Personality and Social Psychology,* Vol. 7: *The psychology of prejudice* (pp. 103-130). Hillsdale, NJ: Lawrence Erlbaum.

Neuberg, S. L., & Newson, J. T. (1993). Personal need for structure: Individual differences in the desire for simpler structure. *Journal of Personality and Social Psychology, 65,* 113-131.

Ng, S. H., & Bradac, J. J. (1993). *Power in language.* Newbury Park, CA: Sage.

Ng, S. H., Moody, J., & Giles, H. (1991). Information-seeking triggered by age. *International Journal of Aging and Human Development, 33,* 269-277.

Nicolini, P. (1987). Puerto Rican leaders' views of English-language media. *Journalism Quarterly, 64,* 597-601.

Noel, P. (1992, February 11). Are you a racist? To find out, take the new racism quotient test. *The Village Voice,* pp. 34-35.

Nogueira, O. (1985). *Tanto preto quanto branco: Estudos de relações raciais* [Both Black and White: Studies of racial relations]. São Paulo, Brazil: T. A. Quieroz.

Noriega, C. A. (Ed.). (1992). *Chicanos and film: Representation and resistance.* Minneapolis: University of Minnesota Press.

No room at the inn. (1994, May 31). *The Advocate,* p. 21.

Nuessel, F. (1982). The language of ageism. *The Gerontologist, 22,* 273-276.

Nuessel, F. (1993). *The semiotics of aging.* Louisville, KY: University of Louisville Press.

Nussbaum, J. F., & Coupland, J. (Eds.). (1995). *Handbook of communication and aging research.* Mahwah, NJ: Lawrence Erlbaum.

O'Keefe, B., & Delia, J. (1982). Impression formation and message production. In M. Roloff & C. R. Berger (Eds.), *Social cognition and communication* (pp. 121-146). Beverly Hills, CA: Sage.

Olson, J. E., & Frieze, I. H. (1987). Income determinants for women in business. In A. H. Stromberg, L. Larwood, & B. A. Gutek (Eds.), *Women and work* (pp. 173-206). Newbury Park, CA: Sage.

Olson, M. D. (1993, Summer). Great expectations: Psychologist Steven Neuberg probes the science of stereotype-tinged self-fulfilling prophecies. *ASU Research,* pp. 6-7.

Omi, M., & Winant, H. (1986). *Racial formation in the United States: From the 1960s to the 1980s* (rev. ed.). New York: Routledge.

Ono, K. A., & Sloop, J. M. (1995). The critique of vernacular discourse. *Communication Monographs, 62,* 19-46.

Opotow, S. V. (1987). Limits of fairness: An experimental examination of antecedents of the scope of justice. *Dissertation Abstracts International, 48*(No. 08B), 2500. (University Microfilms No. 87-24072)

Opotow, S. V. (1990). Moral exclusion and injustice: An introduction. *Journal of Social Issues, 46,* 1-20.

Orbe, M. P., & Strother, K. E. (1996). Signifying the tragic mulatto: A semiotic analysis of *Alex Haley's Queen. Howard Journal of Communications, 7,* 113-126.

Oring, E. (1984). Dyadic traditions. *Journal of Folklore Research, 21,* 19-28.

Ortiz, R. (1985). *Cultura brasileira e identidade nacional* [Brazilian culture and national identity]. São Paulo, Brazil: Brasiliense.

Outlaw, L. (1990). Towards a critical theory of "race." In D. T. Goldberg (Ed.), *Anatomy of racism* (pp. 58-82). Minneapolis: University of Minnesota Press.

Oyer, H. J., & Oyer, E. (1976). *Aging and communication.* Baltimore, MD: University Park Press.

Page, C. (Ed.). (1986). *A foot in each world: Essays and articles by Leanita McClain.* Evanston, IL: Northwestern University Press.

Paim, P. (1988). O racismo disfarcado e o despertar da consciência negra no Brasil [Disguised racism and the awakening of Black consciousness in Brazil]. In *Dia Internacional para a Eliminação da Discriminação Racial* [National Day for the Elimination of Discrimination] (pp. 40-50). Brasilia, Brazil: Centro de Documentãç e Informação, Coordinação de Publicações.

Palmore, E. B. (1990). *Ageism: Negative and positive.* New York: Springer.

Parillo, V. N. (1980). *Strangers to these shores: Race and ethnic relations in the United States.* Boston: Houghton Mifflin.

Parsons, T. (Ed.). (1954). *Essays in sociological theory.* Glencoe, IL: Free Press.

Parsons, T. (1966). *Societies: Evolutionary and comparative perspectives.* Englewood Cliffs, NJ: Prentice Hall.

Passuth, P. M., & Cook, F. L. (1985). Effects of television viewing on knowledge and attitudes about older adults: A critical re-examination. *The Gerontologist, 25,* 69-77.

Pear, R. (1996, September 24). Violent protests at abortion clinics have declined, and new federal law is credited. *The New York Times,* p. A13.

Pech, R. (1995, August 12). Affirmative action. *Vista,* pp. 26, 30.

Pedersen, P. (1995). Simulations: A safe place to take risks in discussing cultural differences. *Simulation & Gaming, 26,* 201-206.

Penn, M. L., Gaines, S. O., Jr., & Phillips, L. (1993). On the desirability of own-group preference. *Journal of Black Psychology, 19,* 303-321.

Perritt, H. H. (1990). *Americans with Disabilities Act handbook.* New York: John Wiley.

Pettigrew, T. F. (1981). Race and class in the 1980s: An interactive view. *Daedalus, 110,* 233-255.

Pettigrew, T. F. (1985). New Black-White patterns: How best to conceptualize them? *American Sociological Review, 11,* 329-346.

Pettigrew, T. F. (1986). The intergroup contact hypothesis reconsidered. In M. Hewstone & R. Brown (Eds.), *Contact and conflict in intergroup encounters* (pp. 169-185). Oxford, UK: Basil Blackwell.

Pettigrew, T. F., & Martin, J. (1987). Shaping the organizational context for Black American inclusion. *Journal of Social Issues, 43,* 41-78.

Pfeil, F. (1995). *White guys: Studies in postmodern domination and difference.* London: Verso.

Philipsen, G. (1989). An ethnographic approach to communication studies. In B. Dervin, L. Grossberg, B. J. O'Keefe, & E. Wartella (Eds.), *Rethinking communication* (pp. 258-268). Newbury Park, CA: Sage.

Pillemer, K., & Finkelhor, D. (1989). Causes of elder abuse: Caregiver stress versus problem relatives. *American Journal of Orthopsychiatry, 59,* 179-187.

Pinderhughes, E. (1989). *Understanding race, ethnicity, and power: The key to efficacy in clinical practice.* New York: Free Press.

Polenberg, R. (1980). *One nation divisible: Class, race, and ethnicity in the United States since 1938.* New York: Penguin Books.

Ponterotto, J. G., & Pedersen, P. B. (1993). *Preventing prejudice: A guide for counselors and educators.* Newbury Park, CA: Sage.

Porterfield, E. (1978). *Black and White mixed marriages.* Chicago: Nelson-Hall.

Pratt, R. H. (1964). *Battlefield and the classroom.* New Haven, CT: Yale University Press.

Prentice, D. A. (1994). Do language reforms change our way of thinking? *Journal of Language and Social Psychology, 13,* 3-19.

Public Agenda Foundation. (1990). *Remedies for racial inequality: Why progress has stalled, what should be done.* Dubuque, IA: Kendall/Hunt.

Pulley, B. (1992, December 21). Culture of racial bias at Shoney's underlies chairman's departure. *The Wall Street Journal,* p. A1.

Quadragno, J., & Fobes, C. (1995). The welfare state and the cultural reproductions of gender: Making good girls and boys in the job corps. *Social Problems, 42,* 171-190.

Quinn, J. B. (1994, June 6). The luck of the Xers. *Newsweek,* pp. 66-67.

Rabbie, J., & Horwitz, M. (1969). Arousal of ingroup-outgroup bias by chance win or loss. *Journal of Personality and Social Psychology, 13,* 269-277.

Rabushka, A. (1974). *A theory of racial harmony.* Columbia: University of South Carolina Press.

Racism prevalent in high school, poll shows. (1990, October 18). *Tempe Daily News Tribune/Chandler Arizonan Tribune,* p. A6.

Radford, A. J. (1987). Ageism: Public prejudice and private preconceptions. *Australian Journal on Ageing, 6,* 4-9.

Rakow, L. F. (1986, August). *Gender is a verb, and other lessons from feminist theory.* Paper presented at the annual meeting of the Association for Education in Journalism and Mass Communication, Norman, OK.

Rakow, L. F., & Kranich, K. (1991). Woman as sign in television news. *Journal of Communication, 41*(1), 8-23.

Ramirez, M., III. (1983). *Psychology of the Americas.* New York: Pergamon.

Ray, M. J., & Lovejoy, F. H. (1986). The generality of racial prejudice. *Journal of Social Psychology, 126,* 536-564.

Reeder, H. M. (1996). *What Harry and Sally didn't tell you: The subjective experience of heterosexual cross-sex friendship.* Unpublished doctoral dissertation, Arizona State University.

Rein, G., Atkinson, M., & McCraty, R. (1995). The physiological and psychological effects of compassion and anger. *Journal of Advancement in Medicine, 8,* 87-104.

Reinhold, R. (1991, December 3). In California, new talk about a taboo subject. *The New York Times,* p. 20.

Reiter, L. (1991). Developmental origins of antihomosexual prejudice in heterosexual men and women. *Clinical Social Work Journal, 19,* 163-176.

Revenson, T. A. (1989). Compassionate stereotyping of elderly patients by physicians: Revising the social contact hypothesis. *Psychology and Aging, 4,* 230-234.

Rex, J. (1980). The theory of race relations: A Weberian approach. In UNESCO (Ed.), *Sociological theories: Race and colonialism* (pp. 117-140). Paris: UNESCO.

Rex, J. (1986). The role of class analysis in the study of race relations: A Weberian perspective. In J. Rex & D. Mason (Eds.), *Theories of race and ethnic relations* (pp. 64-83). Cambridge, UK: Cambridge University Press.

Reynolds, V. (1987). Sociobiology and race relations. In V. Reynolds, V. Falger, & I. Vine (Eds.), *The sociobiology of ethnocentrism: Evolutionary dimensions of xenophobia, discrimination, racism and nationalism* (pp. 208-215). London: Croom Helm.

Reynolds, V., Falger, V., & Vine, I. (1987). Introduction. In V. Reynolds, V. Falger, & I. Vine (Eds.), *The sociobiology of ethnocentrism: Evolutionary dimensions of xenophobia, discrimination, racism and nationalism* (pp. xv-xx). London: Croom Helm.

Rich, A. (1979). *On lies, secrets and silence.* New York: Norton.

Rich, Y., Ben-Ary, R., Amir, Y., & Eliassy, L. (1996). Effectiveness of schools with a mixed student body of natives and immigrants. *International Journal of Intercultural Relations, 20,* 323-340.

Riordan, C., & Ruggiero, J. (1980). Producing equal-status interracial interaction: A replication. *Social Psychology Quarterly, 43,* 131-136.

Roberts, S. (1994). Employers can trim risk of lawsuits with fairness in workplace. *Business Insurance, 28,* 30-32.

Rogler, L. H. (1989). Marital happiness among mixed and homogeneous marriages in Israel. *Journal of Marriage and the Family, 50,* 245-255.

Rohlfing, M. E. (1995). "Doesn't anybody stay in one place anymore?" An exploration of the under-studied phenomenon of long-distance relationships. In J. T. Wood & S. Duck (Eds.), *Under-studied relationships: Off the beaten track* (pp. 173-196). Thousand Oaks, CA: Sage.

Rokeach, M. (1960). *The open and closed mind: Investigations into the nature of belief systems and personality systems.* New York: Basic Books.

Roloff, M. E., & Cloven, D. H. (1994). When partners transgress: Maintaining violated relationships. In D. J. Canary & L. Stafford (Eds.), *Communication and relational maintenance* (pp. 23-43). San Diego: Academic Press.

Romano, D. (1988). *Intercultural marriage: Promises and pitfalls.* Yarmouth, MA: Intercultural Press.

Root, M. P. P. (1992). Within, between, and beyond race. In M. P. P. Root (Ed.), *Racially mixed people in America* (pp. 3-11). Newbury Park, CA: Sage.

Rosenau, P. M. (1992). *Postmodernism and the social sciences: Insights, inroads, and intrusions.* Princeton, NJ: Princeton University Press.

Rosenblatt, P. C., Karis, T. A., & Powell, R. D. (1995). *Multiracial couples: Black and White voices.* Thousand Oaks, CA: Sage.

Ross, L. (1994). Race, gender, and social control: Voices of imprisoned Native American and White women. *Wicazo Sa Review, 10*(2), 17-39.

Ross, M. H. (1991). The role of evolution in ethnocentric conflict and its management. *Journal of Social Issues, 47,* 167-185.

Rothbart, M. (1996). Category-exemplar dynamics and stereotype change. *International Journal of Intercultural Relations, 20,* 305-322.

Rothenberg, P. (1992). The construction, deconstruction, and reconstruction of difference. In R. M. Baird & S. E. Rosenbaum (Eds.), *Bigotry, prejudice and hatred* (pp. 47-64). Buffalo, NY: Prometheus.

Rothschild, M. (1992, September 21). Gay bashing becomes new national pastime. *Arizona Republic,* p. A9.

Rusbult, C. E., Verette, J., Whitney, G. A., Slovik, L. F., & Lipkus, I. (1991). Accommodation processes in close relationships: Theory and preliminary evidence. *Journal of Personality and Social Psychology, 60,* 53-78.

Ryan, E. B., Bourhis, R. Y., & Knops, U. (1991). Evaluative perceptions of patronizing speech addressed to elders. *Psychology and Aging, 6,* 442-450.

Ryan, E. B., & Capadano, H. L., III. (1978). Age perceptions and evaluative reactions toward adult speakers. *Journal of Gerontology, 33,* 98-102.

Ryan, E. B., & Cole, R. (1990). Evaluative perceptions of interpersonal communication with elders. In H. Giles, N. Coupland, & J. M. Wiemann (Eds.), *Communication, health and the elderly* (pp. 172-190). Manchester, UK: Manchester University Press.

Ryan, E. B., & Giles, H. (Eds.). (1982). *Attitudes toward language.* London: Arnold.

Ryan, E. B., Hummert, M. L., & Boich, L. H. (1995). Communication predicaments of aging: Patronizing behavior toward older adults. *Journal of Language and Social Psychology, 14,* 144-166.

Ryan, E. B., & Johnston, J. (1987). The influence of communication effectiveness on evaluations of younger and older adult speakers. *Journals of Gerontology: Series B, Psychological Sciences and Social Studies, 42,* 163-164.

Ryan, E. B., Kennaley, D., Pratt, M., & Shumovich, M. (1996, May). *Responses in the nursing home: Evaluative perceptions by staff, residents, and community seniors.* Paper presented at the Third International Conference on Communication, Aging and Health, Kansas City, KS.

Ryan, E. B., & Kwong See, S. (1993). Age-based beliefs about memory change in adulthood. *Journals of Gerontology: Series B, Psychological Sciences and Social Sciences, 48,* 199-201.

Ryan, E. B., Kwong See, S., Maneer, W. B., & Trovato, D. (1992). Age-based perceptions of language performance among younger and older adults. *Communication Research, 19,* 311-331.

Ryan, E. B., & Laurie, S. (1990). Evaluations of older and younger adult speakers: The influence of communication effectiveness and noise. *Psychology and Aging, 5,* 514-519.

Ryan, E. B., Meredith, S. D., & Orange, J. B. (1995). Changing the way we talk with elders: Promoting health using the Communication Enhancement Model. *International Journal of Aging and Human Development, 41*(2), 89-108.

Ryan, E. B., Meredith, S. D., & Shantz, G. D. (1994). Evaluative perceptions of patronizing speech addressed to institutionalized elders in varied contexts. *Canadian Journal on Aging, 13,* 236-248.

Rynes, S., & Rosen, B. (1994, October). What makes diversity programs work? *HRMagazine,* pp. 68-70.

Sampson, E. E. (1989). The deconstruction of the self. In J. Shotter & K. Gergen (Eds.), *Texts of identity* (pp. 1-12). Newbury Park, CA: Sage.

Sanford, R. N., Adorno, T. W., Frenkel-Brunswick, E., & Levinson, D. J. (1982). The measurement of implicit antidemocratic trends. In T. W. Adorno, E. Frenkel-Brunswick, D. J. Levinson, and R. N. Sanford (Eds.), *The authoritarian personality* (abridged ed., pp. 151-208). New York: Norton. (Originally published by Harper in 1950)

Sarbin, T. R. (1986). *Narrative psychology: The storied nature of human conduct.* New York: Praeger.

Schaefer, R. (1996). *Racial and ethnic groups* (6th ed.). New York: HarperCollins.

Schaie, K. W. (1993). Ageist language in psychological research. *American Psychologist, 48,* 49-51.

Scheibel, D. (1994). Graffiti and the "Film School" culture: Displaying alienation. *Communication Monographs, 61,* 1-18.

Scheier, M. F., Carver, C. S., Schulz, R., Glass, D. C., & Katz, I. (1978). Sympathy, self-consciousness, and reactions to the stigmatized. *Journal of Applied Social Psychology, 8,* 270-282.

Schmitt, E. (1996, September 11). Senators reject gay marriage bill and job-bias ban. *The New York Times,* p. A11.

Schofield, J. W. (1979). The impact of positively structured contact on intergroup behavior: Does it last under adverse conditions? *Social Psychology Quarterly, 42,* 280-284.

Schroeder, C. R. (1992). *Fat is not a four-letter word.* Minneapolis, MN: Chronimed.

Schutte, G. (1995). *What racists believe.* Thousand Oaks, CA: Sage.

Schütz, H., & Six, B. (1996). How strong is the relationship between prejudice and discrimination? A meta-analytic answer. *International Journal of Intercultural Relations, 20,* 441-462.

Schwichtenberg, C. (1989a). Feminist cultural studies. *Critical Studies in Mass Communication, 6,* 202-208.

Schwichtenberg, C. (1989b). The "mother lode" of feminist research: Congruent paradigms in the analysis of beauty culture. In B. Dervin, L. Grossberg, B. J. O'Keefe, & E. Wartella (Eds.), *Rethinking communication* (pp. 291-306). Newbury Park, CA: Sage.

Scollon, R., & Scollon, S. W. (1995). *Intercultural communication.* Oxford, UK: Blackwell.

Sears, D. O. (1988). Symbolic racism. In P. A. Katz & D. A. Taylor (Eds.), *Eliminating racism: Profiles in controversy* (pp. 53-84). New York: Plenum.

Sedano, M. V. (1980). Chicanismo: A rhetorical analysis of themes and images of selected poetry from the Chicano movement. *Western Journal of Speech Communication, 44,* 177-190.

Shafer, R. (1993). What minority journalists identify as constraints to full newsroom equality. *Howard Journal of Communication, 4,* 195-208.

Shalit, R. (1994, July 18-25). The kids are alright. *The New Republic,* pp. 23-31.

Shaner, J. L. (1995, November). *Grumpy Old Men vs. life on Widow's Peak: A comparison of elderly portrayals.* Paper presented at the annual meeting of the Speech Communication Association, San Antonio, TX.

Shao, M. (1995). Affirmative action: Equality still elusive. *Arizona Republic,* pp. A1, A4.

Shaw, M. E. (1981). *Group dynamics: The psychology of small group behavior.* New York: McGraw-Hill.

Shelton, B. A., & Agger, B. (1993). Shotgun wedding, unhappy marriage, no-fault divorce? Rethinking the feminism-Marxism relationship. In P. England (Ed.), *Theory on gender/ Feminism on theory* (pp. 25-42). New York: Aldine de Gruyter.

Sherif, M. (1966). *Group conflict and cooperation: Their social psychology.* London: Routledge & Kegan Paul.

Sherif, M. (1979). Superordinate goals in the reduction of intergroup conflict: An experimental evaluation. In W. G. Austin & S. Worchel (Eds.), *The social psychology of intergroup relations* (pp. 349-356). Pacific Grove, CA: Brooks/Cole.

Sherman, M. F., Smith, R. J., & Sherman, N. C. (1983). Racial and gender differences in perceptions of fairness: When race is involved in job promotion. *Perceptual and Motor Skills, 57,* 719-728.

Shohat, E., & Stam, R. (1994). *Unthinking Eurocentrism: Multiculturalism and the media.* New York: Routledge.

Sidanius, J., Levin, S., & Pratto, F. (1996). Consensual social dominance orientation and its correlates within the hierarchical structure of American society. *International Journal of Intercultural Relations, 20,* 385-408.

Sillars, A. L., Coletti, S. F., Parry, D., & Rogers, M. A. (1982). Coding verbal conflict tactics: Nonverbal and perceptual correlates of the "avoidance-distributive-integrative" distinction. *Human Communication Research, 9,* 83-95.

Sillars, A. L., Wilmot, W. W., & Hocker, J. L. (1993). Communication strategies in conflict and mediation. In J. Wiemann & J. Daly (Eds.), *Communicating strategically: Strategies in interpersonal communication* (pp. 237-261). Hillsdale, NJ: Lawrence Erlbaum.

Simonsen, P., & Wells, C. (1994). African Americans take control of their careers. *Personnel Journal, 73*(4), 99-108.

Sischy, I. (1995, October). bell hooks [interview]. *Interview,* pp. 122-127.

Skidmore, T. E. (1985). Race and class in Brazil: Historical perspectives. In P.-M. Fontaine (Ed.), *Race, class and power in Brazil* (pp. 11-24). Los Angeles: University of California, Center for Afro-American Studies.

Slagle, R. A. (1995). In defense of queer nation: From identity politics to a politics of difference. *Western Journal of Communication, 59*(2), 85-102.

Smith, D., & Evans, P. (1982). *Marx's Kapital for beginners.* New York: Pantheon.

Smith, E. R., Byrne, D., & Fielding, P. J. (1995). Interpersonal attraction as a function of extreme gender role adherence. *Personal Relationships, 2,* 161-172.

Smith, J. P., & Welch, F. (1984). Affirmative action and labor markets. *Journal of Labor Economics, 2,* 269-301.

Smither, R. D., & Houston, M. R. (1991). Racial discrimination and forms of redress in the military. *International Journal of Intercultural Relations, 15,* 459-468.

Smitherman, G. (1994). *Black talk: Words and phrases from the hood to the amen corner.* Boston: Houghton Mifflin.

Smooha, S. (1987). Jewish and Arab ethnocentrism in Israel. *Ethnic and Racial Studies, 10,* 1-26.

Snyder, M., & Ickes, W. (1985). Personality and social behavior. In G. Lindzey & E. Aronson (Eds.), *Handbook of social psychology* (3rd ed., Vol. 2, pp. 883-947). New York: Random House.

Snyder, M., & Miene, P. (1994). On the functions of stereotypes and prejudice. In M. P. Zanna & J. M. Olson (Eds.), *Ontario Symposium on Personality and Social Psychology, Vol. 7: The psychology of prejudice* (pp. 33-54). Hillsdale, NJ: Lawrence Erlbaum.

Soe, V. (producer/director). (1992). *Mixed blood* [video]. (Available from National Asian American Telecommunications Association, 346 Ninth Street, Second Floor, San Francisco, CA 94103)

Sokoloff, N. J. (1988). Evaluating gains and losses by Black men and White women and men in the professions, 1960-1980. *Social Problems, 35,* 36-53.

Solomon, C. (1991). Are White males being left out? *Personnel Journal, 70*(11), 88-94.

Solomon, C. M. (1995). You're going to need them: Unlock the potential of older workers. *Personnel Journal, 74*(10), 56-66.

Solomos, J. (1986). Varieties of Marxist conceptions of "race," class and the state: A critical analysis. In J. Rex & D. Mason (Eds.), *Theories of race and ethnic relations* (pp. 84-109). Cambridge, UK: Cambridge University Press.

Sontag, S. (1978). The double standard of aging. In V. Carver & P. Liddiard (Eds.), *An aging population* (pp. 72-80). Milton Keynes, UK: Open University Press.

Spelman, E. V. (1988). *Inessential woman: Problems of exclusion in feminist thought.* Boston: Beacon.

Spence, J. T., Deaux, K., & Helmreich, R. L. (1985). Sex roles in contemporary American society. In G. Lindzey & E. Aronson (Eds.), *Handbook of social psychology* (3rd ed., Vol. 2, pp. 149-178). New York: Random House.

Spence, J. T., & Helmreich, R. L. (1978). *Masculinity and femininity.* Austin: University of Texas Press.

Spender, D. (1980). *Man made language.* London: Routledge & Kegan Paul.

Sperber, D. (1994). The modularity of thought and the epidemiology of representations. In L. A. Hirschfeld & S. A. Gelman (Eds.), *Mapping the mind: Domain specificity in cognition and culture* (pp. 39-67). Cambridge, UK: Cambridge University Press.

Spickard, P. (1992). The illogic of American racial categories. In M. P. P. Root (Ed.), *Racially mixed people in America* (pp. 12-23). Newbury Park, CA: Sage.

Spillers, H. (1991). *Comparative American identities.* London: Routledge.

Stannard, U. (1977) *Mrs. Man.* San Francisco: Germainbooks.

Starhawk. (1987). *Truth or dare: Encounters with power, authority, and mystery.* San Francisco: HarperCollins.

Starhawk. (1988). *Dreaming the dark: Majic, sex and politics.* Boston: Beacon.

Starosta, W. J. (1984). On intercultural rhetoric. In W. B. Gudykunst & Y. Y. Kim (Eds.), *Methods for intercultural communication* (pp. 229-238). Beverly Hills, CA: Sage.

Staub, E. (1990). Moral exclusion, personal goal theory, and extreme destructiveness. *Journal of Social Issues, 46,* 47-64.

Steedman, C. (1992). Culture, cultural studies, and the historians. In L. Grossberg, C. Nelson, & P. Treichler (Eds.), *Cultural studies* (pp. 613-622). New York: Routledge.

Stepan, N. L. (1991). *"The hour of eugenics": Race, gender, and nation in Latin America.* Ithaca, NY: Cornell University Press.

Stephan, W. G. (1985). Intergroup relations. In G. Lindzey & E. Aronson (Eds.), *Handbook of social psychology* (3rd ed., Vol. 2, pp. 599-658). New York: Random House.

Stephan, W. C., & Stephan, C. W. (1985). Intergroup anxiety. *Journal of Social Issues, 41,* 157-175.

Stephan, W. G., & Stephan, C. W. (1996). Predicting prejudice. *International Journal of Intercultural Relations, 20,* 409-426.

Stephen, T. (1992). Communication, intimacy, and the course of time. In S. A. Deetz (Ed.), *Communication yearbook 15* (pp. 522-534). Newbury Park, CA: Sage.

Stern, F. (1991, August). *Anti-Semitic and philosemitic discourse in postwar Germany.* Paper presented at the Fourth International Conference on Language and Social Psychology, Santa Barbara, CA.

Stevens, A. (1989, April). Disablism: Another form of prejudice. *Social Work Today,* p. 22.

Stewart, C. J., Smith, C. A., & Denton, R. E. (1994). *Persuasion and social movements* (3rd ed.). Prospect Heights, IL: Waveland.

Stewart, M. A., & Ryan, E. B. (1982). Attitudes toward older and younger adult speakers: Effects of varying speech rates. *Journal of Language and Social Psychology, 1,* 91-109.

St. Pierre, M. (1991). Accession and retention of minorities: Implications for the future. *International Journal of Intercultural Relations, 15,* 469-489.

Stronmen, E. F. (1990). Hidden branches and growing pains: Homosexuality and the family tree. In F. W. Bozett & M. B. Sussman (Eds.), *Homosexuality and family relations* (pp. 9-34). New York: Harrington Park.

Study says women face glass walls as well as ceilings (1992, March 3). *Wall Street Journal,* pp. B1-B2.

Sullivan, H. S. (1953). *The interpersonal theory of psychiatry.* New York: Norton.

Sunoo, B. P. (1994). Tapping diversity in America's newsrooms. *Personnel Journal, 73*(11), 104-111.

Szemere, A. (1992). Bandits, heroes, the honest, and the misled: Exploring the politics of representation in the Hungarian uprising of 1956. In L. Grossberg, C. Nelson, & P. Treichler (Eds.), *Cultural studies* (pp. 623-639). New York: Routledge.

Tajfel, H. (Ed.). (1978a). *Differentiation between social groups: Studies in the social psychology of intergroup relations.* London: Academic Press.

Tajfel, H. (1978b). Interindividual and intergroup behavior. In H. Tajfel (Ed.), *Differentiation between social groups: Studies in the social psychology of intergroup relations* (pp. 27-60). London: Academic Press.

Tajfel, H. (1979). Individuals and groups in social psychology. *British Journal of Social and Clinical Psychology, 18,* 183-190.

Tajfel, H. (1981a). *Human categories and social groups.* Cambridge, UK: Cambridge University Press.

Tajfel, H. (1981b). The social psychology of minorities. In H. Tajfel (Ed.), *Human categories and social groups* (pp. 309-343). Cambridge, UK: Cambridge University Press.

Tajfel, H. (Ed.). (1982). *Social identity and intergroup relations.* Cambridge, UK: Cambridge University Press.

Tajfel, H., & Turner, J. C. (1979). An integrative theory of intergroup conflict. In W. Austin & S. Worchel (Eds.), *The social psychology of intergroup relations* (pp. 33-47). Pacific Grove, CA: Brooks/Cole.

Tajfel, H., & Turner, J. C. (1986). The social identity of intergroup behavior. In S. Worchel & W. G. Austin (Eds.), *Psychology of intergroup relations* (pp. 7-24). Chicago: Nelson-Hall.

Tajima, R. E. (1989). Lotus Blossoms don't bleed: Images of Asian women. In Asian Women United of California (Ed.), *Making waves: An anthology of writings by and about Asian American women* (pp. 308-317). Boston: Beacon.

Talbot, M. (1991). *The holographic universe.* New York: Harper Perennial.

Tannahill, R. (1992). *Sex in history.* New York: Scarborough House.

Tannen, D. (1986). *That's not what I meant! How conversational style makes or breaks relationships.* New York: Ballantine.

Tannen, D. (1990). *You just don't understand: Women and men in conversation.* New York: William Morrow.

Taub, N., & Schneider, E. M. (1993). Women's subordination and the role of law. In D. K. Weisberg (Ed.), *Feminist legal theory: Foundations* (pp. 9-21). Philadelphia: Temple University Press.

Taylor, B. C. (1992). Elderly identity in conversation: Producing frailty. *Communication Research, 19,* 493-515.

Taylor, D. A., & Katz, P. A. (1987). Conclusion. In P. A. Katz & D. A. Taylor (Eds.), *Eliminating racism: Profiles in controversy* (pp. 359-369). New York: Plenum.

Taylor, D. M., Wright, S. C., & Porter, L. E. (1994). Dimensions of perceived discrimination: The personal/group discrimination discrepancy. In M. P. Zanna & J. M. Olson (Eds.), *Ontario Symposium on Personality and Social Psychology,* Vol. 7: *The psychology of prejudice* (pp. 233-256). Hillsdale, NJ: Lawrence Erlbaum.

Taylor, V., & Raeburn, N. C. (1995). Identity politics as high-risk activism: Career consequences for lesbian, gay and bisexual sociologists. *Social Problems, 42,* 252-273.

Teboul, J.-C. B., & Correia, M. H. (1985). O luso-tropicalismo: Uma teoria aplicável a colonização portuguesa ou um mito ao serviço de uma ideologia colonial [Luso-tropicalism: A theory applicable to Portuguese colonization or a myth at the service of a colonial ideology]. *Factos e ideais: Revista do Centro de Estudos de Relações Internacionais* [Facts and ideas: Journal of the Center of International Relations Studies], *1,* 239-261.

Terkel, S. (1992). *Race: How Blacks and Whites think and feel about the American obsession.* New York: Free Press.

Text of the appeals court's opinion on affirmative action in admissions. (1996, March 29). *Chronicle of Higher Education,* pp. A28-A38.

Theberge, N. (1993). The construction of gender in sport: Women, coaching and the naturalization of difference. *Social Problems, 40,* 301-313.

Therborn, G. (1980). *The ideology of power and the power of ideology.* London: Verso.

Thomas, I. M. (1994, November). Latinos in the limelight. *Hispanic,* p. 10.

Thornburg, L. (1995, February). The age wave hits: What older workers want and need. *HR Magazine,* pp. 40-45.

Thorne, B., Kramarae, C., & Henley, N. (1983). Language, gender and society: Opening a second decade of research. In B. Thorne, C. Kramarae, & N. Henley (Eds.), *Language, gender and society* (pp. 7-24). Cambridge, MA: Newbury House.

Ting-Toomey, S. (1986). Interpersonal ties in intergroup communication. In W. B. Gudykunst (Ed.), *Intergroup communication* (pp. 114-126). London: Arnold.

Tonight the Battle of the Sexes declares a new war zone in: The Gender Wars [television broadcast]. (1994, November 11). *CNN Presents.* Atlanta, GA: CNN.

Trattner, W. I. (1994). *From poor law to welfare state: A history of social welfare in America* (5th ed.). New York: Free Press.

Treichler, P., & Kramarae, C. (1983). Women's talk in the ivory tower. *Communication Quarterly, 31,* 118-132.

Triandis, H. C., Hui, C. H., Albert, R. D., Leung, S.-M., Lisansky, J., Diaz-Loving, R., Plascencia, L., Marin, G., Betancourt, H., & Loyola-Cintron, L. (1984). Individual models of social behavior. *Journal of Personality and Social Psychology, 46,* 1389-1404.

Trinh, T. M.-H. (1989). *Woman, native, other: Writing postcoloniality and feminism.* Bloomington: Indiana University Press.

Trost, M. R., & Kenrick, D. T. (1993). An evolutionary perspective on interpersonal communication. In S. Petronio, J. K. Alberts, M. L. Hecht, & J. Buley (Eds.), *Contemporary perspectives on interpersonal communication* (pp. 120-124). Madison, WI: Brown & Benchmark.

Trungpa, C. (1973, March). Adapted from the seminar, "Buddhadharma Without Credentials," held at the New York Dharmadhatu. (Reprinted in *Shambhala Sun,* March 1997, pp. 32-35, 66-68)

Trungpa, C. (1976). *The myth of freedom.* Boston: Shambhala.

Tsuno, K. (producer/director). (1991). *The story of Vinh* [video]. (Available from National Asian American Telecommunications Association, 346 Ninth Street, Second Floor, San Francisco, CA 94103)

Tuchman, G. (1978). *Making news: A study in the construction of reality*. New York: Free Press.

Tucker, L. R., & Shah, H. (1992). Race and transformation of culture: The making of the television miniseries *Roots. Critical Studies in Mass Communication, 9,* 325-336.

Tucker, R. C. (Ed.). (1978). *The Marx-Engels reader* (2nd ed.). New York: Norton.

Turner, G. (1990). *British cultural studies: An introduction.* Boston: Unwin Hyman.

Turner, G. (1992). "It works for me": British cultural studies, Australian cultural studies, Australian film. In L. Grossberg, C. Nelson, & P. Treichler (Eds.), *Cultural studies* (pp. 640-653). New York: Routledge.

Turner, J. C. (1985). Social categorization and the self-concept: A social cognitive theory of group behavior. In E. J. Lawler (Ed.), *Advances in group processes: Theory and research* (Vol. 2, pp. 77-122). Greenwich, CT: JAI.

Turner, J. C. (1987). Towards a cognitive redefinition of the social group. In H. Tajfel (Ed.), *Social identity and intergroup relations* (pp. 15-40). Cambridge, UK: Cambridge University Press.

Turner, J. C., Hogg, M., Oakes, P., Reicher, S., & Wetherell, M. (1987). *Rediscovering the social group: A self-categorization theory.* Oxford, UK: Blackwell.

Two men guilty of beating lesbian. (1995, September 14). *Southern Voice,* p. 7.

Tzeng, O. C., & Jackson, J. W. (1994). Effects of contact, conflict and social identity on interethnic group hostility. *International Journal of Intercultural Relations, 18,* 259-276.

Uri, N. D., & Mixon, J. W. (1991). Effects of U.S. affirmative action programs on women's employment. *Journal of Policy Modeling, 13,* 367-382.

U.S. Bureau of the Census. (1994). *Statistical abstract of the United States* (114th ed.). Washington, DC: U.S. Department of Commerce Bureau.

U.S. Congress. (1991). *Civil Rights and Women's Equity in Employment Act of 1991* (Report 102-40, Part 1). Washington, DC: Government Printing Office.

U.S. General Accounting Office. (1988, October). *Equal employment opportunity: EEOC and state agencies did not fully investigate discrimination charges.* Washington, DC: House Education and Labor Committee.

U.S. Government. (1990). *Americans with Disabilities Act of 1990* (P.L. 101-336). Washington, DC: Government Printing Office.

U.S. Government. (1996). *Defense of Marriage Act* (H.R. 3396, S. 1740). Washington, DC: Government Printing Office.

Vaillancourt, D. (1994a, June). The good soldier. *10 Percent,* pp. 72-76.

Vaillancourt, D. (1994b, November/December). Till deportation do us part. *10 Percent,* pp. 52-55, 70-71.

van den Berghe, P. L. (1967). *Race and racism: A comparative perspective.* New York: John Wiley.

van den Berghe, P. L. (1986). Ethnicity and the sociology debate. In J. Rex & D. Mason (Eds.), *Theories of race and ethnic relations* (pp. 246-263). Cambridge, UK: Cambridge University Press.

van der Dennen, J. M. G. (1987). Ethnocentrism and in-group/out-group differentiation: A review and interpretation of the literature. In V. Reynolds, V. Falger, & I. Vine (Eds.), *The sociobiology of ethnocentrism: Evolutionary dimensions of xenophobia, discrimination, racism and nationalism* (pp. 1-47). London: Croom Helm.

van Dijk, T. A. (1984). *Prejudice in discourse.* Amsterdam: John Benjamins.

van Dijk, T. A. (1987). *Communicating racism: Ethnic prejudice in thought and talk.* Newbury Park, CA: Sage.

van Dijk, T. A. (1990). Discourse and the denial of racism. *Discourse and Society, 3,* 87-118.

van Dijk, T. A. (1993). *Elite discourse and racism.* Newbury Park, CA: Sage.

Van Maanen, J. (1988). *Tales of the field: On writing ethnography.* Chicago: University of Chicago Press.

van Oudenhoven, J. P., Groenewoud, J. T., & Hewstone, M. (1996). Cooperation, ethnic salience, and generalization of interethnic attitudes. *European Journal of Social Psychology, 26,* 649-661.

Vargas, G. (n.d.). *As diretrizes da Nova Republica do Brasil* [Speeches of the New Republic of Brazil]. Rio de Janeiro: Livraria Jose Olympio Editora.

Viledot, A., & Giles, H. (in press). Habla condescendiente y ancienidad: Evaluaciones inter-geneerationales en Catalona. *Revista de Psicologia Social Aplicada.*

Villanueva, V. (1993). *Bootstraps: From an American academic of color.* Urbana, IL: National Council of Teachers of English.

Vine, I. (1987). Inclusive fitness and the self-system: The roles of human nature and sociocultural processes in intergroup discrimination. In V. Reynolds, V. Falger, & I. Vine (Eds.), *The sociobiology of ethnocentrism: Evolutionary dimensions of xenophobia, discrimination, racism and nationalism* (pp. 60-80). London: Croom Helm.

Virginia is not for gay lovers, Atty. Gen. says. (1995, August 24). *Southern Voice,* p. 5.

Wackwitz, L. A. (1996a). Sex testing in international women's athletics: A history of silence. *Women in Sport and Physical Activity Journal, 5,* 51-68.

Wackwitz, L. A. (1996b). *The Supreme Court as cultural critic: A textual analysis of decisions and opinions restricting mediated sexual expression.* Unpublished dissertation, University of Georgia.

Wallace, M. (1992). Negative images: Towards a Black feminist cultural criticism. In L. Grossberg, C. Nelson, & P. Treichler (Eds.), *Cultural studies* (pp. 654-671). New York: Routledge.

Wallerstein, I. (1990). World-systems analysis. *Review, 13,* 287-293.

Wallis, J. (1991). Whites' racist attitudes are a serious problem. In W. Dudley (Ed.), *Racism in America: Opposing viewpoints* (pp. 25-31). San Diego: Greenhaven.

Warner, M. (1991). Introduction: Fear of a queer planet. *Social Text, 29,* 3-17.

Warner, M. (1992, June). From queer to eternity. *Voice Literary Supplement,* pp. 18-19.

Waters, H. (1991). Business education: Meeting the needs of the African American student. *Journal of Business Education, 66,* 232-234.

Waters, H. (1992). Race, culture and interpersonal conflict. *International Journal of Intercultural Relationships, 16,* 437-454.

Weaver, G. R., & Gioia, D. A. (1994). Paradigms lost: Incommensurability vs. structurationist inquiry. *Organization Studies, 15,* 565-590.

Weinreich, P. (1986). The operationalisation of identity theory in racial and ethnic relations. In J. Rex & D. Mason (Eds.), *Theories of race and ethnic relations* (pp. 299-320). Cambridge, UK: Cambridge University Press.

Wellman, D. T. (1993). *Portraits of White racism.* New York: Cambridge University Press.

West, C. (1982). *Prophesy deliverance! An Afro-American revolutionary Christianity.* Philadelphia: Westminster.

West, C. (1993). *Race matters.* Boston: Beacon.

West, J. (1991). The social and policy context of the act. In J. West (Ed.), *The Americans with Disabilities Act* (pp. 3-24). New York: Milbank Memorial Fund.

Wex, M. (1979). *Let's take back our space: "Female" and "male" body language as a result of patriarchal structures* (J. Albert, Trans.). Berlin: Frauenliteraturverlag Hermine Fees.

Whillock, R. K., & Slayden, D. (Eds.). (1995). *Hate speech.* Thousand Oaks, CA: Sage.

White, H. (1980). The value of narrativity in the presentation of reality. *Creative Inquiry, 7,* 5-27.

White, J. L., & Parham, T. A. (1990). *The psychology of Blacks: An African-American perspective* (2nd ed.). Englewood Cliffs, NJ: Prentice Hall.

White, M. (1992). *Tele-advising: Therapeutic discourse in American television.* Chapel Hill: University of North Carolina Press.

Whitely, W., Dougherty, T. W., & Dreher, G. F. (1991). Relationship of career mentoring and socioeconomic origin to managers' and professionals' early career successes. *Academy of Management Journal, 34,* 331-351.

Whitman, D., Friedman, D., Linn, A., Doremus, C., & Hetter, K. (1994, October 17). The White underclass. *U.S. News & World Report,* pp. 40-53.

Who's getting rich and why aren't you? (1996, August 8). *CBS Reports.*

Wiegman, R. (1995). *American anatomies: Theorizing race and gender.* Durham, NC: Duke University Press.

Wiese, E. (1994, November 10). San Francisco man shot in brutal hate crime. *Southern Voice,* p. 7.

Wieviorka, M. (1995). *The arena of racism.* London: Sage.

Wilcox, M. (1992, August). How to spot, and fight, age discrimination on the job. *Kiplinger's Personal Finance Magazine,* pp. 87-89.

Wilder, D. A. (1986). Social categorization: Implications for creation and reduction of intergroup bias. In L. Berkowitz (Ed.), *Advances in experimental social psychology* (Vol. 9, pp. 291-355). New York: Academic Press.

Williams, A. (1996). Young people's evaluations of intergenerational versus peer underaccommodation: Sometimes older is better? *Journal of Language and Social Psychology, 15,* 291-311.

Williams, A., Coupland, J., Sparks, L., & Folwell, A. (1997). Talking about my generation: Lifespan positioning, identity and media generations. *Journal of Language and Social Psychology, 16,* 251-277.

Williams, A., & Giles, H. (1996). Satisfying-dissatisfying intergenerational encounters: Views of younger adults. *Human Communication Research, 23,* 220-250.

Williams, A., Giles, H., Ota, H., Pierson, H. D., Gallois, C., Lim, T.-S., Ryan, E. B., Somera, L., Maher, J., & Harwood, J. (1997). Young people's beliefs about intergenerational communication: An initial cross-cultural comparison. *Communication Research, 24,* 370-393.

Williams, C. L. (1992). The glass escalator: Hidden advantages for men in the "female" professions. *Social Problems, 39,* 253-267.

Williams, C. L. (1993). Psychoanalytic theory and the sociology of gender. In P. England (Ed.), *Theory on gender/Feminism on theory* (pp. 131-149). New York: Aldine de Gruyter.

Williams, D. R., & Collins, C. (1995). U.S. socioeconomics and racial differences in health: Patterns and explanations. *Annual Review of Sociology, 21,* 349-386.

Williams, R. (1980a). Base and superstructure in Marxist cultural theory. In R. Williams (Ed.), *Problems in materialism and culture* (pp. 31-49). London: Verso.

Williams, R. (1980b). *Problems in materialism and culture.* London: Verso.

Wilson, B. (producer), with Anderson, E. S. (director). (1992). *None of the above: People of multiracial heritage* [video]. (Available from Filmmakers Library, 124 East 40th Street, New York, NY 10016)

Wilson, C. C., II, & Gutiérrez, F. (1985). *Minorities and media: Diversity and the end of mass communication.* Beverly Hills, CA: Sage.

Wilson, D., & Lavelle, S. (1990). Interracial friendship in a Zimbabwean primary school. *Journal of Social Psychology, 130,* 111-113.

Wilson, P. A. (1992). *Exports and local development: Mexico's new maquiladoras.* Austin: University of Texas Press.

Wilson, W. J. (1978). *The declining significance of race: Blacks and changing American institutions.* Chicago: University of Chicago Press.

Wodak, R. (1991). Turning the tables: Anti-Semitic discourse in post-war Austria. *Discourse & Society, 2,* 65-83.

Wolf, C. (1986). Legitimation of oppression: Response and reflexivity. *Symbolic Interaction, 9,* 217-234.

Wolf, R. (1995, July 26). Experts say benefits outweigh burden. *USA Today*, p. B8.

Wolinsky, H. (1994, June 28). Paging Dr. Jekyll. *The Advocate*, p. 5.

Wolpe, H. (1986). Class concepts, class struggle and racism. In J. Rex & D. Mason (Eds.), *Theories of race and ethnic relations* (pp. 110-130). Cambridge, UK: Cambridge University Press.

Wonsek, P. L. (1992). College basketball on television: A study of racism in the media. *Media, Culture and Society, 14*, 449-461.

Wood, J. T. (1982). Communication and relational culture: Bases for the study of human relationships. *Communication Quarterly, 30*, 75-83.

Wood, J. T., & Duck, S. (1995). Off the beaten track: New shores for relationship research. In J. T. Wood & S. Duck (Eds.), *Understudied relationships: Off the beaten track* (pp. 1-21). Thousand Oaks, CA: Sage.

Wood, L. A., & Ryan, E. B. (1991). Talk to elders: Social structure, attitudes, and address. *Aging and Society, 11*, 167-188.

Wood, P. B., & Sonleitner, N. (1996). The effect of childhood interracial contact on adult anti-Black prejudice. *International Journal of Intercultural Relations, 20*, 1-18.

Work-for-aid idea guides Wisconsin welfare reform. (1996, August 4). *Arizona Republic*, p. A26.

Working dads finding more flexibility on the job. (1991, June 16). *Raleigh News and Observer*, p. E6.

Yamazaki, H. (producer/director). (1989). *Juxta* [video]. (Available from Women Make Movies, 462 Broadway, Suite 501, New York, NY 10013)

Yellin, E. H. (1991). The recent history and immediate future of employment among persons with disabilities. In J. West (Ed.), *The Americans with Disabilities Act* (pp. 129-149). New York: Milbank Memorial Fund.

Young-Bruehl, E. (1996). *The anatomy of prejudices*. Cambridge, MA: Harvard University Press.

Ytsma, J., & Giles, H. (in press). Reactions to patronizing talk: Some Dutch data. *Journal of Sociolinguistics*.

Zandy, J. (1990). *Calling home: Working-class women's writings*. New Brunswick, NJ: Rutgers University Press.

Zatz, M. S. (1987). The changing forms of racial/ethnic biases in sentencing. *Journal of Research in Crime and Delinquency, 24*, 69-92.

Zerbinos, E., & Clanton, G. A. (1993). Minority practitioners: Career influences, job satisfaction and discrimination. *Public Relations Review, 19*, 75-91.

Zorn, T. E. (1995). Bosses and buddies: Constructing and performing simultaneously hierarchical and close friendships. In J. T. Wood & S. Duck (Eds.), *Under-studied relationships: Off the beaten track* (pp. 122-147). Thousand Oaks, CA: Sage.

Zoryan Institute. (1993). The Armenian experience of genocide. In D. Gioseffi (Ed.), *On prejudice: A global perspective* (pp. 86-97). New York: Anchor Books.

Zur, O. (1987). The psychohistory of warfare: The co-evolution of culture, psyche and enemy. *Journal of Peace Research, 24*, 125-134.

Zur, O. (1991). The love of hating: The psychology of enmity. *History of European Ideas, 13*, 345-369.

Index

About the Contributors

Molefi Kete Asante is Professor in the Department of African American Studies at Temple University. He is the leading proponent of the Afrocentric school of thought. He has authored or edited 38 books including *The Afrocentric Idea*.

John R. Baldwin is Assistant Professor of Communication at Illinois State University. He earned his doctorate from Arizona State University. His research interests include communication in intimate intercultural relationships (friendships, romance, marriage) and the social construction of racism in the United States and Latin America. He has coauthored a chapter in the eighth edition of Samovar and Porter's *Intercultural Communication: A Reader*. He also has coauthored "The Layered Perspective of Cultural (In)Tolerance(s)" in Wiseman's *Intercultural Communication Theory*. An underlying goal of Baldwin's research is to bring various methodological and theoretical approaches together to address important social issues, especially issues of intolerance.

Stephanie Brzuzy is Assistant Professor in the School of Social Work at Arizona State University. Her experience in public policy includes a public administration fellowship and employment as a legislative research associate in Washington, D.C. She currently teaches courses on social welfare policy and research.

Julie E. Chalfin is a graduate student in the School of Behavioral and Organizational Studies at Claremont Graduate University. She is interested in intergroup and intragroup relations. Her research focuses on mediation in intercultural and international conflicts.

Frederick C. Corey is Associate Professor in the Department of Communication at Arizona State University. His research focuses on personal narratives and the performance of gay culture. His essays have appeared in *Text and Performance Quarterly, Western Journal of Communication,* and *Canadian Journal of Social and Political Theory.*

Stanley O. Gaines, Jr. is Assistant Professor in the Department of Psychology, Pomona College, and in the Intercollegiate Department of Black Studies, Claremont Colleges. His research interests include the influence of culture, ethnicity, personality, and gender on interpersonal communication processes among interethnic and intraethnic relationships.

Howard Giles is Professor in, and Chairperson of, the Department of Communication at the University of California, Santa Barbara, where he holds affiliated positions in psychology and linguistics. He currently is coeditor of the *Journal of Language and Social Psychology,* which he founded, as he did the *Journal of Asian Pacific Communication.* He has long-standing projects underway in language effects, intercultural accommodation, and bilingualism. His main research activity is on intergenerational phenomena and processes from an intergroup perspective and across the Pacific Rim.

María Cristina González is Director of the Institute for Cocurricular Programs and Service and is Adjunct Professor of Communication at Arizona State University. She received her Ph.D. in speech communication from the University of Texas at Austin in 1986. She is interested in the ways in which various forms of social organization constrain and delimit self-expression and ultimately affect personal and spiritual well-being. She has published numerous essays and poetry, and she teaches a non-Western approach to doing ethnography that she calls "the Four Seasons."

Michael L. Hecht is Professor in the Department of Speech Communication at Pennsylvania State University. He received his Ph.D. from the University of Illinois in 1976 and formerly was a professor of communication at Arizona State University. He has written and edited books on African American communication, nonverbal communication, and interpersonal communication. He currently is completing a book on adolescent relationships and drug use. He has authored or coauthored more than 70 articles and chapters on topics such as interethnic communication, identity, ethnicity, and drug resistance processes; communication effectiveness; and romantic love. He completed a National Institute on Drug Abuse (NIDA)-sponsored study of drug resistance strategies that resulted in an award-winning drug prevention video titled *Killing Time,* and he currently is completing a series of NIDA-supported studies on ethnic and gender similarities and differences in drug resistance as well as cultural sensitivity in drug prevention.

Deborah Wood Holton is Associate Professor at DePaul University, where she teaches interdisciplinary courses in theater, fiction, and creative writing in the School for New Learning, a nontraditional liberal arts college. She received her doctorate from the University of Wisconsin–Madison in American theater studies with an emphasis in art history. She has published essays about cultural pluralism in American theater and drama, Eugene O'Neill, and adult education as well as fiction and poetry.

Mary Kim is a graduate student in the School of Behavioral and Organizational Studies at Claremont Graduate University. She presently is a counselor with the Korean Youth Community Center. Her research interests include acculturation, aggression, and interpersonal relationships.

Sheryl L. Lindsley is Assistant Professor at California State University, Stanislaus. She worked in management and administration in mortgage banking organizations for more than 10 years. She received an M.A. in communication from San Francisco State University in 1992 and an interdisciplinary Ph.D. in communication from Arizona State University in 1995. Her research focuses on increasing understanding of problematic intercultural communication in international organizations. Her professional experiences in the private sector and academe, as well as her international travel, have reinforced her commitment to improving relationships among all members of our "global village."

Flavio Francisco Marsiglia is Assistant Professor in the School of Social Work at Arizona State University. He teaches diversity and social work with groups and coordinates a pilot school social work project in rural Arizona. His areas of interest include social work in the schools as well as substance abuse and HIV/AIDS prevention. He presents in conferences and professional meetings around the nation and has written numerous articles on his areas of interest. He received his Ph.D. from the Mandel School of Applied Social Sciences at Case Western Reserve University.

Dreama G. Moon is a doctoral candidate in the Department of Communication at Arizona State University. She received her M.H.R. degree from the University of Oklahoma. Her areas of specialization include critical intercultural communication studies and feminist theory. She is interested in issues of identity and culture, in particular the ways in which the notion of fractured and intersected identities can inform scholarly inquiry about intercultural communication. Her research areas of focus include anticolonial discourses on Whiteness, class passing, and White identity.

Thomas K. Nakayama is Associate Professor in the Department of Communication and affiliate faculty in the Interdisciplinary Humanities Program and the Women's Studies Program at Arizona State University. He received his Ph.D. from the University of Iowa. He writes in the areas of cultural studies and rhetoric, focusing particularly on issues of race, gender, and sexuality.

Kent A. Ono is Assistant Professor of American Studies and Asian American Studies at the University of California, Davis, where he researches representations of race and gender in media. His chapter in this book grows out of an interest in independent film and video within marginalized communities. His own mixed-race heritage is a personal and political motivation for writing this chapter. He is coeditor of *Enterprise Zones: Critical Positions on Star Trek* and has contributed essays to *Amerasia Journal, Communication Monographs, Philosophy and Rhetoric, Women's Studies in Communication,* and several edited collections.

Lana F. Rakow is Professor of Communication at the University of North Dakota. She is the author of *Gender on the Line: Women, the Telephone, and Community Life* and the editor of two books, *The Revolution in Words: Righting Women 1868-1871* (coedited with Cheris Kramarae) and *Women Making Meaning: New Feminist Directions in Communication.* In addition to her work in feminist communication theory, she has written and spoken extensively about curricular reform in communication studies.

Garry L. Rolison is Associate Professor of Sociology at California State University, San Marcos. He received his Ph.D. from the University of California, Santa Cruz, and has held faculty positions at the University of California, Santa Barbara; the University of Oklahoma; and Arizona State University. His research interests focus on race, social stratification, and urban poverty. He has published a number of articles in both sociology and Black studies journals.

Patrick Taing currently resides in Montebello, California, and teaches English as a second language, social science, and elementary and secondary basic skills. His research interests include cross-cultural perspectives on health behavior and parent-offspring relationships among Asian Americans.

Laura Tohe is Assistant Professor in the Department of English at Arizona State University. She grew up on the Diné (Navajo) reservation in New Mexico and Arizona. Her recent poetry and stories are published in *Reinventing the Enemy's Language; Blue Dawn, Red Earth, Fever Dreams,* and *Southwestern Women: New Voices.* She is the author of *Making Friends With Water.* Her book of poetry, *No Parole Today,* will be published by West End Press in 1998.

Victor Villanueva, Jr. is Associate Professor at Washington State University, where he teaches writing and rhetoric and is Director of Composition. His books include *Cross-Talk in Comp Theory* and the award-winning *Bootstraps: From an American Academic of Color.* He is the Incoming chair of the national organization for college writing and rhetoric, the Conference on College Composition and Communication. His studies concern how writing and the teaching of writing are instances of rhetoric and how rhetoric affects people of color in particular.

Laura A. Wackwitz was Visiting Assistant Professor of Communication at the University of North Dakota at the time her chapter was written. As of the fall of 1997, she is Assistant Professor of Communication at Wayne State University. She received her Ph.D. from the University of Georgia in 1996 with an emphasis in critical media studies. Her research interests include feminist communication theory, media theory and criticism, communication law, and cultural studies.

Angie Williams is Lecturer (Assistant Professor) in the Centre for Language and Communication Research at the University of Wales, Cardiff. She received a B.Sc. degree (honors) in psychology from the University of Bristol (United Kingdom) in 1987. She subsequently studied for an M.A. and then a Ph.D. in communication at the University of California, Santa Barbara. Her primary area of research interest is intergroup communication with a strong emphasis on life span developmental issues, particularly intergenerational communication. She also conducts intercultural research as a collaborator on an international project investigating intergenerational communication across the Pacific Rim. In addition, she has a continuing interest in language attitudes and accent variation.

Gale Young is Professor of Communication at California State University, Hayward, and is Codirector of the Center for the Study of Intercultural Relations. She teaches graduate and undergraduate courses in intercultural communication, conflict, intimacy, and interpersonal relations. She publishes, directs grants, and consults in the areas of intercultural communication, racism, and integrating multicultural perspectives into higher education. She is coauthor (with Benjamin Bowser and Terry Jones) of *Confronting Diversity on College Campuses* and coeditor of *The Inclusive University: Multicultural Perspectives in Higher Education.*